Also by Susan Quinn

A Mind of Her Own: The Life of Karen Horney

Marie Curie

A LIFE

SUSAN QUINN

HEINEMANN : LONDON

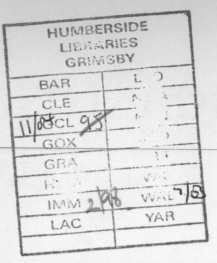

First published in Great Britain 1995
by William Heinemann Ltd
an imprint of Reed Consumer Books Ltd
Michelin House, 81 Fulham Road, London SW3 6RB
and Auckland, Melbourne, Singapore and Toronto

First published in the United States of America
by Simon and Schuster

A CIP catalogue record for this title
is available from the British Library

ISBN 0 434 60503 4

Printed and bound by Mackays of Chatham plc

Acknowledgments

I am grateful to the many readers who have advised me on various aspects of this book, including Elisabeth Crawford, Walter Gilbert, Mario Grignetti, Linda and Michael Hutcheon, Tony Judt, Jaçek Marek, Agnieszka Morawińska, Irwin Oppenheim, Harry Paul, Matt Ramsey, Ruth Sime, Thomas W. Simons, and Jay Winter. Thanks also to members of the Skłodowski and Curie families, Pierre Joliot, Eve Curie Labouisse, Hélène Langevin, Ela Staniszkis, and Jan Szancenbach for their guidance. For their translations from Swedish, Polish, and German, I would like to thank Gudrun Matejka, Ola Gordinier, Anna Sobczinski, and Irene Woods. During my visits to Poland I have been ably guided by my sister, Peggy Simons, as well as Tim Carroll, Krzysztof Cieslak, Wojtek Cejrowski, Kate Jęczmyk, and Jan Rochowski. I am also grateful to Krystyn Kabzińska and Anita Zwolińska, who helped me at the Maria Skłodowska-Curie Museum in Warsaw, and to Barbara Gwiazdowska, who showed me the Warsaw Radium Institute. In France I benefited from the knowledgeable and generous guidance of Monique Bordry, director of the Curie Museum and Archives. Bob Gamble, François Roustang, and Gillie Faure also played crucial roles. Finally, I am enormously grateful to Dominique Pigeon, who has ferreted out information I never could have found without him, and who has been a wonderfully efficient and helpful assistant throughout this project.

Support for this project has come from many sources. I am grateful to the Guggenheim Foundation, which granted me a fellowship, and to the Rockefeller Foundation, which provided a residency in Bellagio. I have also gotten good advice from members of my biography group: Joyce Antler, Fran Molino, Judith Tick, and Lois Rudnick. Megan Marshall, who is also a group member, deserves special thanks for her careful and insightful reading of the manuscript. I also thank Paula Bonnell, Ruth Butler, Judith Cohen, Christopher Corkery, Alice Hoffman, Lexa Marshall, Pam Painter, Sue Standing, and Marjorie Waters for listening and advising. There are a few people who have helped all along the way, both as readers and advisers, and I thank them especially. They are Bernadette Bensaude-Vincent, Georges Borchardt, Evy Davis, Diana Korzenik, Kathryn Kirshner, Fran Nason, Jan Schreiber, and my parents Robert and Esther Quinn. Finally, I thank my husband, Daniel Howard Jacobs, to whom this book is dedicated, and who has believed in me and enthusiastically supported my life as a writer for over thirty years. Like Marie Curie, I have "the best husband one could dream of."

TO DANNY

CONTENTS

INTRODUCTION

MARIE CURIE came from a family of chroniclers. Her father, Władysław Skłodowski, wrote a history of his family in Poland, and her brother Józef recapitulated the story, adding an account of his generation. Marie's sister Helena also wrote her memoirs and published them in Polish. Marie herself wrote a biography of Pierre Curie and a brief autobiography. In addition, both of Marie Curie's children wrote about their famous mother. In 1937, her younger daughter Eve Curie published one of the most popular biographies of all time, *Madame Curie*.

Like all family historians, these members of the Skłodowski-Curie clan had their reasons for setting down the story. For Marie's father, and to a large extent for her brother Józef, keeping a family history was a political act, a means of preserving the precious Polish heritage which foreign oppressors made such brutal attempts to blot out during most of their lifetimes. For Marie's sister Helena and daughter Irène, it was a matter of elaborating one aspect of the story.

But in the case of both Marie Curie and her daughter Eve, one important reason for writing was unspoken. For Marie Curie, writing a biography of Pierre Curie was an act of love, a part of the "religion of memories" she practiced after his tragic, premature death. Her autobiography, written in English and never translated for fear the French would find it immodest, was a means of thanking her American admirers, who had been so generous. But it also provided the outlines for the triumphal version of her life that her daughter would write soon after she died.

After spending seven years working on this biography, I am more astounded than ever at the speed with which Eve Curie was able to gather the facts and put together her mother's story in *Madame*

Curie. Her biography of her mother appeared in 1937, three years after Marie Curie's death. When I asked Eve Curie Labouisse, in an interview in 1988, why she wrote the book so quickly, she told me that she was "afraid that someone else would do it first and not get it right."

For Eve Curie, getting it right meant portraying her mother as a woman of great nobility, tremendously hardworking and dedicated, who often didn't get the credit she deserved. She tells the story so well that it is not immediately obvious that the biography is serving as a defense of her mother. And yet lurking beneath the surface and motivating the undertaking is an event which had had a devastating effect on Marie Curie: her public exposure and vilification because of an affair she had with a fellow scientist, Paul Langevin. Although Marie Curie was a widow at the time, Paul Langevin was married and the father of four children. And reactionary elements in the French press used the incident to drum up xenophobic hatred of the "foreign" woman who was destroying a French home, and to exploit an array of prejudices against godless intellectuals and emancipated women. It was partly to prevent the retelling of that painful episode that Eve Curie wrote her book, which deals with it in a few paragraphs as "a perfidious campaign . . . against this woman of forty-four, fragile, worn out by crushing toil, alone and without defense."

My reasons for undertaking a biography of Marie Curie were as much of our time as Eve Curie's were of hers. I wanted to peel back the layers of myth and idealization which had grown up around Marie Curie's story since her daughter told it over fifty years ago. I have looked for evidence that Marie Curie was not just a singular, exceptional woman (though she was indeed that) but also a woman who experienced the same difficulties as other women with strong opinions and ambitions. That meant exploring more carefully the barriers to women which surrounded her in Poland and in France. It also meant looking more closely at her defeats and humiliations at the hands of the Academy of Sciences as well as the proper bourgeoisie and the outrageous right-wing press.

The triumphal version of Marie Curie's life tends to portray her as impervious to these defeats and humiliations. Of her rejection from the Academy of Sciences, for instance, Eve Curie wrote, "She was not to comment by so much as a word upon this setback which in no wise afflicted her." This is undoubtedly what Marie Curie herself said about her exclusion from the most important scientific institution in France at the time. But the evidence suggests that the rejection had a profound effect: for many years afterward she did not publish her work in the *Comptes rendus,* the official organ of the Academy and the most widely read French scientific publication.

Throughout her life, and particularly after she became the focus of attacks and adulation, Marie Curie tended to present a cool facade to the world. Einstein, though he was fond of her, once went so far as to say that Marie Curie was "poor when it comes to the art of joy and pain." In fact just the opposite was true.

Several important new sources have provided evidence of Marie Curie's intense emotional life. In 1990, a journal that Marie Curie kept during the year after Pierre's death was made available for the first time to researchers at the Bibliothèque nationale in Paris; her entries, addressed to her lost husband, reveal her to be a woman capable of profound joy and deep sorrow.

At the École de physique et chimie in Paris, I found evidence of Marie Curie's passionate attachment to those she cared about. In testimonials which had been closed until I read them, Marie Curie's friends told the story, in detail, of her affair with Paul Langevin and of the scandal that ensued. One friend described her as "capable of going through fire for those she loved." In the Langevin affair, she certainly did. In the end the story reveals Marie Curie as someone who, like the rest of us, didn't always make the wisest choices in love.

The idealization of Marie Curie the scientist has gone in the opposite direction. In general she has been portrayed as passionate, hardworking, dedicated, and a seeker of a cure for cancer. She herself, when she described her work in discovering and then isolating radium, emphasized the dedication and hard physical toil rather than the important scientific ideas upon which the work was premised. But in retrospect, her labor and her association with the search for a cancer cure were far less important than her critical insight that radioactivity was an "atomic property" of her newly discovered elements. It was this idea, put forth almost one hundred years ago, which led to our modern understanding of the structure of the atom. Just as my biography provides new evidence of the range of emotions Marie Curie experienced in her personal life, it also demonstrates, through a detailed examination of her discovery of radioactivity, that her success as a scientist depended not just on her dedication but also on her intellectual clarity.

The distinction between her personal and scientific life was one Marie Curie made during one of her bravest hours. At the height of the Langevin scandal, after it was announced that she had won the Nobel Prize for chemistry, a member of the Swedish Academy wrote to tell her that she would not be welcome in Sweden, because of the Langevin affair, and should refuse the prize until she had cleared her name. Marie Curie wrote back that, in fact, the prize had been awarded for her discovery of radium and polonium and she intended to come to Sweden to accept it. "I believe that there is no connection between my scientific work and . . . private life."

Undoubtedly this is one of many episodes Marie Curie did not want those outside her intimate circle to know about. In general, she tried to hide evidence of her difficulties. Toward the end of her life, she asked several of her friends to destroy her personal letters to them. And when her eyes became clouded with cataracts, she involved Eve in a complicated charade to keep her eye operations secret from her friends and colleagues. No one was to know that she was sick, or that she suffered. And yet, sixty years after her death, it is precisely the evidence of her difficulties, and of her vulnerability, which reveal her as at once human and heroic.

Chapter One

A FAMILY

WITH CONVICTIONS

. . . Poland's fate
Is to enter the Battle
As Mary's Breastplate.
In the thick of the Fight
She succors her Knight,
And Thee, Sweet Fatherland.

IN NINETEENTH-CENTURY Poland, the name Mary was bound, like Catholicism itself, to the national cause. The ancient Polish cavalry, whose plumage made them seem to fly, bore a medallion of the Virgin Mary on their breastplates. And it was said that Mary, the Black Virgin of Częstochowa, had personally intervened to drive off the Swedish invaders and rescue Poland in 1655. She appeared on the ramparts, the embodiment of a revered black-faced icon, "in a shining robe . . . , priming the cannon and tossing shells back in the direction from which they came." And so, even though Władysław Skłodowski was a nonbeliever, it was natural for him and his wife Bronisława, a quietly pious woman, to choose the name Maria Salomea for their fifth and last child. For Władysław and Bronisława Skłodowski, both zealous patriots, Maria was not just the Holy Virgin but also, as Władysław noted, "the patroness . . . of our country."

Born November 7, 1867, near the ancient center of Warsaw, Maria Salomea Skłodowska entered a world in which almost every act, including the naming of a child, bore some relation to the Poles' struggle to survive the systematic and brutal suppression of their nation. Three years before, the Skłodowskis had witnessed the devastating defeat of the January Uprising, the second major attempt in the century to overthrow the rule of the Russian Tzars. In the end, tens of thousands of Poles, among them many of the most talented, were driven by the Tzar's armies in chain gangs to Siberia, most never to return. Władysław himself, though opposed to the tactic of violence, was to suffer along with his wife from the defeat of the insurrection. For the next fifty years, the Tzar's agents in Poland would preside over a "Russification" that was designed to weed out every trace of

Polish consciousness—in education, in government, in intellectual and religious life. And for the rest of their lives, Bronisława and Władysław Skłodowski would fight, as teachers and as parents, to keep the idea of Poland alive.

Three centuries before, Poland had been for a time the largest nation in all of Europe. Later, its Sejm provided an early model for parliaments; its constitution of 1791 was the first enacted in Europe. But the constitution could not prevent political paralysis, and in that last decade of the eighteenth century, the monarchs of Russia, Prussia, and Austria took advantage of Poland's weakness and divided its lands among themselves. For the next 120 years, the Polish nation ceased to exist as a geographic entity. "The name of Poland," the Danish visitor George Brandes wrote in 1885, "is not found on the map of Europe. . . . The freedom and welfare of its sons and daughters are in the power of foreign rulers." Poland became three provinces—of Austria, of Prussia, and of Russia.

Each of the great powers practiced its own form of repression, but Russian rule, in Warsaw and the vast lands to the east which comprised the Russian Partition, was the harshest. And in the nineteenth century, the Poles in the Russian Partition fought back. Two uprisings, in November of 1830 and January of 1863, were so large and so catastrophic that they are embedded forever in the memory of every Pole as the most significant events of that century. The first, the November Uprising, resulted in the exile and imprisonment of Poles on a vast scale and the dispossession of much of Poland's landed gentry.

The January Uprising, thirty-three years later, lasted longer but ended once again in defeat and humiliation. As many as one hundred thousand Poles went into exile at the end of the January Uprising, many taking up residence in France. More than ever before, Paris became the center of Polish intellectual and cultural life. At the same time, women remaining in Poland were required to take on the work their men left behind. In many ways, these consequences of the January Uprising made themselves felt in the life of Maria Skłodowska, just as they had in her parents' lives before her.

The happiest and most productive years of Bronisława and Władysław Skłodowskis' life together coincided with the tumultuous events of this second insurrection. Bronisława Boguska married Władyłsaw Skłodowski in the summer of 1860, as demonstrations in Warsaw started to multiply and alarm the Tzar. That same year, Bronisława assumed the position of headmistress of a private school on Freta Street, one of the best schools for girls in Warsaw. Bronisława herself had graduated from the Freta Street school some years before, and had worked there ever since as an assistant to her mentor and friend Eleonora Kurchanowicz. Now that she was headmistress, she and her new husband could move into apartments adjacent to the classrooms in the stately Freta Street townhouse.

It wasn't always easy living in such close proximity to the school. The Skłodowskis were confined to the rear of the house, away from the tall second-story windows and graceful wrought-iron balcony overlooking the wide, sunny street. Władysław complained when the schoolgirls' noise invaded the couple's private apartments. And even before her own children were born, Bronisława confided to Eleonora that marriage was turning out to be harder than she'd expected. "Don't think that I'm already tired of Władysław," she wrote. "I love him more each day . . . but I must confess that I wouldn't mind being Miss Bronisława again, now that I see how difficult a woman's life is."

During the seven years the Skłodowskis lived on Freta Street, Bronisława bore five children: Zofia in 1862, Józef in 1863, Bronisława (named after her mother) in 1865, Helena in 1866, and, finally, Maria in 1867. She also ran the school, hiring and firing teachers and placating the Russian authorities, who looked with suspicion on any Polish-run enterprise. What's more, during part of this period, the Skłodowskis took in and cared for Władysław's younger brother Przemysław, who was mortally ill with tuberculosis. And yet, despite the demands on Bronisława and the hints of tension, their son Józef wrote later that it was "the happiest time" for his parents, a time free from the money and health worries that would soon enough come to plague them.

Nonetheless, as Józef was quick to add, "political events"—that is, the January Uprising—disturbed their happiness "a great deal." By 1864, when defeat came, the Skłodowskis had brought two children into the world. But family sorrows had darkened their door during the same time. Władysław's brother Zdzisław, twice wounded in the fighting, had escaped, like so many others, to France. Bronisława's brother Henryk, who also fought in the rebellion, had been condemned to four years of exile in Siberia.

The battles had been fought, for the most part, in the countryside. But Russian retribution was dealt out in Warsaw. And the Skłodowskis' townhouse was surrounded on every side by painful reminders of the failure of the January Uprising. Less than a half-mile's walk out Freta Street to the north lay the Alexander Citadel, a red brick colossus built to intimidate by Tzar Nicholas. In peaceful times, Bronisława and Eleonora walked to the citadel and back for exercise. But after the uprising, thousands of Polish resisters were imprisoned there, soon to be sent on to Siberia. And on August 5, 1864, grieving Poles gathered to watch as the leaders of the insurrection were hanged from the ramparts.

Just south of the Skłodowski apartments lay the "Old Town" square, a ramshackle cluster of market stalls surrounded by gaily ornamented narrow medieval houses and filled on normal days with the noise of bargaining. Beyond the market enclosure, a tall porphyry column bearing a statue of King Zygmunt III, sword in one hand and cross in the other, dominated another, grander square. The pious King Zygmunt had once hoped to plant the cross in Moscow. Instead, his stooped silhouette had borne witness as Russian troops fired into an unarmed crowd of Polish demonstrators. Across the way, the gracious front rooms of Royal Castle, once home of a Polish legislature, had become a barracks for the occupiers. In the eighteenth century, the Italian artist-in-residence Bernardo Bellotto had painted sunny views of the castle and of life in the court of the last Polish king, Stanisław August. Now the elegant monarch's residence above the Vistula was home to the Russian viceroy.

Further, along Krakowskie Przedmiescie, the broad main street lined with churches and palaces, the lavish suites of the new Hotel Europejski were impressing travelers from the West. "The ceilings are painted in a style worthy of any palace," an English journalist reported. But the hotel's elegant coffee room already had a bloody history: the bodies of the first five men to fall in the insurrection were brought there. And outside the hotel, in Saxon Square, the Russian infantry lay encamped in low white tents, ready for more trouble.

Even after most of the troops left Warsaw, the mark of Tzarist control was everywhere. The signs on all the shops were written in the required Russian Cyrillic letters—although, according to one visitor, "no bookseller in Warsaw will have a Russian book in his shop, nor even a music-seller a piece of Russian music." Many Poles wore black, in public mourning for their own dead and for the defeat of their cause. And a poet thought the meditative statue of the Pole Copernicus, which dominated the square at the head of Nowy Swiat (New World) Street, was brooding with his compatriots. "Even Copernicus, clutching a hollow globe/Cries vengeance from his pedestal. Revenge! Revenge! It echoes/ Round Warsaw with the ring of cold iron."

The families of Władysław Skłodowski and his wife Bronisława Boguska were of the class most directly affected by these catastrophes. On both sides, they came from the peculiarly Polish form of landed gentry known as *szlachta,* nobles who in previous centuries had fought for the republic but who valued their independent authority and participated with equal voice in the parliament of the land, the Sejm. The *szlachta* were more numerous than the nobles of other countries, and less given to internal distinctions. In Poland, titles like prince or marquis were an alien concept. "Even on making introductions," Brandes noted while visiting Warsaw, "I never heard any titles given among the aristocracy—an agreeable thing when one comes from Germany."

At the same time, the gap between the richest and poorest within the noble class was enormous. The most powerful owned vast estates, and most of the rest owned next to nothing. Landed peasants were better off than forty percent of these minor *szlachta*. And by the nineteenth century, the Skłodowskis and Boguskis, despite noble histories, had been reduced to the position of minor *szlachta*. The uprisings had only worsened their already precarious situation.

On the Skłodowski side, Władysław's father Józef had fought in the artillery in the November 1830 uprising, and was captured by Cossacks near Chmielnik and driven on foot the 140 or so miles north to Warsaw. He arrived there starving and in rags, with badly injured feet. Józef was fortunate, however, compared to many others. He was able, not long after, to resume his career as a teacher, to marry Salomea Sagtyńska, and to father seven children.

Józef Skłodowski, remembered by his grandson (Maria's brother) as a stooping old man with abundant white hair and ever-present pipe, can be seen as a transitional figure in the social history of the family. No longer a landowner himself, he nonetheless avoided and disliked Warsaw, and spent his life teaching in the provinces. His origins were in the *szlachta* class; but without property or authority, he was one of the "déclassé nobles," in the phrase of one historian, "proud élites available for new social roles." Whereas the traditional Polish *szlachta* had studied only war, agriculture, and politics, and scorned foreigners and merchants, men like Józef were drawn to Western ideas, including the egalitarianism of the French Revolution. In his memoirs, his grandson proudly recalls that his grandfather "risked his job" as head of a school when he insisted that "talented peasants" should be allowed to study there alongside the children of the nobility.

The offspring of Józef and Salomea Skłodowski were more cosmopolitan than their parents. Some lived in the country, some in Warsaw, but all were members of the intelligentsia, a group strongly identified in Eastern Europe, in the nineteenth century as in the twentieth, with the national cause.

In Poland, the cause was liberation from the foreign oppressors. But the Skłodowski offspring, like the intelligentsia in general, differed on the means to that end. The family contained within it the two strains of thought which had vied for dominance throughout the Polish nineteenth century: romantic idealism and political realism. The idealists refused to compromise: their goal was national sovereignty, and their means was insurrection. Their most eloquent spokesmen were the romantic poets, calling from exile for a fight to the death; their voices were loudest preceding insurrections.

The political realists were most visible after armed struggle failed; but their ideas persisted throughout the century, beginning with Stanisław Staszic, a leading reformer of the Polish Enlightenment, who told Poles that "science, commerce, and the crafts are the weapons you need, otherwise you will perish." Unlike his brother, who joined the uprising, Władysław Skłodowski espoused the views of the political realists. At age twenty-three, in a poem addressed to his friends on his name day, he exhorted them, with a young man's zeal, to fight the Satan of Russian rule by uniting in selfless hard work:

. . .

Separated, divided, we are individual and helpless,
each looking into the future with apprehension, with fear
each preoccupied with his own small worries
each pursuing a fainthearted course on a narrow road

Our hearts and minds are busy
our souls no longer house great emotion.
All we are is cold, dark, silent, barren.

But suddenly, the storm roars, the thunder cracks
The foundation of the world shakes
Satan's powers cringe, agonized, in fear.
This is the end of the age of error and of treason.

Let us break this armor of ice that binds our chests
Let us begin today, bring stones to build
The temple of truth, the temple of freedom.
Let our willpower cure our crippled souls
Let our hard work prove—to the world,
to God, to our country—our worth . . .

"To the future!" Let us lift our glasses,
Dear brothers. Let us offer our pain
and our lives to that future.
Work, love, and live, brothers!

The poem was written in 1855, more than a decade before Polish positivism emerged as an intellectual creed. But its call for "hard work . . . [to] prove our worth" anticipated the central thesis of the Warsaw positivists: that the future lay in study and hard work, rather than the romantic old *szlachta* dreams of martial glory.

After the failure of the January Uprising, more and more of the intelligentsia came around to the view that work, and particularly the work of educating and training the people, was the only hope for Poland. A new enthusiasm for science and the empirical method developed. Education was seen as "a powerful weapon, an unlimited resource which could fundamentally change and ennoble society."

But to "build the temple of truth," in Russian-occupied Warsaw, was almost as difficult as to plot insurrection. It meant, in the first place, working for the occupiers. A privately circulated "Address from the Inhabitants of Warsaw" following the January Uprising abjured all Polish citizens to "avoid . . . all such as pollute themselves by taking service under the Government." As a teacher, however, Władysław Skłodowski had little choice but to work in a government-run gymnasium. And it was only there that he could hope to influence the young Poles who might rescue his country.

His son Józef found it necessary, in the history of the family he wrote in the 1920s, to explain this at some length. "One might ask: what made the Polish teachers stay in their profession and work in the highly abnormal conditions at the time? The answer would probably be that besides the need to provide for themselves, they acted out of some more or less unconscious impulse to keep teaching and this way stay in touch with the children and help them somehow. Sometimes it was done explicitly . . . [but] more often it was . . . between the lines of the lecture. Besides, by staying . . . Polish teachers were physically occupying the posts which, if they resigned, would have been taken by Russians. The students always recognized a real, honest teacher, and they knew he was their ally in a hostile environment . . . it was difficult and dangerous to keep such relationships from the authorities, especially in the face of widespread spying. Both teachers and students had to be always alert, cautious and sometimes even shrewd to be able to keep the secret."

As it turned out, Władysław Skłodowski paid a price for his principles even while working within the system. Named assistant director of a gymnasium in 1868, he was demoted from his post five years later, probably because he was resented by his tyrannical Russian superior. His departure from the directorship was a terrible blow to his esteem and to the material welfare of his family.

And yet Władysław managed the complicated balance of principle and livelihood better than most of his compatriots. For, as the Danish observer George Brandes noted, a young man in Russian Poland had few options. "For instance, if he studies law[,] he can never become a judge, generally not even an official, without separating himself from all intercourse with his countrymen. [If h]e studies medicine[,] he can never obtain a post at a university, never be at the head of a hospital, never conduct a public clinic, therefore can never attain the first rank in his science. The result is that . . . he goes from one study to another, obtains a smattering of different branches of science, surprises the foreigner by the versatility of his knowledge and information, but has no real mastery of anything."

Brandes could have been describing any number of Władysław's friends and relatives. His brother Zdzisław, who had law degrees from St. Petersburg and Toulouse and taught briefly at the Warsaw University, wound up in the sinecure of public notary in a country backwater, channeling his energies into the task, at once patriotic and literary, of translating Shakespeare's plays into Polish verse. His brother-in-law, Henryk, was a gifted artist but would not have survived, after his return from Siberian exile, without his enterprising wife, who owned a village grocery store. It was he too who brought down the rest of the family, including Władysław, with his plan to build and run a mill in the countryside.

For most of his life, Władysław castigated himself for losing all his savings in this scheme and denying his son and daughters financial support for their education. "He stopped worrying only at the end of his life," Józef explains, "seeing that we were all doing quite well." Perhaps he realized then how much his own example, and his tireless teaching efforts, had contributed to their success.

In a younger photograph Władysław Skłodowski, with his scruffy beard and fiery eyes, might well be taken for a revolutionary. Later, as an old man, posing with his daughters, the beard and lingering hair have turned white and a pale cast of regret seems to have covered the fire in his eyes. His son Józef, with his clinician's eye, notes that his father's features were "quite regular, although a little puffy from obesity." Yet, despite his "heavy construction," he moved with great vigor on long walks in the mountains. Like most of his compatriots, he was drawn to poetry, and often translated verses into Polish. Usually there was a "subtle note of melancholy" in the poems he chose to translate. But he had a playful side as well, most evident in the charming light verse he wrote for special occasions.

His life was ruled by his passion for learning and for teaching. Science, in particular, fascinated him, and he used every opportunity to supplement the poor program in the official schools. "My father," his youngest daughter Maria noted, "enjoyed any explanation he could give us about Nature and her ways. Unhappily, he had no laboratory and could not perform experiments." An avid follower of new scientific developments, he sometimes wrote popular articles about them. He was also a lover of literature, both Polish and foreign. His Russian and French were fluent, his German almost as good, and his English sufficient to translate *David Copperfield* from English to Polish as his wife listened. "Even when we were older," Józef notes, "we still turned to him with all the questions, as to an encyclopedia."

In the classroom and out, Władysław Skłodowski saw nearly every occasion as a pedagogical opportunity. Watching the sun go down on a hike in the Carpathian Mountains with Józef became an occasion for explaining the phenomenon of sunsets. The basics of English were taught during summer vacations. After hours, he used the equipment at the gymnasium to teach biology to his own children. And, even after his youngest daughter Maria left home to become a governess, he worked advanced math problems with her by mail.

Unlike his brother and sister, Władysław Skłodowski never studied abroad or obtained a university degree. After the November Uprising of 1830, the Russians closed Warsaw University. But Władysław studied biology in Warsaw nonetheless, graduating from a "biology department" which continued to operate without official university status. Later, when he did travel, he characteristically used the experience to further his self-education. "Before he went on a trip," Józef remembers, "he would make a detailed plan of activities and places to see, and he would look up information about those places. While traveling, he often took notes about what he saw and learned."

To the often boorish Russian officials sent to Warsaw to operate the public schools, Władysław Skłodowski was likely to have seemed either threatening or incomprehensible. After the tyrannical inspector at one school got him transferred, he worked until his retirement under another, more easygoing Russian who liked to put on occasional all-night vodka parties for his faculty. Władysław Skłodowski was never invited. And once, in a candid moment, the inspector told him why. "You, Władysław Józefowicz," he said, "are a European man; you wouldn't be amused by our company."

As a woman in Russian-occupied Poland, Bronisława Boguska would seem to have had even fewer options than her husband. And yet, paradoxically, the lack of opportunity for women carried certain benefits in a captive society. Women were not on the front lines in the insurrections, and thus were more likely to survive, sometimes taking on their husbands' responsibilities. And because girls were not expected or even allowed to operate in the public sphere, they were less likely to study at public Russian-dominated schools. Their education could be undertaken in private, and passed on—unadulterated by Russian propaganda—to their offspring.

Such was the case with Bronisława Boguska. Her parents, Feliks Boguski and Maria Zaruska, came from long lines of "poor but ambitious szlachta." Because they had no land of their own, they managed other people's estates. Yet they found a way to send Bronisława, as well as her two sisters, to the Freta Street school, the only private girls' school in Warsaw at the time. There, as her daughter Maria later observed, "she had what was, for that time, a very serious education." By her early twenties, she had made the transition from pupil to headmistress.

In the one surviving photograph, probably taken during the headmistress years, Bronisława appears reflective and tranquil. According to her son, she was "rather tall," but her hands and facial features make her seem petite and delicate. Her glistening hair has been worked into perfect coiled braids around her ears. And were it not for her black crepe dress, with its flowing sleeves and white underruffles, we might guess her to be a schoolgirl herself. Yet in a letter she wrote to the former director after she took over, she shows herself capable of carrying out difficult decisions. "It's hard to describe what's happening during the [entrance] exams!" she writes. "The children don't know anything but their mothers think they've brought us Solomons; when they see that their pleas will not help, they cry—sad scenes of which we had only too many this year." Later, in the same letter, she writes that she is dismissing one French teacher who would like to stay because "I prefer a native Frenchwoman, and we couldn't afford to keep two of them."

More difficult than dealing with staff and with ambitious parents was the task of satisfying the Russian officials who watched over the school. "Private schools directed by Poles," Maria wrote later, "were closely watched by the police and overburdened with the necessity of teaching the Russian language even to children so young that they could scarcely speak their native Polish." Under the increased scrutiny which followed the uprising, it may be that Bronisława Skłodowska was relieved when her husband got a promotion, allowing her to give up her difficult post as director and stay home with her five children.

The move from the Freta Street apartments, provided by Bronisława's post, to the Nowolipki apartments, provided by Władisław's, took the young family from the center of Warsaw westward to a neighborhood at the edge of the Jewish quarter. There they would live, in apartments varying with their fortunes, for the next twenty years, always surrounded by the familiar objects of home: a dark mahogany Biedermeier dining-room set with matching chairs and bench adequate for seven; a prized French china cup elaborately painted with Bourbon lilies and the torso of Louis Philippe, the Citizen King; a round table of green marble inlaid with grays, browns, and yellows in the pattern of a chessboard; a portrait of a bishop which, inside the family only, was attributed to Titian; and a large barometer which hung on the wall in Władysław's study and which, it was said, fascinated young Maria from an early age.

Maria was still an infant when the family moved to Nowolipki

Street in 1868. But the two oldest children, Zofia and Józef, were already getting the benefit of private lessons from their mother. And Władysław, though busy with school in the adjoining rooms, was able to keep an eye on everything. "My father," Józef remembers, "was concerned about our health, our physical development, our studies and even our free time, for which he tried to provide us with ideas and games."

Even games, in this household, tended to be educational. Helena remembers that "for history lessons we had our special collage, which we were constantly completing under our father's direction. It became our favorite occupation to look in books and magazines for good pictures for our collage." And then there were the blocks, kept in a chest in the children's room on Nowolipki Street and fondly remembered. "I can still see the colorful blocks of various shapes lying around all over the floor," Helena writes. The children colored the blocks themselves, and used them to represent "continents and countries, cities, mountains and rivers. We traveled among them with our father, who chose that playful and very noisy way of teaching us geography." Their father seems to have tolerated a good deal of disorder. "After such a geography lesson, our room looked just awful!" Helena remembers. But the fact remains that, in the Skłodowski household, play was learning and learning was play. "I still remember how enthusiastically we participated in those lessons," Helena writes, "how our father was happy to see our eagerness, and how well we all knew geography."

Life at the Skłodowskis' was scheduled. Every evening before bed, Władysław gathered the children together to do physical exercises. On Saturday nights, from seven to nine, he read and recited aloud to them, usually from forbidden Polish works. "He had a rare gift," Józef remembers, "of beautiful reading of poetry as well as prose . . . his voice was deep and warm, without a shade of affectation."

In nineteenth-century Poland, as Czesław Miłosz has explained, "the poet was hailed as a charismatic leader, the incarnation of the collective strivings of the peoples." It was through the words of the exiled romantic poets that Władysław Skłodowski passed on "great emotion" to his children. "He implanted in us a hatred for the invaders of Poland," Helena remembers, "especially for the Tzarist regime. . . ." Maria's lifelong "strong taste for poetry," particularly of the exiled Romantic poets Mickiewicz, Krasiński, and Słowacki, grew out of her father's reading of "the masterpieces of Polish prose and poetry. These evenings were for us a great pleasure and a source of renewed patriotic feelings."

Not every moment was given over to edification, of course. Józef recalls hours of playing in the big children's room, using the large blocks to build towers and destroy them, and—best of all—to make a game of recent history and play war. "We would arrange the rectangular blocks in two rows, as the fighting armies. The round blocks . . . served as ammunition . . . the thick cylindrical blocks as cannons . . . All that was naturally accompanied by screams and arguments." The story is told to illustrate the "unusual patience and understanding for children" of Bronisława Skłodowska, who allowed such noisy games even though they went on right next door to her room.

Bronisława Skłodowska is infrequently mentioned in the children's memories of their childhood, and then almost always in such reverential terms as to be beyond believing. Undoubtedly, this is because of the great tragedy which surrounds the children's memory of their mother: her illness and subsequent death, in 1878, from tuberculosis. Bronisława Skłodowska probably contracted TB when Maria was four. By Maria's fifth year she was away from home, "taking the cure," first in Austria, then in the south of France. And yet, despite her absences, she exerted a powerful influence on all her children, including the youngest. She was, as Marie Curie was to write many years later, "the soul of the house."

Unlike her husband, who was a skeptic, Bronisława Skłodowska was a devout Roman Catholic, "religious without exaggeration," in the phrase of her son Józef. She was determined to instill a love of God and of Poland in her children. In her beautiful script, she copied out the *Historical Songs* of Niemcewicz, probably because the printed version was banned. The *Songs* were elegies to the heroes of the Polish past, first published in 1816. They became "a kind of ABC of the Polish nation," Czesław Miłosz has explained, an ideal vehicle for teaching the children their history. A musician with a lovely voice, Bronisława probably sang the Niemcewicz songs to her children as well, accompanying herself on the piano.

Like her husband, Bronisława Skłodowska held advanced ideas for her time about work, as well as the role of women. After she left her teaching job, she decided to economize by making the children's shoes. She set up a little shop in the apartment on Nowolipki Street, acquired the necessary grinding, cutting, and sewing tools, and taught herself shoemaking. Such willingness to do manual work was inherited by her youngest daughter, and was essential to Marie's success many years later in isolating radium. It also defied the conventions of Bronisława's social class, which generally scorned all forms of manual labor. Poles, as Brandes noted, "have cultivated the earth and cultivated their minds for centuries, but they have at the same time obstinately regarded work merely for money as a low, degrading thing. They have nourished the inherited aristocratic contempt for the merchant and the manufacturer, to say nothing of the shopkeeper and the mechanic."

Józef, commenting on his mother's shoemaking, affirms both the prevailing prejudices and the family's independence of them. "I think about it [his mother's shoemaking] with great emotion . . . for it shows my parents' true 'democratic' nature—they didn't resent any form of physical work, even such a 'low' occupation as a cobbler's. Let's not forget that it was the time when Korzeniowski [revolutionary, poet, and father of Joseph Conrad] had just begun writing about the right of a doctor to marry a [higher-class] landowner's daughter. It is true that class prejudices were more common among the village nobility, but there was still a great deal of it among city dwellers who, after all, came mostly from the villages."

WHILE they may not have shared all of the gentry's prejudices, the Skłodowski family held on to their roots in the landowning class. Marie Curie, writing of her childhood, stressed that her parents "continued to keep in close touch with their numerous family in the country. It was with their relatives that I frequently spent my vacation . . . to these conditions, so different from the usual villegiature [summer holiday], . . . I owe my love for the country and nature."

Early in their marriage, the Skłodowskis had owned a modest country house themselves. Józef remembers traveling by train northeast across the flat open Polish landscape to Małkinia, then climbing into "the old waggoner Skrzypkowski's covered break" for the bumpy ride along rutted dirt roads to a wooden manor which was the home of his ninety-year-old great-grandmother. There were fruit trees there, and fields piled high with gravel which were later turned to profit. For the Skłodowskis, however, the place at Prosienica was a losing proposition. The news that they would sell it struck the two older Skłodowski children "like a lightning bolt." They took out their indignation by inventing a rhyming jingle about the new owner, a man named Zochowski. "During our last visit to the farm, Zosia [Zofia] and I ran around in the fields, " Józef remembers, "saying our last goodbye to them and yelling at the top of our lungs: "Zochowski, scoundrel, stole our Prosienica, he deserves the gallows."

By the time the younger girls, Bronia, Helena, and Maria, came along, the Prosienica property was gone. But the historical connection to particular pieces of Polish soil lived on. On both sides, a family coat of arms bespoke *szlachta* origins: the Boguski crest featured a battle-ax (Topór), and the Skłodowskis' was a cluster of horseshoe, arrow, and cross (Dołega). There were also villages, with names corresponding to their own, which had been linked to the families for centuries. The Skłodowskis had roots in a village called Skłody, not far from Białystok, in northeastern Poland. There, on the banks of the small Brok River, a thatched wooden manor house, the home of Władysław's great-grandfather Urban Skłodowski, survived well into the twentieth century. The Boguski name was associated with two towns, both called Boguszyce. Wojciech Boguski, in 1558, built a steep-roofed wooden church in the Gothic style which still stands today on a hill overlooking one of villages. Boguski ancestors as far back as the fourteenth century had served in the Sejm.

After the January Uprising, the manor house in the country, place of origin of both the Skłodowski and Boguski clans, acquired new symbolic power. It was, as art historian Agnieszka Morawińska has written, "a heroic period for Polish manor houses: they provided the soldiers, the hiding places, the command posts, and finally the hospitals. That ill-fated and last of Poland's uprisings was in fact a war conducted by manor houses."

With the failure of the insurrection, the Polish landowning class went into even swifter decline. Many manor houses were burned and plundered by the Russian troops. To divide and conquer, the Russians imposed overdue reforms in Poland which enfranchised the peasants and further impoverished the landed gentry. But for the descendants of these landed gentry, the manor house came to be a kind of embodiment of Poland.

Artists—like Artur Grottger in *The Defense of the Manor House* —depicted it in heroic terms. Poets evoked it lovingly. Adam Mickiewicz begins the epic poem *Pan Tadeusz* with a description of a *szlachta* manor house, "beside a brook, upon a hillock low/ In a birch grove . . . on stone foundations but with frame of wood; Its white walls shone afar; with whiter sheen/ That sheltered it against the winds of fall." Perhaps, during their Saturday readings, the Skłodowski children looked at folios of Grottger drawings—locked in a drawer in many a patriotic Polish household. Certainly, they heard their father recite the forbidden verses of Mickiewicz.

In the summertime, they returned home to the country. "The periods of vacations were particularly comforting," Marie Curie wrote many years later, "when, escaping the strict watch of the police in the city, we took refuge with relatives or friends in the country. There we found the free life of the old-fashioned family estate; races in the woods and joyous participation in the work in the far-stretching, level grain-fields."

Large families and friends provided the Skłodowskis with a variety of retreats. There was Marki, just northeast of Warsaw, where the Boguski grandparents lived and where the Skłodowskis shared a small villa with Aunt Ludwika (Bronisława's sister) and her husband; there the children joined their parents for meals on a glass-enclosed veranda, and climbed up to the tower room to lie in the heat among drying peas. At Zwola, the country house of Uncle Władysław Boguski, they played barefoot for hours in a creek, or took trips to nearby castles. At other times they traveled south from Warsaw to Skalbmierz, the home of Uncle Zdzisław Skłodowski, in the foothills of the Carpathian Mountains.

There were more luxurious country retreats, too, where the Skłodowskis were welcome. Sometimes they visited a more distant cousin, Ksawery Skłodowski, at Zawiepryzce near Lublin. Unlike the immediate family, Ksawery had made a great success of farming his vast properties, governing his workers with a paternalism considered enlightened at the time. "On Saturdays," . . . Józef Skłodowski writes, "he met with his workers and . . . received their reports, gave orders and also held his own 'court sessions,' deciding about conflicts and punishing the guilty peasants. His sentences, even though arbitrary, were always accepted and executed, because they were just and reasonable. . . . This way, everything went smoothly and . . . Ksawery was able to afford not only a relatively high standard of living but also ten children."

Life at the estate of this Skłodowski cousin, whom the children called "Uncle," approximated the life of Polish gentry before the fall. The spacious manor house was constantly open to guests and relatives and was usually "humming with joyous voices and laughter"; there was a crumbling sixteenth-century castle and ancestral chapel on the grounds. And everyone was preoccupied with horses. Guests were expected to ride well, and to participate in hunts which required long hours in the saddle galloping over rough terrain. The Skłodowski siblings applied themselves with their usual assiduity. "Everyone wanted to impress the others, so we all practiced persistently," Józef recalls. "That may be the reason why I and my sisters, including the youngest one, Maria, became quite good riders."

For the Skłodowski children, vacations provided not only relief from the constant surveillance of Russian authorities but a welcome break, as well, from the regimentation (and later the boarding-school crush) of their home life. In the country, they were surrounded by family spendthrifts and eccentrics like Uncle Henryk and Uncle Zdzisław, who didn't measure up to their own parents' high standard, but who were accepted and loved nonetheless. Even when they returned to the city, the Skłodowski children stayed in touch with their country cousins. And it is that correspondence that provides us with a first glimpse of the preoccupations of the youngest Skłodowska, Maria, in early adolescence.

With her closest sister Helena, Maria composed a poem for

Uncle Zdzisław's brood in Skalbmierz, taking them to task for not answering letters. And although it is undated, the references to a vaccination for rabies ("hydrophobia") suggest that it was written around 1880, the year Pasteur's vaccine made news. (The Polish Dr. Bujwid, referred to in the poem, was the first to introduce Pasteur's vaccine into Poland.) Maria would have been thirteen, her sister fourteen, ages which seem to match the poem's sense of humor.

They begin by chastising their country cousins, throwing in a reference to a recent flood:

> *Oh you of Skalbmierz, in mud up to your ears,*
> *A distant call, a moving plea, oh cousins—may you hear!*
>
> *Your staying out of touch with us is hardly a surprise*
> *For all you know is mud, mud, right up to your eyes.*

There is, however, a cure for the lazy nonwriters:

> *In Warsaw there's a doctor, you know he's called Bujwid*
> *Who cures the dogs, the sickest dogs, for he's the man who rid*
>
> *The dogs of hydrophobia, and—cousins—we have news!*
> *A new Bujwid has now appeared and sufferers can lose*
>
> *Their state of "letterphobia," it's such good news, you see*
> *The untold miracles he does, his genius is that he*
>
> *In every case with everyone has always made them better!*
> *They say that one man whom he saw knew not a single letter.*
>
> *He's healed so well he cannot live without his pen and ink*
> *And I am told he never stops, no, not to eat or drink.*
>
> *He writes all day, without a break, a week passed, then another*
> *A month went by, he writes and writes, to sister and to*
> *   brother.*
>
> *His uncles, aunts, his every friend, his cousins of every degree.*
> *He had to add two letter slots, so now he's up to three.*
>
> *Two friends have died beneath the flood of letters he has*
> *   penned.*
> *He went in debt to buy the stamps, and though he never sends*
>
> *Mail registered, his to, his from—they always reach their*
> *   goals.*
> *Oh cousins, may his fine example sink into your souls*
>
> *And make you quickly find your way to visit with us here*
> *So we'll enjoy your company, and cousins, never fear!*

We'll send you to the famous doc who'll cure your dread
    complaint.
Yes, there may still be time—come quick! so you can lose the
    taint.

The theme of "miracle cure" in the girls' poem anticipated, in various ways, the life work of three of the Skłodowski children. Two of them were to become doctors, and one a scientist who would devote a great deal of her energy to the curative powers of her discoveries. But at the moment Helena and Maria wrote the poem, it surely reflected the pain of past events as much as dreams of the future. In play, the Skłodowski girls invented a "genius doctor" who does "miracles" and cures "everyone he works on" from "nasty disease." But in real life, things hadn't worked out that way. By the time they wrote this poem, disease had exacted a terrible toll in their family.

MARIA SKŁodowska was ten years old when her mother died. "This catastrophe," she later wrote, "was the first great sorrow of my life. . . . Her influence over me was extraordinary, for in me the natural love of the little girl for her mother was united with a passionate admiration. For many years," she wrote, "we all felt weighing on us the loss of the one who had been the soul of the house." Of all the children, Maria seems to have been most vocal and insistent in her grief. "She would often sit in some corner and cry bitterly," her sister Helena remembers. "Her tears could not be stopped by anybody." Maria herself later described her reaction to her mother's death as "a profound depression."

It is not clear when tuberculosis began to stalk the Skłodowski household. Helena dates her mother's illness from the year of Maria's birth, 1867. But it seems more likely that it began in Maria's fourth year, 1871; at the time, according to Władysław's account, his wife began taking koumiss, a Tatar drink made from fermented mare's milk, which was thought to be salutary. The following year, on the advice of two of the best doctors in Warsaw, Bronisława, with great reluctance, left home to take her first rest cure.

For the next two years, Bronisława Skłodowska lived away from home most of the time, in the company of her oldest daughter Zofia. The four younger children stayed behind with their father, who cared for them with his sister-in-law Ludwika's help. But "Aunt Lucia," although a great favorite with her nephew and nieces, had four children of her own, and a troublesome husband, to cope with. She could not replace their mother who, despite her ill health, was remembered by Marie Curie years later as "an exceptional personality" who "held in the family remarkable moral authority."

Sometime between or just following their mother's absences from home, the five Skłodowski children posed for a photograph, perhaps so that Bronisława could keep it with her on her journeys. It is a portrait of the children only, without their parents; and unlike many such family photos at the time, in which children are grouped together—some sitting at others' feet, or leaning toward each other— the older children in this photograph stand apart from each other; the somber faces, inevitable in nineteenth-century photographs, are reinforced by their isolation in space. The two oldest girls, with golden light streaming through their long white-blond hair, stand to the right and left of the photo like sentinels, each leaning an elbow on a book. Józef perches on a table, hat in hand. Only the two youngest, Helena and Maria, have been bunched together in an upholstered chair. The littlest girls' legs are too short to reach the ground; Helena's high-topped shoes rest, crossed at the ankle, on a footstool; in her hand she holds a wooden bird, perhaps provided as a distraction by the photographer. Maria, crosses, with effort, her plump little legs in the air. The "moral authority" which Marie Curie ascribed to her mother seems to pervade this portrait of the Skłodowski children. It is a portrait of children with unusual dignity and self-possession. Or else it is a portrait of children trying very hard to look strong.

Besides the silent testimony of the photograph, the only child's view we have of the catastrophe comes from the oldest child in the family, Zofia, always called "Zosia" in the family, who wrote to her godmother Eleonora Kurchanowicz from Nice, where she had accompanied her mother. "I am taking care of [Mother] as best I can," writes the eleven-year-old Zosia. "I help her get dressed, and undressed, I boil water for her herbs and tea morning and evening. She often says that she is pleased with her Małgosia (that's what she calls me now), but I have a feeling that she needs more than just me, and I often worry, seeing her sad and not being able to cheer her up. Each day we count, several times, how many months we will have to stay here, and we are frustrated with time for passing so slowly. In Warsaw a year went by quicker than a month here."

As difficult as the separation must have been for Władysław and the children back in Warsaw, it is hard to imagine their loneliness and despair exceeded that expressed by Zosia and her mother in these letters to Eleonora Kurchanowicz. Eleonora was an important friend to the Skłodowski family. It was she who had headed the school on Freta Street and then turned over the directorship to Bronisława. Later she became Zosia's godmother. Bronisława "loved" her, she wrote from France, "as a daughter would," and included her name "next to all my closest relatives in my prayers." To Eleonora, who shared her faith, she could confide her hope the Virgin Mary would "grant me a recovery."

The seven surviving letters from Bronisława to Eleonora over her two years away from home provide the best insight we have into the woman who, despite her early death, exerted such a powerful influence on her youngest daughter. The letters begin hopefully, in the summer of 1872, when Bronisława journeyed to Hall in the Austrian Alps near Innsbruck, in the company of Zosia and a woman friend named Jozia. Like Hans Castorp in *The Magic Mountain,* Bronisława is full of gossip about the doctors at the spa, the international crowd, the shocking differences in custom. The German doctor Rabl, "the most respected and popular of the six physicians here," has a ready disdain for the "primitive" techniques of Polish practitioners. He has concluded "after a thorough examination that I should benefit greatly from the water here, and that my health should improve." There are few Poles, it seems, among the spa guests, but she is soon spending all her time in company of the "young and nice Miss Rosen," a beautiful Pole who was later to become the piano virtuoso Paderewski's wife.

Bronisława even feels well enough to attend a dance, where she is shocked to find that the men ask women to dance without introducing themselves, a custom which proves that "for all their 'cultural superiority' Germans don't have the best manners." To her delight, the dance leader for the evening is Polish. Ever the Polish patriot, she tells Eleonora that she "would have preferred to see that Pole lead the Germans in more than a dance." Despite a passing reference to her longing for mail—"what an irony that we live right next to the post office, so twice a day we see all the lucky people leaving there with their letters"—Bronisława's tone is upbeat and hopeful. She seems to believe the German doctor's optimistic prognosis.

But a year later, hearing a similar prediction from his French counterpart in Nice, she is more skeptical. "I have been feeling much better lately," she writes Eleonora, "although I still cough a lot.· . . . My doctor says that after a whole summer and winter in Nice I should regain my strength completely and heal my lungs, but I personally don't harbor such a great hope. Different doctors have assured me so many times that it's only natural for me not to have too much faith in their words. God alone can bring me my health back, so I only hope for His miracle; maybe He will take pity on my poor family and spare me for the children."

She was right to be skeptical of the doctors. The conventional medical wisdom at the time held that tuberculosis, the single most important cause of death in Europe, visited those who had an innate susceptibility. The usual treatment was to send patients to warm places to "take the cure." A few years later, in 1882, Robert Koch would isolate the tubercle bacillus and prove to the world that tuberculosis was a contagious disease. But it would take many more years to discover an effective treatment.

What doctors and patients alike knew, however, were the effects of TB. Most often, it began in the lungs, progressed slowly over months or even years, and ended in a galloping consumption, swift wasting and death. Bronisława Skłodowska had had firsthand knowledge of this process. Early in her marriage, when she nursed Władysław's younger brother Przemysław, who subsequently died of tuberculosis. Indeed, in retrospect, it seems possible that she contracted TB from her brother-in-law.

Thus her sense of foreboding, as she embarked on a second year of rest cure in Nice, must have been profound. Nonetheless, she retained a wide-eyed enthusiasm for her new surroundings, at least in the beginning. "Yesterday," she wrote Eleonora in July, "we went to Monaco, where there is the only casino now open in Europe . . . there I saw for the first time in my life the people who spend their time on gambling. Perhaps it was too early [in the day], but I didn't see those burning eyes and impassioned faces that I've read so much about."

It was summertime, and her husband and sister Ludwika were with her. But she anticipated their departure with dread. "I'm afraid even to think what it will be like after [Ludwika's] gone—only Zosia and I all the way to April!" Remembering when they were all together in the country, she writes, "I would gladly have that time back, instead of this stay in Nice. It was a great time, wasn't it? What a joy it was to see our little ones run around in the meadow! Now, when I try to see all of them in my imagination, I have to look for their faces in so many different directions! Not to mention the thought that it is still so long until I will see them all. . . . My only consolation is that line from the poem: 'Like all the things in this world, this too shall pass.' "

As the year progresses, her spirits rise and fall with her health. In October, as the Nice hoteliers spruce up for their season and the roses and oleanders begin to bloom, she feels "very ill" and discouraged as a result. "I can't control my moods even if I wanted to," she confides to Eleonora, "and there are moments when it's almost impossible to resist despair. . . . This very moment I feel a great disdain for myself, for I just received Władysław's letter, the answer to my earlier letter where I was complaining a lot, much to his despair. What an affliction it is to cause sorrow to those to whom one would like to give the whole world!"

Six weeks later, her health is "slowly improving. I feel a little stronger, strong enough to go for long walks on foot; I've been coughing less . . . since mid-October my fever, chills and sweating are gone completely, and I am beginning to look better." There remains, though, an ominous "pain in my side." She is full of hope "that in these few months I have left here my condition is going to improve significantly; otherwise, my disappointment would ruin whatever joy I could feel from the fact that my exile here will be over soon."

The "exile" reaches a climax of loneliness at Christmas—a holiday which, according to Bronisława, the French have no feeling for at all. "Here in Nice," she tells her friend indignantly, "there is no custom of breaking the wafer with the members of your family—the families don't even get together on Christmas eve. There are fewer holidays here than in Poland, and even those that are observed lack the magic and solemnity of ours. . . . On Christmas day everybody here works—women do the laundry just like on any other weekday. It's so much better in our poor Poland: more religion, more morality. . . . May God make this the first and last Christmas away from my family!"

Together, Bronisława and Zosia observed all the rituals of a Polish Christmas: fasting on Christmas eve, then feasting on a meatless supper at a restaurant, then attending the Christmas evening novena at the local Catholic church. "How empty and silent it seemed," she writes Eleonora, "compared to all the previous years! We missed the excited buzz of children waiting to see the Christmas tree; we missed the presence and embrace of everyone dear to us. Zosia set the table with a white tablecloth; she lit the candles, then she put the apples, cookies and the wafer sent to us from Warsaw on the table. At the time when our family in Poland was sitting down to Christmas supper, Zosia and I broke our wafer with tears in our eyes."

Not long after the Christmas letter, there was a "new disaster," followed by a gradual recovery. "I really don't know where all this strength is coming from. Sometimes I even think that I'll never die. . . . And yet, if it weren't for my husband and children, sometimes I feel that I would be glad to finally leave this world." Władisław is now suggesting that she try another resort in the spring. "I wouldn't dare to oppose his will," she writes, "but . . . three more months of this exile!"

Yet Bronisława does "dare" to oppose her husband's will, or at least to change his mind. And in May or June she leaves Nice for home. "Chałubiński [the Polish doctor] agrees with my doctor here that only time can bring me any improvement. They sent me here last year not knowing what to do, and now they see the South hasn't helped me, so they're sending me back home."

Bronisława confides that her joy at returning home is mixed with sorrow. She looks forward to "walks to the citadel" with Eleonora, "just like in the good old days when life was filled with hard work, but was free from these awful sorrows that now bend our shoulders." But she would be happier "if I were going home healthy or at least on the way to improving; . . . is there a greater misfortune than being a constant cause of pain to the people for whom one would give one's own life with joy? . . . And it looks as though that will be my destiny from now on, until the end. God wanted to give me this cross to carry, so let His will be respected. . . . I shouldn't be writing . . . in this sad tone, but I can't help feeling depressed and sad." She ends her lament with a plea to her friend: "Please, don't take this to heart . . . for these moments of despair come and go, at God's will. And don't mention this letter to Władysław—he has had enough sorrows as it is!"

As though the burden of Bronisława's tuberculosis weren't enough, back in Warsaw, in 1873, another misfortune was rocking the Skłodowski family: Władysław had been dismissed from his job as assistant director of the Nowolipki gymnasium. This demotion meant a loss of status and income, and of living quarters, just at a time when Bronisława's rest cure was taxing the family budget. As a result, Władysław had no choice but to turn the family's new quarters into a boarding school.

Life in the Skłodowski family would never be the same after that. "Up until that year, we were a relatively close-knit family, a 'normal' family," Józef remembers. "But when, for financial reasons, our father was forced to open his boarding school . . . it became an integral part of our home. . . . When I think about that time, the impression I have is of some kind of beehive where the noise and commotion never ended. When we [the Skłodowski children] returned from school each day, we ate lunch [in Poland, around 2 or 3 P.M.] all together—about twenty people—and then we would all sit down to study. Every corner of our apartment was then filled with students— not only those who lived with us, but also those who came just to study. First, there were supplementary lessons, and tutoring, then we would do our homework. There were several boys in each room; some were studying quietly, some were humming their lessons to themselves, and some . . . were so loud in their practice that they had to be constantly reminded to lower their voices." Inevitably, there were also "talks and disputes, jokes and sometimes even punches," all of which ceased instantly when the forceful presence of Władysław Skłodowski was felt in the room.

Unfortunately, the boarders did not put the Skłodowskis' money worries entirely to rest. In Nice, Bronisława prayed that "God would grant us enough students who can pay us well this year so we will be able to make up the enormous expenses my illness has been causing." Furthermore, it seems likely, though there is no proof, that the boarding school was the cause of the next, unexpected, tragic event in the life of the family: the death from typhus of the oldest child, Bronisława's beloved companion and nurse, Zosia.

Typhus, in the epidemic form which killed Zosia, was brought to western Russia and Poland by the armies of Napoleon in the early nineteenth century, and took hold there as almost nowhere else. There were several typhus epidemics in Poland in the nineteenth century, including the one that struck the Skłodowski household in 1874. And while everything about the Skłodowskis suggests that they were fastidious in personal hygiene, typhus in general is a disease associated with "filth, overcrowding, famine and poverty." The organism which causes it lives in the blood of mammals (rats, mice, humans) and is usually transferred by lice. It seems quite possible that the crowded conditions of the boarding school brought typhus with them.

Both Zosia and Bronia contracted the disease in January of 1874. Bronia recovered. Zosia, perhaps weakened by a previous illness, died. Józef, who was closest in age to the fourteen-year old Zosia, was devastated. Fifty years later, he wrote that "I still can't think about her without sorrow. January 31st has been since her death the first painful anniversary in my calendar." He remembers her in the last year of her life as "tall, with thick ash-blond hair, gray, dreamy eyes and the large feet and hands of an adolescent." She would often amuse her younger siblings with stories and riddles. "Sometimes she would tell us fantastic tales that lasted for hours," Józef remembers.

Zosia was her mother's pride and joy, as the letters to Eleonora attest. As the oldest child, she was the natural choice to travel with and nurse her mother. But she also seems to have had some health problems which could benefit from the air and waters. Writing from Hall, her mother reports that Zosia "is looking great today" as a result of the fresh air and the waters. And in Nice, the sea bathing is thought to be good for Zosia, replacing her sulfur baths at home.

Whatever Zosia's health problems, they didn't prevent her from taking good care of her mother. "My dear Zosia," Bronisława writes from Nice, "has been giving me so much joy here! I had never imagined that she could bring me so much support and entertainment. She pampers me constantly, comforts me in my sad moments, and even manages to bring a smile to her poor mother's face once in a while." What brought Bronisława the greatest joy of all, however, was Zosia's school performance. In the fall, Zosia begins at the French school and is "very successful." "She wants to be first in her class so much, and she has been so far." Bronisława Skłodowska had none of the modern parent's reluctance to express love conditionally. She let her children know that if they did well in school, she would love them the more for it. Writing to her son Józef on his birthday, she reminds him to "always be good and helpful to your friends, that's your duty. But don't let them beat you in your studies—I would be very ashamed if my son were at the bottom of his class." And when her nephew, Józef Boguski (who would later become an important Polish chemist) is granted a large stipend, she sees it as God's reward to his father Henryk "for his kindness to others."

The happiest passages by far in Bronisława's letters to her friend concern Zosia's triumphs at school. Fortunately, she writes, the head of the school in Nice "has enrolled many ambitious girls this year whose parents expect them to get a solid education," so that Zosia can profit not only from the French but from history, geography, and arithmetic. Zosia herself demonstrates her exquisite penmanship in a letter to Eleonora. She has the feeling, the eleven-year-old Zosia tells her godmother, that her French is now even more fluent than her German. And then, demonstrating her high standards, she laments that she is learning French with the flawed Nice accent.

By November it is clear that Zosia is the best in her class by far, which, as her exacting mother notes, is quite an accomplishment since "she has to do it in French." Indeed, her friends at the school are relieved that Zosia will be leaving before the end of the year, since otherwise she would walk away with all the prizes, and most certainly would be crowned with the laurel wreath awarded to the best student. "I told Zosia that we could stay here longer," her mother writes, "so that she wouldn't lose all the prizes, but she won't hear of it."

Bronisława is pleased with Zosia's spiritual development as well. Preparations for the first communion, she reports, "are having a strong impact on Zosia. I can tell that she is working on her character, and she wants to get closer to God—in large part because we have found a good confessor." Good teaching, religious and secular, is Bronisława's *sine qua non*. Thinking about, planning the future of her children is her obsession.

In Nice, she worries that the inevitable supplementary lessons are irregular because of her illness. "Some things get explained and some are forgotten." Next year, she vows, she will place Zosia in some institute where her knowledge can be better "organized and directed." But how will she find such a place? She asks Eleonora to look around for a good place for Zosia when she returns. Her "only dream," she writes, "is to raise my children well and secure their future."

Never did this mother suspect, in even her gloomiest moments, that one of the children she lived for would die before her. It was, all the children concur, a cruel, perhaps fatal blow. "Our sister's death," Helena recalls, "literally crushed our mother; she could never accept the loss of her oldest child." Maria, too, wrote later that her mother died at forty-two, "cruelly struck by the loss of her daughter and worn away by a grave illness." Józef believed that Zosia's death was "the final blow that killed" his mother. "She had to be almost physically forced to stay home [because she was too ill to go out] on the day of the funeral."

They buried the fourteen-year-old Zosia in the family plot at Powązki cemetery. A last poem was carved on the stone in memory of "our beloved daughter."

> We are lonely here, crying for you
> You, our consolation, pride and adornment;
> And we are strengthened in the hope
> That we will meet again at the feet of our Lord.

Bronisława Skłodowska stayed alive for two years and three months after Zosia died. The family had at least one more summer holiday together in the forested countryside of Gdynska Colony, near Gdańsk. "Cuckoos call all around us," Władysław wrote Józef, who was vacationing elsewhere, "other birds twitter and sing all the time; besides that—silence and the strong, nice smell of resin in the air. After the dust and noise of Warsaw, this is simply delightful." Then he adds, wistfully, "it would be much better if your mother's health improved a little; so far there are no significant changes in her condition."

Yet another attempt at a rest cure seems to have been undertaken in Salzbrunn, in Silesia, in the summer of 1876. But this, too, failed. A friend who saw Władysław at the time reported that "he brought very discouraging news about his wife. He said that her stay in Salzbrunn was of very little benefit. She . . . is scheduled to return to Warsaw in a few weeks. He appears very well himself, but deep sadness pervades every one of his penetrating looks."

On May 8, 1878, Bronisława Skłodowska called her children into her bedroom at the family apartment in Warsaw. "We stood around her bed," Helena remembers, "and she, looking at us with sadness, made a sign of the cross above our heads and said: 'I love you all.' " The next day, she died.

At the foot of the large family tomb, a white marble slab bearing a matter-of-fact inscription was added: "Bronisława Skłodowska, née Boguska, director of a private school, a model daughter, mother, and citizen. Her life, full of sacrifice and merit, ended prematurely on May 9, 1878."

The inscription, so different from the poem on Zosia's grave, with its emotion and hope of an afterlife, must have been the work of the rationalist Władysław. His feelings were expressed elsewhere. In a poem, written ten years later, he described his wife as

> *An angel, whose celestial light brightened my house*
> *And chased every shadow off my forehead.*
> *When she left, my whole world turned into a cemetery.*

Chapter Two

A DOUBLE LIFE

SCHOOL AND HOME were intertwined in the childhood of Maria Skłodowska. Even before she started classes, she lived in the schoolhouse, where the older boys knew her as the teacher's child. Then, when she went off to first grade, she walked across town to the Freta Street school in the building where she was born and where her mother had been headmistress. Most of the teachers would have known Bronisława Skłodowska, and felt a special sympathy for the little girl whose mother was now so ill with tuberculosis. Then, when her parents decided to enroll Maria, along with her sister Helena, in another private school a little closer to home for the third grade, school came home for Maria in the person of a math and history teacher there named Antonina Tupalska, who moved in with the Skłodowski family to take over some of the tasks of the ailing Bronisława. "Tupcia," as the girls nicknamed her, seems to have been both severe and a little ridiculous—hardly a replacement for their mother. But every morning, when Maria and Helena set out from Nowolipki Street for school, they walked there alongside the dour Miss Tupalska.

Many mornings during the long Polish winters, the teacher and small girls, aged nine and ten, bundled up and left for school in the dark, heading south along narrow streets to the broad, gaslit Leszno Street, turning east past the imposing new Reform Church, with its lacework neo-Gothic steeple, and then south again through a busy square before turning onto paths that meandered among the statuary and frozen fountains of the Saxon Gardens. In summer, the French-style gardens were filled with promenaders enjoying the paths shaded by grand chestnut trees, the patterned flower beds, and the social commerce in what Baedeker called "one of the finest parks in Europe." In midwinter, the gardens were the quickest route to the door-step of a remarkable institution: the private school of Madame Jadwiga Sikorska.

It must have provided Bronisława Skłodowska some consolation, in the last year of her life, to know that her two youngest daughters were under the wing of Jadwiga Sikorska. She worried most, as she grew increasingly ill, about how her children would get a decent Polish education before they were forced, for practical reasons, to enroll in the government-run gymnasium. The government schools, as the Skłodowskis knew firsthand, were an educational travesty. But only they could award the diplomas her children would need in the world. She worried about Józef. "I get so anxious," she wrote Eleonora from the south of France, "when I realize that he will be ready for gymnasium so soon! I would like so much to be able to teach him at home for at least another year, but it seems very unlikely." And she worried about Józef's younger sisters: "All of my girls will be needing a solid education soon," she lamented, "and I don't think I will be able to teach the children myself even a few subjects . . . what trouble it is to educate children these days!"

Jadwiga Sikorska, a broad-bosomed, round-faced woman with kind eyes behind her black-rimmed pince-nez, was equal to the task. When necessary, she could challenge the Russian authorities, pointing out all the ways her girls' education was far superior to what they required. But most of the time she was engaged, along with everyone else in her school, in a complicated cover-up, a two-tier educational program which taught one thing and professed, on crucial inspection days, to teach another. It was, Jadwiga Sikorska wrote in her diary, "a hard life, a double life. We had to do our best to protect and cultivate all that was dear and sacred to us, and at the same time we had to be able to satisfy the authorities in order to be allowed to keep working. I don't think I ever lied to the authorities in the presence of my students, but they were all used to lying anyway, living in a constant state of conspiracy."

The conspiracy took the form of a double schedule: "one for the authorities, with all the required subjects," Sikorska explains, "and the real one for the students, with the maximum hours of Polish language, history and geography. All the students knew . . . that home economics on the official schedule meant Polish history in real life . . . and that the phrase 'German language' should be read sometimes as 'Botany,' and so on."

Drawing up the double schedule was logistically complicated and time-consuming, "almost like solving a puzzle." For strategic reasons Sikorska always sent the schedule in to the authorities late, provoking reprimands. "The delay was helpful," she explains, "because from the day the schedule was finally confirmed, we had to be ready for the inspections." From that moment on, "the tension rose and we were on constant alert."

"Something as small as a sudden animation in the hallway," a teacher remembers, "or a bell rung in the middle of a class would force everyone to change the language of the lecture, and often the subject of it as well . . . All the participants had to collaborate—starting with the principal and ending with the domestic servants."

Teachers debated from time to time whether the strain of the double life wasn't too much for young children. "The pedagogue," as one teacher put it, "questioned the Pole, but the Pole would always win, for in times of servitude the first duty of a teacher is to prepare the children to fight for their nationhood."

Sometimes, however, the pressure overwhelmed the young students. Once, during an examination in Russian geography, a young girl fainted while answering geography questions up by the map. Another time, when an inspector named Krylow asked the girls to pray, they were too frightened to respond, since they knew their prayer only in Polish. "Only when I said calmly: 'Please, pray girls,' did they dare to do it," Sikorska remembers. "Krylow stood there somber like Jupiter, then he asked me why I allowed the prayer to be said in Polish. I answered that the religion class was always taught in Polish, and the prayer belonged in that domain. He didn't say anything to that."

Inspector Krylow was generally agreed to be "a real brute." Fortunately for Maria Skłodowska, her year at the Sikorska school coincided with the reign of the relatively benign inspector Mikolaj Hornberg, a man who was said to be fond of expensive bribes, particularly Persian carpets, but who was generally "quiet" and "harmless" as long as his job was safe. He even helped Sikorska out once, warning that the superintendent was coming the next day and that the children should leave their Polish books at home.

Nonetheless, Maria felt the strain of this "abnormal" situation keenly. Because she was the brightest and best at speaking Russian, as well as "the youngest and smallest in the class," Maria was often called upon to recite on the dreaded day when the Russian inspector came to visit. "This was a great trial to me, because of my timidity; I wanted always to run away and hide." "Timidity" was the word Marie Curie chose in the final draft of her *Autobiographical Notes.* But an earlier draft suggests that she was enraged as well by the official intrusion. In that version she wrote that she "wanted always to raise my little arms to shut the people away from me, and sometimes, I must confess, I wanted to raise them as a cat its paws, to scratch! . . ."

"With my mind's eye," Maria's sister Helena writes, "I can still see little Maniusia [Maria], a plump girl with fair, curly hair bound up with a black velvet ribbon, wearing her apron trimmed with flounces; her eyes were pale gray, and they looked at the world with a smile, kindness and unusual seriousness. Although the youngest, she influenced her classmates with her unusual intelligence, abilities and great memory. . . . All of her friends respected her and often asked her for help in math and other difficult subjects."

Although Helena was a year older, she shared a third-grade class with her precocious sister. Despite Helena's insistence that she and Maria "loved each other deeply," it mustn't have been easy to have a younger sister who was always first in their class. Years later, recalling one of Maria's intellectual feats, a hint of envy still came through. Maria had forgotten to memorize a long passage in German from Schiller's "Der Ring des Polykrates" at home. Since German was her third class of the day, she used the two ten-minute breaks between classes to do it. "I had to spend several hours to do the same thing!" Helena protested. With Maria, she notes, "everything was always 'so easy, so beautiful, so interesting!' "

There is a great temptation to invent, after the fact, childhood anecdotes which presage a brilliant career. But these stories of Maria's remarkable memory are specific and detailed enough to be convincing. Maria herself, who was not given to exaggeration, once wrote her sister about a feat of memory at a party when she was in her late teens or early twenties. One of the guests had delivered a poem she admired, and she asked for a copy. He, challenging and perhaps a little flirtatious, responded that since she was known to have such a great memory, he would read it one more time and then she could reproduce it herself. " 'I'll try,' said Maria, 'but I don't know if I can do it.' " After hearing the poem a second time, she went into another room to try to write it out. In a half hour she returned and read the poem aloud, to the astonishment of the guests, without a single error.

Józef insists that Maria's abilities were not much remarked upon in the very bright Skłodowski family. "Since none of us had trouble learning and obtaining good grades," he notes, "Maria's progress was considered a natural thing." Still, the earliest family story about Maria suggests that she was even brighter than her older siblings. Maria, the story goes, was looking on one day as her sister Bronia struggled with a long sentence during her reading lesson. Maria, who was two years younger, suddenly read the sentence with ease, surprising her parents, who didn't know she could read at all. The family reaction caused complicated feelings in the youngest Skłodowska. "Seeing our parents' astonished faces and the expression of shame in Bronia's eyes, [Maria] burst into tears, sobbing 'I didn't know I wasn't supposed to do that . . . but it was so easy!' "

Cumulatively, the stories about young Maria Skłodowska begin to form a picture of a child of strong and quickly aroused emotions. Later, when she was old enough for self-observation, she wrote, "I feel everything very violently, with a physical violence." Relatively minor events, like the inspector's visit, or her parents' reaction to her surprising abilities, stirred up storms of emotion. That the reservoir of emotion was so readily available, and so quickly tapped, may have had to do with the far graver events which stalked her childhood: since age five, she had lived with the frightening reality of her mother's illness, and the ache of her absence. At age nine, she had lost her oldest sister to typhus. And in the spring of her year at Madame Sikorska's school, her mother died too.

The death of a parent, according to psychologists who have worked with surviving children, is often too painful and too frightening for a child to accept. Unlike adults, who gradually grow to live with the fact of the loved one's absence, children as young as Maria was may not have the necessary psychic tools to truly mourn. And while they acknowledge the death on one level, at the same time they may cling to secret expectations of the parent's return. They are depressed, but they fail to link their sadness with the loss. And when they do grieve, they have a "short sadness span" because they fear that the painful feelings will increase to an intolerable intensity. Maria, who wept long and uncontrollably, seems to have allowed painful feelings to surface more than many children. But there are hints that she "mourned at a distance," in the phrase of one psychologist, throughout her girlhood, experiencing generalized feelings of depression and emotional volatility.

Maria's dark moods after her mother's death would have been noticed by Jadwiga Sikorska, whose empathy with her students sometimes led her to cry herself after the inspector visited. Undoubtedly it was Maria's emotional state at the end of that year which led Sikorska to suggest to Władysław that he wait a year before enrolling her in fourth grade. Maria was, after all, a year younger than her classmates. Władysław, however, chose not to follow the headmistress's advice. Indeed, he went to the opposite extreme and removed Maria from the nurturing atmosphere of Sikorska's school to the hostile environment of a government-run gymnasium.

No one knew better than Władysław Skłodowski just how bad a Russian-dominated gymnasium could be. His son Józef, who attended the gymnasium where Władysław taught, is grimly amusing on the subject. There were a few good teachers (including his father), particularly in math and science, where it was easier to maintain one's integrity. But "they were replaced more and more by the newcomers, chosen according to their political correctness and not their teaching abilities." Even the "privileged subjects" (Russian subjects for which teachers were paid higher salaries) were taught badly: Russian history was taught "one-sidedly" from a "notorious" textbook which was "the object of contempt and jokes." Polish history, of course, was not taught at all, except as part of the triumphal Russian past. One had to "suppress shame and outrage" while reciting that the Polish King Jagiello won the battle of Grunwald (a great Polish victory) commanding Russian troops. The classics teacher knew Latin and Greek well but couldn't keep order in his classroom. Another teacher was "unstable and unpredictable." And a third, who was fond of pronouncing that "only God deserves an A and the B is reserved for me," had to be retired to the country because he turned out to be a "sexual degenerate." The French teacher was an alcoholic; another, just out of university, was "still learning the languages himself" as he taught them.

Worse than the poor teaching, and worse than the distortion of Polish history, was the prohibition against speaking the Polish language. It was a prohibition carried to absurd lengths: even the teaching of Polish as a language had to be carried out in Russian. And whereas children in private schools were allowed to speak Polish among themselves, in the government-run gymnasia even private conversations between classes were supposed to be conducted in Russian.

In some schools, this rule seems to have been regularly broken. "All that Russification," Józef writes, "was basically a formality . . . the rule that required [students] to speak Russian even between classes was never taken seriously—not only by the numerous Jewish students, but by Poles and even some Russian boys. The teachers spoke Polish between classes, avoiding only being heard by the school director or the inspector, direct representatives of Russian law." But other schools were stricter than Józef's. Maria remembered an atmosphere at her gymnasium in which children were "constantly held in suspicion and spied upon," and in which they "knew that a single conversation in Polish, or an imprudent word, might seriously harm, not only themselves, but also their families."

The battle over language was deeply emotional on both sides. By the latter nineteenth century, as historian Norman Davies explains, Russians had come to view their language as "the touchstone of Nationality" and the principle of Russian nationality had become "as intense and as exclusive as its Polish counterpart." Russian, its advocates argued, was superior to other languages. "The Russian language," wrote Bulgarin, "which . . . holds first place in melodiousness and in the richness and ease of word construction, is the language of poetry and literature in all the countries of the globe."

The Polish language, however, had been "an essential touchstone of Polish nationality" for much longer. "In strict contrast to the English-speaking world, where Irish, Scots, Australian, or American nationalisms have less to do with language, families who ceased to speak Polish, ceased to be regarded as Poles." As a result, nothing in the Russian program "riled so much as the compulsory use of the Russian language."

In the Skłodowski family, the Polish language was viewed as a sacred trust. Władysław, writing to fourteen-year-old Józef during the boy's summer vacation, turns serious on the subject of Józef's Polish. "In your letter you made one mistake which violates the purity of our language: you wrote 'in the first time'—that's a Russianism. In Polish it's 'for the first time.' Please, try to do your best to use our language correctly; our language should mean more to us than to any other nation. It is like a precious gem that we have retained from the modest heritage of our ancestors."

It was this forced use of the Russian language in the government schools which led the Polish intelligentsia, including the Skłodowskis, to postpone gymnasium as long as possible. And yet, in the fall of 1878, Władysław Skłodowski decided to enroll Maria at the girls' Gymnasium Number Three in downtown Warsaw. It may be that he was too overwhelmed with his duties as single parent and teacher to contemplate alternatives for his youngest child. But given the family's predilections, it seems likely that he believed that a new challenge was the best consolation, and that the gymnasium, for all its weaknesses, might provide it. It may also be that Maria, eager to follow in the footsteps of Józef and Bronia, pushed him toward the decision. One mechanism often invoked by the grieving child is to strongly idealize and identify with the lost loved one; Maria's push forward may have been impelled by her mother's ghost.

And so, in the fall of 1878, just a few months after the death of her mother, the youngest Skłodowska set out for Gymnasium Number Three. It must have been lonely at her new school at first: even though she repeated third grade, she was still younger than her classmates. And her sister Helena, her classmate and constant companion the year before, had stayed behind at Madame Sikorska's. Fortunately, Gymnasium Number Three, although stricter than her brother's school, had better teachers. A German-speaking school before Russification, it benefited from "a traditional [German] respect for learning." Unlike Józef's school, Maria's gymnasium had a good physics teacher and, even, an excellent teacher of Russian literature, as well as a very demanding teacher of German.

Nevertheless, Marie Curie, looking back decades later on her gymnasium years, speaks darkly of them. The teachers were "hostile to the Polish nation" and "treated their pupils as enemies." What was taught was "of questionable value, and the moral atmosphere was altogether unbearable." In such an atmosphere, children "lost all joy of life, and precocious feelings of distrust and indignation weighed upon their childhood." Marie's grim memories of these years, so different from Józef's farcical rendition of a similarly oppressive situation, were surely colored by her own sadness. She herself links the personal and the political when she writes of "this period of my early youth, darkened . . . by mourning and the sorrow of oppression."

Writing forty years after the fact, Marie Curie has forgotten or overlooked more positive feelings she expressed about school at the time. "In spite of everything," Maria wrote her friend Kazia Przyborowska during her thirteenth summer, "I like school. Perhaps you will make fun of me, but nevertheless I must tell you that I like it, and even that I love it. I can realize that now. Don't go imagining that I miss it! Oh no; not at all. But the two years I have left to spend there don't seem as dreadful, as painful and long as they once did. . . ."

Kazia Przyborowska, Maria's "chosen sister," helped to make school bearable. The daughter of the librarian to Count Zamoyski, scion of an important Polish magnate family, Kazia lived with her parents in the count's residence, the Blue Palace, a repository of the art and elegance of Poland before the fall. Every morning, Maria walked to school by way of the palace, a grand, sprawling neoclassical monolith along the edge of the Saxon Gardens. There she rendezvoused with Kazia, and the two cut through the gardens, passed under the colonnade connecting the buildings of the Saxon Palace, and came out onto the cobblestones of the vast Saxon Square.

Nowhere in Warsaw was the Russian military presence more palpable than in Saxon Square. The Saxon Palace, once a royal residence, was now a Russian military headquarters; low-lying buildings surrounding the square were given over to barracks. Sometimes there would have been military reviews in progress when Maria and Kazia passed by. And always towering over the buildings and the people coming and going in the square was the graceless bronze obelisk, surrounded by horrific two-headed eagles, erected by the Tzar after the November uprising.

The obelisk celebrated the bravery of those Poles who remained faithful to the Tzar during the uprising. To Poles, of course, these "brave" men were traitors, and the monument was a provocation. Indeed, for some time after the January Uprising a sentinel protected the obelisk from vandals day and night. Kazia and Maria, for their part, made a point of spitting on the obelisk every time they passed by.

At the edge of Saxon Square, the girls emerged onto Krakowskie Przedmiescie, the broad main street of Warsaw, a place visually dominated by churches and palaces, but alive, in between the edifices, with coffeehouses, stores, and shoppers. Every kind of horse-drawn conveyance rattled along Krakowskie Przedmiescie—water-barrel wagons pulled by bony country nags mixed with shiny closed carriages led by well-groomed teams driven by coachmen in livery. In the middle of the street, a horse-drawn trolley glided north and south on steel tracks, picking up passengers at kiosks along the route.

Maria and Kazia had to cross the broad, busy street to arrive at their school, which was housed in the former convent of the adjacent Church of the Visitation, a seventeenth-century edifice with a rococo facade of pillars stacked on pillars. On the ground floor of the rectangular convent building, Mr. B. Wosiński's shop sold watches from Geneva. Upstairs, schoolgirls moved from class to class of Gymnasium Number Three.

One positive side effect of the Russian oppression was that it provided girls like Maria an outlet to express anger and indignation that would otherwise violate the social rules for young ladies of the era. Even during school, under the close watch of the authorities, Maria and Kazia found ways to show their defiance. In 1881, after Tzar Alexander II was killed by a terrorist bomb in St. Petersburg, Maria and Kazia were discovered by a teacher dancing in an empty classroom. In general, according to Helena, Maria's "independence was too well-developed" for some of her teachers. "She always had her own opinion, which she knew how to defend." The little girl who wanted to scratch like a cat had now learned to fight back with her wit instead. This seems to have been especially annoying to Mademoiselle Mayer, the diminutive home economics teacher, who undertook several attempts at reform. She particularly objected to Maria's very curly and unruly hair, which she tried to subdue into smooth braids. Maria's mildly superior air on such occasions aggravated her; once, she forbade Maria to "look down" on her, and Maria, who was a head taller than her teacher, replied that "the fact is I can't do anything else!"

After school, Maria and Kazia often returned to the warm atmosphere of Kazia's family apartments at the Blue Palace, which provided a respite for Maria from the noisy boarding school which was home, and from disliked housekeepers, hired by her father to help him manage without a wife. Five years after she graduated, working at a lonely governess post, Maria fondly remembered the "lemonade and chocolate ices" provided by Kazia's mother during afternoons spent at the Blue Palace.

Maria Skłodowska graduated from Gymnasium Number Three in 1883. She had reason to feel triumphant: like her brother Józef and sister Bronia before her, she finished first in her class and was awarded the gold medal. Yet graduation was a troubling event as well: it meant that formal schooling might well be over forever. Józef could, and did, proceed directly from gymnasium to medical school at Warsaw University. But Warsaw University didn't admit women. For the sisters Skłodowska, there were two career options: they could study abroad, in Paris or St. Petersburg, or they could teach, as their mother had before them, in private schools. What's more, it was not clear that Władysław Skłodowski, poorly paid and impoverished by his bad investment in his brother-in-law's business, would ever be able to afford to send any of the girls abroad.

There was of course a third option: marriage. According to their brother Józef, the Skłodowska sisters didn't "fit the role of a 'young marriageable girl,' so typical for that time." One look at Maria's photo, taken at the time of graduation, affirms this. Her face is still round and pudgy, but her eyes look out at us defiantly, even angrily, with the forcefulness which must have rattled Mademoiselle Mayer. All his sisters, Józef noted, "dreamed of higher education and of an independent career," and such dreams meant postponing marriage or forgoing it altogether. Most certainly, the sisters had no intention of following in the footsteps of the numerous aunts in the family, including Aunt Lucia, who were chained to boorish, inferior husbands.

Nonetheless, since youth can have it both ways, there was a good deal of talk about boys, matches, and weddings among the sisters as they entered their teens. For a time, Maria and Helena shared a crush on one of the exceptional boarders on Nowolipki Street, a young man named Witold Romocki who lived with the Skłodowskis for six years and was allowed to sit in on the family's Saturday literary readings. According to Helena, he so "distinguished himself with elegance and good manners" that both she and Maria "fell in love with him." Their love was "often watered with tears of jealousy" so intense that Helena contemplated writing a novel about it, to be entitled *Sisters—Rivals*.

Maria was only fifteen when she finished gymnasium, still younger than her class and hardly old enough to marry. But it was not too early, in her circle, to begin thinking about a match. Within five years, several of Maria's contemporaries would marry. And the possibility of a good match may have contributed to the surprising conclusion Władysław Skłodowski came to that spring: Maria, it was agreed, should abandon all intellectual pursuits and spend a year in the country. Maria's father may have been concerned as well about her emotional state. There are hints that depression still persisted five years after her mother's death. In her *Autobiographical Notes,* Marie Curie writes that "the fatigue of growth and study compelled me to take almost a year's rest in the country." In her lexicon, however, fatigue can mean many things. Later, when she suffered depression, she and others always described it as fatigue or "exhaustion."

Probably for both reasons—to meet and socialize with eligible young men and to recover from fatigue and early sorrows—Maria boarded a train not long after graduation and left Warsaw for an extended visit with her maternal uncles to the south. The "year's rest," an unending round of all-night dances and general hilarity, was about to begin.

POLES in the nineteenth century had a near-mystical faith in the healing powers of the land. "The land," art historian Agnieszka Morawinska notes, "was the one certain thing left. It was a bit of the mother country, all the more important because the mother country in its full political meaning did not exist. The theme of the nation as an orphan, of the nourishing mother earth that sustains its life, and of the soil . . . for which exiles abroad continually yearn occurs again and again in Polish literature and art."

Except for the Carpathian Mountains, which define the southern border, the land the Poles invested with so much symbolic power was a vast, open continuation of the Asian plain. Landscape painters like Maksymilian Gierymski celebrated its simple beauty: fields, groves, sandy plains and roads gutted by carriage tracks, and pale diffused light. Gierymski, whose impression was colored by his participation in the January Uprising, saw in the plains a "picture of smiling melancholy. The landscape of Ophelia."

The melancholy countryside of Mazovia surrounded Maria Skłodowska as she traveled south, first by train and then by horse and wagon along jaw-rattling rutted roads. Around her was the pastoral landscape described by Brandes: "Rich it is, cornfield beyond cornfield, and pleasant, for poplars and birches, willows and lindens shade the roads . . . the flatness is only broken by windmills, trees, and now and then far away by a church or a wood." But she would also have passed through small towns with square wooden synagogues and narrow churches, and through lively market squares where everything from live pigs to flax to balls of whitewash were bought, sold, and bartered. There would have been groups of Jewish traders in long black coats, and peasant women dressed in bright regional costume for the trip to market. Along the country roads, she would have seen evidence of the extreme hardship of peasant life: men and women plowing the fields in their bare feet with or without oxen; peasant villages in which large families lived in low log houses with thatched roofs and earthen floors, clustered around a rough-hewn wooden cross.

Compared with these shaggy peasant dwellings, the manor houses of Uncle Henryk and Uncle Władysław Boguski, where Maria was to spend the first part of her summer, were palaces, "oas[es] of civilization in a land of rustics." Their houses were full of books, and talk, and music: both uncles were talented violinists, and one had been a serious student of art. Yet within the family the two brothers of Bronisława were known as ne'er-do-wells. Uncle Henryk, who had spent four years in Siberia after the uprising, was viewed by Józef Skłodowski as "a typical dilettante, . . . good at everything and nothing in particular; presumptuous and hasty, full of grandiose ideas," a man entirely dependent on the income from the village store run by the "rather simple woman" he married. It was Uncle Henryk who convinced Władysław Skłodowski to invest all his savings in construction of the infamous mill. The other Boguski uncle, Władysław, started out well, marrying a woman with a dowry and buying the estate, Zwola. But he too got caught up in his brother's moneymaking scheme and things ended badly.

The money worries of the Boguski clan, however, don't seem to have dampened the celebratory mood Maria Skłodowska encountered that summer. "Ah how gay life is at Zwola!" she wrote her friend Kazia. "There are always a great many people, and a freedom, equality and independence such as you can hardly imagine."

Probably Maria's cousin Józef Boguski, a student of chemistry who later encouraged her scientific pursuits, was among the crowd of summer guests. But Maria seems to have been more excited about the visit of a well-known dramatic actor of the time, Józef Kotarbiński. "He sang so many songs," she wrote Kazia, "and recited so many verses, concocted so many jokes and picked so many gooseberries for us, that on the day of his departure we made him a great wreath of poppies, wild pinks and cornflowers; and just as the carriage was starting off we flung it at him with shouts of Vivat! Vivat! M. Kotarbinski! He put the wreath on his head immediately, and it seems that afterward he carried it in a suitcase all the way to Warsaw." Also of interest were the two young priests at the local church. "Every Sunday the horses are harnessed for the trip in to Mass, and afterward we pay a visit to the vicarage. The two priests are very clever and very witty, and we get enormous amusement from their company." In Poland, an independent young skeptic like Maria could look to clerics for intellectual, and undoubtedly political, stimulation.

The "freedom, equality, and independence" Maria refers to was not just political, however. It was also, as her spirited, freewheeling letter to Kazia attests, a freedom from the seriousness of her life in Warsaw. "I can't believe geometry or algebra ever existed. I have completely forgotten them," she writes, ". . . aside from an hour's French lesson with a little boy I don't do a thing, positively not a thing —for I have even abandoned the piece of embroidery that I had started . . . I have no schedule. I get up sometimes at ten o'clock, sometimes at four or five (morning, not evening!). I read no serious books, only harmless and absurd little novels. . . . Thus, in spite of the diploma conferring on me the dignity and maturity of a person who has finished her studies, I feel incredibly stupid. Sometimes I laugh all by myself, and I contemplate my state of total stupidity with genuine satisfaction."

One of Maria's Skłodowska's consistent virtues was her inability to dissemble. Later, she would learn to hide her emotion behind an impersonal mask. But in the letters of the young Maria to her friends and family, all the genuine feelings of the moment come out: deep sadness, outrage, and pleasure are simply, and wonderfully, there in every word—even a century after they were written, and a half-century after they were translated into another language. In the best Polish tradition, the country seems to have truly banished melancholy. There were not to be many times as happy as this.

"We swing a lot," Maria wrote her friend, "swinging ourselves hard and high; we bathe, we go fishing with torches for shrimps. . . . We go out in a band to walk in the woods, we roll hoops, we play battledore and shuttlecock (at which I am very bad!), cross-tag, the game of Goose, and many equally childish things." Accompanying her, as she rollicked about, was the family dog Lancet, a rather large, short-haired creature, given to fits of barking.

The Polish mother earth herself contributed to Maria's improved spirits. "There have been so many wild strawberries here," she writes Kazia, "that one could buy a really sufficient amount for a few *groszy* —and by that I mean a big plateful heaped high. Alas, the season is over! . . . But I am afraid that when I get back my appetite will be unlimited and my voracity alarming."

But Maria was not to return for some time. For the winter months, she traveled further south to the home of her paternal uncle Zdzisław Skłodowski, near Skalbmierz in the foothills of the Carpathian Mountains. Maria had visited Skalbmierz many times before, and was on friendly terms with her cousins there. Her father, in one of his occasional verses, described the home of his brother Zdzisław and wife Maria as the family epicenter. "Your home," he wrote Zdzisław, "is the heart of our family/ With the family banner fluttering on your roof/ Its sons and daughters come there from all over the world/ The poor adore it/ the kind praise it/ its gates are watched with reverence."

Uncle Zdzisław had obtained a law degree in St. Petersburg before rushing home to participate in the January Uprising as a lieutenant of the cavalry. Afterward, forced into exile in France, he obtained a doctorate in law from the University of Toulouse, and on his return to Poland was named adjunct professor of law at Warsaw University. According to Józef, he prepared one brilliant lecture. "Unfortunately, it was one of very few prepared lectures." He left the university under a cloud, and practiced small-town law for ten years before becoming Skalbmierz public notary, a job which left him with plenty of time for his life's work: translating Shakespeare into Polish verse. A lover of cards and women, he sometimes forgot to pay his debts, but was generous to a fault when in the money. "During his life," Józef wrote, "he was close to having a fortune, but he could never keep it," and he died, like the uncles on the Boguski side of the family, in poverty.

Uncle Zdzisław's wife, Maria Rogowska, was even more unusual than he—a liberated woman before her time. A tall, beautiful blonde, Aunt Maria didn't care for child care and cooking, and so assigned those duties to an "aunt" (not really a relative) so that she could spend her time managing the family estates. She started a lace-making school and a furniture factory near the couple's home, Kielce, and flaunted convention along the way by scorning dresses and smoking cigarettes. "She didn't like dancing and other 'feminine' forms of entertainment," Józef recalls, "preferring the company of men."

Maria Skłodowska, about to turn sixteen when she arrived in Skalbmierz, must have been intrigued by both these relatives—the uncle who had studied abroad and the aunt who launched factories (something she herself would do later on). But it was the freedom and beauty of the place which impressed her most.

Skalbmierz, which was on the edge of less repressive Austrian Poland, was even less constrained than Zwola had been. "We could speak Polish in all freedom," Marie Curie wrote in her *Autobiographical Notes,* "and sing patriotic songs without going to prison." It was probably during that winter in Skalbmierz that she got her first real exposure to the Carpathian Mountains, not far to the south. "My first impression of the mountains," she wrote in her *Notes,* "was very vivid, because I had been brought up in the plains. So I enjoyed immensely our life in the Carpathian villages, the view of the pikes [sic], the excursions to the valleys and to the high mountain lakes with picturesque names such as: 'The Eye of the Sea.' "

It was in Skalbmierz too that Maria encountered the *kulig,* the subject of her most ecstatic letters home to Warsaw. The *kulig,* or sleigh party, was a centuries-old Polish tradition in which horse-drawn sleighs of revelers, with torches flaring and sleigh bells jangling, traveled from one manor house to the next. Sometimes they took their hosts by surprise. But at each stop, the partygoers improvised a feast and danced to the music of the small band of musicians who traveled with them. The costumes, and the dances, were a celebration of Polish custom, at once gay and deeply political. After the defeat of the uprising, dance, "one of the Polish graces," became an expression

of defiance. "In Poland," George Brandes reported in 1885, "the mazurka is . . . a long, difficult, and impassioned national dance . . .
the Russian government has forbidden the dancing of this dance in
the national costume; and the fourth or fifth question the foreigner is
asked in Warsaw is this: 'Have you seen our national dance?' In every
other country it would at least be the thirtieth or fortieth."

Maria's letters glowed with enthusiasm for the *kuligs,* the costumes, and, above all, her handsome and nimble partners. "I have
been to a *kulig,*" she wrote Kazia. "You can't imagine how delightful
it is, especially when the clothes are beautiful and the boys are well
dressed. My costume was very pretty. . . . After this first *kulig* there
was another, at which I had a marvelous time. There were a great
many young men from Cracow, very handsome boys who danced so
well! It is altogether exceptional to find such good dancers."

It was, she told her sister Bronia, the Polish costume which made
the *kulig* so gay. "Ordinary balls, with evening clothes and dresses,
don't inspire the same gusto, the same mad gayety." The boys,
dressed in Cracow style, would have worn blousy pants, usually
striped in red and white, the Polish national colors, tucked into boots;
a loose overblouse, gathered at the waist with an ornamental belt,
sometimes with dangling brass discs that jingled to the dance steps;
and a felt hat with a spray of peacock feathers. Maria and the other
girls would have worn full, brightly printed skirts; and white aprons
bordered in eyelet lace; white blouses; and vests that descended to the
waist, then flared out in a short peplum over their full, petticoated
skirts. The vest was laden with beads and embroidery, in patterns and
colors which varied from one village to the next.

Perhaps Maria and her friends, playing at country customs, embroidered their own gorsets in preparation for the *kuligs.* Maria,
whose unruly hair had bothered her teacher at gymnasium, now delighted in doing up her hair and everyone else's. "I improvised my
own hairstyle," she wrote Bronia, "and I curled all the young girls'
hair for the *kulig,* very prettily, I must say!"

Then it was time to go. "There were various incidents along the
way: we lost and refound the musicians, one of the sleighs tipped
over, etc. . . . When the leader of the dance, Mr. Penot, arrived, he
told me that I had been chosen 'maiden of honor' of the *kulig* and
presented me to my boy of honor, a young man from Crakow, very
handsome and very elegant." The evening vibrated with the three-
quarter time and syncopated beat of the Polish dances: the running
step of the mazurka, legs moving briskly and steadily while the upper
carriage maintains perfect stillness and poise; the faster one, two,
three of the oberek, with a drum or euphonium maintaining the
steady beat while violins sang the sweet, familiar melodies. Maria

danced "an exquisite oberek with figures"—a variation in which she
followed her partner through a series of improvised high kicks and
show-off steps. Maria's competitive spirit persisted in her dancing.
"You should know," she wrote Bronia, "that I now dance the oberek
to perfection. I danced so much that, during the waltzes, I had several
dances reserved in advance. If I happened to go out for a second to
catch my breath, my partners posted themselves in the doorway in
order to watch for me and wait for me."

At eight in the morning, "in broad daylight," the *kulig* ended
with a "white mazurka," one in which the ladies traditionally choose
their partners. "This *kulig*," she told Bronia, "was sheer rapture from
beginning to end . . . perhaps never ever again in my whole life will I
have as much fun." Was there a particular partner who made her feel
"a great longing" afterward for that night of dancing? Perhaps not.
But the idea of marriage came up, as she talked over the wonderful
evening with her aunt. "We have decided with Aunt that, if I should
marry one day, we will have a marriage in the Cracowian style, something like a *kulig* wedding. Of course, this is all in jest—but it is
certain that this would amuse me enormously!"

By spring, it looked as if the idyll might end. But then a reprieve
came from an unexpected source: an old student of Bronisława Skłodowska's offered Maria, and her sister Helena, a final summer of
indolence at her luxurious country estate northeast of Warsaw, Kępa.
Kępa was a small replica of a French château, situated on the watery
alluvial plain near the junction of the Narew and Biebrza Rivers. It
was surrounded by meadows of deepest green grass, cut and sold as
hay to the Russian military for their horses. Its owner, the French-
born Count Ludwik de Fleury, had married into wealthy Polish aristocracy, been widowed, and married a second time to a much
younger woman, the gay countess who had been Bronisława Skłodowska's pupil. The two of them, the aging count, an aesthete and a
gourmet, and his young wife, a talented musician, held court to a
seemingly unending stream of visitors, including the two young and
wide-eyed Skłodowska sisters. "That summer," Helena wrote years
later, "was the best time I remember in my whole life."

For the first time in her year of wandering, Maria, accompanied
by her sister, headed north, first by a train which took them out of
the dirty, noisy city and deposited them halfway to Kępa, in Małkinia. For once they would not have to endure a rough ride in a
public coach. "At the station a splendid carriage drawn by four horses
was waiting for us. We were absolutely impressed! A coachman in a
splendid uniform took us to our destination."

The manor house stood near a grove of oaks and lindens, surrounded by a beautiful garden. "I have never seen so many flowers in

one place," Helena writes, "so well grouped according to color and shape." Just across the meandering river Bierbrza, there was an orchard where "we fought the sparrows for the best cherries." Nearby was a forest "with berries and mushrooms and cool shade."

Inside the manor house, Maria and Helena delighted in space and ease they had never known before. "Our room," Helena remembers, "was clean, sunny, full of flowers." What's more, it was "all ready, prepared by the housekeeper Mrs. Rogowska. It had a large veranda, so thickly covered with vines that it could have served as another room. . . . And when on the colorful tablecloth in the kitchen we saw a pot of coffee with delicious cream, rolls, cookies, fresh butter, honey and jam—our joy became almost unbearable. We hugged each other, feeling happier than ever before."

Several weeks later, Maria wrote Kazia, "I ought to give you an account of our existence here—but as I haven't the courage, I shall only say that it is marvelous . . . there is plenty of water for swimming and boating, which delights me. I am learning to row—I am getting on quite well—and the bathing is ideal. We do everything that comes into our heads, we sleep sometimes at night and sometimes by day, we dance, and we run to such follies that sometimes we deserve to be locked up in an asylum for the insane. . . ."

The "follies" involved not only the septuagenarian host and his young wife and the house guests but also the gardener and the housekeeper, Mrs. Rogowska, "who kept feeding us with all kinds of country delicacies." Maria, according to her sister, was the "principal organizer of the most irresponsible and funny practical jokes."

One target was the twenty-seven-year-old Jan Moniuszko, brother of the hostess, described by Helena as a "young man without big ambitions, but with an enormous appetite." Helena and Maria conspired to dilute, slowly and over time, the quart-sized pot of fresh milk he consumed at dinner. Finally, as the sisters waited impatiently, he noticed the change, and complained to his sister. "This milk is not white anymore; it's kind of grayish, and to be honest, it doesn't taste very good." Madame de Fleury became alarmed, suspecting someone was trying to poison him. But Helena and Maria's giggles gave them away and "we all laughed uncontrollably for a long time."

The amount of time and energy Maria and Helena spent on teasing this particular young man are surely telltale signs of their keen interest in him. And indeed, Helena writes that "each of the three young men" among the guests "chose one of us to be his lady." The sixteen-year-old Maria was chosen by Madame de Fleury's twenty-year-old nephew, Józef Szajbo. And Helena was "chosen" by Madame's darling brother "Janek," the one who seemed to bring out the devil in the Skłodowska sisters.

Another time, the sisters devised a more elaborate practical joke on Janek. They sent him off to the nearby town of Łomza with an impossible list (including "thirty pounds of cinnamon" and a quarter inch of ribbon a foot wide), and proceeded to "cure his obsessive neatness" by undoing the "perfect order" of his room. "Helped by our devoted friend, the gardener," Helena writes, "we hung all the furniture, including the bed and wash basin, on huge nails driven into the ceiling. Even the table was hanging up there, all four legs dangling in the air. We put lots of little objects on it. The effect was reinforced by poison ivy bouquets placed in the hanging shoes. . . . The always perfectly clean room looked quite shocking."

Janek returned exhausted, ate a big lunch, and repaired to his room for a nap, "watched secretly by those who knew about the plot. He opened his door, not without some trouble because of the suitcase hanging behind it, looked around, spit with rage, and shouted: 'What the hell?' He forgot about his nap and threw all the things out the window that belonged to his roommate, thinking he was the traitor." For the next few days, Helena remembers, he was "mortally offended" but, "seeing our indifference, he finally gave up and stopped avoiding us."

The parties that summer were even more elaborate than the practical jokes. A three-day ball, with guests from as far away as Warsaw, was held in the salon. Maria and Helena, who didn't have ball dresses, dressed up their everyday ones with ribbons and danced "for three days until we could hardly move." In mid-August, the young guests orchestrated an elaborate celebration of their hosts' fourteenth wedding anniversary. "We sat them on two old, ancestral chairs, under a canopy, and we gave them a splendid wreath made out of beautiful carrots, onions, turnips, cauliflowers, tomatoes, cabbage . . . decorated with colorful ribbons."

Together, the younger generation composed a poem which looked toward the day when "following your example, we may walk . . . up to the altar."

> Kind sir, beloved lady too,
> Our hearts arrayed we offer you,
> Without false phrases to endear,
> (The sort you wouldn't want to hear.)
> Your silver anniversary
> Draws near. We wish you joy! And we,
> When every girl has found a beau,
> Each boy a sweetheart he can show,
> Will come back for a festive dance
> Hosted with "pomp and circumstance"!!!

Once, a few years after this, Maria Skłodowska contemplated a marriage which would have made her mistress of a Polish manor. But she would never return, except in memory, to the pleasures of that sixteenth summer. "The summer passed as quickly as a dream," Helena wrote, "but the memory of it has been lasting. How many times did Mania and I talk about Kępa . . . and every time we would smile, and even shed a tear of nostalgia. It is good when a person has had at least one such crazy summer in her life."

Chapter Three

SOME VERY HARD DAYS

I N LATE SUMMER, Maria and Helena returned to the noise, dirt and sultry air of their small apartment on Nowolipki Street. Their father, for the first time in ten years, had decided not to take in boarders, forcing the family to move from the broad and open Leszno Street to smaller and dingier quarters nearby. Life was more tranquil without the din of students at work. "The plants are healthy, the azaleas are in flower," Maria wrote a friend. "Lancet sleeps on the carpet." But peace and quiet had a price. Instead of a new dress, Maria had to settle for a dyed and refashioned one. "I have written to nobody," Maria noted. "I have so little time, and even less money." Probably, Maria was rationing stamps, as she was to do repeatedly over the next seven years.

Remarkably, even though women were excluded from university in Poland and faced formidable barriers elsewhere, the sisters Skłodowska assumed higher education was their right. But the family's straitened circumstances made it seem unlikely that any of the sisters would ever be able to afford university studies abroad. Władysław Skłodowski, his savings depleted, was only a few years from retirement. Józef, now pursuing medical studies at Warsaw University, might be able to help them one day, but by then it would probably be too late. The most likely future, outside of marrying, was sometimes foreseen by Maria: "I shall install myself in Warsaw, take a post as teacher in a girls' school." She added, "It is all I want. Life does not deserve to be worried over."

But in truth Maria wanted more. Deprived of university in Poland, she divided her time during that first year after gymnasium between giving lessons and self-education, reading widely and responding in her diary. She illustrated the fables of La Fontaine, she copied out long passages of Renan's iconoclastic *Life of Jesus*, as well as an excerpt from Max Nordau's recently published attack on institutional hypocrisy, *Conventional Lies of Civilization*, and she translated the poems of François Coppée, who vividly portrayed the poor of Paris, into Polish verse. In Russian, she read Goncharov and Dostoevsky; in German, she read and copied out the poems of Heine.

Interspersed in her reading of the romantic poets, known and loved since childhood, were the voices of a new group of Polish writers who were rebelling against the high emotion and impossible dreams of the old poet heroes. Instead of calling for armed insurrection, as the exiled poets had, these writers of prose called for the more prosaic "organic work." "We have learned how to die intelligently," as one of their number observed, "but never how to live intelligently."

The antecedents of this pragmatic point of view appeared in the late eighteenth century, and reemerged between the two uprisings. But it was only after the defeat of the January Uprising that the currents of pragmatism gained enough force to be described as a movement and given a name: Polish positivism. Like the original positivism of Auguste Comte, Polish positivism embraced empiricism and rejected the metaphysical. But unlike Comte, who conceived of positivism as a sort of religion, the Poles viewed it as a method of solving the socioeconomic and political problems of their society. Bolesław Prus, novelist and important positivist, used an appropriately scientific metaphor to explain:

> When a bullet strikes a wall, it halts and generates heat. In mechanics this process is called the transforming of mass motion into molecular, of what was outward into an inner force. Something like this happened in Poland after the cruel quelling of the insurrection [of 1863]. The nation as a whole woke up, ceased to fight and to conspire, and began to think and to work.

The impact of Polish positivism was not so great as Prus suggests. In the beginning, it was espoused by a small cadre of the Warsaw intelligentsia, particularly the younger generation at Warsaw University. These young people, led by the "stubborn, clear-eyed" Aleksander Swiętochowski, were ready to burn bridges with the older generation. "The ideals of the past," declared Swiętochowski, "are not the ideals of the present." The poets were no longer relevant, these shocking youths asserted. "Poets," asked a *Weekly Review* writer rhetorically, "what do you give to humanity? Faith, strength, an ideal? Do you open new paths? No! For such things you do not have time, for you are suffering!!!"

"We believe," positivist convert Józef Kraszewski explained, "neither in revolution nor in radical utopias which profess to change society overnight and to cure all its social ills. . . . We believe in slow and gradual progress [which] through reforming individuals, increasing enlightenment, encouraging work, order and moderation should accomplish the most salutary revolution, or rather evolution in the social system." Implicit in the positivist program was the importance of science, industry, and commerce—areas of activity which had long been considered beneath the dignity of the Polish *szlachta* class.

The Skłodowski children had been raised with many of these ideas, if stated less stridently, and were natural converts to the positivist cause. Indeed, Maria would continue to live by parts of the positivist credo for the rest of her life. She was stringent about empirical proofs, believing with the positivists that all statements should be "supported by evidence which can be checked." And she shared the positivists' ingenuous faith in the power of education to change and ennoble society. "I still believe," Marie Curie wrote in 1923, "that the ideas which inspired us then are the only way to real social progress. You cannot hope to build a better world without improving the individuals."

Unlike Comte, a believer in the "natural inferiority" of women, Polish positivists were enthusiastic supporters of women's rights. Swiętochowski decried the drawing-room education given upper-class girls and insisted they should be studying mathematics and the natural sciences. And Eliza Orzeszkowa, a novelist admired by Maria, insisted that "a woman possesses the same rights as a man . . . to learning and knowledge . . . on the basis of her humanity." Orzeszkowa deplored comparisons of women to flowers, dolls, or angels, and glorification of woman in the role of wife, mother, and housekeeper. An aging teacher in one of her stories finds fault with a mother who dresses up her daughter like a model in a magazine. "You should be ashamed, Madam, ashamed," scolds the teacher. "Do you want to bring up your daughters as parasites and contribute to the loss of women's emancipation when it's in its embryonic stage? To have the obstruction of humanity's progress on one's conscience, that's a fine thing!"

The Skłodowska sisters' style would have been much more to the old teacher's liking. Posing together for a photograph in 1886, Maria and Bronia wear black from head to toe. Bronia, at twenty-one, wears a dress with velvet trim, a gold bracelet, and gold clasp at the neck. She is womanly and conventionally feminine, with her tiny corseted waist and grown-up hairstyle. Maria, at eighteen, looks as though she's nearly outgrown her plainer dress. She is still plump and schoolgirlish compared to her sister, although she is the prettier of the two. Yet their features and their purposeful gaze identify them as sisters and kindred spirits. When they gave this photograph to their friend and fellow believer Maria Rakowska, they added an inscription which played on the Polish countercurrents of realism and idealism: "To an ideal positivist," they wrote, "from two positive idealists."

The Skłodowska sisters could look to their own family for examples of female independence. There had been their mother, the forceful headmistress. And there was Uncle Zdzisław's wife, Maria Rogowska, the tall blonde who founded factories and ran the family estates, defying the rules of dress and decorum along the way. But the most pertinent example, at that moment in their lives, may well have been Aunt Wanda Skłodowska, "the most educated of all" the women, according to Józef; she had attended university in Geneva and developed a "literary career."

By the time Maria graduated from gymnasium, another remarkable woman, Jadwiga Szczasińska-Dawidowa, was beginning an experiment which would become an important influence. Davidowa, responding to the yearnings of young Polish women for higher education, began then to organize a clandestine academy for women. At its beginning in 1882, the academy involved perhaps two hundred young women meeting secretly in the private apartments of supporters, where they were taught by prominent Warsaw scientists, philosophers, and historians of Polish literature and culture. Dawidowa, the guiding spirit of the organization, took pride in outwitting the Russian police. But in 1883, the year Maria graduated from gymnasium, most of the teachers in the academy were forced to leave Warsaw.

Like most such efforts at suppression, however, the action merely led to greater defiance. By 1886, so many women wanted to participate that Dawidowa formalized the academy into what became known as the Flying University. A regular curriculum, with a broad spectrum of courses each meeting for two hours a week, was set up. There was tuition (waived for those who couldn't afford it), and the promise of a degree after six years of study. By the 1889–90 school year, a thousand women were enrolled in the Flying University, and the classes, which no longer fit into living rooms, were being held clandestinely in several supportive institutions around Warsaw.

Maria apparently was involved in the secret academy almost from its inception. She and her family moved in the circles which supported it. One of the homes used for laboratory courses, for instance, was that of her former headmistress, Jadwiga Sikorska, and books for the school were provided by the subversive priest who was Bronia's godfather. Soon after graduation Maria herself, along with Bronia, Maria Rokowska, and other friends, began to take courses. And among these young women, the talk often turned to the possibility of careers and study abroad.

Even without the influences of relatives and of Jadwiga Dawidowa's Flying University, the Skłodowska sisters were exposed, because of Poland's struggles, to other forceful women. Among the twenty-one Poles who were tried publicly at the citadel after the January Uprising, four were women who had harbored revolutionaries and supplies and passed along key messages. And many women, widowed or left behind by exiled husbands, learned out of necessity how to run the family estate and manage the family assets.

The Danish visitor George Brandes was both amazed and charmed by this forcefulness, which he observed in Polish women on his several trips to Poland in the late nineteenth century. "The men in Poland are certainly not wanting in passion, in courage and in energy, in wit, in love of freedom, but it seems as if the women have more of these qualities. In Poland's great uprisings they have been known to enter into conspiracies, to do military duty, and frequently enough of their own free will to accompany their loved ones to Siberia." Once, while visiting a Polish manor house, Brandes overheard a Pole "who had been brought up in England" suggesting that patriotism was now on the wane. "The gentlemen contradicted him," Brandes noted, "but the ladies—it was quite a spectacle to see them. With flaming eyes and blazing cheeks they stood round him, and their voices trembled in refuting him. In a perfect fury one of the youngest ladies exclaimed: 'I promised you to take you home in my carriage, but now you may go on foot.' "

The Skłodowska sisters had neither carriage nor manor house, but they had both the patriotic fervor and the sense of their own importance which Brandes observed in "these women of the higher and lower aristocracy." "They are women," he wrote, "who even in narrow and straitened circumstances preserve the grand self-esteem which runs in their blood."

This "grand self-esteem" was probably what allowed Bronia and Maria to sustain their belief, despite the hardships of the present, that they would make it to university. And even though they accepted the need to earn money, it also made them unwilling to accept slave wages or unpleasant employers. "A person who knew of us through friends came to inquire about lessons," Maria wrote a friend during this period. "Bronia told her a half ruble an hour, and the visitor ran away as if the house had caught fire. . . ."

When, after a year of giving lessons from home, Maria signed on as a governess, she found her post in a "family of lawyers" unbearable. "It was one of those rich houses," she explained to her positivist cousin Henrietta Michałowska, "where they speak French when there is company—a chimney-sweeper's kind of French—where they don't pay their bills for six months, and where they fling money out of the window even though they economize pettily on oil for the lamps.

[We may imagine this particularly troubled Maria, the night student.] They have five servants. They pose as liberals and, in reality, they are sunk in the darkest stupidity. And last of all, although they speak in the most sugary tones, slander and scandal rage through their talk— slander which leaves not a rag on anybody. . . . I learned to know the human race a little better by being there. I learned that the characters described in novels really do exist, and that one must not enter into contact with people who have been demoralized by wealth."

Being a governess, as the English Lady Elizabeth Eastlake noted, placed a young woman in an innately contradictory position: "There is no other class which so cruelly requires its members to be, in birth, mind, and manners, above their station, in order to fit them for their station." The governess, she notes, is "a needy *lady.*"But Maria Skłodowska, needy as she was, couldn't and wouldn't suppress her growing dislike for her employers. "I shouldn't like my worst enemy to live in such a hell," she wrote Henrietta that December. "In the end, my relations with Mme. B—— had become so icy that I could not endure it any longer and told her so. Since she was exactly as enthusiastic about me as I was about her, we understood each other marvelously well."

By the time Maria broke off her relationship with the hateful "B——"s, she and Bronia had hatched a plan that could, eventually, get them the university education they dreamed of. They would work as a relay team. Bronia would depart for study in Paris within the year. Maria would work as a governess, helping out her father and supporting Bronia. Then, once Bronia was established in a profession, she would help Maria to follow her.

Perhaps it was this plan which gave Maria the courage, despite that disastrous first experience as a governess, to try again. "I shall not be free long," Maria told her cousin that December. "I have decided, after some hesitation, to accept a place in the country." The family were not satisfied with their current governess. "It is quite possible," she noted, "that I shall please them no better than the other one." She might have added that it was possible they would please *her* no better than her first employers. The pay was good, however: five hundred rubles a year, starting that January. So in the midst of winter, at the age of eighteen, Maria Skłodowska set off from Warsaw for the manor house of the Zorawski family, some fifty miles to the north, in a place called Szczuki.

In her memory, this was a momentous departure. "That going away," she wrote in *Autobiographical Notes,* "remains one of the most vivid memories of my youth. My heart was heavy as I climbed into the railway car. It was to carry me for several hours, away from those I loved. And after the railway journey I must drive [by horse and sleigh] for five hours longer. What experience was awaiting me? So I questioned as I sat close to the car window looking out across the wide plains." In an earlier draft, she had continued: "Once I arrived to my destination, if I wanted to turn and run away, how could I ever be able to retrace that last five-hour stretch and regain the railway?"

In the summer, the fields would have been bright green with the leaves of the sugar beet, a large tan root second only to cane as a source of the world's sugar. But in the winter, sleigh horses pulled her along a narrow corridor of wet-black trees, infested with mistletoe, through a desert of snow to her grim destination. Szczuki consisted of a brick factory for processing sugar beets, right next to the manor house of her employers. The red brick chimney of the sugar-beet factory was just a few yards from Maria's bedroom window.

And yet, in her *Autobiographical Notes,* Maria emphasized the pleasures of being in the country again. "Loving the country," she wrote, "I did not feel lonesome, and although this particular country was not especially picturesque, I was satisfied with it in all seasons. . . . I remember the marvelous snow house we made one winter when the snow was very high in the fields; we could sit in it and look out across the rose-tinted snow plains. We also used to skate on the ice of the river and to watch the weather anxiously, to make sure that the ice was not going to give way, depriving us of our pleasure." Maria, true to positivist ideals and to her own scientific bent, took an active interest in the farming of the estate, which was considered a model for the region. "I knew the progressive details of the work, the distribution of crops in the fields; I eagerly followed the growth of the plants, and in the stables of the farm I knew the horses."

This picture of quiet, contented country living, however, hides the truth about Maria's four years as a governess. What began pleasantly enough became, as time went on, a cruel personal trial she would never forget. In her last months in Szczuki Maria wrote to Henrietta: "Everybody says that I have changed a great deal, physically and spiritually, during my stay at Szczuki. This is not surprising. I was barely eighteen when I came here, and what have I not been through! There have been moments which I shall certainly count among the most cruel of my life."

Maria's employers, the Zorawskis, were estate administrators, as Maria's paternal grandfather had been. They were charged with the supervision of sugar-beet farming and processing on one of the many estates of the Czartoryskis, the wealthiest of the Polish magnate families. Compared with the Skłodowskis her employers were very well off indeed. But their manor house was far from grand: a stuccoed brick house with a central two-story section, flanked to right and left by low-lying wings. Maria's room, on the second floor, was, as she wrote Henrietta in an early letter, "big, quiet and agreeable."

In the beginning she found much to admire in the family as well. There were, as she explained to Henrietta, "a whole collection of children . . . three sons in Warsaw (one at the university, two in boarding schools). In the house there are Bronka (eighteen years old), Andzia (ten), Stas who is three, and Maryshna, a little girl of six months." The parents she found to be "excellent people." "The Z. household," she told Henrietta, "is relatively cultivated. M. Z. is an old-fashioned man, but full of good sense, sympathetic and reasonable. His wife is rather difficult to live with, but when one knows how to take her she is quite nice. I think she likes me well enough."

Maria compared the Zorawskis favorably to others in their social set. "In this part of the country," she wrote Henrietta, "nobody works; people think only of amusing themselves; and since we in this house keep a little apart from the general dance, we are the talk of the countryside." Right from the start, she had a special affinity for the eighteen-year-old daughter, Bronka (a diminutive of Maria's mother's and sister's name, Bronisława), who compared favorably to the other girls of the village. "The young people here are most uninteresting," she wrote Henrietta. "Some of the girls are so many geese who never open their mouths, the others are highly provocative. It appears that there are some others, more intelligent. But up to now my Bronka (Mlle. Z.) seems to me a rare pearl both in her good sense and in her understanding of life."

The use of the phrase "my Bronka" here hints at the complexity of Maria Skłodowska's situation. In a certain sense, Bronka was her charge. Out of the seven hours she spent teaching each day, four were given over to Andzia, the ten-year-old girl, and three to Bronka. Thus although Bronka and Maria were the same age, Maria was her superior in education. And Maria's role as governess in the household made her Bronka's inferior in status. Bronka and Maria managed to overcome these contradictions and remain friends. But eventually, the ambiguous status of governess in the Zorawski family led to other difficulties.

Maria tried hard to behave as a governess should. "If you could only see my exemplary conduct!" she boasted to Henrietta. "I go to church every Sunday and holiday, without ever pleading a headache or a cold to get out of it. I hardly ever speak of higher education for women. In a general way I observe, in my talk, the decorum suitable to my position."

And, as always, she took her responsibilities very seriously. "I still don't know if my pupil, Andzia, is going to take her examinations," she wrote Józef sixteen months into her stay, "but I am in torment over them already. Her attentiveness and memory are so uncertain. . . . It is the same thing with Julek [Andzia's brother, apparently home from boarding school]. To try teaching them is truly to build on sand, because when they learn one thing they have already forgotten what one taught them the day before. At times this is a sort of torture."

Not all her dealings with the children were so difficult. She delighted in the baby Stas. "His *nyanya* told him God was everywhere. And he, with his little face agonized, asked: 'Is he going to catch me? Will he bite me?' He amuses us all enormously." And at times, her letters convey a deep satisfaction with her busy routine: "With all I have to do," she wrote Henrietta, "there are days when I am occupied from eight to half-past eleven and from two to half-past seven without a moment's rest. From half-past eleven to two there are a walk and lunch. After tea, I read with Andzia if she has been good, and if not we talk, or else I take my sewing, which by the way I also have by me during the lessons."

But other times her struggles with Andzia left her miserable. "The arrival of new guests constantly upsets the normal employment of my time. Sometimes this irritates me a great deal, since my Andzia is one of those children who profit enthusiastically by every interruption of work, and there is no way of bringing her back to reason afterwards. Today we had another scene because she did not want to get up at the usual hour. In the end I was obliged to take her calmly by the hand and pull her out of bed. I was boiling inside. You can't imagine what such little things do to me: such a piece of nonsense can make me ill for several hours. But I had to get the better of her. . . ."

With great difficulty, Maria managed during these years to maintain two projects which gratified her as her governess duties never could. One was teaching a group of Polish peasant children how to read. The other was her continuing self-education, which she hoped, in optimistic moments, would bring her closer to the level of French lycée students when she began her studies at the Sorbonne.

"At nine in the evening," Maria reported to Henrietta, "I take my books and go to work, if something unexpected does not prevent it. . . . I have even acquired the habit of getting up at six so that I work more. . . . At the moment I am reading:

1. Daniel's *Physics,* of which I have finished the first volume;
2. Spencer's *Sociology,* in French;
3. Paul Bers' *Lessons on Anatomy and Physiology,* in Russian.

I read several things at a time: the consecutive study of a single subject would wear out my poor little head which is already much over-worked. When I feel myself quite unable to read with profit, I work problems of algebra or trigonometry, which allow no lapses of attention and get me back into the right road."

Sometimes her duties interfered. "A very nice old man, Andzia's godfather, is staying here just now, and Mme Z. asked me to ask him to teach me how to play checkers—to amuse him. I also have to make a fourth at cards, and that drags me away from my books." And sometimes she felt she was getting nowhere. "I am very much afraid for myself," she complained to Józef, "it seems to me all the time that I am getting terribly stupid—the days pass so quickly and I make no noticeable progress."

Nonetheless, it was during these years of self-education that Maria decided she would pursue science. "I was as much interested in literature and sociology as in science," she wrote later. "However, during those years of isolated work, trying little by little to find my real preferences, I finally turned towards mathematics and physics, and resolutely undertook a serious preparation for future work." And, through her efforts, she "acquired the habit of independent work," a habit that was to assume enormous importance later on.

Balancing Maria's program of self-improvement were her efforts to educate a group of local peasant children. With the approval of her employers, she and their daughter Bronka embarked on this project not long after her arrival. "Bronka and I give lessons to some peasant children for two hours a day," she wrote Henrietta some months into her first year. "It is a class, really, for we have ten pupils. They work with a very good will, but just the same our task is sometimes difficult. What consoles me is that the results get better gradually, or even quite quickly."

The positivists considered the Polish peasantry, a group the Tzars had attempted to pit against the *szlachta,* as an untapped source of national strength who must be integrated into the Polish nation through education. And this educational task, with the *noblesse oblige* of intellectuals, they took upon themselves. Since village schools taught only Russian, a language the peasants did not know or wish to know, illiteracy was almost universal. Maria's little school, teaching peasants to read in their own language, was an admirable piece of positivist "work at the foundations."

In her letters to Henrietta, Maria longs for the give-and-take her cousin enjoyed with intellectual peers in the freer atmosphere of Galicia. "For the girls and boys alike," she explains in an early letter, "such words as 'positivism' or 'the labor question' are objects of aversion—supposing they have ever heard the words, which is

unusual." And later, with more irony: "You are probably unaware
that in our provincial hole the frost and the advantages it brings us
are at least as important as a discussion between conservatives and
progressives in your Galicia . . . it is a real satisfaction for me to learn
that there exist some regions . . . in which people move and even
think."

Although she may have missed the political talk, Maria derived
"great joys and great consolations" from her political action. And this,
too, became a lifetime characteristic; she was always more comfortable with doing than with debating. "The number of my peasant
pupils is now eighteen," she wrote Henrietta in December of that first
year. "Naturally they don't all come together, as I couldn't manage it,
but even as it is they take two hours a day. On Wednesdays and
Saturdays I am with them a little longer—as many as five hours con-
secutively. Of course this is only possible because my room is on the
second floor and has a separate entrance on the stairway to the courtyard—thus, since this work doesn't keep me from my obligations to
the Z.'s, I disturb nobody."

Maria never mentions, in her letters to Henrietta, the dangers of
what she was doing. To Henrietta it would have gone without saying.
But in her *Autobiographical Notes* years later, she noted that "even
this innocent work presented danger, as all initiative of this kind was
forbidden by the government and might bring imprisonment or de-
portation to Siberia." George Brandes, in his contemporary account,
tells of "a young lady, who on her own estate was privately teaching four or five peasant children" and who received "an injunction
from the highest judicial officer of the district to desist immediately,
since he . . . was very unwilling to be the cause of her being sent far
away."

Nonetheless, despite the great risks involved, Maria lamented to
Bronia, after reading an inspiring novel by Eliza Orzeszkowa, that
she wasn't doing nearly enough:

> I've been shaken by reading a novel by Orzeszkowa, *On the
> Banks of the Nieman.* This book haunts me, I don't know any
> more what to make of myself. All our dreams are there, all the
> impassioned conversations which brought fire to our cheeks. I
> cried like a three-year-old. Why, why have these dreams faded?
> I was determined to work for the people, with the people, and
> I've scarcely been able to teach a dozen children of the village
> to read. As for making them aware of who they are, of their role
> in society, that hasn't even come up. Ah! my God, how hard it
> is. . . . I feel myself becoming so petty, so common. And then
> all of a sudden, an unexpected shock, like reading this novel,
> tears me from my suffocating life, and I suffer horribly.

The letter provides stronger evidence than any other of Maria Skłodowska's intense involvement with ideas of social change. But it is interesting that the novel to which she responded so passionately, Orzeszkowa's *On the Banks of the Nieman,* tells the story of a cross-class romance. Because at the time the letter was written, in January of 1888, Maria was in the midst of a profound personal crisis growing out of a love relationship with her employer's son. And it seems likely, as so often happened, that her tears flowed not only for Poland but also for herself, surrounded, as she confided to her brother around the same time, by "an icy atmosphere of criticism. . . . If only you know how I sigh and long to go to Warsaw for only a few days.!"

Only the simple outline of what happened between Maria Skłodowska and Kazimierz Zorawski is known. Kazimierz, the oldest son of the family and a year older than Maria, was studying mathematics at Warsaw University, but sometime during one of his vacations he and Maria met and fell in love. Eventually, they made plans to marry. The Zorawski parents, however, when they learned of the young couple's intentions, refused absolutely to allow their son to marry a penniless governess. Maria's intelligence, obvious refinement, and *szlachta* origins didn't make up, in the Zorawskis' view, for her current low status and, perhaps even more importantly, her impoverished state.

Maria's contempt for such a petty, materialistic attitude is evident in her letters. And yet she was deeply hurt by it. What must have been more painful still was that Kazimierz Zorawski eventually went along with his parents, choosing his duty to them over his love for her. This decision, however, seems to have been made and unmade numerous times, with wrenching effects. Repeatedly, in her letters, Maria swears she will never love and has no plans to marry. And yet, even at the long-awaited moment when Bronia wrote inviting her to come to Paris, Maria hesitated, still hoping she and Kazimierz might overcome their difficulties. By that time, the relationship with Kazimierz had preoccupied her for at least four years.

Unfortunately, almost no evidence exists of the pleasure this love match must have, however briefly, provided. Socially, in Szczuki, Maria seemed for the most part to hold herself aloof, feeling at once timid and superior. "One week after my arrival," she told Henrietta, "they were already speaking of me unfavorably because, as I didn't know anybody, I refused to go to a ball at Karyacz, the gossip center of the region." The girls "all dance perfectly" and "certain ones are even intelligent, but their education has done nothing to develop their minds, and the stupid, incessant parties here have ended by frittering their wits away." As for the young men, there were very few who were "even a bit intelligent."

Rare, in the excerpts of these letters that survive, are signs of the great enthusiasm with which she had danced and reveled during her year of vacation in the countryside. At a ball on Twelfth Night, where she was "treated to the sight of a certain number of guests worthy of a caricaturist's pencil," she admitted to "enjoying myself hugely." And in the *Autobiographical Notes,* a memory returned of going for "long sleigh rides" on which at times "we could hardly see the road. 'Look out for the ditch!' I would call to the driver. 'You are going straight into it,' and 'Never fear!' he would answer, as over we went! But these tumbles only added to the gayety of our excursions."

In the letters that survive, however, there is scarcely a hint of such pleasure. It is perhaps a little surprising that she chooses, that first summer, to stay in Szczuki, despite the chance to go elsewhere. "I could have had a holiday this summer," she explains to Henrietta, "but I didn't know where to go, so I stayed in Szczuki. I didn't want to spend the money to go to the Carpathians." Could she be staying because of Kazimierz? We can only guess so.

Indeed, the first indication that something has occurred comes the following December, in the form of a denial in a letter to Henrietta. Maria begins by describing her study regimen, moves on to her plans for the future, which are "so commonplace and simple that they are not worth talking about," then arrives finally at the subject of romance: "Some people pretend that in spite of everything I am obliged to pass through the kind of fever called love. This absolutely does not enter into my plans. If I ever had any others, they have gone up in smoke; I have buried them; locked them up; sealed and forgotten them—for you know that walls are stronger than the heads which try to demolish them. . . ."

Around this time, too, Maria wrote a touching letter to Władislaw Skłodowski which may be related to the disappointment over Kazimierz. Maria is responding to a letter from her father in which he has lamented the family's poverty, probably because it has prevented Maria from marrying her employer's son. Writing in the formal, third-person style in which a respectful Polish daughter addresses her father, Maria insists that he should not blame himself:

> Above all, and beyond all, my beloved father must stop despairing about not being able to help us. It is inconceivable that my father could do more for us than he has done. We have a good education, a solid cultural background, character which is hardly the worst. . . . Therefore my father shouldn't be discouraged: we'll make out all right, without doubt. As for me, I will be eternally grateful to my dear father for what he has done for me, because he has done so much.

To her father she is gently reassuring and hopeful. But in her letters to her brother and close friends the tone shifts, after that December. The optimism of her first year at Szczuki disappears, to be replaced by waves of despair, indignation, and longing for escape. To Józef, who is contemplating a move from Warsaw, she insists that he mustn't "bury" himself in the provinces, as she has. "I think that if you borrowed a few hundred rubles you could remain in Warsaw. . . . You see, darling, everybody says that to work in a small town would prevent you from developing your culture and doing research. You would be thrust into a hole and would have no career at all. Without a pharmacy, without a hospital, or books, one gets very dull, in spite of the best resolutions. And if that happened to you, darling, you will not be surprised to hear that I should suffer enormously, for now that I have lost the hope of ever becoming anybody, all my ambition has been transferred to Bronia and you. You two, at least, must direct your lives according to your gifts. These gifts, which, without any doubt do exist in our family, must not disappear. . . . The more regret I have for myself the more hope I have for you."

Shortly after, when Henrietta writes to tell her she has had a stillbirth, Maria writes of pain and of her longing for the consolation of faith. "What suffering it must be for a mother to go through so many trials for nothing! If one could only say, with Christian resignation, 'God willed it and his will be done!' half of the terrible bitterness would be gone. Alas, that consolation is not for everybody. I see how happy are the people who admit such explanations. But, strangely enough, the more I recognize how lucky they are the less I can understand their faith, and the less I feel capable of sharing their happiness. . . . So far as I am concerned, I should never voluntarily contribute toward anybody's loss of faith. Let everybody keep his own faith, so long as it is sincere. Only hypocrisy irritates me—and it is as widespread as true faith is rare. . . . I hate hypocrisy."

In May, she learns from Józef that her sister Helena, who had been on the brink of marriage, has been rejected, apparently for the same reason she was. She is outraged. "I can imagine how Hela's self-respect must have suffered. Truly, it gives one a good opinion of men! If they don't want to marry poor [impecunious] young girls, let them go to the devil! Nobody is asking them anything. But why do they offend by troubling the peace of an innocent creature?" Later in the same letter she reports "There are always more petty annoyances with the *babas* [roughly, "busybodies"]—but I, even I, keep a sort of hope that I shall not disappear completely into nothingness."

Perhaps sometime during that spring or summer, Maria and Kazimierz Zorawski renewed their romance. Otherwise it is difficult to explain a letter to Henrietta in December 1887, fully a year after she renounced the "fever of love," about rumors of marriage. "Don't believe the report of my approaching marriage," she writes. "This tale has been spread about the countryside and even at Warsaw; and though this is not my fault, I am afraid it may bring me trouble. My plans for the future are modest indeed: my dream for the moment, is to have a corner of my own where I can live with my father. The poor man misses me a lot; he would like to have me at home; he longs for me! To get my independence again, and a place to live, I would give half my life."

For fifteen more months, however, Maria would continue to work for and live with employers who considered her unworthy of their son. Judging from her letters, they were months of nearly unrelieved misery. Even her birthday letter to her brother, usually an occasion for good cheer, is a long complaint. She is using the last stamp she owns, "since I have literally not a penny—not one!—I shall probably not write to you again until the holidays, unless by some chance a stamp should fall into my hands." "My darling Jozio, if you only knew how I sigh and long to go to Warsaw for only a few days! I say nothing of my clothes, which are worn out and need care—but my soul, too, is worn out."

She complains that Bronia doesn't write from Paris, and that her father and Helena, who do write, send her "nothing but laments. . . . I ask myself if everything really is so bad; and I am in torment; and to these worries there are added quantities of worries I have here, of which I could speak—but I don't want to. If I only didn't have to think of Bronia I should present my resignation to the Z.'s this very instant and look for another post, even though this one is so well paid."

Toward the end of her long stay with the Zorawskis, anger begins to take the place of despair. Her resentment toward her brother and sister at university surfaces: "I am learning chemistry from a book," she writes Józef in October of 1888. "You can imagine how little I get out of that, but what can I do, as I have no place to make experiments or do practical work?" She adds, "Bronia has sent me a little album from Paris. It is very elegant."

Her resentment of her gymnasium friend Kazia, who has written to announce her engagement, is more obvious. She assures Kazia that "nothing you could ever confide in me could ever seem excessive or ridiculous. How could I, your chosen little sister, not take to heart everything that concerns you, as if it were my own?" But later she confesses, "I write with some bitterness, Kazia, but you see . . . you tell me you have just lived through the happiest week of your life; and I during these holidays, have been through such weeks as you will never know."

The saving grace, as Maria acknowledges to Kazia, is that, whether she intends to or not, she speaks her mind in the end. "There were some very hard days, and the only thing that softens the memory of them is that in spite of everything I came through it all honestly, with my head high. (As you see, I have not yet renounced, in life, that carriage which brought me Mlle. Mayer's hatred of old.)"

In this letter to Kazia, her co-conspirator from gymnasium days, Maria Skłodowska admits, more than elsewhere, that she fights back. "I often hide my deep lack of gaiety under laughter. This is something I learned to do when I found out that creatures who feel as keenly as I do, and are unable to change this characteristic of their nature, have to dissimulate it at least as much as possible. But do you think it is efficacious. . . . ? Not at all! Most often the vivacity of my temperament runs away with me gradually, and then—well, one says things that one regrets, and with more ardor than is necessary." In other words, despite putting on a conventionally girlish facade, her true indignation bursts forth in the end.

There is a tragic fictional counterpart to Maria Skłodowska in a Polish short story, "Miss Antonina," written by Eliza Orzeszkowa in 1881. Like Maria, Miss Antonina goes to work as a governess in a "strange house" while still in her teens, falls in love with a young man, devotes herself whenever possible to teaching poor children and "keeps the lamp . . . burning all night in her room." "Self-education was her ambition, her passion, the second longing of her whole youth," writes Orzeszkowa. Unlike Maria Skłodowska, however, Miss Antonina "drifted from one landowner's home to another," accepting worse and worse treatment. In the end, she died alone, with only her small box of keepsakes, including "the discolored, half-faded photograph" of "a young man's face . . . ."

" 'You see,' " declares Miss Antonina, " 'everyone in the world has some little poem in his past. And I have him.' "

Increasingly, as the time comes for her to leave Szczuki, Maria shows the resilience and fire which will save her from Miss Antonina's fate. Even though she feels things intensely, she writes Henrietta in November of 1888, "then I give myself a shaking, the vigor of my nature conquers, and it seems to me that I am coming out of a nightmare. . . . First principle: never to let one's self be beaten down by persons or by events."

Her excitement about the future has returned with a vengeance: "I count the hours and days that separate me from the holidays and my departure to my own people," she writes toward the end of 1888. "There is also the need of new impressions; the need of change, of movement and life, which seizes me sometimes with such force that I want to fling myself into the greatest follies, if only to keep my life from being eternally the same. Fortunately I have so much work to do that these attacks seize me pretty rarely."

By March of 1889, she can "think only of Easter," when she will leave her post in Szczuki for good. "My head is so full of plans that it seems aflame," she writes Kazia. Adding to her excitement and increasing her hopes of coming to Paris was the news, which arrived from Paris around this time, that Bronia was engaged to marry a fellow medical student named Kazimierz Dłuski.

Kazimierz Dłuski was a man of aristocratic bearing whose parents had fought in the January Uprising and who, while still very young, had become a revolutionary spokesman for the most radical ideas of the socialists. Ten years earlier, while still living in Warsaw, he had launched a notorious diatribe against the "huckster" patriotism of the positivists. "The idea of socialism," he argued, "is wider and greater than any form of patriotism." Dłuski's association with Ludwik Waryński, the first socialist organizer in Warsaw, got him in trouble with the authorities and forced him to flee Poland for Geneva. There he wrote for socialist magazines under a pen name, and continued to associate with the leading Polish socialists of the period. Finally, unable to realize his dream of diplomatic service because of his politics, he enrolled in medical school in Paris, where he met Bronia Skłodowska, ten years his junior. Somehow, the couple managed to reconcile philosophical differences and fall in love.

Within a year Bronia, on the brink of marriage, would ask Maria to come join them in Paris. In the meantime, Maria signed on as a governess with the Fuchs family, beginning her tenure auspiciously at a resort on the Baltic coast. "My journey went off all right," she wrote Kazia after her arrival, "in spite of my tragic presentiments. . . . Nobody robbed me, or even tried to; I did not take the wrong train at any of my five changes, and I ate up all my *serdelki* [a Polish sausage]: only the rolls and the caramels were too much for me. . . . M. and Mme. F. were waiting at the station for me. They are very nice, and I have been attracted to the children. Everything will therefore be all right—as indeed it must be."

Things didn't always go smoothly with the Fuchs family. At one point, Maria wrote that "Mme F., her husband, her mother . . . are in such temper that I should like to hide in a mousehole, if I could." Anything would be better than the humiliation she had experienced at the Zorawskis', however. Besides, she was nearing the end of her years as a governess.

That spring, Bronia began to make final plans for her wedding. More than anything, she explained in a letter to an old family friend who was her godfather, the priest Władysław Knapiński, she would like to be married in Poland instead of "this awful Paris, which I haven't been able to like at all." But there was a problem: Kazimierz couldn't return to Warsaw without risking arrest. The plan was to marry in Cracow, in Austrian Poland, because Dłuski had "never been involved with any anti-Austrian activities." Bronia wanted the whole family to gather in Cracow in August for the wedding, at which Father Knapiński, himself a political refugee from Warsaw, would officiate.

At around the same time Bronia wrote Father Knapiński about her wedding plans, she wrote Maria the letter she had hoped for and despaired of ever receiving for the last four years:

> If everything goes as we hope, I shall surely be able to marry when the [summer] holidays begin. My fiancé will be a doctor by then, and I shall have only my last examination to pass. We shall stay another year in Paris, during which I shall finish my examinations, and then we shall come back to Poland. I see nothing in our plans that is not reasonable. Tell me if you think I am not right. Remember that I am twenty-four—which is nothing—but he is thirty-four, which is more serious. It would be absurd to wait any longer. . . . And now you, my little Manya: you must make something of your life sometime. If you can get together a few hundred rubles this year you can come to Paris next year and live with us, where you will find board and lodging. It is absolutely necessary to have a few hundred rubles for your fees at the Sorbonne. The first year you will live with us. For the second and third, when we are no longer there, I swear Father will help you in spite of the devil. You must take this decision; you have been waiting too long. I guarantee that in two years you will have your master's degree. Think about it, get the money together, put it in a safe place, and *don't lend* it. Perhaps it would be better to change it into francs right away, for the exchange is good just now, and later it might fall. . . .

Maria's reply to this invitation is, at first glance, astonishing. Within days she writes back:

> Dear Bronia,
> I have been stupid, I am stupid and I shall remain stupid all the days of my life, or rather, to translate into the current style: I have never been, am not now and shall never be lucky. I dreamed of Paris as of redemption, but the hope of going there left me a long time ago. And now that the possibility is offered me, I do not know what to do. . . . I am afraid to speak of it to Father: I believe our plan of living together next year is close to

his heart, and he clings to it; I want to give him a little happiness in his old age. And on the other hand my heart breaks when I think of ruining my abilities, which must have been worth anyhow something.

The letter continues in this vein, with a litany of other people's needs and her own need to help them. There is Hela, recently spurned in love, and working in the provinces; Maria has promised to find her a post in Warsaw. "You have no idea how sorry I felt for her! She will always be the minor child of the family, and I feel it is my duty to watch over her—the poor little thing needs it so. . . ." And there is Józef, still in danger, it seems, of burying himself in the provinces; Bronia must find a way to get money for him. "Even if it seems to you that it is not your part of soliciting help from that Mme. S, who can extricate him," Maria lectures, "conquer the feeling. After all, the Bible says literally: 'knock and it shall be opened to you.' Even if you are forced to sacrifice a little of your self-esteem, what does that matter? An affectionate request can offend nobody. How well I should know how to write that letter! You must explain to the lady that there is no question of a large sum, only of a few hundred rubles so that Józef can live in Warsaw and study and practice; that his future depends on it; that without this help such wonderful abilities will be ruined. . . . In a word, you must write all that, and at length; for, darling Broneczka, if you simply ask her to lend the money, she will not take the business to heart: that is not the way to succeed. And even if you have the feeling of being a nuisance, what of it? What's the difference, so long as the end is achieved? And besides, is it such a big request? Aren't people often greater nuisances than that? With this help Józef can become useful to society, whereas if he leaves for the provinces he is lost." Later in life Maria Skłodowska would follow her own fund-raising advice many, many times.

Only at the end of the letter, after this long digression into what Bronia should do for Józef, does Maria return to herself, and then with no further mention of Paris.

My heart is so black, so sad, that I feel how wrong I am to speak of all this to you and to poison your happiness, for you are the only one of us all who has had what they call luck. Forgive me, but, you see, so many things hurt me that is hard for me to finish this letter gaily.

I embrace you tenderly. The next time I shall write more cheerfully and at greater length—but today I am exceptionally unhappy in this world. Think of me with tenderness—perhaps I shall be able to feel it even here.

Maria's reluctance to go to Paris after dreaming of it for so long is partially explained by the fact that her long, tortured romance with Kazimierz Zorawski was still lurching on. But Kazimierz may not be the whole story. For one thing, Maria always had trouble traveling to strange new places. Just as her departures for Szczuki and the Baltic Sea in her governess years filled her with dread, all her travels in later years, except for the familiar summer trips to the seashore or the mountains, were undertaken reluctantly. Indeed, it seems likely that, had Bronia not gone first and created a nest for her in Paris, Maria, like her younger sister Helena, would have remained forever in Warsaw and become an educator.

Then too, as is so often the case for women, connection to loved ones was central to who she was. Her concern for her father, Józef, and Hela was not selflessness, but the basis of her sense of self in the world. At the moment when connections were threatened, it was natural for her to return, obsessively, to those concerns. And Bronia, knowing this, wisely advises her not to act on them and lend her money, but to put it right away into French francs for the trip.

Since Bronia and Kazimierz had decided to stay on in Paris, Maria had some extra time to make up her mind. She spent the next year in Warsaw living with her father, who finally, having put in two difficult years beyond his retirement at a "tiring and unpleasant" job directing a correctional agricultural colony in Studzieniec, outside Warsaw, had returned to his apartment and to a life of ease. "Together," she remembered, "we passed an excellent year, he occupying himself with some literary work, while I increased our funds by giving private lessons."

Perhaps the year spent with her father satisfied Maria's powerful sense of duty, and allowed her to reconsider her refusal of Paris. But that year also provided intimations of what it might be like to study at the Sorbonne. By then, the Flying University was at its height, and Maria had the opportunity to study with many of her peers, instead of in the lonely isolation of a governess post.

At the same time, her efforts at self-education took a new and exciting turn: for the first time in her life, she had access to a laboratory. Maria's cousin Józef Boguski, fourteen years older than she, had returned to Poland after studying in Russia with Mendeleev, and was now director of a private, positivist-influenced institution called the Museum of Industry and Agriculture, right near the center of Warsaw. The museum was devoted, as Bolesław Prus explained in his "Chronicles," to the "scientific development of agriculture and industry." Founded in 1875 with the backing of Poland's wealthiest landlords and industrialists, the museum soon opened a chemistry lab under the supervision of prominent Polish chemist Napoleon Milicer. Some of the Flying University's courses were held at the Museum of Industry and Agriculture, and Maria may have attended them there. But her family connection through her cousin Józef Boguski allowed her "to my great joy [to be] able, for the first time in my life, to find access to a laboratory. . . ."

"I found little time to work there," Marie Curie wrote in her *Autobiographical Notes,* "except in the evenings and on Sundays, and was generally left to myself. I tried out various experiments described in treatises on physics and chemistry, and the results were sometimes unexpected. At times I would be encouraged by a little unhoped-for success, at others I would be in deepest despair because of accidents and failures resulting from my inexperience. But on the whole . . . this first trial confirmed in me the taste for experimental research in the fields of physics and chemistry."

It may have been this experience in a chemistry lab which caused Maria to choose chemistry and physics over biology when she arrived in Paris. Her sister Bronia, after all, had chosen medicine, as had her brother. And an early hero of hers had been the French biologist Claude Bernard. But the event which turned her toward Paris was probably much more deeply personal.

In the summer of 1891, there was one last attempt, on a trip to the Tatra Mountains, to overcome the difficulties in the relationship with Kazimierz. Once again, very little direct information exists about what happened. But there is intriguing indirect evidence from two sources: a letter from Władysław to Bronia in Paris, and a reminiscence from a day's walk in the Tatra Mountains.

Władysław's letter, written in September from Warsaw, explains that Maria has stayed in the Tatra Mountains in part because of her health ("a bad cough and a grippe") and in part because she "has a secret about her future, of which she is to speak to me at length, but only on her return. To tell the truth," he adds, "I can well imagine what it has to do with, and I don't myself know whether I should be glad or sorry. If my foresight is accurate, the same disappointments, coming from the same persons who have already caused them to her, are awaiting Manya. And yet if it is a question of building a life according to her own feeling, and of making two people happy, that is worth the trouble of facing them, perhaps." Later, in another reference to the affair, Władisław notes "how funny it would be if each of you [i.e., Bronia and Maria] had a Kazimierz."

But the difficulty with Kazimierz is not the only thing troubling Maria. "Your invitation to Paris," he writes, "which fell upon her in such unexpected fashion, has given her a fever and added to her disorder. I feel the power with which she wills to approach that source of science, towards which she aspires so much."

Quite naturally, after the loss of his wife and oldest daughter, he worries about Maria's health. "If Manya does not come back to me completely cured, I should oppose her departure, because of the hard conditions she would find herself in during the winter in Paris—without speaking of all the rest of it, and without even taking account of the fact that it would be very painful for me to separate from her, for this last consideration is obviously secondary." But then, a little wistfully, he notes that "if she remained in Warsaw, even if she could find no lessons, I should certainly have a bit of bread for her and for myself for a year." In an attempt to raise her spirits, Władysław has written Maria a light-hearted letter in verse and sent it to her in the mountains.

One other document, a long, reminiscing poem written by a childhood companion, Maciej Szukiewicz, gives us a glimpse of Maria Skłodowska's state of mind that summer as she tried to decide what she should do. It seems that Maria, Szukiewicz, and a second young woman, with whom he was in love, took a walk one fine day along a valley road high up in the Tatras. "It was slowly getting dark, the sun was going down in a red glow and the pale circle of the moon was discernible in the eastern sky," when the young people's talk turned to Shakespeare's *Othello*—the plot, the origins of the characters, the bard's sources. "Suddenly I heard Skłodowska, who was seriously upset, attack her friend":

> "Damn it! What kind of person was that 'sweet Desdemona' who let herself be slapped on the face without a word of protest! It takes a stupid lamb to allow that!'

> "But dear Mania," answered her friend, "a loving wife can take more than that, if that's what it takes to appease her husband. . . . "

> "I don't believe you," said Mania, "for even an absolute nullity has some limits! A person, insulted to the deepest, chooses death! . . . And if you think more about it, you have to agree that the issue there was not only her dignity, but the whole country's pride. The Moor's insult touched the whole kingdom! I can bear an insult, and even forgive it, if someone does it to me only, but I could never forgive an offence to my fatherland!"

Maria Skłodowska's analysis reverberates with the anger she must have been feeling about her own humiliation at the hands of a man she loved. Unlike Desdemona, she refuses to be a "stupid lamb" and a "nullity." There are limits to what she will take. We may be sure that Maria offered more than "a word of protest" in her own situation. Perhaps, too, she considered the "death" she decrees preferable to the deepest insults.

Most surprising is Maria's view that Desdemona is responsible not just for herself; to wrong her, it seems, is to wrong her nation. This is an interpretation more romantic than positivist. But it reveals Maria Skłodowska's deep belief that there is a transcendent life-purpose beyond the personal. She had always been taught that she was part of something larger than herself, a national cause that commanded pride and action. And she drew on this sense of a larger mission throughout her life to temper and overcome personal anguish. For the fatherland, as well as for herself, Maria now set her sights on Paris.

At the end of that summer in the Tatra Mountains, and just weeks before the opening of classes at the Sorbonne, she wrote Bronia, now pregnant, a second letter:

> . . . Now Bronia, I ask you for a definite answer. Decide if you can really take me in at your house, for I can come now. I have enough to pay all my expenses. If, therefore, without depriving yourself of a great deal, you could give me my food, write to me and say so. It would be a great happiness, as that would restore me spiritually after the cruel trials I have been through this summer, which will have an influence on my whole life—but on the other hand I do not wish to impose myself on you.

> Since you are expecting a child, perhaps I might be useful to you. In any case, write me what about it. If my coming is just possible, tell me, and tell me what entrance examinations I must pass, and what is the latest date at which I can register as a student. I am so nervous at the prospect of my departure that I can't speak of anything else until I get your answer. I beg of you then, write to me at once, and I send all my love to both of you. You can put me up anywhere; I shall not bother you; I promise that I shall not be a bore or create disorder. I implore you to answer me, but very frankly.

Bronia wrote back telling her to come.

Chapter Four

A PRECIOUS SENSE
OF LIBERTY

Bronia, who had always mothered her little sister, returned to Warsaw that fall to help Maria prepare for her journey to Paris. By that time, the older sister knew well what was required for success. Bronia had graduated from the School of Medicine that July, one of three women in a class of several thousand to do so, and now contemplated practicing in Paris with her physician husband Kazimierz Dłuski. Because Kazimierz was *persona non grata* in Poland, the couple had settled into a comfortable apartment in a working-class district of Paris, and gathered a community of Poles around them. In a few months, Bronia would be giving birth to their first child.

In the meantime, however, Bronia had Maria to attend to. Probably Bronia brought the course catalogue *(annuaire)* for 1891–92 with her from Paris, so that the two of them could go over the curriculum at the Faculté des sciences. In the *annuaire*, Maria could learn exactly what to expect in her pursuit of a *licence ès sciences* at the Sorbonne over the next several years: not only which courses were required, with which professors, but also what she would be required to know at the end of each semester. Although she had been a medical student, Bronia would have known the reputations of some of the professors Maria would encounter. Most certainly, she could prepare Maria for the challenges of being a Pole and a woman in a predominantly French, male world.

All of that, however, was several months off: registration didn't open until November 1. Meanwhile, there was the question of what to bring. Warm wool dresses were a must, since Maria would be taking the hour-long omnibus ride from the Dłuski apartment to the Sorbonne each day. Paris would be milder in winter than Warsaw, but the damp could penetrate, especially in the cheap open seats on top of the horse-drawn omnibuses. And then, the sisters reasoned, some things, like a mattress, could be transported from Warsaw for less than they would cost in France.

The railroad trip itself, a forty-hour, thousand-mile journey across Russian and Prussian Poland, Germany, and eastern France on jerky, noisy trains, required careful planning. Passengers in the better-class cars could draw warmth from the coal-fired iron boxes under their seats, and enjoy hot lunches on the Berlin–Cologne line. But Maria's budget was small, and she would be traveling fourth class, sitting on the stool she provided and keeping warm through the long, chilly night with her own blankets. She would need to bring along plenty of food as well, to avoid the costs of station restaurants. And she had to be sure that all her documents were in perfect order: the border police, particularly the Russian ones at Alexandrovo, the Russian–Prussian border, were always looking for trouble.

Departures had never been easy for Maria. When she first left Warsaw to become a governess in Szczuki, she traveled with a "heavy heart." Later, when she took another train to the Baltic for a last stint as a governess, she had fears of being robbed or of taking the wrong train at the changes. This time, however, when she said goodbye to her father, her brother Józef, and her sister Helena, she had the reassuring knowledge that Bronia would be joining her before long at the other end. What's more, the second half of the sisters' shared dream was at last coming true: Maria really was going to study in Paris.

The train carrying twenty-three-year-old Maria Skłodowska west toward Paris left the Vienna–Warsaw station in midafternoon one day early in November of 1891. For the first few hours of the journey, it was still light enough to take a farewell look at the familiar countryside of Poland. The train meandered south along an uneven track, passing little clusters of crooked log houses with their thatched roofs, and small trading towns, sometimes with a castle, always with churches. Then, at Skierniewicz, the Berlin-bound tracks turned northwest, cutting through deep woods along the Vistula and angling up, as night descended, toward the Russian–Prussian border. All through the next day, with her companions in the fourth-class ladies' carriage of the German railway car, Maria traveled across northern Germany, passing through Berlin and bypassing the cathedral city of Cologne. It wasn't until late that night that she reached the French border. And it wasn't until the next morning that her train pulled under the great glass roof of the Gare du Nord.

Suddenly, after three days of numbing travel and countless days of anticipation, Maria was in Paris. There to greet her was her new brother-in-law, Kazimierz Dłuski. Before long, under his guidance, she and her belongings had been transported to her first home, a second-floor apartment not far from the Gare du Nord.

Rue d'Allemagne, where Bronia and Kazimierz lived, was one of the broad avenues created by Baron Georges Eugène Haussmann, who replaced the old crooked streets and irregular architecture of Paris with a far grander style worthy of the imperialist ambitions of his employer, Louis Napoléon. Small trees lined both sides of the rue d'Allemagne, and seven-story stone apartment buildings with mansard roofs and lacy wrought-iron balconies faced each other across it. Similar streets, closer to the center of Paris, were filled with elegant carriages and top-hatted coachmen. But rue d'Allemagne, like most streets on the outskirts of the city, was a place of carts and wagons. Slaughterers from the nearby stockyards, la Villette, lived there, and factory workers, people who spent their days, in the words of one disdainful chronicler, "in the atmosphere of blood or of fire." In fact, by his account, this was a "somber *quartier* of unhealthy factories" which had been even more disreputable in the past. "The neighborhood is gradually improving," he wrote; "broad avenues are being constructed; healthy and cheerful apartment houses are going up everywhere, driving out the sordid hovels and exiling their inhabitants. Some years hence it will be transformed into a purely working-class quarter."

To the Dłuskis, however, the neighborhood was already improved enough. Kazimierz, an aristocrat by birth, was proletarian in spirit; it suited his politics to live among the working people. What's more, the rent was manageable, and the men and women in the neighborhood were in need of doctoring. From one to three o'clock each day, the apartment on rue d'Allemagne turned into a doctors' office. In addition, free consultations were offered from seven to eight two evenings a week.

Between visits from patients and the constant coming and going of fellow Poles, the Dłuski apartment was rarely quiet. Although he could appear stiff and haughty at first, Kazimierz was in fact the most gregarious of men. And Bronia was willing and able, it seemed, to play hostess. Artists, musicians, scientists, and above all Polish activists gathered frequently at the Dłuskis'. The urologist Bolesław Motz, editor of the Polish-language *Socialist Review,* came to call, as did Jan Danysz, the director of microbiology at the Pasteur Institute. Two future presidents of Poland, Ignacy Jan Paderewski and Stanisław Wojciechowski, were part of the Dłuskis' circle. Paderewski, though a passionate Polish patriot, was pursuing a romantic interest and his brilliant career as a concert pianist at the time. Wojciechowski, on the other hand, was organizing: that year, he helped to form the

Union of Workers, and the following year became a cofounder of the Polish Socialist Party. There were Polish women in the circle as well, including two who were studying math at the Sorbonne.

Since Bronia was still away in Warsaw with her family, Kazimierz may have hoped that Maria would help him entertain his friends. But he quickly learned otherwise. "Mademoiselle Marie," he reported in a letter to her father in Warsaw, "is a very independent young person . . . she passes nearly all her time at the Sorbonne and we meet only at the evening meal." He yearned for the more sociable and domestic Bronia. "I await Bronia's arrival with impatience," he wrote. "My young lady does not seem to be in a hurry to get home, where her presence would nevertheless be very useful and where she is much in demand."

Kazimierz insisted that he and Maria "understand each other very well and live in the most perfect agreement." But Maria came to feel otherwise. Writing home to her close confidant Józef, she complained that "my little brother-in-law" had the habit of "disturbing me endlessly" and was unable to "endure having me do anything but engage in agreeable chatter with him" whenever she was home. "I had to declare war on him on this subject."

It must have provided some comfort to Maria to know that she could return at night to a Petite Pologne, where the language, the food, and the faces were familiar. But it was the unfamiliar world beyond the Dłuski apartment which now commanded her attention. Everything was new out there, including her name: she now signed herself Mlle. Marie Skłodowska. And things which would have been simple in Warsaw were a challenge. The horse-drawn omnibus ride to the Sorbonne was the first test: the ascent, difficult in long skirts, up the spiraling iron steps to the upper deck, the hour-long, jerky ride in a crushing crowd, the commands and explanations from the omnibus *contrôleur,* barked out in a French that school hadn't prepared her for.

On sunny days, though, the *impériale* (upper deck) provided a wonderful seat from which to view the marvels of Paris. The *omnibus brun* traveled directly south into the commercial heart of the city, skirting les Halles, and crossing the bustling rue de Rivoli. In the morning the streets were full of vendors and porters of every kind: market women in long white aprons; itinerant sellers of baskets and flowers, their wares heaped around them; porters carrying slabs of meat piled high on one shoulder or bread in square baskets on their heads. As the omnibus neared the pont Notre Dame, broad vistas opened: on a clear day, there was a view of the chain of bridges over the Seine, extending east and west as far as the eye could see. And then, all at once, the horses were trotting past the magnificent, densely peopled facade of the cathedral of Paris, Notre Dame, across a second little bridge, and onto the Left Bank. From the boulevard St. Germain, where Marie got off, it was just a short walk up rue St. Jacques to the bright new stone buildings of the Sorbonne.

For all those who had grown up under the Tzarist régime, there was a sense of freedom in Paris which was even more amazing than the city's beauty. A Russian who visited during this period wrote of his astonishment at hearing people sing "La Marseillaise" on the street without being arrested. "The first times I was very upset. I was careful not to sing it myself, but I trembled that I would have to explain my presence in a place where someone was singing the Marseillaise. . . . The Frenchman sings the Marseillaise and feels good about it, while for us it is death."

Like the Russian, Marie Skłodowska was most impressed by the latitude she was given when she "came to France as a simple student to seek a scientific education." Once issued a certificate equivalent to the *baccalauréat* (essentially the graduating certificate for the French lycées), she was free to do as much or as little as she wanted. There was no charge for study at the Sorbonne (except small fees for qualifying tests and diplomas). Moreover, students were free to attend classes as frequently or infrequently as they wanted, to choose when to take the exams for a diploma, or indeed not to take the exams at all.

Reflecting many years later on the quality of French education, she described feeling a bit disoriented ("un peu dépaysée") at first by the system, so different from the "strict supervision" of her Polish-German gymnasium. But she quickly picked up the "general spirit," and came to feel that it would be difficult to return to a system in which "personality would be allowed less free expression. . . . The student who comes to France," she observed, "should not expect to find direction towards a utilitarian goal right at the start. The French system consists essentially of awakening the student's confidence in his own abilities and fostering the habit of using them." At the Sorbonne, "the goal of the teachers is to create large possibilities for free work rather than to form disciples. Required exercises and scholarly discipline don't play an essential role."

The freedom she felt at the Sorbonne was soon matched by the exhilarating experience of living alone, answerable to no one, for the first time in her life. After six months at the Sorbonne, she decided to escape the noise of the little Poland on rue d'Allemagne and move to a garret apartment in the Latin Quarter. She wrote her brother Józef in March:

You have no doubt learned from Father that I decided to live
nearer to the schools, as it had become necessary for several
reasons, above all for the present quarter. The plan is now
realized: I am writing to you, in fact, from my new lodging, 3
rue Flatters. It is a little room, very suitable, and nevertheless
very cheap. In a quarter of an hour I can be in the chemistry
laboratory, in twenty minutes at the Sorbonne. Naturally without the Dłuskis' help I should never have been able to arrange things like this.

She adds that she is "working a thousand times as hard as at the
beginning of my stay," now that she is free of constant interruptions
from "my little brother-in-law." Bronia and Kazimierz had come to
her place for a visit. "We drank tea, bachelor fashion," she reports,"and then we went downstairs to see the S's, who also live here."

Marie would continue to live, "bachelor fashion," in four different apartments over the next two and a half years. It was a life which,
as she wrote later in *Autobiographical Notes,* "gave me a very precious sense of liberty and independence. Unknown in Paris, I was lost
in the great city, but the feeling of living there alone, taking care of
myself without any aid, did not at all depress me. If sometimes I felt
lonesome, my usual state of mind was one of calm and great moral
satisfaction."

Marie Skłodowska lived in six-story stone apartment buildings
typical of Paris in the era after Haussman, buildings of uniform height
and facade, made distinct from each other by shops and cafés on the
ground floor. She rented one of the single attic rooms, a *chambre de
bonne* underneath a zinc slanted roof.

An American woman who studied at the Sorbonne and lived in
such a room during this period noted that "social cleavage in Paris is
horizontal as well as lateral. . . . And a fixed line is drawn at the sixth
story . . . , for the sixth story in houses of this type is not divided up
into the usual three sets of flats like those below, but consists of separate rooms . . . theoretically used as bedrooms by . . . servants, in
reality frequently let to separate tenants. . . . Inhabitants of the sixth
are outside the pale. . . . And even the friendliest of hostesses will
wonder naively after the first shock is over 'What is it like up there?' "

One advantage of living on the top floor was that it afforded marvelous views of Paris. The other, and the one that Marie Skłodowska
cared most about, was that it was cheap. Many foreign students rented
a furnished room, and engaged a *femme de ménage,* all of which
could be managed for less than fifty francs a month. But Marie lived
for half that by doing her own chores and furnishing the rooms herself. "Today I begin the installation of my little corner for this year,"

Marie wrote Józef the following fall, "—very poorly, but what am I to do? I have to do everything myself; otherwise it's all too dear. I must get my furniture into shape—or rather what I pompously call my furniture, for the whole thing isn't worth more than twenty francs."

The disadvantages of a top-floor abode became apparent as soon as one entered the dank hallway and began to climb, grasping the iron railing, the hundred or more wooden stairs, past five landings, to reach home. "The room I lived in," Marie Curie wrote in her *Autobiographical Notes,* "was . . . very cold in winter, for it was insufficiently heated by a small stove which often lacked coal. During a particularly rigorous winter, it was not unusual for the water to freeze in the basin in the night; to be able to sleep I was obliged to pile all my clothes on the bedcovers. In the same room I prepared my meals with the aid of an alcohol lamp and a few kitchen utensils. These meals were often reduced to bread with a cup of chocolate, eggs or fruit. I had no help in housekeeping and I myself carried the little coal I used up the six flights."

Nonetheless, Marie Curie looked back on this "period of solitary years exclusively devoted to the studies . . . for which I had waited so long" as "one of the best memories of my life." In a poem she wrote in Polish for fellow student Jadwiga Dydyńska, the little room became an exalted place:

> Higher, higher, up she climbs.
> Past six floors she gasps and heaves.
> Students shelter near the sky
> Up among the drafty eaves.
>
> This is no elegant abode
> The cold in winter chills the face,
> The room in summer's stuffy, close.
> But it's a tiny, quiet place.
>
> It sees the student's restless toil,
> The hours of work without a break;
> It's there when she returns from school
> To cook herself a leather steak.
>
> And when the time for sleep is come,
> When streets and shops are shut up tight,
> The room awaits her, quiet and calm,
> Libraries closed now for the night.
>
> But still she studies in her cell,
> Spending long hours on lab or test
> Before her cheap sheets cast a spell
> And grant her a brief moment's rest.

How hard the life of her young years,
How rough her day till she retires
While, looking round, she sees her peers
Seeking new bliss with new desires.

Yet she has joy in what she knows
For in her lonely cell she finds
Rich air in which the spirit grows,
Inspired by the keenest minds.

Ideals flood this tiny room;
They led her to this foreign land;
They urge her to pursue the truth
And seek the light that's close at hand.

It is the light she longs to find,
When she delights in learning more.
Her world is learning; it defines
The destiny she's reaching for.

Jadwiga Dydyńska was one of the few women Marie knew who shared her fervor. For the most part, her classmates were men. Yet never, in her several accounts of her student life, does Marie Curie take note of the fact that she was a singular woman in a nearly all-male world. She writes of "conversations about our studies" with "student companions." And she explains that she had to work harder because "despite all my efforts, I had not succeeded in acquiring in Poland a preparation as complete as that of the French students following the same course." In fact she should have written "French *male* students." French women students, for the most part, were not even able to qualify for the Sorbonne. Maria Skłodowska, like other pioneering women, was so intent on fitting into this male world that she preferred not to dwell on just how unusual she was.

But implicit in the "precious sense of liberty and independence" and the "moral satisfaction" she felt living alone in her garret is an awareness that such autonomy was a rare accomplishment for a woman in fin de siècle Paris, a city in which proper young Frenchwomen didn't even leave their houses without an escort. "The worst fate for a woman was to live alone . . . ," wrote historian Jules Michelet. "She could hardly go out in the evening; she would be taken for a prostitute. There are thousands of places where only men go, and if some business should take the woman there, one would be astonished. . . . For example, if she were late, far from home, and became hungry, she would not dare enter a restaurant. . . . She would make a spectacle of herself." Michelet wrote this in 1860, but attitudes had changed very little by 1891. And yet, here was the dimin-

utive Marie Skłodowska, returning home late at night from the Bibliothèque Ste. Geneviève, descending narrow streets alone, then
climbing the dark staircase to her single room.

France, in the last three decades of the nineteenth century, was
moving toward some republican ideals, but equality for women was
not prominent among them. The first president of the Third Republic
was a monarchist who wanted to restore the Pope's temporal power.
In reaction, republicans took control of French government and, in
1877, passed a series of anticlerical laws. That was the beginning of a
democratization and secularization of French life which brought
some benefits to women.

Yet in 1891, when Marie Skłodowska came to France, women
still couldn't bear witness in a civil suit and could not spend their
own earnings without their husband's permission. And in some ways,
independent women had fewer opportunities in the Third Republic
than in the days of Louis Napoléon. "The decline of the aristocratic
salon," writes historian Jo Burr Margadant, "and the emergence of
the all-male bourgeois club [cercle] had undercut the one respectable
arena for such women in the nineteenth century."

Just venturing out alone to a cultural event required pluck.
"Women without men friends," an American woman noted in 1900,
will be shocked almost anywhere at first." Nonetheless, women "can
go anywhere alone nowadays; for . . . the customs of the English and
the Americans have modified the French criticisms, as their numbers
have intimidated the boulevardier. One lady can even go to the best
theaters, if she is quiet in her dress, and is careful not to loiter nor
stroll in the foyers. People in Paris have begun to discriminate between two kinds of lone ladies."

But when women tried to move from audience to inner circle,
they incurred the wrath of the powerful. The Belle Époque writer
Octave Mirbeau, on learning of two women's desire to join the Society of Men of Letters, responded with a stern tongue-lashing:
"Woman is not a brain, she is a sex, and that is much better. She has
only one role in this world, to make love, that is, to perpetuate the
race. She is not good for anything but love and motherhood. Some
women, rare exceptions, have been able to give, either in art or literature, the illusion that they are creative. But they are either abnormal
or simply reflections of men. I prefer what are called prostitutes because they at least are in harmony with the Universe."

Mirbeau's view was not unusual in fin de siècle Paris. It reflected
a deep-seated cultural conviction that male-female difference was at
the core of a truly civilized society. Henri Marion, lecturing on the
psychology of women at the Sorbonne in the 1880s and 1890s, reduced this belief to a formula: "the more advanced a society's civiliza-

tion, the more pronounced the division of labor between men and women becomes. . . . In the large cities of the great nations of the West where civilization is at its height, gender differentiation is at a maximum."

Even republicans like Michelet, supposed adherents of liberty and equality, clung to the notion that the respectable woman's place was at home, as inspiration. Unlike the man, who "passes from drama to drama," the woman "follows the noble and serene epic that nature chants in her harmonious cycles, repeating herself with a touching grace of constancy and fidelity." Needless to say, such an angelic presence would have been unbearable had she not been supplemented by a mistress or the occasional prostitute. It says a great deal about the Belle Époque that a wife's adultery was treated as a crime, while a husband's was not even a misdemeanor.

Some republican initiatives did benefit women, particularly in the realm of education. In 1880, the Camille Sée law was passed, extending secondary school education to girls for the first time. But the French belief in *la différence* cast its shadow even over this reform. Boys, in their lycées, got physics and biology, along with the Latin and Greek necessary to pass the *baccalauréat* exam and gain entry to the university; girls, in their newly established schools, got domestic and applied science. Thus, the doors to university remained closed to all but a few exceptional women. It would take fifty-seven years before the girls' *lycées* created by the Camille Sée law adopted the same program as the boys'.

As a result of these constraints, Frenchwomen had greater difficulty entering their own universities than foreign women did. As in other countries, they managed to succeed first in medicine: the Faculté de médecine granted its first degree to a Frenchwoman in 1875. A rationale could be found for medical training in the very difference between the sexes which so often kept women down: women doctors, after all, could address themselves to the special mysteries of the female body. A *nouvelle doctoresse* in medicine was praised by *l'Illustration* because she had the "tact" to prepare her dissertation on menorrhagia, a menstrual complication "specific to the weaker sex."

Women's entry into letters, the sciences, and the law, however, continued to meet with opposition into the 1880s and beyond. Jeanne Chauvin, the first woman to defend her dissertation in the law, was so harassed by the spectators that she had to finish up her examination in private. And in every field of study at the Sorbonne, Frenchwomen were outnumbered by foreigners. Indeed, it wasn't until 1912 that the number of Frenchwomen surpassed that of foreign women in their own universities.

Marie Skłodowska, as one of those foreign women, drew less

attention and opprobrium than her French counterparts. The foreign contingent at the Sorbonne was often thought of as a group apart, with different rules of conduct. It was said of the Russians, with whom Marie might have been lumped, that they were "different from Parisians, and not susceptible to the enticements of Cupid, at least not during their college life." This fact allowed several of them of both sexes to "take an apartment together," using one bedroom for the men and one for the women. "For students with less Siberian blood in their veins this arrangement could not be thought of."

Besides the protective coloring of foreignness, Marie had a tradition to rely on. She came from a family in which women led independent lives, and from a country in which women were often outspoken and independent, even if they were denied access to higher education. And then, too, she had the freedom which travel brings. To be abroad, away from those we know and whose opinion matters to us, is always liberating.

But even foreign women like Marie were not immune to cruel stereotyping by chroniclers like Henri d'Almeras. "What distinguishes the serious female student, almost always a foreigner, is that almost no one takes her seriously," he wrote. "If she is treated with a certain courtesy, she should consider herself lucky. The jokes that are made about her are not always in the best of taste. . . . These female students work with great patience, as though they were doing embroidery. Their study makes them ugly. They usually look like schoolteachers and wear glasses. In the examinations, they recite with admirable exactitude what they've learned. They don't always understand it."

Men like d'Almeras would have been happier if women had continued to fit into the usual two categories: prostitute and wife/mother. Indeed, until late in the century the word *étudiante* (female student) had been one of the many names for the mistresses of male university students. These *étudiantes,* as Henri d'Almeras quipped, were not the kind who prepared for exams but "the kind who distracted you from preparing." Alternatively called *grisettes, lolottes, filles galantes,* and a host of other sobriquets, they were thought to be a perfectly natural solution to the sexual cravings of young males, who took up with them and passed them on with the greatest of ease. A caricaturist of the time has one young student telling his friend as he leaves on vacation, "I'm entrusting you with my pipe and my woman. Take good care of my pipe. . . ."

A remarkable young American woman, newly married and studying at the Sorbonne with her husband during this period was troubled both by the phenomenon of the "girls in the Boul' Mich' cafés" and the reason given for them, "the absolute necessity of the one type of

woman in order to preserve the virtue of the other . . . of me in fact.
. . . Let the point of view shift," suggested Mrs. A. Herbage Edwards,
"as it is shifting, question the undisputed kingship, admit woman's
equal right as a human being, and man's needs become his own
problem." Yet Mrs. Edwards understood why the women came, out
of "desire for life and pleasure . . . just exactly as it brought the men."
But the women were different, she noted, because they were working-
class. For them, "the alternative was not different pleasures, but
none, and the hard, monotonous, grinding life of the workshop to fill
to exhaustion their waking hours."

The number of genuine *étudiantes* at the Sorbonne had been
increasing gradually since the first woman attended classes there in
1867. In 1887, the year that Bronia enrolled in the school of medicine,
there were 215 women in attendance, most foreign and most in medical school. Five years after that, when Marie enrolled in the science
faculty, the number of women had actually decreased slightly, to 210,
a small minority indeed in an overall university population of over
9,000. The number of women seriously pursuing degrees at the Sorbonne, and not just attending classes, was much smaller still. In 1893,
the year Marie Skłodowska received the *licence ès sciences,* she was
one of two female *licence* recipients in the entire university. In 1894,
when she received the *licence ès mathématiques,* she was one of five.

As Sorbonne historian Henri Bourrelier remembered it, the
"presence of women at the University caused a profound transformation of the Latin Quarter, both in personal lives and in the picturesque life on the streets. The behavior of the male students became
more refined through regular contact with this less dissipated, less
boisterous and more delicate element."

And yet in 1891, when Marie Skłodowska stepped down from her
omnibus onto the boulevard St. Germain, there was still a powerful
feeling that the Latin Quarter was male territory. It was not uncommon in the nineties for male students to organize a *monôme,* a long,
snaking single-file parade of students in a holiday mood, waving their
canes and tossing their top hats in the air while holding up traffic on
the "boul' Mich'." And in July of 1893, as Marie studied furiously to
pass the *licence ès sciences,* thirty thousand troops were called in to
quell violent demonstrations in the Latin Quarter which grew out of
protests over a police crackdown on nudity at the Bal des Quat'z Arts
in Montmartre.

What's more, it was impossible to walk up the rue St. Jacques
without noticing what one American visitor called the "spectacular
diversions" of the *étudiants.* "Does it not seem strange," wrote Stuart
Henry in 1896, "that both St. Séverin and the Sorbonne . . . appear
to take no notice of the notorious fact that the apartments, whose

windows look in upon them, are occupied by *filles galantes,* who live in the most open manner possible with the students, and flourish elbow to elbow with the Church and the University?"

It wasn't easy, in this atmosphere, for a woman to feel entirely sure just how she might be treated. "The cafés of the Boul' Mich'," as the astute Mrs. Edwards observed, "gave much to think about. . . . There was always just that element of uncertainty. I have seen the apparently innocent passer-by suddenly, and for no obvious reason, become the target for all manner of loud-voice and uncomfortable jests, even equally suddenly and without reason surrounded by a ring of café habitués of both sexes and sometimes escorted in this manner halfway along the boulevard. One never quite knew. So much loose force and energy were lying all round and any untoward spark might fire them." Mrs. Edwards saw herself as "an unsophisticated, well-brought up person," a description which might apply equally well to Marie Skłodowska. As she walked alone along the broad boulevards, past the noisy cafés, Marie too must have felt that "loose energy" and braced herself for the possibility that it would spill over rudely in her direction.

Yet in the classroom, the same mentality which divided women into prostitute and lady worked in women students' favor. Young men who were crude and boisterous "in the very different atmosphere of the cafés" were the soul of courtesy inside the walls of the Sorbonne. "No attempts were ever made," Mrs. Edwards writes, "to launch billets-doux into my pockets, and an atmosphere of severe respect which took no notice of such incidents as sex pervaded the inside of the classrooms and all the students with whom I came in contact."

Marie Skłodowska too had "pleasant memories of my relations with my student companions." One of 23 women among over 1,825 students enrolled in the Faculté des sciences in 1891, she was "reserved and shy" in the beginning. But before long she "noticed that the students, nearly all of whom worked seriously, were disposed to be friendly."

At this stage of her life, Marie Skłodowska was only interested in friends who "worked seriously." For a while, after she moved to her garret apartment, she had socialized with the "small colony" of Polish students "in one another's bare rooms, where we could talk over national questions and feel less isolated. We would also go for walks together, or attend public reunions, for we were all interested in politics." But by the end of the first year, "I was forced to give up these relationships, for I found that all my energy had to be concentrated on my studies." And so, increasingly, she prized "conversations about our studies" with science classmates which "deepened our interest in the problems we discussed."

"All my mind," she wrote, "was centered on my studies. I divided my time between courses, experimental work, and study in the library. In the evening I worked in my room, sometimes very late into the night. All that I saw and learned that was new delighted me. It was like a new world opened to me, the world of science, which I was at last permitted to know at all liberty."

IT WAS A GOOD TIME to be a science student at the Sorbonne. For over a century, the fate of the University of Paris, the Sorbonne, had been tied to the struggle between the republicans, arguing for separation of church and state, and the royalists, who yearned for some form of monarchy allied with the Church. Founded and named after a thirteenth-century royal chaplain, Pierre de Sorbon, the university took on its modern outlines in the seventeenth century, when Cardinal Richelieu made the Sorbonne a symbol of both personal and ecclesiastical power. He renovated its buildings at his own expense and oversaw the construction of a sumptuous domed chapel which would eventually house his imposing tomb. But when revolution came, the tomb of Richelieu was sacked and his chapel was renamed the "temple of Reason." The university itself, associated as it was with the forces of repression, fell into disuse; classrooms and lecture halls, as well as the chapel itself, were rented out as artists' studios.

Over the next hundred years, the Sorbonne's fate improved only slightly, as France vacillated between parliamentary government and the central control of a succession of emperors and monarchs. Then events of the late nineteenth century conspired to bring about a renaissance. In 1870–71, the French Second Empire suffered a swift and humiliating defeat at the hands of Prussia. In the period of self-examination which followed, leaders of the Third Republic argued that superior German education, particularly in the scientific realm, had put France at a military disadvantage. The key to ultimate triumph over the Prussians, they insisted, was an overhaul of the French educational system. "The survival of France . . . ," notes historian Harry Paul, "was made contingent on the development of science."

The leaders of the Third Republic chose to make the Sorbonne the centerpiece of their educational reform. Once a clerical stronghold, the new Sorbonne was to preach republican anticlerical gospel, insisting on the primacy of the rational over the irrational. And the republicans, like Richelieu before them, decided to make their dominance manifest by undertaking a major building program. They would erect a new Sorbonne which would be "above all an homage to science."

By the time Marie Skłodowska arrived in 1891, the reconstruction

of the Sorbonne was well under way. The grand amphitheater, dominated by a sweeping Puvis de Chavannes mural portraying the Sorbonne as a "secular virgin" *(vierge laïque)*, was complete, as were
many of the lecture rooms. The science classrooms and laboratories,
however, were still being built. Marie's classes had to be held in makeshift quarters nearby, while architect Henri-Paul Nénot oversaw the
creation of lavishly equipped laboratories which were to make the
Faculté des sciences "one of the best housed in Europe." When finished, the west side of the rectangular block of Sorbonne buildings
would be crowned with whimsical chimneys and towers devoted to
scientific inquiry. An observatory dome for charting the stars and a
physics tower for studying falling bodies would now overshadow the
dome of the Richelieu chapel, the only remaining structure of the old
Sorbonne.

The science towers were an outward symbol of a revolution
within. Theology was banished from the new Sorbonne, and letters
were deemphasized. Science was the order of the day. As a result of
new and generous subsidies, the science faculty doubled between
1876 and 1900, and the number of supporting laboratory assistants
and technicians quadrupled. Greater emphasis was placed on original
research in hiring faculty, with a resulting explosion in fundamental
and applied research production. Scholarships were initiated, increasing the number and quality of science students. A greater variety of
subjects was introduced into the curriculum, and classes grew
smaller. Informal seminars became available to students for the first
time. More importantly, there was a new emphasis on laboratory work
as a part of the students' learning experience.

Most importantly of all, a brilliant young roster of faculty members assembled at the Sorbonne, a group able to inspire by example,
rather than to just doggedly teach the known science necessary to
passing the exams. "In the life of the laboratories," Marie Curie wrote
later, "the influence of the professors on the students is due to their
own love of science and to their personal qualities much more than
to their authority. One of them would say to his students: 'Don't trust
what people teach you, and above all what *I* teach you.' "

During those three years, from 1891 to 1894, in which Marie
Skłodowska prepared first for the *licence ès sciences* and then for
the *licence ès mathématiques,* she was exposed to some of the most
important scientific minds of the age. Among the sixteen professors
who taught her during those years, eight made a contribution significant enough to earn them a place in the current *Dictionary of Scientific Biography.*

One of her physics professors was Gabriel Lippmann, who would
win a Nobel Prize in 1908 for developing a method of photographic

color reproduction. Lippmann, who had worked in Germany, was a practical physicist adept at instrument design; he developed a number of sensitive measuring devices which were useful in seismology and astronomy. A second physics teacher, Joseph Boussinesq, was Lippmann's opposite: one of the last of the classical physicists, an author of imaginative and pioneering works who until his death in 1929 remained adamantly opposed to relativity theory and all its implications.

Others were daring adventurers in the larger world: Pierre Puiseux, who taught analytic geometry, was a passionate mountain climber who would later author a two-volume work on climbing without a guide. Paul Painlevé, also a mathematician, would become an early aviator and, eventually, the French minister of war. And Émile Duclaux, who taught Marie biological chemistry, was a man of "wit and verve" who combined "the logic of the scientist and the style of a poet." Duclaux had been one of the first to believe Pasteur's microbe theory and became one of its most important advocates. His courses in microbiology at the Sorbonne were the first of their kind anywhere. Marie Skłodowska's course with Duclaux was called biological chemistry, but there can be little doubt that the still-new ideas of Pasteur, who was still at work in a Paris laboratory, made their way into his impassioned lectures.

And then there was Paul Appell, an Alsatian whose brother was jailed in Alsace for anti-German activity at the time Marie Skłodowska attended his class in *mécanique rationelle.* His scientific contribution would consist of "a series of brilliant solutions of particular problems, some of the greatest difficulty," though he didn't manage, as he had hoped, to "open new doors." In this he stood in starkest contrast to his friend, the man who without a doubt was the most brilliant among Marie Skłodowska's teachers, Henri Poincaré. Poincaré was the preeminent mathematician of the late nineteenth century, a prolific writer of books and papers who made historic contributions to mathematical theory and to celestial mechanics. Still in his early thirties when Marie attended his classes, Poincaré was already world renowned.

Given this array of teachers, it is not surprising that Marie Skłodowska, who had hungered so long to study unencumbered, should put aside all other pleasures. "It is difficult for me to tell you about my life in detail," she wrote Józef in the spring of 1894, as she neared the end of her studies for the *licence* in mathematics. "It is so monotonous and, in fact, so uninteresting. Nevertheless I have no feeling of uniformity and I regret only one thing, which is that the days are so short and that they pass so quickly."

There were some diversions, of course. In the spring of 1893, as she prepared to take her first *licence* exams, she traveled one Sunday to Le Raincy, and wrote home of the beauty of spring in France. "The lilacs and the fruit trees, even the apples, were in full bloom and the air was filled with the scent of flowers. In Paris, the trees get green as early as the beginning of April. Now the leaves have sprung out and the chestnuts are blooming." She worried that she might not be ready in time for exams. "At the worst," she wrote, "I shall wait until November, but that will make me lose my summer, which doesn't appeal to me."

But in fact she didn't lose that summer, or the other long summers of those three undergraduate years: every July, she left Paris to stay with her family in Warsaw, and to travel with them in Poland and Switzerland.

And unlike the ideal student she evoked in her poetry, the lonely scholar immune to "new bliss" and "new desires," Marie Skłodowska did find time for at least one suitor during these years, a young man by the name of Lamotte. His farewells are all that survive from which to imagine their relationship. In June of 1894, as Marie prepared to take her last series of examinations at the Sorbonne, he wrote:

> Mademoiselle, it is likely I won't have a chance to see you again; it is painful not to see you once again before you leave Paris: especially because on Sunday you seemed so sad that I have an unpleasant memory of our last encounter. But I don't know whether it would be asking too much, given all you have to do right now, for you to give me a few minutes, and for that reason I won't ask.

> I want to thank you for the kindness you have shown me: if at times I have been too forward, forgive me for the sake of my friendship which might be indiscreet but has always been sincere and without ulterior motive.

> Allow me to wish you all the happiness you deserve in the future—I hope in particular that the coming month brings you the success you hope for and will be the just recompense for all your efforts.

> One small word still of reproach: you insisted that I would quickly forget you when I had lost sight of you. I fear that you are mistaken. Without doubt we won't meet again. However, if you ever should need it, remember that you have left somewhere a friend ready to do everything possible for you. Adieu! M. Lamotte

Marie Skłodowska must have cared about M. Lamotte. She had confided in him about her ambitions, and she seems to have found their parting difficult. But the pull was not powerful enough to change the course she had set for herself three years before, when she left home. She told him, as she told her family, that she was going back to Warsaw, where she would live with her father and earn her living as a teacher.

Władysław Skłodowski had been looking forward to the day of her return ever since she left. When, early in her stay in Paris, she dressed as "Polonia" for a soirée with Polish friends, he became alarmed about the possibility that such activity would prevent her return to Poland and wrote her a letter full of carefully worded warnings:

> Your last letter saddened me. I deplore your taking such active part in the organization of this theatrical representation. Even though it be a thing done in all innocence, it attracts attention to its organizers, and you certainly know that there are persons in Paris who inspect your behavior with the greatest care, who take note of the names of those who are in the forefront and who send information about them here, to be used as might be useful. This can be a source of very great annoyance, and even forbid such persons access to certain professions. Thus, those who wish to earn their bread in Warsaw in the future without being exposed to various dangers will find it to their interest to keep quiet, in a retreat where they may remain unknown. Events such as concerts, balls, etc., are described by certain correspondents for newspapers, who mention names. It would be a great grief to me if your name were mentioned one day. This is why . . . I have . . . begged you to keep to yourself as much as possible. . . .

Undoubtedly, her father had reason to worry. After all, Maria was associating with Kazimierz Dłuski and other known "troublemakers" at the time. But his severe tone may also reflect his concern that such frivolity could lead not just to political censure but to romance, depriving him of the company of his youngest daughter just as it had of his eldest, Bronia.

Two years later, when he heard that Marie was taking the *licence* exam in science, he wrote to Bronia that he was going to "keep the lodging that I occupy for next year: for myself and for Manya—if she comes back—it is perfectly suitable. . . . Little by little Manya will work up a list of pupils, and in any case I am ready to share what I have with her. We shall manage without trouble. . . ."

Marie, like her father, continued to cast herself in the role of faithful daughter. It had been concern for her father's feelings which had almost kept her from coming to study in Paris three years before. Now, in her letters to Józef, she played at being jealous of his wife: "Is your wife taking care of Father, as she promised me? Let her take care, just the same, not to cut me out altogether at home! Father is beginning to speak of her a little too tenderly, and I am afraid that he will be forgetting me soon. . . ."

And yet, when her friend Jadwiga Dydyńska managed to arrange a six-hundred-ruble Alexandrovitch scholarship for her after she passed the *licence ès sciences* exam, Marie decided to return to Paris for a second degree despite the pull of home. "I hardly need say that I am delighted to be back in Paris," she wrote Józef, soon after her arrival. "It was difficult for me to separate again from Father, but I could see that he was well, very lively, and that he could do without me—especially as you are living in Warsaw. And as for me, it is my whole life that is at stake. It seemed to me, therefore, that I could stay on here without having remorse on my conscience."

Marie's academic success in Paris had been nothing short of spectacular. The previous July she ranked first among those taking the *licence ès sciences* exam. And now she was on her way, with her usual assiduity, to a second triumph. "I am studying mathematics unceasingly," she wrote Józef that September, "so as to be up to date when courses begin." In July of 1894, the Polish girl who was poorly prepared in math at the Warsaw gymnasium ranked second in her examinations for the *licence ès mathématiques*.

Certainly she had credentials now which would place her in great demand as a teacher in Poland. And until a few months before her departure, she still had every intention of returning home to work and keep her father company. But sometime that spring, she was introduced to Pierre Curie. Very soon, her sense of duty had to compete with the exciting possibility of love. When she left Paris in August, having finished her last exam, everyone in the family, along with the admiring M. Lamotte, fully expected that she would never return. Only Pierre Curie had reason to hope otherwise.

Chapter Five

A BEAUTIFUL THING

YEARS LATER, Marie vividly recalled the first time she saw Pierre Curie. He was standing in a French window opening on a balcony.

> He seemed to me very young, though he was at that time thirty-five years old. I was struck by the open expression of his face and by the slight suggestion of detachment in his whole attitude. His speech, rather slow and deliberate, his simplicity, and his smile, at once grave and youthful, inspired confidence.

Both Marie and Pierre came to their first meeting with painful memories which made them reluctant to love again. Marie had told her sister, when her hot-and-cold relationship with Kazimierz Zorawski finally ended three years earlier, that "the cruel trials I have been through . . . will have an influence on my whole life." Pierre's traumatic experience, as he confided eventually to Marie, had to do with the death of a young woman he had known and loved since childhood. He was twenty at the time. "I lack the courage to tell you about that," he wrote. "I was very guilty, I had and will always have great remorse about it. I spent many days and nights afterward with an *idée fixe*. I took pleasure in torturing myself. Then I made a resolution that I would live the life of a priest and I promised that I would take an interest only in things and would think no more of myself or of other people."

Given Marie's scars and Pierre's oath of abstinence, it was fortunate that the first meeting between the two was arranged for scientific purposes, with little hint of matchmaking. It came about through a Polish physicist named Józef Kowalski, a professor at the University of Fribourg, and his new wife, who had met Marie during her governess years at Szczuki. The Kowalskis, who were on their honeymoon in Paris, may have had thoughts of a possible romance. But that winter Marie Skłodowska was preoccupied, as she would be for much of her life from then on, with the need for more laboratory space. She was well along, at that point, in the preparation for her second undergraduate degree at the Sorbonne. And she had had the good fortune, probably through her professor, Gabriel Lippmann, to be hired by one of those organizations formed after the Franco-Prussian War to promote the cause of French science: the Society for the Encouragement of National Industry had commissioned her to conduct a study of the magnetic properties of various steels. When the Kowalskis came to call on their countrywoman, she lamented the small space she had to work in in Professor Lippmann's laboratory at the Sorbonne. Kowalski thought of Pierre Curie, who was doing important work on magnetism at a new, lesser-known institution nearby; he suggested the four of them get together to talk about Marie's problem.

Thus the first encounter of Marie Skłodowska and Pierre Curie hung on two improbable threads. One was a chance meeting between Marie and the future Mrs. Kowalski in a remote Polish crossroads called Szczuki. The other was Mr. Kowalski's acquaintance with the work of Pierre Curie.

Pierre Curie's work should have been well known at that point in scientific circles. Already his study of crystals had led him to postulate important laws of symmetry. And for some years, he had been conducting experiments which would form the basis of laws of magnetism which are still invoked today. Also, he had invented a number of delicate measuring instruments, one of which had drawn the praise of Lord Kelvin, highly respected for his own inventions and his contribution to the understanding of heat and work.

But, as Curie's colleague Paul Langevin later observed, "we quickly forget the best people when they live apart." And Pierre Curie was the ultimate outsider. Instead of attending one of the *grandes écoles,* the best path to success in French academia, he had studied at home with his brother, and then with a gifted tutor. He hadn't bothered to seek a Ph.D., the *sine qua non* of advancement in the French system, even though he had done the original work required several times over. What's more, he taught at a fledgling, industrially oriented school, the École municipale de physique et chimie industrielle, where he had to make do with improvised laboratory space that was a far cry from the superb new laboratories at the Sorbonne.

Even when he was sought out for honors, Pierre Curie was likely to decline. Early on, the founder/director of the École de physique et chimie, Professor Schützenberger, had thought of submitting his name for the honorific *palmes académiques*, and had received this letter from the proposed honoree:

> I write to beg you not to do anything. If you obtain this honor for me, you will obligate me to refuse it, because I have decided never to accept any decoration of any sort. I hope that you wouldn't want to put me in a position which would appear ridiculous to many people. If your intention is to give me testimony of your interest you have already done so, and in a fashion much more effective by which I have been very much moved, in giving me the means to work at my leisure.

Pierre Curie might have attributed his extreme diffidence to his trauma at age twenty, which made him resolve to abandon self-interest forever. But then again, as he himself astutely observed, "I have often wondered . . . if this renunciation of existence wasn't simply a ruse that I made use of in order to have the right to lose myself." Pierre Curie's wish had always been to lose himself: to work, as he had told Schützenberger, "at my leisure," to be free of conventional pressures and expectations, to devote himself entirely to the excitement and wonder of discovery.

In part, his extreme aversion to academic politics and to self-promotion may have grown out of his own awkwardness and inwardness. He lacked small talk, was easily embarrassed by any sort of special attention, and had the kind of mind which required stillness. Then too, like many capable people, he believed he should be able to succeed on his merits, without self-advertisement, and tended to associate academic politicking with mediocrity. To his partner in irony Georges Gouy, he wrote contemptuously of a "cherished child" in Gabriel Lippmann's lab, a "chouchou" who rushed to popularize every one of Lippmann's discoveries. "He's a young man of little talent . . . very fawning with everyone and hungry for honorific and other positions." At the same time, and most significantly, Pierre Curie's refusal to play the usual game was deeply rooted in family history. He was the son and grandson of men who lived by strong, often unpopular convictions.

Pierre Curie was born on rue Cuvier in Paris on May 15, 1859, the second son of Sophie-Claire Depouilly and Eugène Curie. His mother was the daughter of a prominent manufacturer from Puteaux, near Paris, who had suffered serious reversals during the economic crisis of 1848. Her father and her brothers were commercial inventors. Eugène Curie, Pierre's father, came from Alsace, and trained as a physician, like his father before him. But both Eugène and his father, Paul, were also advocates of revolutionary ideas.

Paul Curie, Pierre's grandfather, had been a churchgoing, socially prominent doctor in the city of Mulhouse, in Alsace, until he publicly professed his conversion to a new, secular alternative to Christianity called Saint-Simonianism. The year was 1831, just after the revolution which routed the last Bourbon king, and Dr. Curie believed he had found a new way to save the people. "We can do in this life," Dr. Curie promised the citizens of Mulhouse, "that which Christianity expects only of the next life."

The doctrine of Saint-Simon captivated some of the most important intellectuals of that time, including the founder of positivism, Auguste Comte. Like positivism, Saint-Simonianism advocated a new faith, one that produced the social cohesion Catholicism had lacked. Followers of Saint-Simon developed a cult which emphasized love and stressed the spiritual importance of women. In the new society, war and antagonism would be no more, because each person would be performing his true calling. Anticipating Marx and Engels, the Saint-Simonians' cry was "From each according to his capacity."

As Dr. Curie explained it in his several public statements on the subject, Saint-Simonianism, unlike traditional Christianity, would lead to the social betterment of the most numerous and impoverished class. All privileges of birth would be abolished and society would be reorganized into a hierarchy based on ability.

Predictably, Dr. Curie's pronouncements brought a rebuttal from the local pastor, who noted that "the poor should be the object of general compassion" but that "in most cases they are in their unfortunate position through their own fault." Dr. Curie was demoted from his prominent position in the local Protestant church. Ultimately he left Mulhouse for England, where he became a much-sought-after practitioner of homeopathic medicine.

Eugène Curie, the oldest of Paul Curie's four children, grew up with his mother in Paris, with little knowledge of his father, who seems to have been less magnanimous toward his offspring than toward humanity in general. Nonetheless, Eugène followed in his father's ideological footsteps, espousing the republican ideals of anticlericalism and egalitarianism. His early years, following medical studies, were spent working as an assistant to Louis Pierre Gratiolet, an important descriptive anatomist at the Museum of Natural History in Paris. According to his older son, Jacques, he would have preferred to continue in academic medicine, but was compelled by straitened circumstances to become a practitioner.

As the dramatic events of the nineteenth century unfolded, Eugène Curie seems to have seized every opportunity to act on his convictions. In the 1848 revolution he manned the barricades, had part of his jaw shattered by fire from government troops, and was decorated, during the brief reign of the republicans which followed, for his service to wounded insurgents. When a cholera epidemic invaded Paris, he set up in an area of the city deserted by other physicians in order to treat the victims. And in 1871, when the people of Paris rose up against the conciliatory government at Versailles, Eugène Curie allied himself once again with the rebels. He turned the family apartment on rue de la Visitation into an emergency clinic for wounded Communards from the barricades nearby. Pierre, who was twelve at the time, remembered expeditions with his brother into the neighborhood to seek out and bring back victims of the bloody street fighting.

It was maintained in the family that Eugène Curie's radical past made it difficult for him to attract a bourgeois clientèle, and obliged him to work for less pay as a school doctor in the employ of the republican government. According to Jacques, "the family lived in relative financial difficulty," and it was this situation which forced both him and his brother Pierre to make some "regrettable decisions." Pierre, because he needed to "be able to support himself as early as possible," was denied a "regular and complete development" and "had much less time to consecrate to personal research."

Nonetheless, there were great advantages to growing up in the Curie house. Because of their father's fervent republicanism, neither Pierre nor Jacques was baptised or exposed to religion. But they were imbued from an early age with a sense of awe. The brothers learned the careful study of flora and fauna from their father; they took long walks together out into the wilds surrounding Paris and brought back specimens for him. On summer vacations in the nearby countryside, there were tramps along the Seine, sometimes lasting days, interrupted by swimming and diving. Pierre, who was understood to be meditative, was allowed to go off on his own as well, and to lose himself in beautiful surroundings: at twenty, he looked back with near ecstasy on his times alone in the country:

> Oh, what a good time I have passed there in that gracious solitude, so far from the thousand little worrying things that torment me in Paris. No, I do not regret my nights passed in the woods, and my solitary days. If I had the time I would . . . describe my delicious valley, filled with perfume of aromatic plants, the beautiful mass of foliage, so fresh and so humid, that hung over the Bièvre, the fairy palace with its colonnades of hops, the stony hills, red with heather, where it was so good to be. Oh I shall remember always with gratitude the forest of the Minière; of all the woods I have seen, it is this one that I have loved most and where I have been happiest. Often in the evening I would start out and ascend again this valley, and I would return with twenty ideas in my head.

Fortunately for Pierre, his parents were quick to perceive that he needed latitude in his education as well. On principle, Eugène had decided to educate his sons at home, where Pierre was allowed to progress at his own pace, and following his own interests. The result, as Jacques noted, was an "irregular and incomplete" foundation, with "certain parts neglected" and "certain parts quite developed." Pierre had practically no literary and classical training, for instance, while he was very precocious in his understanding of natural sciences and geometry.

Everyone in the Curie family seems to have been aware, however, that Pierre's unusual intellectual strengths and weaknesses were not simply the product of home schooling. He thought of himself, in fact, as having a "slow mind." Unlike his brother Jacques, a more conventional learner, Pierre needed to focus exclusively and deeply on one thing at a time. Further, while his writing is thoughtful and expressive, his penmanship would have displeased a lycée teacher. The o's are consistently written like a's, thoughts are run together without the guideposts of capitals and periods, and he sometimes makes errors in agreement which are unusual in an educated Frenchman. (Jacques, despite a similar training, had none of these writing difficulties.)

Later, Marie, anticipating modern views of learning disability, wrote that "his dreamer's spirit would not submit itself to the ordering of the intellectual effort imposed by the school." He needed, she explained, "to concentrate his thought with great intensity upon a certain definite object, in order to obtain a precise result." Nor was it possible for him to "interrupt or to modify the course of his reflections to suit exterior circumstances." Pierre would have been unhappy and unsuccessful in a formal school setting, since "no system of education has been especially provided by the public school for persons of this intellectual category, which nevertheless includes more representatives than one would believe. . . . Very fortunately for Pierre, who could not . . . become a brilliant pupil in a lycée, his parents had a sufficiently keen intelligence to understand his difficulty, and they refrained from demanding of their son an effort which would have been prejudicial to his development."

Paul Langevin wrote later that Pierre's "quite irregular" education gave him "time to look, to see everything around him with his own eyes, to form a complete and intimate bond with things which he retained for the rest of his life, and which rendered him incapable of this hasty, superficial and insipid understanding one acquires from books." Indeed, even in books (his father had a large library), Pierre chose depth over surface brilliance. He once told someone who was objecting to his weighty choice of reading matter, "I don't dislike tedious books."

It is easy enough, in retrospect, to see the advantages of Pierre's haphazard education. But at the time there must have been an uneasy feeling about it, even in the laissez-faire atmosphere of the Curie family. That, at least, would seem to be implied in brother Jacques' account of the arrival on the scene of a tutor named Albert Bazille. Until he was fourteen, Pierre had been taught by his parents and by Jacques, who was four years older. Then "a wonderful transformation in his education took place. He was placed under the tutelage of an excellent professor of mathematics, M. Al. Bazille, who taught him elementary and special mathematics and who, having understood and appreciated him as he deserved to be, became strongly attached to him and pushed him to develop himself. It seems certain that it was through these lessons that the mind of Pierre Curie was opened up and developed and it is due to the remarkable teaching of M. Bazille that he owes his intellectual transformation, the deepening of his faculties and the birth of his scientific abilities."

Once awakened, the "slow" mind of Pierre Curie became prodigious. Two years later, he passed the *bachelier ès sciences* which allowed him to enter the Sorbonne. At eighteen, he received the *licence ès sciences* and was offered the job of assistant *(préparateur)* in the Sorbonne physics laboratory set aside for student experiments. Very soon, he began to publish original work, first in collaboration with one of his teachers, Paul Desains, with whom he studied heat. After that, he joined forces with his brother Jacques, who was also working as a *préparateur,* in the laboratory of mineralogy at the Sorbonne.

The subject of the Curie brothers' research together harked back to their years of exploration of natural wonders: they undertook a systematic study of crystals, a group of mineral substances in which molecules are arranged in repeating patterns of varying complexity. Nature is replete with symmetry, much of it obvious to the naked eye. Snowflakes, for instance, are a crystalline form of observable symmetry. "An object possesses a plane of symmetry, or a plane of reflection," as Marie Curie later wrote in explaining Pierre's work, "if this plane divides the object into two parts. . . . It is this, approximately, that occurs in the external appearance of man and of numerous animals . . . a regular flower of four petals has [a plane of symmetry] and an axis of symmetry of the order four. . . . Crystals like those of rock salt or of alum possess many planes of symmetry and many axes of symmetry of different orders."

It was these "hemihedral" crystals, with their multiple planes and axes of symmetry, which interested the Curie brothers. And it was in the study of this group that Pierre and Jacques Curie happened upon a remarkable discovery. It had already been observed by Charles Friedel, Jacques' teacher, that heat caused such crystals to become charged; this was a phenomenon called "pyroelectricity." Jacques and Pierre established that the underlying cause of the charge was not heat but pressure: when the shape of certain of these hemihedral crystals was altered by pressure, they gave off an electric charge. In 1880, when Pierre was twenty-one, the brothers published their first brief communication of the discovery they called "polar electricity" in the *Bulletin of the Mineralogy Society.* Subsequently, Gabriel Lippmann predicted, and the Curie brothers bore out experimentally, that the inverse was also true: that such complex crystal forms would change shape in response to the application of an electric charge.

All together, the brothers published nine papers on the phenomenon, which came to be called piezoelectricity (from the Greek *piezein,* "to press tight"). And then, out of their discovery, they devised an instrument called the piezoelectric quartz balance *(quartz piezoélectrique)* which allowed the measurement of extremely small amounts of electric charge through the known relationship between pressure exerted on the crystal—quartz in this instance—and electrical response.

The piezoelectric quartz balance, which was the subject of Jacques Curie's doctoral thesis in 1889, led a short but significant life: it proved essential to the delicate measurements which resulted in the discovery of radium. The phenomenon of piezoelectricity, on the other hand, has continued to find useful applications into the present. During World War I, Pierre Curie's friend Paul Langevin used quartz resonance to produce high-frequency sound waves, the "sonar" which enabled the location of enemy submarines; and the principle of piezoelectricity has application in radio broadcasting and measurement of pressure variations as well.

In the course of his work on piezoelectricity, Pierre Curie demonstrated a versatility that might not have been possible had he been raised to think in narrow categories of accomplishment. He had begun, as in childhood, with the observation of a remarkable natural phenomenon, the structure of crystals. Then came a period of close physical relationship with the objects in question. This, as Paul Langevin observed, was a critical part of the process for Pierre Curie. He and Jacques began in the mineralogy laboratory, subjecting a wide variety of intriguing rocks—topaz, tourmaline, calamine, salt, quartz —to their pressure test. Then, drawing on their knowledge of geometry and on previous knowledge of the behavior of crystals subjected to heat, that is, pyroelectricity, they made their way to the discovery of the underlying cause.

While he worked in the realms of mineralogy and chemistry, Pierre was also inventing. He and his brother devised an electrometer adapted to measuring the minute charges involved in the piezoelectric phenomenon, and a number of other scales and measuring instruments, as well as the piezoelectric quartz balance. He oversaw the design, machining, the patenting, and distribution of a number of these instruments, tinkering and testing all along the way. Despite his lifelong abhorrence of taking profit from scientific discovery, Pierre seems to have enjoyed selling his inventions. "Thanks to you," Pierre wrote gaily to his friend Georges Gouy after he ordered several Curie instruments, "the city of Lyon is going to be the one where our important firm will run up its biggest profits!"

In 1883, when Pierre was just twenty-four, economic necessity forced a physical separation of the brothers. Jacques had accepted a position in mineralogy at the University of Montpellier in 1883, and the two had had to limit their collaboration to the summer months. Around that same time, Pierre had moved to a new position outside the Sorbonne, at the École municipale de physique et chimie industrielles (EPCI). The EPCI was a brand-new school, coaxed into existence by Jacques' mentor Charles Friedel. It was housed in ancient buildings and had none of the sumptuous facilities of the Sorbonne. It was a step aside, rather than a step up the academic ladder for Pierre Curie, and one that made others indignant on his behalf. "From the scientific point of view," his brother Jacques argued, "it is certain that his appointment to this school . . . slowed by several years his experimental research. At the time that he was appointed, nothing existed in this school; everything had to be created. . . . He had to spend significant amounts of time . . . putting it in place. He did it . . . with characteristic precision and originality. The experiments of the many students were also very difficult to oversee for a young man assisted only by a laboratory helper. These were hard years of assiduous work, which were useful mainly to the students he formed and educated."

And yet, Pierre Curie made use of his early years at the EPCI for his important nonexperimental work on symmetry. And those who knew him best during that time remember how happy and fulfilled he seemed as a teacher. Paul Langevin, who would go on to become an important scientist in his own right, remembered "the time when, with beginner's timidity and awkwardness, I began my experimental education with him." Pierre Curie, who was then twenty-nine, had "the laugh of a child" and a "clear flame of enthusiasm" which he transmitted to his pupils. "The mastery afforded by ten years passed entirely in the laboratory, the assurance of his movements and explanations, and his easy attitude, tempered by timidity, impressed us students despite our ignorance. . . . One returned with joy to this laboratory, where it was good to work near him because we felt that he was working near us. . . . He loved to stand in front of the blackboard and talk with us, to awaken interesting possibilities in us, and to speak of the work which was developing our taste for science." It was, according to Langevin, a "milieu conducive to research" and one in which Pierre was "perfectly happy." "No one knew better how to intertwine his work and his joy."

Pierre himself was always grateful to the EPCI, and in particular to its director, Paul Schützenberger. "In all scientific work," Pierre observed, "the influence of milieu . . . is of great importance. . . . Schützenberger allowed us a great deal of freedom, and made his influence felt by communicating his own passion for science. The professors of the EPCI and the graduates of the school have created a positive and productive atmosphere that has been extremely useful to me."

One incident alone suggests Pierre's intense involvement in teaching. He was working out a problem at the blackboard with two advanced students one afternoon, and they all became so absorbed that they lost track of time. When they tried to leave, they found that the custodian had locked the door of the second-floor classroom. Pierre and his students, as he later recalled with amusement, had to climb out a classroom window and shinny down a drainpipe to escape the building.

Pierre Curie seems to have concluded perhaps because of the early traumatic incident with a girlfriend, that his intense and deep involvement with his work made romance impossible. And while he may have excelled, as Paul Langevin noted, in combining work and joy, he saw no way to combine work and love. "Women of genius are rare," the young man told his diary thirteen years before meeting Marie Skłodowska. Most women "love life for life's sake . . . when we give all our thoughts to some work which removes us from those immediately about us, it is with women that we have to struggle, and the struggle is nearly always an unequal one. For in the name of life and of nature they seek to lead us back."

Despite his father's prohibition on religion, Pierre's journals reveal him to be a young man with the sensibility of a priest: a near-mystical faith in science and a strong conviction that pleasure and sensuality are digressions from the true path.

To drink, to sleep, to caress, to kiss, to love [Pierre wrote at age 21], that is to say to partake of the sweetest things in life and at the same time not succumb to them, it is necessary while doing all that to keep the anti-natural thoughts, to which I'm devoted, dominant and active on their impossible path in my poor head; one must make life into a dream and make the dream into a reality.

Pierre seems to have had the usual young Frenchman's experience of sex, but, perhaps because of that mysterious early trauma, more than the usual fear of attachment. Even his love for his mother, and her displays of affection to him, stir up feelings which make him uncomfortable and distract him from his work. "A kiss given to one's mistress," he maintains, "is less dangerous than a kiss given to one's mother, because the former can answer a purely physical need."

Weak as I am [he wrote] I can't allow my mind to follow every wind, yielding to the smallest breath it encounters. Everything must be immobile around me so that my mind can take off and spin like a top. A mother never seems to understand such a thing. When I'm in the process of turning slowly inward upon myself in order to take off, a little nothing, a word, a story, a newspaper, a visit stops me in my tracks and keeps me from becoming a gyroscope or a top. No, a mother doesn't understand that a kiss she gives me at certain moments can delay or destroy the instant when I've reached a sufficient acceleration to concentrate within myself, despite what's going on around me.

Pierre's attachment to his family, and his isolation within it, are both apparent in a family photograph from this period. Marie Curie wrote of Pierre in this photograph: ". . . his head is resting on his hand in a pose of abstraction and reverie, and one cannot but be struck by the expression of the large, limpid eyes that seem to be following some inner vision. Beside him the brown-haired brother offers a striking contrast, his vivacious eyes and whole appearance suggesting decision." And yet there is no mistaking the intimate connection between the brothers. They look and dress alike: both wear blousy rumpled work shirts, both have full beards and long faces. Pierre is the taller of the two and the thinner, with sharp shoulders and thin, long-fingered hands. In a gesture of long familiarity, Pierre is leaning his elbow laconically on his brother's shoulder.

Seated in front of the two tall brothers are their parents, a couple Pierre would describe to Marie as "exquisite." The plump mother, enveloped in a large polka-dot dress, has her sewing box before her, and one hand fisted in a sock she is mending. The father, tanned and vigorous, has on a straw hat, with the broad brim turned up comically. Like his sons, he wears a loose work shirt. Everything about the photograph—the country setting, the casual unstudied clothes, the slouching poses, the mending—bespeaks a family without pretension, at ease in the country, preferring to be photographed living the simple life.

At age thirty-five, Pierre Curie continued to live in the comfortable embrace of this family. In the summertime, when Jacques returned from Montpellier and the two brothers resumed their research, it was possible to believe that the foursome might stay together forever. And even though Jacques had married, it seemed likely that Pierre would live out his life as a bachelor, teaching and experimenting in the familiar surroundings of the École de physique et chimie, returning home each night to his parents' small, charming house and garden in Sceaux, on the outskirts of Paris. Then, in the spring of 1894, Pierre met Marie Skłodowska. Very soon, the intensity he had reserved up to then for his work was turned to the task of winning her.

"We began a conversation," Marie Curie wrote of that first night, "which soon became friendly. It first concerned certain scientific matters about which I was very glad to be able to ask his opinion. Then we discussed certain social and humanitarian subjects which interested us both. There was, between his conceptions and mine, despite the difference between our native countries, a surprising kinship, no doubt attributable to a certain likeness in the moral atmosphere in which we were both raised. . . ."

Indeed, the similarities were astonishing. Both Marie and Pierre had grown up in families with more education than means. Both fathers had been idealists whose convictions hampered their careers. Both Pierre and Marie had been educated to an important degree by their parents. And in both families, the father's love of science, and yearning to be a scientist, had been passed on to the children. There was a difference, of course, between being anti-establishment in France, where the enemy was entrenched power, and in Poland, where the enemy was the Russian oppressor. Yet both Marie and Pierre had been raised with similar doses of skepticism toward that other establishment, the Catholic Church. "I have just read *Lourdes* by Zola," Pierre reported to Marie in an early letter, "and I have found your own views on religion there." Pierre promised to pass on the book, in which Zola presented the miracles of Lourdes as "a blasphemy against the scientific spirit," but not until his parents had finished it.

Qualities which would have driven others away attracted Pierre and Marie to each other. Both were obsessed with their work, and considered it the main source of life's happiness. "I hope, my dear friend," Pierre wrote Georges Gouy, "that you are well and that you have some work underway." "If your life is filled with work," Marie Skłodowska wrote her friend Kazia at the time of her engagement, "I won't be worried about you. Work gives life the sweet taste of happiness." One of Pierre's first billets-doux to Marie was a copy of his 1894 paper on "symmetry in physical phemonena," dedicated

"to Mlle. Skłodowska, with the respect and friendship of the author."
And while other suitors, like M. Lamotte, might have been a little put
off by Marie Skłodowska's drive to excel at the Sorbonne, Pierre,
who had despaired of finding a "woman of genius," took pride in it.
Not long after they met, Pierre, who never concerned himself with
such things, was totting up her scores on the *licence ès mathé-*
matiques exam to figure out whether she would place first, second, or
third.

Sometime that spring as well, Pierre paid a visit to 11 rue des
Feuillantines, up the hill from the Sorbonne, where Marie was living
at the time. Her top-floor garret, and her unchaperoned state, would
have shocked a proper bourgeois suitor. But it warmed Pierre's heart.
"Pierre Curie came to see me," Marie recalled, "and showed a simple
and sincere sympathy with my student life."

Indeed, the more they got to know each other, the more perfectly
suited they seemed. Marie had some of the "vivacity and energy"
Pierre had relied on in Jacques. Although an idealist, Marie had a will
to succeed in this world, and an understanding that self-promotion
could sometimes help pay the bills. Pierre, for his part, contributed
his delight in the natural world, an antidote to Marie's overserious-
ness. Soon it would become apparent that they complemented each
other, in complex and important ways, as scientists.

By the time Marie left for Poland, just a few months after they
met, Pierre had clearly pinned his hopes on marrying Mlle. Skłodowska. Later, he would tell her that it was the only time in his life that
he acted without hesitation, because he was convinced that he was
doing the right thing. Marie, however, had reservations. Probably she
was still feeling cautious, because of the Zorawski business. But the
more immediate obstacle was her feeling of loyalty to Poland. "I
wished," she explained later, "like many other young people of my
country, to contribute my effort toward the conservation of our national spirit." In the past, she had considered marriage to a non-Pole
to be a kind of betrayal. When her friend Kazia became engaged to a
German, Marie, who carried on the family tradition of writing occasional verse, gave her a gentle scolding in rhyme:

> *Godspeed then, sister, though you choose*
> *To sign on with a foreign crew.*
> *This precious land you'll never lose*
> *That first revealed the world to you.*
>
> *And our mistreated mother tongue*
> *Which others scorn, attack, and spurn,*
> *Hold in your heart and speak among*
> *Family and friends where home fires burn*

For only in our hearts can we
Nurture and keep this land we share
Therefore your heart cannot be free
But must be Polish everywhere.

Whatever her reservations about marrying a foreigner, Marie couldn't just walk away from Pierre Curie the way she had from M. Lamotte. Within ten days of her departure from Paris to spend the summer with her family in Switzerland and Poland, she wrote him of her whereabouts. Pierre's response was immediate, and grateful. Without salutation, he begins: "Nothing could give me more pleasure than having news of you. The prospect of waiting for two months without hearing about you was extremely unpleasant to me, which is to say that your little note was most welcome.

"I hope," his letter continues, "that you are taking in the good air and that you will return in the month of October." Twice, in his first three sentences, Pierre manages to mention the great *desideratum* of his letters to Marie that summer: in two months, as he sometimes assumed, sometimes pleaded, she would return to Paris.

"We have promised (isn't it true?) to have at least a great friendliness toward each other!" Pierre writes in his eccentrically punctuated but efficient prose. "Provided that you don't change your mind! because there are no promises that have to be kept these are the kinds of things which cannot be forced. . . ." Then, having given Marie the room he supposes she needs, he proceeds to make the idealistic argument which is most likely to capture her heart. "It would be a beautiful thing, a thing I dare not hope, if we could spend our life near each other hypnotized by our dreams: your patriotic dream, our humanitarian dream and our scientific dream."

Subtly, indirectly, Pierre then makes the point that the science dream (unlike the Polish one) has at least some chance of success. "Of all these dreams the last [science] is the only one I think is legitimate. I mean by that that we are powerless to change the social situation and even if this were not so, we wouldn't know what to do and in taking an action in one direction could never be sure that we weren't doing more harm than good by interfering with some inevitable evolution. —from the scientific point of view, on the contrary, we can hope to achieve something; the terrain here is more solid and every discovery, no matter how small, lives on."

It is a statement which takes on irony in view of the destructive powers the Curies' discoveries would subsequently unleash. Even scientific discoveries, Pierre was obliged to acknowledge then, could "do more harm than good." "It is possible to conceive," he said in his

Nobel speech nine years later, "that in criminal hands radium might prove very dangerous, and the question therefore arises whether it be to the advantage of humanity to know the secrets of nature, whether we be sufficiently mature to profit by them, or whether that knowledge may not prove harmful." But Pierre concluded, as he had in his pre-radium letter to Marie, that "humanity will obtain more good than evil from future discoveries."

Marie, with her positivist belief in science as salvation, would have liked Pierre's argument. She must have been touched too by the care he took in raising the marriage question. "You see how everything points to the fact that we are going to be great friends, but if you leave France after a year this will be truly too platonic a friendship, a friendship of two beings who won't see each other again. Wouldn't it be better if you stayed here with me? I know this question angers you and I don't want to speak further of it, since I feel myself so unworthy of you from all points of view."

Pierre ends with a hint that he would like to meet her somewhere "perhaps by chance at Fribourg" (where she must have been paying a visit to the Kowalskis, who had introduced them). "But you're only staying there one day, aren't you, and that day certainly should be devoted to our friends."

The charm of Pierre's letter worked. Very soon, he received an invitation from Marie to meet him in Switzerland, where she would be spending some days with her father.

Pierre's response proves his tendency to overthink a problem. Sometimes his "spinning" could produce profound insights, as with symmetry. But other times, as he acknowledged, it could keep him almost nightmarishly anchored to one spot, unable to take action. "I couldn't decide to come join you," Pierre writes.

> I hesitated for an entire day before coming up with a negative result. The first impression I got in reading your letter was that you would prefer that I not come. The second was that you all the same were very kind to give me the possibility of spending three days with you and I was on the point of leaving. Then a sort of shame came over me about pursuing you in this way almost in spite of you and finally what made me decide to stay was the quasi-certainty that my presence would be disagreeable to your father and would spoil his pleasure in going about with you. Now that it is too late I regret that I didn't go, because wouldn't it perhaps double the friendship we feel for each other if we spent three days together and gathered the strength not to forget each other during these two and a half months that separate us?

Pierre senses he may have lost Marie through his indecisiveness.

Do you remember the day of the mid-Lenten festival? I lost you suddenly in the crowd. It now seems that our friendly relations are going to be severed without either one of us wishing it. I am not a fatalist, but this will probably be the consequence of our characters. I won't know how to act at the crucial moment.

Then, with an unconvincing shrug, he allows it's probably for the best.

I don't know why I got it into my head to keep you in France and to exile you from your country and your loved ones without having anything worthwhile to offer you in return for this sacrifice.

Pierre ends his letter on a despondent note. Marie, apparently, had written that she was free to make choices in her life. Pierre responds somewhat peevishly:

I find you a little pretentious when you say that you are perfectly free. We are all more or less slaves of our affections, slaves of the prejudices of those we love. We have to earn our living and in that become a cog wheel in the machine, etc.

And then, in a finale both profound and self-pitying:

The worst are the concessions one must make to the prejudices of the society around us. One makes more or less depending on whether one feels weaker or stronger. If one doesn't make enough, one is crushed; if one makes too many, one is vile and one feels disgusted with oneself. I'm far away these days from the principles I lived by ten years ago. I believed then that it was necessary to be excessive in everything and to make no concessions to the society around me. I believed that one must exaggerate one's faults as well as one's virtues. I only wore blue shirts, like the workers, etc. Now you see that I have become very old and I feel very weakened.

His farewell, after such belittling of himself, sounds almost sarcastic: "I wish you much pleasure. Your devoted friend, P. Curie."

Not surprisingly, Pierre's letter had a chilling effect. Because only Pierre's side of this first correspondence survives, it is impossible to know exactly what Marie wrote in response. But there seems to have been a period of silence. And someone in the Curie family must have convinced Pierre, in hopes of diverting him, to go off into the country with his brother Jacques, who was pursuing a new interest in map-making in the mountains of Auvergne.

When he returned, Pierre found a letter from Marie so "troubled" and "indecisive" that it angered him. "Why write that way?" he asks her. Having been cheered by his travel with Jacques, he is much firmer (perhaps with a little push from his brother) about the fact that Marie, who seems to be having second thoughts, must return to Paris. "As you can imagine, your letter disturbs me. I advise you strongly to return to Paris in the month of October. It would cause me great pain if you didn't come this year."

Marie has written of "egoism," and apparently it has stung him. "It is not the egoism of a friend which makes me say you must return. I believe simply that . . . you will do more solid and more useful work here."

If Pierre wanted to avoid entanglement in the past, he is hungry for it now. Even his account of his travels with Jacques echoes with a longing for a new companion.

> I was very happy to pass some time with my brother; we were far from all cares and so isolated by our style of living that we couldn't even receive a letter, since we didn't know where we'd be staying from one day to the next. Sometimes, it seemed as though we had gone back to the period when we were constantly together: we came to have, during that time, the same opinions on everything, to a point where, since we thought alike, it wasn't necessary for us to speak in order to understand each other. That was all the more astonishing since we have entirely different personalities. But even though we gave ourselves over to this agreeable illusion, we were not fooled, and we know well that this perfect communication can never return.

Then, once again, he insists there's no point in trying to change the world. No mention is made of Poland, in part because, as Pierre observes, their letters are probably being read by the authorities and "could be misinterpreted and cause trouble." But it is clear that he is arguing once again for science, and for Paris, over Polish patriotism.

> What would you think of someone who was the first to smash his head against a wall with the hope of breaking it down. That might be an idea born of beautiful sentiments but in fact this would be ridiculous and stupid. . . . I believe furthermore that justice is not of this world and that the strongest system or at least the most efficient will prevail.

Dropped furtively into a postscript is Pierre's boldest stroke thus far:

> I wrote you a second letter in Lemberg [Lvov, then a city in Prussian Poland where the Skłodowskis had gathered] which you probably didn't get—nothing in particular in it. However, I asked you if you would like to rent an apartment with me on rue Mouffetard with windows overlooking a garden. This apartment is divided into two independent parts.

With the hope of winning her, Pierre has been shopping for apartments!

Perhaps this more forceful letter, with its open (if highly irregular) suggestion that they live together, changed Marie's mind. In any case, Pierre's letter ten days later is triumphant. "So you are going to return to Paris and that gives me great pleasure. I want very much for us to become at the very least inseparable friends. Are you not of the same opinion?"

Marie has written to him of practical things, including how she will earn a living. He, reluctantly, responds in kind. "I haven't initiated my candidacy for a professorship, because there isn't a vacancy at the moment. Certain of my friends have come to me to let me know that one professor may resign abruptly in early October. But I don't believe it one bit and I regret having mentioned it to you. I believe also that nothing is more unhealthy for the spirit than getting caught up in these sorts of preoccupations and listening to all the gossip people pass on."

Then, about her career possibilities: "If you were French [which she would be if she married a Frenchman] you could easily become a professor in a lycée or a Normal school for girls. Does this profession appeal to you?"

Marie has sent him her photograph, for which he thanks her "with all my heart." Then, in a postscript, he mentions that he has shown the photograph to his brother Jacques. "Was I wrong to do so? He finds you very fine. He also said, 'she has a very decisive look, maybe even stubborn.' "

As though to prove him right, Marie did not do as Pierre proposed and move in with him when she returned to Paris that fall. Instead, she took an apartment on rue de Chateaudun, next door to her sister Bronia's medical office. Nor did Pierre's plan that they would be constantly together materialize. His mother became ill, necessitating his spending more time than he would have liked in Sceaux.

"I'm not coming to see you tonight," he wrote Marie one Thursday. "My father has rounds to make and I will stay at Sceaux until tomorrow afternoon so that Maman won't be alone." He adds, in his self-deprecating mode, "I sense that you must be having less and less esteem for me while at the same time my affection for you grows each day."

But the relationship was developing on both sides. The word "affection" had been introduced; Pierre now began with the salutation "chère amie" and ended, familiarly, with the promise that he would "come to your place Monday evening, if that's convenient."

Marie met Pierre's parents: the tall father, "with beautiful blue eyes of a clearness and brilliancy that were striking," and the ailing mother, a woman who "even though raised for a life of ease . . . accepted with tranquil courage the precarious conditions which life brought her."

Pierre, after refusing for years to bother, wrote up a doctoral thesis and petitioned for his doctorate from the Sorbonne. Pierre, anticipating marriage and family responsibilities, could have decided on his own to take the steps necessary to his advancement. But it seems more likely that he was able to do it because Marie very much wanted him to.

Just about a year after Marie and Pierre first met, Pierre defended his doctoral thesis before examiners from the Faculté des sciences of the Sorbonne. It was a period in which the standards for the doctorate were extremely high. Erudition and elaboration were no longer enough: candidates were expected to present "true discoveries." But even in this exacting atmosphere, Pierre Curie's thesis, "Magnetic properties of bodies at diverse temperatures," had unusual sweep and significance.

"Magnetic properties" was the product of a series of investigations begun four years before in which he subjected a diverse group of materials to magnetic fields of varying intensity at elevated temperatures. The work was difficult: it involved working in high heat measuring very small, easily distorted, differences in magnetism. His question, when he began, was whether heat could cause the many substances which had virtually no magnetic properties to behave like the smaller number of substances which did. Heat, he found, had little effect on the first group, called "diamagnetic" substances, which had no magnetic properties. But among those substances which *had* magnetic properties, heat did make a difference. At a certain temperature, which is still called the "Curie temperature," the properties of these materials underwent a transformation which continues to be the subject of experimental study. Those which magnetized strongly, the "ferromagnetic" substances, began to behave like the substances which magnetized less strongly, the "paramagnetic" group. What Curie demonstrated experimentally was much later explained quantum mechanically, and still constitutes the basis of modern theories of magnetism. Ferromagnetism and paramagnetism are properties of the aggregate arrangement of atoms in substances, an arrangement which is altered by thermal excitation.

Marie Skłodowska was present when Pierre presented his thesis at the Sorbonne in March of 1895. Since she too was working on magnetism at the time, it was a subject she understood well. And it is interesting to note that Pierre Curie's methods, which involved a survey of the behavior of a vast array of substances, bore a resemblance to the method Marie would soon use in her doctoral work on Becquerel's rays. "I was greatly impressed," she remembered afterward. "It seemed to me that the little room that day sheltered the exaltation of human thought." However muddled Pierre Curie might have been at times in wooing her, his presentation of his work was a model of "clarity and simplicity." The jury was composed of three men who had been her teachers. "The esteem indicated by the attitude of the professors, and the conversation between them and the candidate . . . reminded one of a meeting of the Physics Society."

Not long after Pierre obtained his Ph.D., a professorship was established for him at the École de physique et chimie. Also, perhaps because of the attention all this brought, Pierre and his brother Jacques were belatedly awarded the Prix Planté for their work together on piezoelectricity. And finally, sometime during that triumphant spring, Marie overcame her reservations about leaving Poland. "After my return from my vacation," she wrote later, "our friendship grew more and more precious to us; each realized that he or she could find no better life companion."

That summer, Marie wrote a series of letters to friends and family announcing her engagement to Pierre Curie. From Józef, to whom she was always most candid, she received a warm endorsement, assuring her that "you are right to follow your heart, and no just person can reproach you for it." She was not, he assured her, being disloyal to her country. "Knowing you, I am convinced that you will remain Polish with all your soul, and also that you will never cease to be part of our family in your heart. And we, too, will never cease to love you and to consider you ours." It was much better for her to be "happy and contented" in Paris than back in Poland, a "victim of a too-subtle conception of your duty." Józef ended by welcoming Pierre into the family. "I offer him my friendship and sympathy without reserve. I hope that he will also give me his friendship and esteem."

To her "chosen sister" Kazia, whom she had chided for her engagement to a German, Marie had now to explain that *she* had chosen a Frenchman.

When you receive this letter your Manya will have changed her
name. I am about to marry the man I told you about last year
in Warsaw. It is a sorrow to me to have to stay forever in Paris,
but what am I to do? Fate has made us deeply attached to each
other and we cannot endure the idea of separating.

Rather apologetically, Marie explains to Kazia that she had "hesitated
for a whole year" before deciding, and assures her that she will "bring
him to Poland so that he will know my country," adding that she will
"not fail to introduce him to my dear little chosen sister, and . . . ask
her to love him."

Surprisingly, considering earlier farewells, she wrote also to Monsieur Lamotte, who apparently still had hopes. She expressed the wish
that they remain friends. But Lamotte wrote back that that was entirely impossible, and that they must now "consider each other dead."
He concluded, quoting de Musset: "I came too late into a world too
old."

In her dancing days back in Poland, Marie had imagined one
day getting married in colorful Cracowian style. Instead, she married
Pierre Curie without fanfare on July 26, 1895, at the Town Hall in
Sceaux, wearing a simple navy suit and a lighter blue blouse she had
had made for the occasion. The reception was held in the garden of
the Curie family house, a short distance from there.

It was a beautiful day, and the garden was overflowing with the
irises and climbing roses of late July. Marie's father and sister Helena
had come from Warsaw. And of course Marie's sister Bronia was
there, along with Kazimierz, mixing with the more numerous members of the Curie family. It was, Helena remembers, a "joyous atmosphere," complete with simple food. A giant turkey was brought out
and skillfully carved by old Dr. Curie, and there were "delicious
peaches the size of oranges," unlike any Helena had seen before or
since. After lunch, the guests played *boules* in the meadow near the
house. Then Pierre and Marie went off to Brittany to make use of
their wedding gift to themselves. With money from a cousin, they had
purchased a pair of shiny new bicycles.

Chapter Six

EVERYTHING HOPED FOR

As SOON AS she married, Marie began to keep a complete and tidy record of expenses, a habit she continued all her life. In time, the notebooks she used for this purpose would be small and plain. But in the beginning, she purchased an imposing, scrapbook-sized ledger with a gold script *Dépenses* slashed across the front. The notebook's cost—1.90 francs—was conscientiously recorded within, in one of the numerous columns provided for the purpose.

The *dépenses* notebook reflected all the usual needs of a French bourgeois household of the 1890s: there were categories for heat and light, for rent, for illnesses, for "expenses of the table," and of course for wages of employees. And there were separate columns for the expenses of *Monsieur, Madame,* and *les enfants.* One column, which showed the expense book to be absolutely up-to-date, was headed *Voitures/Fantaisies.* Here the new Madame Curie allowed herself a moment of whimsy: she crossed out *Voitures* and entered instead, in an ornate script with a final flourishing *s*, the word *Bicyclettes.*

In her letters home to Poland and in her memoirs, Marie Curie insisted that her life with Pierre was taken up entirely with work. "Our life is always the same, monotonous," she wrote Józef during the second year of her marriage. "We see nobody but the Dłuskis and my husband's parents in Sceaux. We hardly ever go to the theater and we give ourselves no diversion."

But this was a slight exaggeration. Certainly the Curies took no part in the café life and the lavish entertaining which characterized fin de siècle Paris. In an era of spectacle, they had no wish to see or to be seen. Yet they routinely attended the dinners of the Physics Society. They were not entirely oblivious, either, to the innovations which were the talk of Paris. In 1896, one year after the Lumière brothers perfected a technique for turning photographs into moving pictures, they bought tickets and took a look at the new *cinémato-graphe.* There are fairly regular entries in the expense book for the-ater tickets as well. They were subscribers to the Théatre de l'Oeuvre, where anarchists and symbolist poets gathered to see the latest plays of Ibsen, Strindberg, and Hauptmann.

Marguerite Borel, the wife of a professor and later a close friend, once encountered them after an Ibsen play and was "amazed" by their modest clothes. ("One dressed up in those days," she explained, "even for the Théatre de l'Oeuvre.") Marie spoke with vivacity about the play's heroine. When Margaret Borel agreed, Marie embraced her. "You remind me of students in my youth," Marie told her. "You are passionate about things, as they were and I was in those days."

Time was taken, always, to admire the flowers, and to adorn the house with them. "At Sceaux," Marie wrote home to Poland, "simple violets were showing themselves already in February, . . . the rockery in the garden is full of them. In the streets of Paris they sell masses of flowers at very possible prices, and we always have bunches of them at home."

And then there were the bicycles. The bicycle had been around, in various forms, for much of the nineteenth century. But in the 1890s, the sport of cycling was taken up, like jogging and running in our time, with enormous zeal. At first there were arguments about its effect on the human body: some believed it vitiated the system. But others soon argued the opposite more vehemently. "The idea of rup-ture being produced by it [cycling] is simply nonsense," wrote one enthusiast. "Taken . . . judiciously and in moderation, it is one of, if not the, best exercise of the day . . . an almost infallible remedy for a sluggish liver." Bécane, a meat-based fortifying drink especially for cyclists, appeared on the market. And a two-volume scientific treatise scrutinized the cycling phenomenon—both the machine and the rider—in immense detail.

It was not possible, in fin de siècle Paris, to be indifferent to the bicycle, the machine which made humans faster than horses. According to one convert, cycling was nothing short of "a revolution in the locomotion of men," and "a religion which inspires . . . more than a million happy believers." Women in particular associated cy-cling with liberation. "To the many who earnestly wish to be actively at work in the world," wrote Maria E. Ward in *Bicycling for Ladies,* "the opportunity has come." And Maria Pognon, addressing the Women's Congress in Paris in 1896, raised a glass to the bicycle, "which will liberate us."

The lady's cycling costume, and most especially the knickers *(cu-lottes),* were the outward symbol of this new freedom. "It is the bicycle which will lead to the emancipation of women," wrote Georges Mont-orgueil in *les Parisiennes d'à présent.* "The leveling and egalitarian bicycle has created a third sex.

"This is not a man," he expostulated, "this passerby in blousy knickers, calf exposed, torso set free and crowned with a boater. . . . Is it a woman? The vigorous step, the lively walk, hands in the pockets, moving about at will and without a companion, settling in on café terraces, legs crossed, speech bold: this is a *bicycliste.*"

Pierre and Marie Curie were hardly the slaves of fashion. But when they took up something, they did so wholeheartedly. And this was certainly the case with bicycling. Soon after their wedding, they posed in the garden of the Curies' house in Sceaux with their bicycles. Their *vélos* are of the latest style: "safety bicycles" with front and rear wheels of the same size, instead of the traditional high-wheeler, which left the rider "in constant fear of plunging either forward or sideways from a height." Their tires are the very new air-filled ones, instead of the usual thin bands of rubber. Marie's handlebars are decorated with a garland of flowers, to honor the occasion, and both she and Pierre are dressed from head to toe in the recommended *costumes.*

Pierre's suit has a short sack-style jacket and loose-fitting pants. Marie wears a straw boater with a narrow brim, "a hat that will stay on under any conditions" (as advised by a ladies' cycling manual) and a shirtwaist with some breathing room and a detachable collar. On her feet are low rubber-soled shoes like Pierre's. And instead of a long skirt she wears knee stockings and a pair of knickers, "full at the knees, finished with a band and button."

Over the next few years, the *bicyclettes* column in Marie's expense book gives regular evidence of money spent on fixing, replacing, and outfitting. There are multiple entries for valves and spokes and cotter pins and grease for making their own repairs. An oil lantern was needed for each bike, to light the way at night. There was a bicycle tax to pay each year, since ownership was still considered a luxury, although in fact it had already become a proletarian passion. And there were cycling clothes: cycling shoes, cycling rubbers for wet days, a cycling outfit fashioned for Marie by a dressmaker. Bike maps, newly available, were purchased for longer trips.

After their wedding in the summer of 1895, Marie and Pierre put their bikes on the train and traveled north to the sea, where they cycled from one fishing village to the next. "We loved the melancholy coasts of Brittany," Marie wrote later, "and the reaches of heather and gorse, stretching to the very points of Finistère, which seemed like claws or teeth burying themselves in the water which forever rages at them."

The next summer, they traveled in the opposite direction to the strange volcanic mountains and calcified gorges of Auvergne, scene of Pierre's tramps with his brother Jacques. In the nineties, Auvergne was becoming a fashionable destination for the growing numbers of city dwellers who sought thermal cures and pleasures in the country. But Marie and Pierre stayed away from the spa at Mont Doré, preferring to rent a peasant hut in a tiny village and take long bike excursions through the surrounding terrain, climbing and descending the slopes of the gentle volcanic mountains of the massif Central, "some with their heads rounded like a dome," as a contemporary traveler observed, "others pointed like a cone, some wearing a thick coat of green, others leaving exposed their ancient wounds . . . an army of giants in repose."

Sometimes, as used to happen when the two brothers were together, Marie and Pierre lost track of time. At least once they had to stay out all night as a result. "Lingering until twilight in the gorge of the Truyère," Marie later recalled, "we were enchanted to hear a popular air dying away in the distance, carried to us from a little boat that descended the stream. We had taken so little notice of the time that we did not regain our lodging before dawn. At one point we had an encounter with carts whose horses were frightened by our bicycles, and we were obliged to cut across ploughed fields. At length we regained our route on the high plateau, bathed in the unreal light of the moon. And cows that were passing the night in enclosures came gravely to contemplate us with their large, tranquil eyes."

Even when they were in Paris, Pierre and Marie used their bicycles whenever possible. On weekends and shorter holidays, they explored the countryside around Paris, traveling south to Fontainebleau, where "the banks of the Loing, covered with water buttercups, were an object of delight for Pierre"; and north, on another occasion, to Compiègne, which "charmed us in the spring, with its mass of green foliage . . . and its perwinkles and anemones." Weekly, Pierre and Marie biked the seven and a half miles from their apartment near the Sorbonne to the Curies' house in Sceaux. "We only take the train when it is raining cats and dogs," Marie informed Józef.

In Paris, they had taken an apartment on rue de la Glacière, within blocks of the series of rooms Marie had rented as a single student. It was a modest place, furnished simply with hand-me-downs from their families. But it was a palace compared to Marie's garrets: three rooms with a view out over a large garden. "Everything goes well with us," she wrote Józef soon after they moved in, "we are both healthy and life is kind to us. I am arranging my flat little by little, but I intend to keep it to a style which will give me no worries and will not require attention, as I have very little help: a woman who comes for an hour a day to do the heavy work. I do the cooking and housekeeping myself."

Pierre and Marie's combined income during those first years together (from salary plus prizes, commissions, and fellowships) was six thousand francs, about three times that of a schoolteacher and four times that of a laborer. And while Marie later wrote that "our means did not permit having servants," she might have been able to afford a little more help than she allowed herself. Certainly there was enough money left over to send considerable sums to Pierre's brother Jacques on a fairly regular basis.

Perhaps it was her wish to be wifely, like her sister Bronia, which made her decide against the more usual complement of servants. All through these years—and even after her time was taken up with children and with research on radioactivity—there are regular seasonal entries in the expense book for fruit with which to make jam. In July of 1898, one month after discovering a new element, she wrote a careful note on the making of a large batch of gooseberry jelly in the margin of her cookbook: "I took eight pounds of fruit," she wrote, "and the same weight in crystallized sugar. After an ebullition of ten minutes, I passed the mixture through a rather fine sieve." Her satisfaction in the result was evident: "I obtained fourteen pots of very good jelly, not transparent, which 'took' perfectly."

At the same time, the idea of depending on Pierre's income, even temporarily, seems not to have occurred to Marie. If she had, as other wives certainly did, it might have been possible for her to begin work right away on the doctorate she had been contemplating. But instead, she spent her first year of marriage studying for the *agrégation*, the teacher's certificate which would allow her to teach in a girls' secondary school.

Along the way, she managed to keep learning: she took two courses for her own satisfaction, one with Marcel Brillouin, a theoretical physicist with wide-ranging interests who was also an inspiring teacher. And the research on magnetism was at least, as Marie told Józef, "work I can do in the laboratory. It is a half-scientific, half-industrial occupation, which I prefer to giving lessons."

Pierre, meanwhile, was charged for the first time with a formal teaching assignment. In addition to his duties as a lab instructor he had been asked to give the course at the EPCI on electricity. "To satisfy his need for thoroughness and clarity," Paul Langevin later wrote, "he had to give himself completely to the task . . . careful to draw a faithful picture of the state of ideas and knowledge, not to exaggerate the degree of certainty of results and to emphasize clearly all the hypotheses, he constructed a course full of originality, full of his sense of experimental facts." The course on electricity was, according to his wife, "the most complete and modern in Paris." At the same time, however, he had undertaken more work on crystals—this time studying their growth—and was beginning to come up with some interesting results.

Regardless of the need to earn a living, which occupied much of their time, Pierre and Marie seemed to see themselves as a team of researchers right from the start, sharing their careful notes on scientific articles in French, German, and English, and taking an active interest in each other's work. Marie, describing the couple's frequent visits to Sceaux, assured her brother that the visits did not "interrupt our work; we have two rooms on the first floor there, with everything we need; we are therefore perfectly at home and can do all the part of our work that cannot be done in the laboratory." Commenting on their collaboration, Henri Poincaré once said of the Curies that theirs was not just an exchange of ideas, but also "an exchange of energy, a sure remedy for the temporary discouragements faced by every researcher."

Because they were together almost constantly, there is scant evidence of just how this "exchange of energy" took place. But once, in the summer of 1897 when Marie was pregnant with her first child, she left for the Brittany coast ahead of Pierre. And Pierre's letters to her give a sense of how completely they shared everything in their lives.

Marie had been miserable that spring, during the early months of pregnancy. "I am going to have a child," she wrote her friend Kazia in March, "and this hope has a cruel way of showing itself. For more than two months, I have had continual dizziness, all day long from morning to night . . . although I do not look ill, I feel unable to work and am in . . . very bad . . . spirits." At the same time, Pierre's mother was fatally ill with breast cancer. "We are very depressed," she confided to Józef at the end of March. "I am afraid, above all, that the disease will reach its end at the same time as my pregnancy. If this should happen my poor Pierre will have some very hard weeks to go through."

In July, it was decided that Marie, now seven months pregnant, should leave Paris for the seashore. Pierre would stay behind to finish his teaching duties and to help care for his ailing mother. When his brother Jacques arrived from Montpellier to take over his mother's care, he would join Marie in Port-Blanc on the Brittany coast.

With their usual penchant for finding out-of-the-way places, Marie and Pierre had chosen a village so tiny it escapes mention in the guidebooks. Port-Blanc was a typical small fishing village along the unique and spectacular northern coast of Brittany, where, as another visitor noted at the time, "the moorland country reaches to silver sands, sprinkled with gigantic masses of orange rock of the most extraordinary and picturesque forms, and between them the sea rushes up in deep blue and brilliant green waves of indescribable transparency." The village itself consisted of a cluster of stone houses, built solid and low to the ground, and a chapel said to house the skull of St. Gildas, a sixth-century Breton martyr. The women in Port-Blanc, as all over Brittany, still went about in traditional costume, crowned by the immense starched lace bonnets that made them seem to be sailing on land. There was at least one hotel, appropriately named the Hotel of the Gray Rocks, where Marie established herself, soon to be joined by her father and by her friend from student days at the Sorbonne, Jadwiga Dydyńska.

Pierre wrote to Marie almost daily, and she seems to have replied at least as often, though only one postcard of her side of the correspondence survives. Pierre's letters alone, however, attest to their intimacy. Whether he is writing about academic politics, about complicated family problems, about science, or about his feelings, Pierre's underlying assumption is that Marie will understand as no one else could.

When his parents' house is inundated with Sunday callers, he writes Marie about the "terrible" day he has endured. "Taken as individuals, the people who came weren't altogether disagreeable," he concedes. "But this was a procession of people coming to visit us . . . you can imagine how fed up I was!"

When a thorny problem comes up at work, he wishes Marie were there to help him handle it. A new man has replaced Pierre's friend Schützenberger as head of the École de physique et chimie, and has written "a rather disagreeable note" requiring professors to get permission from him before receiving visitors. Pierre has written him a letter calculated to appeal to his elitism and patriotic pride, "explaining to him that the prestige of professors would be seriously eroded" if he doesn't permit free visiting, and that "this prestige is already quite weak in France since the lowliest office employee seems to think he has the right to give orders to professors." Pierre shows his letter to his father before sending it, but wishes Marie had been there "to give me your advice on the situation."

Pierre longs for Marie's presence. "I think of my dearest who fills up my life and I would like to have new powers," Pierre writes. "It seems to me that in concentrating my mind exclusively on you, as I have just done, I should be able to see you, to follow what you are doing and also to make you feel that I am entirely yours at this moment. But I can't manage to call up the image." And later, "I need your caresses and need to hide my head in your arms and to feel you very close to me."

Because he had, in Marie's words, "a touching desire to know all that was dear to me," Pierre had decided early in their marriage that he wanted to learn Polish. When he was with Marie's Polish family, and on a visit to Poland the previous summer, he had managed to acquire a small vocabulary which he now practiced by adding postscripts to Marie's letters home and also in his letters to Brittany. "My little darling small and dear, that I love very much," Pierre wrote in his rudimentary Polish, "I have received your letter just today and I'm very happy."

Marie wrote a postcard back to him in Polish, kept simple so that he could understand it: "My dear husband!" she begins. "The weather is beautiful today, the sun is shining and it's warm." She is "doing fine, working as much as I can, but Poincaré's book is more difficult than I thought. I need to talk to you . . . and we need to see together what's hard to understand, but important." She misses him very much, is "waiting for you from morning until evening." And finally, "I kiss you with all my heart and fold into your arms."

Pierre too is longing to join Marie, but work and family obligations keep delaying his departure: there are exams to grade, and a patent document to rewrite. Jacques is slow in coming, and Pierre is reluctant to leave his ailing mother. "Maman is so sad when I talk of going," he explains to Marie, "that I haven't had the heart to fix the date." Finally, at the end of July, Pierre leaves Paris for Brittany.

Pierre liked to express his affection for Marie in diminutives. In his letters she was "My darling little child," or my dear little *enfanticule* or *chéricule,* words of his own coining, and his favorite photograph of her was as "the good little student." Yet he never seemed to think she needed the pampering that usually accompanies such tenderness. Even though she was nearly eight months pregnant, Pierre showed very little solicitude. Once, when she wrote him of *malaise* on a boat trip, he wrote back sternly: "Have you found out where the nearest doctor lives and how to get him there?" It must have occurred to him that she could give birth any day. And yet he arrived in Port-Blanc fully expecting that he and Marie would tour on their bicycles just as they had in the past.

Pierre had been preparing himself in Paris, "training on the coasts of Fontenay [near Sceaux] in anticipation," as he wrote, "of the coast of Brittany. I've changed my outfit and the new one pulls a little in the back." Marie, who must have been large and awkward by then, felt well enough to mount her bike and wheel along with him. And the two of them set off to explore Brest, on the southern coast of Brittany.

Apparently they biked at about their usual pace, despite Marie's condition. And yet they could not have felt quite as free that summer as they had the previous one, when they stayed out all night in Auvergne. And after the Brittany trip, although they continued to ride their bicycles, they would never again be able to lose all touch with the world. Because on September 12, shortly after their return to Paris, Marie gave birth to a 6.6-pound baby girl, whom they named Irène. They celebrated, as the *dépenses* notebook shows, with a bottle of champagne.

Both Marie and Pierre had been making practical preparations for the baby all summer. Marie, while in Port-Blanc, bought flannel and a diaper pattern so that she could make diapers. She asked Pierre to find out about undershirts for her. And Pierre, who didn't care about the conventional distinctions between male and female concerns, engaged in detailed conversations with his mother's friends to find out just what would be required. "I've sent you a package," he wrote, "with two knit undershirts from Madame P. It's the small size . . . which is good for undershirts in elastic knits, but you must make them a little larger in . . . cotton. You need to have undershirts in two sizes. But Madame D., a friend of Maman's, has promised to make some and send them. . . ."

After Irène was born, the *dépenses* book reflected a new fact of the Curies' life: employee wages jumped from 27 francs in September, the month of her birth, to 135 in December. Sadly for Marie, in addition to a nurse to care for Irène, it became necessary to hire a wet nurse after two months to take over the feeding. Marie had written to her father about her concerns on November 10.

> I am still nursing my little Queen, but lately we have been seriously afraid that I could not continue. For three weeks the child's weight had suddenly gone down, Irène looked ill, and was depressed and lifeless. For some days now things have been going better. If the child gains weight normally I shall continue to nurse her. If not, I shall take a nurse, in spite of the grief this would be to me, and in spite of the expense; I don't want to interfere with my child's development for anything on earth.

Ten days after she wrote this letter, Marie made a note: "we have taken a nurse for Irène."

To observe and to record was Marie Curie's way of being and of understanding, at home as much as in the laboratory. And the development of the children was no exception. Shortly after Irène's birth, she began a new notebook in which she recorded all the important milestones in her children's lives over the next fifteen years. Early entries of Irène's weight, sometimes even before and after feeding, gave way as the baby grew to bulletins about her own initiatives. "She is nursing very well," Marie wrote in the notebook in January, "and she's beginning to change her position on the bed by rolling." Later that month, Irène was able "to hold objects in her hand," and early in February she began to be "afraid of unknown people and objects, loud voices and so on." By early March she was jumping in her chair. And then, on March 31, Irène sprouted her very first tooth.

Even if Irène had not been born in the fall of 1897, it would have been a momentous time in the lives of Pierre and Marie Curie. Just as Marie had feared, Pierre's mother died, on September 27, only two weeks after Irène was born. Pierre, with characteristic intensity, vowed to mourn unceasingly. One day, not long after, he inadvertently laughed about something and then reproached himself for it. "The bear cub laughed," he told Marie in disbelief, as she tried to console him. Pierre's father, who was now alone, moved in with Pierre, Marie, and his new grandaughter.

In their professional as well personal lives, things were about to change dramatically. Marie had finished her teacher-preparatory work with top ranking the previous summer, and was now in the process of assembling the photographs and charts to accompany her article on the magnetism of tempered steels for the bulletin of the Society for the Encouragement of National Industry. It would be her first published article, and, equally importantly, it would bring fifteen hundred francs. Now the time had come—or so she and Pierre decided—for her to reach higher and begin original research in pursuit of a doctorate.

She decided to look into a curious phenomenon which had turned up in the laboratory of the eminent physicist Henri Becquerel at the Muséum d'histoire naturelle. Uranium compounds, it seemed, gave off "rays of a peculiar character" somewhat akin to X rays. Eighteen months had gone by since Becquerel had made this discovery, in March of 1896, and only a few attempts had been made to pursue it further. The excitement at the time was focused elsewhere. And in the Paris in those days, everyone, including scientists, tended to get caught up in the latest sensation.

PARIS in the 1890s was the city of innovation in art, in style, and in technology. The world watched Paris, and imitated Paris. And Paris grew increasingly conscious of and fascinated with itself. The number of daily newspapers in Paris grew in the nineties into the hundreds, and mass circulation took over from distribution to a small and cultivated elite. The press, as cultural historian Eugen Weber observes, "replac[ed] Parliament as the chief site and instrument of public debate." Much of the time, the press was not so much a forum for debate as an amplifier of the new and shocking.

The sensation which symbolized the age was without doubt the

Eiffel Tower, the tallest structure in the world when it was erected for the Universal Exposition of 1889, and one of the least conventional. Its exposed skeleton stood in starkest contrast to the lavish Paris Opéra, encrusted with the work of seventy-three sculptors and thirteen painters and illuminated with a six-ton chandelier. The Opéra, the largest theater in the world when it opened in 1875, was a dream left over from the reign of the last Napoléon, a grand setting for France's most brilliant social set. The Eiffel Tower, on the other hand, was a fitting symbol of the democratic ideals of the nineteen-year-old Third Republic, conceived by an engineer who also built railroad bridges. It drew the curious of every stripe, and served as setting not for grand opera but for dazzling innovation.

Electricity, the new sensation, powered the elevators of the Eiffel Tower in 1889, and began to replace gas lighting in the streets of Paris two years later. Other innovations—the telephone, indoor plumbing, electrification of streetcars, the moving picture, the introduction of standard time—made their appearance in the daily lives of Parisians in the 1890s as well, along with bicycles and steam-powered road-building machines. And all of these changes contributed to a sense that Paris was the most modern city in the world.

The "modern" had arrived in art as well. The French impressionists, first vilified, were now admired and collected in certain advanced circles. The symbolist verse of Mallarmé and Verlaine was recited in Montmartre; Debussy was composing *Prélude à l'après-midi d'un faune.*

The shameless, often ostentatious, pursuit of pleasure gave Paris another sort of claim to modernity. Elegant *rentiers* (who lived on fixed incomes) spent their days and nights strolling the boulevards, in lavish restaurants, in cabarets and cafés, and afterward in the arms of a great variety of women, from expensive and stylish mistresses, *les grandes horizontales,* to ballerinas and shopgirls.

While aristocratic Paris continued to conduct its social life discreetly behind closed doors in the Faubourg Saint-Germain, there was a new social set eager to see and be seen, and to take part in the cultural excitement around them. In the winter of 1895, Alexandre and Misia Natanson gave a party for three hundred in their sumptuous new home on the avenue de Bois de Boulogne which was the talk of Paris. The occasion was the unveiling of a series of decorative panels by Vuillard. Toulouse-Lautrec, his small form dressed in a white barman's suit with a waistcoat made of an American flag, served up drinks. He had shaved his head for the occasion, and concocted libations of layered liqueurs in bright colors.

To certain social critics, such ostentation and prodigality were evidence that the end of the century was bringing the decline of civilization. Max Nordau, whose earlier work on hypocrisy Marie had read during her governess years, published a jeremiad in 1895 which predicted "imminent perdition and extinction." In his widely read *Dégénération*, Nordau laid the blame for the decline of humanity on a wide range of evils, including alcohol, overwork, pornography, and overexposure to the paintings of the impressionists and the plays of Ibsen.

Nordau's exaggerations aside, there was an undercurrent of anxiety beneath the surface gaiety of the nineties. "Doom loomed more clearly in *fin de siècle* France," Eugen Weber has observed, "than almost anywhere else at the time." The Third Republic had failed, in the eyes of many Frenchmen, to provide national direction following the ignominious defeat at the hands of Bismarck's armies and the bloody Commune uprising. Evidence of plotting and corruption sullied members of the government, and anarchist violence endangered it. When a French company ran into financial difficulty in its ambitious attempt to cut a canal through the isthmus of Panama, members of parliament became embroiled in a conspiracy to prop it up. The Compagnie du Canal interocéanique went bankrupt anyway, and many small investors lost their life savings. In the pages of *l'Illustration,* dignified men in top hats and fur-collared coats were seen stepping, with downcast eyes, into the back of a horsedrawn paddywagon.

Three years later, in 1894, another scandal shook the republic to its foundations: Captain Alfred Dreyfus, a trainee of Jewish origin attached to general staff of the French army, was accused of treason.

Many years and several governments would come and go before the reverberations of the Dreyfus affair abated. But even before it took hold, the anti-Semitism to which Dreyfus fell victim, as well as more general xenophobia, was widespread. Prejudice against foreign workers, especially the most numerous Italian contingent, resulted in violent rioting in the provinces. In Paris, in 1895, *la Libre Parole* sponsored an essay contest on the subject of how best to annihilate the power of the Jews in France. Even *le Figaro* joined in the general malice: the day after the Natansons' party in honor of Vuillard, the newspaper predicted that the couple's next invitation would be written in Hebrew.

The burgeoning popular press also played up all that was sordid and criminal in French society. When a wave of anarchism threatened public safety and ultimately the government, the papers reported the resulting anarchist trials in great detail. Between the spring of 1892 and the summer of 1894, eleven anarchist bombs exploded in Paris. The climax of anarchist activity came in June of 1894, when the president of the Republic, Sadi Carnot, was assassinated by an Italian anarchist.

Despite their violence, the anarchists were seen as martyrs in certain artistic quarters; their challenge to the smugness of the Third Republic set a standard for outrageous behavior. In the *café chantants* and the cabarets of the nineties a new aesthetic surfaced—gay, mischievous, and antirational.

The historian Fierens-Gevaert, noting that many writers and artists had anarchist sympathies, chose to lump anarchy and "modernism" together, and to condemn the whole package as fundamentally decadent. "Every philosopher, writer, poet, dramatist and artist is today a latent anarchist," he wrote in his 1899 essay *la Tristesse contemporaine*. There was corruption everywhere: people were losing respect for institutions, they were mocking tradition and the heritage of the past. Indeed the whole of contemporary France was infected with anarchy.

Science and scientists were not immune from these criticisms. But here the charge was not decadence but impotence and soul-destroying materialism. The positivists, and other true believers, had made inflated claims for science and technology. "The cult of reason and science provided . . . the central *mystique*" for the anticlerical leaders of the Third Republic. Zola, one of the most ardent of the cult, claimed that science should rule the world: the methods of physics and chemistry, he argued, should be applied to the "investigation of human suffering and feelings." To science alone, he wrote, "belongs mystery, for she marches continually to its conquest." The guardian of morality is not religion but science, which eliminates the error and superstition of the Church.

And yet all the advances of science and technology, including the "god of the day, electricity," had ushered in an industrial age in which cities were dirtier, poverty was more pronounced, and the pace of life more frantic. In 1895, the same year that Zola delivered his ode to science before an audience of true believers, Max Nordau's *Dégénération* warned that everyone, before long, was going to be required to "read a dozen square yards of newspaper daily, . . . be constantly called to the telephone . . . think simultaneously of five continents of the earth," and "live half their time in a railroad carriage or in a flying machine." That same year, a prominent literary critic named Ferdinand Brunetière weighed in with a more measured critique of scientism. Following a faith-affirming visit to the Vatican, he published an article in the *Revue des deux mondes* arguing that science had failed to explain either the origins of man or the mysteries of the universe. Science, Brunetière pointed out, does not give men the means to live morally. Indeed, science, if not bankrupt, had had its credit severely shaken.

The "bankruptcy" of science became the rallying cry of the conservatives and the Church. Scientism and positivism undermine morality. "Bring up a woman in the positivist school," one critic warned, "and you make of her a monster, the very type of ruthless cynicism, of all engrossing selfishness, of unbridled passion." The teaching of science endangers not only the family, but also religion. Socialism and anarchy are the result.

Republicans and a few prominent scientists issued rebuttals. Henri Brisson, a sometime visitor to Eugène Curie's house who was now president of the Chamber of Deputies, warned that the "bankruptcy" charges were an attack not just on science but on republicanism and free thought. Marcelin Berthelot, the high priest of French science at the time, went to extremes, insisting that "the world is now without mystery."

Though most scientists chose not to take on the critics directly, the charges of Brunetière et al. affected the way they defined their work, and the way they viewed the future. In general, as historian of science J. L. Heilbron has observed, there was "a withdrawal from big questions and relaxation of claims to knowledge of truth." A modest approach to science, which Heilbron calls "descriptionism," took over. Predictions for the future were scaled back. "Who knows whether the limit has been reached?" asked one cautious physicist in 1893. The physicist A. A. Michelson maintained that "the future truths of Physical Science are to be looked for in the sixth place of decimals."

The brilliant Henri Poincaré, whose interest ranged over physics and mathematics, supported this humble approach. Scientists, he argued before an assembly of physicists, could not hope for unified explanations of the physical universe, nor should they seek them. Theories and principles are not true or false, but only more or less useful. And physical models are mere visual aids, bearing no absolute relation to the physical universe.

By the time Poincaré delivered these remarks at the International Congress of Physics in 1900, however, real events were conspiring to contradict him. Beginning in 1895, the year Brunetière wrote of scientific bankruptcy, a surprising discovery in Germany set in motion a chain of events which would ultimately lead to certain knowledge of the invisible structure of the material world.

Wilhelm Conrad Roentgen, who made the discovery, was a shy, secretive experimenter who worked all by himself in a laboratory in Würzburg, Germany. He was a "descriptionist" par excellence: when asked by a reporter what he thought about a discovery, he responded "I did not think; I investigated." Like Pierre Curie, he was interested in crystals, and spent time exploring Pierre and Jacques's piezoelectricity. He was also, like Pierre, a gifted mechanic who preferred to make his own apparatus. And it was in the process of tinkering with his own version of a vacuum tube, while attempting to duplicate an experiment outside his normal field of research, that Roentgen made a discovery which astonished the world.

Roentgen's work was contingent on two fairly recent inventions, the all-glass vacuum tube and the Rhümkorff coil. The tube, perfected by Johann Geissler in the 1850s, was a long glass bulb attached to a hose and a pump which could evacuate the gases within, creating an excellent vacuum. The Rhümkorff coil, which also came into use for the first time in the 1850s, provided an efficient means for generating high-voltage currents. Because of these two inventions, it became possible to watch cathode rays (which we now know to be electrons) in action. In a vacuum free of interfering gases, a torrent of electrons could be observed as they raced from a cathode source to a positively charged plate (anode). Sometimes the streaming electrons showed as blue streaks, sometimes they were invisible. And wherever the rays touched the glass wall of the tube, they created a green or blue luminescence.

Another German researcher, Phillip Lenard, had begun observing the behavior of cathode rays which *escaped* the vacuum tube, and discovered that they would illuminate a surface some distance from it which was coated with a material that phosphoresced. It was this experiment that Roentgen was trying to duplicate when he noticed something remarkable. Although Roentgen's vacuum tube was entirely encased in black cardboard, he could still produce rays which illuminated a phosphorescent screen outside it. But, more significantly, the rays would illuminate the phosphorescent screen "regardless of whether the coated [phosphorescent] surface or the other side is turned toward the discharge tube." The rays seemed to have penetrating power.

Soon, Roentgen began to experiment with the effects of these new rays on photographic plates, and discovered that he could use them to produce shadow pictures of the interiors of objects. Then, on December 22, 1895, six weeks after he began his experiments, Roentgen used the rays to "photograph" his wife's hand. The result was a fuzzy but unmistakable image of the dark skeleton of her left hand, with her ring making a dark blot on her fourth finger.

What were these new rays? They weren't like cathode rays, because they couldn't be deflected by a magnet. They didn't seem to be light rays, since they couldn't be refracted. Roentgen decided to call them X rays, since they weren't yet understood. X rays caused an immediate sensation among scientists and the general public. Within weeks, the fashionable *Illustration,* which generally favored colonial conquests and royal visits, featured the full-bearded Dr. Roentgen on its front page, along with X-ray images of a fish and a frog, their delicate skeletal structures revealed beneath shadowy flesh. An X-ray float was added to the carnival parade of 1897, and a huckster took to the streets with an X-ray machine which could serve, for ten centimes, as a "barometer of love."

Within a year, several scientists had guessed the true nature of X rays: they are electromagnetic rays identical in nature to, but shorter than, those of visible light. But it would be another eighteen years before the true nature of X rays was established beyond doubt. In the meantime, conjecture was rife. There was a run on vacuum tubes and induction coils, as other scientists set out to duplicate Roentgen's findings. In the year following the discovery of X rays, 49 books or pamphlets and 1,044 papers were published on the subject. Two French scientists attempted to jump on the bandwagon by discovering "rays" of their own. Gustave LeBon, an amateur who had written about group psychology, reported in January of 1896, just two months after Roentgen's discovery, that he had discovered a new radiation he called "black light." Some years later, a well-known physicist named René Blondlot claimed to have found yet another kind of rays, which he named N rays after his native city of Nancy.

LeBon's and Blondlot's rays turned out to be specious and unimportant, except to historians of science. But another incorrect notion led to a chance discovery of even greater significance than Roentgen's.

On January 20, 1896, just weeks after Roentgen made his discovery, Henri Poincaré reported on it to the French Academy of Sciences. Included in his explanation was the fact that the new rays caused phosphoresence, both on the glass wall of the vacuum tube and on a screen outside the tube which was coated with a phosphorescent substance. Phosphorescence is the glow which light excites in certain substances, a glow which continues for a time even after the light source has been removed. In France, it had been extensively studied by a scientist named Alexandre-Edmond Becquerel. Among other things, Alexandre-Edmond Becquerel had invented a *phosphoroscope* which made it possible to identify many new substances which had phosphorescence of extremely short duration. Alexandre-Edmond Becquerel died five years before Henri Poincaré made his report to the Academy on X rays. His son Henri Becquerel, however, was in attendance at the meeting that day. And the mention of phosphorescence, his father's specialty, caught his attention.

Henri Becquerel belonged to a scientific dynasty of a kind familiar in France. Both his grandfather and his father had been directors of the esteemed Muséum d'histoire naturelle. He had obtained his doctorate from the Sorbonne at thirty-five, entered the Academy at

the early age of thirty-nine, and become essentially inactive in research five years before he heard Poincaré's report on the new X rays.
The talk of phosphorescence, however, inspired him to return. "I
thought immediately," he recalled, "of investigating whether . . . all
phosphorescent bodies could not emit similar rays." In other words,
might the phosphorescence observed on the glass wall of the vacuum
tube, and on the phosphorescent screen, be the *source* of X rays,
rather than simply the reflector of them? Maybe phosphorescent substances could produce X rays, even without the cathode ray tube.

It seems a weak idea in retrospect, and hardly worth investigating. But Henri Becquerel, along with three other scientists who
learned about the hypothesis indirectly through Poincaré, went back
to their labs to try it out. Fairly quickly, three of the four found
evidence of what they wanted to find, and presented papers to the
Academy in support of the entirely false notion that phosphorescent
substances produce penetrating rays like X rays. Meanwhile, Henri
Becquerel had stumbled quite by accident on something else.

Because he was "a man of assured position who could afford the
risk of mistakes," Becquerel reported every step of his research to the
Academy. The first few phosphorescent substances he tried showed
no X ray–type action, contrary to the findings of others. Then he
tried a sample of uranium salts, a powdery white substance he had
prepared some fifteen years before while assisting his father. These
phosphorescent salts produced immediate results.

On February 24, Becquerel made his first written report to the
Academy: "One wraps a photographic plate . . . in two sheets of very
thick black paper . . . ," Becquerel explained, "so that the plate does
not fog during the day's exposure to sunlight. A plate of phosphorescent substance is laid above the paper on the outside and the whole
is exposed to the sun for several hours. When the photographic plate
is subsequently developed, one observes the silhouette of the phosphorescent substance, appearing in black on the negative. If a coin,
or a sheet of metal . . . is placed between the phosphorescent material and the paper, then the image of these objects can be seen to
appear on the negative." Becquerel concluded that this particular
substance, potassium uranyl disulfate, did emit rays which could penetrate paper impervious to light.

At this point, Becquerel assumed that it was the sunlight which
was causing the uranium salts to phosphoresce and penetrate to the
photographic plate. After the first paper, he went back to his lab to
prepare a corroborating experiment. This time, Becquerel placed a
thin copper cross between the black paper covering the photographic
plate and the uranium salts. He had reason to expect that this combination, when exposed to sunlight, would produce the pattern of a

cross on the photographic plate. But February in Paris is not a very sunny month. And by the time he was ready to try his experiment, there was no sunlight coming in the windows of his laboratory at the Muséum. So the photographic plate, the copper cross, and the uranium salts sat ready to go in a dark cupboard, awaiting a change in the weather.

The English scientist William Crookes, who happened to be in Becquerel's lab at the time, describes what happened next. "The sun persistently kept behind clouds for several days, and, tired of waiting (or with the unconscious prevision of genius), Becquerel developed the plate. To his astonishment, instead of a blank, as expected, the plate had darkened as strongly as if the uranium had been previously exposed to sunlight, the image of the copper cross shining out white against the black background." The uranium salts didn't need sunlight to penetrate the paper and leave their impression on the photographic plate. Something else must be at work. The very next day, Becquerel made his second report to the Academy. "I shall particularly insist on the following fact," Becquerel wrote, "which appears to me very important and quite outside the range of the phenomena one might expect to observe. The same crystalline lamellas [of potassium uranyl disulfate] placed opposite photographic plates, under the same conditions . . . but . . . kept in darkness, still produce the same photographic impressions."

Becquerel deduced, correctly, that it was the uranium in his preparation that was causing the reaction. In his next four papers, he continued to explore the phenomenon, drawing some correct and some incorrect inferences. One thing was absolutely clear: uranium, and only uranium, produced the penetrating rays. And it didn't matter whether the uranium was in a phosphorescent state or not. Uranous salts, which are not phosphorescent, still produced images on the photographic plates.

And yet, perhaps out of loyalty to the memory of his father, Becquerel never entirely gave up the idea that phosphorescence was somehow involved in the phenomenon. "All that he could say at present," historian of science Alfred Romer has noted, "was that energy was somehow stored in the uranium, and the best language he had to express that fact was to call it a form of phosphorescence." In May of 1896, three months after he began his investigation, Becquerel concluded that "the emission produced by the uranium . . . is the first example of a metal exhibiting a phenomenon of the type of an invisible phosphorescence."

In fact, as his son Jean was later to point out, Henri Becquerel had "discovered radioactivity." But Becquerel would not be the one to give it that name, nor to explain its source. The physicist Jean

Perrin, looking back on the history of radioactivity, noted that Becquerel was "a prisoner of the hypothesis that had served him so well at first." Before the uranium rays could be understood, "a second major step would have to be taken."

For a variety of reasons, however, few showed much interest in taking the next step. Becquerel himself seems to have concluded that the subject was exhausted: after his initial papers in 1896, he published only two in 1897 and none the following year. By early 1898, as science historian Lawrence Badash has noted, the subject was "something of a 'dead horse.'" Other than Becquerel's papers, only four were devoted to the uranium rays at the Academy in the year of their discovery. In contrast, Gustave LeBon's false claims for "black light" were the subject of fourteen papers. And Roentgen's X rays got the most attention of all. Nearly one hundred papers were delivered at the Academy in 1896 concerning X rays.

X rays, not uranium rays, held everyone in their thrall. Their dramatic effects—and potential usefulness—were a rebuttal to those who claimed science was bankrupt. X rays could produce shadow photographs of the bones in the hand. Uranium rays were too weak to make good bone pictures. X rays were easily produced by anyone who had a vacuum tube and a high-voltage coil. Uranium was almost impossible to obtain. Furthermore, uranium rays shared some characteristics with X rays and were discovered *because* of X rays. It was natural to lump the two kinds of rays together. It would take fresh eyes, and more careful quantitative methods, to establish that uranium rays were part of another phenomenon altogether. X rays might reveal hidden bones. Uranium rays were pointing the way to an understanding of the building blocks of all matter.

The relative neglect of Becquerel's rays was one of the reasons Marie Curie decided to study them. "The subject," she wrote later, "seemed to us very attractive and all the more so because the question was entirely new and nothing yet had been written upon it." In addition, the Curies may have been influenced by the work of Lord Kelvin, who came closer than anyone else in Pierre's life to being a mentor.

Marie and Pierre certainly had no personal connection to Becquerel as mentor. Heir to a scientific dynasty and member of the inner sanctum, Becquerel was associated with the pomp and circumstance Pierre Curie disdained; he was the ultimate insider to Pierre's outsider. Indeed, when Pierre sought and was refused admission to the Academy some years later, he suspected Becquerel of voting against him.

On the other hand, William Thomson, Lord Kelvin, had taken a lively interest four years before in the work of Pierre and Jacques

Curie on piezoelectricity. In 1893, Pierre had sent him one of his instruments, and Kelvin had responded with praise for "the beautiful experimental discovery of yourself and your brother" and with questions about its use. A collegial correspondence ensued, and in the fall of 1893, Lord Kelvin took advantage of a trip to Paris to call on Pierre at his laboratory.

In December of 1897, about nine months after Becquerel's discovery of uranium rays, Lord Kelvin presented the first of a series of papers to the Royal Society of Edinburgh which were "the best and most serious investigations of this period" on the subject. Kelvin's purpose was to test whether uranium rays, as well as X rays, "have any electrifying effect on air." He obtained a small quantity of uranium from Becquerel's source, Henri Moissan. Working with two research fellows at the University of Glasgow, Kelvin found that both kinds of rays did "electrify" the air, as Roentgen and Becquerel had claimed. Though he offered no explanation for the phenomenon, the seventy-three-year-old Kelvin made careful measurements using his electrometer to confirm this "wonderful fact."

Becquerel, under the influence of X rays, had concentrated on uranium's effect on photographic plates. It was Kelvin's direction which would lead to the next big breakthrough. It seems very likely that Pierre and Marie's extensive article-reading in German and English would have included these articles by Lord Kelvin on the "electrification of air by uranium and its compounds." When Marie Curie started her research, in the winter of 1897, she began where Lord Kelvin had left off.

Chapter Seven

DISCOVERY

THE ROOM in which Marie Curie began her work on Becquerel rays was a gritty, brick-walled storage space on the ground floor of the school where Pierre taught. Instead of the state-of-the-art equipment of the Sorbonne labs, she started off with a few wooden worktables and a rickety chair or two in a room where the temperature descended on a cold day to forty-three degrees Fahrenheit. Still, Marie Curie had autonomy there she could never have achieved at the Sorbonne, working in the lab of one of her professors. At the same time, she had the respectful guidance of her more experienced partner, Pierre Curie.

Even though the project was agreed to be hers in the beginning, she was never alone with it. The lab notebook she began on December 16, 1897, was one Pierre had already used for some of his work on crystals. And the first task recorded in it was a test, with Pierre's help, of one of his inventions. Indeed, though Pierre was supposed to be busy with his crystals, the work of the first six weeks seems to have been at least as much his as hers. During these early weeks, the Curies arrived at "a new method of chemical analysis" based on a very precise measurement of what we now call radiation. It was a breakthrough which bore the imprint of the maker of highly sensitive measuring instruments, Pierre Curie.

Becquerel had already noted that uranium had the ability to turn air into a conductor of electricity. Others had found that the air could carry only a certain quantity of charge—that it reached a "saturation point." But no one had yet tried to quantify the energy given off by the uranium, or to test other elements. To do this, the Curies built an "ionization chamber" from leftover wooden grocery crates. Inside, they placed two circular metal plates eight centimeters in diameter, one above the other and separated by three centimeters. On the lower plate, they placed a thin layer of the substance in question. Then they charged the lower plate with a high-voltage battery. If the substance on the plate was a conductor through air, the upper plate would become charged. The speed with which this happened was relative to the energy being emitted by the substance in question. It was by measuring these energies that the Curies would come to their most important conclusions.

In the beginning, Marie Curie's experiment fit the "descriptionist" paradigm: she intended, for her Ph.D. dissertation, to measure a known phenomenon with greater precision, to look for "future truths," in A. A. Michelson's famous phrase, in the "sixth place of decimals." It was an exercise not unlike her careful testing and graphing of the magnetic properties of a variety of tempered steels, which appeared in the *Comptes rendus* around this time. The precision was due in large part to the use of Pierre's inventions—both the electrometer and the piezoelectric quartz balance—as part of an ingenious method Pierre and Marie arrived at during the first six weeks.

A photograph conveys the complex interplay of experimenter and apparatus involved in these delicate measurements. The apparatus, a gawky-looking collection of cylinders, wires, and poles, is spread out over the length of a worktable. Marie Curie sits at one end of the table with a stopwatch in her left hand, her eyes fixed on the needle of an electrometer, her right hand holding a weight which she releases to produce a charge from the *quartz piezoélectrique,* with which she counteracts a charge given off by the substance in the ionization chamber. The relative ionizing power of the substance is judged by the amount of time it takes to produce "saturation," the point at which no more charge can be transmitted through the air.

For the first two months of the investigation, there was every reason to believe that Marie Curie's task would be a descriptionist one. After she and Pierre established a method of measurement together, Marie placed the disc of white uranium powder she had obtained from Henri Moissan on the plate, charged the plate, and measured the uranium's ionizing current. Then she began, somewhat haphazardly at first, a survey of other elements. Here Marie Curie displayed for the first time her gift as a scavenger: she got some of her samples from a chemist in the building, others from a colleague at the Museum of Natural History. On one day, February 10, 1898, she tested thirteen elements, including gold and copper, all of which gave off "no rays" or "nothing clear."

Had she stayed with the testing of simple elements, Marie Curie would have missed the next, surprising, turn of events. But on February 17, 1898, she tested a sample of the heavy, black pitchy mineral compound known as pitchblende. Pitchblende had been mined in the mineral-rich Joachimsthal region, on the German–Czech border, for over a century. In 1789, a self-taught chemist named Martin Heinrich Klaproth used pitchblende to extract the gray metallic element he named uranium, after the newly discovered planet Uranus.

Until Marie Curie placed it in her condensation chamber that day in February 1898, pitchblende had been valued principally as a source of uranium, which provided a superior coloring agent in ceramic glazes. Now it turned out to have another mysterious potential: it produced a current much stronger than that produced by uranium alone.

There is no comment in Marie Curie's notebook about this surprising development. Instead, she undertakes new tests of her equipment—suggesting she is puzzled and preoccupied by it. The next day, February 18, she tries again, measuring several uranium compounds, as well as pure uranium and pitchblende. The compounds are less active than pure uranium, but the pitchblende is, once again, more active.

The next few days are taken up with comparisons of pitchblende and various substances, seemingly picked up at random from around the lab, or perhaps provided by other chemists. Then, on February 24, there is a second surprise. The mineral aeschynite, which contains thorium but no uranium, is also more active than uranium.

Suddenly, Marie Curie is faced with not one but two surprising results. Thorium, a mineral element discovered by the Swedish chemist J. J. Berzelius in 1828, is more active than uranium, and pitchblende is more active than either of them. The "rays" which Becquerel named "uranic" are not simply an anomaly of uranium: they are part of some sort of more general phenomenon which requires naming and explanation.

Ironically, just as their research began to show great promise, Pierre learned that he had been turned down for a professorship at the Sorbonne. Marie and Pierre had discussed the possibility of a Sorbonne appointment in their earliest correspondence. Pierre, characteristically, had insisted then such preoccupations were unhealthy. Nonetheless an appointment to the faculty of the Sorbonne would have been a move up for Pierre in both salary and status, and would have provided the Curies access to a much better laboratory for their research. So it must have come as a disappointment to them when the chair vacated by a death was given to Jean Perrin, a younger scientist who had the advantage of an education in one of the *grandes écoles.*

Certainly it was a disappointment to Charles Friedel, who had proposed Pierre's name. Friedel, the chemist in whose labs Pierre and his brother Jacques did some of their earliest work, wrote Pierre Curie a consoling letter:

> My dear friend,
>
> We are beaten, and I feel nothing but regret for having encouraged you in a candidacy which has been so unsuccessful, since the discussion of you was so much more favorable than the vote. But despite the efforts of Lippmann, of Bouty, and of Pellat, as well as my own, despite the praises with which even your adversaries have spoken of your fine work, what can one do against a *normalien* and against the preconceptions of the mathematicians.
>
> I send you herewith the vote count. Console yourself and continue despite everything to do good work in physical chemistry in order to show these *messieurs,* who refuse to admit that one can change jobs at age 40, that you have sufficient flexibility of mind to do it.

There is no evidence that either Pierre or Marie lingered much over this rejection. All Marie's attention at the time was focused on verifying the energy given off by thorium and by pitchblende. Increasingly, as the implications of the findings became clear, Pierre's scribbled notes appeared in the notebook alongside Marie's. On March 16, Pierre drew up an untidy graph of a whole series of minerals containing uranium and thorium, comparing their density and composition. This was followed by a long, orderly recapitulation by Marie of the results of measurements of many minerals, active and inactive.

On March 18, Marie and Pierre Curie begin a second lab notebook together. Pierre, as Marie recounted, "abandoned his work on crystals (provisionally, he thought) to join me in the search."

By this time, the Curies were operating on the hypothesis that pitchblende's dramatic ionizing power was caused by an unknown element, giving off much more energy than uranium. The problem with pitchblende, however, was that it contained an enormous variety of minerals and could not be easily simulated in the lab. Around this time the Curies discovered another mineral that was simpler to reproduce artificially: chalcite. Chalcite from natural sources registered a strong current like pitchblende, suggesting that it, too, contained the mystery element. If this was true, then there should be a difference between chalcite made in the lab, with known ingredients, and chalcite in nature. Marie Curie proceeded to make it, combining uranium and copper phosphate. She then tested this artificially synthesized chalcite and found it showed no greater activity than uranium. The conclusion was unavoidable: the natural chalcite, like the pitchblende, contained an element more active than uranium.

Within two weeks of the chalcite experiment, Marie Curie would submit her first report to the Academy on her findings. Meanwhile, probably with publication in mind, the Curies made several attempts to link their discoveries to those of past experimenters. Using Becquerel's methods, they made impressions with their compounds on photographic plates. They tried a variety of experiments involving X rays, still puzzling over how their rays and X rays overlapped. On Saturday, April 9, three days before the report to the Academy, Marie Curie made repeated measurements, once again, of pure uranium and of pitchblende from three different sources. The results were undeniable: pitchblende was two, three, or four times as active as uranium alone.

On Tuesday, April 12, the members of the Academy heard a report written by Marie Skłodowska Curie on "Rays emitted by uranium and thorium compounds." It came toward the end of the weekly session, following presentations on everything from astronomy to hydraulics and just before a brief communication on frog larvae. Because neither Marie nor Pierre was a member of the Academy, it fell to Gabriel Lippmann, Marie's teacher and advocate, to deliver it.

At the time, the academicians were probably most intrigued by Marie Curie's finding that two uranium minerals, pitchblende and chalcite, were much more active than uranium itself. This, as she herself notes, "is very remarkable and leads us to believe that these minerals may contain a much more active element than uranium." In retrospect, as Abraham Pais has noted in his history of physics, *Inward Bound,* two other revelations in this first paper are even more important. The first breakthrough is implicit in Marie Curie's conjecture about a new element. She suspects there is one because of the "rays" (i.e., radioactivity) pitchblende and chalcite were giving off. With this, Pais notes, she introduced a "novelty into physics: radioactive properties are a diagnostic for the discovery of new substances." Even more important is Marie Curie's intimation that this activity she is measuring is an *atomic* property, proportional to the amount of uranium or thorium being measured. "All uranium compounds are active," she states, "the more so, in general, the more uranium they contain."

Other researchers had already touched on some of the findings in this first paper. An Italian, E. Villari, had also used pitchblende to measure the activity of uranium. And in Germany, unbeknownst to the Curies, Gerhard Carl Schmidt had actually reported the activity of thorium to the Deutsche Physikalische Gesellschaft on March 24, nineteen days before Marie's announcement to the Academy. What distinguished the Curies' work, and propelled it forward, was their precise and systematic approach. Had Villari had a measuring instrument for comparing the activity of substances, he might have discovered that pitchblende was more active than uranium. And Schmidt, for whatever reasons, didn't try to measure the great variety of elements and minerals that Marie Curie did, and therefore didn't happen upon chalcite and pitchblende.

The next step for the Curies was obvious: they must try, by chemical means, to isolate this hypothetical new element. "I had a passionate desire to verify this hypothesis as rapidly as possible," Marie wrote later. The news that someone else had anticipated her discovery of the activity of thorium must have added some urgency to the pursuit. Pierre, as Marie noted admiringly, claimed that it didn't matter whether he or someone else announced a discovery first, as long as the discovery was made. Marie, however, was not so selfless.

On the Thursday after Marie's paper was read at the Academy, she and Pierre were back at work on pitchblende, pulverizing one hundred grams so that they could begin to isolate the very active mystery element. They attacked the pitchblende with various chemicals, then measured the activity of the breakdown products. The more active substance was then attacked again. Two weeks later, the Curies thought they had a product pure enough to attempt spectroscopy.

Spectroscopy, the study of characteristic color patches produced when elements are heated and the light refracted through a prism, had been a source of information about the universe since the eighteenth century, when Newton studied crude spectra of sunlight. In the 1860s, R. Bunsen and G. R. Kirchhoff had developed a method of determining the chemical content of substances by heating them and analyzing the spectra produced by the refraction of their flames. Since then, eight hitherto unknown elements had been identified by spectroscopy alone. The Curies hoped that their new element would produce characteristic spectral lines, thus corroborating their own findings.

Ultimately, spectroscopy would prove an important tool. But at this point, the Curies were much farther from a pure product than they suspected, and no definite spectral lines appeared. Realizing, perhaps, that they needed more chemical expertise than they could muster between them, they called on Gustave Bémont, a laboratory chief at the EPCI, for help.

Bémont, a quiet, unassuming chemist who was a sort of fixture at the school, began by heating a fresh sample of pitchblende in a glass tube. Very quickly, this approach yielded results: the product distilled in small quantities on the glass was strongly active. This heating, combined with chemical treatment, began by early May to result in products more active than pitchblende.

By mid-May, the notebook seems to indicate that Pierre and Marie have divided forces and are working with two different samples —sometimes chemicals. Soon, there are products 17 times as active as uranium—now their standard of comparison. On June 25, a chemical treatment of the sulfurs Marie is working with results in a product 150 times as active as uranium. Then, after a precipitation with ammonium, a product 300 times as active. At the same time, Pierre has come up with a product 330 times as active as uranium.

Already, the Curies' chemical treatments and distillations were suggesting that pitchblende contained not one but two unknown, highly active, elements: one that accompanied bismuth in the breakdown from pitchblende and one that accompanied barium. They concentrated first on the element that accompanied bismuth.

Once again, they tried to corroborate their findings through the use of spectroscopy, this time calling on the expert spectroscopist Eugène Demarçay. The results were again disappointing: the highly active substance accompanying bismuth produced no clear spectral lines. Nevertheless, by early July, the Curies had decided their own evidence could lead to only one conclusion: the active bismuth was harboring a new element. On July 1, as on previous occasions, they tested a series of known elements to make sure they weren't missing something. Then, on July 13, in Pierre's hand, comes the first indication that they have given their new element a name: alongside the symbols for bismuth and lead in the lab notebook, Pierre has written "Po"—an abbreviation for the name he and Marie have chosen, in honor of her country: polonium.

Five days later, within the domed sanctuary of the Institut de France, the academicians heard Henri Becquerel read the Curies' report on the new element polonium. "We have not," the Curies acknowledged, "found a way to separate the active substance from bismuth." Their inability to identify spectral lines for their product was, they conceded, "not favorable to the idea of the existence of a new metal." But they had "obtained a substance which is 400 times as active as uranium" and had found nothing comparable among known elements. "We thus believe that the substance we have extracted from pitchblende contains a metal never before known, akin to bismuth in its analytic properties. If the existence of this metal is confirmed, we propose to call it *polonium* after the name of the country of origin of one of us."

The Curies' paper introduced another new word: "radio-active." They used it only once, in the paper's title, "On a new radio-active substance contained in pitchblende," but it would soon be taken up by scientists everywhere. They also laid claim, with a nod to Becquerel, to the discovery of a new method of element hunting. "Permit us to remark," the Curies concluded, "that if the existence of a new element is confirmed, this discovery will be due entirely to the new method of investigation provided us by the Becquerel rays."

The Curies' second laboratory notebook ends around the time of the paper on polonium. There is no evidence that they did any further work for the next three months. In part, this may be because they were waiting for a new shipment of pitchblende. But it was the usual thing for academics to leave Paris in the summer for the *grandes vacances*. Apparently the Curies saw no reason to make an exception in the summer of 1898, despite their knowledge that they were on the brink of more new revelations.

A NOTEBOOK of Irène's progress during this period serves as a sort of domestic counterpoint to the lab notebooks. Here are another sort of measurements, recorded with equal care, of Irène's weight, and length, of the diameter of her head, and of the small changes and reversals so absorbing to a mother. In May, Irène's vaccination button became inflamed and made her ill. In June she had learned to say "merci" with her hand. By July Irène was getting around on all fours and saying "gogli, gogli, go."

That summer, the Curies returned to the volcanic mountains of Auvergne, where they had bicycled together before Irène was born. Now, they spent time watching the baby bathe in the river and play with a cat. But they also seem to have toured on their bicycles as energetically as ever, leaving Irène behind with a nurse.

Even on vacation, though, the Curies were preparing for the next step in their research. On October 15, Marie's expense notebook showed payment for a shipment of pitchblende from Joachimsthal alongside a purchase of shirt material for Pierre. A month later, on November 11, they were back in the lab at the École de physique et chimie, ready to look for a second new radioactive element.

Once they returned to their small lab, things moved very rapidly. A series of trials and errors led them, by the end of November, to a very active product which was carried off by barium. With the help of Gustave Bémont, they were able to make the barium product's radioactivity grow and grow, until its radioactivity was 900 times that of uranium. Hoping, this time, that the mystery element was present in enough quantity to produce spectral lines, they sent it off to Eugène Demarçay. This time he got results: a distinct spectral line showed up which could be attributed to no known element.

Around December 20, just six weeks after their return to the lab,

Pierre scrawled a name for the new element in the middle of a page in heavy ink: radium.

Only one task was left to absolutely clinch their proof: the isolation of the new element, and the assignment of an atomic weight, the basis for placement on the periodic table. For several weeks, they compared samples of active barium (containing radium) with simple barium, hoping that their active barium would be measurably heavier. But there was no significant difference, a fact which led them to guess—correctly—that they were dealing with an enormously radioactive substance present in the barium in very small quantities.

Fortunately, the Curies didn't linger long over this effort at establishing atomic weight. It would require another three years, and herculean labor, before Marie Curie could establish just how radioactive the radium was, and how tiny the quantity (less than a millionth of a percent!) was present in their active barium. In the meantime, toward the end of December, 1898, they sent off their next report to the Academy.

The Academy had already started to sit up and take notice of the Curies' research. In July of 1898, they had awarded Marie the 3,800-franc Prix Gegner, citing her "lengthy work" on magnetic properties of steel, as well as her work on radioactivity. "The result of this curious work seems to be that the properties of pitchblende are due to a new element," the Gegner citation notes, concluding that "whatever the future of this scientific view, the research of Madame Curie deserves the encouragement of the Academy."

While the academicians were willing to depart from usual practice and award the prize to a woman, they were not willing to go so far as to inform her of it *directly*. Instead, both Henri Becquerel and Marcelin Berthelot wrote letters to Pierre Curie, informing him that his wife had won the prize. "I congratulate you very sincerely," wrote Becquerel, "and beg of you to present my respectful compliments to your wife."

The paper read to the Academy on December 26, 1898, brought news of the most exciting development thus far in the Curies' research. It was authored by the Curies and Gustave Bémont and entitled "On a new strongly radio-active substance contained in pitchblende." This time, in addition to their own evidence, they had Demarçay's report that he had picked up a spectral line which "intensifies at the same time that the radioactivity intensifies . . . a very serious reason for attributing it to the radioactive part of our substance."

Demarçay's note, appended to the Curies' report, added weight to their findings. "This ray does not appear to me to be attributable to any known element," Demarçay observed, concluding that its presence "confirms the existence, in small quantity, of a new element in the barium chloride of M. and Mme Curie."

THE ANNOUNCEMENT of the discovery of radium, at the end of 1898, marked a turning point in the Curies' research partnership. Until then, their roles in the work were nearly interchangeable; Marie's careful script and Pierre's scrawl intermingle on the pages of the laboratory notebooks. But in 1899, that changed. Marie took on the formidable task of isolating radium. Pierre, working nearby, focused on the phenomenon of radioactivity, attempting to understand its meaning. For the first time, Marie became primarily the chemist, and Pierre primarily physicist.

Some have suggested that this division of labor was based on intellectual aptitudes—that Pierre was the more abstract thinker, and Marie the more concrete. This casts them in the expected male and female roles. In fact, Marie was better at abstract mathematics than Pierre, and nothing interested Pierre more than such very concrete tasks as designing and building instruments. The division had more to do with predilections than abilities. "Pierre Curie," as their daughter Irène has noted, "was attracted above all by the fascinating problems posed . . . by the . . . mysterious rays emitted by these new materials. . . . Marie Curie had the stubborn desire to see salts of pure radium, to measure radium's atomic weight."

Both the Curies were already convinced that radium and polonium existed. But Marie was concerned, in a way that Pierre probably wasn't, with the opinion of others. "There could be no doubt," she explained later, "of the existence of these new elements, but to make chemists admit their existence, it was necessary to isolate them."

Pierre Curie once confided to a friend that he would never have taken on the task of isolating radium. "I would have gone another way," he told Jean Perrin. His daughter Irène endorses this view. "One can discern," she writes, "that it was my mother who had no fear of throwing herself, without personnel, without money, without supplies, with a warehouse for a laboratory, into the daunting task of treating kilos of pitchblende in order to concentrate and isolate radium."

In her accounts of the undertaking, Marie would always emphasize that she was "extremely handicapped by inadequate conditions, by the lack of a proper place to work in, by the lack of money and of personnel." But the fact was that she not only managed, over three years, to isolate radium, but also to establish a method for extracting radium which was adopted by industry. Far more than the diffident Pierre, Marie proved capable of seeking out and persuading others to give her the help she needed.

Since radium was present in tiny quantities in pitchblende, it was first necessary to find space for large-volume chemical treatments. The Curies were given use of a cavernous hangar at the EPCI which had been a dissection room for medical students. As Marie pointed out later, it was inadequate in many respects—"a wooden shed with a bituminous floor and a glass roof which did not keep the rain out, and without any interior arrangements. The only objects it contained were some worn pine tables, a cast-iron stove, which worked badly, and the blackboard which Pierre Curie loved to use. There were no hoods to carry away the poisonous gases thrown off by our chemical treatments, so that it was necessary to carry them on outside in the court, but when the weather was unfavorable we went on with them inside, leaving the windows open."

Still, it *was* a workable space, and just across a courtyard from their original laboratory. They also managed, probably at Marie's instigation, to persuade Eduard Suess, a Viennese geologist who was a corresponding member of the French Academy, to intervene on their behalf with the Austrian government. With the first of many financial donations from Baron Edmond de Rothschild, they were able to procure over ten tons of pitchblende residue left after extraction of uranium, considered by everyone but the Curies to be nearly worthless.

"How glad I was when the sacks arrived," Marie recalled years later, "with the brown dust mixed with pine needles, and when the activity proved even greater than that of the primitive ore! It was a stroke of luck that the residues had not been thrown far away or disposed of in some way, but left in a heap in the pine wood near the plant."

By the spring of 1899, Marie Curie had what she needed to begin. "I had to work with as much as twenty kilograms of material at a time," she recalls, "so that the hangar was filled with great vessels full of precipitates and of liquids. It was exhausting work to move the containers about, to transfer the liquids, and to stir for hours at a time, with an iron bar, the boiling material in the cast-iron basin."

Fairly soon, it became clear that it was going to be easier to tease radium apart from barium than it would be to isolate polonium from bismuth. "I extracted from the mineral the radium-bearing barium," she explained, "and this, in the state of chloride, I submitted to a fractional crystallization. . . . The very delicate operations of the last crystallizations were exceedingly difficult to carry out in the laboratory, where it was impossible to find protection from the iron and coal dust."

Despite all the difficulties, there is evidence that Marie Curie was extremely happy during this period, more invigorated than enslaved by the challenge of her work. Together, as she later wrote, she and

Pierre "were . . . entirely absorbed in the new field that opened before us, thanks to the discovery so little expected. And we were very happy in spite of the difficult conditions under which we worked. We passed our days at the laboratory, often eating a simple student's lunch there. A great tranquillity reigned in our poor shabby hangar; occasionally, while observing an operation, we would walk up and down talking of our work, present and future. When we were cold, a cup of hot tea, drunk beside the stove, cheered us. We lived in a preoccupation as complete as that of a dream."

If there were sadnesses for Marie, they had to do most often with missing home. When Bronia and Kazimierz left Paris for Poland in the fall of 1898, Marie was stricken. "You can't imagine what a hole you have made in my life. With you two, I have lost everything I clung to in Paris except my husband and child." A series of questions followed about how to cope: Should the green plant Bronia left behind be watered "and how many times a day. Does it need a great deal of heat and sun?" Irène was being difficult about her food, refusing everything but tapioca. "Write me what would be suitable for persons of her age."

The Dłuskis had embarked on a great experiment of their own: the founding of a modern tuberculosis sanatorium on the outskirts of Zakopane in the Carpathian Mountains. To raise funds, they had enlisted the support of some of Poland's most illustrious leaders, including Paderewski and Henryk Sienkiewicz (best known outside Poland as the author of *Quo Vadis*). Bolesław Prus reported in his weekly "Chronicles," much read in Warsaw, that the Dłuskis were traveling to the famed Davos in Switzerland in order to learn the very latest approaches, thus enabling them to "introduce the open-air treatment for tuberculosis in the new sanatorium in Zakopane."

It wasn't too long after the Dłuskis' departure, though, before Marie was writing more hopeful letters. "I miss my family enormously," she wrote Bronia, "above all you, my dears, and Father. I often think of my isolation with grief. I cannot complain of anything else, for our health is not bad, the child is growing well, and I have the best husband one could dream of; I could never have imagined finding one like him. He is a true gift of heaven, and the more we live together the more we love each other."

Marie's letters home, especially those to her brother Józef, emphasize worries and difficulties even in good times. "We have to be very careful and my husband's salary is not quite enough for us to live on," she writes in March of 1899. But then she adds that "up to now we have had some unexpected extra resources [i.e. prizes] every year, which keeps us from having a deficit." Then there is fact that "at the moment we have so much work with our new metals that I cannot prepare my doctorate." But even here Marie's proud proprietary feelings about "our new metals" peek through.

One unexpected property of the "new metals" had particularly delighted the Curies. "We had an especial joy," Marie recalled, "in observing that our products containing concentrated radium were all spontaneously luminous. My husband who had hoped to see them show beautiful colorations had to agree that this other unhoped-for characteristic gave him even greater satisfaction."

Sometimes, after dinner, the Curies would walk the five blocks from their apartment on rue de la Glacière back to rue Lhomond "for another survey of our domain. Our precious products, for which we had no shelter, were arranged on tables and boards; from all sides we could see their slightly luminous silhouettes, and these gleamings, which seemed suspended in the darkness, stirred us with ever new emotion and enchantment."

Later, it would be this understandable pride in the luminous new substances which made Marie Curie reluctant to acknowledge their deadly potential. But in 1899, no one had reason to believe that the usual precautions, such as working outside in the courtyard to avoid noxious fumes, weren't perfectly adequate. And it seemed quite natural, as the excitement about the new metals grew, to mail them out to fellow scientists all over the world.

A scientist in Iceland wrote thanking the Curies for a sample of their active barium in October of 1899. "We have abandoned all methods hitherto employed . . . and are using only your radiant powder," reported Adam Paulsen. Responding to a request, Marie sent two samples to Warsaw with an explanation in Polish. One sample, she explained, "is a very active substance, very concentrated" and "sends photo and electric energy through the glass of the test tube for quite a distance." Pierre's friend Georges Gouy wrote to thank him for "your shipment, which inspired the admiration of all the personnel of the laboratory. I already had some samples, but they were less luminous." Gouy added: "I am following with extreme interest your triumphal march in the study of the 'Curie rays' (for so I've baptised them) and I congratulate you on having left the kitchen a bit in order to harvest the fruits of your discovery."

The "fruits" the Curies were harvesting were their favorite kind: the interest and respect of colleagues. Later, after the Nobel Prize, they would find popular fame a nuisance and a burden. But in this period, they were sought out because others were captivated by their work. Henri Becquerel, for instance, borrowed a sizable quantity of their active barium in order to renew his research on the subject. And others began to work closely with the Curies on various aspects of radioactivity. With the physicist Georges Sagnac, Pierre produced a paper on X rays and radioactivity. And, at Pierre's request, a young chemist, André Debierne, began to work on radioactivity. Although he worked in a lab at the Sorbonne, he was a frequent visitor to the Curies' hangar and "was soon an intimate friend."

The closest collaboration of all, however, continued to be between Pierre and Marie. In 1899 and 1900, Marie wrote two papers alone updating her effort to isolate radium, and Pierre wrote one alone on the effect of a magnetic field on radium emissions. But three papers, including groundbreaking reports on "induced" radioactivity and on the electric charge of certain radium "rays," were authored jointly by Marie and Pierre.

As usual, the Curies, since they were not members, couldn't report their research to the Academy in person. Pierre, however, had been presenting their work to the Physics Society all along. And in 1900, an International Congress of Physics in Paris provided the Curies an opportunity to pull all their research on radioactivity together and to present it to an illustrious gathering of scientists from all over the world.

The International Congress of Physics was called on the occasion of the Universal Exposition of 1900, an immense celebration of art and technology which drew nearly fifty million visitors to Paris. The Eiffel Tower was surrounded for the occasion by pavilions exhibiting fine arts and domestic designs, and a Palace of Electricity sponsored a brilliant light show. The "magic fluid," electricity, was the star of the Exposition; the American sensation Loie Fuller danced in her own small building "through beams of electric light colored by moving cellophane filters." Visitors moved through the fair on an electrically powered sidewalk. And the American essayist Henry Adams confessed to sitting "by the hour over the great dynamos watching them run noiselessly and smoothly as planets." He judged them "marvelous," adding "the Gods are not in it. Chiefly the Germans."

For the many scientists who gathered for the International Congress of Physics, however, radioactivity, not electricity, was the fascinating topic. They came from the United States, Italy, Russia, Scandinavia, Britain, Austria, Germany, Switzerland, and Hungary, as well as Japan and India, to join the most illustrious physicists of France. Lord Kelvin, Pierre Curie's friend, was there, as were future Nobelists H. A. Lorentz and J. H. van't Hoff of Holland, and S. A. Arrhenius of Sweden. It was, as Marie Curie wrote later, "an opportunity to make known, at closer range, to foreign scientists, our new radioactive bodies. This was one of the points on which the interest of this Congress chiefly centered."

In their longest paper to date, "The new radioactive substances," the Curies brought together all the research and findings on radioactivity, giving credit to concurrent work in England and Germany. As the paper amply demonstrated, a fair amount was by then known about the behavior of these strange "Becquerel rays." It was known that the rays varied: some could be deflected by a magnet and some couldn't, some penetrated thick barriers and others didn't. It was known that the elements could "induce" radioactivity in other substances—and indeed had turned the Curies' lab radioactive. It was known that they could color glass. What wasn't known was why and how. What was the source of this strange energy?

"The spontaneity of the radiation," the Curies noted, "is an enigma, a subject of profound astonishment." Radioactivity seemed to violate the first law of thermodynamics, i.e., that energy can be converted from one form to another but cannot be created or destroyed. In radiation, there seemed to be no evidence of conversion: radium just emitted energy without seeming to undergo any change. The Curies' paper concluded with questions: "What is the source of energy coming from the Becquerel rays? Does it come from within the radioactive bodies, or from outside them?" Every possible answer to this question violated one assumption or another of nineteenth-century science.

Until the discovery of radioactivity, two forces had sufficed to explain all the phenomena occurring in nature. One was the gravitational attraction between massive objects, first elucidated by Newton in the seventeenth century. The second was the electromagnetic force, whose laws were formulated by James Clerk Maxwell in the nineteenth century. Over the first four decades of the twentieth century, the "enigma" of radioactivity would lead to an understanding of new forces contained within the nucleus of the atom, forces of such potency that knowledge of them has changed our world forever.

Chapter Eight
A THEORY OF MATTER

IN FRANCE, the discovery of X rays had raised questions which led to the discovery of radium, polonium, and, more importantly, to the phenomenon of radioactivity. In England, Roentgen's amazing rays provoked different questions. J. J. Thomson, the newly appointed head of the preeminent Cavendish Laboratory at Cambridge University, put together his own cathode ray tube in order to duplicate Roentgen's results. But right from the start, according to his young protégé Ernest Rutherford, Thomson had different goals than Becquerel and the Curies. "The Professor, of course, is trying to find out the real cause and nature of the waves," Rutherford wrote home in 1895, "and the great object is to find the theory of matter before anyone else."

By 1897, Thomson had, if not a "theory of matter," at least a first step in that direction. He had focused his attention on what were then called cathode rays, those streams of light which traveled rapidly from the negative to the positive anode inside a vacuum tube, and had come to the conclusion that they were made up of very small, negatively charged particles. These particles were smaller than "ordinary atoms or molecules," and were, he maintained, basic building blocks of all matter. "Thus on this view," he wrote in *The Philosophical Magazine* of October 1897, "we have in the cathode rays a new state, a state in which the subdivision of matter is carried very much further than in the ordinary gaseous state; a state in which all matter —that is, matter derived from different sources such as hydrogen, oxygen, &c.—is of one and the same kind, this matter being the substance from which all chemical elements are built up." Thomson's particles came to be called electrons. They were the first subatomic particles to be identified, and their discovery marked the beginning of modern particle physics.

But Thomson was at least one and in some cases two steps ahead of many of his colleagues. First of all, it was necessary to accept the corpuscular idea of matter, the idea that all things are made up of discreet invisible molecules composed of even smaller atoms. This required a leap of faith some were unwilling to take. Though the idea of atoms had been around since the British scientist John Dalton proposed it in 1809, and though the work of others had made the corpuscular scheme increasingly plausible, many serious scientists were still debating the proposition as the century came to a close. There were, in fact, two theories of matter current at the time: the corpuscular or atomist view held that matter was discontinuous, consisting of extremely small discrete particles. The other view posited a continuous aether, a sort of glue which held everything together and which existed, in most versions, in an elusive other dimension.

According to those in the aether camp, the atomist theory had not earned the right to be taken seriously. Skepticism about Dalton's atom was part of a wide-ranging distrust of scientific claims about the unseen. Marcelin Berthelot, eminent French chemist and opponent of the corpuscular theory, asked rhetorically, "Who has ever seen a gas molecule or an atom?" Pierre Duhem, one of the most articulate opponents, disdained a theory which bypassed the visible. "The bodies which senses and instruments perceive," he noted, "are resolved (in this conception) into immensely numerous and much smaller bodies, apprehended by reason alone. . . ."

Those who accused science of being "bankrupt" were likely to favor the aetherial view. Philosophers like Henri Bergson were calling on modern science to "reestablish . . . [the] continuity of the universe." They disliked the atomists' mechanistic, billiard-ball conception.

In England, where the idea of the atom was born, the argument over corpuscular versus aether theory was lively enough so that J. J. Thomson began his historic 1897 paper on the cathode rays with a recapitulation of it. "The most diverse opinions are held as to these rays," he noted. "According to the almost unanimous opinion of German physicists they are due to some process in the aether to which . . . no phenomenon hitherto observed is analogous: another view of these rays is that, so far from being wholly aetherial, they are in fact wholly material, and that they mark the paths of particles of matter charged with negative electricity." He concluded, magnanimously, that "amongst the physicists who have most deeply studied the subject can be found supporters of either theory."

But even "atomists" weren't necessarily easy converts to Thomson's theory of the electron. "The assumption," Thomson admitted, "of a state of matter more finely subdivided than the atom is a somewhat startling one." Having placed their faith in the atom as the elemental building block of all matter, some atomists were reluctant to see it coming apart. The great Mendeleev, creator of the periodic table, insisted on "the immutability of the atoms forming the elements. . . ." "The elements are indivisible and intransmutable," Mendeleev continued to argue some years after Thomson proposed the electron. To think otherwise would be to suggest that elements are not themselves elemental. This, to his mind, was something akin to alchemy. About this Mendeleev was correct: Thomson's electron was leading toward a new alchemy, the transmutation of elements.

By the time of her first publication on radioactivity, Marie Curie was clearly in the atomist camp, as was Pierre. Indeed, the École de physique et chimie, where Pierre taught, had been founded by breakaway atomists. Schützenberger, the director of the school Pierre was so grateful to, and Charles Friedel, his teacher and friend, were both outspoken advocates of the corpuscular view.

In her first solo paper on radioactivity, Marie Curie noted that radioactive substances have high *atomic* weights, and that their radioactivity seems to be independent of chemical states (implying activity on an atomic level). And in the Curies' joint paper announcing the discovery of radium, Marie is credited with having shown that radioactivity is related in some way to the atomic makeup of the substances. "One of us has shown," the paper states, "that radioactivity seems to be an atomic property, persistent in all the physical and chemical states of the material." This, as historian of physics Abraham Pais has noted, marks "the first time in history that radioactivity is linked to individual atoms."

The question of *how* radioactivity was linked to atomic makeup was much more difficult to answer. What confounded the Curies and others right from the beginning was that there seemed to be no source for radioactive energy. "The emission of the uranic rays," Marie Curie wrote in a lucid overview of the problem in 1900, "is very constant, it does not vary noticeably with time, nor with exposure to light, nor with temperature. That is the most troubling aspect of the phenomenon. When we observe the production of cathode rays or of Roentgen rays, we ourselves are furnishing . . . the electric energy. . . . But at the time of the uranic [radioactive] emission, no change occurs in this material which radiates the energy . . . in a continuous fashion. The uranium shows no appreciable change of state, no visible chemical transformation, it remains, in appearance at least, the same as ever, the source of the energy it discharges remains undetectable. . . ."

In their attempt to explain the phenomenon, the Curies proffered two incorrect hypotheses. One was that the law of conservation of energy (sometimes called the Carnot principle by the French) had to be revised; perhaps radioactivity represented an exception to the general rule that energy cannot be created or destroyed. It was a suggestion that Pierre Curie's brilliant friend Georges Gouy had made ten years earlier in connection with another phenomenon, and Pierre was inclined to go along with it. "The truth is," Pierre wrote a colleague in 1898, "there is a contradiction of the Carnot principle [the law of conservation of energy] and wasn't it Gouy who was right? Some years ago already he told me that there were going to be some exceptions to the Carnot principle. . . ."

Another idea, proposed by Marie Curie in her very first paper on the subject, was that the energy was brought to the radioactive substances from *outside* them. Perhaps, she suggested, "all of space is traversed by rays . . . which can only be absorbed by certain elements of high atomic weight, like uranium and thorium."

This conjecture led two German gymnasium teachers and gifted part-time scientists, Julius Elster and Hans Geitel, to a series of outdoor experiments. If the radioactive element was collecting energy from the surrounding atmosphere, they reasoned, then it would lose energy if buried in the ground. They placed a radioactive source under 300 meters of rock in the Harz mountains and waited for forty-eight hours; then they put a source down at the bottom of an 850-meter mine shaft. They found no decrease of radioactivity in either case. "From this research," Elster and Geitel concluded, "the hypothesis that the [radioactivity] is excited by other rays in the surrounding air appears highly unlikely to us." Within the year, they conducted a second experiment, exposing a radioactive source to cathode rays and to sunlight, and concluded even more forcefully that the energy in radioactive bodies must be emanating "from the atom itself." Because of this early insight, Elster and Geitel have been called, with slight exaggeration, the *Entdecker der Atomenergie,* discoverers of atomic energy.

Their work made a strong impression on Pierre Curie. "Elster and Geitel," he wrote to a Swiss colleague in December of 1898, "are certainly the ones who have worked best on the question of the uranic rays. . . . and I wouldn't be surprised if they provide us with something very good." Parenthetically, Pierre Curie noted in mock horror that they were "foreigners!"

In the end, it would not be necessary to abandon the law of

conservation of energy or to find a mysterious source of radiation in the atmosphere. The explanation of radioactivity required an even greater leap of imagination than either of these two hypotheses. Radioactivity is a manifestation of the disintegration of atomic nuclei. When radium gives off radiation, it is sending out subatomic particles: tiny electrons and larger, but still extremely small, particles with positive charges which we now know to be helium nuclei, as well as gamma rays (electromagnetic rays with wavelengths much shorter than visible light). All the heavier elements, it turns out, are inherently unstable and continously transmuting. An atom which started out as uranium or radium repeatedly alters itself, sometimes after seconds or minutes and sometimes after thousands of years. We now call this process "decay," and have detailed knowledge of chains of decay. For instance: uranium becomes thorium, thorium decays into radium, radium into radon, radon into polonium, which ultimately decays into lead.

Because in most of the elements the Curies were working with the transmutation was slow, and because the energy available in the nucleus was enormous, the Curies and others had difficulty at first detecting a change in their radioactive sources. But change was occurring. Indeed change, transmutation, causes radiation.

By 1903, just five years after Marie Curie's first paper on radioactivity in pitchblende and five years as well after J. J. Thomson proposed electrons, the theory of transmutation was in place. The Curies and Becquerel made critical contributions, as did some German researchers. But the great theoretical leaps on the path to a transmutation theory were made by the British, and particularly by a young man of unbounded ambition and enormous talent, Thomson's protégé Ernest Rutherford. Like Marie Curie, Rutherford was an outsider, a New Zealander who came to England on a scholarship and was eager to make his mark. "I am now busy writing up papers for publication and doing fresh work," Rutherford wrote his mother in New Zealand early in 1902. "I have to keep going, as there are always people on my track. I have to publish my present work as rapidly as possible in order to keep in the race. The best sprinters in this road of investigation are Becquerel and the Curies in Paris, who have done a great deal of very important work on the subject of radioactive bodies during the last few years."

The sports metaphor came naturally to Rutherford, who had been a powerful cricket player back in New Zealand. It stands in starkest contrast to the sensibility of Pierre, who, as Marie later wrote, "could never accustom himself to a system of work which involved hasty publications, and was always happier in a domain in which but a few investigators were quietly working." But the lively, sometimes testy, play of ideas back and forth between France and England during the next few years shows that the Curies were not so unambitious, nor Rutherford quite so ungracious, as these extremes suggest. Everyone working on radioactivity wanted to get to the right answers first. The difference was not in desire but in focus.

Marie and Pierre Curie, quite understandably, concentrated on the properties of the strange and awe-inspiring new elements they had discovered and which they had on their shelves. Rutherford, on the other hand, was excited not so much by the elements—of which he had, in any case, very limited quantities—as by the possibilities he saw in them for continuing his professor's search for a "theory of matter." Predictably, the Curies made critical contributions to the understanding of the substances. But it was Rutherford who arrived at an explanation of the phenomenon of radioactivity.

The first step had been taken by Rutherford's teacher J. J. Thomson when he proposed the electron in 1897. By 1899, Thomson had gone further, asserting (correctly) that electrons were the source of electricity. "Electrification essentially involves the splitting up of the atom," he asserted, "a part of the mass of the atom . . . becoming detached." A few months later Thomson estimated, with reasonable accuracy, the value of the negative charge of a single electron.

Meanwhile, Ernest Rutherford had accepted a job at McGill University in Canada, where he was taking a closer look at the emissions from radioactive substances. In January of 1899, he published a paper, lengthy even by relatively verbose British standards, which a historian suggests was "the masterpiece by which this research student qualified for admission to the guild of working physicists." The key new finding, in this elaborate, fifty-four page debut, was that radioactive emissions are made up of at least two different kinds of "rays." One kind, which Rutherford labeled "beta rays," penetrated thick barriers. The other kind, which he called "alpha rays," carried a much larger charge but were deflected by even a fairly thin layer of aluminum foil.

It would be some years before the alpha and beta rays would reveal the internal geography of the atom. But German researchers soon discovered that Rutherford's beta rays responded to a magnetic field in the same way as Thomson's cathode rays (electrons). And over the next ten months Pierre and Marie Curie, and Henri Becquerel, published a series of papers which led inexorably to the conclusion that Rutherford's beta rays were in fact identical with his professor J. J. Thomson's negatively charged particles. Thomson's electrons, it turned out, were one of the components of the Curies' radioactivity.

What happened next was a dramatic example of the way in which research goals influence outcomes. It involved thorium, the element which in 1898 was discovered, independently by Gerhard Carl Schmidt and Marie Curie, to be radioactive. Way back in March of 1897, when Marie Curie was measuring substances in her makeshift ionization chamber, she had noticed a slight buildup in activity in the course of measuring the ionizing power of thorium. She was intrigued enough to open the chamber up, renew the air, and make further measurements. Once again, she noted a slight increase in activity within the chamber. Her results, however, were not very clear, and the trials were not pursued. Irène Curie, writing about her mother's work many years later, noted that "had these experiments been more clearcut, the entire orientation of future work might have been changed."

Nearly two and a half years later, an electrical engineer named R. B. Owens who was working with Rutherford at McGill was troubled by the same effect. When he attempted to measure the ionizing power of thorium oxide, his data was puzzlingly uneven. Thorium's radiation seemed to change "in response to events as irrelevant as the opening of a door." Only by enclosing the thorium in a metal box could he obtain consistent measurements.

Rutherford was intrigued. In the summer of 1899, he set out to study the unusual behavior of thorium. He found that it was possible to detect a gaseous substance given off by thorium but different from it. This gas, which he labeled an "emanation," had "the power of producing radioactivity in all substances on which it falls," a radioactivity which lasted for "several days." He concluded, in the first of two papers published early in 1900 in the British *Philosophical Magazine and Journal of Science,* that "the radiation is of a more penetrating character than that given out by thorium . . . the emanation from thorium compounds thus has properties which the thorium itself does not possess."

Between the publication of Rutherford's first "emanation" paper in January of 1900 and his second, in February, he read Pierre and Marie Curie's paper on the same phenomenon, published November 6, 1899, and entitled "On the radioactivity induced by Becquerel rays." Somewhat in advance of Rutherford, the Curies had observed that radioactive substances in their laboratory "can communicate their radioactivity and that this induced radioactivity persists during a rather long time." Unlike Rutherford, however, the Curies attributed this "induced radioactivity" to a transfer of energy, a kind of "phosphorescence," provoked by the original substances. Becquerel, always ready to find a new phosphorescence, weighed in with a brief addendum, suggesting that the phenomenon was "a persistent activity of a kind of phosphorescence," which he attributed to the "prodigious radiant activity of the substances discovered by M. and Mme. Curie."

Perhaps because of the Curies' paper, Rutherford's second report on the thorium emanation was a little more tentative than the first. In a footnote, Rutherford addressed some of the news from France. Displaying what was probably a quite unconscious sexism, Rutherford referred to "Curie" in the singular, blotting out one half of the team. Unlike "Curie," Rutherford noted, he had been able to observe "the power of exciting radioactivity" only in the thorium compounds. However, his specimens of radium and polonium are very weak compared to Curie's. "No mention is made," Rutherford continued, "of . . . whether there is an 'emanation' from radium and polonium, as there is from thorium compounds. Curie concludes that the results obtained are due to a kind of phosphorescence excited by the radiation; while in the case of thorium the author has shown that such a theory is inadmissible."

The key question had been defined. Was the temporary radioactivity, which both Rutherford and the Curies had observed in objects placed in proximity to radioactive substances, caused by a transfer of energy of some kind from the substances themselves, or was it caused by a breakdown product, an offspring which differed in makeup and in behavior from its parent? If another radioactive substance could be found to produce an "emanation" different from itself, as thorium did, then perhaps such emanations were a general phenomenon of radioactivity.

In May of 1900, just two months after Rutherford's emanation papers, Sir William Crookes chanced upon corroborating evidence. Crookes was a consulting chemist and editor of a weekly paper, *The Chemical News,* a man of affairs who took a lively interest in the latest developments. There were few subjects on which Sir William did not have an opinion, from the grain supply to spiritualism. He had already gone on record early in 1899 in the *Comptes rendus* in support of the theory that radioactive energy came from an external source, citing "the enormous quantity of energy imprisoned in the aether." Sometime after that, Crookes decided to conduct his own investigation of the subject in his well-equipped private lab. He cut through a slice of pitchblende and sent a "radiographic impression" to Pierre Curie, and he "went through every mineral in my cabinet— a somewhat extensive collection, numbering many fine specimens" searching for radioactivity. In the process of preparing his own sample of pure uranium, he made an unexpected discovery: he found that it was possible to part uranium from its radioactivity. By a series of chemical treaments of uranyl nitrate, he arrived at a substance which was chemically different from uranium and highly radioactive. He named it "uranium X."

It was beginning to look as though radioactive elements were less stable, less elemental, than elements were supposed to be. In October of 1900, the Curies' colleague and friend André Debierne announced and named a new element "actinium," and suggested that it might in fact be the thorium emanation Rutherford had observed. But then Debierne made a discovery that echoed Crookes's. If he prepared a solution of actinium and barium and precipitated the barium, the barium turned out to be radioactive. What was going on? Early in 1901, Becquerel understated the case when he wrote in *Nature* that "recent studies on induced radio-activity appear to open still new horizons."

By March of 1901 Pierre Curie appeared to be agreeing with Rutherford that the radioactive substances were producing another substance. In a paper written with André Debierne and entitled "On induced radioactivity and the gas activated by radium," Curie noted the "deplorable situation in the lab, where everything has become radioactive. This deplorable situation does not seem to us to be explained by the direct radiation of radioactive dust spread about the lab; it is probably due in large part to the continual formation of radioactive gas."

Was not this gas akin to the thorium "emanation" Rutherford had written about the year before? Rutherford thought so. "M. and Mme. Curies," he wrote in *Nature* not long after, "stated that they had obtained a radio-active gas which preserved its activity for several weeks; this is possibly identical with the emanation." He added that "quite recently . . . some light has been thrown on these emanations . . . the results point to the conclusion that the emanation from radium is in reality a radio-active gas."

By this time, Rutherford had enlisted a junior member of the McGill chemistry department, an Oxford graduate named Frederick Soddy, in his continuing study of thorium emanation. And in January of 1902, they published the most detailed paper to date on the phenomenon, concluding that the emanation, which they now called thorium X, was a substance independent of and different from its parent element thorium; thorium X was a gas which actually carried off (temporarily) thorium's radioactivity.

Within less than two weeks of the appearance of Rutherford and Soddy's paper in England, the Curies replied from across the Channel with a paper entitled "Sur les corps radio-actifs" in which they resisted, more adamantly than ever before, the "transformation theory" which was gaining momentum all around them. True, some substances may lose energy temporarily, but it is always restored over time. There were still, as far as they were concerned, two hypotheses on the table: either "each radioactive atom possesses in the form of potential energy the energy it releases," or "the radioactive atom is a mechanism which at each instant draws in from outside itself the energy it releases." They noted that "the experience of several years" had shown no indication of a loss of energy in their radioactive substances. "One may conceive that radioactive atoms are in the process of transformation," but "experiments made so far to verify this have given negative results."

Their brief paper ends with an astute observation about science which is also clearly an indirect criticism of Rutherford and others who, they believe, are rushing too quickly to conclusions. "In studying unknown phenomena we can make quite general hypotheses and advance step by step in concordance with experience. This sure, methodical progress is necessarily slow. In contrast, we can make bold hypotheses in which the mechanism of phenomena is specified. This procedure has the advantage of suggesting certain experiments and above all of facilitating the thought process, making it less abstract by the use of an image. On the other hand, we cannot hope to imagine *a priori* a complex theory which agrees with experience. Precise hypotheses almost certainly contain a portion of error along with a portion of truth."

But the hypothesis of transmutation—or transformation, as early researchers called it—had come to stay. In April of 1902 Rutherford and Soddy sent off a paper to London entitled "The cause and nature of radioactivity" in which they concluded that radioactivity "is at once an atomic phenomenon and the accompaniment of a chemical change in which new kinds of matter are produced. The two considerations force us to the conclusion that radioactivity is a manifestation of subatomic chemical change."

Such subatomic changes, Rutherford and Soddy noted, differ from ordinary chemical changes in that they are "not among those that are yet under our control." They ended their historic paper by acknowledging that "nothing can yet be stated of the mechanism of the changes involved, but . . . it seems not unreasonable to hope that radioactivity affords the means of obtaining information of processes occurring within the chemical atom."

Pierre Curie published another paper in early 1903 in which he, once again, argued with Rutherford about the "material nature of the emanation." "I don't think there is sufficient reason to accept the existence of a material emanation with ordinary atomic form." In February, Rutherford sent off a rejoinder to the *Philosophical Magazine,* claiming that his most recent results made it "very difficult to explain such phenomena except on a material hypothesis." He reminded Curie that he was not claiming *"ordinary* chemical change" but that "the radioactivity of the elements is a manifestation of *sub-atomic change.*"

Though many, including the Curies, still had doubts, it is clear in retrospect that by 1903, Rutherford and Soddy had established transmutation. The study of radioactivity had brought scientists from a quarrel about the existence of atoms to the threshold of nuclear physics.

GEORGES GOUY, writing to his friend Pierre Curie from Lyon in July of 1903, expressed amazement at the behavior of "the so-called cor-puscles" acting "each individually" in the experiments of J. J. Thom-son and others. "To use M. Poincaré's expression, one is astonished that the atoms are so highly-developed as that!" He adds: "The general public is often amazed at how uncertain scientific theories are. I'm amazed, on the contrary, to see them so often verified. When we imagined the atomic structure of matter, it was basically a logical artifice used to escape the difficulties raised by the concept of a *con-tinuum.* That we have been led, from this altogether artifical hypothe-sis, to . . . nearly prove [the atoms'] real existence, that is for me a subject of profound astonishment."

If the "real," "material" existence of subatomic particles came as a surprise to Gouy, who had early on declared himself a "partisan of the materialist or ionic hypothesis," it is understandable that the Cu-ries, given the "descriptionist" and "positivist" traditions they were heir to, would be reluctant to accept Rutherford's transformation theory without more empirical evidence.

Thus it is not surprising that the British, rather than the French, were the first to understand radiation as a release of subatomic parti-cles. The astute Sir William Crookes, addressing a Berlin Congress in 1903, noted that the dream of "resolving the chemical elements into simpler forms of matter . . . has been essentially a British dream, and we have become speculative and imaginative to an audacious extent, almost belying our character of a purely practical nation."

And yet it remains surprising that the Curies were as resistant as they were, for as long as they were, to the idea of transmutation. After all, as Rutherford and Soddy rather graciously pointed out in their 1902 paper, "The cause and nature of radioactivity," "all the most prominent workers in this subject are agreed in considering radioac-tivity an atomic phenomenon. M. and Mme. Curie, the pioneers in the chemistry of the subject, have stated that this idea underlies their whole work from the beginning and created their methods of re-search."

Then too, the Curies showed signs early on that they were attracted to the idea of some sort of transformation. Marie Curie, in an article published in the *Revue scientifique* in July of 1900, wrote so convincingly of this possibility that one suspects she herself was persuaded of it: Radioactive substances, she explained, may be "substances in which there is a violent interior movement of substances in the course of breaking up. If this is the case, radium should constantly lose weight. But the smallness of the particles is such that, although the electric charge sent out into the atmosphere is easy to detect, the corresponding mass is absolutely insignificant . . . it would take millions of years for radium to lose . . . milligrams of its weight." Thus it is impossible to measure the loss. "The materialist theory of radioactivity is very seductive," she continues. "It explains the phenomena of radioactivity well."

Why, given this early sympathy for the theory, were the Curies so reluctant to embrace it? In part, it was their careful, empirical approach: after all, even with their delicate measuring instruments, they truly could not find evidence that radium was losing weight or energy over time. And Rutherford's theory was, as a modern historian acknowledges, based on "decidedly limited knowledge, mostly derived from thorium and its derivatives." "Even more surprising than this [transmutation] theory," another historian has noted, "was its rapid acceptance."

Another underlying reason for their resistance undoubtedly had to do with the threat Rutherford's theory seemed to pose to their recently discovered, and still largely unproven, new elements. As it turned out, the radioactive elements assumed their place on the periodic table despite their instability. But as events unfolded at the time, with thorium losing its radioactivity to thorium X and uranium to uranium X, it must have seemed to them that all the hard work establishing the existence of the new elements might be undone, or hopelessly muddled. If Rutherford's transformation theory proved true, it would not only contradict the inviolability of the atom, it would also threaten the inviolability of their new elements.

Marie Curie, in particular, must have felt herself to be working at cross-purposes with Rutherford et al. during this period. Beginning in 1899, around the time he started his investigations into radiation, she undertook the daunting task of isolating radium in order to prove its existence beyond doubt. It was an exhausting, and exhilarating, task. "Sometimes," she recalled, "I had to spend a whole day mixing a boiling mass with a heavy iron rod nearly as large as myself. I would be broken with fatigue at the day's end. Other days, on the contrary, the work would be a most minute and delicate fractional crystallization, in the effort to concentrate the radium. I was then annoyed by the floating dust of iron and coal from which I could not protect my precious products. . . . The feeling of discouragement that sometimes came after some unsuccessful toil did not last long and gave way to renewed activity."

There were two progress reports published in *Comptes rendus* along the way, in November of 1899 and August of 1900. Then finally, in July 1902, Marie Curie announced that she had successfully isolated one decigram of radium. "It had taken me almost four years," she noted later, "to produce the kind of evidence which chemical science demands, that radium is truly a new element." Marie Curie's paper for *Compte rendus* announced that the atomic weight of radium was 225 (very close to the current agreed value of 226) and concluded that "according to its atomic weight, it [radium] should be placed in the Mendeleev [periodic] table after barium in the column of alkaline earth metals."

The isolation of radium was an enormous personal and important professional accomplishment. Frederick Soddy, in 1904, observed that only in the case of radium was there "evidence of a material character of the specific elementary nature of the [radioactive] substance. In the other cases, such evidence is lacking, for all exist in such minute quantity that, apart from the radioactivity, there is no other evidence of their existence." As time went on, this radioactivity would become the accepted means for distinguishing between radioactive substances. But in the beginning, the isolation of radium was critical to making the entire field credible. "It is not an exaggeration," physicist Jean Perrin noted twenty-two years later, "to say today that [the isolation of radium] is the cornerstone on which the entire edifice of radioactivity rests."

Around the time that Marie Curie succeeded in isolating and determining the atomic weight of radium, Rutherford was discovering that all the radioactive elements were in perpetual flux, going through a complicated and initially confusing chain of transmutations. Nowhere was the confusion more pronounced, nor Marie Curie's proprietary feeling about the elements she had discovered more in evidence, than in a dispute which arose at the time over the first element she and Pierre laid claim to, polonium.

It all began, ironically enough, with a footnote in the Curies' 1902 critique of Rutherford's work on thorium X. The Curies were insisting that they had observed no changes over time in the radioactivity of their elements. Since polonium, which lost radioactivity very rapidly, was a dramatic exception to this claim, they suggested that it might not in fact be an element but merely a "species of active bismuth."

In June of 1902, a professor of chemistry at the University of

Berlin named Willy Marckwald presented a paper in which he took note of the Curies' doubts about polonium, and proceeded to describe a substance which he believed to be a possible new element. Marie Curie read Marckwald's paper and became convinced that he was talking about the substance she had already described. She wrote and published a paper in German which asserted as much. Her previous remarks, she insisted, were not intended to imply that polonium did not exist, only that it had been impossible thus far to isolate it. "Marckwald's polonium," she concluded in December of 1902, "appears to be the same as ours."

Marckwald replied that "it lay far from my thoughts to diminish the immortal merit which the Curies, husband and wife, have earned for the discovery of the new radioactive elements," and insisted that the element he had isolated was different from polonium; he named it radiotellurium.

It is possible that Marckwald was merely ambitious and wanted to lay claim to an element of his own. But it seems more likely, as historian of science Alfred Romer suggests, that the confusion resulted from the fact that no one yet understood that the materials they were working with changed from one day to the next, and behaved differently each time they transmuted.

In the end Soddy and Rutherford concluded that Marie Curie was right: the substance Marckwald called radiotellurium was her polonium, or something very close to it. And, with further irony, it was through an understanding of transmutation that Marie Curie ultimately was able to win over her colleagues. In 1906, she published the results of a ten-month study of polonium which showed that it lost half its radioactivity in 140 days. "There can be no question . . . ," she wrote, "that . . . the substance prepared by Marckwald is simply the same as I discovered earlier and have described as polonium." Since, by now, the time a substance took to reach half-life (half its initial radioactivity) had become its identifier, and since radiotellurium had the same half-life as Marie Curie's polonium, Marckwald didn't have any arguments left.

His capitulation, however, was grudging. After quoting, in English, from *Romeo and Juliet:* " 'What's in a name? that which we call a rose, By any other name would smell as sweet,' " he concluded that "the great services of Mme. Curie in the discovery of radioactive substances justify us in considering her wishes in a question of no wide-ranging importance. For this reason I propose in the future to replace the name of 'radiotellurium' by 'polonium.' "

Marie Curie would not have agreed with Marckwald that the issue was unimportant: polonium was the first element she and Pierre discovered, and it was named after her beloved Poland besides. But by 1906, when it was finally settled, the issue may have lost some of the urgency it possessed for the Curies three years earlier, when she and Pierre were beset by personal trials and professional disappointments.

MARIE and Pierre Curie always considered themselves to be outsiders. Pierre, son of a Communard and product of a highly unconventional education, continued to mock the establishment even after the establishment, ever so reluctantly, allowed him in. Marie was not so anti-establishment as Pierre. But she had been raised on the heroic poems of Mickiewicz, and on the exhortations of the Polish patriots. She tended to view life as a heroic struggle against great obstacles. In almost all her nonscientific writing, overcoming adversity is the template imposed on experience. And since Marie Curie's biography of Pierre and *Autobiographical Notes* have been the source for subsequent biographers, struggle has always been the central theme of the Curies' story. In particular, it has been generally accepted that the Curies were badly treated by the French scientific establishment, that they were celebrated abroad but prophets without honor at home.

This is an oversimplification. In fact, the Académie des sciences of the Institute provided quite a bit of early financial support for the Curies: Marie Curie was thrice recipient of the Prix Gegner, beginning in 1898, and in 1903 Pierre won the coveted 10,000-franc biannual Prix La Caze. In addition, in March of 1902, the Institute made a 20,000-franc credit available to the Curies for their work in isolating radium.

Further, there were influential members of the Institute who actively supported the Curies. As early as 1899, when Pierre made it known to some of his colleagues that he was thinking of finding a commercial solution to their financial woes, Henri Becquerel wrote that he had spoken to the physicist Éleuthère Mascart on Pierre's behalf. Already, Becquerel informed Pierre Curie, there was a 2,000-franc grant available through Mascart. "He deplores that you should be obliged to put your products on the market and will help you find still more funds in order to avoid this necessity." And, insisted Becquerel, there are others who are "full of admiration for your beautiful work and that of Madame Curie."

For some reason which remains unclear, both Pierre Curie and his friend Georges Gouy thoroughly distrusted the powerful Becquerel, and were suspicious of his offers of help. "You will be pleased to know," Pierre wrote Gouy at one point, "that it's Becquerel . . . we are most fed up with." But the fact remains that the Institute in general and Becquerel and other powerful academicians in particular came through with rather generous financial support.

The problem was not that there was no help from the French scientific establishment, but that the help wasn't the kind the Curies really needed. Mascart's 2,000 francs is a case in point. Becquerel's letter informing Pierre of the gift went on to advise him that he "would do well to go and see Mascart to thank him and to show him at the same time your luminous substances." Pierre Curie, who was both shy and proud, was absolutely undone by the prospect of such errands. "His sincerity," Paul Langevin observed, "prevented him from exploiting useful connections or powerful friendships" and he "didn't belong to any established family or group." Henri Poincaré put it more succinctly: "He was what one calls a 'poor candidate.' " The one group Pierre Curie did join around this time was the new Association of Professors, pledged to remove the influence of "politics, of schools and of families" from academic life in France—just the sort of organization most likely to alienate the powerful.

What the Curies needed, rather than piecemeal grants, was a home for their work: a well-equipped laboratory, generous salaries, and freedom from the need to cultivate connections and play politics. The French establishment, however, was unwilling to bestow such a gift upon this odd, and seemingly ungrateful, couple.

Thus it is not surprising that Pierre and Marie Curie were initially tempted by an offer which came to them in 1900 from the University of Geneva. If Pierre joined the faculty there, he would be given a chair at the university; a laboratory, to be equipped according to his requirements; and two assistants. There would also be an official position for Marie, although her exact title seems not to have been specified. At first, the Curies decided they would accept the offer. "The University of Geneva," Pierre wrote his Swiss friend Charles Edouard Guillaume in July of 1900, "has offered me the chair in physics . . . and I have accepted. . . . Your compatriots have been extremely kind and have very much insisted on having me, the dean M. Chodat is in particular an extremely charming man. We are just now going to Geneva to take a closer look at the situation." He added: "It seems to me it would be an excellent thing to live in your beautiful land of mountains."

Even after accepting, however, Pierre confessed he was "not without uneasiness about the consequences of this change of existence. Now that I have embarked on it, the task seems immense." Perhaps it was during the visit to Geneva, or perhaps it was in August, while Marie and Pierre were vacationing with Irène on the lush Île de Noirmoutiers off the southern coast of Brittany. But sometime during that summer of 1900, they changed their minds and decided to return to their still-difficult existence in France.

Earlier that year, they had moved from their apartment in the

Latin Quarter to quieter streets on the southern outskirts of Paris, where they rented a boxy two-story stucco house with tall shuttered windows opening out onto a terrace and garden. They were protected there from the noise and bustle of the city, tucked in behind the barrier of a wall and several rows of trees. And they had room there to better accommodate Pierre's father, Dr. Eugène Curie, who now lived with them.

In their more spacious quarters, Pierre and Marie had room for the Curie family sofas, mahogany with upholstery of well-worn green velvet, as well as Restoration armchairs. But the young Sèvrienne Eugénie Feytis was most struck, when she came to baby-sit, by the "deliberate ordinariness" of the interiors. Dr. Eugène Curie's room, where he had "assembled the memories of his life," was the one notable exception to this austerity. A large reproduction of Ingres's *The Source* greeted visitors who entered Dr. Curie's room. Within, there was a library rich in medical texts and in the works of Victor Hugo.

The rent at 108 boulevard Kellerman was 4,020 francs a year, considerably more than they had paid at the apartment on rue de la Glacière. Even with the help of Institute grants, Pierre's salary seems to have been inadequate to the increased costs of their new suburban existence.

At the time of the move to boulevard Kellerman in March, Pierre took an additional job teaching at the École polytechnique to add another twenty-five hundred francs to their income. Then, in the fall of 1900, after they turned down the offer from Geneva, two new appointments eased the financial pressures somewhat. Marie became the first woman named to the faculty of the École normale supérieure at Sèvres, France's best preparatory school for women teachers. And Henri Poincaré, alarmed that Pierre might leave the country, intervened on his behalf and got him appointed to teach a course in physics preparatory to the *certificat d'études* in physics, chemistry, and natural history (P.C.N.). This made Pierre, for the first time, a member of the faculty of the Sorbonne. But, truth to tell, the course was attended primarily by medical students and was peripheral to the Faculté des sciences, where Pierre rightfully belonged. Aside from the additional salary and a small office and workroom, it only meant he had to spend more time teaching, and more time shuttling back and forth on his bicycle between the École de physique et chimie on rue Lhomond, his new office at 12 rue Cuvier, and the couple's woefully inadequate, makeshift laboratory. Pierre, as Marie later lamented, was forced to "face the many anxieties . . . of a complicated system of work when his happiness depended on his being able to concentrate his efforts on a single determined subject."

More humiliations and frustrations were to follow. Already, in 1898, Pierre had tried and failed to attain a faculty appointment at the Sorbonne. In 1902, the chair in mineralogy became vacant and he tried again. Pierre Curie was qualified in mineralogy because of his pioneering work with crystals. But, according to Marie Curie, he had "few illusions about his chances of obtaining an important chair in the University of Paris, which would . . . have . . . enabled us to live without a supplementary revenue." As always, his not being a *normalien* put him at a disadavantage, since he "lacked the support, often decisive, which these . . . schools gave their pupils." As a result, Pierre Curie was refused a second time.

Then, sometime in the spring of that same year, Pierre was encouraged by his colleagues to apply for membership in the Académie des sciences. Pierre's attitude toward this august and self-important French institution was highly ambivalent. But in this he was no different than the members themselves, as Marcel Proust shrewdly observed them in *The Guermantes Way*. Institute member de Norpois, Proust wrote, "repeatedly dismissed his brother Academicians as old fossils. Other reasons apart, every member of a club or academy likes to ascribe to his fellow members the type of character that is the direct converse of his own, less for the advantage of being able to say: 'Ah! If it only rested with me!' than for the satisfaction of making the honour which he himself has managed to secure seem less accessible, a greater distinction."

And yet, as Proust's Monsieur de Norpois knew well, the Institute was the seat of power and influence. For scientists, it was also *the* source of funding, giving out about 150,000 francs a year in grants during this period. And so, when all the physicist members of the Institute vowed to support his candidacy, Pierre overcame his dislike of pomp and applied for membership.

On June 9, he reported the unhappy result to Georges Gouy. "My dear friend," he wrote. "As you had foreseen, the election turned in favor of Amagat [Émile Amagat, a physicist eighteen years Pierre's senior] who had thirty-two votes while I had 20 and Gernez [physicist Désiré Gernez] six. I regret, all things considered, having lost the time and made the visits for this brilliant result. The [physics] section presented me unanimously as first choice and I allowed them to do it. But Amagat made a great effort, he stressed his seniority, his age, and also he set himself up as a persecuted man. Ultimately, Becquerel, even though declaring for me, I am convinced played a double game. In any case I am sure that he was delighted that I didn't get in and I think also that he must have voted for Amagat. Amagat also had all the clerical votes and all those of senior academicians.

"I tell you all this gossip," Pierre hastened to add, "because I know that you rather enjoy all that, but don't think that I'm much affected by these minor events."

Georges Gouy encouraged Pierre to look on the experience as a first step. "After all, you don't have too much to complain about; now, you are the presumptive heir and the next vacancy is bound to arrive one day or another. You should not regret the time lost making your visits, because all that will make things easier the next time." It was true, as Proust's Monsieur de Norpois observed, that "the Academy likes to keep a postulant waiting for some time before taking him to its bosom."

But Pierre was not inclined to listen to friends who urged him to "play the game." The next year, when the mathematician and dean of the faculty of the Sorbonne Paul Appell plotted to have Pierre named to the Legion of Honor, he knew enough to enlist Marie in the effort. Appell's letter to her reflects the way in which success in France was tied at the time to hierarchy and ritual.

> Madame [Appell began], allow me to put you *au courant* of a question which preoccupies me and which is going to perhaps arise one of these days. I have spoken several times with the Rector . . . about the recent work of Monsieur Curie, and about the inadequacy of your installation, about the wisdom there would be in giving him a larger laboratory. The Rector spoke of Monsieur Curie to the Minister and he [the minister] took the opportunity to offer him the presentation for the fourteenth of July of the Legion of Honor.

> The Minister seemed to be very interested in Monsieur Curie. Perhaps you might, to begin with, reveal [to Pierre Curie] his interest in decorating Monsieur Curie. If you should do so, I ask you to use all your influence to make sure Monsieur Curie *does not refuse.* The thing itself is obviously of no interest—but from the point of view of practical consequences (laboratory, credits . . .), it has *considerable* interest. What's more, whether Monsieur Curie wears or doesn't wear his ribbon is up to him.

> I repeat: if my suppositions prove true, I ask you to insist with Monsieur Curie, as I already have, that he allow himself to do it, for Science, for the greater interest of the faculty."

Pierre Curie, however, was unmoved. Soon after this entreaty, he wrote Appell asking him to inform the minister that "I do not desire to be put on the list for decoration. It seems to me that if the Minister is truly convinced that that is my wish, he will not insist."

Twice denied a chair at the Sorbonne, denied membership in the

Académie des sciences, refusing the Legion of Honor, Pierre Curie struggled along on the periphery, attempting to fit in his research where he could. For a man who required stillness, it was a difficult existence. "I'm studying induced radioactivity," he reported to Georges Gouy in late 1902, "but I have a daily course which comes unfortunately to trouble my existence." To make matters worse, people were beginning to take notice of the Curies' work. On another occasion that year, he reported to his friend that "as you have seen fortune favors us at the moment; but these favors of fortune bring with them a lot of bother. Never have we been less tranquil than at this moment. There are some days where we don't have time to breathe. And to think that we had dreamed of living as savages far from other human beings!"

When both Marie and Pierre began around this time to have problems with their health, they saw overwork as the culprit. "The physical fatigue due to the numerous courses [Pierre] was obliged to give was so great," Marie later wrote, "that he suffered from attacks of acute pain." Marie, too, seemed weakened by overwork. In the five years following the discovery of radium in 1898, she lost ten pounds.

Friends counseled the Curies to take time off, and to take better care of themselves. Georges Sagnac, a younger colleague, wrote to Pierre that spring of 1903 that he had been "struck in seeing Madame Curie at the Physics Society with the change in her appearance" and proceeded to deliver a lecture:

> [Madame Curie] does not have enough physical resistance to lead the purely intellectual life that you two lead; and what I say about her goes for you too.
>
> . . . You hardly eat at all, either one of you. I've seen more than once, when I have had the pleasure of sitting at your table, Madame Curie nibbled on a piece of sausage and swallowed a cup of tea with it! Please, reflect a little. Do you think even a robust constitution wouldn't suffer from such *insufficient nourishment.*

Sagnac's prescription is simple: Stop eating at all hours; have lunch and dinner regularly and take time for them. Stick to this for a year with "a thousandth of the will and the tenacity that you show in the pursuit of scientific discoveries," and you will return to health. Above all, he adjures, you must not think of science "every instant of your life, as you are doing. You must allow the body to breathe. You must sit down in peace at your meals and swallow them slowly, keeping away from discussion of distressing or dispiriting events. *You must not read or talk physics while you are eating."*

Even if they didn't take Sagnac's advice, the Curies probably agreed with it. They worked too many hours, and took too little time over that *sine qua non* of French life, the leisurely repast. But in retrospect, it seems likely that their health complaints had more to do with exposure to massive doses of radioactivity during this period than with overwork.

It had been obvious early on that radioactive substances caused superficial burns. In 1901 Pierre Curie had published a paper with Henri Becquerel in which they described the burns caused on their skin by contact with various radioactive materials. Two Germans, named Walkoff and Giesel, had been the first to report on the phenomenon in print. Pierre Curie attempted to reproduce their experiment: he placed a thinly wrapped quantity of radioactive barium on his arm for ten hours and observed, when it was removed, that his skin had become red in the place where it had lain. After several days, the redness grew in intensity, and on the twentieth day a crust formed, then a wound which he covered with bandages. On the forty-second day the skin began to re-form around the edges of the wound, and on the fifty-second day there remained a small spot which had turned gray, "indicating a deeper injury."

Becquerel's experience was similar: he had incurred a skin burn from a very active sample of barium, in a glass tube wrapped in paper and enclosed in a cardboard box. The wound, which resulted from carrying around the radioactive barium for about six hours in his coat pocket, was the exact oblong shape of the glass tube.

In addition, the Curies reported that they had experienced various problems with their hands as a result of working with "very active products." "The ends of fingers which had held tubes or capsules containing very active products become hard and sometimes very painful; for one of us the inflammation of the ends of the fingers lasted 15 days and ended with the shedding of skin, but the pain has not disappeared completely after two months."

Both the Curies and Becquerel tended to make light of these injuries. Marie Curie reported that Becquerel was both "delighted and annoyed" by the discovery that the tube of radium had burned his skin. "I love it," he told the Curies, "but I owe it a grudge!"

Despite the fact that one of their colleagues had found that laboratory animals died after exposure, it did not seem to occur to anyone that radiation might be causing systemic as well as superficial damage to their bodies. In retrospect, it seems clear that many of the complaints which plagued both Marie and Pierre in coming years were the result not of overwork but of overexposure.

Indeed, throughout this period of extreme hard work, they took time both in spring and in summer to escape Paris with Irène. In the spring of 1900, for instance, they traveled by boat along the rocky coast of Normandy, beginning at le Havre and heading eastward to St. Valéry sur Somme, a bathing resort at sea level with a lovely promenade leading up to medieval ruins and fortifications along the cliffs above. And that summer, they stayed on l'Île de Noirmoutiers, off the south coast of Brittany.

From her entries about Irène, it is clear that Marie considered these summer vacations essential to her daughter's health and well-being, if not her own. In fact, Irène was sometimes sent away first, to spend time in Jouy en Josas, south of Versailles on the Bièvre. It is unclear whether her grandfather Curie went with her, or whether she was with a nanny only. In the summer of 1901, Marie noted in her little book that Irène, now nearly four, spent a month and a half in Jouy en Josas and then almost two months with Marie and Pierre in Brittany. The little girl's skin rashes responded to "sea baths" and she finished the summer "in very good health."

Le Pouldu, where the Curies went that summer, was on the calmer, more protected southern coast of Brittany. It was a small, quiet resort, with only a few hotels and rooming houses. In summer, the Breton light, and the plain white plaster and gray stone of the low-lying houses, deepened and intensified the purple of the hydrangeas, the orange-red of the geraniums, and the deep pink of the abundant climbing roses. Undoubtedly, when they felt energetic, the Curies walked along the well-worn paths high above the beach, at the edge of the cliffs that skirt the coast.

The Curies returned to the sea the following year, 1902, this time settling in for two months on the rougher, more dramatic Normandy coast in a little village called Arromanches-les-Bains. There, Marie reported in her book that Irène was once again in "very good health." Marie wrote nothing about her own health, but it seems likely that she was extremely tired. In July, she had completed the exhausting task of isolating a decigram of radium. And whatever satisfaction that might have brought had been dampened by a great loss. In May, her father had died before she could get back to Warsaw to say a last goodbye.

Fortunately, there had been several trips back to Warsaw before Władysław Skłodowski became ill. In 1899, Marie and Pierre had journeyed to Zakopane in the Carpathian Mountains for a joyous reunion with Bronia and Kazimierz, as well as Helena, Józef, and their father. It was a hopeful time: the Dłuskis' new sanitorium was under construction. When complete, it was to be one of the most modern treatment centers in Europe as well as an exquisite exemplar of a particularly Polish style of regional folk decoration called *styl Zako-piański*. Władysław Skłodowski, who had lost his wife to tuberculosis, must have felt proud that his daughter Bronia would now help to cure other victims, in this beautiful place perched on a mountainside in the Carpathian Mountains. Undoubtedly, he was pleased too that the board of the sanitorium included his old friend, the patriotic priest and godfather to Bronia, Władysław Knapiński, as well as important Polish leaders.

In Zakopane, everyone in the family was charmed by Pierre, who had taken the trouble to learn some Polish. "Maria was so happy to show Pierre the beauty of her native country," Helena remembered. "She was happy to see that he liked it, that he felt at home with her family." They all took long walks together, climbing Rysy, the highest mountain in the Tatra chain. Helena remembered Pierre's exclaiming, "What a beautiful country. No wonder you love it so much!" Pierre's kindness made a deep impression on Helena. Once, she saw him coming up the road carrying a heavy pack. "It turned out that he was helping some old woman who was carrying her sheets to the mangle. He brought them there, explaining, 'I couldn't have let her carry such a heavy load.' "

Not too long after that visit, Marie's father suffered a complicated fracture when he was struck by a truck as he got off a tram in Warsaw. He recovered enough, however, to continue corresponding with Marie. In 1902, after she reported to him that she had isolated radium, he wrote a response which revealed the family bias toward the pragmatic:

> And now you are in possession of salts of pure radium! If you consider the amount of work that has been spent to obtain it, it is certainly the most costly of chemical elements! What a pity it is that this work has only theoretical interest, as it seems.

The letter was written on May 8, 1902. Within days afterward, Władysław Skłodowski had a gallbladder attack, followed by surgery to remove large gallstones. On May 14, at age seventy, he died. Marie took a train from Paris to Warsaw as soon as she heard of his illness, but she learned en route that she was too late. She sent word ahead asking that they delay the funeral until she got there. When she arrived, the coffin was opened so that she could look on his face one last time. "My father," she later wrote, "who in his own youth had wished to do scientific work, was consoled in our separation by the progressive success of my work. I keep a tender memory of his kindness and disinterestedness."

There was at least one happy event wedged in among the sadness and difficulties of these years. After she isolated a decigram of radium,

Marie finally felt free to write the dissertation which she had set out to prepare five years earlier. On May 11, 1903, her manuscript was approved by dean of the faculty Paul Appell. And in June of 1903, in the students' hall of the Sorbonne, she defended it. The mood was celebratory. Bronia had come from Poland, and had managed to get Marie to a dressmaker's to order a new dress. The proud family party, including Dr. Eugène Curie, Pierre, and Bronia, was augmented by a group of young women from Sèvres, who admired their teacher "profoundly."

By this time, the examiners hearing Marie Curie's presentation, Gabriel Lippmann, Edmond Bouty, and Henri Moissan, had become colleagues: Moissan had supplied the uranium with which Marie Curie made her initial measurements, and Lippmann had sought funds for her work. As Marie Curie pointed out in her dissertation, "our researches upon the new radioactive bodies have given rise to a scientific movement." As a result, the thesis was treated as an important document of the new science of radioactivity, published in England in Crookes's *Chemical News* over the summer and in France in the *Annales de physique et de chimie* in September of 1903.

Marie Curie was not yet willing to accept Rutherford's theory of transmutation. "We think, M. Curie and I," she wrote, "that the supposition that radium emits a gas is not yet justified." Yet her dissertation was a lucid, beautifully organized presentation of the research in radioactivity to date. Needless to say, Marie Curie was awarded the title of doctor of physical science *(docteur ès sciences physiques)*, with the mention *très honorable*. Georges Gouy sent his "congratulations on the defense [of the dissertation], which was one of the most brilliant and celebrated, if I am to believe the papers. I join my applause to that of the public."

The triumphant day ended with a surprise encounter. Ernest Rutherford, in Paris with his New Zealand bride, dropped by the Curies' lab that day on rue Cuvier, only to discover that everyone was at the students' hall listening to Marie defend her dissertation. Fortunately, he also called on Paul Langevin, who had been a fellow research student at the Cavendish Laboratory eight years before. Langevin, who lived with his wife and child in a pleasant villa facing the Parc Montsouris, invited the Rutherfords, along with the Curies and the Perrins, to dine with him. After dinner, Rutherford remembered, they all went out into the garden, where Pierre Curie "brought out a tube coated in part with zinc sulphide and containing a large quantity of radium in solution. The luminosity was brilliant in the darkness and it was a splendid finale to an unforgettable day."

By the time Marie presented her dissertation, she and Pierre were anticipating another much-desired event: the birth of a second child.

But this was not to be. In August of 1903, in her fifth month of pregnancy, she had a miscarriage which devastated her. "I am in such consternation over this accident," Marie wrote to Bronia on August 25, "that I have not the courage to write to anybody. I had grown so accustomed to the idea of the child that I am absolutely desperate and cannot be consoled."

Now Marie wondered if her friends had been right about her not taking good enough care of herself. "Write to me, I beg of you, if you think I should blame this on general fatigue—for I must admit that I have not spared my strength. I had confidence in my constitution, and at present I regret this bitterly, as I have paid dear for it. The child—a little girl—was in good condition and was living. And I had wanted it so badly!"

Whatever caused the loss, Marie's disappointment was compounded not long after by tragic news from Poland. Bronia's second child, a five-year-old son, died suddenly of a meningitis. "I am quite overwhelmed," Marie confided to Józef when she heard the news, "by the misfortune that has fallen upon the Dłuskis. That child was the picture of health. If, in spite of every care, one can lose a child like that, how can one hope to keep the others and bring them up? I can no longer look at my little girl without trembling with terror. And Bronia's grief tears me to pieces."

Marie remained ill through that summer and a good part of the fall. She was well enough, though, to travel with Pierre to St. Trojan les Bains, a village on the southern end of the lush Île d'Oléron, to convalesce. Marie had asked Eugénie Feytis, a student of hers at Sèvres, to recommend a spot in her native Saintonge where they might vacation. Eugénie, who had been invited to come along, learned of Madame Curie's illness and feared that she would no longer be welcome. "But Pierre Curie asked me very simply to stay," she later remembered, "saying that my presence would be a distraction for the convalescent. Madame Curie insisted too that I could replace her around little Irène who was then six." And so the young student "lived for some days with the great *savants.*"

In the morning, she read to Marie Curie, while Pierre worked and "Irène and her good grandfather, Dr. Curie, went fishing and collected shellfish. But in the afternoon, Madame Curie had decided to get her husband outside for some hours, and to oblige him to exercise she had asked him to teach me to ride a bicycle."

The lessons were occasions for "beautiful rides on the road that led across the forest from the west coast of the island, where the village is, to the wild wind-battered coast that faces America." They were also the occasions for long discussions of the science of crystals and magnetism, which the young student (who later became the director of the École normale at Sèvres and married the physicist Aimé Cotton) never forgot, even though she was struggling all the while to keep her balance on a "man's bicycle," which "greatly complicated my apprenticeship."

Despite Marie's illness, there were jolly times that summer. Eugénie Feytis remembered visits from André Debierne which sparked lively scientific discussions. Georges Urbain, another colleague who was vacationing on the island, used to "enter with a leap through the open window of the dining room" to participate. The young Sèvrienne was shocked by such informality. "Raised in a little village, I was astonished to see men so simple in their manners, having so much independence of spirit and of character and so little concern for traditional ways of thinking and for social hierarchy."

Despite her claim in late September that she was "almost cured," Marie Curie's illness lingered on. She spent some time recuperating on her own that fall at Villers-Cotterets, a town in the forest not far from Paris. In November, she had a "sort of grippe" and cough. A trip to the doctor revealed that her lungs were clear (always there was the nagging concern about tuberculosis). "On the other hand," she confided to Józef, "he accuses me of being anemic." Anemia, of course, is common in women, but it might also be a sign of changes in blood chemistry brought on by exposure to radioactivity.

It would be months before Marie Curie would gain enough strength to go back to work. But that fall, the Curies' fortunes began to change dramatically in other ways. On November 5, they learned that the Royal Society of London had awarded them the Humphrey Davy medal, given out annually for the most important discovery in chemistry. Pierre and Marie had already visited England earlier in the year, when Pierre gave a lecture at the Royal Society which received "a most enthusiastic reception." This time, since Marie was still not entirely well, Pierre returned to London alone. Afterward, Marie wrote a spirited letter of thanks to Pierre's hostess in England, Lady Margaret Huggins. Sir William and Lady Huggins, like the Curies, were partners in science, and Marie wrote that her husband "was very moved to see you two, Mr Huggins and you, in the place where you have spent your work life. It is truly a beautiful existence which serves as a worthy example, and it is wonderful to devote one's entire life to the accomplishment of a beautiful piece of work." Marie enclosed a picture of Irène and added that the little girl had been almost as happy with the gold Davy medal as her mother.

The letter is unusual for Marie Curie, who always wrote politely but seldom with such ebullience. Perhaps she was responding to

Pierre's enthusiasm about the Hugginses. But perhaps her bouyant mood was also inspired by a wonderful secret she was keeping: in mid-November, a letter had come from the Swedish Academy, informing Marie and Pierre Curie in "strict confidence" that they, along with Henri Becquerel, had won the Nobel Prize.

Chapter Nine

THE PRIZE

THE FIRST PERSON to suggest Pierre and Marie Curie for a Nobel Prize was not a physicist or chemist but a pathologist who was an influential member of the *Académie de médecine,* Charles Bouchard. As it turned out, Bouchard's endorsement, in 1901, the first year the prize was given, and again in 1902, was critical: without it, the Swedish Academy would have lacked the official nomination they needed to award the prize to Marie Curie, along with Pierre and Henri Becquerel.

In 1902, the first year there was any substantial support for the Curies, Marie Curie was very much in the picture. Among the two dozen European physicists asked that year to name candidates for the Nobel Prize, two—Jean-Gaston Darboux, dean of the Faculty of Sciences at the Sorbonne, and Emil Warburg, an influential German physicist—proposed that the prize be awarded to Pierre and Marie Curie, along with Becquerel. The only person who nominated Pierre Curie alone in 1902 was the physicist Éleuthère Mascart.

Mascart notwithstanding, had the award been given for the discovery of radioactivity in 1902, there would have been little justification for leaving Marie Curie out. But in 1903, in what appears to have been a concerted effort to deprive her of the prize, four members of the Académie des sciences wrote a nominating letter which completely ignored Marie Curie's contribution. One of the four who signed the letter, Gabriel Lippmann, had been an early mentor of hers. Another, Gaston Darboux, would later be an outspoken advocate of her candidacy to the French Academy. So it is difficult to understand why in their letter these two, along with Mascart and Henri Poincaré, presented a completely false picture of the events surrounding the discovery of radioactivity, a picture which obliterated Marie Curie.

In fact, the letter was a fiction almost from start to finish. Pierre alone was said to have studied the "different minerals of uranium and thorium" and to have isolated two new bodies, polonium and radium. Pierre and Henri Becquerel together were said to be in competition with foreign "rivals" for the radium supply and to have "procured with great difficulty some decigrams of this precious material," carrying on their study "sometimes together, sometimes separately." The letter concluded that "it appears impossible for us to separate the names of the two physicists, and therefore we do not hesitate to propose to you that the Nobel Prize be shared between Mr. Becquerel and Mr. Curie."

The decision not to nominate Marie Curie must have been a deliberate one. Three of these four nominators knew the work of the Curies well. Lippmann had presented the first paper on the discovery of radioactivity, written by Marie Curie alone, to the Académie des sciences. He had been one of the three professors who heard Marie Curie defend her dissertation. He knew that Marie alone had happened upon the surprising radioactivity in pitchblende. They all knew that the isolation of a decigram of radium was the accomplishment of Marie Curie alone. The final line, asserting that "it is impossible for us to separate the two physicists," suggests a guilty secret about the inseparable work of Pierre and Marie Curie.

Fortunately for Marie Curie, one of the most influential members of the Swedish Academy of Sciences, a mathematician named Gustav Mittag-Leffler, came to her defense. No Swedish scientist, except for the physical chemist Svante Arrhenius, had more influence over Nobel Prize decisions than Mittag-Leffler. Both Arrhenius and Mittag-Leffler, according to Nobel historian Elizabeth Crawford, were "more adventurous, and also closer to science in the making, than the majority of the members on the committees." At the same time, Mittag-Leffler was an improbable ally for Marie Curie. An elitist and a monarchist with extravagant tastes, he wielded power from his country estate through his use of influential connections at home and abroad. Yet Mittag-Leffler was very sympathetic to women scientists. It was he who invited the Russian mathematician Sonya Kovalesky to spend the last years of her life at Stockholm's Högskola. And it was he who, on two important occasions, spoke up for Marie Curie.

When Mittag-Leffler learned during the summer of 1903 that only Pierre had been nominated, he wrote to inform him. On August 6, Pierre wrote back:

If it is true that one is seriously thinking about me [for the prize], I very much wish to be considered together with Madame Curie with respect to our research on radioactive bodies.

After pointing out the important role she had played in the discovery of polonium and radium, he added "Don't you think it would be more satisfying, from an artistic point of view, if we were to be associated in this manner?"

If they wanted to nominate Marie Curie, however, the Nobel Physics Committee had to overcome one difficulty: no one had nominated her for the prize in 1903! This was the moment at which the earlier nominations from Dr. Charles Bouchard became important. Because Bouchard was a foreign member of the Swedish Academy of Sciences, he was judged to have permanent nominating rights. Thus, with a little stretching of the statutes, his 1902 letter was resurrected and used to nominate Marie Curie.

On August 29, 1903, three and a half weeks after Pierre wrote his letter, the report of the Nobel committee on the work of Becquerel and the Curies was delivered to the physics section of the Swedish Academy. It showed a much better understanding than the French academicians' letter of the work of all three scientists, and it gave full credit to Marie Curie. "A completely new field of greatest importance and interest has opened up for physics research," Swedish physicist Knut Angström told his colleagues. "The credit for these discoveries belongs without doubt in the first place to Henri Becquerel and Mr. and Mrs. Curie. . . . The discovery by Becquerel of the spontaneous radioactivity of uranium . . . inspired diligent research to find more elements with similar remarkable qualities. The most magnificent, methodical and persistent investigations in this regard were made by Mr. and Mrs. Curie." Angström was up-to-date on the latest research of Rutherford and Soddy, including the possibility of transmutation. But he insisted that the fact that the Curies "have sometimes been overtaken by other scientists can by no means diminish the honor due them for the first discovery of the phenomenon."

In the end, the Swedish Academy of Sciences accepted the physics committee's recommendation and named Becquerel and both Curies for the physics prize. But there was still one question to be resolved: what was the prize to be given for? Chemists in the Academy pointed out that the discovery of radioactivity was as much a chemist's as a physicist's accomplishment. In order not to preempt a future prize in chemistry, they persuaded the members to give the award not for the discovery of the radioactive elements but for "their joint researches on the radiation phenomena."

With this decision Marie Curie became the first woman to receive a Nobel Prize. For many years—indeed, until her daughter won the prize in 1935—she would be the only woman Nobel laureate in the sciences. The medal she received was a reminder of just how unusual it was for a woman to be recognized for tangible work rather than for powers of inspiration. Embossed above Marie Curie's name on the round gold medal was the kneeling female figure of Scientia, lifting the veil from the face of the half-nude female figure of Natura.

Pierre and Marie Curie first learned they had won the Nobel Prize in mid-November of 1903, in a letter from Charles Aurivillius, secretary of the Swedish Academy of Sciences. He invited them to come to Stockholm in December, to receive the prize and also to give the "public lecture" about their work which was required of recipients.

Pierre's response was swift and predictable. He thanked the Swedish Academy, but explained that, what with their teaching obligations and his wife's health, he and Madame Curie couldn't possibly come to Sweden for the ceremonies.

> We can't be gone from our classes at this time of year without incurring great difficulties in the teaching which is entrusted to us. Even if we should go to the meeting we could only stay a very short time and we would barely be able to make the acquaintance of the Swedish scientists. Further, Madame Curie has been sick this summer and is still not entirely recovered.

Pierre suggested they could come and give a talk at Easter, or better yet in June.

Marie's ill health *was* a consideration. "We did not go to the ceremonial meeting," Marie wrote Józef, "because it was too complicated to arrange. I did not feel strong enough to undertake such a long journey (forty-eight hours without stopping, and more if one stops along the way) in such an inclement season, in a cold country, and without being able to stay there more than three or four days: we could not, without great difficulty, interrupt our courses for a long period." Yet Georges Gouy also rightly suspected that Pierre "didn't much want to waste time on such a trip."

But what seemed a perfectly good excuse to the Curies must have seemed an affront to the Swedish Academy. After all, even though Madame Curie was sick, it was still possible for Pierre to go to Stockholm; he could have accompanied Henri Becquerel. And the idea that their teaching couldn't be interrupted to go and accept a Nobel Prize suggests an incomprehension of the enormity of the event. It is true that Aurivillius's letter to the Curies was understated: he didn't mention that the king of Sweden would present them with gold medals, nor that their half of the Nobel Prize would amount to some one hundred fifty thousand crowns, the equivalent of what the Académie des sciences gave out to all prize recipients in a year. Yet it is also true that receiving the Nobel Prize in science was not quite as momentous in 1903 as it has since become.

Ironically, no one is more responsible for increased public awareness of the science prize than the publicity-shy Curies. "There is no doubt," historian Elisabeth Crawford has written, "that the 1903 physics prize awarded to Becquerel and the two Curies represented a watershed." That year, the amount of news coverage of the prize increased dramatically. The first year the Nobel Prize was given, in 1901, it went to Roentgen. Although that had sparked some interest, X rays were already a bit passé by then. The work of Lorentz and Zeeman, who won the prize in 1902, was difficult to explain to general readers, with the result that the press paid much more attention to the prizes for peace and in literature. But all that changed in 1903.

If the Nobel committee had sought to make the science prize famous, they could have done no better than to award it to the Curies, and particularly to Marie Curie. The prize not only established her legendary popular status in twentieth-century science but also made the Nobel Prize in science newly fascinating, especially in France.

Mass-circulation dailies had become a phenomenon of French life in the two decades preceding the Curies' Nobel, and had discovered the public's appetite for the sensational. Such events of the 1890s as the anarchist bombings and the Panama Canal scandal had been found to boost circulation. But the event which had most excited the public imagination and established the new power of the press to shape public opinion was the Dreyfus affair. "For the first time," writes Jean-Denis Bredin, "the press exercised a major influence on the political life of the nation, dramatizing and fueling the event, supporting or denouncing the authorities, exercising pressure and various forms of blackmail."

In 1894, the right-wing press had played a decisive role in convicting the Jewish captain Dreyfus, falsely accused of spying, by exploiting anti-Semitism and chauvinism left over from the Franco-Prussian war. And later, by exposing the miserable conditions of his imprisonment, the Dreyfusard press was instrumental in bringing about a retrial. It was through the press that Émile Zola issued "J'accuse," his *cri de coeur* on Dreyfus's behalf, which helped eventually to bring about Dreyfus's pardon.

The Dreyfus affair was still a major story in December of 1903, when the news broke that the Curies and Becquerel had won the

Nobel Prize. "This tale of the Curie couple," noted *la Vie parisienne,* "one barely knows it in France. But we have an excuse: they have reopened the Dreyfus Affair . . . one can't do two things at once."

When the French press did turn its gaze on the "Curie couple," it used the same hyperbole that had characterized its coverage of the Dreyfus affair. And if the story lacked the conflict and drama of the affair, French journalists found ways to introduce it.

What fascinated the press, and the public, were the Curies and their amazing radium. Henri Becquerel, mustachioed bearer of an old family name who posed with pride in the green brocaded costume of the Institute, was too familiar a figure to make good copy. Even Becquerel's journey to Stockholm and his address to the Swedish Academy were given only passing notice.

Instead, much was made of the fact that the Curies, unlike Becquerel, were virtually unknown. Some had thought at first that they were English or American. Thanks to the Swedish Academy, the press chorused, France discovered its own geniuses. "It is from the North, without a doubt," noted *le Figaro,* "that light comes to us."

The fact that the Curies had toiled in a "miserable wooden hangar" without public funds became the basis for exaggerated cries of outrage. "Eh bien!" exclaimed Alphonse Berget in *la Grande Revue.* "During seven years, no one in our country thought to reward these admirable scientists who have made this new conquest. . . . It took the generosity of a foreigner." For the French, he concluded, the Nobel prize to the Curies was both "a glory and a disgrace."

Endless scoldings in this vein appeared in the French press. *Le Rapide de Paris,* calling for public support for the Curies, complained that "even today, the public powers, ministers, senators, deputies, don't know about radium. It illuminates, it heats, it burns everything it touches and everything it comes near. Only the public official is unaffected by its rays."

But the same writers who deplored France's reluctance to recognize its own prophets were quick to claim that the Curies' discoveries were entirely French. The "supremacy of France," wrote Lucien Corpechot in *l'Éclair,* "is not due to the organization or the assistance that scientific work receives in our country. It relates uniquely . . . to the special form of intelligence, to the ability to doubt methodically and disinterestedly which characterizes the French mind." Marie Curie's Polish origins were mentioned only in passing, often to insist that she was now as good as French. "Madame Curie," noted *les Dimanches,* "was born Polish and . . . is French by adoption. She . . . has acquired a doctorate in physics here and has worked as a professor at the Normal School at Sèvres. So let's not quibble about nationality."

Cooler heads, in other countries, came closer to an accurate critique of the situation. "The truth is," the *Chicago Evening Post* noted, with some exaggeration, "that the Institute now stands in the way of scientific research. It is a caste and extremely conservative and at bottom its bent is rather artistic than scientific. It wants neat and elegant statement and demonstration. It likes well-dressed *savants,* who can invite their acquaintances to well-appointed dinner tables. Had M. Curie married the only daughter of wealthy parents, and been able to take her to the Opera Francais on subscription nights, the Academy of Sciences would not have turned a deaf ear."

Marie Skłodowska Curie was a far cry from the conventional wife of a *savant.* And it was this, more than anything else, which intrigued the press and public. The idea that a man and a woman could have a loving *and* working relationship was exciting to some, threatening to others. "The case of Monsieur and Madame Curie, working together in the field of science is certainly not the usual," observed *les Dimanches.* "An idyll in a physics laboratory, that's something that's never before been seen."

Some writers ignored Marie Curie entirely, ascribing all the research findings to either Becquerel or Pierre Curie. Those who did mention her most often cast her in a supporting role. "Mrs. Curie," the *New York Herald* reported, "is a devoted fellow laborer in her husband's researches and has associated her name with his discoveries." "M. Pierre Curie," noted *The Vanity Fair* of London, "was ably seconded by his wife." Even sympathetic portraits had Pierre doing, Marie inspiring. Mademoiselle Skłodowska, according to an English publication, "assisted him" at the EPCI, and "he soon discovered that he could not do without her. . . . She fanned the sacred fire in him whenever she saw it dying out."

Feminists tended to overstate the case in the other direction. "Radium," insisted *le Radical,* "was discovered by Madame Curie. . . . In defiance of the dogma that woman is inferior, public homage was rendered to Madame Curie in awarding her with a striking sum. Then, since it is the rule in matrimony that the husband has the pleasure, the benefit and the full ownership of all that belongs to his wife, Monsieur Curie was associated with Madame Curie in sharing the 100,000 crowns of the Nobel Prize with Monsieur Becquerel."

Only a few observers, like a writer in the *Nouvelles illustrées,* seemed capable of understanding the mutuality of the Curies' relationship. "It would be a mistake," the *Nouvelles illustrées* claimed, "to believe that it is because of a feeling of conjugal gallantry that Monsieur Curie wanted to associate his wife with the honor of his discovery. In this household of married scientists . . . the woman is not an auxiliary but, with all the strength of the word, a collaborator and often indeed the inspirer of her husband."

Journalists sought out Marie Curie at home to reassure themselves that she retained feminine virtues. Marcel Villain, who paid a visit for the publication *Familia,* reported that even though her sitting room bore no resemblance to "our opulent bourgeois salons" and was on the whole "rather cold," Madame Curie herself was proof that "one can be a part of the elite while retaining the exquisite feelings of a woman and a mother."

Other journalists worried over the "delicious sentiments of love and maternity," the "minute attentions" to the *ménage* and to the children which a career woman might neglect. A writer using the pen name Verax worried in *Paris Sport* about the "example of Marie Curie." Was "the woman . . . to abandon her traditional household occupations from now on to give herself over to the concrete or abstract studies which, until now, have been the privilege of the man?" He was willing to concede that women were capable of working "manually or intellectually in order to support their material or moral needs." But such abilities were of value for "the minority, the tiny minority" of unmarried women, those "bizarre heroines who abdicate feminine character altogether."

The roles of wife and working woman, however, were "absolutely incompatible." "The woman who works," Verax maintained, "is usually obliged to abandon, to neglect her household, her children . . . because unrewarding work, earning a living, takes up all her time." What's more, women "in their ardent desire to liberate themselves through work have caused a considerable lowering of salaries. They have taken, in many industries, the place of men . . . their husbands often walk the pavement, searching for some kind of work . . . it is the women who have made their work disappear, by accepting lower wages for the same labor." For this reason, Verax concludes, "feminism will fail. Man and woman will perceive, a little late . . . that they are competing against each other and harming each other." One must consider women like Marie Curie as "exceptions to the general rule."

But a writer using the pen name Diogène took the opposite view, seeing the Curies' collaboration as a precedent which could liberate men and women. "It seems that it was Madame Curie, of Polish origin, who took the initiative in the first research, but for the outside world there is only this unity, Monsieur and Madame Curie. No feminism, no masculinism. . . . How far we are here from the concept of the woman necessarily alone because she is a scientist, of the man of depth hampered in his valuable work by a companion who is an idle social butterfly!" In the past "superior women" like George

Sand and Rosa Bonheur had dressed as men to avoid importunities, and "isolated men" had turned feminine in the precious atmosphere of the salon. Now "the *ménage* equalizes aspirations, maintaining each in his/her place and preventing a tug of war. There is neither Monsieur nor Madame Curie . . . but Monsieur and Madame Curie, whom the Swedish Academy and humanity is pleased to crown with the same, single prize."

Another way of dealing with the unfamiliar collaboration of the Curie couple was to turn their story into a delicious, and familiar, romance. "I hesitate to speak of 'falling in love,' to use the language employed in all the romance novels," wrote "Christiane" in *le Matin*. The Curies' "first encounters, in the midst of the vapors of the laboratory, surrounded by alembics, retorts, the instruments of physics, are a far cry from the flirtations . . . which go on in our *salons.*"

"I see in my imagination," wrote Flammarion, "She and He, in the age of dreams, both impoverished but rich in hope and seeking I know not what magic talisman to cure the world of its miseries. . . . With ardour they mix, in the same crucible, the gold of their hearts, of their science, of their experience; then they throw in, without counting, the money which, with great difficulty, they have earned as professors. . . . They labor in silence, marching, without ever looking back, to conquer the sparkling chimera. . . . And one day, at the bottom of their crucible—joy intense and unforgettable—they find the treasure they were searching for. With some scraps wisely combined, they mould, with anxious hands, a little ball, so small that it seems to be a grain of sand, so powerful in its effects that one believes it to be a force of nature."

The romance of the Curies with each other was only slightly more stimulating to the purple-prose writers than the romance between the Curies and radium. It was the "métal conjugal," and the "bimétal," because they discovered it together. Unlike radioactivity, a complex and incompletely understood phenomenon, radium could be seen and celebrated and appropriated by anyone and everyone. Within weeks of the announcement of the Nobel Prize, radium was enjoying a "singular and extra-scientific vogue." And by 1905, "scarcely a person in the civilized world was unfamiliar with the word 'radium' or the name of its discoverer ('Our lady of radium')." In Paris, a Montmartre revue was entitled *Medusa's Radium,* while a revue at Fischer's in San Francisco featured "fancy unison movements by eight pretty, but invisible, girls, tripping noiselessly about in an absolutely darkened theater, and yet glowingly illuminated in spots by reason of the chemical mixture upon their costumes." In New York, a musical comedy boasting radium dances called itself *Piff!Paff!!Pouf!!!*

In London, according to a visiting reporter from New York, the Nobel announcement inspired society to become "quite scientific."

Mr William Gillette has been giving afternoon parties at the Bachelor's Club at which the great attraction was the exhibition of a minute particle of the fascinating element discovered by M. and Mme. Curie. . . . Rumors are abroad that several fashionable hostesses will provide lectures on radium with their afternoon teas. Already it is the smart thing to carry in one's pocket a spintharoscope. This is a small brass tube [recently invented by William Crookes] . . . from one-half to two inches long. At one end is a magnifying glass; at the other, held by a tiny lever in front of a screen of sulphide of zinc, is an infinitessimal particle of radium bromide. It was claimed that with this instrument one could create a sensation in a drawing room and everybody was talking of buying these articles as Christmas presents. The supply ran short however, perhaps fortunately, because there have been several cases where the spinthariscope has been the cause of certain troubles to which inexpert handling of radium frequently gives rise.

The dangers of radium were merely titillating. An American popularizer, William J. Hammer, told packed audiences around the country that Pierre Curie had personally told him that he "would not care to trust himself in a room with a kilogram of pure radium, as it would doubtless destroy his eyesight and burn all the skin off his body, and probably kill him." But at the same time, curiously, radium was touted everywhere as the answer to every ill. Hammer himself advised that "if I were the Kaiser's physician I would gargle his throat with radium."

The usual tendency of the popular press to exaggerate the practical benefits of a scientific discovery was carried to wild extremes in the case of radium. Clever Americans were said to be perfecting new ways to extract radium and get rich. Charles H. Gage in San Francisco, a man who "has a laboratory and calls himself professor," claimed that he could "run a big automobile filled with passengers a distance of three hundred miles" on batteries charged with his "new radium preparation." And a French newspaper reported that Edison, "the great American inventor, is buying up, at no matter what price, all the pitchblende he can find."

Reports abounded on the ability of radium to cure cancer and other diseases. A woman at Charing Cross Hospital with a "rodent ulcer" was expected to enjoy "complete recovery." Radium was thought to be beneficial in the treatment of lupus. And cancer treatment was so promising that le Petit Journal asked in a rhetorical headline: "Is the Monster Conquered?" Even George Bernard Shaw took note of the excitement. "Just at present," he wrote in his introduction to *The Doctor's Dilemma,* "the world has run raving mad on the subject of radium, which has excited our credulity precisely as the apparitions at Lourdes excited the credulity of Roman Catholics."

Pierre Curie, the most modest of men, was himself turned into a mountebank in the excitement. The "Comtesse d'Alemcourt," reporting in the *New Orleans Picayune* on a visit with the Curies, had Pierre claiming that "after the physicians have finished their investigations of radium, and when they are through with the necessary experiments, sufferers from cancer, lupus and paralysis will be healed by radium rays, no doubt. As to cancer, I am particularly positive. Radium rays, employed in good season, will destroy the evil growth once and for all. . . . I am positive in what I assert. I never yet asserted anything that I could not prove, and never will."

YEARS LATER, looking back on all the attention which followed the awarding of the Nobel Prize, Marie Curie described it as "serious trouble." She added, not wishing to seem ungrateful: "Of course, people who contribute to that kind of trouble generally mean it kindly." However, the French press's treatment of the Curies and their work does not seem so much "kindly" as high-handed and exploitative. With a few exceptions, writers were too busy spinning theories and romances to pay much attention to the work. And the Curies, who had seen the power of the press in the Dreyfus affair, must have sensed how empty the admiration was, and how little it would take for them to be turned from darlings into scapegoats. Indeed, eight years later Marie Curie would learn firsthand about the cruel underside of such adulation.

But worse by far than the distortions and exaggerations were the intrusions. Writing home to Józef the day after the Nobel ceremony, Marie reported that they were "inundated with letters and with visits from photographers and journalists."

> One would like to dig into the ground somewhere to find a little peace. We have received a proposal from America to go there and make a series of lectures on our work. They ask us what sum we wish to receive. Whatever the terms may be, we intend to refuse. With much effort we have avoided the banquets people wanted to organize in our honor. We refuse with the energy of despair, and people understand that there is nothing to be done.

Pierre was even more aggrieved than Marie about the situation. Writing to Georges Gouy, he railed against "the stupid life we are living just now. . . . this infatuation with radium . . . has earned us all the advantages of a moment of popularity.

> We have been pursued by journalists and photographers from all the countries of the world, they have gone so far as to reproduce the conversation of my daughter with her maid and to describe the black and white cat who lives with us. Then we have received letters and visits from all the eccentrics, from all the unknown inventors, and from all the unknowns in general —then we have had requests for money in great numbers, and finally collectors of autographs, snobs, worldly people and even sometimes people of science have come to see us in the magnificent setting of rue Lhomond with which you are familiar. With all that, not an instant of tranquillity in the laboratory and a voluminous correspondence to take care of every evening. With this routine, I feel mindlessness invading me."

Two months later, when Marie sent birthday greetings to her brother in Poland, it was still going on.

> I send you my most affectionate greetings for your birthday. I wish you good health and success for all your family—and also that you may never be submerged by such a correspondence as inundates us at this moment. . . . I regret a little that I threw away the letters we received. . . . There were sonnets and poems on radium, letters from various inventors, letters from spirits, philosophical letters. Yesterday an American wrote to ask if I would allow him to baptize a race horse with my name. . . . I hardly reply to these letters, but I lose time by reading them.

Journalists insisted on calling on the "happy laureates," only to discover that the Curies wanted to be left alone to do their work. When a reporter from *la Liberté* came to call, Pierre politely offered him a seat but remained standing. "I sense that my visit annoys him. . . . 'Well,' he says to me after a pause, 'you want to write an article about us? But we're not worth an article. We have only existed since yesterday.' "

Reporters wouldn't take no for an answer. "Fontaine" of *le Gaulois* was told by Marie Curie that an interview was impossible because she was working in the lab all day every day. Fontaine therefore "took advantage of the Sunday day of rest" to pay a visit to Marie at her home on boulevard Kellerman. Marie's reception was understandably icy: "What can I say that nobody knows?" she asked her persecutor.

Some who came expecting a warm reception grew testy when they didn't receive it. "I had to ring the bell three times," noted

Gaston Rouvier of *le Temps.* Even then, the door was answered by a maid who informed him that Pierre was at the lab and Marie was teaching her course at Sèvres. Rouvier was obliged to wait in a "sort of parlor in which the principal ornament was a lamp on the fireplace. Two pieces of furniture were remarkable, two couches, deep like those in Baudelaire's poem, but older." There was no fire in the fireplace, so the door had been left ajar to allow heat to enter from the stove in the next room. There the child Irène was being told to sit down to supper by the maid. "And Mlle. Irène," wrote Rouvier, nastily, "ate all alone, so that her mother could win the Nobel Prize."

Things went from bad to worse when Pierre arrived. "Monsieur Curie," Rouvier complained, "does not have experience with interviews. He . . . answers only the questions one asks, and in two words. I know people who have not invented radium and who know better the art of talking about themselves."

By the end of their interviews, most reporters got the message that they were not welcome. " 'I can give you fifteen minutes,' " Pierre Curie told a reporter, pulling out his watch. "He leaned his elbows on the lab table, resigned to the suffering. . . . He said yes, he said no, he inclined his head, and that's all."

Another interviewer came to "see a house invaded by happiness," a "dwelling illumined all at once by money and glory." Pierre provided him with the information he required, "gently, deliberately," while Marie looked on approvingly. Then followed an uncomfortable silence. "No one said another word," the visitor from *la Presse* reported. "They were waiting for me to leave."

The Curies' cold, sometimes almost rude, response to inquiring reporters was their defense against "the frittering away of our time . . . a question of life or death from the intellectual point of view." But it also grew out of their extreme discomfort with fame. For Pierre, who had refused the Legion of Honor and apologized for even speaking of academic promotions, the Nobel Prize was a threat to his view of himself as an outsider. Marie, a stellar student who had been collecting prizes all her life, probably felt this less. But she too seems to have been uncomfortable with such dazzling success, particularly in writing to family who had stayed behind and lived a much more modest life in Poland. Writing to Józef the day after the news became public, she started off with greetings to his daughter: "Don't forget to thank Manyusya for her little letter, so well written, which gave me great pleasure. I shall answer her as soon as I have a free moment." Then followed a detailed description of her recent illness. Only then did she get around to mentioning, in the bleakest of terms, the Nobel Prize. "We have been given half of the Nobel Prize. I do not know exactly what that represents; I believe it is about seventy thousand francs. For us, it is a huge sum. I don't know when we shall get the money, perhaps only when we go to Stockholm." This announcement is followed by a much longer paragraph complaining about the onslaught of journalists they have to put up with as a result.

Despite the impression the Curies gave their friends and family, the Nobel Prize did bring some benefits. But it took several years for the most important ones to materialize. Of course there was the money, which came sooner. In addition to the Nobel Prize funds, Marie Curie was awarded, along with telegraph innovator Edouard Branly, the Prix Osiris, which added sixty thousand francs to the pot. The prize monies alleviated the Curies' financial worries and allowed them to indulge a little. They spent some of it to hire a lab assistant, some to paper a room at boulevard Kellerman and to install a modern bath.

Characteristically, they also gave a lot away. A donation of ten thousand Austrian crowns went to Bronia and Kazimierz for the sanitorium in Zakopane. There were loans and outright gifts to Pierre's brother Jacques, who supported his family of four on a professor's salary, and to Marie's sister Helena, a private school teacher in Warsaw. There was some aid for Polish students and for a student in need at Sèvres; and Marie, who understood homesickness, provided funds for a French friend who had married a Pole and lived in Poland to come back to France for a visit.

But the more important rewards of the prize—a decent laboratory and salaries and jobs that would allow the Curies to pursue their research—did not come easily or quickly. In the interim, the prize often seemed more of a curse than a blessing. And because Marie was cast in a supporting role by a sexist society, the most cursed aspects of celebrity fell more heavily on Pierre.

There was, for instance, the expectation that Pierre Curie would give a public lecture at the Sorbonne. This led him, as he confided to his Swiss friend Charles Edouard Guillaume, "to wish for a calmer time spent in a tranquil country where lectures would be outlawed and journalists persecuted." But in February, Pierre, dressed in formal clothes, made his way to the long lecture table of the Sorbonne's magnificent new grand amphitheater. "It was evident," wrote a Philadelphia reporter in the audience, "the instant the professor put his foot upon the platform that he was trembling with shyness; that he had probably never before worn an 'afternoon semi-dress suit'; that the massed thousands in the university amphitheatre were terrible as lions to him, and that could he have escaped without disgrace he would have . . . leaving his precious atom of radium imprisoned in its blankets of lead. But once he found his lips ready to respond to his thought, the modest professor captivated the throng by the lucidity of his explanations, the clarity of his experimentations."

The Nobel publicity had also made it impossible for the Institute of France to refuse Pierre Curie membership. "Here is an absolutely unknown fact," *la Presse* reported incredulously in January of 1904. "M. Curie was presented previously to the Academy of Sciences and he wasn't elected. Yes, five years after discovering radium . . . he was not judged worthy to enter the Institute." Fortunately, the Institute was now hurrying to correct this "bizarre" situation.

When a place became available some sixteen months after the Nobel Prize was announced, Pierre was informed by Éleuthère Mascart that "you are naturally placed on the first line, without serious competition and the nomination is not in doubt." But what was an honor in the eyes of most was just another onerous duty to Pierre, who was required once again to go through the courtesies he found so empty and difficult. "It is *necessary* for you to screw up your courage and make a round of visits to the members of the Academy," Mascart told him sternly, "if only to leave an visiting card *with a note* if you find no one at home." Apparently, Pierre replied with a litany of excuses. Mascart wrote again: "Arrange it however you can, but it is necessary that before the twentieth of June you make the sacrifice of a final round of visits to the members of the Academy of Sciences, even if you have to rent an automobile for the day to do it. The reasons you give me are excellent," Mascart added, "but one owes some concessions to practical exigencies. You must also reflect that the title of Member of the Institute will allow you to more easily render service to others."

In the end, Pierre made just enough visits, it seems, to get himself elected. "As for the Academy," Pierre wrote Georges Gouy in the summer of 1905, "I find that I am in it without wanting to be and without the Academy wanting to have me." Rather apologetically, Pierre explained to his friend that "I didn't feel I could refuse to present myself this time. I made one single round of visits, leaving cards with those who weren't home. . . . When I made my visits, everyone told me that it was agreed that I would have 50 votes. That's the reason I almost didn't get elected. People mounted a campaign for Gernez in the following fashion: 'It is certain that Curie will win, Gernez will have only the seven votes of his intimate friends . . . so vote for him and that will make eight, and that will make him so happy' and this eight votes wound up being 22 . . . that was a general surprise, even for those who voted for him. Several of these felt obliged to make excuses to me."

Pierre was disdainful of the whole enterprise. "What do you

want? In that place they can't do anything simply and without intrigue. . . . As for me, I very much regret that Gernez wasn't elected; I had nothing to lose, and the Academy would have been placed in such a bad light that it would have been a good and very entertaining lesson."

Insisting that he repeated all this "gossip" only because it interested Gouy, he noted that "besides this little intrigue, I also had against me the lack of sympathy of the clerical group and of those who found that I hadn't made enough visits. The young Schlösing questioned me about which academicians would vote for me and I told him, 'I have no idea, I didn't ask them.' 'That's just it, you didn't *deign* to ask them.' And the word is going around that I am *arrogant.*"

The French press saw Pierre's election to the Institute as another opportunity to celebrate, and misrepresent, the Curies. On July 5, 1905, *la Patrie* recounted yet another visit to the Curies' "little house, tucked away in greenery and yet crowned with sun" on boulevard Kellerman.

> Unfortunately, at the hour when we presented ourselves, the eminent scientist had gone off on visits of thanks to his new colleagues. In his absence we were received by his admirable collaborator, Mme. Sklodowska Curie.

The reporter proceeds to quote Marie Curie at length: she "rejoices enormously at [her] husband's success" and is sure that "this new mark of distinction is going to convince him to pursue his scientific work more determinedly than ever. . . ." Her husband was "even more affected by the honor conferred on him by the members of the Academy because, in times past, he hadn't perhaps received all the encouragement he had a right to." But Madame Curie was magnanimous: "Why invoke these rather painful memories since the Academy opened its doors to him yesterday?"

And what of Madame Curie, asked the reporter? Madame Curie dismissed the question. " 'Oh! me, I am only a woman,' she told us smiling, 'and no woman, ever, has sat under the Cupola [of the Institute].' Madame Curie told us in closing that her only ambition is to aid her husband in his work."

There is no way of knowing how Marie Curie really felt about the fact that her husband, not she, was given a chair at the Sorbonne and a seat at the Académie des sciences. Probably, judging by later events, she saw it as appropriate, since he was older and more experienced. But she would never say that her "only ambition" was to assist her husband. Nor would she have portrayed the proud Pierre as grateful.

The next day, a letter appeared in *la Patrie* from the "admirable" Madame Curie:

> I read, to my great astonishment, in yesterday's issue of *la Patrie,* an account of an interview that I had yesterday morning with a reporter from your paper. This interview is purely imaginary. I had no conversation with any person coming from *la Patrie,* and, furthermore, I have not said anything to anyone resembling the account contained in this interview.

La Patrie was only mildly repentant, explaining that the article was written by an "occasional collaborator," and accepted without question since "there was nothing in the text but compliments."

Press accounts to the contrary, the only thing the Curies really wanted was a laboratory to work in and time to work in it. This desire alone made Pierre Curie bold. Early in 1904, when the president of the Republic, Émile Loubet, paid a visit to the Curies' lab, Pierre made a "discreet allusion" to the inadequacy of their present laboratory and his wish for a better one. When the state tried, for a second time, to confer the Legion of Honor, Pierre replied, "I pray you to thank the minister, and to inform him that I do not in the least feel the need of a decoration, but that I do feel the greatest need for a laboratory." And writing to Georges Gouy a few weeks after the Nobel was announced, Pierre avowed that "all this noise will not perhaps have been useless . . . if it gets me a chair and a laboratory."

The first step in that direction was taken shortly after the Nobel Prize was announced. On December 15, 1903, the Chamber of Deputies created a chair in general physics at the Sorbonne for Pierre Curie. The chair, however, came without any explicit reference to a laboratory. As a result, Pierre announced (perhaps with a little urging from Marie) that he would have to hang on to his P.C.N. teaching post so that he could retain the small lab on rue Cuvier that went with it. This ploy led the deputies to add a fund for a laboratory, and to offer the job of *chef des travaux,* laboratory chief, to Marie.

Pierre and Marie were given a large room at rue Cuvier where Pierre taught in the P.C.N., as temporary space, with plans for additional rooms to be built in a nearby courtyard. "They are going to create a chair for me," Pierre explained to Georges Gouy, "and in the beginning I won't have a laboratory. I would have preferred it the other way around; but Liard . . . wants to profit from the present moment to create a new chair which will then be acquired for the university."

And so a new burden, preparation for teaching a new course at the Sorbonne, was added to Pierre's already heavy load. "What with my courses, the students, the equipment to install," Pierre complained to Gouy early in 1905, "and the interminable procession of people who come to disturb me without good reason, life passes without my accomplishing anything really useful."

A look at Pierre Curie's oeuvre confirms his lament. The months which preceded the Nobel announcement had been remarkable ones in the history of radioactivity, thanks in part to his work. In November of 1902 and again in February of 1903, he had published notes in the *Comptes rendus* about "induced radioactivity," the temporary radioactivity observed in the vicinity of radioactive elements. This "induced radioactivity" was in fact a gas produced by the transmutation process, but Pierre Curie was still skeptical about Rutherford's transmutation theory. Nonetheless, he made an important discovery about the phenomenon. He demonstrated that the "induced radioactivity" caused by radium disappeared at a fixed rate. This was the seed from which archeological and geological carbon-dating grew. If radioactivity disappeared at a fixed rate over time, then the age of a substance could be determined by measuring its radioactivity. Pierre Curie, by establishing that "induced radioactivity" (what Rutherford called the "emanation") diminished in an exact amount of time (in this case, 5,752 days), "defined a standard for the absolute measurement of time on the basis of radioactivity."

Soon after, in March 1903, Pierre Curie published a paper which astounded his colleagues. In collaboration with Albert Laborde, he measured the heat spontaneously emitted by radium and found it to be enormous. It was possible, he found, for one gram of radium to heat about a gram of water from freezing to boiling in one hour. This finding, as Marie Curie has noted, "defied all contemporary scientific experience." A historian of science identifies it as "the first appearance, in human affairs, of atomic energy in the familiar form of heat."

Pierre's paper aroused new curiosity about the source of radium's remarkable energy. Lord Kelvin was still arguing for an external source: "somehow ethereal waves may supply energy to radium." But others used Curie's finding to buttress the argument that the source of radium's energy came from within the atom. Frederick Soddy argued that it was difficult, given the enormity of energy produced, to imagine an external source; "the hypothesis," he maintained, "involves far greater difficulties than the effects it is designed to explain."

Pierre Curie was still unwilling to give up the possibility of an external source, insisting that "this release of heat could still be explained by supposing that radium uses an external energy of an unknown nature." But he was clearly leaning toward the Rutherford/ Soddy idea. What gave him pause, quite understandably, was the enormity of the energy which that hypothesis implied. "If one searches for the origin of the heat production in an internal transformation, this transformation must be . . . due to a modification of the atom of radium itself." It follows that, since the transformation of radium is extremely slow, only a tiny emission from the atom is accompanied by a large release of energy. "Therefore, if this hypothesis . . . were correct, the energy put in play in the transformation of atoms would be extraordinarily great."

Writing to Pierre shortly after the paper was published, the prescient Georges Gouy elaborated: "When an atom of radium explodes, sending off its parts with enormous speed and producing a significant heat, the constituents must be exposed, during this explosion, to colossal forces." The enormity of these forces, which have so powerfully influenced world events in the twentieth century, was first suggested by this 1903 paper of Pierre Curie.

Some months after Pierre published his paper on energy, Frederick Soddy, following a hunch of Rutherford's, made a discovery which pretty much clinched the transmutation hypothesis. Rutherford had guessed that the large amounts of helium in the atmosphere might be products of radioactive decay processes. By the summer of 1903, Soddy, in collaboration with the discoverer of helium, William Ramsay, established that radium emanation, confined in a glass over time, did indeed produce a gas whose spectra corresponded to those of helium. This, as Pierre Curie noted, was "a new fact of fundamental importance. . . . The birth, little by little, of helium in their tube could be one of the products of the disintegration of radium."

The Soddy/Ramsay discovery not only reinforced transmutation theory, it also led the way to an understanding of atomic structure. Rutherford came to the correct conclusion, fairly quickly, that helium was the same thing as the alpha particle emitted by radioactive bodies, and that it was probably one of the essential building blocks of all atoms. "I feel *sure*," Rutherford wrote the American chemist Bertram Boltwood in 1905, "helium is the alpha particle of Ra [radium] and its products but it is going to be a terrible thing to prove *definitely* the truth of this statement."

But while Rutherford, Ramsay, and Soddy's research in radioactivity promised to explain central mysteries, Pierre Curie's work in the years after the Nobel Prize retreated to relatively minor issues on the periphery. Between 1904 and 1906, he published two more papers on the time constant in radioactive decay, and one which elaborated the Soddy/Ramsay finding on helium as a disintegration product of radium. But two other papers, written with Albert Laborde, measured the relative radioactivity of various thermal waters in Europe. And another, written in collaboration with physiologists, focused on the effects of exposure to radium on mice and guinea pigs.

One reason for the change in Pierre's output was undoubtedly all the unwanted attention that followed the Nobel Prize. But it wasn't just the prize which was draining away his energy. Pierre's hands were so damaged by exposure to radium that for a time he had trouble dressing himself. Increasingly, he was troubled by debilitating bone pain, in his legs and in his back, which kept him from working.

As early as March of 1899, Marie was concerned about Pierre's "rheumatism" and was treating it with a diet free of wine and red meat. In the summer of 1904, he had a "violent crisis," severe pains in his legs and back, which kept him from going to Sweden to give his Nobel address. And in the spring of 1905 he told Georges Gouy that physical activity tired him so much that "work in the laboratory is barely progressing at all." Doctors first diagnosed rheumatism, then decided that "a kind of neurasthenia" was causing the pains. Their prescription of small amounts of strychnine (a common palliative at the time) didn't help. By the fall of 1905 Pierre was doubting that he would "ever be able to work seriously in the laboratory again."

Nowhere does Pierre give any hint that he saw a connection between his pains and radioactive exposure. And yet, the focus of three of the papers he wrote during this period suggests that it was on his mind. The papers would seem to contradict each other. The two on thermal waters conclude that their health-giving properties may be directly related to their radioactive content. At the same time, and more ominously, laboratory animals breathing in the emanation of radioactive substances in a confined space died within a matter of hours. "We have established," the paper concluded, "the reality of a toxic action from radium emanations introduced into the respiratory system."

Pierre Curie's curiosity had always ranged widely; Marie marveled at his ability to move in "very varied directions" and to "change the object of his research with surprising ease." But also, as she observed, he preferred to walk on untrodden paths. And "the considerable vogue of radioactivity made him wish to abandon this field of research for a time, and to return to his interrupted studies of the physics of crystals." In his lectures at the Sorbonne, where he could develop whatever themes he wanted, Pierre did return to his crystals and symmetry.

It seems quite possible that the same impulses caused him to take up, with more energy than ever before, an old fascination with the paranormal. It was Pierre's brother Jacques who had introduced him to these questions a decade earlier. "My brother," he wrote Marie in September of 1894, "is very much occupied with spiritualism at the moment," adding that "these spirit phenomena also intrigue me a great deal."

Pierre Curie was not the only scientist who took an interest in psychic phenomena at the turn of the century. The chemist William Crookes told an audience of distinguished colleagues that he considered his researches into "psychic phenomena" to be "the weightiest and farthest reaching of all." In addition to his duties as editor of *Chemical News* and officer of various scientific societies, Crookes was president of the Society for Psychical Research.

Charles Richet, physician, member of the Institute, and professor at the Sorbonne, wanted to put paranormal research on the same plane as other sciences. His *Traité de metapsychique* offered abundant evidence of the three psychic phenomena which he believed to be proved beyond doubt: telepathy, telekinesis (causing objects to move without touching them), and *ectoplasmie* (the materialization of objects, human bodies or body parts). Richet insisted that "science, severe and inexorable science, must admit to these three strange phenomena which it has thus far refused to recognize."

For some in the antimaterialist camp, psychic phenomena were proof of the bankruptcy of science. There were more mysteries in heaven and earth, they could claim, than were dreamt of in the laboratories. But for others, including Crookes, Richet, and Curie, psychic phenomena did not seem far-fetched or inexplicable. On the contrary, the study of them grew out of the wish to impose science on all experience. "All the phenomena of our universe," William Crookes wrote in 1898, "are presumably in some way continuous and it is unscientific to call in the aid of mysterious agencies when with every fresh advance in knowledge it is shown that aether vibrations have powers and attributes abundantly equal to any demand—even the transmission of thought."

Henri de Parville, writing about the Curies' Nobel Prize in *le Correspondant,* insisted that "everything around us is but vibration and thence radiations. Luminous radiations, caloric, electric, sonorous . . . why doubt telepathy, the influence from a distance of thought on thought? . . . The rays which escape from the nervous cell are very capable of exciting other nervous cells from afar."

Pierre Curie would never have made such wild claims. But he and Marie did observe, in arguing for a possible external source for the energy given off by radium, that "we know little about the medium that surrounds us, since our knowledge is limited to phenomena which can affect our senses, directly or indirectly." Among the religious, such a statement might argue for humility before an all-knowing God. But for Pierre Curie, it meant only that nature was full of surprises yet to be studied and explained. It was in this spirit that he and Marie began to attend, around this time, the séances of a woman named Eusapia Palladino.

Eusapia Palladino was one of a handful of mediums, those "intermediaries between the world of the living and the world of the dead," who traveled the world conducting séances. Born in an Italian mountain village, "Eusapia," as she was widely known, was a neglected, and perhaps abused, child. Given over to neighbors by her widowed father, she fell on her head as a child and sustained an injury which left a "hole." One of the less believable claims about her was that, when she was in a trance, this hole emitted a "cold breeze." Her psychic powers came to light one evening, when she was about to be sent to a convent by her caretakers. It was discovered, in the midst of a parlor game, that Eusapia could make the table rise, the chairs dance, the curtains swell, and the glasses and bottles walk about. Since then Eusapia had been "studied by all the *savants* of Europe."

As early as 1896, she had caused a stir in Paris. "Eusapia is within our walls," reported Georges Montorgueil. "Her presence communicates a sort of incoherent life to material objects, and peoples the void with phantoms." By the time Pierre and Marie Curie encountered her in a series of séances in 1905, Palladino was a full-bosomed matron in her fifties, dressed in black crepe; her face was broad and plain, her mouth turned downward rather severely. She had sad, penetrating eyes.

"We have had a series of séances with Eusapia Palladino at the Society of Psychology," Pierre reported to his friend Georges Gouy.

> It was very interesting, and really the phenomena that we saw appeared inexplicable as trickery—tables raised from all four legs, movement of objects from a distance, hands that pinch or caress you, luminous apparitions. All in a locale prepared by us with a small number of spectators all known to us and without a possible accomplice. The only trick possible is that which could result from an extraordinary facility of the medium as a magician. But how do you explain the phenomena when one is holding her hands and feet and when the light is sufficient so that one can see everything that happens?'

Pierre was eager to enlist Gouy. Eusapia, he told him, would return in November, and "I hope that we will be able to convince you of the reality of the phenomena or at least some of them." Though it wasn't easy to conduct experiments in this setting, Pierre was planning to undertake them "in a methodical fashion."

Marie Curie attended the séances with Eusapia Palladino, but she does not seem to have been as intrigued by them as Pierre. Her energies were directed elsewhere. She published even less than Pierre did in the years immediately following the Nobel Prize. Even though she wasn't expected to become a public figure like Pierre, she too was bombarded by requests and interviews which kept her from her work.

But the more important reason for the hiatus in her scientific work during these years was personal. Marie Curie was thirty-six in the year of the Nobel Prize. She had completed her doctorate, she had isolated a decigram of radium, and she had been recognized and rewarded for her work. And that spring, she became pregnant once again. Because she had lost a baby the previous year, she wanted to take good care of herself. She was also deeply worried about Pierre, whose health seemed to be getting worse as hers got better. And to add to her sense of vulnerability, Irène kept coming down with various childhood illnesses. Everything conspired to turn her attention toward home.

Chapter Ten

TURNING TOWARD HOME

IN THEIR EARLY YEARS together, Marie and Pierre Curie had been drawn to wild and remote vacation places—tiny towns on the rocky coast of Brittany; a peasant hut amid the volcanic mountains of Auvergne. More recently, there had been summers on islands off France's western coast. But in the hectic year of the Nobel Prize, they chose the tamest setting possible: a farmhouse in the tranquil village of St.-Rémy-les-Chevreuse, just a short train ride from Paris.

There were good reasons. For one thing, by August of 1904 Marie, now thirty-six, was five months pregnant. This time she was taking every precaution so as not to lose her baby. The year before, when she miscarried in the fifth month, she and everyone else blamed overwork. A long vacation on a "farm" in the country, not too far from Paris doctors, seemed the sensible choice.

Also, there was the growing concern about Pierre's health. Pierre (once again Marie was exempt) had intended to go to Stockholm during the summer of 1904 to deliver the required Nobel speech. But a series of "crises violentes" prevented the trip. "We are," he lamented to Georges Gouy, "completely out of line regarding the Swedish Academy."

For Pierre, who also needed rest in a quiet place, the vacation in St. Rémy was a return to the terrain he had loved best in his youth. It was in the "lovely jungle through which the Bièvre flowed" that Pierre had wandered so happily then, alone or in the company of his brother. St. Rémy, just a few kilometers farther south in the valley of the Yvette River, was familiar ground, a place "cut through with wooded vales, watered with fresh brooks and dotted with old castles and magnificent country-houses." Here were meadows full of wildflowers in spring, farms where Pierre and Marie could fetch fresh milk, little towns to walk to like Milon-la-Chappelle, with its fifteenth-century chateau. And, above all, here were strings of ponds like those along the Bièvre, full of the waterlilies and the richly varied aquatic life that Pierre loved to investigate. A contemporary guidebook described the area near St. Rémy as "the monotonous region of ponds." But for Pierre, nothing could have been less monotonous. To complete the picture, Jacques Curie, with his wife and two children, joined Marie, Pierre, and Irène that summer at St. Rémy.

Over the next several years, St. Rémy became Pierre and Marie Curie's country retreat. At Easter, they went there to greet the spring. And in summer, they returned for many weeks. St. Rémy's proximity —it was only about an hour by train from Paris—allowed them to negotiate a growing difference between Pierre's wish to be at the lab and Marie's to be with the children. As Pierre acknowledged in a letter to a benefactress who wanted to build the Curies a lab in the country, "children and the laboratory require the constant presence of those concerned with them." In general, Pierre chose the laboratory. His increasing inability to work seemed to make him feel more urgency about trying. And though he was a loving father, he deferred to Marie on child-rearing matters as small as the scheduling of playmates. Marie, on the other hand, juggled. Sometimes, as Pierre acknowledged, "she finds her double task beyond her powers." With the birth of a second child, the tasks at home intensified.

Eve Denise Curie, a "very chubby" baby with a "very full head of black hair," was born on December 6, 1905. The expense notebook reflects an expenditure of 8.45 francs that day for telegrams, most undoubtedly sent to Poland. Marie had had a prepartum rather than a postpartum depression. Before the birth, she was morose, perhaps remembering the traumatic miscarriage of the previous summer. To Bronia, who came to help, she lamented about bringing a new creature into the world. "Existence is too hard, too barren. We ought not to inflict it on innocent ones. . . ." But even though the birth itself was difficult, Marie recovered quickly and was soon singing the praises of babies.

"Don't you find it delicious to have a little tiny being to love?" she wrote Tatiana Jegorow, a friend from schooldays in Warsaw who also had a young family. "As for me, I adore little babies, but that doesn't prevent me from also loving my big seven-year-old daughter."

When Irène was an infant, Marie had kept a careful record of her weekly weight, of the dimensions of her head, of each new tooth. In the separate section of her notebook reserved for Eve, she was more casual—several teeth might appear before she got around to making note of them. Her entries about Eve concerned her body less and her behavior more. At the same time, her enjoyment of Eve's progress was more evident, though still tempered by the carefulness of the scientist.

Because she had been unable to successfully nurse Irène, Marie hired a wet nurse for Eve right away. "She nurses well and doesn't cry," Marie wrote in her book. By Christmas eve, just eighteen days after Eve's birth, her mother noted that she could "follow movements with her eyes." And at five weeks, despite some difficulties with digestion, Eve was capable of "very beautiful radiant smiles." Already a personality was emerging: Eve was "very active," "very alert," slept "very little" during the day, but was also "grumpy and impatient."

At three and a half months, Marie wrote Józef that Eve "protests energetically if I leave her lying awake in her cradle. As I am not a stoic, I carry her in my arms until she grows quiet." Eve was "conducting conversations in gutturals" by then. Later in the spring, Marie noted that she "knows all the people in her entourage well," and "gives her hand when one asks for it." And although sometimes "difficult," she was a chubby, healthy-looking baby. "She does not resemble Irène," Marie told her brother. "She has dark hair and blue eyes, whereas up to now Irène has rather light hair and green-brown eyes."

Irène seems to have been the child more worried over, as first children often are. She was, by several accounts, jealous of her mother's attention to others, and especially to the new baby in the house. Her mother sometimes went to great lengths to please her—traveling across town for bananas or apples she knew Irène would eat. Her notes about her older daughter during this period fluctuate between pride and concern. On the one hand, Irène took quickly to riding her new bicycle during the summer of 1904, and the next spring went on a sixteen-kilometer bike trip. But by the following summer, Marie worried that Irène lacked "flexibility and decisiveness" when it came to other kinds of exercise. Mostly, however, Marie worried, with good reason, about Irène's health.

The array of childhood diseases Irène (and sometimes Eve too) contracted during this period would discourage any mother, and must have been particularly alarming to one who had lost her own sister and mother to illness as a child. In the early months of Marie's pregnancy with Eve, Irène contracted a flu which turned into whooping cough, followed by a ten-day fever and a cough which persisted through the summer in St. Rémy and into September. In October, she was in bed for ten days with a "benign" scarlet fever. In December, probably because of the persistent cough, she had an X ray (by now a part of the medical arsenal) which showed her lungs to be clear, but soon after she had a four-day fever. Around Easter, she was sick again. And so on.

Fortunately, Pierre's father helped out with his grandchildren, and was particularly close to Irène. Had it not been for his steady support, plus the help of a nanny and a maid, as well as the wet nurse and occasionally a cook, it would have been difficult for Marie to continue her life away from home. Even with help, she found it a challenge. "I have a great deal of work," she wrote Józef, "what with the housekeeping, the children, the teaching and the laboratory, and I don't know how I shall manage it all."

Yet it does not seem to have occurred to her that she could do less. The Nobel Prize money, for instance, might have made it possible for her to give up teaching at Sèvres. But she liked working with these sisters of her younger self. "These pupils were girls of about twenty years who had entered the school after severe examination and had still to work very seriously to meet the requirements that would enable them to be named professors in the lycées," she later wrote. "All these young women worked with great eagerness, and it was a pleasure for me to direct their studies in physics."

Sèvres, founded in 1881 to provide girls with the quality education so long enjoyed by their brothers, was housed in the eighteenth-century factory used in the first manufacture of the celebrated Sèvres porcelain. Its faculty was a distinguished collection of professors brought in from the Sorbonne and the Collège de France. Marie was the first woman among them.

Though her pedagogical roots ran deep, Marie was inexperienced at teaching when she began at Sèvres. According to one observer of the twentieth *promotion,* her first class, it showed. "The twentieth *promotion* detested her," Marthe Baillaud recalled years later, and they proclaimed it in a song, set to the tune of "la Paimpolaise."

> And while the prof is stuttering
> The . . . the . . . the . . . foot in the air
> The girls in class are muttering,
> Sketching her awkward pose up there;
> Saying under their breath
> "Oh God, I'm bored to death!"
> Wouldn't she be better off
> Cooking for her husband-prof
> Instead of talking in a stream
> To a class that's bored enough to scream?

Most people who knew Marie Curie took little notice of her Polish accent. If they did mention it, they emphasized how slight it was and what excellent French she spoke. But her Sèvres students that first year found her accent "shocking," and went around quoting one of her most awkward sentences. Probably, as their song suggests, the appearance of a woman in an unfamiliar role made them uncomfortable and inclined them to ridicule.

But Marie Curie came to understand that there were difficulties which went beyond her accent or her style. The students didn't understand her presentations, in large part because the formulas and equations which accompanied them went beyond their mathematical knowledge.

Somehow, between her first and second year of teaching, Marie Curie figured out how to reach her students. And "as spontaneously as the twentieth promotion had detested her the twenty-first loved her." Most who taught at Sèvres arrived there from Paris on the train and strolled from the train stop along a corridor of chestnut trees to the main entrance. The moment the professor passed through the elegant iron grille of the entryway and crossed the threshold into the school building, a bell announced his presence. "But in the case of Madame Curie," a Sévrienne remembers, "we didn't wait for the ringing of the bell. We watched from our windows for the arrival of the professor, and as soon as we saw her little grey dress at the end of the allée of chestnut trees we ran to take our seats in the conference room."

Lucienne Goss Fabin, a pupil who dreamed of a career in the laboratory but became a lycée professor, considered Marie Curie's courses at Sèvres "the essential reference during the entire length of my career. She didn't dazzle us, she reassured us, attracted us, held us with her simplicity, her desire to be useful to us, the sense she had of both our ignorance and our possibilities."

Eugénie Feytis, the Sévrienne who worked as a baby-sitter for the Curies and who later became director of the school, was most impressed by the "experimental skill" of the petite professor. "Until we came to Sèvres," she explained, "we had thought that physics was learned entirely from books in which we found the pictures of the apparatus they used to establish the laws we were studying. The collection rooms of the lycées contained some bright brass instruments mounted on polished mahogany stands. Our professors took them out to . . . reproduce a qualitative experiment sometimes, but we never touched them."

That changed in Marie Curie's classes. The solution was to double the length of the physics classes, "adding interesting manipulations. Often she brought us equipment made or modified by her which we used with her. It was very simple equipment but our guide was so skilled that we ended by achieving our measurements, and nothing was more fascinating than discussing the results we had in common with her after the bell. . . . Experiments done in common are an occasion for spontaneous ideas . . . and it would happen that the pretty face of our teacher, so grave ordinarily, would brighten into an amused and charming smile after certain of our remarks."

Marie Curie also taught by example. She invited her physics classes from Sèvres to hear her defend her dissertation in June of 1903 at the Sorbonne. The Sévriennes were "proud to hear their professor respond with certainty to the questions that were posed to her . . . and they rejoiced to learn that Marie Curie was received with *mention très honorable* and that she had merited the congratulations of the jury. What a great example and what encouragement for other women!"

On another occasion, vividly recalled by Eugénie Feytis Cotton, Marie took them to the modest lab on rue Cuvier to meet Pîerre Curie and observe his work.

It was during the period when he was attempting to measure the quantity of heat given off by radium . . . and he had decided to use a Bunsen calorimeter to do it. He performed for us . . . the measure of the specific heat of a small sample of copper. We were struck by the clarity of his explanations, spoken slowly and gravely, by his luminous expression and by the deftness of his long artistic hands, which operated before us with astonishing confidence.

Afterward, back at Sèvres, she had her students repeat Pierre Curie's experiment.

Marie Curie also took an interest in curriculum issues at Sèvres. It was she who convinced Faculty of Sciences dean Gaston Darboux that differential calculus should be taught to Sévriennes. She also joined with other professors to argue for the elimination of an additional, and difficult, test given to the women at Sèvres but not to their male counterparts.

Such a life left little time for dalliance. Yet there was a small amount of that too during these busy years. Marguerite Borel, the young, slightly giddy wife of mathematician Émile Borel, remembered seeing the Curies at some of her "evenings." They were, she recalled, "like two shadows. He spoke little. She, looking very young, attractive with her curly hair, entered quickly into a scientific conversation and gave her point of view at length. They intimidated me." On at least one occasion, the Curies visited the great sculptor Auguste Rodin in his studio home at Meudon, and Marie, for her part, promised to visit him again.

More was spent, according to Marie's expense record, on clothes, especially for Pierre and the children. Even she, judging from a 1904 photograph, sometimes got dressed up for evening. The photograph must have been taken in the first half of the year, before her pregnancy showed. In it, she wears a dress with a scooped neckline finished in delicate black ruching, which gathers in folds at her shoulders. Her pretty, slightly plump arms are bare, and she is leaning on her elbows, head tilted to one side against both hands. She has pulled her hair back into a twist, but frizzy ash-blond strands have already escaped, creating a sort of halo effect. There may be a hint of something coquettish around her mouth. Perhaps Marie wore this dress when she and Pierre went to see Eleonora Duse in Gorky's *The Lower Depths* at the innovative Théâtre de l'Oeuvre.

Another time, probably because of some visitor from abroad, there was an extravagant day in Paris, complete with a hired car, lunch and dinner out, and a trip up the Eiffel Tower. This, however, was an exception. Despite the Nobel's infusion of money into the Curies' budget, Marie continued her careful ways: umbrellas were repaired, not replaced, and accounts were reconciled at the end of every month. When she lost her change purse on the street one day, she made note of the resulting deficit in the expense notebook. Yet sometimes, on the way home from the laboratory with Pierre, Marie would stop and buy caviar, a delicacy which reminded her of Poland.

Pierre's tastes were as modest as Marie's. Most of the time, he ate lunch in a second-floor bistro at the corner of rue Monge and rue Censier. It was a short, pleasant walk there from the laboratory, across the Jardin des Plantes into an industrial neighborhood, then up a spiral staircase to the modest, clean little restaurant, where tanners and other workers mixed with students and researchers from the École de physique et chimie and the Museum of Natural History. In a Paris where such things mattered, a journalist found it "touching" to see this man "whose name was celebrated in every language, from one pole to the other, take his turn at the cash register, where the café owner reigned, armed with a chalk and blackboard, and recite 'One cutlet plate, one brie, two sous-worth of bread, no wine,' and settle up for his meal, which barely exceeded forty sous!"

On boulevard Kellerman, there were occasional dinner parties, especially when a respected colleague like H. A. Lorentz came to town. Then Marie would forgo her usual habit of shopping at Felix-Potin, a grocery store, and repair instead to an open market for fresh cheeses, vegetables, and flowers. Once, the American dancer Loie Fuller, the Paris sensation who danced with veils illumined by colored lights, put on a show for the Curies at their house. But this production, which required the assistance of a team of electricians, appears to have been thrust upon them by Fuller, whose admiration for the Curies knew no bounds. Generally, social gatherings on boulevard Kellerman were much more informal and spontaneous.

Paul Langevin, who lived nearby, liked to "go in the evening and find them, always ready for long conversations in the second-floor room where they worked together, above the garden that the grandfather cultivated. We pursued their continual work of examining ideas and facts, work guided by the keen mind of [Pierre] Curie, sustained by his wife's insistence on clarity."

Eugénie Feytis Cotton remembers many such "fruitful conversations" at the Curies', "the hypotheses flowing, numerous and varied, followed by long silences in which everyone was absorbed in reflection." Besides Paul Langevin, the Curies' longtime collaborator André Debierne was often in attendance, as well as Pierre's Swiss friend Charles Edouard Guillaume and Georges Sagnac, author of the long letter admonishing the Curies about their health. Georges Urbain, an artist as well as chemist whose collection of minerals was much admired by Pierre Curie, often joined in. And the neighbors, Jean and Henriette Perrin, were likely to drop by as well.

The Perrins, who had moved in next to the Curies on boulevard Kellerman, were ideal neighbors. Irène and the Perrins' children, Aline and Francis, became playmates, and could pass easily back and forth through the rusty iron fence which separated the two houses. When reporters came snooping, Irène could escape to the Perrins' house (although this was not always a successful strategy, since the reporters followed her there). Henriette Perrin became Marie Curie's closest woman friend during this period. And Jean Perrin was a worthy member of the little group that gathered at the Curies' to talk science.

Perrin was a man of many parts: a social animal who loved to receive his friends for dinner, he possessed, "the gaiety of an exuberant child." Sometimes he would burst into Wagnerian song. He was also a political activist. Along with Paul Langevin, he was among the first scientists to sign the petition on Dreyfus's behalf in the wake of Zola's "J'accuse." In the gatherings at the Curies' house, he was likely to be found engaged in passionate political debate with Dr. Eugène Curie.

At the same time, Perrin was an early student of electrons who suggested, as early as 1901, that the atom was constructed like a miniature solar system. Himself the winner of the Nobel Prize in physics in 1926, Perrin had a gift for explaining science to the world. His book *les Atomes* remains a model of lucidity. A pettier man than Pierre Curie might have resented Perrin: it was he who was named to the vacant chair at the Sorbonne Pierre had applied for in 1898. Instead,

Perrin became a regular member of the "little colony" that formed around the Curies—sometimes in their workroom, sometimes at the dining room table, and often, when the weather was good, outside in the garden.

"We touched on everything," Paul Langevin remembered, "but we returned by preference to the wonderful events which were happening at that moment in physics and in which their [the Curies'] work together had such an important role." Undoubtedly, they talked of the work of Rutherford and Soddy in England, as well. The peccadilloes of the Institute, Pierre's belief that there was too much Greek and too little science in the lycée curriculum, the strange phenomena produced by the medium Eusapia—all these must have come up for consideration at the roundtable. Undoubtedly, the scientists talked too of some of the dubious research on radiation that radium had spawned.

It was during this period that the physicist René Blondlot claimed to have discovered a new kind of ray, which was emitted by a wide range of materials and which he named the N ray after his native city of Nancy. The popular press got quite excited about these N rays, concluding that they were another in a whole "pile of mysterious things which would have made us smile in the past but which could well be explained tomorrow." The possibility that another sort of radiation might indeed exist led Pierre Curie, and some of his colleagues, to cross the street from his lab to a blackened room in the Museum of Natural History, where a demonstration of N rays took place. Curie and the others, however, couldn't see much evidence of the rays.

In Lyon, Georges Gouy was also having trouble seeing N rays. "I just read his [Blondlot's] last note in the *Comptes rendus,*" Gouy wrote Curie, "in which an old tempered steel knife resembles radium because it has been emitting N rays for centuries. I would certainly like to see these famous rays, but I haven't succeeded; it seems that certain eyes are not sensitive to them." Pierre replied that he had just come across a note in the *Comptes rendus* in which a colleague "measures the rotatory power of sugar for N rays of various wavelengths with an astonishing precision. There is a whole page of figures and they have left me stupefied." Later, Gouy told Pierre that he had "announced to my acolytes that we are soon going to undertake research in L rays in order to bring glory to our town [Lyon] and that I'm going to set up a black chamber for that purpose." In the atmosphere of "frank gaiety" which reigned around the table at boulevard Kellerman, there must have been plenty more of such badinage.

IN THE SPRING of 1905, Pierre Curie felt well enough to journey with Marie to Stockholm for the much-postponed Nobel lecture. Despite their misgivings. the trip turned out to be, as Pierre wrote Georges Gouy, "very agreeable." Sweden was a "rather uniform but very pretty and very restful place," made up of lakes and of ocean sounds with a little land around them, of pines, of moraines and of houses of red wood."

To the Curies' relief, they were received without fanfare. "We were delivered of all care," Pierre explained, "and that made it a rest for us. What's more there is almost no one in Stockholm in June, so that the official aspect was much simplified."

Pierre's lecture to the Swedish Academy was a typical performance. It was brief: a mere seven printed pages as opposed to Henri Becquerel's fifteen. It relied heavily on demonstration, which came easier to him than words. And it was tremendously, perhaps even excessively, modest. At the same time, it ranged far and wide, like Pierre's curiosity, exploring the significance of radioactivity not just for physics, the field in which the Curies' Nobel was awarded, but also for chemistry, geology, meteorology, and biology. And it ended with a paragraph so prescient that his continues to be one of the most quoted Nobel speeches of all time.

In all, Pierre Curie cites "Madame Curie" ten times in his address, while referring to himself only five. "We," the team of Pierre and Marie Curie, is mentioned five times. Other scientists, most notably Rutherford and Soddy, are frequently acknowledged. At the same time, Pierre's reluctance to wholeheartedly embrace Rutherford's theory of transformation peeks through. He still cites it as one of two possible hypotheses (the other being that radioactive substances derive their energy from outside themselves). The transformation hypothesis, he admits, "has shown itself the most fruitful for explaining the properties of radioactive bodies . . . it permits in particular an immediate explanation of the disappearance of polonium and the production of helium by radium." This theory, he adds with just a hint of skepticism, "has been developed and clarified with great boldness by Messieurs Rutherford and Soddy." It is, if true, "a veritable theory of the transmutation of elements, but not as the alchemists understood it. Organic matter would necessarily evolve across the ages, following immutable laws."

Pierre Curie's final observations would seem to assume that radioactivity *is* in fact a small manifestation of colossal subatomic forces. "One can imagine," he told the Swedish Academy,

> that in criminal hands radium could become very dangerous and here one can ask if humanity is at an advantage in knowing nature's secrets, if it is mature enough to make use of them or if this knowledge might not be harmful to it. The example of

the discoveries of Nobel is a case in point; powerful explosives have allowed men to do admirable work. They are also a terrible means of destruction in the hands of great criminals who lead people into war. I am among those who think with Nobel that humanity will derive more good than bad from new discoveries.

Pierre Curie's concluding words have always been considered, quite rightly, to be a statement about the relationship between scientific discovery and humanity in general. But it is interesting to reflect on their implications in his own life. As he continued to suffer the effects of radiation on his fingertips and to lie awake in pain with a mysterious illness, did he perhaps wish to believe that radium, that strange and wonderful discovery, would do more good than harm to him as well?

The summer of 1905 was to be a restful, restorative time, with July and August spent in St. Rémy, followed by several weeks on the coast of Normandy; Marie's sister Helena, and her seven-year-old daughter Hania, were to come from Poland and travel with the Curies to the seashore. Irène, now eight, was already excited about the summer when she wrote to her father in Sweden in early June. "On what date do we leave for the country" she wrote in her large, deliberate script, "and when will you come back?" Eve, Irène reported, was up to her usual tricks in their absence: "Little sister wants to grab everything that comes in front of her."

Soon after Pierre and Marie returned from Sweden, parts of the family began making their way to St. Rémy for the start of the long summer break. The children and their entourage (grandfather, nanny) were there by the end of June, and Marie, it would seem, not long after. Pierre, however, stayed in Paris, where his candidacy for the Institute was under consideration. It wasn't until the end of July that he joined the rest of the family in St. Rémy. Not long after that, they all returned to Paris to meet Helena and Hania, who had made the long train journey from Warsaw.

That summer was one of the most memorable summers of Helena's life, vividly recalled in a memoir published in Polish some forty-five years later. "The trip seemed very long, because my excitement was so great," she remembered. "I was going to spend a whole summer with Maria and Pierre, whom I loved enormously; I was going to see them every day, to hear their melodious voices; and Hania was going to have little Irène for company! I was going to spend the summer at the ocean, which I had never seen before!"

Pierre and Marie were waiting when the train pulled into the vast glass-ceilinged Gare du Nord. Pierre, "calm, smiling, slightly stooped," greeted Helena in his best beginner's Polish: " 'Dear sister, very good, came to see us from so far.' " Marie was "very moved and joyous."

Marie had everything planned. Knowing that times were hard for Helena because of reverberations from the strikes and rebellion in Russian Poland, she made sure that her sister wouldn't have to spend any money in France. Before Helena arrived, she had bought clothes for Irène and Hania to take to the beach: matching red outfits, as well as matching swimsuits and bathrobes. She had also rented a house that she and Pierre had spotted on an earlier bike trip along the Normandy coast. It was in the tiny seaside village of Carolles, right on a wide, isolated beach of coarse-grained sand. At high tide, waves crashed and thundered against the front porch.

A week of sightseeing in Paris "passed like a dream" for Helena. Then everyone except Pierre headed north by train to the sea. "We traveled like a king's court," Helena remembers, "Maria and I, three children and one nanny and one cook. Pierre was supposed to join us in a couple of weeks, after finishing some urgent project in Paris." Helena was disappointed when she first arrived at the house. Instead of the ocean, "all I could see was a gray, boundless plain, stretching to the horizon. . . . Maria only laughed. She knew the ocean very well by then; she knew that in a few hours the water would come back with impossible noise, making it difficult for us to talk with the windows open." When the sea did appear, it was "splendid and formidable, shining with all the colors of the rainbow, leaving snow-white foam on the shore." At night, several lighthouses blinked their signals across the water.

Every day, they walked down the steps that led from their house to the ocean's edge to swim. Helena was frightened at first of the enormous waves. " 'Let the wave carry you, relax,' " shouted Marie. But every time I saw a wave coming, I would turn around and let it push me back on the sand. My knees were very sore from those harsh landings on the coarse sand." In time, however, Helena learned to follow her sister's advice.

After Pierre arrived, he and Marie spent several hours of every day working. The rest of the time Pierre spent on the beach. "We went for walks at low tide," Helena remembers, "collecting beautiful little rocks, seaweed. . . . The girls always accompanied us, constantly bringing their 'treasures' for us to admire. . . . Pierre took every single object that the girls had brought in his hands, examined it attentively and put it in his pocket." Whether by design or lucky circumstance, however, Pierre's pocket had a hole in it. "He couldn't have possibly kept all of those 'gifts' that the girls were giving him. The girls never noticed anything, though, and we grownups had fun watching them."

Because of his leg pains, Pierre wouldn't walk out onto the damp sand at low tide, but he had all kinds of advice and instructions for Helena when *she* did. "We were most interested in the life of the little hermit crabs who carried stolen shells on their backs which contained colorful anemones. They looked so beautiful moving in the water like blue, purple or pink flower petals."

Helena brought the crabs back to the house in order to "observe the symbiosis of the two species. We would put the crabs in basins full of water and watch them for hours." Helena was struck by the breadth of Pierre's knowledge. "He knew so much geology and biology! I learned so much from him that summer!"

Marie, meanwhile, seems to have been tending to more practical matters. One day, as Helena and Pierre were bent over their basins of crabs, she appeared in the doorway, smiling. "Could you perhaps lend me one basin so I can wash up? There is not a single one left in the house." According to Helena, she and Pierre "looked at each other and decided to comply with the request. Naturally we chose the smallest basin."

In early August, Pierre, Marie, Helena and the two older girls set out in a large carriage drawn by two horses in tandem for Mont-St.-Michel, just a few kilometers to the south along the Normandy Coast. Mont-St.-Michel, a magnificent Benedictine abbey dating back to the tenth century, perched at the apex of a jutting rock and surrounded completely by water when the tide is high, is one of the Western world's great marvels. But on this occasion the travelers were anticipating an additional marvel: a complete eclipse of the sun.

"Before the eclipse," Helena recalls, "we managed to visit the castle, the prison from the time of Louis XI, the amazingly beautiful cathedral and the tiny village of one hundred inhabitants which clings to the rocky slope." Then they walked out onto one of the terraces where visitors go to look down on the coming and going of the tides. There they trained their eyes on the sky.

It was a perfect day for observing an eclipse. Around one in the afternoon, it started to get dark. "The surface of the sun became more and more overshadowed," Helena remembers, "until finally it disappeared. Birds were flying around us in panic." Pierre had brought special lenses from Paris which made it possible to observe the eclipse more closely. Just as Władysław Skłodowski had explained the sunset to his children, Pierre explained the eclipse to everyone "from a scientific point of view." Irène and Hania were "absolutely amazed; they kept inundating us with questions." An hour later it was over; everything returned to normal.

After the tide receded and they could leave Mont-St.-Michel by road, Pierre returned with the girls to Carolles. But Helena and Marie tarried, visiting St. Malo and the beautiful rose gardens of Dinard nearby. That night, in Dinard, they sat on a restaurant terrace, "ate a delicious supper with great appetite, and talked for a long time, looking out at the sea before us."

"It was a wonderful evening," Helena recalled much later.

> The sea undulated quietly in the dark; remote lights glittered far away, reflected on the water. . . . All the memories of childhood, our youthful dreams, all the pain and disappointment, our longtime separation and our adult life—all that came alive passing in front of our eyes. We went to bed very late that night, and we didn't get too much sleep, either.

They returned to find Eve quite sick with a high fever. Helena remembers how guilty Marie felt for having left her, and how worried she looked as she asked Pierre, "What do you think? She's going to get over it, isn't she?" Within a few days, Eve had recovered.

Of all the children, Eve was the one who attracted the most admiration from strangers. "Marie and I grew annoyed with this attention," Helena recalls, "but there was no place on the beach where we were safe from it." One day, as Eve was playing charmingly on her blanket, three women approached. "Looking at her in ecstasy, they asked me: 'To whom does this superb baby belong, Madame?'

'I have no idea,' I answered. 'She's an orphan.'

"That did it!" Helena remembers. "The women went away, indignant, and Maria laughed so hard that tears ran down her face. From that day on, she often stroked Eve's hair and said, 'My poor orphan!' "

When August came to an end, Helena had to return with Hania to Warsaw, where she ran a school. With great sadness, Marie accompanied her to the little train station at Granville. On their way there, as they bumped along in a carriage, Marie confided tearfully that she was seriously worried about the health of Pierre, then age forty-six. "She told me that the last few nights he had spent sleeplessly because of the pain in his back. The pain was getting stronger all the time, and the attacks were getting more frequent. 'Maybe it's some terrible disease that doctors don't recognize,' she confided. 'Maybe Pierre will never be well again.' "

Helena tried to comfort Marie, "but I couldn't stop myself from crying either." Just as the train was about to pull out of the station, Marie touched her sister's cheek, looked her in the eyes, and said 'I love you.'

'For what?' asked Helena.

'Because you are good and wise,' Marie answered.

"How good it felt to hear her say that!" Helena wrote many years later. "I can still hear those words, which have given me strength in moments of depression and weakness. Even . . . after all these years, I have tears in my eyes thinking about it."

DESPITE Marie's worst fears, things seemed to be going better when the family returned to Paris that fall. Irène, according to Marie's notes, "benefited greatly" from her time by the ocean. She exercised, she ran around barefoot, and she "came to have a good appetite and a healthy look."

Back in Paris, Irène had a busy schedule for a ten-year-old. She spent her mornings in school, and in the afternoon went to classes in gymnastics, drawing, Polish, and music. But her mother noted that she "likes all her occupations and does it all with pleasure."

Marie felt strongly that children should lead a balanced life, and later wrote a critique of *surmenage* (overwork) in the French school system. She bristled when a reporter suggested to her that Irène would grow up to be a scientist like her mother. "Oh, she will be whatever she wants to be," Marie was reported to reply. "All I ask of her right now is that she be healthy."

Already, though, Irène loved to visit the natural-history collections at Sèvres with her baby-sitter, Eugénie Feytis. She was particularly excited by the enormous size of a cast of a mammoth's tooth, and gravely quizzed her baby-sitter about whether she had ever seen a mammoth. When Eugénie explained that the mammoth had lived a very long time ago, Irène declared, "Well then, I will ask grandpa."

Eve was prospering too. By her first birthday, in December of 1905, her mother noted that she "walks very well . . . parades alone around the whole house" and "climbs the stairs." She had begun to eat tapioca pudding, and on December 14 she ate her first egg. A few months later, she was eating an egg every day, had twelve teeth, could drink on her own, had begun to run, and was in general "lively, gay and imprudent."

Marie's own energy seems to have been entirely restored. "My wife . . . ," Pierre reported to Georges Gouy that November, "leads a very active life between her children, the École de Sèvres and the laboratory. She doesn't waste a minute and she occupies herself much more regularly than me with the ongoing work of the laboratory, where she spends the better part of her day."

Despite Pierre's middling health, a colleague remembers that he and Marie were sometimes in the lab together during this period. When they were, Albert Laborde detected little signs of their interdependence and intimacy.

In the laboratory in the rue Cuvier I was working with a mercury apparatus. Pierre Curie was there. Madame Curie came, grew interested in a detail of the mechanism, and at first did not understand. The detail was, for that matter, very simple. Nevertheless, when the explanation was given she insisted upon refuting it. Then Pierre Curie burst forth with a happy, tender, indignant 'Well, really, Marie!'

A few days later, when several workers in the lab asked Pierre Curie to help them disentangle a complicated mathematical problem, he advised them to wait for his wife, who knew integral calculus better. "And in fact Madame Curie found the difficult solution in a few minutes."

Pierre had been buoyed that fall by visits from his brother Jacques and Georges Gouy. "Unless one acts sometimes," Pierre had noted in a letter to Gouy, "one ends up losing sight of one's best friends and frequenting others simply because one encounters them easily." Pierre continued to complain to Gouy about the time he wasted at the Institute. "I don't have a relationship with any of the members, the interest of the meetings is nil. I feel very much that this milieu is not mine and . . . that it's entirely because of a misunderstanding that I'm a member of the Academy."

And yet some good things came of it that fall. Because he was a member, Pierre was able to argue on behalf of others he cared about. Although he felt "scarcely competent" to write about Georges Gouy's work in optics, he agreed to contribute a report to the Academy on Gouy because "at least your reporter will be driven by good intentions and won't slip in these little perfidious phrases which are the joy and the amusement of the academicians." That December, largely as a result of Pierre's advocacy, his friend Georges Urbain won the Prix Hughes and Georges Gouy won the coveted Prix La Caze. A month later, Pierre experienced another of the genuine advantages of membership in the Institute. Rather than having a paper read by an intermediary, he himself presented Marie Curie's final paper in the Marckwald polonium controversy: "On the diminution of the radioactivity of polonium over time."

Around that same time, it also began to look as though the long-delayed dream of a laboratory was going to come true. Several new, highly sensitive instruments for the new lab were completed according to Pierre's specifications, and there was a detailed plan for new space on rue Cuvier.

Even though he tired easily, Pierre had enough energy to pursue ideas and causes that interested him. He regularly attended meetings of the Association of Professors of the Science Faculties, an organization he hoped would fight the entrenched power of the "gros bonnets" and the "normaliens."

Pierre's interest in Eusapia Palladino during this period seems almost to have superseded his interest in radium. In a letter to Georges Gouy in the spring of 1906, he mentioned his efforts with radium in a single sentence, then proceeded to write, at length, about a recent series of séances.

> We have had some more séances with the medium Eusapia Palladino. The result is that these phenomena really exist and it is no longer possible for me to doubt it. It's improbable but this is so and it is *impossible to deny it* after the séances we have had in perfectly controlled conditions. A kind of fluid members detach from the medium (mostly from her arms and legs . . .) and push objects forcefully. (Richet calls these *exoplasmes*). These fluid members form as a rule on a piece of black material . . . but sometimes they jump out into the open air.

Pierre finds these conclusions "extremely troubling," since the admission of some of these phonemena can "lead little by little to the acceptance of everything, even the ghosts [free-floating body parts] of Crookes and Richet."

Pierre wants Gouy to join him in this new adventure. "I don't doubt that after some good séances you would be convinced too. . . . You who have such great intuition so often about phenomena, how do you explain these displacements of objects from a distance, how do you conceive that the thing is possible? There is here, in my opinion, a whole domain of entirely new facts and physical states in space of which we have no conception."

Pierre wrote this letter on Saturday, April 14, 1906. That same day, he took the train to St. Rémy to join Marie and the children for a few days in the country. It was early spring, and the weather was fine. On Monday, Marie sat leaning against Pierre in a meadow near the house, watching Irène chase butterflies. "We were happy," she remembered afterward. Though she had "a little heartache" about Pierre's fatigue, she also "had this feeling I had had recently a lot, that nothing was going to trouble us."

For Marie, who had spent so much time over the last several years worrying about everyone's health, it was a rare moment of optimism. But her confidence in the future was about to be cruelly undermined. Three days later, Pierre Curie was dead.

Freta Street in Warsaw in the nineteenth century. Maria Skłodowska was born in the building with the balcony, in the left foreground. The family apartments were in the rear, behind the private school of which Maria's mother was headmistress.

Władysław Skłodowski, Maria's father.

Bronisława Skłodowska, Maria's mother.

The Skłodowski children. FROM LEFT:
Zosia, Helena, Maria, Józef, and Bronia.

Józef in his student uniform.

Maria (left), age twenty-two, and Helena,
age twenty-three.

Kazimierz Zorawski, who was romantically involved with Maria while she worked as a governess to his younger siblings.

Maria during the governess years.

The house in Szczuki where Maria served as a governess from 1886 to 1889.

Władysław Skłodowski with his
three daughters in 1890, the year
before Maria left for Paris. FROM
LEFT: Maria, Bronia, and
Helena.

Maria, now called Marie, on
the balcony of Bronia and
Kazimierz's apartment on rue
d'Allemagne in Paris. Pierre
Curie loved this photograph of
her as, in his words, the "good
little student."

Pierre Curie.

*ABOVE RIGHT: Pierre
Curie in 1878 at age
nineteen.*

*Pierre with his family.
CLOCKWISE FROM UPPER
LEFT: Jacques, Pierre,
his father, Dr. Eugène
Curie, and his mother,
Sophie-Claire
Depouilly Curie.*

Pierre and Marie Curie with their newly purchased bicycles and cycling costumes, at the time of their wedding in the summer of 1895.

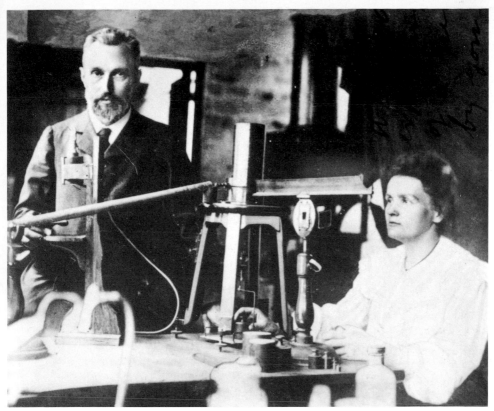

Pierre and Marie Curie with the quartz piezoélectrique used to measure radioactivity.

The storage room on rue Lhomond where polonium and radium were discovered.

Henri Becquerel, wearing the
green brocade costume and sword
of a member of the Académie des
sciences.

Marie and Pierre Curie in 1904,
the year after they won the Nobel
Prize.

Ernest Rutherford.

Georges Gouy.

Marie with Irène and some of her pupils at Sèvres in 1903. Eugénie Feytis (later Cotton) is at the far right and Henriette Perrin is third from the right.

Marie with Irène in 1904.

Irène, age eight, with Eve, age two.

Eve at age three.

Marie with her children in 1908, two years after Pierre's death. It was probably this photograph that prompted Jacques Curie's comment: "The two little girls are a pleasure to see, but you! How sad you look! . . . You must rally a little, if it is only for your children. . . ."

Paul Langevin.

*Paul Langevin with his bride,
Jeanne Desfosscs, in 1902.*

Marguerite Borel, who came to Marie Curie's defense at the time of the scandal.

Jean Perrin.

Hertha Ayrton, the scientist who provided Marie Curie with an anonymous refuge in England.

Marie Curie in Birmingham in 1913.

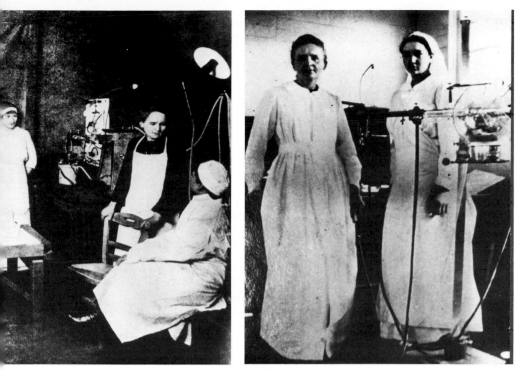

Marie Curie with fellow X-ray workers at the front.

Marie Curie and Irène with X-ray equipment installed at the hospital in Hoogstade, Belgium, 1915.

Marie Curie at the wheel of one of the radiology cars she equipped, October 1917.

Marie Curie's Radium Institute.

Marie Curie and Irène in 1921.

Marie Curie with her daughters on a balcony at the rear of the institute in 1918. Marie Curie's laboratory was on the other side of the glass doors.

TOP: *Marie Curie during her visit to a radium manufacturer in Pittsburgh in 1921.*

CENTER: *Marie Curie with Missy Meloney, Irène, and Eve shortly after her arrival in the United States for her first visit in 1921.*

BOTTOM: *Marie Curie with her family during a visit to Poland.* FROM LEFT: *Marie, Helena, Bronia, and Józef.*

Marie Curie on the balcony outside her laboratory.

Eve Curie.

Irène Curie and Frederick Joliot.

Chapter Eleven

DESOLATION AND DESPAIR

THAT MONDAY EVENING, despite Marie's wish that he stay, Pierre ate a hurried dinner and took the train back to his obligations in Paris. Marie lingered with the girls in St. Rémy, to take advantage of the sunshine. But on Wednesday, she too returned to the city. By then the weather had turned raw, cold and rainy, so that there didn't seem much point in staying on. Besides, there was a dinner meeting that night of the Physics Society which she and Pierre planned to attend.

Over dinner at Foyot's restaurant, where the society met, Pierre spoke excitedly to Henri Poincaré of his current preoccupations: the need for more science education, and the phenomena of Eusapia Palladino. "Poincaré made some objections" about Eusapia, Marie remembered, "with his smile of the skeptic, curious about new things." Pierre "argued for the reality of the phenomena." Poincaré was struck by "the fecundity and the depth of [Curie's] thought, the new aspect which physical phenomena took on when looked at through that original and lucid mind."

The next day, Pierre had another meeting, this time with the recently formed Association of Professors of the Science Faculties. The association was the first organization Pierre had belonged to that excited him. He saw it as a possible counter to the establishment, a way to wrest decision making from the "one or two powerful people" who now determined who did or did not advance in the system. To the man who had vowed in his youth to be "extreme in everything," the fact that vice-rector Louis Liard and "most of the tenured faculty" already viewed the association with a "hostile eye" was a promising sign.

Pierre Curie's only fear, as he confided to Georges Gouy, was that the association would be too timid. His idea was to make "a burning demonstration against the *literati* and the *philosophes,"* a "declaration that teaching of science should be the dominant teaching in the boys' and girls' lycées." Also, he wanted promotion to be based on merit rather than seniority, and to be decided by the faculties rather than the deans. But already the president of the association, a mineralogist from Lille named Charles Barrois, was warning that they didn't want to "offend anybody," and that "secondary teaching isn't our business." It looked as though the association might confine itself to petty grievances about salaries and procedures, rather than the "general questions" Pierre preferred. There was also a danger that the struggle would degenerate into a battle between the provinces (represented by the association) and Paris, the seat of power; this, in Pierre Curie's opinion, would be "nearly fatal."

Other members found Pierre Curie impressive enough that they wanted to elect him president of the organization. But this, as Pierre wrote Gouy, was a terrible idea, "a diabolical invention to trouble the tranquillity of the world." When Gouy rescued his friend from this fate, the association elected Curie vice president instead. And it was in this capacity that he argued his causes when the group met on Thursday, April 19, at the Hôtel des Sociétés des savants.

Pierre left his laboratory a little before ten and traveled the mile or two across Paris in the rain to the meeting on rue Danton. Despite his wishes that the association take on large issues, his pleas that day focused on smaller ones. He argued that junior faculty too often were trapped in unrewarding positions, without opportunity for advancement. He also suggested (interestingly, in view of his own experience with radium) that new legislation needed to be drafted on dealing with accidents in laboratories. He promised to "conduct a campaign toward this goal."

Pierre Curie's new activism seemed to agree with him. "Never," Paul Langevin remembered later, "was he more lively and gay than at this meeting." Along with Langevin, Perrin, and others he saw all the time, Pierre was reunited that day with Joseph Kowalski, the Polish-born physicist from the University of Fribourg who had introduced him to Marie Skłodowska twelve years before. Kowalski was to join the Curies at their home for dinner, and Pierre, in an expansive mood, invited others in the luncheon party to reconvene on boulevard Kellerman that evening.

When the meeting broke up, some time after two, Pierre made his way back to the Latin Quarter in the company of Jean Perrin. Then, with his umbrella up for protection against the continuing downpour, he headed off alone in the direction of the Institut de France. He had some proofs to read at Gauthier-Villars, the publisher of *Comptes rendus,* whose offices were located on the quai des Grands Augustins. And he was planning to pay a visit to the Institute library, a little farther along the Seine in the same direction.

Huddled under his umbrella, Pierre Curie hurried toward Gauthier-Villars along the quais, passing the large open square of the place St. Michel, with its rococo, water-spewing dragons; walking along opposite the *bouquinistes,* their books and prints barely sheltered from the rain under the flimsy roofs of their small wood booths. At Gauthier-Villars, he found to his surprise that the doors were closed because of a strike. So he continued on along the quai toward the Institute.

As Pierre approached rue Dauphine, just a block from his destination, the rain and the traffic were heavy. The point of convergence of the pont Neuf, the quais and the rue Dauphine was one of the busiest intersections in all of Paris. Hackneys, trams, automobiles, horseback riders, and pedestrians all passed through there in large numbers as they made their way through Paris. Pierre was beginning to cross the street when a thirty-foot wagon, fully loaded with material for military uniforms and pulled by two large Percherons, came rumbling down off the *pont Neuf* into the intersection. When the driver, a former milkman named Louis Manin, saw a tram coming from his right along the quai Conti, he began to pull up his horses to allow it to pass. But the tram conductor, knowing that it was difficult for a heavily loaded wagon to stop on the downgrade, signaled the wagon driver to go forward.

According to the wagon driver, he had just passed through the intersection when a horse and carriage going in the opposite direction brushed by. Quite suddenly, out from behind the carriage appeared the figure of Pierre Curie, hurrying to cross the street. Curie collided with the front flank of one of the Percherons, and tried to hang on to the horse to keep from falling. But both horses, which the driver later acknowledged were young and unused to Paris traffic, reared, and Curie fell onto the pavement. The driver then jerked his horses to the left, in a frantic attempt to steer clear of the fallen body. The front wheels of the heavily laden wagon missed Curie completely, but the left rear wheel rolled into line with his head. The wagon, with its full load, weighed close to six thousand kilograms. The wheel crushed Pierre Curie's skull, killing him instantly.

Very quickly, a crowd gathered. Seeing the mortally wounded gentleman on the pavement, they turned their wrath on the wagon driver. Policemen on the scene had to surround the driver to protect him. But ultimately, after the driver was interrogated repeatedly and at length, along with other eyewitnesses, the police concluded that the accident was not his fault. Instead, it resulted from a combination of bad weather, poor visibility, and Pierre Curie's inattention.

Pierre Clerc, the lab assistant from the Sorbonne who tearfully identified Curie's body, said he had often told Pierre Curie that "he wasn't careful enough when he was walking in the street, or when he rode his bicycle. He was thinking of other things."

"Pierre Curie," wrote Academy president Emile Gautier, "was a Parisian, a Parisian of Paris; he had a good walk, a good eye and the habit of the pavement. But alas! as often happened to him, he was probably thinking of other things—of something less banal. . . . No one, in truth, could have been more distracted, more detached from material life, than this great bearded boy, who looked more like an old student, a bohemian sculptor or a nihilist than a professor and member of the Institute. He was always 'out of it' . . . chasing after some transcendent problem."

What Gautier didn't know was that Pierre Curie was not as sure-footed as he once had been. It may be that his weakened condition made him less able to stay on his feet after he collided with the big horse. It may be, too, that Pierre, who worried about the effect of damp weather on his leg and back pains, was just hurrying to get in out of the rain, rather than preoccupied with some great problem. Or the explanation may have been simpler yet: perhaps Pierre's large umbrella momentarily blinded him to the approach of the wagon.

No explanation, however, could undo the catastrophe. Very quickly, from the calling cards in his pockets, the police at the scene learned that the profusely bleeding man was Pierre Curie. Because no ambulance could make its way through the congestion, they put his body on a stretcher and walked with it to a nearby pharmacist, who said there was no first aid he could administer. At the police station a block away, in the Hôtel des Monnaies, a doctor pronounced Pierre Curie dead. The police went to the Sorbonne to inform Faculty of Sciences Dean Paul Appell of the tragedy. He was given, as a friend of the family, the terrible task of traveling to boulevard Kellerman to inform Pierre Curie's father and wife.

When Appell arrived at the house, accompanied by Jean Perrin, he discovered that Marie had gone to Fontenay-aux-Roses for the day with Irène. Only the baby Eve and Dr. Eugène Curie were at home. So it was the old man who first had to sustain the terrible shock. According to one account, he suspected the worst as soon as he opened the door and saw Perrin and Appell's stricken faces. "My son is dead," he pronounced, before they spoke a word. Over and over he repeated, mournfully, "What was he dreaming of this time?" For the next three hours he kept vigil with the others, waiting for his daughter-in-law to return. Finally, at around seven, Marie Curie learned the awful news.

Her first reaction, as she recalled in her journal, was disbelief.

> I enter the room. Someone says: 'He is dead.' Can one comprehend such words? Pierre is dead, he who I had seen leave looking fine this morning, he who I expected to press in my arms this evening, I will only see him dead and it's over forever. I repeat your name again and always 'Pierre, Pierre, Pierre, my Pierre,' alas that doesn't make him come back, he is gone forever, leaving me nothing but desolation and despair.

The next morning, front pages all over the Western world relayed the news: Pierre Curie, world-renowned scientist, killed in an accident on the streets of Paris. Pierre Curie, one journalist wrote, had "brushed up against death in his sparse laboratory . . . where the most dangerous experiments were conducted." But in the end he died "like an ordinary man," sliding under a heavily loaded wagon. "Physical forces," Paul Langevin wrote some weeks later, "affirmed once more their power over the most beautiful of all their creations, over human goodness and intelligence." Physical forces, in more awesome dimensions, visited the western United States that same terrible day. The papers which reported Pierre Curie's accidental death also brought news of the San Francisco earthquake, which reduced much of the city to ruins, killed hundreds, and left many thousands without food or shelter.

For Marie Curie, the loss of Pierre was a cataclysmic event which would reverberate through all her days and nights. It echoed the painful loss of her mother and sister in childhood. And because Pierre was her collaborator as well as her husband, it left her with a feeling that she could not continue as a scientist. Twenty-four years later, when she sat down to reconstruct a chronology of her life, Marie wrote that on April 19, 1906, "I lost my beloved Pierre, and with him all hope and all support for the rest of my life."

Until recently, all those outside the family could know of Marie Curie's reaction to the terrible event came from excerpts of a diary published in Eve Curie's 1937 biography, *Madame Curie*. But in January of 1990, the diary itself was made available to researchers. This mourning journal, kept sporadically for a year after the fateful day, is an eloquent and profoundly moving document. In it, we learn not only of Marie Curie's suffering but also of some of the pleasures and the tensions in her life with Pierre, and with their two young children. The journal also allows us to know Marie Curie intimately, away from those curious eyes which led her to develop a stiff public persona.

The mourning journal gives us the keen emotion under the dignified mask.

She began it on rue Cuvier on April 30, 1906, eleven days after the accident. "Dear Pierre," she wrote, "who I will never more see here, I want to speak to you in the silence of this laboratory, where I never thought I would have to live without you."

To understand what has happened, and to comfort herself, she starts by returning to the days leading up to the terrible event. She remembers the time in St. Rémy: her leaving Paris with the girls on Friday, believing it would be "good for Irène" and that Eve, who was being weaned, could manage it more easily away from the wet nurse. "You left for the laboratory as we were going to the train station," she recalls, "and I reproached you for not saying goodbye to me."

A mild tension lurks beneath the surface. Marie wants more attentiveness from Pierre, wants him to work less and spend more time with the family. "I made you promise," she recalls, "that you would join us Saturday evening." And yet, when she sends Irène off on her bicycle to meet the Saturday evening train, she is "not entirely sure" that Pierre will be on it. "The two of you arrived [at the house] together," she remembers, "Irène in tears because she had fallen and skinned her knee. Poor little girl, her knee is almost cured, but her father who cared for it is no longer with us."

Then, as sometimes happens when she is brought up suddenly against the reality of his death, she shifts from addressing Pierre as *tu* and talks about him in the more distant third person. "I was happy to have Pierre there," she writes. "He warmed his hands in front of the fire that I had lighted for him in the dining room, and he laughed to see Eve bring her hands up to the fire to rub them the same way."

That night, Pierre and Marie slept "pressed up against each other, as usual." But there was more worry than romance in the air. Marie gave Pierre one of Eve's little scarves "to cover your head," and Eve, who was sleeping in a basket in the same room, woke in the night and had to be rocked back to sleep. "I didn't want you [Pierre] to wake up," Marie remembered, "though you had wanted to."

That Sunday, Easter Sunday, turned out to be glorious, and Pierre and Marie took pleasure in the early signs of spring everywhere, in the children, and in being together. Pierre was outside as soon as he got up, taking a look at the countryside. Then Marie and the children joined him for a walk to the farm below to fetch milk. "You laughed to see Eve go in all the ruts in the road and climb up on the stony places along the way."

"Oh! how badly I remember," Marie laments in her journal, "the details escape me." And yet her memory of that day is rich with vivid details.

We were astonished to see broom in flower. Then you raised
the seat of Irène's bicycle and after lunch we all three went on
our bicycles into the Port Royal valley. The weather was exquisite. We stopped by a pond which is in the hollow where the
road passes from the other side of the valley. You showed some
plants and some animals to Irène, and we regretted that we
didn't know them better. Then we went through Milon-la-
Chappelle and stopped in the meadow on the other side. We
collected flowers and we examined some of them with Irène.
We had also cut some branches of flowering mahonia, and
made a large bouquet of the big marsh marigolds you loved so
much.

A painful paradox interrupts her reminiscence. "You brought
this bouquet back to Paris with you the next day," she writes, "and it
lived still when you were dead."

Marie returns to her reminiscence of the time in St. Rémy. Back
at the house that day, a variation on a familiar difficulty arose between
them. Pierre was tired, wanting to remain with the family, but also
worried about his obligations in Paris. Marie prevailed upon him to
stay; the next day was even more blissful than the day before.

In the morning you sat in the meadow that one comes to along
the little road to the village. . . . Irène ran after butterflies with
her pesky little net and you discovered that she wasn't catching
any. But she caught one to her great delight, I led her off to
give it back its freedom. I sat up against you and I lay across
your body. We were happy. . . . I felt calm and full of a sweet
tenderness toward the excellent companion who was there with
me, I felt that my life belonged to him . . . my heart overflowed
with affection for you, my Pierre, and I was happy to feel that
there, near you, in this beautiful sun and facing the divine view
of the valley, I lacked nothing.

As they sat watching Irène run in the meadow, "happy about her
grace and beauty," Marie covered Pierre "so you could rest." But
Pierre insisted on walking with her to the farm above for milk. "I was
a little worried that you might tire yourself, but I was happy all the
same because I didn't want to leave you. We went slowly." Then,
deciding to look for the ponds with water lilies they remembered from
the previous summer, they sent Emma (the maid) and Irène to the
farm and turned off in another direction, taking turns carrying Eve.

The ponds were almost dry, and there weren't any water lilies,
but the broom was in flower, we admired it a lot. . . . We sat
next to a millstone, and I took off my underskirt so that you
wouldn't stay seated on the ground with nothing under you,

you told me I was crazy and you scolded me but I didn't listen to you, I was afraid that you would get sick. . . . Emma and Irène finally came to join us. We saw Irène's . . . blouse from afar, it was getting late. We descended by the road through the woods and found some ravishing periwinkle there and some violets.

When they returned to the house, the little family idyll was quickly over. "Once we got back you wanted to leave," Marie remembers. "I was very unhappy, but I couldn't oppose you." In retrospect, Marie regrets that she didn't return with Pierre. "I wanted to give the children one more day in the country. Why was I so misguided? I lived one day less with you." She stayed until Wednesday, returning in "nasty cold and rain. . . . It was already the weather that was to cost you your life."

Back in Paris, familiar tensions resurfaced. Both Marie and Pierre resented having to go to a meeting of the Society of Physicists that night, and Marie wondered if she shouldn't perhaps have stayed at home. Nonetheless, she made the trip into the city to meet Pierre and go. "I came to get you . . . at the laboratory," she remembers. "I saw you by the window with your smock and your hat . . . in front of the barometer. . . . You said to me that you had thought that with the bad weather I wouldn't have regretted leaving St. Rémy. I answered you that in fact that was true. . . . You went to get your overcoat and your hat. . . . We left for Foyot Restaurant. It was the last time I was to dine with you."

At dinner, seated on either side of Henri Poincaré, the Curies argued for "the need to replace literary education with an education closer to nature." Marie "spoke to him of an article that had pleased us . . . (wasn't it at St. Rémy that we read that?). Then a little annoyed at having talked so much, I tried to pass the word to you, obeying this feeling that I so often had that what you could say would be more interesting than what I could say myself. . . . I always had this unshakeable confidence in you, in your worth."

On the way home on the train, the conversation about education continued.

In front of our house we were still speaking about this question of education that interested us so much. I told you that the people we spoke to didn't understand our idea, that they viewed the teaching of the natural sciences as a presentation of the usual facts, that they didn't understand that we were talking about giving children a great love of nature, of life, at the same time as a curiosity about understanding it. You agreed with me, and we felt that there was a rare and wonderful mutual understanding between us. Did you say it then? I don't remember, but how many times have you said to me, my Pierre: 'we really have the same way of seeing everything.'

The next morning, the strains of daily living surfaced again. Emma, the maid, wanted a raise, and Pierre, in response, reproached her for not keeping up the house well enough. "You were in a hurry," Marie remembers, "I was taking care of the children, you left, asking me from below if I was coming to the laboratory. I answered you that I had no idea and I begged you not to torment me. And that is when you left, and the last sentence that I spoke to you was not a sentence of love and tenderness. . . . Nothing has troubled my tranquillity more."

At this point in the journal, an entire page is torn out. It is unclear who tore it out, or why. But it is likely that it was either Marie, or someone in Marie's family after her death. Whoever did the censoring of this and subsequent passages in the journal seems to have been concerned about revealing too much of both the tensions and the intimacies in the marriage. In this instance, one can guess that Marie elaborated on her desire to be with the children (it was school vacation time, and Irène was at home) and Pierre's wish that she spend more time with him at the laboratory. As it turned out, she decided to go on an outing with Irène to Fontenay-aux-Roses, despite Pierre's wishes. Undoubtedly, this sharpened her anguish when she returned home to learn that Pierre was dead.

That evening, after she learned the news, Marie sat "for some deathly hours" waiting for the wagon carrying Pierre's body to arrive at boulevard Kellerman. "They brought me objects they found on you: your fountain pen, your calling cards, your wallet, your keys, your watch, this watch which didn't stop when your poor head received the shock which crushed it." Those things, she laments, are "all that I have left of you, along with some old letters and some papers . . . all I have in exchange for the beloved and tender friend with whom I planned to spend my life."

When they arrived with his body, Marie remembers, "I kissed your face in the wagon, so little changed!" After stretcher-bearers carried the body into a downstairs bedroom, "I kissed you again, and you were still supple and almost warm, and I kissed your dear hand which still flexed."

Someone told her to go away while they took off Pierre's clothes and she, "numb," obeyed. Afterward, she regretted it, feeling that "it was my job to pull off your poor bloody rags . . . no one else should have touched you. Afterward . . . I was less and less able to detach myself from you, and I stayed in your room more and more, and I caressed your face and I kissed it."

> Pierre, my Pierre, there you are calm like a poor wounded one, sleeping with his head wrapped up. And your face is still sweet and serene, it's still you enclosed in a dream from which you cannot emerge. Your lips that I used to call *gourmande* are pale and discolored. Your little graying beard; one can barely see your hair, because the wound begins there, and on the right one can see the bone sticking out from under the forehead. Oh! how you were hurt, how you bled, your clothes were all inundated with blood. What a terrible shock your poor head, that I had caressed so often, taking it in my hands, endured. And I still kiss your eyelids which you closed so often so that I could kiss them, offering me your head with a familiar movement which I remember today, and which I will see fade more and more in my memory. . . . I should have the memory of a painter or a sculptor so that . . . your dear image will never fade away."

The days that followed were "gloomy and frightful." The next day, Pierre's brother Jacques arrived from Montpellier. He, more than anyone else, understood Marie's grief. "The first word that Jacques said beside your bed was 'he had all the qualities; there was not another like him.' . . . his presence was a comfort to me. Together we stayed near to the one we had the deepest affection for, together we mourned, together we reread the old letters and what remained of his journal."

On Saturday, they buried Pierre at the cemetery in Sceaux, not far from the house he had lived in with his parents.

> We put you in the coffin . . . and I held your head for this move. Isn't it true that you wouldn't have wanted anyone else to hold this head? I kissed you, Jacques also, and also André [Debierne], we put the last kiss on your cold face which was still so precious. Then some flowers in the casket and the little picture of me, "petite étudiante bien sage" as you said, that you loved so much. . . . it was the picture of the one you chose as your companion, of the one who had had the happiness to please you so much that you didn't hesitate to make her the offer of sharing your life, even when you had only seen her a few times. And you had said to me many times that it was the only time in your life when you acted without any hesitation, because you were absolutely convinced that it was right. My Pierre, I believe you were not mistaken . . . our union was meant to be. But, alas, it was meant to last longer.

Marie refused to allow the usual black chiffon to be draped over the closed coffin, covering it instead with flowers and watching over it in the downstairs bedroom until it came time to go with it to the cemetery. It was then, sitting alone with the coffin, that she believed she felt Pierre's presence.

> I put my head against [the coffin] . . . and in great distress . . . I spoke to you. I told you that I loved you and that I had always loved you with all my heart. . . . I promised that I would never give another the place that you occupied in my life and that I would try to live as you would have wanted me to live. And it seemed to me that from this cold contact of my forehead with the casket something came to me, something like a calm and an intuition that I would yet find the courage to live. Was this an illusion or was this an accumulation of energy coming from you and condensing in the closed casket which came to me . . . as an act of charity on your part?

Marie had decided on a very small ceremony at the grave, knowing that Pierre would have wanted it that way. Even so, there was "a frightful line of people" who wanted to greet her at the cemetery in Sceaux. She and Jacques escaped them in order to watch the gravediggers cover the coffin with dirt. "They packed the ditch, then put on some bundles of flowers, everything was over, Pierre sleeps his last sleep under the ground, it's the end of everything, of everything, everything."

Marie had succeeded in avoiding the "noise and ceremonies that you hated" at the funeral. But for many weeks, there would be letters and speeches in tribute to him. Some were pro forma expressions of condolence from public figures, sometimes revealing complete ignorance of Pierre Curie. At the Institute, a member spoke of a great scientist who accepted fame only because it "brought glory to France." This of a man who hated nationalism and had twice refused the Legion of Honor!

Many of the tributes, however, were genuine and deeply felt. "All those who knew him," wrote Henri Poincaré, "knew . . . the delicate charm that was exhaled . . . by his gentle modesty, by his naive directness, by the fineness of his spirit. . . . Who would have thought that so much gentleness concealed an intransigent soul? He did not compromise those general principles on which he was nourished, nor the particular moral ideal he had been taught to love, that ideal of absolute sincerity, too high, perhaps, for the world in which we live."

Charles Cheveneau, who had been Pierre Curie's student, wrote of his students' "worship" of him. "His immense kindness extended even to his most humble helpers, who adored him. I have never seen more sincere and more heartbreaking tears than those shed by the laboratory boys on the news of his sudden death."

Even those who had disagreed with him paid heartfelt tribute. Marcelin Berthelot, the influential chemist who had sometimes doubted Pierre, wrote that the news that this "genial inventor" was dead hit him "like a thunderbolt." And Ernest Rutherford wrote from England that "although I only had the pleasure of a few hours' acquaintance with Prof. Curie, yet our scientific connection has been so close that I feel as if I had lost a personal friend, as well as an esteemed colleague. . . . I think that only those who were early engaged in investigations in Radioactivity can form a true estimate of the magnitude of the work he accomplished in the face of so many difficulties."

Of all the tributes, none was more eloquent than that written by Paul Langevin, two months after Pierre Curie's death and published in the *Revue du mois.* "Very near here," Langevin began, "in the depths of a valley full at this moment of flowers and fragrances, the great physicist and excellent man who was Pierre Curie now rests."

It has been two months since we led him there to sleep an eternal sleep, in the tranquil cemetery, overlooking the hills of Sceaux and of Fontenay where he so often walked immersed in lively thought. It has been two months since . . . blind matter, mother of life and of pain, destroyed the brain which understood it, dominated it and loved it. . . . It has been two months, and yet those who lived close to him, who were accustomed to sharing their ideas and their doubts with him, are scarcely able still to accept the loss. . . . The hour when we knew we could meet him, when he loved to talk about his science, the walk that we often took with him, these bring back his memory day after day, evoke his kindly and pensive face, his luminous eyes, his beautiful expressive head, shaped by twenty-five years spent in the laboratory, by a life of unrelenting work, of complete simplicity, at once thoughtful and industrious, by his continual concern with moral beauty, by an elegance of mind which produced in him the habit of believing nothing, of doing nothing, of saying nothing, of accepting nothing in his thought or in his actions which was not perfectly clear and which he did not entirely understand.

Langevin, a promising physicist of thirty-four, had first met Pierre Curie when he arrived at the École de physique et chimie as "a timid and often clumsy beginner" of only seventeen. Later, he became one of Pierre's closest friends. When Pierre went to the Sorbonne, Langevin assumed his teaching duties at the EPCI. "It is in the laboratory," Langevin wrote, "that my memories, still so fresh, are most likely to bring him back to me. . . ."

I see him, tall and thin, a little bent usually with the weight of some difficult task, thick hair whitened prematurely above his broad forehead, fine features, a little thinner recently because of physical pains endured without any complaint, his face illuminated by a smile that reflected his exquisite goodness, brightened by his child's laugh, or attentive with his constant desire to observe and understand.

Sadly, Langevin observed, at his death Pierre Curie was about to have the freedom he had longed for. "Liberated for the year from the only teaching he still did, at the Sorbonne, feeling better also than he had for a long time, he was just arriving at a time when he would be able to devote himself exclusively to the laboratory." Now it was Marie Curie alone who must pursue their work, "coming every day, as in the best times, to the laboratory where memories evoked by objects and by familiar places at once sustain her and sadden her. She knows that she is rendering thus the most pious homage to the one who is no more and whose spirit survives in her."

It would be a month before Marie could bring herself to return to work in the lab, with all its painful reminders. In the beginning she withdrew entirely into the embrace of the family. Within a few days after the burial, Józef and Bronia arrived. "They are good," she reports in her journal, "but they talk too much in this house. . . . Around me they forget. As for me, I have some moments of nearly complete forgetfulness, and what amazes me very much, I can work for a few minutes. But the moments of calm are rare, and the feeling of obsessive distress reigns, with some moments of anguish, and also uneasiness, and sometimes the absurd idea that all that is an illusion and that you are coming back. Yesterday, hearing the front door close, I had the absurd idea that it was you!"

The children reacted in ways appropriate to their ages. Eve, sixteen months old, played with her uncles Józef and Jacques, "trotted around the house in unknowing gaiety." Nine-year-old Irène was more sober, staring "with big worried eyes at the black clothes we were wearing."

At first, Marie told Irène only that her father had hurt his head badly and couldn't come home. But on Sunday, the day after the burial, she went next door to the Perrins', where Irène was playing, and told her the truth. "She didn't understand at first and let me leave, without saying anything." Afterward she cried and asked to see her mother. "She cried a lot at the house, then she went back to her little friends' house to try to forget. She didn't ask any details and was afraid at first to speak of her father."

After sleeping the night in her mother's bed, she awoke

> half asleep, looking for me with her arms, she said in a plaintive voice, 'Mé [the children's word for their mother] isn't dead?' Now she no longer seems to be thinking about it, but she asked for the picture of her father that we had taken from the window in her bedroom. Today, writing to her cousin Madeleine, she didn't speak of her father. . . . She will soon forget him completely. . . . But the loss of this father will weigh on her existence and we will never know the harm this loss has done. Because I dreamed my Pierre, and I said it to you often, that this daughter, who promised to resemble you in her grave reflection and calm, would become as soon as possible your companion in work. . . . Who will give her what you would have been able to give her?

One by one, the visiting family departed—Jacques and Józef first, followed soon after by Bronia. But before she left, Bronia helped Marie with the gruesome task of disposing of the clothes Pierre was wearing at the time of the accident. Marie's account is unsparing: "Into a big fire I throw the tatters, cut up, of material with the clots of blood and the pieces of brain. Horror and misery, I kiss what remains of you in all that, I would like to intoxicate myself with my suffering, drink the cup down to the lees, so that every bit of your suffering would reverberate in me, stop my heart from bursting."

This entry is followed immediately by the most despairing of all those in the journal. "In the street," Marie writes, "I walk as though hypnotized, without care about anything. I will not kill myself, I don't even have the desire for suicide. But among all these carriages, isn't there one which will make me share the fate of my beloved?"

For weeks, everything Marie and Pierre had enjoyed together brought pain. On Sunday, April 22, just three days after the accident, she returned with Jacques, to the laboratory. "I tried to take a measurement for a curve on which each of us had made some points. But after some time I felt the impossibility of continuing. The laboratory had an infinite sadness and seemed a desert." After that, she returned only to make "the most pressing" measurements. "It seems at one moment that I feel nothing," she writes, "and that I can work and then the anguish returns. . . ."

To work, to laugh, to see the coming of spring bloom—all of this reminds her that she is alone. "My Pierre," she writes on May 7, "life is atrocious without you, it is anguish without a name, a desolation without limits."

> Since you ceased to exist, it has been eighteen days, the thought of you hasn't left me a single instant, except when I was sleeping. . . . I have more and more difficulty thinking of other things and as a result working. Yesterday, for the first time since the terrible day, a funny word spoken by Irène made me laugh, but I felt badly as I was laughing. Remember how you reproached yourself for laughing a few days after the death of your mother? . . . My Pierre, I think of you without respite and without end, my head bursts with it and my reason is troubled. I don't understand how I can live as I used to without seeing you, without smiling at the sweet companion of my life. . . . For the last two days I've seen that the trees have leaves and that the garden is beautiful. This morning I admired the beautiful children there. I thought that you would have found them beautiful also and that you would have called me to show me the periwinkles and the narcissus in flower.

At the cemetery, which she visited often, she sometimes found a measure of peace. "I am closer there to Pierre," she writes, "and more tranquil for living with my thoughts." But even there she feels regret. "Yesterday, I was at the cemetery," she writes two and a half weeks after the accident. "I couldn't comprehend the words Pierre Curie engraved on the stone. The sun and the beauty of the countryside made me feel bad and I put my veil on in order to see everything through my crepe. . . .

> Pierre, how my heart aches with the memory of the dear image, it seems to me that the effort of my suffering should suffice to break it and to finish my life from which you have departed. . . . Oh the longing to see you, to see your good smile, the sweet face, to hear the grave and gentle voice, and to press up one against the other as we often did. Pierre, I can't, I don't want to endure this. Life isn't possible. To see you sacrificed like this . . . never will I have enough tears to cry for this. . . .

During the first month, Marie refuses not to mourn; everything else seems a betrayal. "I am aware . . . that if I am to have the least chance in my work," she writes after three weeks, "it is necessary that I not think of my unhappiness while working. But not only can I not succeed at this right now, but even the idea that that could happen is repugnant to me. It seems to me that after losing Pierre, I will not ever be able to laugh genuinely until the end of my days." A few days later, she writes that she slept well and rose feeling fairly calm. "And there is a quarter hour of that and here I am once again wanting to scream like a savage beast."

As spring ripens into summer, her sadness seems to deepen. "My little Pierre," she writes in mid-May, "I would like to tell you that the false ebony trees are in bloom, the wisterias, the hawthorns, the iris are starting up, and you would have liked to see all that and to warm yourself in the sun. . . . I want to tell you that I no longer love the sun nor the flowers . . . I feel better in the gray weather like the day of the death, and if I don't hate the beautiful weather it's because my children need it."

Slowly and inevitably, the needs of the children, the possibilities of research begin to call Marie back to the land of the living. "I work in the laboratory all my days," she reports in this same entry. "I am better there than anywhere else. I feel more and more that my life with you, Pierre, is irrevocably over. . . . I can't conceive anymore of anything that could give me true personal joy except perhaps scientific work." But she quickly adds, "And still not that, because if I should succeed, I would be desolate that you knew nothing of it."

> Still this laboratory provides me with the illusion that I am holding on to a piece of your life and the evidence of your passage. I found again a little picture of you next to the scales, a picture by an amateur certainly and not at all a work of art, but of such a nice smiling expression that I can't see it without sobs rising in my chest.

Nearly a month goes by before Marie writes in her journal again. Then, on June 10, she reports that she is crying less. "My pain is less acute . . . I have . . . tried to create a great silence around me, and to make the entire world forget me. In spite of that I can scarcely live with my thoughts. The house, the children and the laboratory preoccupy me constantly. But at no moment do I forget that I have lost Pierre, only I often can't concentrate my thought on him, and I wait with impatience for the moment when I can . . . I endure life, but I believe that never again will I be able to enjoy it. . . . Because I don't have a gay or serene soul by nature and I leaned on the sweet serenity of Pierre . . . and the source is gone."

Very shortly after Pierre's death, the question arose as to what would happen to the chair at the Sorbonne that had been created for him. The obvious solution was to offer it to his wife and chief collaborator. But at the time, this was a revolutionary idea. No woman had ever been appointed to teach at the Sorbonne, let alone to hold a chair. On May 3, just two weeks after the accident, a commission of the Faculté des sciences proposed a compromise solution: the chair would be left vacant, and Marie Curie would be named *chargé de cours* and director of the laboratory. In other words, Marie Curie was asked to assume Pierre's duties without assuming his chair.

Friends, knowing that work was essential to Marie Curie's recovery, urged her to accept. Georges Gouy, suffering from "unrelenting pain" about the loss of his friend, pointed out that "the chair was created for Pierre; the creation was the end result of his discoveries and yours. . . . The traditions connected with it, the instruments created, the supply of precious materials, all of that carries his imprint. Wouldn't it be infinitely preferable that all that should be conserved with pious care, that a stranger shouldn't have it and that the name Curie should continue to be attached to it? Isn't it the only way to save what can be saved out of this ruin? . . . Don't you think that Pierre would have been happy to think that his work would be continued by you, his collaborator, who alone knows the inner workings of his projects and methods?"

In her journal, Marie talked with her lost Pierre about the situation:

> They have offered that I should take your place, my Pierre . . . I accepted. I don't know if it is good or bad. You often said to me that you would have liked for me to teach a course at the Sorbonne. Also I would like to at least make an effort to continue the work. Sometimes it seems to me that that's the way it will be easiest for me to live, other times it seems to me that I am crazy to undertake that. How many times have I said that if I didn't have you, I probably wouldn't work anymore? I put all my hope for scientific work in you and here I dare to undertake it without you. You said that it was wrong to speak that way that 'it was necessary to continue no matter what' but how many times did you say to me yourself that 'if you didn't have me, you might work, but you would be nothing more than a body without a soul.' And how will I find a soul when mine has left with you?

On May 14, not quite a month after Pierre's death, she reported in her journal she had been officially named Pierre's successor, adding "there are some imbeciles who have actually congratulated me."

Between June and November, Marie wrote nothing in the journal. She continued to work in the laboratory, and as fall approached spent more and more time preparing to teach Pierre's course at the Sorbonne. Dutifully, she entered progress reports on the children in her notebook: Irène learned to swim in June at the municipal pool, but didn't dare jump in the water. Eve was in very good health. In the summertime, Marie returned to St. Rémy with the children and was joined there by Jacques and his family.

On November 5, 1906, Marie Curie became the first woman in history to teach at the Sorbonne. It was a historic occasion, and turned out to be a fashionable one as well. The lecture was to begin at one-thirty, but several hundred had gathered in front of the closed iron gate of the Sorbonne well before noon that day. When the doors opened, the crowd rushed through, filling every bench of the physics amphitheater and every inch of standing room, until guards had to close the gates to prevent overcrowding. A young Sévrienne in attendance saw "men-about-town, artists, reporters, photographers, French and foreign celebrities, many young women from the Polish colony, and also some students." Because she had had to leave Sèvres precipitously, Marie Curie had managed to obtain permission for her advanced class from Sèvres to attend her Sorbonne lectures. They sat in the front rows. Nearby, in dramatic contrast, were women of fashion in enormous hats. The Countess Greffulhe, a patron of the arts whose *salon* was much in fashion, was among those who came to see and be seen. "Fortunately," one journalist observed acidly, "the amphitheater was terraced."

The main attraction that day, however, was Marie Curie, who was scheduled to walk out one of the wooden doors at the front of the amphitheater at one-thirty and take her place before the long table on which her husband used to perform his spectacular demonstrations. Most in attendance undoubtedly hoped for drama: a tearful tribute to her late husband, perhaps, or at the very least some acknowledgement of this historic day, of the courage of those who had dared to appoint a woman to the faculty of the Sorbonne. But Marie Curie gave them none of this.

Instead she entered "almost furtively" at the appointed hour, to an enormous ovation. "She looked very pale to us," the Sèvres student remembered, "her face impassive, her black dress extremely simple; one saw only her luminous, large forehead, crowned by abundant and filmy ashen blonde hair, which she pulled back tight without succeeding in hiding her beauty." With her gaze fixed on the Sévriennes in the front row, she began right away to summarize the research of the last decade in physics. "When one considers the progress in physics in the last decade," the lecture began, "one is surprised by the changes it has produced in our ideas about electricity and about matter."

Probably anything Marie Curie had said or done would have moved such a primed audience. According to one observer, all of the women and many of the men were moved to tears by this impersonal opening sentence. What they didn't know was that this occasion, which they found so thrilling and fascinating, was sheer torture for Marie Curie. The next day, she sat down to write about it in her journal:

> Yesterday I gave the first class replacing my Pierre. What grief and what despair! You would have been happy to see me as a professor at the Sorbonne, and I myself would have so willingly done it for you—But to do it in your place, my Pierre, could one dream of a thing more cruel. And how I suffered with it, and how depressed I am. I feel very much that all my ability to live is dead in me, and I have nothing left but the duty to raise my children and also the will to continue the work I have agreed to. Maybe also the desire to prove to the world and above all to myself that that which you loved so much has some real value. I also have a vague hope, very weak alas, that you perhaps know about my sad life and the effort and that you would be grateful and also that I will find you perhaps more easily in the other world if there is one. . . . That is now the only preoccupation of my life. I can no longer think of living for myself, I don't have the desire nor the faculty, I don't feel at all lively any more nor young, I no longer know what joy is or even pleasure. Tomorrow I will be 39. . . . I probably have only a little time to realize at least a part of the work that I have begun.

The morning before giving that first lecture, Marie had paid a visit to Pierre's grave in Sceaux. She had decided by then that she would move to Sceaux with the girls and Dr. Curie in the spring, partly because it was Pierre's family home and the site of his grave. "I would like to go often [to the cemetery] when I live in Sceaux," she wrote, "because I believe that there I will be able to think of you more peacefully than elsewhere where life constantly distracts me."

As much as possible during that year, Marie Curie kept to herself. To her former student, Eugénie Feytis, who felt neglected, she explained:

> Don't think that I'm no longer interested in you and what concerns you. I have the same warm feelings for you as in the past, but . . . I no longer am able to devote any time to social life. All our friends in common will tell you that I never see them anymore except for business: for questions concerning work or education of the children. No one visits me, and I don't see anyone and I haven't been able to avoid offending some people in my circle and my laboratory who don't find me sufficiently friendly. . . . I have completely lost the habit of conversations without a set goal.

A year after the accident Marie Curie's depression was still so profound that it prompted a gentle lecture from Jacques. "I believe that many years will pass before you will get used to this loss and this separation. Nonetheless I hope that, forced to take charge of all your daily duties, you have found a little energy to overcome your despondency; you are the center of a little world and your responsibility is great. You must revive and carry on in spite of everything."

But when she returned to her journal on the anniversary of Pierre's death to make one last entry, Marie Curie was still in despair. "It has been a year," she wrote in April 1907. "I live, for your children, for your old father. The grief is mute but still there. The burden is heavy on my shoulders. How sweet it would be to go to sleep and not wake up. How young my dear ones are. How tired I feel!"

Chapter Twelve

A NEW ALCHEMY

> *For I am every dead thing, in whom*
> *love wrought new alchemy.*
> —*John Donne*

After Pierre died, Marie rarely spoke his name. "Until the end of her days," according to Eve Curie, "it was with the greatest difficulty that [she] could pronounce 'Pierre' or 'Pierre Curie' or 'your father' or 'my husband,' and her conversation, in order to get round the little islets of memory, was to employ incredible stratagems." But if his name was rarely uttered, Pierre Curie's spirit filled the silences.

In the first four years after his death, Marie sustained herself by living for his sake, and by his ideals. Her first new scientific publication after his death was a paper he had started on the effect of gravity on radioactive materials. The first sentence began, "Pierre Curie observed some years ago. . . . " Soon after that, she wrote a loving introduction to the Gauthier-Villars publication of Pierre Curie's complete works, emphasizing his "power to exercise a profound influence, not only through his great intelligence but also through his moral integrity and the infinite charm that he radiated and to which it was difficult to remain indifferent."

For Marie, clearly, Pierre's power to influence continued beyond the grave. Unlike her husband, she was not averse to public recognition. But when France proposed to offer her the prized Legion of Honor four years after Pierre's death, she wrote back explaining that it was impossible for her to accept "decorations in general and the Order of the Legion of Honor in particular. . . . For me this is not a matter of a personal opinion," she explained, "but a real case of conscience, growing out of the respect I owe to the memory of Pierre Curie, who did not want to be decorated. It is a question of a religion of memories [*une religion de souvenirs*] which it is not possible for me to compromise under any circumstances."

Marie Curie's "religion of memories" was one of the reasons why she decided, in the spring of 1907, to move from the boulevard Kellerman to the small house in the more remote western suburb of Sceaux. The train ride to the Sorbonne was longer, but she could more easily visit Pierre's grave beneath the chestnut trees in the Sceaux cemetery. Sceaux was also the home of Pierre's youth, and familiar ground for her father-in-law, who would have more room there to cultivate his garden. What's more, in Sceaux the girls had more chance to play outdoors. Soon after moving to a "house without charm," at 6 rue Chemin de fer in Sceaux, Marie installed a crossbar with a trapeze, rings, and a rope so that Irène and Eve could practice their gymnastics.

When it came to raising the children, Marie did not necessarily adhere only to Pierre's ideas. The child of educators, she had strong views of her own. Interestingly, given her own tendency to overwork, she had a particular horror of educational programs which kept children too long at their books; fresh air, exercise, and free time were essential in her opinion to healthy development.

It was partly the wish to limit the hours spent in school which inspired Marie to organize an unusual education experiment in the year after Pierre died. A cooperative in which parents did the teaching, it was an elaboration of the home schooling Pierre had experienced as a boy. Its curriculum was in keeping with the Curies' conviction, the topic of one of their last conversations, that more time should be spent on the sciences and less on classics in early education.

"It is rather curious," Irène noted in retrospect, "that my mother, who was the good student *par excellence,* succeeding in everything, had such distrust of the educational program in the lycées; one must infer there perhaps in part the influence of my father . . . who would never have been able to be a normal good student because he . . . couldn't move rapidly from one subject to another, as one is obliged to do in classes." Perhaps Marie guessed that Irène, who had her father's meditative qualities, would have struggled as well in a conventional classroom.

The "school" which Marie organized involved about ten children, offspring of the Perrins, the Langevins, and Edouard and Alice Chavannes, and Henri Mouton of the Pasteur Institute. Alice Chavannes, whose husband was a professor of Chinese at the *Collège de France* and who was to become a good friend, taught the children English, German, and geography. Henriette Perrin taught history and French. There was a sculptor named Magrou for modeling and drawing. Henri Mouton introduced the children to natural science, and Paul Langevin, Pierre Curie's good friend and successor at the École de physique et chimie, taught mathematics.

For the most part, the cooperative, like the "Flying University" Marie had attended in Warsaw, met in living rooms. But physics and chemistry, taught by hands-on practical experiments in the manner Pierre and Marie preferred, took place in the laboratory. Jean Perrin taught the children physics in his small lab at the Sorbonne and Marie Curie taught chemistry on Pierre Curie's old turf at the École de physique et chimie.

Marie could be a stern taskmaster, especially when it came to questions of orderliness in the lab. "If one of the apprentices created a disorder or dirt in constructing an electric pile, Marie grew red with anger. " 'Don't tell me you will clean it *afterward*. One must *never* dirty a table during an experiment.' " But such rigor came with a playfulness in the experiments themselves. Bicycle bearings were dipped in ink and rolled on an inclined plane to study the law of falling bodies. A thermometer was constructed by the pupils and found to work like a manufactured one. Marie, who was very good at doing arithmetic in her head, coached her students in the technique. The secret, she explained, was not to go too fast. "You must get so you *never* make a mistake."

According to Eugénie Feytis, the Sévrienne who was a sometime baby-sitter, the little traveling band seemed to enjoy this impromptu school they attended. "One had only to see their joy," Feytis wrote, "before brilliant combustions of oxygen or the successful measure of electrolysis." Afterward, traveling back toward the western suburbs on the train, they got Irène to translate from Sienkiewicz's *Quo Vadis,* which she was reading in Polish. Often, they got off at the Sceaux-Ceinture stop for their classes with Henriette Perrin. Other times, they would travel farther out for classes with Madame Chavannes in Fontenay-aux-Roses. Sometimes, instead of class, they visited museums in Paris: the Louvre, the Musée Carnavalet.

The cooperative's hours left plenty of time for extracurricular activities. Irène and, later, Eve were encouraged to pursue them all. "My mother," Irène recalled years later, "tried to give us every opportunity for physical exercise, either through outings or sports. We did gymnastics, swimming, bicycling, horseback riding, we rowed, we skated." Because she began to ski before it became a fashion, Irène boasted in later life that she was "one of the oldest skiiers in France."

Eve, who was too young to attend the cooperative school during its two-year existence, remembered early-morning tutoring by her mother, after which she and Irène were "sent into the open air." There were long walks and physical exercises "in all weather. . . . hands and limbs were constantly on trial. Marie," wrote Eve, "however tired she might be, compelled herself to accompany them in their jaunts on bicycles."

As this last sentence suggests, Marie's daughters were keenly aware from an early age that things were not easy for their mother. After Pierre's death, she watched over their development with even greater vigilance. Often, she took the train home from the laboratory at lunchtime to see them, sometimes bringing a delicacy for Eve, who was a fussy eater, and making sure that everything was going according to plan in the household. Her entries in the notebook she kept to record their progress were longer than ever, and filled with pride over her daughters' accomplishments.

But the great, unmentioned loss cast a pall over the household. Marie's niece, who came from Poland to study in Paris during this period and lived in the house, remembered long after that Marie Curie wanted to be involved in every detail around the house, from making preserves to fittings of her daughters' dresses. And yet when she came home from work she was "mostly silent and tired" and moved around the house "almost without a sound, in her soft, gray wool robe resembling a nun's habit." Eve wrote years later that one of her earliest memories was "of my mother collapsing on the floor in a faint, in the dining room at Sceaux—and of her pallor, her mortal inertia." Despite her eagerness to give her daughters the best possible upbringing, Marie was unable to give them the thing they would have liked best: a mother unencumbered by grief.

Writing to her childhood friend Kazia in 1907, Marie confessed that her life was "upset in such a way that it will never be put right again. . . . I want to bring up my children as well as possible, but even they cannot awaken life in me. They are both good, sweet and rather pretty. I am making great efforts to give them a solid and healthy development. When I think of the younger one's age, I see it will take twenty years to make grown persons of them. I doubt if I last so long . . . grief does not have a salutary effect on strength and health."

Fortunately for the children, Pierre's father Eugène Curie was an important presence in the household. It was he, along with a series of Polish governesses, who provided companionship to the little girls during Marie's long days at the laboratory. A rationalist *par excellence,* the old doctor saw no reason to linger in the past; he refused to join Marie in her pilgrimages to Pierre's grave. "The father and the wife of Pierre Curie had a thousand reasons to understand each other," Eugénie Feytis Cotton noted, "having both had a great love for the . . . one who was gone." But while both were determined "not to allow themselves to be defeated," they approached the challenge differently—she with "desperate courage," he with a sort of "smiling serenity." "The presence of Dr. Curie," Eve has written, "was a joy for the girls. Without the old man with blue eyes, their childhood would have been smothered by grief."

Irène, who was "slow and timid" in the way Pierre had been, became the grandfather's special charge. When they were apart, he wrote her loving, playful letters. As early as the summer of 1906, only a few months after his son's death, he wrote Irène in the words of her baby sister. "Eu,eu,eu," read the letter, signed by Eve and followed by an explanation. "My dear Irène, my dear big grandchild. I am sending this letter from Eve who is telling you that she has received the postcards that you have sent her. I think that you will recognize her style."

Such playfulness, foreign to Marie even in the best of times, delighted Irène, who begged for more: "My good grandfather. I would very much like you to send me one of your amusing letters." Several years later, when Iréne signed a letter to him, "Your little Irène of nothing at all," he responded with a lecture: "No, you are not a little Irène of nothing at all. You are . . . my big Irène. Irène of everything. My big Irène of six slices of bread and butter who would smother a little Irène of nothing at all. My big Irène with her certificates of study, who has just crossed the Beauce and its fields of wheat dotted with poppies. My big Irène who writes regularly to her old grandfather, something the little Irène of nothing at all didn't often do."

According to Eve, the grandfather's influence on Irène's intellectual life was "decisive." "Her horror of grieving, her implacable attachment to the real, her anticlericalism, even her political sympathies, come to her in a direct line from her grandfather." Irène stresses her grandfather's "literary" influence: "He had me read many things, memorize poetry of which I understood only half the meaning but of which I felt the beauty. As a result I have always loved poetry very much."

Eugène Cune's most important role, however, was without a doubt emotional. One visitor to the Curie household described a humming, happy little universe, with the grandfather at the center. "Rising at dawn," wrote Alice Chavannes, "[the grandfather] cultivated his garden until the children's steps sounded in the house; his daughter-in-law, no less a morning person than he, gave orders, looked over the smallest details of her house, then took the 7:55 train to Paris leaving the direction of the household to a governess and that of the children's occupations to her father-in-law."

The cooperative school ended in 1909, partly because of the too great demands it placed upon the teachers, and partly because its students needed the training official programs could provide for the *baccalauréat* exam. Marie Curie sometimes stayed home in the mornings to tutor Irène and her friend Isabelle Chavannes in mathematics. On such occasions, another happy family scene would occur at lunch. "The students dined gaily with their teacher," Alice Chavannes remembered, "and it was then that the good grandfather gave, *à propos* plants of the garden, a fish brought back from the market, a frog collected in a jar, one of his luminous insights into natural history, insights which brought back to the old doctor the time when he studied botany and anatomy."

But Alice Chavannes, who painted this idyllic picture of family life, was only an occasional visitor. Eve Curie remembers home differently. "The struggle against sorrow, active in Irène, had little success in my case," she writes. "My young years were not happy ones." Under two when her father died, and preceded by Irène in the affections of her grandfather, Eve was keenly aware of her mother's absence, both physical and emotional. She remembers that her mother was "ever away from home—always kept at the laboratory of which the name was endlessly rumbling in their ears," and that the Polish governesses, hired after Józef's sister-in-law Maria Kamienska returned to Poland, were "less reliable and less charming" than she had been.

Just as she suppressed Pierre's name, Marie suppressed her grief. But "her near ones watched uneasily when her dull gaze was vaguely fixed on nothing." Silence and withdrawal could come at any time. Once, according to Eve, Marie decided to punish Irène for an impertinence by not speaking to her for two days. Irène wrote of another occasion, when her mother was teaching mathematics to her and Isabelle Chavannes. "I think," Irène recalled, "that I must have been on the moon sometimes during these lessons. . . . One day my mother, having asked me a question to which I should have been able to answer easily and getting no result, was overcome with impatience that she manifested by throwing my notebook out the window, into the garden. I went down two floors without a word, came back with my notebook and responded to the question." The reprimand was given, and accepted, in silence. "My mother," Eve remembers, "would not allow anybody to raise his voice, whether in anger or in joy."

It was this silent, depressed house which Marie's niece and namesake (Józef's daughter) remembers from the year she lived with her aunt Marie and her cousins Irene and Eve. "I will never forget those solemn evenings," Maria Skłodowska wrote years later. "Every night, again and again, both the thirteen-year-old Irène and the five-year-old Eva tried to win [their mother's] attention and her favors. Irène, who was very possessive of her mother, spoke seriously about her successful studies; and Eva, warbling like a little bird, moved around the table trying to get her beloved Mé to pay some attention to her too."

The hunger for Marie Curie's attention and affection, the need to engage her and cheer her, as well as a certain solicitousness, recur in the letters Irène wrote to her mother from the seashore during long summer vacations.

In 1906, the summer just after Pierre's death, the family had returned to the familiar St. Rémy. But for the next three years Marie chose seaside places, free of painful memories, for the long vacations of summer. Two of those years, she took the children to Arromanches, a small fishing port tucked into a dip in the cliffs of Normandy coast. The beach at Arromanches, as Marie explained to a colleague, was "on the shore of the Channel, surrounded by green fields and enclosed by equally green cliffs. The air is very gentle and very good there." Marie herself spent part of the summer at the beach, taking warm baths and writing. But for much of the time, Irène and Eve were there without her, staying in the house of a local couple in the company of their governess and various family visitors. And it was from there that Irène wrote some of her earliest letters to her mother.

They are charming letters, written in ink in a child's deliberate script, sometimes illustrated with country subjects, sometimes embellished with ink blotches. Irène's tenderness toward her mother, always called Mé by her children, is apparent in the salutations: "sweet Mé," "good Mé," and "dear good Mé."

A letter written in the summer of 1907, when Irène was nine, is typical. "My dear good Mé," she begins. "I have caught lots of prawns, and yesterday I shared a pretty little lobster with Madeleine. I am very happy to be at the sea and I am making some very beautiful forts in the sand and some very beautiful scratches, scrapes and grazes on my arms and legs. Every morning I come to eat breakfast in bare feet. But all in all, I am very well."

Except for a few minor complaints about a loose tooth or two, Irène's letters are filled with reassurances about how healthy she is. Her mother's wish, expressed in a letter to her childhood friend Kazia, that her children should grow up "solid and healthy" is Irène's command. Most of all, she emphasizes all the swimming she is doing in the health-giving waters of the ocean. "I am taking some very nice swims," she reports in one letter, and "I bathe in the sea as often as possible." After Marie has come and gone the first summer, she writes that she has "only missed one bath since you left." The next summer, at age ten, she reports that "I have a good appetite, the bathing is doing me good."

Besides swimming, the other recurring theme of young Irène's letters is "work." "I love Mé very much, I am working, and I am happy," is a typical conclusion. "I read every day in Polish," she writes at age nine, "and I understand fairly well, but it is very difficult." Two years later, writing from yet another seashore on the southwest coast, near Royan, Irène reports that during a visit from a young Polish woman "who barely knows ten words of French" she has been obliged "to speak to her in Polish. That makes for some very good lessons for me," notes the eleven-year-old, "but I breathe great sighs of happiness when I have finished a sentence." In fact, both Irène and Eve learned their mother's native language fairly well; Eve's Polish, according to one visitor, was impeccable, and Irène's allowed her, at age eleven, to write a letter in Polish to her Uncle Józef.

For Irène, however, the favored "work" was mathematics, perhaps in part because it provided a direct and exclusive link to her mother. Like her father before her, Marie included math problems in her letters to her daughter. Irène could sometimes solve them, sometimes not. "I couldn't do problem number two," the nine-year-old Irène reports to her mother, "that is the two equations with the two unknowns, but I am sending you numbers three and four. M. Hornois [the husband in the family they were staying with] helped me with three, I did four by myself." And at age eleven, from another seashore, "I've forgotten a little what you have to do to get the derivation of a radical and of the two numbers that divide it. You would do well to send me the rules of derivations and some examples."

Irene's letters are full of thoughts of home, especially of animals and flowers. From Palais-sur-mer near Royan in the summer of 1909, she writes a letter in the form of ten questions. She wants to know if Filou and Tigrette (who may have been mice or guinea pigs) have escaped. "If they are still in the house," she adds, "that's dangerous. If you see them, write me if they are fat, and if they are being given anything to eat." She wants to know too if "my palm tree" and "my monkey puzzle tree" are doing well, if "the peaches in my garden are getting ripe," what flowers are "blooming in my garden." Her last questions seem intended to reach out to her mother in her grief: "What are the flowers on Pé's [Pierre Curie's] tomb?" she asks. And "which ones are in flower?"

There is a kind of longing in these letters reminiscent of the young boy's longing for his mother's kiss at bedtime in Marcel Proust's *Remembrance of Things Past*. "I would like to know," she writes in one letter, "if Mé will take some [sea baths] and what day you will come, on what train and if that will be soon." Or, another time, "It has been a long time since I have received a letter from the good Mé and I would like to have one." "Come back soon, my good Mé." "I would like to know the exact day of your arrival." And "I will be very happy when you come because I have great need to cuddle someone."

Probably Marie Curie believed, like the family of Proust's hero, that it was a mistake to respond to such longings in a child, and that bearing them was part of growing up. There is no evidence that she worried about the effect of these long summer separations from her daughters. On the contrary, she was pleased that the girls could be at the seashore all summer, and regularly recorded the benefits in her progress notes. In 1907, she reported that Irène had a "superb appearance" after her summer in Arromanches, and that "she is becoming a good swimmer." After the summer of 1908 she wrote of Irene: "Looks very good. Good swim and bath daily. Bicycle trip of 50 kilometers." The next year, it was "Excellent health. Takes 71 swims in the sea. Swims very well." There are similar entries for Eve, who by age five "takes regular baths in the sea," is in "excellent condition," and "grew several centimeters during the summer." Marie's concern was that her children should get the best possible upbringing. It didn't occur to her that her presence was required.

Marie's behavior during this period was strikingly like her own mother's at around the same age. Bronisława Skłodowska, knowing that her years were numbered, was forced to spend her time far from her children, but poured a great deal of energy into watching over their education and upbringing. Marie, who believed she wouldn't live long, also spent much of her time away, while remaining involved in every aspect of child rearing.

Like Bronisława Skłodowska's children, Marie Curie's daughters performed spectacularly in almost every sphere despite the sadness that surrounded them. In June of 1909, Marie recorded in her journal that Irène, with the informal schooling her mother had provided, received the "certificate of primary studies." As for Eve, she began early on to show remarkable musical abilities. Marie, who did not have her mother's musical gifts, took careful notes as Eve began to display them. "She begins at three years and four months to pick out an air, 'Au clair de la lune,' on the piano. She takes singing lessons with Madame Chavannes and plays at the house. At three and a half, she knows how to play some airs and recognizes all the others. . . . At four years, she knows how to play around thirty airs and songs. She goes from piano to piano playing a new air that she hears and picks it out perfectly, makes few mistakes and knows when she does. At Christmas . . . she also picks out the 'Marseillaise.' Before she is four and a half she recognizes the notes without a mistake and can play the corresponding note on the piano." In other words, Eve has perfect pitch.

By the time she was six, Eve's "astonishing musical abilities" led Marie to ask her countryman Ignacy Jan Paderewski to listen to her play. Afterward, she wrote about it in her notebook as only a proud mother could:

June 9, 1911. Eve is presented to Paderewski; she plays "Marlborough" and *"Il pleut, il pleut bergère."* Paderewski thinks that
she has exceptional ability. . . . I felt great emotion in hearing
these words from the mouth of the great pianist and musician,
words which give hope that my little child has a marvelous gift.
I had an intuition about it, I who understand nothing of music,
I felt very much that she didn't play like just anyone, . . . but I
wouldn't have dared to put forward such an opinion. And still I
was the one in the whole group who understood best that there
was something more than ordinary ability, *something altogether different.* When I heard her play "Marlborough," I always said to myself, "A child doesn't play like that."

Though she kept a certain emotional distance, Marie was not the
kind of mother who cared only for her children's outward successes.
Particularly at times of great loss and suffering, she could be empathic
and caring. Such was the case when Dr. Curie, *grandpère* to all in
the family, became seriously ill with a pneumonia. Knowing how
close Irène was to her grandfather, Marie watched her older daughter
carefully. "The year 1909 is that of the illness of *grandpère,*"she wrote
in the notebook. "Irène is concerned, takes care of him, stays near
him. She is devoted and affectionate. At the end of the year [as his
condition worsens] she is very unhappy and suffers."

Marie too was devoting all her spare time to her ailing father-in-
law, a "difficult" and "impatient" invalid whom she tried to amuse.
"The little packets that she brought from Paris," Alice Chavannes
remembers, "were always destined for *grandpère* . . . delicacies, illustrated newspapers, reviews." When he became gravely ill, at the end
of 1909, Marie moved his bed to the living room and slept on a cot in
the dining room, so that she could be nearby when he needed her.

When the end came, in February of 1910, Marie recorded Irene's
reaction in her notebook. "She is very shaken. Her pain is deep. She
saw her grandfather dead and was present at the burial. During the
entire year after she cried a lot, thought of her father, worried about
losing me too, attached herself to me even more than ever. She suffers and matures."

For months after, Irène's grief was often palpable. On one spring
day, Marie wrote in her notebook, "I see her eyes fill suddenly with
tears at the table where we are alone. I ask her what's the matter.

"Are you thinking of your grandfather?"
"Yes, I am thinking that he also loved the sun and the flowers."

Marie too was "preoccupied and saddened" after Dr. Eugène
Curie died. But this loss was nothing like the death of her beloved
Pierre at an unnatural age. Before the burial of *grandpère,* Marie had

the gravediggers perform a task which re-evoked that tragedy. In the bare, frozen cemetery, they dug up the coffin of Pierre and placed it to one side, lowered the coffin of his father, then replaced that of Pierre above it. Marie wanted to lie on top of her husband when she died.

To those who loved her, Marie seemed to be leaning toward the grave. Jacques Curie, reacting to a photograph she sent him two years after Pierre died, noted that "the two little girls are a pleasure to see, but you! How sad you look! My wife cried so much when she saw how thin and drained you were. You must rally a little, if it is only for your children who need for you to last a long time still!"

In her introduction to Pierre's complete works, Marie concluded that Pierre Curie had been about to enter "a new era" in his work when he died. "Fate did not wish it to be so," she wrote, "and we are forced to bow before its inexorable decision." To many who knew her, Marie Curie herself seemed to bow almost to breaking under fate's terrible blow. "Everybody said," noted Marguerite Borel, " 'Mme Curie is dead to the world. She is a scientist walled in behind her grief.' "

But in the spring after her father-in-law's death, Marie Curie appeared for after-dinner coffee at the Borels' house one night looking suddenly rejuvenated. Instead of her usual black, she was dressed "in a white gown, with a rose at the waist. She sat down, quiet as always, but something signaled her resurrection, just as the springtime succeeding an icy winter announces itself subtly, in the details."

The next day, Jean Perrin, who had witnessed this astonishing change, returned to talk it over with Marguerite Borel. "What's happened to her?" he wondered aloud. Neither Marguerite Borel nor Jean Perrin knew what to make of it.

PAUL LANGEVIN'S friends worried about him in much the same way that Marie Curie's worried about her. "His emotional state concerned us," Marguerite Borel remembers. "We thought about it a lot, I, my husband, Jean Perrin . . ." Besides long bouts of depression, Langevin suffered from chronic stomach problems, which sometimes became acute enough to interfere with his work. Everyone's fear, according to Borel, was that " 'Paul's nerves are going to give out on him.' " More than once, an entire evening's amusement was organized around the need to "distract Paul."

Among his friends, it was generally understood that the reason for Langevin's unhappiness was his troubled marriage. "They can't comprehend at his house," Borel explains, "that he refuses magnificent situations . . . in private industry to dedicate himself to science, he says he will die of these struggles, but can't give up research."

Early on, Langevin confided to Jean Perrin that the marriage had been a mistake and that he was paying for his "inexperience."

Paul Langevin married Emma Jeanne Desfosses, the daughter of an artisan who specialized in making ceramic copies of artworks, in 1898. He was twenty-six and his bride was twenty-two. Problems seem to have arisen very early. Henriette Perrin remembers that there were "terrible scenes" at the time of the birth of the first child, Jean, in 1899, largely because of the "stupid interference" of Jeanne's mother.

"Terrible scenes," scenes which in the retelling sound like farce, seem to have been a staple of Paul Langevin's married life. He told Jean Perrin that two months before his first son was born, his mother-in-law and sister-in-law "stole" letters from his pockets—letters in which his own mother expressed concern about his marital situation. When he asked for them back, his wife told him she was keeping them for "ammunition" in case of divorce. Later, he came upon the letters one day "hidden under a chandelier," at which point his "wife and sister-in-law pounced on him and took them back by force."

One of Langevin's closest confidants, Jean Perrin, got his next indication of trouble in the marriage when Paul came to see him at the lab and asked him to keep eight hundred francs he wanted to give to his relatives. He told Perrin that he didn't feel the money was safe at home. "He complained of the spitefulness of the three women who tormented him (his wife, . . . his sister-in-law and his mother-in-law), citing many facts which I have now forgotten."

For a little while after that, it seemed things were going better. A second child was born in 1901, and Langevin told Perrin that though he had thought of divorce, he couldn't bring himself to it because of the children. Then one day Langevin appeared in the laboratory with his face covered with bruises. When Jean Perrin asked him what had happened, Langevin said, "I told the others that I fell off a bicycle, but in fact I was hit at my house by iron chairs." He explained that he and his wife had had an argument over their respective mothers. According to Langevin, his mother had decided never to come to the house again because of his wife's insults. Then he had insisted that Jeanne's mother should never come. When he came home unexpectedly one day, found his mother-in-law there, and insisted she leave, a quarrel ensued. Perhaps Langevin's mother-in-law was retaliating for his attempt to banish her. Whatever the reason, the mother-in-law "armed herself with an iron chair and threw it at him, assisted by her daughters." From time to time, Langevin also complained about his wife's "crude" insults and "brutalities," but "it was extremely disagreeable to him to go into detail and I didn't question him."

Despite all the difficulties, Langevin seems still to have cared about, or at least depended on, his wife. In 1902, when she left him after one of their blistering arguments, he begged her to return. And after she became ill following the birth of a third child, Madeleine, he "cared for her with solicitude."

For some time after that, relations between the Langevins seemed to be more peaceful. "We found ourselves," Perrin remembers, "in frequent and very cordial contact with the Langevin household. . . . Madame Langevin . . . was always agreeable and smiling to my wife and me, while Paul often appeared to be in a somber mood. As I had, after all, never witnessed the violence I had been told about, I came to think the wrongs must have been committed by both equally."

Perrin's view was reinforced by the fact that Jeanne Langevin complained to Henriette Perrin about her husband's "harshness." What's more, Paul Langevin "didn't defend himself . . . , as though admitting implicitly certain wrongs." When Henriette asked him one day to be gentle and patient, he replied that his wife was "insolent." Perhaps Langevin expected subservience, as husbands were wont to do in France of the Belle Époque, and reacted angrily when he didn't get it. Perhaps Jeanne Langevin was simply a woman who refused to submit to her husband's will.

In any case, sometime in 1907 another blowup occurred, over the cooperative school that Marie Curie was organizing with the Langevins, the Perrins, and others. Because of the school, Henriette Perrin found herself at the Langevins' house in Fontenay-aux-Roses more frequently. "I grew more and more attached to M. Langevin and his wife," she recalled some years later. "I thought only minor misunderstandings separated them." Then one day she learned that "a huge scene had exploded regarding the setting up of a study room for the children. Madame Langevin told me the story, and I was especially moved by her telling me that little Jean [aged eight] had cried a lot, saying 'Maman, I love you a lot. Papa, I love you a lot. Don't fight.' " Paul Langevin also spoke to Henriette about the scene, asking her to try to persuade his wife to be less "insolent." He complained that she said things to him like "you will die crazy" and "you're the son of an alcoholic."

During the week following this scene, Henriette Perrin went to the Langevins' almost every day. "Often, during meals, M. Langevin, cruelly wounded by the words of his wife, left the table. The meal continued; no one even sent a child to find M. Langevin."

Henriette Perrin's sympathies, after this week in the house, shifted toward the husband. "I was very sad to see the unhappiness of a friend that I liked with all my heart and who had become one of my greatest preoccupations. He said to me, 'I don't know who I can lean on, I have only my children and they are very small.' " It was the kind of plea for mothering and sympathy which few women could resist. Least of all Marie Curie.

Henriette Perrin shared her concerns about Langevin with Marie Curie, who was "still plunged in her great grief." And sometime around 1907, Paul Langevin himself began to talk more intimately with Marie Curie about his difficulties. He said later that he was drawn to her "as to a light, in the sanctuary of mourning in which she was enclosed, with a fraternal affection borne of the friendship for her and her husband, brought close because of the common lessons we were giving to our children. . . . Little by little, I got in the habit of talking to her of the difficulties of my existence, which I had always kept quiet from my friends, and I began to seek from her a little of the tenderness which I missed at my house."

Marie Curie's life had been intertwined with Paul Langevin's for many years before she became his confidante. Langevin had first encountered Pierre Curie in 1888 when, at seventeen, he came to study under him at the École de physique et chimie. When Pierre finally left the EPCI in 1904, the young Langevin took over his job. Langevin and Marie Curie taught together at Sèvres, and Langevin —eager for work as the Curies had been at an earlier stage of their lives—succeeded Marie there when she was appointed to Pierre's post at the Sorbonne in 1906. Pierre Curie once wrote admiringly to Georges Gouy of Langevin's energy: "Langevin is standing in for Mascart at the College, my wife at Sèvres [when she was ill] and me at the *École de physique;* what's more he has a family, numerous students and he has been preparing a number of papers." Langevin had studied with J. J. Thomson in England, and the experience had made him, in Pierre's words, "a believer: he believes in ions [electrons] and knows everything about this new religion. And he is succeeding with all this; he is certainly the best physicist we have here right now."

According to those who attended his classes, Langevin was a brilliant and passionate teacher. Einstein remarked that "In his scientific thinking Langevin possessed an extraordinary vivacity and clarity. . . . [His courses] influenced more than a generation of French theoretical physicists in a decisive fashion." In Einstein's view, Langevin would have "developed the special theory of relativity if it hadn't been done elsewhere." And when Einstein came to France to discuss relativity, it was Langevin who stood by his side and supplemented Einstein's explanations. "Reason," Einstein noted, "was his religion; it was supposed to bring not only illumination but also redemption."

At the same time, Langevin was capable of strong and deep attachments. Langevin's grief at the loss of Pierre was apparent in his tribute, and must have been one of the reasons Marie drew closer to him. It must have helped, too, that he and Pierre thought so much alike: Langevin was also the son of a republican, a critic of French education, and a fierce adversary of tradition. Indeed, he had been more vocal than Pierre about his political beliefs: he was one of the signers of a petition circulated by Zola in 1898 in support of Dreyfus. And throughout his life, his devotion to causes meant that, as Einstein observed, "the fruit of his work appeared more in the publications of other scientists than in his own."

By 1907, at age thirty-five, Langevin had already made what is now considered his most important and original contribution to physics: his application of electron theory to the phenomena of magnetism. Characteristically, his work brings together the ideas of two of his most important mentors: J. J. Thomson, and Pierre Curie, whose 1895 experimental findings on magnetism it explained. As historian of science Bernadette Bensaude-Vincent has observed, Langevin had a talent for uniting seemingly unrelated research. He "produced new insights by astutely joining separate circuits." Marie Curie "greatly appreciated [Langevin's] wonderful intelligence," Henriette Perrin noted, "and pitied with me the way he was misunderstood by his entourage."

A trim, rather tall man, Langevin wore his dark hair in a brush cut and cultivated a broad handlebar mustache; in early photographs his eyes are blank and his face a broad plane. Only later, in informal pictures, do we see the transformation which occurred in good company. "When he talks about science," Marguerite Borel wrote many years later, ". . . about literature, about philosophical theories—he understands everything and is interested in everything—his very beautiful chestnut eyes and his whole face light up."

Marie Curie, too, liked his eyes. In the summer of 1910, she wrote him from the seashore:

> My dear Paul, I spent yesterday evening and night thinking of you, of the hours that we have spent together and of which I have kept a delicious memory. I still see your good and tender eyes, your charming smile, and I think only of the moment when I will find again all the sweetness of your presence.

It is not clear when the mutual sympathy between Marie Curie and Paul Langevin turned into love. For some years after Paul began to confide in Marie, relations between Marie and Paul and Jeanne Langevin seem to have continued to be simply friendly. Marie and her daughters vacationed with the Langevins at Arromanches in the summer of 1908. And as late as the spring of 1910, Jeanne Langevin still felt free to complain to Marie about her husband's harsh treatment of her. That may in fact have been the critical moment, because when Marie Curie reproached Paul Langevin, he exploded in anger and told her that his wife had broken a bottle over his head. This report of violence shocked Marie, and she mentioned it to Jean Perrin, who was also "troubled."

By mid-July of 1910, all the evidence suggests, Marie and Paul had become lovers. On July 15, they rented an apartment together near the Sorbonne—a two-room place on the fifth floor at 5 rue Banquier—and repaired there whenever they could spare time from work and family to be together. In their letters to each other, they called it "our place" *(chez nous)*. A note from Paul Langevin to Marie Curie began, "I write you in haste to tell you that, if you don't come in the morning, I will come back to our place in the afternoon after two."

> . . . I am so impatient to see you, much more than I am uneasy about the difficulties to come. It will be so good to hear your voice again and see your dear eyes. . . . Until Saturday, my darling, I will not stop thinking of you. I embrace you tenderly. . . . I am trying to obtain acceptable conditions of existence for us two and I agree with you about what we must do to obtain them. We will speak of that tomorrow. In any case, I'll pass by our place about eight o'clock.

Around this time, Jeanne Langevin began to show a "very lively" and—as it turned out—justified jealousy of Marie Curie. To Henriette Perrin, she complained that Marie and her husband often took the train together to work. Jean Perrin hadn't given the reports of jealousy much thought, but "toward the end of August 1910, I perceived that . . . the situation had become very grave." Jean Perrin's family was vacationing in Brittany at the time, and he came back alone from the seashore to Paris to finish up some work that he was preparing for the International Congress of Radiology and Electricity, to be held in Brussels in September. Marie Curie, hearing that he was in town, came to tell him that she was extremely concerned about Paul Langevin. "She had been without news of [him] for several days and feared that a letter from him might have been intercepted."

What she was in fact telling Jean Perrin indirectly was that she feared that Paul's letter to *her* had been "intercepted" by Jeanne. She told Perrin the letter in question was purely scientific in content, but was written "in a fraternal fashion." But it seems likely that by that time Paul Langevin's letters to Marie were openly romantic.

Something else Marie Curie told Perrin was even more disturbing than the theft of the letter. She said that "their great friendship angered Mme. Langevin," and "that she had declared to her husband that she was going to get rid of this obstacle." When Marie asked what this meant, Paul Langevin answered, "That means that she would kill you." Langevin thought his wife capable of murder, and considered the threat to be very serious.

The next day, Jean Perrin went to visit Paul Langevin at his home in Fontenay-aux-Roses and found him "very beaten and sad. [Perrin] learned from him that they were making his life impossible because a letter written by him to Madame Curie had been taken from the letter box by a servant . . . and given to his wife."

Jeanne Langevin was extremely excited. As soon as Perrin entered the house, she greeted him with: "Well, now, Monsieur Perrin, this is not a pretty picture, you are going to see quite a scandal in the newspapers." She continued her harangue at the table in front of the children, "even involving them, asking for example of her son Jean [aged eleven] if he was going to have a 'mistress.' "

It must have been clear at this point to Jean Perrin, as it was to Paul Langevin and Marie Curie, that Jeanne Langevin had it within her power, by means of this letter, to publicly disgrace both Paul and Marie, and that she was probably willing to do so, despite the pain and embarrassment she and her children would also suffer as a result. Good friend that he was, Perrin began to spend a part of each day trying to calm down Jeanne Langevin.

"I returned to Fontenay on the following day," Perrin later wrote, and "tried to convince Madame Langevin that . . . she was overexcited." On the fourth day of visiting with her, "Madame Langevin spoke to me more calmly and promised me to be gentle and I left a little bit reassured." But that night, Perrin found out that the dispute had escalated to a new and more dangerous level.

"I dined out and came back to my house after midnight," Perrin recalled. "I was astounded to see Madame Curie run to me as I was entering the house. She had been waiting for me for several hours on the fortifications on the boulevard [boulevard Kellerman], near my house. She said that she had been insulted in the street in crude terms by Madame Langevin and by her sister, Madame Bourgeois, that this woman had threatened her," told her "to leave France." Marie Curie explained to Perrin that she was afraid to return to her house in Sceaux, and that she didn't know where to go. "I think I will never forget the emotion I felt," Perrin later wrote, "seeing the distress to which this illustrious woman had been reduced, reduced to wandering like a beast being tracked."

The next day, and "all the days after," Perrin visited Madame Langevin. She was in a highly agitated state, "shouted threats for everyone to hear, that if Madame Curie didn't leave in eight days she would kill her." It was during this time that Perrin "got a sense of how difficult the marriage was and how the friendship of a woman like Madame Curie would have been a comfort and a support for my friend."

Perrin advised Marie Curie to leave France until things cooled down; but she, more courageous than on the day of the street encounter, refused to go. So instead, Perrin sat down with Jeanne and Paul Langevin, and Jeanne's brother-in-law Henri Bourgeois (an editor of the *Petit Journal* who was to play a more mischievous role later on), to work out a truce: it was agreed that Paul Langevin wouldn't see Marie Curie any more, even for scientific purposes. In exchange, Jeanne Langevin was to stop her threats of both physical violence and public scandal.

That was where matters stood when, in mid-September, Jean Perrin, Paul Langevin, and Marie Curie left for the International Congress of Radiology and Electricity in Brussels. Perhaps because of the stress at home, Marie "fell seriously ill." Ernest Rutherford, who had come from England, reported to his friend Bertram Boltwood that he sat next to Marie Curie at the opera "and found she was not well, and took her home halfway through. She was very miserable the next day and could not attend the Dinner; but was well enough next morning to leave with Perrin for Paris. I think she had been overworking, and some of the medical fraternity consider she is in a very bad nervous state."

Despite the distractions at home, Jean Perrin managed to present his groundbreaking work on Brownian movement, the mysterious activity of tiny particles suspended in liquid. "Perrin," Rutherford wrote, "gave a good paper . . . was very lively and jumped about like a jack-in-the box. I made the only joke of the meeting by saying that Professor Perrin himself was an admirable example of the Brownian movement." Rutherford was impatient with the rest of the French contribution: "Perrin, Becquerel, and some of the other Frenchmen took a whole hour talking of work about three years old," he reported. "They are incorrigible in the matter of length."

The most important decision of the congress was to establish an international standard for radium, a standard in which all results would be expressed. On the recommendation of an international committee which included Marie Curie, Rutherford, and other pre-eminent researchers from Europe and the United States, it was decided that Marie Curie should be charged with preparing a twenty-milligram sample of radium, to be kept in Paris, against which all other radium samples would be measured. It was also suggested that the unit of measurement (probably the amount of radium emanation equal to one gram of radium) be called a "curie," "in honour of the late Prof. Curie." Rutherford, reporting on the Congress in *Nature*, wrote that "thanks of all workers in this subject are due to Madame Curie in undertaking the full responsibility of preparation of a standard, and for the large expenditure of time and labour its preparation will involve."

But back in Paris, Marie Curie's private life threatened to overwhelm her professional duties. Jean Perrin's efforts to contain Jeanne Langevin turned out to have been in vain. Perhaps she realized that her husband's pledge not to see Madame Curie would be easy to violate in Brussels. Or perhaps she simply couldn't control her impulses, despite her promises. In any case, Perrin and Marie Curie learned on their return that Madame Langevin had repeated her murder threats against Marie to at least two other people in their absence.

Before returning to the laboratory, Marie Curie traveled north from Paris to join her family for a much-needed respite on the Brittany coast. That summer, and the summer before, Marie's sister Helena had come from Poland with her daughter Hania to accompany Eve and Irène to the the southwest coast. But in the late summer of 1910, it was decided that Helena would travel with the three girls to the Brittany coast for the latter half of the summer, to be joined by Marie at a place called l'Arcouëst.

L'Arcouëst was a little cluster of houses on the side of the cliffs that skirt the jagged red rocky shore of Brittany, not far from the town of Paimpol. Two academics, Charles Seignobos and Louis Lapicque, had come upon the site while hiking in the summer of 1895. By 1910, when Marie and her family visited, l'Arcouëst had become a magical place to the small group of Sorbonne professors, family, and friends who gathered there each summer. It was, in the words of Marguerite Borel, the "nucleus of a second family, this one of choice."

It would be several summers before Marie Curie and her daughters were accepted as regulars at l'Arcouëst. But eventually, it became a second home for them, as it did for the Perrins and the Borels. L'Arcouëst is linked to some of Irène and Eve's happiest memories. They remembered that their mother was often happy there as well.

By the time Marie Curie arrived there in the late summer of 1910, she was tired, sick, and preoccupied. But for the first time since Pierre's death, she was also excited about the future. Apparently, both she and Paul viewed the agreement not to see each other as temporary. It seemed possible, as she wrote to Langevin from l'Arcouëst, that she and Paul could find a way to live out their lives together.

> It would be so good to gain the freedom to see each other as much as our various occupations permit, to work together, to walk or to travel together, when conditions lend themselves. There are very deep affinities between us which only need a

favorable life situation to develop. We had some presentiment of it in the past, but it didn't come into full consciousness until we found ourselves face to face, me in mourning for the beautiful life that I had made for myself and which collapsed in such a disaster, you with your feeling that, in spite of your good will and your efforts, you had completely missed out on this family life which you had wished to be so rich in abundant joy.

The instinct which led us to each other was very powerful, since it helped us to overcome so many unfortunate impressions about the very different way in which each of us had understood, organized our private life.

What couldn't come out of this feeling, instinctive and so spontaneous and so compatible with our intellectual needs, to which it seems so admirably adapted? I believe that we could derive everything from it: good work in common, a good solid friendship, courage for life and even beautiful children of love in the most beautiful meaning of the word.

So began a very long and remarkable letter that Marie Curie wrote to Paul Langevin from l'Arcouëst that September. Clearly, she had allowed herself to hope that he might separate from, or divorce, Jeanne Langevin. But as the rest of the letter makes clear, she was also afraid of the forces arrayed against her: Paul Langevin's attachment to his wife; his susceptibility to her tears; his strong affection and concern for his four young children; and, finally, leaving the familiar for the unknown. The rest of Marie's letter was both a rumination and an attempt to fortify him. She begins by pointing out that she "must be tied to you by a very strong link," since she is risking her standing and indeed her life. "Think of that, my Paul, when you feel too invaded by fear of wronging your children; they will never risk as much as my poor little girls, who could become orphans between one day and the next if we don't arrive at a stable solution."

And what is a stable solution? "A separation which is as peaceful as possible." Marie doesn't believe that the arrangement which exists in some French households, in which the husband has a mistress, will ever be possible between Jeanne and Paul Langevin:

Your wife is incapable of remaining tranquil and allowing you your freedom; she will try always to exercise a constraint over you for all sorts of reasons: material interests, desire to distract herself and even simple idleness.

And even if Marie were not in the picture, she reminds Paul, his marriage would be full of conflict:

Don't forget either that you have constant disagreements about the education of the children or the life of the household; they are the same disagreements which have troubled your life since your marriage began and to which I am a complete stranger. A stable regime based on reciprocal liberty . . . making it possible for the children to have an atmosphere in which they could breathe, will never exist at your house. If she [Jeanne Langevin] committed herself to it, she would never be able to keep her promise, being too violent and too used to getting her way by violent means, then also too crude and too devoid of scruples to understand the harm she is doing to her children.

It may be that Marie had decided to go to l'Arcouëst because she needed the support of friends. Henriette Perrin said later that Marie "came to find me in Brittany" to talk about what was going on. Since the Perrins and Marie Curie were sharing the same house, and since their children played together, there were plenty of opportunities to talk. And much of what Marie Curie wrote she had discussed with the Perrins.

There was, for instance, the question of the custody of the Langevin children. After discussing it with the Perrins, Marie was convinced that it is "entirely illusory on your part to want to argue for joint custody of the children," since it would result in "hostilities with their mother over them, which is detestable." She adds that "that is also the opinion of Perrin."

Even leaving the children, as long as they are young, principally with their mother and her family, would be less bad than . . . the continual example of a family in a state of war. . . . If the separation took place, your wife would very quickly stop paying attention to her children, who she is incapable of guiding and who bore her, and you could take up little by little the preponderant direction.

Marie's final argument for the separation has to do with Langevin himself:

Finally, my Paul, there are not only your children to consider. There is you, your future as a scientist, your moral and intellectual life. All that has been in great danger for some years. All your friends know it, even if they don't know the reasons. You have seen what Perrin thinks. All those who love you: Perrin, Weiss, Bernard, Urbain, have been worried about your state for years; I have heard the same thing said by Seignobos. Your students at the College speak with uneasiness of your visible fatigue for whatever reason. You must realize all that. You can neither live nor breathe nor work in the atmosphere which you're in.

You haven't been able to work recently except when your wife was in the hospital. I speak of *preparatory reflection* for the paper that you wrote in August. *Your family is a milieu of irresistible, destructive power, and, I believe, altogether exceptional.* You can't live in this family without being manipulated by it to its own purpose, contrary even to the interest of this family, which should value you more than it does. Even your children become in this group an instrument of your oppression *and not at all in relation to their mother, who is too much of an egoist to allow herself to be exploited.*

The rest of Marie Curie's long letter is about strategy: what Paul should do to effect a separation. It sometimes sounds imperious, sometimes even cruel. It is clearly written with the understanding that Paul Langevin needs guidance, needs someone strong and hard-headed to counteract the pressures of his wife and her entourage.

It is certain that your wife will not readily accept a separation, because she has no interest in it; she has always lived by exploiting you and will not find that situation as advantageous. What's more, it is in her character to stay, when she thinks that you would like her to go. It is therefore necessary for you to decide, no matter how difficult that is for you, to do all that you can, methodically, to make her life insupportable. . . . the first time she proposes that she could allow you to separate while keeping the children, *you must accept without hesitation* to cut short the blackmail that she will attempt on this subject. It's enough for now that Jean continues to board at the lycée and that you live in Paris at the School [EPCI] [i.e., Paul will be able to visit his son Jean in Paris]; you could go to see your other children at Fontenay or have them brought to the Perrins'; the change wouldn't be so big as you think and *it would certainly be better for everyone.* We could maintain the same precautions we do now for seeing each other until the situation becomes stable.

Marie even suggests that they could agree not to see each other for a time (as they had in the earlier negotiation), if that would speed things along. "That would look better even to people outside," she notes, "who would [otherwise] go around saying that you left your wife for another woman. Really it would be better if you left her for the reason of emotional incompatibility."

Sometime during these difficult days, Marie Curie told Henriette Perrin that Paul Langevin had said, "Without your affection, I can't live." Marie asked Henriette, "When you know that a man is one of the most intelligent there is . . . should you refuse to do what you can to help him?" Characteristically, Marie Curie had cast herself in the role of rescuer, without owning up to her own desires. But in her long letter to Langevin, she reveals both her wish to rescue and her wish to possess, to have and to hold Paul Langevin. "We can't go on living in the current state," she writes, and goes on to urge him not to return to the marital bed. "One of the first things to do is to regain your room. . . . I still worry because I can't speak to you of unforeseen events." Quite understandably, Marie fears that Langevin's wife will try to hold on to him by becoming pregnant again. She fears "crises of tears which you resist so badly, ambushes in order to make her pregnant. . . . You must mistrust all of that. . . . I beg of you, don't make me wait too long for the separation of your beds. I could then watch with less fever the progress of your separation."

All of this seems quite rational and sensible. But the length and passion with which she pursues the subject reveal her jealousy.

> But when I know that you are with her, my nights are atrocious, I can't sleep, I manage with great difficulty to sleep two or three hours; I wake up with a sensation of fever and I can't work. Do what you can to be done with it.

> Don't ever come down [from the upstairs bedroom] unless she comes to look for you, work late, . . . As for the *pretext* that you were looking for, tell her that, working late and rising early, you absolutely have need of rest in order to be able to do your work, that her requirement of a common bed unnerves you and makes it impossible for you to have a real rest and that if you perhaps had given in out of lassitude during the vacation, you refuse absolutely to continue and that, if she insists, you will sleep in Paris with Jean.

> Do that, my Paul, I beg of you (you can speak of it with Perrin) and don't let yourself be touched by a crisis of crying and tears; think of the saying about the crocodile who cries because he has not eaten his prey; the tears of your wife are of this kind. It is necessary absolutely that she understand that she can expect nothing from you. When she has understood, she will no longer be unhappy, since you will give her the means to live largely as she pleases; she will be able then to look for pleasure and even affection elsewhere and find it.

The final pages of this very long letter deal with social relations, and encourage Paul to limit them so that his wife can't spread gossip further about the affair. Marie urges him especially not to move his wife and family into the apartments of the École de physique et chimie, where he teaches, since that would further complicate the situation.

> You know well that your wife, even if she promises and if it is in her interest, will not be able to control her violence and you know also that I can't encounter her. It will be impossible to avoid stories at the School. . . . But what's more there would always be the fear of a scandal.

In closing, Marie asks Paul to read her letter carefully and to discuss any or all of it with the Perrins (who seem to be traveling with it to Paris), "except for the phrases of personal tenderness." She ends: "Goodbye, my Paul, I embrace you with all my tenderness; I will try to return to work, even though it is difficult, when the nervous system is so strongly stirred up. . . . I await the joy of seeing you with impatience and I hope to have news of you tomorrow by way of Henriette."

Compared with Marie, who clearly spent many hours over her letter, in his reply Paul Langevin sounds harried and preoccupied back in Paris. He has "read and reread" her letter but doesn't have "time to respond in detail today." "To the extent that I am still able to judge our situation, I believe also that a separation will be better and I will do all that I can to make it happen without violence." His existence at the house is "extremely difficult for me and must be also for everyone. I try only to imagine what the change will be like for the children." He ends by assuring Marie of his conviction that his "entire moral life will be profoundly changed thanks to you." It cannot have been a very reassuring response.

At about the same time that Marie was writing to Paul Langevin, Jean Perrin was too, informing Paul that the Perrins would no longer welcome Jeanne Langevin at their house. "Without speaking of the incidents of violence, regrettable but at least not premeditated, which have sometimes troubled your household, your wife has recently made threats of murder serious enough so that we all have been afraid that she is capable of acting on them."

> By this brutal means, she has been able to get almost exactly what she wants, but I have received a terrible impression of her. . . . I have sometimes hidden this impression, because I wanted to develop . . . a well-considered opinion and also because I wanted to talk at length with Henriette, who had always shown your wife so much friendship . . . she [Henriette] is as incapable as I am of continuing to display sentiments that she can't feel. . . .

Perrin's letter was an attempt to end his involvement not only with Jeanne Langevin but with the whole marital quarrel.

I very much want you to understand that it is not a question at all of taking your wife's side or your side concerning the issues which have divided you (and which I don't want to be involved in any more). She may be right, she may be wrong, I am not concerned with that . . . it is the means that she employs much more than the end that she seeks which seems unacceptable to us. The single fact of comtemplating a premeditated murder, and even more daring to act through incessant threats of premeditated murder, creates between her and us *such a difference of moral structure* that it would be laughable to speak any more of friendship.

To Paul Langevin, Perrin promises continuing friendship:

As for you, we will see you as much as you wish, without speaking further of these things. . . . Excuse me once again, my dear friend if I increase your domestic difficulties with this letter, but truly there is no other way, there is no other way.

Perrin concludes that they are willing to resume their relationship with Jeanne Langevin if her threats turn out to be caused only by "fatigue and pain" and if she shows "by *actions* and not by words, that she is other than she has shown herself to be during these sad days."

In October, after everyone had returned to Paris, Henriette Perrin received a visit from Jeanne Langevin. "She was very changed, appeared very excited." Henriette told Jeanne of "my pain at all that had happened," including the bottle incident. "Madame Langevin didn't deny the incident, and assured me that if her husband saw Marie Curie, she would kill her. I made a great effort to dissuade Madame Langevin from this plan, I told her that she was at one of those turning points in life where one can keep one's friends or alienate them, save what one loves or lose it forever." To this, Madame Langevin answered " 'Madame Perrin, I don't have your temperament.' "

It would be another year before the explosive Langevin household finally blew apart, with disastrous effects for all concerned. And during that year, another event, seemingly unrelated, placed Marie Curie in greater jeopardy. After she returned to Paris from l'Arcouëst in the fall of 1910, Marie was approached by some of her colleagues about the possibilty of advancing her candidacy to fill the chair in the physics section of the Academy of Sciences vacated by the death of the chemist and physicist Désiré Gernez. The reasons for electing her seemed obvious. There were at the time three living Nobel Prize winners in France; all but Marie Curie, one of the first to be so honored, had long been members of the Institute. Marcel Brillouin had determined there was no legal reason why a woman couldn't become a member. After seeking the advice of Pierre's friend Georges Gouy, she agreed to be nominated. With her candidacy to the Institute, Marie Curie was to learn what trouble can come to a woman alone, if she is suspected not just of passion, but of ambition.

Chapter Thirteen

REJECTION

FAIRLY SOON after Pierre's death, Marie Curie began to play a leadership role which would not have been available to her had he survived. Within three years after the accident, the number of workers in her small laboratory on rue Cuvier had grown from seven to twenty-four. Using funds from the Carnegie Foundation, she was able to offer stipends to promising researchers from Poland and elsewhere. And she had extracted a financial commitment from the University of Paris and the Pasteur Institute to build a laboratory—the laboratory that had been promised to Pierre—according to her needs and specifications. Like her mother and sisters before her, Marie was proving an able administrator.

A case in point was her decision, in June of 1909, to place practicality above sentiment and fire the man who had been Pierre's lab assistant before he became her own. "For three years," she wrote Jacques Danne in June of 1909, "I have not asked you to give all your time or your service, and I have thus been deprived of assistance I have a right to . . . I hope that you will be willing to recognize that your situation with my husband . . . had very fortunate consequences for you . . . was privileged from all points of view and has remained so during these three years. . . . I think that you will understand the necessity . . . of reestablishing normal relations concerning the services of a lab assistant."

At the same time that she was asserting herself as an administrator, Marie Curie was increasingly taking on an international role as the keeper of the record in the field of radioactivity. To a certain extent, she had played this role even during Pierre's lifetime: when her discovery of polonium was challenged by Marckwald, she undertook the writing of a series of papers in German in response. But in

1908, in a paper entitled "Action of radium emanation on solutions of copper salts," she took on one of the most respected chemists of the day, Sir William Ramsay. Ramsay, as one Paris newspaper pointed out, "discovered five new gases in the atmosphere in less than five years: argon, helium, neon, krypton and xenon." In 1903 Ramsay had teamed up with Frederick Soddy to establish that helium was produced by radium, providing strong confirmation of Rutherford's disintegration theory.

Unfortunately Ramsay decided, after the success of the Soddy collaboration, to continue working in radioactivity on his own. An expert on detecting inert gases in the atmosphere, Ramsay was a neophyte in radioactivity. And experienced researchers in the field watched in disbelief as a whole series of new "discoveries" issued from his laboratory. He claimed that not only helium but also neon and argon were produced by radium. And he claimed that when radon, the emanation produced by radium, was combined with copper, the copper itself began to disintegrate or "decay" in much the same way that radioactive elements did. He claimed to have combined radon and copper and produced lithium, an element in the same series as copper but of lower atomic weight.

"If R[amsay] is right," Rutherford noted in a letter to his friend the American chemist Bertram Boltwood, "the subject of radioactivity enters a new phase." Many took Ramsay seriously. But Rutherford and Boltwood were skeptical in the extreme. "Why," Boltwood asked Rutherford in April of 1905, "doesn't Ramsay have one of his students rediscover radium? It offers lots of interesting possibilities!" Two years later, Rutherford reported to Boltwood that Ramsay "is very anxious to convert me & showed me all his methods. He is quite sure about it but he always is. I shall not be sure of them until I try it myself but at present intend to take a negative position." Ramsay's claim that he can obtain lithium from copper is, Rutherford writes, "rather more than I can momentarily swallow." He laments that "no one has any Ra[dium] to test his results." Almost a year later, Boltwood and Rutherford were still complaining about Ramsay. "I wonder," Boltwood wrote in May of 1908, "why it hasn't occurred to him that radium emanation and kerosine form lobster salad!!"

Unlike Rutherford, Marie Curie did have enough radium to test Ramsay's claims about copper turning into lithium. By the spring of 1908 she was trying to reproduce his results. What she found was that the glass vials in which Ramsay was combining radium and copper sulfates were introducing lithium into his final product. When platinum containers, free of lithium, were used to perform the same experiments, the amount of lithium was reduced to nearly nothing.

Ellen Gleditsch, a young Norwegian who had come to work in the lab and who was to become a friend and significant worker in the field, assisted Marie Curie in the experiments. "The work turned out to be laborious," Ellen Gleditsch remembered, "since everything, the copper salts . . . the distilled water, contained lithium in quantities recognizable with the spectroscope. Also, once one finally got a certain quantity of copper sulfate free of lithium, the introduction of the emanation into the little platinum container . . . was a delicate operation. . . . During the course of these experiments, I was able to see and appreciate Marie Curie at work on a scientific problem. She was very precise in manipulations, she judged everything which resulted with a lively critical intelligence, and she evaluated the results with perfect lucidity. I saw how much she took the success of an experiment to heart. She was devastated when she saw that the introduction of the emanation hadn't succeeded; when everything went well, she was happy, her eyes were luminous, and a smile transformed her ordinarily sad face."

Even at the seashore that summer, Marie continued to worry over her results in the copper/lithium experiments. "I decided anyway to publish the paper," she wrote Ellen Gleditsch from Arromanches, "but I am still a little bothered, and maybe I will redo one experiment after vacation." The brief paper, co-authored by Gleditsch, appeared in the *Comptes rendus* of August 10, 1908. It concluded that "the residue [of lithium] that we obtain is in all cases much weaker than that obtained by MM. Ramsay and Cameron, and this probably results from the suppression of the use of glass. . . . In summary, we can say that we have not succeeded in confirming the experiments of MM. Ramsay and Cameron . . . we believe in any case that the fact of the formation of these elements cannot be considered to have been established."

Undoubtedly, it was the fact that the copper/lithium claim had been "riddled by Madame Curie," as Rutherford put it, that led Ramsay to concede at a scientific meeting that September that the transformation was "difficult." In an exultant mood, Boltwood wrote in October that Ramsay "has been treed" and encouraged Rutherford not to "call off the dogs. . . . He should be absolutely discredited in all matters radioactive, for he entered the field under false colors and has been playing to the grandstand ever since." Boltwood was always reluctant to give Marie Curie credit, but in this instance he was impressed. "I must acknowledge . . . that I liked the way she summed up the situation in her "copper-lithium" paper. She certainly left no doubt in the mind of the reader as to where *she* stood in the matter."

For the rest of her life, Marie Curie would be the source of reliable information about radioactivity. It had been she who first isolated radium; it was she who, in 1907, established its atomic weight (226.45, within .55 of its currently accepted weight). After the Ramsay paper, her work for the next several years addressed questions of equivalents between radium and radium emanation, equivalents which would form the basis for the unit of measurement to be called the curie. It was she who was charged by the international commission with preparing a radium standard. And somehow, amidst the turmoil of the Langevin affair, Marie Curie also managed to write and publish the first work attempting to bring together all the research in radioactivity to date, in a two-volume *Traité de radioactivité*.

The memory of Pierre permeates Marie Curie's well-organized and lucid presentation of the "extremely rapid" development of the science of radioactivity in the *Traité*. A grave but handsome photograph of him is the frontispiece. And his name is mentioned often in the text. Rutherford in fact complained to Boltwood that at times Marie Curie was "very anxious to claim priority for . . . herself and her husband."

But Rutherford also concedes that "she has got a great deal of useful information collected together." Though he suspects she has included too much, and done so too uncritically, he admits that "she has been reasonably generous in the recognition of those outside of France. At any rate, I should judge I have not been neglected." Indeed, the *Traité de radioactivité,* which Marie Curie describes as "the collection of the lessons which have made up . . . the course in radioactivity taught at the Sorbonne," shows great respect for the work of the English scientists and its implications. She describes the discovery of the production of helium from radium, for instance, "one of the most important facts in the history of Radioactivity." Helium, she writes presciently, "forms, in all probability, one of the constituents of all or almost all the radioactive atoms, and is perhaps, in general, a constituent of the atomic edifice."

Rutherford commented, condescendingly, that "the poor woman has laboured tremendously, and her volumes will be very useful for a year or two." But Rutherford's judgment was colored by a certain pique that Marie Curie got there first. "In reading her book," he confided to Boltwood, "I could almost think I was reading my own [yet to be published] with the extra work of the last few years thrown in to fill up. Some of the chapters start in very much the same way, and the subject-matter is divided in much the same manner." He added, "I am glad to see that she has shown great discrimination in dealing with Ramsay's discoveries."

In a later letter, Rutherford reported that he had slowed down on his own book, "as there is no object in coming out so soon after Mme.

Curie's book." Subsequently, both Rutherford and Boltwood cited "Madame Curie's book."

Eugénie Feytis Cotton, who knew her well, believed that Marie Curie kept going during the years after Pierre's death not only because she was "a passionate researcher," but also "to prove, to those who kept insinuating it, that she was not simply Pierre Curie's assistant in their common work." Given her achievements before Pierre's death, it should have been necessary for Marie Curie to have to prove herself again afterward. But by 1910, as her colleagues prepared to nominate her for membership in the French Academy of Sciences, she had done it nonetheless.

IT IS NOT entirely clear why Marie Curie decided to place her name in nomination to the Academy in 1910, rather than before or after. The death of chemist and physicist Désiré Gernez on October 31 had left a position open. But members of the Academy, though sometimes called "the Immortals," died at regular intervals; it was not the first nor would it be the last opportunity. Probably her colleagues urged her to it because they felt an increasing discomfort about the fact that she was *not* a member, given her Nobel Prize, her pivotal role on the International Radium Standard Committee, and her membership in the Swedish, Dutch, Czech, and Polish Academies, the American Philosophical Society, and the Imperial Academy in St. Petersburg, among others.

Then too, as permanent secretary Gaston Darboux pointed out in a letter to *le Temps,* the Academy needed her. "A seat in our Academy, . . . if it gives legitimate satisfactions and some rights, also imposes extended duties. . . . For distributing all the prizes, all the grants, for rapidly evaluating the worth of the communications which come to it, the Academy obviously needs to draw on all its abilities. Where would the Academy find a scientist with greater authority than Madame Curie to give it an opinion on these works about radioactivity, whose number is growing so rapidly?"

Further, Darboux argued, the researchers in "the prosperous laboratory of Madame Curie" should have her as their advocate at the Academy. "Is there not an obvious interest in having the chief who inspires their work be admitted, like her other colleagues at the Sorbonne, to present their works, to defend them in the prize committees, to propose them for grants; in a word, to fulfill in all its breadth the role of titular member of the Academy of Sciences?"

In the beginning, Darboux and other supporters expected Marie Curie's candidacy to run up against the usual obstacles. It was assumed that her only serious challenger for a chair in the physics section would be a sixty-seven-year-old inventor named Edouard

Branly. And Branly, who had been a candidate before, and who had in fact shared the Prix Osiris with Marie Curie in 1903, had certain predictable allies.

Branly's career as a physicist had begun in 1869, two years after Marie Curie was born. But his most important discovery was made twenty years later, as he experimented with Hertz's recently discovered radio waves. He was the first, at his laboratory at the Catholic Institute, to discover that it was possible to effect a radio communication without a conducting wire. The receiver he fashioned came to be called a coherer, and was essential to Marconi's success in 1889 in establishing wireless communication between Bologna in Italy and Douvres in France, and later in sending signals across the English Channel. When he made the Douvres connection, Marconi sent a telegraph message thanking Branly, pointing out that "this beautiful result" was "due in part to [Branly's] remarkable work."

Branly was by all accounts a modest, quiet man. But others often made patriotic claims on his behalf. "We are happy," his eulogist remarked, "that such a great discovery as the wireless telegraph, like photography and cinematography, all inventions which have profoundly altered conditions of human life, has had its origins in the work of a Frenchman." Because he was a teacher at the Catholic Institute, Branly had the support of the generally conservative clerical faction. Pierre Curie, writing to Georges Gouy about Gouy's chances in competition with Edouard Branly for the 1905 Prix La Caze, had noted that "Branly would have all the clerics and nationalists on his side (according to them, the wireless telegraph is a French discovery!!)" Undoubtedly, nationalist sentiment for Branly was heightened by the fact that in 1909 Marconi, without Branly, had won the Nobel Prize.

When Marie wrote asking advice about her own candidacy for the Academy of Sciences, Pierre's old friend Gouy saw things in much the same way. "I can't but encourage you to accept the overtures," he wrote. "The struggle between you and M. Branly will arise most strongly on the clerical issue and it is clear that your adversary can count . . . on a good number of votes, but I believe . . . they will remain a minority. Against him will be the forward-looking and university elements of the Academy, which will hardly forgive him for having abandoned the Sorbonne some time ago for the Catholic Faculty. And then his work has little in it to compare to your qualifications."

Gouy's assessment was partly right. The clerical issue would play some role in the debate. But he overlooked the obvious fact which would transform the debate into a front-page story and "the joy of hostesses who don't want the conversation to languish": Marie Curie was a woman. If elected, she would be the first woman to become a member in the 215-year history of the Institut de France.

According to Darboux, whose long letter to *le Temps* on December 31, 1910, opened the debate, Madame Curie "has expressed the desire that her candidacy not give rise to any commentary in the press." But this, as Marie Curie should have known from her experience with the Nobel Prize, was wildly unrealistic. In the month between the first news of Marie Curie's nomination to the Academy and the vote, all the lively and opinionated penny newspapers of Paris, from the right-wing *Action française* to the socialist *l'Humanité,* took up the issue. And unlike her supporters, who saw it as a simple question of merit, most of the French press saw the candidacy as a symbol, or as a symptom, of the whole direction of the nation. All the familiar oppositions—between the masculine and the feminine, of course; but also between Church and Republic, between clerical educators and the Sorbonne, between foreigners and the true French; and of course, because it was an issue that wouldn't go away, between the pro-Dreyfus and anti-Dreyfus factions—were evoked by those who took up their pens to write, at length, about Marie Curie's candidacy to the Institute.

Marie Curie's supporters tried to keep the focus narrow. Gaston Darboux stressed her scientific accomplishments. "Your readers," wrote Darboux in *le Temps,* "know the name and reputation of Madame Curie, but perhaps it will be of use to recall the qualifications that she has acquired in recent times. For fourteen years she has pursued with tireless ardor, either alone or with her husband, an admirable number of research projects. . . . To those who might believe that she has simply been the helper to her husband, we can counter with the very touching testament which was made to her by Pierre Curie himself . . . in his [Nobel Prize] presentation. . . . Furthermore, since his tragic death, the productivity of Madame Curie has not slowed in the least. We cite only her recent success in isolating radium in a pure state and also the two beautiful volumes that she has just published [the *Traité de radioactivité*] in which she reviews, with admirable clarity and precision, not only her own research but also that of her emulators and her collaborators."

Darboux noted that other academies in other countries had allowed women in their midst, and that France, "which often marches in the avant-garde of nations," must follow their lead in this instance. And even though Marie Curie didn't want contention, Darboux was prepared to do battle on her behalf. "Now that the moment has come," Darboux wrote, "we will not hesitate to defend the cause which appears to us to be just."

To feminist writer and activist, Marguerite Durand, Gaston Darboux's long, forceful letter to *le Temps* was an "admirable plea, a precious document." Darboux, noted Durand, on January 4, 1911, "is one of those who believe that brains have no sex." Durand insisted that the issue was not as momentous as "the brutal impact of a stray comet" or "the end of the world." It simply meant that "the principle of masculine supremacy is going to crumble because nothing justifies it in a time when the power of brains is happily more important than that of muscles." To Durand, who didn't disguise her contempt for the "milieu of mediocrities" which was the Institute, it almost didn't matter whether Marie Curie won or lost. If the Academy admitted her, it was a triumph; if not, the Academy "will have furnished feminism with one of the most precious pieces of ammunition for its campaigns." She cited Jean de La Bruyère, who advised that 'when you see science and reason united in the same person, don't worry about the gender, admire.' Feminism, concluded Durand, "doesn't ask so much: it isn't admiration that it claims, it's equity."

But in Belle Époque France a woman who wanted equity rather than special treatment, respect rather than admiration, was flying in the face of strongly held beliefs about the feminine ideal. Woman as symbol was pervasive: the republicans had their Marianne, a symbol of the French Revolution who was reviled by the right as "the slut," and the conservatives engaged in emotional defenses of Joan of Arc. And as these symbolic uses suggest, woman was supposed to inspire, not perspire. The quietly influential Julia Daudet, widow of the novelist Alphonse Daudet and mother of the right-wing journalist Léon Daudet, articulated the conventional feminine ideal: A woman should be "serious and seductive, less instructed than intuitive and sensitive," . . . pouring herself "a little of the wine of science with which she dares to lightly intoxicate herself rather than to fortify herself. . . . Science is useless to women, unless they are the exceptions who are inclined to a masculine career, and that is always too bad . . . this excessive independence of ideas, quest for liberal careers, usurpation and intrusion in the role of lawyer or of intern in the hospitals . . . all that seems to me the fantasies and ambitions of those with dormant hearts, women without children or households who . . . could use even greater gifts in simple and useful tasks."

For women like Julia Daudet, and for the men who depended upon them, the candidacy of Marie Curie to the Institute, a male bastion, did seem cataclysmic. Léon Bailby, editor of the right-wing *l'Intransigeant,* noted that "Fifty years ago we would have greeted the idea of women in the Institute with a burst of laughter. Today one fervently discusses the idea. . . . Can sentences stop an idea on the march? Soon the brook will become a torrent. And it will carry away the dike."

Bailby had a certain sympathy for this new woman, who, "obliged to provide for her own needs, . . . has become a maker of boots, a couturière or a woman of genius. . . . It is entirely natural today that woman would want to claim her place in the circles which are charged with recognizing talent and making reputations. Isn't the work of Madame Curie equal to that of another scientist wearing trousers and a full beard?"

But like many of his contemporaries, Bailby seemed to believe that equality meant incompatibility, that once woman no longer needed to be "taken care of," men and women would part ways, fulfilling "the prophesy of Baudelaire": 'Throwing angry looks across the divide/The two sexes will live each on their own side.' "

The idea that liberation would divide the sexes was borne out by a reporter for *le Figaro* who paid a visit to the United States, said to be "a paradise for women," around this time, and found separate waiting rooms for men and women in train stations, separate universities, and even, in New York, "a bank for women." His dispatch ended on a rhetorical note: "What do you prefer *mesdames?* Do you want to retain your privileges and continue be protected by the man, or share his rights and become his adversary?" Women, he insisted, "will not succeed in changing nature's plan. . . . they will succeed in providing themselves with their own waiting rooms in train stations . . . their universities and their special banks. . . . What else? Perhaps their own exclusive academies . . ."

Men weren't the only ones who saw Marie Curie's candidacy as a threat to future harmony. One of the most vivid protests came from the pen of a prolific and popular novelist of the period, Marie Louise Antoinette Regnier. Madame Regnier, whose husband, Henri de Regnier, was also a novelist, wrote under the male pen name of Gérard d'Houville, but insisted that she wanted everyone to know her novels were a woman's work: "A woman's book should be feminine like a sachet; and the only excuse that it can have for being signed sometimes with a man's name . . . is that this name should be placed at the bottom of the pages, with the coquetry of a mask, without preventing one from seeing . . . the sly ingenuous smile of a little mouth."

Her novels, with titles like *The Slave, The Inconstant Woman, The Seducer,* were full of the kind of coquetry she advocated. In the opening paragraph of *A Time to Love,* for instance:

> I began to laugh, because my hair tickled me and I regained the sense of my personality: laurence,—or rather Laurette,—23 years old; beautiful, men say; graceful, admit women; with a little talent, according to the public . . . with some independence, some wisdom, some illusions . . .

Madame Regnier's long essay about Marie Curie's candidacy appeared in *le Figaro* just three days before the final election. In a reference to the green ceremonial costume worn by members of the Institute, the headline above it read: THE GREEN TRAVESTY:

Is Madame Curie going to be called to carry through this green travesty? Will she be elected Monday to be a member of the Academy of Sciences? Will a woman sit for the first time at the Institute? And will the disturbing novelty of this fact create a dangerous precedent for the security of the Immortals, until now undisturbed and sheltered from the eternal feminine under the coupola? . . . This is the question which, since two weeks ago, has been asked of us so often and which, I don't know why, I have the wish to respond to a little this morning.

If Madame Regnier is writing on a whim, she nonetheless has strong feelings on the subject. In answer to those who claim that science has no sex, she points out that "science" is a feminine word (in French), and that not only is science feminine but so too are the Muses and "most of the gifted and beautiful things in the world." Madame Curie, she believes, is too magical a person to stoop to membership in the Academy. She is "a sort of fairy and sorceress who has torn from silent and frightening matter some of its most mysterious secrets." And isn't this "more astonishing and more miraculous than being a member of the Institute? Can the magic sceptre be replaced by the frivolous sword of an académicienne?" Madame Regnier would be happier if Marie Curie "remained independent and solitary, possessing only her own glorious accomplishments which double and reinforce her femininity."

Equality, from Madame Regnier's point of view, is the enemy:

One must not try . . . to make of woman the equal of the man!
The more we differ from him, the more we are ourselves. . . .
The "equal of the man." These words alone are terrible! They
destroy all that which makes for grace, charm, beauty, fantasy;
they abolish all privileges; they ban our tyranny, they give us
rights, these famous rights which forbid us to have caprices.
. . . *Mesdames,* you *must not* become part of the Academies.

It is telling that when the radical suffragist Christabel Pankhurst passed through Paris for a few days in the midst of this debate, *le Figaro* spent the first three paragraphs of its front-page article about this leader of hunger strikes discussing her appearance. Inevitably, questions of dress and decorum came up in connection with Marie Curie's candidacy as well. Gaston Deschamps, writing in *le Figaro,* acknowledged that many women were worthy, "but what difficulties! There is the question of dress. There is the question of required visits, since it is not the custom, in France, for women to go and make visits to gentlemen."

Madame Regnier too was concerned about how all this would look. If the new *académiciennes* were older, and plain, there might not be a problem. Women could, after all, wear ceremonial robes like the bishops in the Academy, instead of the embroidered green suits and swords. But what of

> the women yet young, all the pretty ones, all the beauties, all the primping ones, say, say, what would they do there? One of two things: either they would overwhelm this important gathering with their frills and their charms, or they would be sober, serious, dignified, not women for two *sous*. . . . I can see now the youngest *académicienne* seated on the dictionary, making the Thursday meetings agreeable with cups of tea, smiling from mirrors under the table and chairs, a cloud of rice powder rising around the Immortals and the prize of virtue, alas! sometimes a little neglected.

It used to be, Madame Regnier goes on, rather nastily, that women only envied their friends' dresses. "Now they want to be 'like the men.' They must have red ribbons in the buttonhole, they who possess all the ribbons!" They want "the prerogatives and the distinctions and the green costume!" To this, Madame Regnier replies: "Don't change so much! Stay, ah! stay yourselves! you were so nice, often! and it has never been forbidden to you to have talent." But this talent must be kept private, "a charm which belongs to you, like very beautiful eyes, a supple body and a great head of hair."

Women, she concludes, are made for love. "May they not denature themselves! May they not demand from masculine ambitions the satisfactions which would not fulfill them. . . . They are created only for love, they can live only by it; let them not try to forget. . . . It is to love that they owe, as much as to maternity, their talent or their genius. . . . The most illustrious women of past times, who still shine, have been the lovers. The most surprising glory is to love and to be loved and it is by love alone that some women can hope to be numbered one day among the immortals."

Five days after *le Figaro* published this lengthy exhortation, a journalist known as "Séverine" responded in *l'Intransigeant*. Séverine was herself a feminist and suffragist, a woman whose journalistic reputation was built on her passionate defense of the weak and the oppressed. A wit had dubbed her "Our lady of the tear in the eye." And indeed, in her reponse to Madame Regnier, she managed to find an oppressed group to champion.

Séverine begins with praise for her colleague Marie Louise Regnier, who has written "one of the most pretty pages ever traced by a feminine pen, . . . a vaporous tulle of illusion." As a novelist, Séverine notes, Madame Regnier is "very popular among men. Her type of heroine is the one they approve of . . . the victim blessing her irons and cherishing her martyrdom. It is more flattering to their self-love." But, as in her novel *The Slave,* Madame Regnier is still the "happy passive one" in her essay in *le Figaro,* resembling "the women of the harem, freed of all material care, separated from all moral responsibility, receiving all the liberality of the master in exchange for her beauty alone."

But not everyone, argues Séverine, can lead such an existence.

> What of those whom love neglects, or who have never encountered it, those who have neither elegance nor attractiveness nor charm, nor very beautiful eyes, nor supple bodies, nor a great head of hair: the ugly, the old, the isolated, the damaged—and who have however a brain? . . . They are legion, the girls left to cope because they have no dowry, the widows whose household remains empty because their heart remains faithful. . . . If the desire comes to them to seek glory, so much the better! It is a goal, an element of interest, something which gives company— poorly, certainly, but there is no other!—to the solitude of their heart. It is just not to deny them.

Such an argument suggests just how bold Marie Curie must have seemed, even to feminists like Séverine. For Marie, after all, had known the love of a husband, the joys of children, and she was not unattractive. Certainly she had suffered with the loss of her husband, but, Séverine notwithstanding, being a young widow was not necessarily a terrible fate in Belle Époque France; as an experienced woman, a widow had certain freedoms. And yet, despite all this, Marie Curie was still claiming a place for herself in the lofty Academy; she wanted to be an *Immortelle* among the *Immortels.* No wonder the Institute traditionalists were gathering votes to try to keep her out.

The academy system in France began in the seventeenth century, when Richelieu founded the Académie française, a company of scholars devoted primarily to the promotion of French language and literature. According to historian Londa Schiebinger, several celebrated women of the seventeenth century had been proposed for membership at the time, and "it was here that women were first excluded from modern institutions of learning." After the French Revolution, three academies that had been independent of each other were united to form the Institut de France. By the time Marie Curie became a candidate, there were five academies in the Institute, and the designations had shifted.

The Academy of Science, which would decide Marie Curie's fate, had become an institution of enormous power and influence in French life. It was the central agency which defined, reported, rewarded and generally controlled French science. And membership in it was, even for some very great scientists, one of the great *desiderata*. Louis Pasteur wrote in 1866 that "for twenty years . . . I must plead guilty to living only to deserve the approval of the Academy."

There were sixty-eight members of the Academy of Sciences when Marie Curie sought admission. They were divided into eleven sections, including chemistry and physics, and it was the physics section which proposed to place Marie Curie's name in nomination. But three times a year, all five academies assembled for a plenary session. And it happened that one of these plenary meetings was to take place before the Academy of Sciences could meet to consider Marie Curie's candidacy. As soon as the news got out that a woman might be elected to the Institute, the idea of bringing the question before the plenary session began to gather momentum.

By Wednesday afternoon, January 4, 1911, when the members of the five academies gathered at the Mazarin Palace, most of the academicians arrived knowing that the assembly was going to address the issue of a *candidature feminine*. Instead of the usual seventy or eighty in attendance, there were 163, including not only intellectuals but also such celebrated members as the Prince of Monaco, Baron Edmond de Rothschild, and Prince Roland Bonaparte. "Never in memory," reported *l'Intransigeant,* "had there been such a flood of embroidered suits under the Cupola."

When the meeting opened, each side in the debate rose in turn to argue that tradition favored them. Émile Lavasseur, head of the Academy of Moral and Political Sciences, gave a lengthy disquisition on the laws and traditions of France and other countries, coming to the conclusion that it "had never been the intention of the founders of the Institute to admit women among us." Lavasseur's final plea, "not to violate the unity of this elite body which is the Institute of France," was drowned out in lively applause. Then Monsieur Viollet, of the Academy of Inscriptions and Belle-lettres, used historic examples to prove the opposite, that women *did* belong in the Institute.

For the most part, members of the Academy of Sciences chose not to argue for or against women, but to focus on the question of procedure. Henri Poincaré, Paul Appell, and the mathematician Charles Picard, supporters of Marie Curie, rose to insist that it was a violation of the tradition of autonomy of the five academies for the assembly to vote one way or the other on the question. At one point, Poincaré pointed out that the Académie française had rejected the candidacy of a woman, Pauline Savary, without consulting the larger Institute. Why should the Academy of Sciences be obliged to ask permission of the Institute when the Académie française hadn't?

The argument that the academies should be left to make their own decisions had wide appeal. As a result, when Monsieur Bétolaud, member of the Académie des sciences morales et politiques, put together his motion against women, he acknowledged it. The motion read: "The assembly, consulted on the question of the eligibility of women for the Institute, without claiming the right to impose its decision on the various Academies . . . , merely notes on this question, which is of general concern, there is an immutable tradition which it appears to the Institute to be altogether wise to uphold."

Bétolaud, lawyer and former president of the bar, "produced very clever arguments" in support of his motion. Among the most far-fetched: Marie Curie might be elected president of the Academy of Sciences, and if that happened, she would become eligible for a tour of duty as president of the entire Institute. It seemed to go without saying that this was a terrifying prospect.

"The vote! The vote!" came the cry from some of the academicians, who had been listening long enough. At that point, there was pandemonium. Everyone began shouting at once, demanding the floor, and Monsieur Artur Chuquet, the robust, heavily bearded member of the Academy of Sciences who was presiding over the meeting, desperately rang his bell to gain order. Finally, "at the risk of losing all his majesty," he climbed onto his presidential chair and proceeded from there to organize the voting. The result, by a vote of 85 to 60, was to uphold the "immutable tradition" of the Institute.

The next day, most of the papers pronounced the result "a victory for the antifeminists." The most ironic response came from the socialist paper l'Humanité, which declared Marie Curie's rejection from the "misogynous Institute" a blessing in disguise. The writer for l'Humanité addressed his remarks directly to Madame Curie:

> Immutable tradition, it seems, is opposed to your presence under the Cupola. The green costume must be uniquely masculine or it cannot be. . . . You will not be in the Academy and

I rejoice without false irony. . . . You will know nothing of the petty intrigues, the base jealousies, the perfidious gossip which hide in the shade of academic laurels. But you will pursue, in the silent glory of your laboratory, the research begun with the collaborator who was so brutally destroyed . . . you will conserve intact the deferential friendship of those who were your defenders yesterday. . . . And that I imagine is a greater satisfaction than Mr Bertolaud, president of the bar, could ever imagine.

If Marie Curie read this, she might have smiled. *L'Humanité* used many of the same words Pierre had in complaining about the goings-on at the Institute. Marie Curie's supporters, however, were not yet ready to declare defeat. Indeed some of them seemed to think that the assembly vote would work in their favor. One claimed that the election of Madame Curie was assured because those who "want to respect the autonomy of the academies" would be added to her partisans. Gaston Darboux declared the result much better than expected. And academician Gaston Bonnier told the *Petit Parisien* that "Madame Curie would be wise to order her academic costume soon from a good tailor."

Such optimism, however, was premature. Five days after the assembly, a committee of the Academy of Sciences met in secret to decide on their nominations to fill the seat vacated by Gernez. Despite the assembly's opposition, they nominated Marie Curie on the "first line." On the "second line" were six other candidates, including Edouard Branly. On Monday, January 17, the nominations were made public at a meeting of the Academy of Sciences. At that meeting, each nominee's work was presented by a current member. Marie Curie's accomplishments were reviewed by Gabriel Lippmann, who had (with the exception of the Nobel nominating letter) supported her work since her student days. The members had a week to make up their minds before the final vote.

Those in the Academy who knew Marie Curie's work were aware that there was simply no comparison between her contribution and Branly's. But some just didn't want a woman in their midst. The engineer Jules Carpentier probably spoke for many when he told *le Temps,* "No matter what you say, something will change at the Institute when a woman invades it." Other members were more circumspect. The astronomer Henri Deslandres, for instance, conceded that a woman should be elected "if she has incontestable worth." But he added that in the present case, it seemed to him "very difficult to judge the works of Madame Curie and to separate her research from the inspired work of [Pierre] Curie."

The conservative and right-wing press, which was uniformly opposed to admitting her, echoed these sentiments. "Madame Curie had never done anything in physics before her marriage," an anonymous scientist was quoted as saying, "and since her husband's death she hasn't done anything alone." Another paper damned with faint praise: "In the opinion of competent people, Madame Curie was a helper and assistant of the first order to her illustrious husband," adding that she "has never worked except in collaboration, first with her husband, then with M. Bémont and Debierne, who are themselves scientists of true value."

Another astonishing argument was that Marie Curie had already been given too many prizes: "Madame Curie has had all the possible rewards, numbers of prizes of the Academy, nominations to a great number of organizations, a laboratory and a chair at the Sorbonne where she has only had to ask to obtain what she thinks she needs, while so many . . . can't get what they need for their laboratories."

In general, however, the opposition press preferred not to focus on Madame Curie. Attacks on a blameless woman could seem cowardly and ungallant. Instead, they championed Edouard Branly, whose contribution of a coherer was "the most beautiful discovery of our era." Sentiment favored him as well. Branly had tried for election twice before; at sixty-seven, he had "a whole long scientific career behind him," while Madame Curie at forty-four was "only at the dawn of her career."

By far the most vituperative attacks on Marie Curie came from the right-wing *Action française,* and in particular from the truculent pen of a rising star on the right, Léon Daudet. Daudet was both a fanatic nationalist and a libertine, a monarchist, an anti-Semite, a practicing Catholic and champion of the Church, "a master of invective who could give literary shape and expression to a mass of disorganized hatreds and resentments." In 1908, using his wife's money, he had turned *l'Action française* into a daily newspaper, and used it to exploit French fears of internal and external enemies, fears which by 1910 had resulted in a perceptible turn to the right in France, and which would lead, within four years, to war with Germany.

Daudet's paper was highly visible, not only because of its outrageous and unremitting campaigns, but also because Daudet had the ear of a group of young toughs called the *camelots du roi.* Purportedly charged with distributing the newspaper, they were combative and angry young men, spoiling for a fight and often finding one.

In the two years before Marie Curie's nomination to the Academy, the *camelots du roi* had been involved in an ongoing action against a professor at the Sorbonne named Thalamas—the name of a "half-breed," according to *l'Action française.* Thalamas had given a lecture in which he dared to doubt the purity of Joan of Arc, viewed by *l'Action française* as a sort of patron saint. Thalamas was said to have claimed that Joan of Arc had had auditory hallucinations since childhood and may been more of a camp follower than a leader of the troops. Egged on by *l'Action,* about fifty *camelots* turned up at the Sorbonne every Wednesday to disrupt Thalamas's lectures, throwing rotten eggs and shouting insults until the Sorbonne had to bring in the police. To Daudet and *l'Action française,* Thalamas was just part of the problem; the entire Sorbonne was the enemy, infested as it was with godless foreigners and republicans.

For reasons which were peculiarly French, the one group that *l'Action française* was reluctant to criticize was women. It had long been believed, by both the right and the left, that the women of France were the last best hope of the Catholic Church. It was the reason that republicans, despite giving lip service to women's rights, were reluctant to advocate women's suffrage. "Attendance at Mass," note historians Steven Hause and Anne Kenney, "was a secondary sexual characteristic of French women. As agents of the 'black peril,' they would elect a clerical government."

Because so many women were supporters of the Church (which generally meant the right), and because powerful women backed *l'Action française,* the paper chose an indirect way of attacking Marie Curie's candidacy. Marie Curie, they claimed, was being used as a pawn by a "cabal of Dreyfusards" against the Catholic Edouard Branly.

Though the Dreyfus case was officially closed, it was still used on the right and left as a rallying cry. The socialist *l'Humanité* railed against the Republic's treatment of a labor leader by calling it "The New Dreyfus Affair." And *l'Action française,* for whom Dreyfus, as a Jew, was a traitor by definition, saw the candidacy of Marie Curie to the Institute as "feminine and eccentric," and in truth an attack on Branly, "who doesn't associate with either grand Jews nor the protestant oracles."

On the day the Academy of Sciences was to take its vote, Léon Daudet took up most of the front page of *l'Action française* with an invective under the heading *Dreyfus contre Branly:*

But yes . . . Dreyfus against Branly. Such is, in fact, the bizarre struggle which is going to take place today at the Academy of Sciences, under this false cover: Marie Curie versus Branly. . . . The imbeciles who go around insisting that the Dreyfus affair has been buried should take notice: it is so unburied, this epic struggle of the national genius versus the foreign demon, that on every fashionable, sportive, literary, dramatic, musical, scientific, social, political, and economic occasion it begins again in a thousand forms, with actors who are always basically the same . . .

Daudet insists that Marie Curie's credentials aren't anywhere near as impressive as Branly's and that failure to give him a place in the Academy will puzzle "the scholars of the entire world—who have already been stupefied by the attribution of the Nobel Prize [to the Curies, not to Branly]." As Pierre Curie would have predicted, Branly is held out by this ultranationalist as the patriotic choice. "We have . . . the duty to represent and defend French science," insists Daudet. "The invention of the wireless telegraph is an absolutely French invention. Our verdict . . . should say it loyally."

But, claims Daudet, "the Dreyfusards, in their rage" still insist on supporting Marie Curie. Why? Because Branly, "tired of the stupid quarrels and the tyranny of official education," left the Sorbonne to teach in the Catholic Institute.

> In the eyes of the fanatic Dreyfusard Darboux, permanent secretary of the Academy of Sciences, of fanatic Dreyfusard Poincaré—a man of genius, they say, in mathematics, but stupid and hateful when it comes to the rest—in the eyes of the Jew of color photography Lippmann, of fanatic Dreyfusard Appell, dean of the Faculty of Sciences . . . this exit from the Sorbonne, this entry into the Catholic Institute—yes sir CA-THO-LIC—constitutes a double and inexpiable crime.

Daudet accuses Marie Curie's supporters of being "steeped in the most inane, the most narrow, the most blind of all prejudices: the anticlerical." They are "a somber clique, basically semite and huguenot," who "dress up their ferocious partiality in great honorable works or in seemingly scientific falsehoods. In our time the true Tartuffe [Molière's religious hypocrite] is in the laboratory and the library. . . . They hide no longer behind the life of the Saints, but behind algebra, physics and chemistry treatises. . . . They intend in fact to chase from the house . . . all those who don't think like them, don't feel like them, who have the audacity not to deny God, not to insult Rome, to go to mass, to raise their children as Christians."

The "hypocrisy" of these Sorbonne professors, according to Daudet, lies in their decision not to attack Branly head-on, but to "redirect the question toward feminism." Permanent secretary Darboux "hoped to thus confuse the issue, throw the public onto a false trail and, thanks to the confusion, to quietly defeat Branly. Lousy calculation, Monsieur Permanent Secretary, . . . for a mathematician of your ability. . . . Because what is worse than having anti-French sentiments is disguising them behind a . . . feminist generosity." Winding down to a conclusion, Daudet "hopes, for the good name of the Academy of Sciences, that these miserable ruses will fail, that Branly will be named this afternoon." He adds that he has heard that "many academicians . . . propose to give a lesson to the bizarre knights serving Madame Curie, and behind her, Dreyfus. Let's hope so."

The circulation of *l'Action française* was a small fraction of that of the "quatre grands" Parisian newspapers—only about twenty-three thousand, as compared with well over a million for the republican newspapers, *le Journal* and *le Petit Parisien.* Yet *l'Action française* had plenty of readers in the literary and intellectual world. It is interesting to note, for instance, that *l'Intransigeant,* a less rabid right-wing paper which was at first rather sympathetic to Marie Curie's aspirations, later adopted the rhetoric of Léon Daudet and contended that "Madame Curie . . . has been embroiled, to her great misfortune," in the plot of a protestant "and two Israelites" to deny the Catholic Branly.

On Monday, January 24, 1911, the question which had "caused so much ink to run and so many words to be spoken" was put to a final vote. The number of guards at the Institute was doubled for the meeting that day, and crowds of spectators gathered outside the large hall hours before the members of the Academy of Sciences began to arrive and take their places. At first, only members were allowed admission to the hall. Then Academy president Gautier ruled that everyone else should be allowed in—everyone else, that is, except women.

By tradition, all women were barred from the Institute, and this day was to be no exception. The only female who gained entry was the editor of a morning newspaper, who was given a special dispensation after her male colleagues pleaded on her behalf. A large crowd of women spectators was turned away.

Those who managed to get inside the hall learned that the vote they had come to witness couldn't take place, by tradition, until four o'clock; meanwhile, they would have to endure scientific presentations in the overheated, overcrowded room. "One talks, one mixes, one bumps," reported *le Figaro.* An assistant fainted, done in by the heat; a doctor rushed to his side, two guards carried him out through the crowd. Meanwhile, Monsieur Deslandres reported on the discovery of a new star, and the Curies' friend Charles Edouard Guillaume spoke about a curious metal. "No one listens; they are waiting for four o'clock."

Finally, the little clock on the desk at the front of the room struck four times. The hour of the vote had arrived. The guards passed the urns and the members deposited their ballots. As President Gautier read out the ballots one by one, everyone counted. The president counted in a loud voice, the vice president counted more softly, the secretaries counted in writing, and the members and audience kept count in their heads.

All but a handful of members had come for the historic vote. Charles Bouchard, Marie Curie's first Nobel advocate, came up from Cannes just to vote for her once again. Altogether there were fifty-eight in attendance. An absolute majority would be thirty. On the first vote, Edouard Branly received twenty-nine votes and Marie Curie twenty-eight, with one vote going to Marcel Brillouin. On the second vote, Branly received thirty votes and Marie Curie twenty-eight. Branly had won. The following Monday, the *Comptes rendus* noted that Monsieur E. Branly, at the invitation of Monsieur Président, took "his place among his confrères."

Predictably, *l'Action française* hailed the vote as "the defeat of Dreyfus." In electing Branly, the Academy "refused to bend under the yoke of the judeo-huguenot coterie," and proved itself once more "worthy of the country." Cooler heads were more inclined to see it as a sort of victory in defeat for Marie Curie. It was "a personal victory and a victory for feminism . . . in the future this barrier will fall and [Madame Curie] will take the place of which she is worthy in every regard." *Le Temps* declared pompously that "the vote doesn't leave wounds" but "gives equal honor to the two scholars as well as to the illustrious assembly."

But Marie Curie's friends were outraged. Charles Edouard Guillaume, who had made a presentation at the Academy meeting the day of the vote, wrote her that he had "suffered more than you can imagine with the abominable denial of justice of which you've been the victim; I've passed some sleepless nights, asking myself how the Academy could be carried away into such aberrations. . . . The election of M. Branly was achieved by methods which would embarass monkeys . . . and which very much lessen the stature of the Academy itself."

Others dismissed the importance of the Academy. "I think you are of too noble a character," wrote Georges Urbain, "to be affected the least bit by this affair at the Institute. . . . In affirming to you that the best academy is still a circle of devoted friends and enthusiastic students, I would be preaching to the converted."

These sympathetic letters from friends are as close as it is possible to come to Marie Curie's feeling about the entire affair. There are no references to it in what remains of her correspondence. Eve Curie, in her biography of her mother, insists that the loss "in no wise afflicted her," and that her lab assistants and colleagues were far more unhappy than she was about it. Certainly she would have agreed with Georges Urbain's view that colleagues and friends were the "best academy." Probably she thought too of Pierre, who was first rejected by the Academy and who fairly actively disliked belonging once he was voted in. According to her "religion of memories," membership in the Academy was not something one should care much about.

And yet Marie Curie didn't like to lose. When her findings were challenged, she fought hard in their defense. Whatever her view of the Academy, once she undertook something, she liked to succeed at it. Furthermore, even if she didn't care about membership in the Academy, she did care about her reputation and her dignity. Just as she despised all the attention and distortion in the press when she and Pierre won the Nobel Prize in 1903, she must have been pained much of the time by the way her name was taken up by strangers who had little understanding of her work and who merely wanted to stir up their readers.

Throughout the whole process, she had remained steadfastly behind the scenes. She didn't address a letter to the Academy declaring her candidacy; she did pay some of the customary visits to members, though it is not clear how many. Others, most notably Gaston Darboux, also made visits on her behalf. But this did not mean she was indifferent. Given the attitudes toward women at the time, any open show of ambition on her part would have been held against her.

As it turned out, it didn't matter that she had been so retiring; the very act of allowing her name to be put in nomination proved offensive enough. Even before the vote, some accused her of a "lack of nobility and dignity" for allowing her name to be used. After she lost, others joined in. Jean Bernard, in his running commentary on Parisian life, claimed that it would have been a "beautiful gesture, an elegant gesture very much in the character of this race of Frenchwomen to which the scientist belongs" for Marie Curie to withdraw her name after the first vote, to "efface herself before her rival" as "an homage rendered to an older man by a woman who can wait and who has just triumphed in principle regarding the admission of women to the Institute." He adds, "the gesture was not made. It's a shame."

An even harsher judgment of Marie Curie came from Léon Bailby, the editor of l'Intransigeant. "In posing her candidacy herself, in protesting to the newspapers that she was indeed a candidate, she has displayed a lack of reserve that was not of her own sex. She has thus offended some scientists who otherwise admired her work." And he concluded, more ominously: "As to the general public, one must say also that they have become hostile to the candidate. This woman who had formerly been so popular, they have judged that she has pushed her taste for recompense and honors a little too far. They have applauded the lesson in patience and modesty that the Institute has just inflicted."

There were harsher "lessons" to come.

Chapter Fourteen

SCANDAL

WHAT MADE the liaison between Paul Langevin and Marie Curie dangerous was that it didn't conform to Belle Époque conventions. Bourgeois men were allowed, even expected, to keep a mistress; but a mistress stayed in the background, allowing the wife to be at her husband's side in polite society. As long as a married man was discreet, and chose wife and mistress who dutifully played their roles, he could carry on an affair with impunity. The Napoleonic Code, enforcer of male privilege, was indulgent toward the husband in such cases.

But Marie Curie was not an anonymous mistress, a woman of humble origins grateful to be "kept" by a man of means. She was a woman who had her own career, her own means, her own aspirations. This made her an object of envy and resentment, someone others wanted to expose and discredit. And because Marie Curie was so famous, Paul Langevin's jealous wife could threaten her with public exposure as she never could have the usual mistress. It was this, as Perrin noted, which made this triangle "singular." "Madame Curie should have been left completely out of this," he wrote later. It was because she was "illustrious" that she became a "precious hostage."

Public exposure was a powerful threat in the Belle Époque. If private affairs were generally condoned, an affair which became public knowledge was almost universally condemned. "Like venial sins in the confessional," Edward Berenson observed in *The Trial of Madame Caillaux*, "private transgressions could be readily forgiven. . . . But once made public, the sin became far more serious because it was now more difficult to dismiss as a mere aberration." Middle-class women in particular dreaded public exposure, which could turn them into pariahs and bring shame even to their daughters, who could no longer be assumed to be innocent.

Marie Curie was not immune to these fears of public shaming. Writing to Paul about his sexual relationship with Jeanne, she noted that she wouldn't be able to bear it if Jeanne had another child, since it would be "judged very severely by all those, alas already numerous, who know [about us]." If that should happen, it would mean "a definite separation between us . . . because I can risk my life and my position for you, but I couldn't accept this dishonor in the face of myself, of you and of people I esteem." She added, "if your wife understood this, she would use this method right away, and someone may suggest it to her."

Marie worried about other methods Madame Langevin might employ as well. She worried that she might have her husband followed. She cautioned Paul when she wrote to him in the summer of 1910 that he should "be very careful in going to our place and also to the post office, where people you know often come." She worried that one of his children was being used to spy on him, and was being interrogated afterward by Jeanne.

Given these concerns, it is astonishing that Paul and Marie kept letters which had passed between them in a drawer in their pied à terre in Paris. Perhaps they saved them for sentimental reasons. Perhaps they simply couldn't conceive how far Madame Langevin would go in her pursuit of her rival. Around Easter of 1911 they found out: someone, apparently hired by Jeanne Langevin, broke into the apartment and stole the letters. Shortly after, Jeanne Langevin's brother-in-law Henri Bourgeois, the newspaper editor, paid a visit to Madame Curie. He informed her that Madame Langevin had the letters and that a scandal was imminent. It was the beginning of a long nightmare for both Paul Langevin and Marie Curie.

As she often did in times of crisis, Marie turned to Jean Perrin. She told him about the letters, "which Madame Langevin could use as dangerous ammunition." And she told him that she found it impossible to deal with people who had decided to act through threats and blackmail. She felt "drained." Just as he had during Jeanne's murder threats the previous summer, Perrin suggested Marie leave town for a while. This time she took his advice. Émile Borel, the mathematician, and his wife Marguerite were traveling to Genoa during the Easter recess for a scientific conference. Marie accepted their invitation to come along. She could attend the conference and escape Paris at the same time.

Until then, the Borels had seen Marie Curie only occasionally. Once or twice, Marguerite Borel remembered, Pierre and Marie had come, "like two shadows," to the scientific soirées for which the Borels were famous. At the time, the young hostess had found the Curies intimidating. There had been occasional encounters since then, including that time, not long before, when Marie had appeared at the Borels' in white, mysteriously rejuvenated. But never until the Italian trip had Émile and Marguerite Borel and Marie Curie had a chance to take each other's measure, to get to know each other. Traveling together, along with Marie's children, walking together along the water, sharing ravioli at their modest hotel and planning boat excursions, the Borels and Marie Curie formed a strong—and crucial—friendship.

The Borels were a remarkable couple. Émile, son of a Protestant minister, had been recognized as a prodigy in his native village and graduated first in his class at the elite École normale supérieure in Paris. At the time of the trip to Genoa, he was vice-director of the École normale, a position which among other things conferred a residence at the school. A gifted mathematician, he also held the chair, newly created for him, in theory of functions at the Sorbonne. Marguerite, thirteen years younger than her husband, had been born into the scientific elite: her father was Paul Appell, mathematician and longtime dean of the Faculty of Sciences at the Sorbonne. Though she had married at only seventeen, Marguerite was a forceful woman and an intellectual in her own right; with her husband, she founded the *Revue du mois,* a monthly which published in-depth essays by France's leading thinkers. Both Paul Langevin's and Marie Curie's tributes to Pierre Curie appeared first in the *Revue du mois,* as did writings on contemporary education, literature, theater, science, and politics.

The Borels had no children of their own, so all of their remarkable energies could be devoted to their lively social, political, and intellectual pursuits. Besides maintaining a large circle of friends among the Parisian intelligentsia, both were prodigious writers. Émile Borel's writing, and activity, reflected his interest in public affairs as well as mathematics. Eventually he would become mayor of the small town where he was born. Marguerite Borel, using the pen name Camille Marbo, published more than thirty novels. Most importantly, from Marie Curie's point of view, the Borels were people who stood by their friends and by their principles.

In Italy, the Borel/Curie entourage took over a small hotel on the seashore at Santa Margherita Ligure, paying a modest six francs per person. There, Marguerite Borel remembered later in her novelistic fashion, they quickly warmed to each other. Irène, shy and standoffish at first, talks with Émile Borel about mathematics. She "asks questions about everything, in her shy reflective voice." Mornings they stroll together on the beach, take boat rides to Portofino, which Madame Curie finds "too fashionable," and Rapallo. Eve "prances about, wants to try to row." In the afternoons, a hired car takes Marie Curie and Émile Borel to the conference in Genoa.

After two days, Marie Curie, who is in the habit of going to her room after dinner, asks Marguerite Borel to come visit. Thus is established a nightly routine vividly recalled by the visitor: "How could I forget that lime-whitened bedroom, that bed with its ornate ironwork, with the crucifix above, and the reclining woman speaking to me." Marguerite keeps silent, "so as not to scare off confidences," and Marie speaks to her of Paul Langevin's unhappiness. "I discover, evening after evening, under the austere scientist, the tender and lively woman, capable of walking through fire for those she loves." Marie is afraid that Langevin will yield to pressures and "renounce pure science" or sink into despair. " 'And he is a genius!' . . .

"She agitates her narrow hands, grabs mine. 'Marguerite, it is necessary to save him from himself. He is weak. You and I, we are tough. He needs understanding, gentle affection. . . . ' "

Meanwhile, back in Paris, life in the Langevin household had gone from bad to worse. When the letters were stolen, Paul Langevin left home for the Perrins' in protest, returning only during the day. But after two weeks, he returned home "out of fatigue and because of the children." Once again, according to Perrin, "an approximate equilibrium was reached," but this time life was even more difficult for Paul Langevin because "they threatened him without end with publishing the stolen letters." When the Langevins' daughter was ill that summer, Jeanne Langevin told her husband that this was just the beginning of his punishment.

On July 26, a rupture finally came. According to Jeanne Langevin, her husband struck her in the face because of a badly cooked compote. According to Paul, his wife hurled vulgar insults at him in front of the children, upsetting him and them. Whatever the cause, when Jeanne ran to the bedroom, Paul left the house, with the two older boys in tow, and turned up once again at the Perrins' doorstep. This time, instead of returning to his house, he decided he would take the two boys off with him for a month's vacation. After checking with an attorney to make sure it would not prejudice his case if there were a separation and divorce, Langevin wrote to his brother-in-law, informing him that he was leaving with the boys, and asked Perrin to dispatch five hundred francs to his wife.

Paul Langevin later defended his sudden departure with the two boys, arguing that he had been planning to go off with the family on vacation anyway and that he simply went "a little more quickly." But Jeanne Langevin had reason to be upset when she heard nothing of her husband and sons until the next day. His departure prompted her to file charges. Notwithstanding his lawyer's advice to the contrary, Madame Langevin was able to charge Paul Langevin with "abandoning" his home and to forbid him, at least provisionally, from returning.

At this point, Henri Bourgeois, the scheming brother-in-law behind much of the trouble, wrote to inform Jean Perrin that there was going to be a trial. This meant, as everyone knew, that the Curie/Langevin letters could be made public. "They saw there," Perrin wrote afterward, "the means to make [Langevin] yield unceasingly on all points under pain of seeing Madame Curie dishonored. The odious blackmail profoundly revolted me."

Although Perrin doesn't say it, it seems likely that in fact blackmail was paid during this period. On August 17, Marie Curie lent Paul Langevin two thousand francs "to pay life insurance," and five days later she lent him another thousand. In October, there was another loan of two thousand francs, for a grand total of five thousand francs. This was a considerable amount of money; it amounted, in fact, to more than ten percent of Marie Curie's annual salary. Later Paul Langevin was to complain that he had not been repaid by his brother-in-law Henri Bourgeois for loans of which there was no written record.

Perhaps the payments succeeded in buying time. For eight months after the letters were stolen, Madame Langevin and her supporters did not go public with them. Paul Langevin's sons returned home to their mother, while he kept his distance, first vacationing with the Borels, then attending a scientific conference in Germany. Marie Curie, meanwhile, was deeply engaged in her work. In July, she traveled to Leiden, in Holland, to join Heike Kamerlingh Onnes in his cryogenic laboratory studying the behavior of radioactive bodies at very low temperatures. She continued, as she wrote Rutherford, to try to establish the decay series of polonium. She was also in the midst of preparing the first international radium standard and planning her new laboratory.

All the while, she watched her daughters develop and recorded their progress in her notebook. Irène, she noted, got her period that spring. "She doesn't lose much [blood] and scarcely suffers." By summer Irène was taller than her mother. "Irène's physical development is very rapid," her mother noted. "She grows, becomes strong, even too strong in the stomach. . . . She requires lots of activity."

As for the six-year-old Eve, in addition to her remarkable musical ability, she displayed an empathy for others which astonished her mother. "I had just reproached Irène for I don't know what, and Eve dissolved into tears."

"You don't like it when Irène gets scolded?"

"No." (Eve cries)

"You love her even though she pushes you around?"

"Yes, anyway I like that better than if it was me who pushed her."

"My little girl, are you sometimes unhappy?"

"Yes, when others are in pain" (suffering expression on her face)

"Then you worry more about others than yourself?"

"Yes, because myself, I like it better when others are more happy than me." (the little face tenses. Eve is ready to dissolve in tears.)

"Surely," Marie comments, "no one taught her to talk like that." But it is striking how much Eve's concern for others' pain parallels her mother's embroilment in Langevin's unhappiness.

The momentous event of that summer of 1911 was the girls' first trip to Poland. They went ahead of their mother to Zakopane, the mountain village in Austrian Poland where the Dłuskis had their sanitorium, and were soon introduced to delights Marie remembered from her own childhood—gathering strawberries and blueberries, riding horseback, and being indulged by relatives. "We eat ice cream two times a week," Irène reported to her mother in Paris. "When you come here, I hope you will keep Aunt Helena from trying to make me eat, eat, eat because I can't eat so much."

Marie was eager for her daughters to love her country, and to experience the love of their aunts and uncles, who didn't think of Marie as a famous woman but as a sister. Irène, however, was preoccupied with thoughts of home. "I find that it is sweet as you say," Irène writes, "to be considered by my aunts to be the daughter of their sister, but I think that M. and Mme Perrin and M. and Mme. Chavannes consider me to be the daughter of an intelligent and likeable woman and not the daughter of a famous man and woman." As for her mother's beloved homeland: "I love Poland, the Poles and the Polish language because it is your country, your countrymen and your language. But as for me, I love France more."

There is an undercurrent of concern in Irène's incessant and eloquent longing for her mother. "I kiss you with all my heart on your beautiful tired forehead," she writes in one letter home, "Perhaps that will do it some good." And in another:

When I see the sun burning in the sky and making beautiful reflections in the water of the brook, I think that all that would be more beautiful if a sweet Mé were there, near me to look at it.

When it rains, I think that these moments spent in my room waiting for a lightning flash would be sweeter if you were in a chair near me.

Finally Mé did arrive, and they all set out on excursions of several days' duration in the Carpathian Mountains surrounding Zakopane. Marie, who led the way in her hobnailed boots with a sack on her back, wrote with pride afterward of the six-year-old Eve's endurance in the mountains. "Eve very much adored by everybody and very happy," she wrote. "She goes into the mountains with us. . . . She bears up well and walks well. . . . She carries her backpack and is very happy with the excursion and the camping."

That fall, the girls returned with a Polish cousin, Helena's daughter Hania, who was to spend the year in Paris with them. School began. Marie wrote in her notebook that Irène, "in spite of an appearance of not being intelligent, is really gifted in mathematics. She also begins to be very interested in it." Then at the end of October, with the girls installed in their program for the year, Marie left Paris once again, this time for Brussels, where she would attend the first of what was to become a regular and important event in physics, the Solvay Conference.

The Solvay Conferences grew out of the interest and enthusiasm for science of a Brussels manufacturer and chemist named Ernest Solvay, who had made a fortune from a new process he developed for producing sodium carbonate. From the German physical chemist Walter Nernst, Solvay learned of the puzzling contradictions posed by new quantum concepts of Max Planck and Albert Einstein. Together, Nernst and Solvay worked out a plan for a conference on the subject. It was to be, as Solvay wrote, "a personal exchange of views on these problems between the researchers who are more or less directly concerned with them."

Solvay, who admitted that he was "a stranger to such special questions because of . . . other activities," underwrote the conference. A total of twenty-one European and English scientists, including Einstein, Planck, and Rutherford, attended. The French contingent included Jean Perrin, Henri Poincaré, Marcel Brillouin, and Paul Langevin, as well as Marie Curie.

Eleven papers were presented, followed by lively debate. The chairman of this and subsequent Solvays, the Dutch physicist H. A. Lorentz, "needed all his vast scientific knowledge, mastery of languages, and incomparable tactfulness, to keep the discussions focussed. . . . and yet allow each participant's views to come through." Einstein, who gave the last paper and pulled together much of what had gone before, told a Geneva colleague that the conference had been "most interesting."

> Lorentz is a miracle of intelligence and subtle tact—a living work of art. In my opinion he was the most intelligent of all the theoreticians present. Poincaré was altogether simply negative about the relativity theory . . . and showed little understanding for the situation. Planck is untractable about certain preconceived ideas which are, without any doubt, wrong . . . , but nobody really knows. The whole thing would have been a delight for the diabolical Jesuit fathers.

Marie Curie did not give a paper, but she was a lively participant in the discussions, questioning, conjecturing, and adding information from her own work. At one point, she engaged in a lengthy discussion with Rutherford on the nature of Beta-ray decay. According to Einstein, she also participated in the informal socializing that went on between meetings. "I spent much time together with Jean Perrin, Paul Langevin and Madame Curie," he reported, "and I am just delighted with these people. The latter even promised me to visit us with her daughters." Einstein was impressed with Marie Curie's "passionateness" and her "sparkling intelligence."

As it turned out, the Solvay Conference would be the last time for many months that Marie Curie would be able to function as a scientist. On November 4, the day after the conference ended, one of Paris's largest-circulation dailies, *le Journal,* carried a front-page story with a photograph of Marie Curie under the headline: A STORY OF LOVE: MADAME CURIE AND PROFESSOR LANGEVIN. The siege had begun. The story began:

> The fires of radium which beam so mysteriously . . . have just lit a fire in the heart of one of the scientists who studies their action so devotedly; and the wife and the children of this scientist are in tears . . .

Perhaps the fact that Marie Curie and Paul Langevin attended a conference together in another city upset Jeanne Langevin and made her decide to go to the papers. In any case, the *Journal* reporter, Fernand Hauser, seems to have gotten most of his information from Jeanne Langevin's mother, who provided him with abundant half-truths and innuendos. "At Fontenay-aux-Roses," Hauser writes, "in the pretty center of the little town of enchanting gardens, I knocked at the door of the house inhabited, until three months ago, by M. Langevin, professor . . . at the *Collège de France.*" There he met "an aging woman with a very small child on her knee. It was the mother of Mme. Langevin." Hauser said he had come to hear "you yourself deny" that "Professor Langevin has left his home to follow Mme. Curie."

> The mother of Mme. Langevin looked at me for an instant, then, letting the child who was playing with her slip off her lap:
> —What? They know already? . . .
> —This is true then?
> —It's unimaginable, isn't it? . . . The widow of Pierre Curie, the great scientist, who collaborated in the discovery of radium, who is a professor at the Faculty of Sciences, who almost gained entry to the Institute of France, the celebrated, the illustrious Mme. Curie has carried off the husband of my daughter, the father of my little children [her grandchildren]! . . . M. Langevin was a student of Curie. With the death of his master, he put himself at the disposition of his widow . . . to help her in her work; little by little, M. Langevin got in the habit of being more often at Madame Curie's than at his house; very quickly —the instinct of a woman is never wrong—my daughter suspected something; and then, one day, she knew all. Ah! The frightful scenes! The terrible days! . . . Finally, one morning three months ago, M. Langevin left with his children . . .

> [The *Journal* reporter finishes the sentence]
> —And with Mme Curie.

> The mother-in-law answers: I don't know; but one fact is certain, at the same time that he left, she also left Paris.

The reason her daughter went to the judge, she explains, is because she "wanted at least to find her children." They "don't know" where Langevin is at present, she claims, but her daughter doesn't want to start a divorce action because she still hopes her husband will return. "You understand that when one has children—six children— one hesitates to do the irreparable."

The reporter saved his most tantalizing piece of information for last:

> It is said that you have some letters of Mme Curie at hand.

> —Ah! they say that also; very well, yes, we have these letters. And they constitute the proof of what we suspected. . . .

This revelation is followed by an exchange of shocked exclamations. Then, "as though to cut short this painful conversation," the mother of Madame Langevin produces a photographic portrait of Marie Curie. "There is the great scientist, her forehead heavy with ideas, leaning on her hand." Fernand Hauser ends his story as dramatically as he began it: "I would have liked to know what Mme Curie and M. Langevin say of this sad story; I would have liked to hear them cry out to me: 'They are wrong, they abuse us, there is not a true word in what you've been told.' But Mme Curie can't be found and no one knows where to find M. Langevin."

Those who were intimate with the parties to this quarrel would have realized immediately what a web of lies the *Journal* reporter had woven, with the help of Paul Langevin's mother-in-law. Jeanne Langevin was hardly an innocent victim, nor was her husband "carried off" by Marie Curie. There were four, not six, children, and the two boys Langevin had taken with him to England in August had long since returned home to their mother. Nor was there any mystery as to the whereabouts of Paul Langevin and Marie Curie; anyone who worked with them knew they were in Brussels.

There was so much wrong in the story that it was easy for Marie Curie to issue an immediate denial, which appeared in *le Temps* the next day. "I would just like to say," she told the paper, "that I came to Brussels . . . along with 20 French and foreign scientists to a scientific meeting of the greatest importance." Suspecting what others might say about her being with Langevin in Brussels, she went on to say that the meeting "has necessitated a great expenditure of effort and has completely absorbed the time of all the scientists who attended to the point that . . . my colleagues have frequently asked me if I didn't feel tired." As proof that her whereabouts were well known, she noted that she had sent back to her laboratory for charts and films. "Thus they knew in Paris where I was." The story is "pure folly."

Colleagues in Paris verified that Marie Curie and Paul Langevin, far from running off together, had spent the summer miles apart. Langevin was in England, then with the Borels in Aveyron, then at a meeting in Karlsruhe, Germany. And all that time, "Mme Curie didn't stop working in her laboratory on rue Cuvier," *le Temps* reported. "Her collaborators saw her there each day, even in the evening after dinner, as well as Sundays. She almost always took her noonday meal there." Then at the end of August she left to join her children and family in Poland, returning only a short while before the Solvay Conference. *Le Temps* concluded that the whole story was "pure invention."

But to the unrestrained French press and its audience, the story of illicit love at the Sorbonne was just too good to give up. Readers of Parisian newspapers had an insatiable appetite for tales of adultery and betrayal, power, jealousy, and revenge. No paper was complete without its serialized romance, the *feuilleton*. Even the staid *le Temps* ran a *feuilleton* below the fold. And if fact imitated fiction, so much the better.

The day after *le Journal* ran its interview with the aggrieved mother-in-law, *le Petit Journal* weighed in with a front-page story under the headline A ROMANCE IN A LABORATORY: THE AFFAIR OF MME CURIE AND M. LANGEVIN. Running alongside the story was a photograph of Marie Curie among her test tubes. Conservative and anti-Semitic, *le Petit Journal* had lost a large portion of its readership because of its virulent anti-Dreyfus campaign. But it was still, along with *le Journal,* one of the four largest-circulation papers in Paris. Most importantly, in the case of the Curie-Langevin story, it numbered Henri Bourgeois, Madame Langevin's brother-in-law, among its editors. And even though newspapers generally stopped short of publishing private letters, Bourgeois's knowledge and possession of the letters gave him power, and allowed him to pace the drama.

The unsigned story which appeared on the front page of *le Petit Journal* on November 5 began by taking the high ground concerning the Curie-Langevin affair. "We had known about it for several months," the writer acknowledges. "We would have continued to maintain the secret, if the gossip hadn't spread yesterday that the two actors in this tale had taken flight, the one abandoning his household, his wife and his children, the other renouncing her books, her laboratory and her glory." This, admits *le Petit Journal,* is untrue. But the fact of the liaison and the resulting legal action demanding "physical separation" are attested to by Madame Langevin. She also claims to have "proofs of her husband's betrayal."

The rest of the story consists of a long interview with Madame Langevin, who was visited by *le Petit Journal* at her home in Fontenay-aux-Roses. "We found a woman in tears," the newspaper reported, "terrified of the fuss that her conjugal misfortune was causing. . . . " Madame Langevin, displaying the modesty expected of her sex, went on to explain how much she disliked all the publicity. Nor would she have pursued her husband in the courts if it were only a question of an affair with another woman: "I was always hoping to lead him back to me." Had it not been for Langevin's flight with her two sons after an argument, she would never have acted. "If I had been the woman that they are trying to make me out to be in certain circles—a stupidly jealous madwoman—I would have . . . shouted the betrayal of my husband and of the one who has destroyed my home. I have kept silent, because it was my duty as a mother and wife, to hide the faults of the one whose name I bear. I was waiting thus, always hoping for a reconciliation, for my husband's return to reason."

Then, on July 26, she and her husband argued, and he went off with the two boys. "You can understand my anxiety, my fever, my mother's pain when I understood that my children had been carried off. It was only the next day, through a letter received by my brother-in-law, that my husband let me know indirectly that he had gone abroad, taking my sons. Some days after, I learned by intermediary . . . that his correspondence should be addressed to him in England." Although she had "endured martyrdom" for her children's sake, Madame Langevin could bear it no longer when "they were taken from me." It was only this that caused her to initiate legal action. As for the public scandal, she had nothing to do with it.

The story ended with a heart-rending touch: "While this poor and unhappy woman whose heart is ravaged by undeserved misfortune was thus expressing herself, her smallest little girl, an adorable baby, was pressing close against her and stammering, 'Don't cry, *maman, petit père* will come back!' "

Eventually, this story—the saga of the mother in tears, desperately defending home and hearth, mortified by the public attention, willing to forgive and forget, suing only for the sake of her little ones —became the basis of a campaign against Marie Curie. Though patently false to those who knew the real situation, it was perfectly constructed to win the sympathy of the French public. Madame Langevin, in this version, was everything a French woman should be: passionate, indulgent of her husband's dalliances, fiercely protective of her children, but never selfish or aggressive. She was not the sort of woman, in this "script," who would ever go to the newspapers; she had consulted a lawyer not for her own sake but for the sake of her children.

The portrait was as notable for what it left out as for what it included. The fact that Madame Langevin's brother-in-law and ally was an editor of *le Petit Journal* was never mentioned. Nor was there even a hint that Madame Langevin might be looking for a financial settlement from her husband—a fact which would make her sound calculating and "unfeminine." As for the rival woman, she was portrayed as someone whose only attachment was to "masculine" pursuits: "books, laboratory, glory." The fact that she too was a mother of young children was never mentioned, in this account or any other.

For the first few days after the story broke, the papers which would eventually turn on Marie Curie weren't sure whom to believe. *L'Intransigeant* reported that people in Fontenay were "saying softly that Madame Langevin has spoken of nothing but creating trouble for Madame Curie from the moment she went to present herself at the Institute." As for the letters, "we know that M. Langevin . . . allowed all his letters to fall into the hands of his wife, including those from Madame Curie. One can assume therefore that they are hardly compromising."

On November 8, the fourth day after the initial story in *le Jour-*

nal, a strong statement by Madame Curie, coupled with a retraction by the *Journal* reporter Fernand Hauser, fueled more doubts about the story. Marie Curie, who had had time to return home from Brussels and seek legal advice, sent a letter to *le Temps.*

> I consider abominable the entire intrusion of the press and the public into private life. This intrusion is particularly criminal when it involves people who have manifestly consecrated their life to preoccupations of an elevated order and general utility.

> . . . The mad extravagance of the allegations about my claimed disappearance with M. Langevin obliges me to assert the most express reservations about the exactitude or authenticity of all that which one may be able to attribute to me.

> There is nothing in my acts which obliges me to feel diminished. I will not add anything. Whatever may be the suffering that I have felt, I refuse to engage in lawsuits right now, because of the formal retractions and apologies which have been addressed to me. But from now on I will rigorously pursue all publication of writings which are attributed to me or tendentious allegations regarding me. Since I have the right, I will demand damages and interest of considerable sums which will be used in the interests of science.

Probably, even though this letter was signed "M. Curie," it was composed with the help of friends and perhaps of Alexandre Millerand, the lawyer and former socialist cabinet minister who had agreed to represent her. Later, Marie Curie's attackers would accuse her of lying about her relationship with Paul Langevin, but a close reading reveals that she doesn't deny the liaison. She only says what she clearly believed: that she has done nothing which diminished her. The haughty tone of the letter, for which she was also taken to task, was designed to intimidate and shame her pursuers. But for the most part, it didn't succeed.

The one exception was Fernand Hauser, the writer of the initial story in *le Journal.* Within twenty-four hours after its appearance, he completely reversed himself and publicly apologized in abject terms. "I am in despair," Hauser wrote in a letter addressed to Marie Curie, "and I come to present to you my most humble apologies. On the faith of corroborating information, I wrote the article you know of: I was wrong; . . . and I can't understand now how the fever of my profession could have led me to such a detestable act."

> I am cruelly punished, Madame, by the tortures that I endure, at the thought of the harm that I have done you. There is only

one consolation left to me, that is that the humble journalist
that I am will not be able . . . to tarnish the glory which surrounds you, nor the respect which surrounds you. Never again,
Madame, will I write a word, signed or not, about this sad
affair. . . . In bowing respectfully before you, I authorize you,
Madame, to make whatever use you need to of this letter, notably to publish it. Your very afflicted, F. Hauser.

Anyone reading Hauser's extreme apologies would think that he
was in danger of being sued for libel. But in France, such a suit would
have had almost no chance of success. Louis Depoully, a cousin on
the Curie side who wrote Marie to express his sympathy, lamented
that "private life is safeguarded by nothing in our stupid Republic; in
England no one would dare to mount such a campaign because the
courts would award enormous damages." Depoully was right. The
French legal system placed almost no restraints on the content of
newspapers. Editors and columnists in the penny press felt free to
engage in polemics "whose violence shocks us today" without fear of
legal action. Libel and slander suits were very rare, successful ones
even rarer. "In the name of liberty, license was tolerated." Indeed, it
is not much of an exaggeration to say that the only way to silence the
French press in the era was to bribe it.

Despite the paucity of legal remedies, Marie Curie's letter and
Fernand Hauser's apology, which were widely reprinted, sufficed,
along with the quiet pressure of Marie Curie's allies on influential
people, to keep the story out of all but the extreme right-wing papers
from then on. But the absence of the story did not mean that those
papers had forgotten. What happened next demonstrated that Marie
Curie, once tainted, remained suspect, as far as "respectable" newspapers were concerned.

On November 7, by an uncanny coincidence, Reuters sent out a
bulletin that Marie Curie had just been awarded the Nobel Prize in
chemistry for 1911. The decision in 1903 to award the prize to Becquerel and the Curies in physics for the discovery of radioactivity had
left open the possibility of awarding another prize in chemistry for the
discovery of the radioactive elements. And in the intervening eight
years, the momentous implications of those discoveries had become
much clearer. In addition, Marie Curie had accomplished feats of
chemistry since the last prize. In 1907, as the Nobel chemistry committee report pointed out, she had obtained a pure enough sample of
radium to make public the atomic weight—a weight subsequently
confirmed by other researchers. And in 1910 she had succeeded in
obtaining radium in a metallic state.

The report also noted that the Curies' "discovery" of induced radioactivity in 1899 had been a "point of departure" for Rutherford's and others' study of emanations and of "the nowadays generally accepted disintegration theory." And furthermore, the committee pointed out, there was now the possibility that radium might be used in cancer treatment. All of this meant that radium was something "much greater than the discovery of other elements." Indeed, it had led to the establishment of a "special branch of science." For these reasons, the committee urged the Swedish Academy to take the unprecedented step of awarding a second Nobel Prize to the same person. After all, the report pointed out, "it is works, not persons" for which the prize is given. It was an observation which would take on added irony as events unfolded.

The suggestion of scandal had worried the Academy, which had asked Swedish ambassador to France August Gyldenstolpe to look into it. On November 5, the day after *le Journal* broke the story, he cabled the Academy: "The said lady and professor who have been interviewed both protest against the information [in the paper]. Seem to have been together at a scientific meeting in Brussels." Two days later, on November 7, he cabled twice again, reporting "further protests and explanations from prominent scientists" and "further denials and protests from credible sources" in the newspapers. This was enough to persuade Swedish Academy secretary Carl Aurivillius to go ahead with the voting. That same day, in plenary session, the Swedish Academy voted to award Marie Curie the prize.

The French press, however, was not so forgiving as the Swedish Academy. The same newspapers which had made so much of the Curies' 1903 Nobel Prize greeted the news of this one with silence, or with minimal, inside-page reports. Even though Reuters carried the story on November 7, the relatively sympathetic *le Temps* waited until November 9 to mention it, in a brief dispatch buried on page four. "Madame Curie, who has been very exhausted by the cruel incidents that everyone knows of . . . has received warm congratulations from her admirers in Stockholm and Paris," *le Temps* reported, implying that not everyone could be numbered among her admirers. Six days later, *le Temps* ran a front-page article under the heading "The Nobel Prize" which was devoted entirely to Maurice Maeterlinck, the Nobel winner in literature that year; there was not a single mention of the prizewinner in chemistry. Marie Curie was being given the silent treatment.

Fortunately, many of Marie Curie's friends and colleagues were as quick to support her as the papers were to write her off. Jean Perrin, Henri Poincaré, and Émile Borel wrote letters to the editor on her behalf, decrying the newspaper campaign. Albert Einstein wrote his friend Heinrich Zangger within days that "the thriller spread around in the newspapers is nonsense. That Langevin wants to get a divorce has been known for some time. . . . I also don't believe that Madame Curie is either domineering or has some other such affliction. She is a straightforward, honest person whose duties and burdens are just too much for her."

In Einstein's opinion, Marie Curie was an unconvincing *femme fatale*. "She is not attractive enough to become dangerous for anyone," he declared. Nor did he believe there was anything "special" between Langevin and Marie Curie; they simply "enjoyed being together in a harmless way." But one gets the impression that he wouldn't have condemned them in any case.

When the public attacks mounted, Einstein wrote Marie Curie that he was "so incensed over the way in which the rabble dares to react to you that I absolutely had to vent these feelings."

> I am convinced, however, that you hold the rabble in contempt, whether they feign reverence or seek to satisfy their lust for excitement through you.

> I feel the need to tell you how much I have come to admire your spirit, your energy and your honesty. I consider myself fortunate to have made your personal acquaintance in Brussels. . . . I will always be grateful that we have among us people like you—as well as Langevin—genuine human beings, in whose company one can rejoice. If the rabble continues to be occupied with you, simply stop reading that drivel. Leave it to the vipers it was fabricated for.

> With cordial regards to you, Langevin and Perrin.

> A. Einstein

Ernest Rutherford was immediately concerned for his "old friend" Langevin as well as Marie Curie when he heard about the *Journal* article. Marie Curie wrote him gratefully before leaving Brussels. "I know that you spoke of me again yesterday in sympathetic terms and I want to thank you for it." To his friend Bertram Boltwood he wrote that he was "sure it is all moonshine; but it must be rather a miserable business for both of them." When she won the Nobel Prize, he seemed to be genuinely pleased, and wrote to tell her so. And he asked Perrin to keep him informed about developments in the Langevin-Curie affair.

Many other friends and colleagues wrote to express sympathy and indignation, in styles ranging from dancer Loie Fuller's "I love you, I take your two hands in mine and I love you. Pay no attention to the lies, *c'est la vie*" to more formal expressions of "disgust and indignation." "May the vibrant sympathy of your friends," wrote Pierre Weiss, "and the profound esteem of those who know you from a distance provide you with some comfort." Some wrote to congratulate her for winning the Nobel Prize, noting that it was a kind of vindication. Émile Picard, who had participated in the Institute battle, wrote that it was "just recompense for the admirable series of works that you have conducted recently on the isolation of radium. If terrible hours have not been spared you this year, the esteem of those who know you will surely console you."

Of all the letters Marie Curie received, the most indignant came from Jacques Curie, who wrote immediately after the *Journal* article appeared, and kept on writing with heartfelt and adamant support. "What a story this is in the *Journal!*" he wrote, "what rabble, what pigs, what filthy swine!"

Doesn't one have the right to sue newspapers for damages . . . when they try to defame you and mix in private affairs that are none of their business?? This must have troubled you considerably, this business, and Langevin as well—the reality from the point of view of said Langevin is that he should have left his wife several years ago—she's a plague who has been profoundly harmful to him during his entire existence since his marriage.

When it was suggested to Jacques that he should write of his support to a newspaper, he sent a tribute that surely heartened Marie:

To the Editor:

Living in the provinces, I have learned somewhat belatedly that certain people have been astonished by my silence regarding the odious attack launched against my sister-in-law, and that they have made use of it to deny the affection that I have for her and that we have always had for her in my family . . .

It is hardly necessary to say to what extent the ignoble articles written against her have excited my indignation: that is the unanimous feeling of all honest people, and the letters of MM. Poincaré, Borel and Perrin express extremely well the opinion that we all have in this regard. . . . In the name of the Curie family, it may be useful to say that my sister-in-law has always been in her private life as perfect and remarkable as she has been distinguished from the scientific and general point of view.

She was the happiness of my brother during the ten or eleven years of their marriage up to the time of his death. It is impossible to imagine two natures which would understand each other more perfectly.

She was the happiness of my father, during the last years of his life, which he spent alone with her and her children. The affection that they bore for each other was real and complete.

And as for me, the attachment that I feel to her is as profound as for a true sister. I believe I can say that we have full confidence, coming from the bottoms of our hearts, in each other, she and I, and that nothing in the future will ever part us.

Jacques implied, and later demonstrated, that he would support Marie Curie even if it turned out that she and Langevin were lovers. All of those closest to her—some of whom were already privy to the affair—felt the same way. But Marie Curie and her close friends knew that others, including colleagues at the Sorbonne, would desert her if the letters confirming the liaison became public. As the least responsible of the Parisian newspapers continued to pursue the story, the great worry was that one of them would defy convention and publish the letters.

Le Petit Journal, the paper of Henri Bourgeois, seemed to be threatening as much on November 6 when it quoted Jeanne Langevin as saying that she could "by publishing one single one of the letters that I possess reduce their plan [to discredit me] to nothing. I haven't wanted to do it until the present; I still don't want to do it." The story ended ominously: "We have learned from elsewhere that a very grave incident is going to occur which will throw a great deal of light on this sensational affair."

It may have been this warning, or one like it, which caused Jean Perrin and Émile Borel to request a meeting with the powerful and popular prefect of police, Louis Lépine. Perrin later claimed that he had wanted to speak with Lépine about Jeanne Langevin's murder threats. But even if that was his intention, the prefect of police had another agenda in mind. He had already conferred with Jeanne Langevin and her allies, and informed Perrin and Borel that a "huge scandal was going to erupt" if Langevin didn't give up custody of the children unconditionally and agree to pay his wife one thousand francs a month for their support.

Perrin rose in indignation, declaring that "children shouldn't be turned into goods in a market." He felt it wrong that "they were trying to completely take away the children of a man who, having married a young woman without resources, had worked unceasingly and to the point of exhaustion (in a way damaging to his scientific research) to give his children (and his wife) not only the necessities but also the luxuries. . . ."

Borel, calmer than Perrin, asked Lépine for a second meeting, to which he could bring Langevin's response. Borel then discussed Lépine's offer with Langevin and with Marie Curie, whose interests were also at stake. According to Perrin, Marie Curie "left Langevin completely free to make a decision which, however favorable to the children of Langevin, was enormously dangerous for Mme Curie (*and her daughters*)." The next day Borel met again with Lépine, in the presence this time of Henri Bourgeois. He told them that Paul Langevin would not accept the terms.

As Perrin feared, this refusal brought a retaliation more directly damaging to Marie Curie than anything that had gone before. Jeanne Langevin charged her husband with "consorting with a concubine in the marital dwelling"—a charge which would be heard in criminal court. This meant that Marie Curie would be involved in a public trial and that, in all likelihood, the letters would come out. "I witnessed the emotion that this . . . produced on Madame Curie," Perrin later wrote, "an emotion so powerful that we feared for her life."

Her lawyer, Alexandre Millerand, tried to reassure her, insisting that the trial would "dishonor those who initiated it and not those who were its object," and that in any case "a favorable result was not in doubt"; that Madame Curie would not have to attend and could go in confidence to receive the Nobel Prize in Sweden, even though the date set for the trial coincided with that of the Nobel ceremony.

The effect of Jeanne Langevin's charges, however, was felt even before the trial took place. In drawing up the accusation against her husband and his "concubine," Jeanne Langevin's lawyer prepared a document which quoted at length from the Langevin-Curie letters. And it seems to have been this document which circulated among members of the press in mid-November. Very soon after that, *l'Action française* launched an attack in its front pages.

Léon Daudet, the contentious editor of *l'Action,* had been disposed to believe the rumors from the beginning. Two days after the *Journal* story appeared, he wrote a front-page essay entitled "Science and Virtue" in which he attacked the notion that scientists are above carnal desire. "The shock and indignation of certain people at the idea that a celebrated laboratory could harbor a love story—whether it be true or not—is a very amusing thing," wrote Daudet, a former Sorbonne medical student and a libertine. "We find here, in concrete form, one of the superstitions most cherished in a democracy . . . Science (with a capital S) confers virtue."

> Nothing is more stupid, nothing is more false. If I consult my memories, which are numerous and precise, I realize that . . . crises of the heart are extremely frequent among male and fe-

male scientists. That is understandable. Hard studies and the
ardors of physics, chemistry, natural history, mathematics and
medicine take up the passion of youth, above all among
women. . . . Then when the woman scientist is past thirty—
and forty for the male scientists—nature reclaims its rights with
all the more impetuosity because it has been so long held back.

After that, very little was written about the affair in *l'Action française* for ten days. Then, following the secret circulation of the letters,
the paper began to publish daily front-page attacks on Marie Curie
under the headline FOR A MOTHER *(POUR UNE MÈRE)*. The articles,
many of which were written by Daudet's lieutenant Maurice Pujo,
went to great lengths to establish a conspiracy theory involving powerful government and university figures. There was Jean Dupuy, a sena-
tor and former minister, who had tried to silence newspapers in his
role as president of the Parisian press syndicat. There was the attorney
Raymond Poincaré, cousin of Henri Poincaré and future president of
France, who represented the conflicting interests of both Paul
Langevin and the syndicat. Prefect of Police Louis Lépine, according
to this theory, was also trying to bury the evidence, with the help of
Professor Émile Borel, who was using the university's influence to try
to get the letters back. As with all conspiracy theories, there was
enough truth in this one to arouse suspicions; Marie Curie's well-
placed friends *had* used their influence to keep the story out of the
papers, though hardly in a concerted way.

L'Action française was not to be deterred by powerful lawyers
and bureaucrats. The only reason to hesitate would be that the story
concerned a woman.

Even though this woman is not of our race, even though she is
a public functionary . . . , even if in any case she has been
willing to benefit from the prerogatives of men—we were quite
naturally disposed to offer her also the immunities of her sex.
We would have offered them indefinitely if an interest of the
same order but much more sacred had not entered into the
situation. . . . There is not one woman in this affair, there are
two, and the second is infinitely more worthy than the first.
But if the first fears for her reputation, which she has risked
appallingly,—the second, the irreproachable woman, the
mother of a family whose home is being destroyed, can fear, if
we keep silent, . . . that her children, her supreme consolation,
will be taken from her. . . . If we cannot stay silent . . . if we
disobey therefore the instructions of MM. Dupuy and Poincaré, it is because the scandal's strength has become the only
saving grace of the mother.

In fact, the interests of "the mother" are so important that *l'Action française* may not be able "to keep to ourselves the documents that we have. . . . If we are forced, it will be necessary to publish them."

Pujo ended his long diatribe with the larger point the ideologues of *l'Action* never failed to make: the source of all this evil was the immoral Dreyfusards. Among those who played "an odious role," were Perrin, Borel, and Paul Painlevé, as well as other professors of the Collège de France, the Sorbonne, and the École normale supérieure. "As it happens, these intellectuals are almost all old acquaintances from the Dreyfus Affair." They are advocates of "Ibsenian and Dreyfusard morals, preferring anarchy to order, who have in this instance launched an attack on the family." Theirs is the "official morality of the Republic. . . . It is not Science, it is this Morality which they want to save, by imposing silence . . . while depriving an honest woman of her children."

The next day, *l'Intransigeant* followed the lead of its more outrageous counterpart and ran a front-page story entitled A NEW AFFAIR. *L'Intransigeant* had been skeptical of early reports, and had even quoted neighbors who blamed Madame Langevin. But now Madame Langevin's cause had taken on a symbolic meaning which made it "impossible for the independent press to keep silent." *L'Intransigeant* will "respect private life" (that is, not publish the letters) but will not be intimidated by the Sorbonne clique. "Their threats are indeed in vain." That France will "lose a genius who will go off to live under other skies" is a bluff, since everyone knows that Marie Curie's scientific work is "overrated."

> On the other side there is a mother, a French mother, who . . . wants only to keep her children. . . . It is with this mother, not with the foreign woman, that the public sympathizes. . . . This mother wants her children. She has some ammunition. She has some support. She has above all the eternal force of the truth on her side. She will triumph.

From then on *l'Action française* and *l'Intransigeant* kept up a daily barrage, sometimes quoting each other, often echoing each other. "Priggish pedants, in league with the republican powers," are trying to muzzle a "simple mother of a family," treated as unintelligent "because she is not a *doctoresse.*" The powerful establishment of the Sorbonne has forced the hapless Madame Langevin to pursue her cause in the criminal courts, and in the press. "What recourse remained to Mme L . . . in her struggle against the two formidable outside pressures interfering abusively in her private affairs: that of the University and that of the Government? . . . There was nothing left for her but to call on the influence of the press, on . . . enlightened public opinion." The Frenchwoman has "only one piece of ammunition with which to make herself heard, some letters that she found last April, which she had always refused to make public and which she is only using today because all other usual recourse is closed to her," writes Léon Bailby in *l'Intransigeant.* "Those who are displaying such righteous indignation about the possible publication of these incriminating documents can only do one thing: let genuine justice prevail. All French mothers are on the side of the victim and against her persecutors."

IN THE END, neither *l'Intransigeant* nor *l'Action française* published the letters, despite all their threats. Instead, they turned the job over to a maverick outsider who was only too happy to defy the rules. His name was Gustave Téry and he was founder, editor, and principal writer for *l'Oeuvre,* a vitriolic weekly which promised to "say out loud what everyone thinks to themselves." In fact, *l'Oeuvre* said out loud what Gustave Téry thought.

Téry was a man of extremes. In his years as a teacher, he had been a satirist of the Catholic Church and a Dreyfusard, a man who attacked everything sacred, including the flag, the faith, and the crucifix on the wall behind him in the classroom. He said of himself that he was a founder of the National Association of Free Thinkers and above all "applied myself to free thinking." While teaching, he worked as a journalist on *la Fronde,* the feminist newspaper of Marguerite Durand.

But Téry's relationships in academia and in journalism soured. He decided that he was "nothing but a negligible accessory to a woman of talent" at *la Fronde* and then accused Durand of plotting against him. A campaign he launched at another paper, *le Matin,* precipitated a rare lawsuit and seems to have caused his dismissal from the university. In 1909, he founded *l'Oeuvre* and used it as a platform for his new views, which, like Léon Daudet's, had taken a very sharp turn to the right. Formerly anticlerical, he now defended Catholic dogma and accused the teaching establishment of destroying patriotism. He was now viciously anti-Semitic, and used the covers of *l'Oeuvre* to warn against the "Jewish enemy." "How the Jews ruin us," was one headline. "If war breaks out, the Jews will betray us," was another. In the Curie-Langevin affair, Téry saw an opportunity to discredit the academia which had rejected him, and which he now characterized as the "German-Jewish Sorbonne."

On Thursday, November 23, Gustave Téry's pamphlet-sized weekly included ten pages of the correspondence between Marie Curie and Paul Langevin. He claimed that he was not actually publishing private correspondence, but rather the text of the charges

Madame Langevin had brought against her husband and his mistress. "We thus do not commit . . . any indiscretion," wrote Téry, "unless it is that of making the legal document known to the public some days earlier."

What appeared in *l'Oeuvre* were excerpts from the letters Marie Curie and Paul Langevin had written each other in the summer of 1910. There were brief exchanges, with expressions of tenderness and references to "chez nous." All were written using the familiar form, *tu,* and left little doubt that Marie Curie and Paul Langevin were having an affair. Most of the ten pages, however, were taken up with the extremely long letter Marie Curie wrote to Paul Langevin during her vacation at l'Arcouëst that summer, in which she laid out the steps by which he could extricate himself from his unhappy marriage.

Later, when Jacques Curie read these letters, he wrote to assure Marie that what she had written was "very beautiful and very remarkable . . . written in the great scientific spirit; and the advice that you give in them is the most precise, the most exact and the best that you could give to help out the one to whom they were addressed. . . . From the absolute moral point of view, you can only be proud of what you have written."

But the French public didn't share Jacques's view of morality. And with the publication of the letters, the campaign entered a new, more vicious phase. Before, the focus had been on the need to support a defenseless French mother. Now it turned into a xenophobic attack on the other woman, the "foreign woman" who was destroying a "French home." The Curie-Langevin story, as viewed by Gustave Téry, was the Dreyfus affair in a new form. "It no longer divides two Frances, but it shows . . . France in the grip of the bunch of dirty foreigners, who pillage it, soil it and dishonor it."

> They have brought out all that they could find to intimidate us. First it was the respectability of the Sorbonne, the good name of French science . . . now on all occasions, they say "France, it is us." And they say it with such a cold impudence that one hesitates an instant before laughing in their faces.

When "independent journalists" were not intimidated, the powers that be argued for gallantry. And when that didn't work, "Israel mobilized all its levites, its hired killers and its knuckle busters. They multipied the cries, the visits: 'If you speak, you will be a boor, a scoundrel!' . . . I said to myself, 'What is it then that makes them protest so loudly? What is the truth of which they have such great fear?' "

Now that Téry has discovered the truth, he will not hold back but will "shout it out."

> The truth is that, deliberately, methodically, scientifically, Mme Curie has applied herself, through the most perfidious advice, through the most vile suggestion, to detach Paul Langevin from his wife and to separate his wife from her children. All that is recounted with cynicism or revealed unconsciously in the letters.

In scientific circles, Téry reports cattily, Paul Langevin is being called the "chopin de la Polonaise."

It was the cool, dispassionate tone of Marie Curie's letter that came in for the most criticism. Women could be forgiven a great deal if they were overcome by passion. But in this letter, according to *l'Action française,* "what is shocking to people of our country is the absence of sincere cries, always excusable. There is only cold reasoning."

> This foreign woman, who pushes a hesitant father of a family to destroy his home, claims to speak in the name of reason, in the name of a morally superior Life, of a transcendent Ideal underneath which she hides her monstrous egoism. From above, she disposes of these poor people: of the husband, of the wife, of the children. . . . And she applies her scientist's subtlety in indicating the ingenious means by which one can torture this simple wife in order to make her desperate and to force the rupture.

Even more alarming than this "unfeminine" rationality is the morality of the "right to happiness," the right to "live one's life," which hides beneath it. According to Gustave Téry, Marie Curie is really advocating a "scientific morality . . . utilitarian, Ibsenien and Nietzschean." She isn't brave enough to say it, but she scorns French traditions. She is "a foreign woman, an intellectual, emancipated."

Predictably, Téry reminded his readers that Marie Curie had had the audacity to seek admission to the Academy of Sciences. "Strange double standards of these women who proclaim feminist principles at every opportunity! When it comes to forcing open a door, obtaining an advantage, a place, a title, a chair at the Institute, they don't admit to any distinction between the sexes." But when the going is rough these same women resort to appeals to "French gallantry."

The right-wing extremists who attacked Marie Curie were a noisy minority that only seemed to dominate Paris society. There were strong countervailing forces of pacificism and internationalism as well, which tended to be sympathetic. *Gil Blas,* a newspaper of the left with a libertine past, was quick to defend Marie Curie. And the socialist *l'Humanité* made one of the few humane observations about the whole affair, pointing out that "we have passions within us" which are too strong to overcome. "There are always victims in these crises," observed *l'Humanité,* "but does it . . . soothe the suffering of the one to degrade and inflict pain on the other?"

But such sympathy for Marie Curie was rare. And the silence of the moderate press, coupled with the noise on the right, reflects the social and political atmosphere of 1911, a time not only of increasing conservatism and xenophobia, but of growing discomfort about changing sexual mores.

In 1910, the national elections had resulted in a marked swing to the right in France's Chamber of Deputies. And in 1911, the international situation, "which had never been more than a minor sub-plot in the history of the Third Republic," claimed center stage. For some time, there had been friction between Germany and France over territorial rights in Morocco. In July of 1911, a French column was ordered to march on Fez to "impose respect." The mood in Paris by this time was coming to resemble that which preceded the Franco-Prussian war. In the end of June, the old unhealed wounds of that war were revived in a demonstration in the Latin Quarter, where shouts of "Vive l'Alsace, Vive la Lorraine" rang out. November 4, 1911, the very day on which the Curie-Langevin story erupted, is the date one historian believes marks "the birth of nationalism as a widespread, chauvinistic feeling." On that day, a Franco-German treaty was signed on Morocco, the Congo, and Cameroon which was viewed by the French public as a capitulation to Germany. From that time on, French newspapers of the left and right vied with each other in their displays of patriotism, and many thought war with Germany was imminent. This was the atmosphere in which *l'Oeuvre* and *l'Action* launched their attacks on the "foreign woman."

Marie Curie's "foreignness," however, was not nearly so threatening as her gender. The Langevin-Curie affair coincided with the time in which French feminists were becoming more vocal in their pursuit of their rights. When it came to women's rights in France, as Hubertine Auclert once ironically remarked, "revolutionaries and reactionaries, believers and atheists" all joined together in opposition. But beginning in 1908, with the Congrès nationale des droits civils et du suffrage des femmes, the scattered voices which had long been calling for the vote swelled to a chorus. In 1909 a national suffrage league was formed. And in 1910, both Marguerite Durand and Hubertine Auclert tried, unsuccessfully, to run for office. Although French suffragists were still far behind their more militant sisters in England, the fact remains they were more threatening to the status quo in 1911 than they had ever been before. And while Marie Curie might not have called herself "feminist," the right-wing newspapers did, and treated her accordingly.

Among conservative critics in particular, all of France's problems, and most particularly its perceived weakness vis à vis Germany, could be traced to the emancipation of women and the changes which followed in its wake. The change in relations between the sexes—men's emasculation and women's new strength—were seen as symptoms of national decline. "Many of France's most pressing political concerns," Berenson has noted, ". . . were regularly expressed as aspects of an intensified war between the sexes." The passage of the Naquet law in 1884, reestablishing the right to divorce, was thought to be weakening the family, and therefore the nation. "Again and again in these early years of the new century," Berenson has noted, "publicists of the right identified the fate of the nation with the fate of the family."

Concerns about the family were especially prevalent because France, unlike nearly every other industrialized society, was in a period of population stagnation. The steadily falling birth rate, barely exceeding the death rate, was a cause of great concern: eighty-two books on the subject were published between 1890 and 1914. And particularly on the right, one of the reasons set forth, for the falling birth rate was a general decline in morals, a desire by men and women alike to place happiness above duty.

Given these concerns and prejudices, it would be hard to imagine a letter more likely to offend than the long one Marie Curie wrote to Paul Langevin in the summer of 1910. A respectable woman, first of all, was not supposed to enjoy sex, much less to talk about it. And here was Marie Curie giving advice about the marital bed and revealing, barely below the surface, her own passion for Paul Langevin. What's more, the substance of her counsel was that Paul Langevin should withhold sexual favors from his wife—thus denying France the progeny needed for its resurgence in the struggle with Germany. Finally, she was aiding and abetting in the breakup of that most sacred and endangered of institutions, the French family. Her letter, and her behavior, were tantamount in this scenario to treason. All of this helps to explain (if not excuse) the immediate, outraged reaction of the French public to *l'Oeuvre's* publication of the letters.

ALMOST no evidence survives of Marie Curie's own reaction to the tumultuous events of 1911; if there were letters, or journals, they were probably destroyed. Aside from the statement and letter published in the newspaper, there is no document in Marie Curie's own words about the affair, and certainly nothing which reveals her intimate thoughts and feelings. Only the accounts of her friends, written later to set the record straight, provide glimpses of what she was enduring. And among these, the one that brings us closest to Marie Curie is the account Marguerite Borel wrote, more than fifty years later, about the tumultuous days following the publication of the letters.

Marguerite Borel tells the story with her novelist's flair for the dramatic. She is sometimes inaccurate, and there are, undoubtedly, embellishments. Furthermore, in all of her stories, she casts herself in a heroic role. But because she is a novelist, she provides the details. Her vivid retelling allows a glimpse of how Marie Curie, and her daughters, experienced these difficult days.

On the morning *l'Oeuvre* published the letters, according to Marguerite Borel, she receives a visit in her apartments at the École normale superieure from Jean Perrin and André Debierne. They tell her that they are alarmed for Marie Curie, who is virtually a prisoner in her house in Sceaux. A crowd has gathered outside the house and is shouting "Down with the foreigner, the husband-stealer." Marguerite Borel, who has been spending the morning in bed, dresses quickly and sends for her husband.

Émile Borel, when he hears the news, "trembles with indignation" and announces that they will offer Madame Curie the spare room in their apartments in the École normale, where she and her daughters will be protected from insults. Marguerite, along with André Debierne, is dispatched to Sceaux to extricate Marie and bring her back to the Borels' apartment in Paris. "At Sceaux," Borel recalls, "I pass before some groups of the curious" outside the house. "Madame Curie allows herself to be convinced, follows us, holding Eve by the hand." On the way to the Borels', she "sits petrified, white as a statue." Silently, and "with dignity," she crosses the courtyard and enters the Borels' apartment.

Irène, meanwhile, is at a gymnastics lesson with her friend Isabelle Chavannes, who happens to see a copy of *l'Oeuvre* lying around the room. Glancing at the names of Langevin and Curie in large letters, she calls to her friend, "Irène, they're writing about your mother!" Then, seeing the substance of the article, she tries to hide it from Irène. But Irène reads it, and is extremely upset. André Debierne arrives and leads her back to rue d'Ulm to join her mother.

"At rue d'Ulm," according to Borel's account, Irène "glues herself to this mother for whom she feels such adoration." Neither mother nor daughter cries, but Marie caresses her daughter's hair. When friends try to take Irène away to a friend's house, she is adamant: "I can't leave Mé," she insists. But finally, her mother convinces her to go to the Perrins', where she will be with her friend Aline. Eve stays with her mother.

Very quickly, the Borels learn that the letters in *l'Oeuvre* have turned even their friends and colleagues against Marie Curie. The phone rings constantly and "they *all* are saying:"

Who would have believed it? We can't support her. It will be
terrible to stop seeing her. And yet . . . She is so much compro-
mised. . . . Have you read? . . .

Marguerite Borel, who has been "delegated" to answer the
phone, insists to everyone that it is "a sordid cabal," and informs them
that Madame Curie "is here, with us, and we are supporting her."
The callers are incredulous. "At the École normale? . . . Are you
crazy?"

At lunchtime, Marie Curie eats in her room with Eve, "who
doesn't understand much of this turmoil except that they have
changed houses, that Mé is sad, a little sick, and that she needs
cuddling." Downstairs, the noontime meal is interrupted when Émile
Borel receives a call from the minister of public instruction demanding a meeting. The minister upbraids Borel for using his apartments, which are an extension of the École Normale, to harbor
someone who is a discredit to the school. He threatens Borel with a
demotion. Borel refuses to back down.

Soon after, Marguerite Borel is called to the apartments of her
father Paul Appell, dean of the Faculty of Sciences at the Sorbonne,
for a dressing-down. "His gray eyes are flashing," Marguerite Borel
reports, "as always in fits of anger, rare but violent." Appell has heard
from the head of the École normale and the director of Pierre's old
school, the École de physique et chimie, that Marguerite and her
husband have taken in Marie Curie. "Why mix in this affair which
doesn't concern you?" Appell asks his daughter. "Scandal makes a
stain of oil." Marguerite Borel is steadfast. She argues that Marie
Curie has been slandered.

Appell's response reveals that he and others in power are already
contemplating a solution: Marie Curie should be asked to leave
France. "The Council of Ministers is going to speak about it this
evening," he says. He is planning to ask Marie Curie to his office to
"explain it to her gently." An argument ensues. Marguerite reminds
her father that he has stood up to gossip in the past, and he counters
that he is "responsible for order in the faculty." Marie Curie, he
notes, "will have a chair and a laboratory in Poland. She can leave at
her own pace . . . Her situation is impossible in Paris . . . I've done
everything for her, sponsored her candidacy at the Academy. But I
can't hold back the sea which is drowning her. . . ."

Marguerite Borel, who has "never had an argument" with her
father, is trembling: "If you yield to the idiotic nationalist movement,
if you insist that Madame Curie leave France . . . I swear to you that
I will not see you again in my entire life. Because . . . this isn't you."
Her father, who has been putting on his shoes, is so enraged that he

throws one of them against the door of his office. Though he insists that she is courting disaster and that Marie Curie will be "swept away and you with her," he agrees to hold off.

Marguerite Borel, who views the attack on Marie Curie as a product of "xenophobia, jealousy, and antifeminist reflexes," continues her defense. She tells the wife of an influential minister that the university is "an old lady hypocrite," which looks the other way when the offenders are French and male. Slowly, some who were reluctant at first are brought around by Marguerite Borel and other allies, including Marie's good friend Henriette Perrin. The mathematician Paul Painlevé gives a speech to the Association of Students on the "intellectual and moral influence of the woman" in which he compares Marie Curie to the heroines of classic antiquity. People pay visits to Marie Curie in the second-floor room where she spends her days, attending "minutely" to Eve. Some bring flowers for her and candy for Eve. Others come frequently to noonday meals. "During this period," Marguerite Borel writes, "we didn't know how many of us there would be at the noonday table, nor who would be our companions. The table leaves were added permanently." Poles, including Ignacy Paderewski, come to pay their respects. And Józef and Bronia arrive from Poland to support their sister.

Józef and Bronia, understandably outraged by the way their sister has been treated, try to convince her to return to Poland. But she, according to Marguerite Borel, is adamant. "I am French," she says. "My daughters also. Like Pierre. I will stay here and I will continue if I'm allowed to, if not I will come to you."

Shortly after the letters were published, Paul Langevin, still living apart from Jeanne Langevin, had appeared at the Borels' house looking "pale" and wearing a "buttoned frock coat." He announced to the Borels, out of Marie Curie's hearing, that he had "decided to challenge Téry to a duel." He added, "It's idiotic, but I must do it."

The immediate reason Langevin decided he must fight was Gustave Téry's pointed insult, in the article accompanying the letters in l'Oeuvre. Téry had written, in his diatribe addressed to Marie Curie, that "There is . . . a man one can address to cut short this jesuitic farce; you will not succeed in hiding this man in your skirts: he is named Paul Langevin." A man who allows "the woman who carries his name, the woman who remains the mother of his four children, to be dragged in the mud by all his friends, this man, even if he is a professor at the Collège de France, is nothing but a boor and a coward." In the code which governed middle-class behavior in Belle Époque France, these words could only be understood as a challenge to a duel.

Although dueling is often associated with earlier eras, more duels were fought in France during the years following defeat in the Franco-Prussian war than at any time since the seventeenth century. The resurgence seems to have had many causes, including concern over France's "virility" following that humiliating defeat. "Duelling became the emblem of a masculine revival," Edward Berenson has noted, "destined to restore the national will through a new spirit of combat." As sociologist Gabriel Tarde observed, duels were the result of the collision of the Belle Époque's obsession with the opinion of others and a newly ascendant penny press, which he called "a steam engine for the fabrication and the destruction of reputations on an immense scale." In a time of increasing democratization, those who belonged to the aristocracy no longer felt secure that birth assured status, and might duel to protect their reputations. Non-aristocrats viewed dueling as a way to climb the social ladder. One left-wing deputy noted that "the easiest way to appear to possess good blood lines . . . is to endanger one's own blood." And finally, since there was so little recourse in the courts for those who felt dishonored, the duel was one way to redress a grievance.

For all these reasons, hundreds of duels were fought in Paris between the end of the Prussian War and the beginning of World War I. Journalists seem to have been the most frequent combatants, but other writers, including Marcel Proust and Guy de Maupassant, dueled as well. Politicians and statesmen dueled; Georges Clemenceau fought twenty-two duels. And a 1906 handbook entitled *The Laws of the Duel,* written by Emile Bruneau de Laborie, enjoyed a wide readership.

The male ritual of the duel was always the same. The wronged party found two friends, "seconds," to support his cause. They paid a visit to the offending party, informing him that he was being challenged. A time and place were agreed upon, and the weapon of combat—either sword or pistol—was chosen. On the day of the duel, the combatants either stood fifty feet apart and aimed their pistols at each other or battled hand to hand with swords.

Whatever the weapon, duels were not nearly as dangerous as they sound. A joke went around Paris about a journalist's wife who couldn't find her husband and was worried about him until she learned that he had journeyed to the country to fight a duel. "Thank heaven!" she exclaimed. "Then he is safe." This is a slight exaggeration: some died in duels, and others were seriously injured. But generally, the ritual requirements of the duel were met if blood flowed. When that happened, everyone, including the doctors attending the combatants, could go home.

Amazingly enough, the Curie affair provoked not one but at least five duels. Three of them involved writers for the newspaper *Gil Blas,* a defender of Marie Curie, and her two most vituperative detractors, Léon Daudet and Gustave Téry. In one of them, fought the day after the letters were published, Pierre Mortier of *Gil Blas* was wounded by Gustave Téry in the biceps and the forearm. Afterward, Mortier received a letter of condolence from Marie Curie, and wrote back that Gustave Téry had behaved like a "scoundrel" and that he was "happy to tell him so." The duel which attracted the most attention by far, however, took place three days after the letters were published, on November 26, between Téry and Paul Langevin.

According to Marguerite Borel, who rode around Paris in a carriage with him to look, Paul Langevin had a hard time finding seconds. The director of the École de physique et chimie, expressed sympathy but refused, as did several others. Finally, they went to visit Paul Painlevé, who agreed. With Painlevé's endorsement, Langevin was able to convince the director to agree too. This done, Marguerite Borel and Paul Langevin shared lunch in a workingmen's bistro, then continued on to Gastinne-Renette, the well-known supplier of firearms to dueling Parisians. There, the physicist tried his hand at discharging a pistol in the store's firing range.

At eleven in the morning on November 26, Paul Langevin and Gustave Téry convened with their seconds and doctors in the Bois de Vincennes, the large park east of Paris. A few photographers and reporters were there too, and although the rules of combat kept them at a distance, they were close enough to see and report on what happened.

That same day, *le Petit Journal* and *l'Intransigeant* gave detailed accounts to their readers. Paul Langevin arrives first. "Nervously tugging on his mustache," he paces back and forth with his seconds at his side. Langevin is "tall, thin," and wears a soft hat. "A black mustache cuts across his blemished face." A black scarf around his neck conceals the whiteness of his false collar. Some minutes later, a second group appears. Gustave Téry also wears a soft hat and an overcoat with the collar turned up against the November damp.

The seconds mark off the field of combat, counting out the twenty-five meters that will separate the combatants. Then they load the pistols. Paul Painlevé hands Langevin a pistol. Urbain Gohier, the journalist who is one of Téry's seconds, does the same for him. Painlevé has been chosen by lot to direct the combat. He informs the adversaries of the rules. Then, in a loud voice that "bites through the fog," he shouts, "Are you ready?" He counts rapidly, "one, two, three." And then "fire!" Langevin lifts his arm halfway up, as though to discharge his gun. But Gustave Téry keeps his pistol barrel pointed toward the ground. Langevin, seeing that Téry does not plan to fire, lowers his pistol as well.

There is a long silence, followed by a gathering of the seconds to discuss the situation. The tension eases as it becomes clear that the "duel" is over without a shot being fired. A statement is signed by both combatants. Urbain Gohier takes the pistols and fires them into the air, providing the photographers with a chance to take pictures of a nonevent.

Afterward, in *l'Oeuvre*, Gustave Téry gave, in his usual overblown style, an explanation of his behavior:

I have no personal animosity toward my former colleague and my comrade from the École normale Paul Langevin . . . furthermore, the defense of Mme Langevin does not oblige me to kill her husband. That is quite simply the reason, not having a thirst for blood, I didn't feel it was my duty, the other morning, to use the firearm which they placed, a little imprudently, in my hands. I add, but this is secondary, that Paul Langevin has a reputation as a scientist . . . however grave may be the errors made by Langevin in his domestic life, I obviously had scruples about depriving French science of a precious brain. . . . You say to me that . . . it would have been enough simply to fire. What do you know? I am so clumsy that I could very well have killed him. I admit that I wouldn't have been able to forgive myself, because to my mind, in this adventure, the most pitiful victim, after Mme Langevin, is her husband.

It is not clear when and to what extent Marie Curie was informed of Paul Langevin's duel. Marguerite Borel claims they kept it from her. But given that she knew about the duel of Téry with Pierre Mortier several days earlier, it seems likely that she knew of Langevin's duel as well. Certainly, it was the talk of Paris. Indeed, news of the duel even reached the Nobel committee in Sweden. And it was this, along with the publication of the letters, which led to one of the cruelest of all the humiliations she was to suffer.

On November 22, the day before the letters were published, Marie Curie wrote to Svante Arrhenius, the member of the Academy who had so enthusiastically advocated her candidacy for the Nobel, in order to discuss the "delicate matter" of the "attacks by the family of M. Langevin." She explained that she would like to come to thank the Academy in person "for the very great honor." But she feared that the ceremony might be "disagreeably troubled by rumors of the press scandal that they are trying to stir up." She asked him to tell her "if you think I should come or whether it would be better to stay away."

Arrhenius's response was reassuring. He told her the "chicanery" and "lies" of the French press were well known but no one believed them. He assured her that the press would be free of any mention of the Langevin affair during her visit, when she would be considered the "guest of the nation." Arrhenius went on to respond to her questions about the lecture she would be giving.

But six days later, following the publication of the letters and Langevin's duel, another, very different, letter arrived from Arrhenius. He was writing again, he explained, because things had changed.

> A letter attributed to you has been published in a French newspaper and copies have circulated here. . . . I have therefore asked some colleagues what they thought should be done in the new situation, which has furthermore been considerably aggravated by the ridiculous duel of M. Langevin. The duel gives the impression, I hope incorrect, that the published correspondence is not false. All my colleagues have told me that it is preferable that you not come here on December 10. . . . I therefore beg you to stay in France; no one can be sure what might happen here with the distribution of the prize.
>
> If the Academy had believed that the letter in question might be authentic, it would not, in all probability, have given you the prize before you had given a plausible explanation that the letter is false. . . .
>
> I therefore hope that you will telegraph M. Aurivillius [secretary of the Academy] or even me that it is impossible to come . . . and that you will then write a letter saying that you do not want to accept the prize before the Langevin trial has demonstrated that the accusations made toward you are absolutely without foundation.

The pain that this letter caused Marie Curie surfaced in a letter she wrote a few weeks later to another member of the Academy, Gustav Mittag-Leffler. "You know," she wrote, "that I considered M. Arrhenius a friend." But even though she found Arrhenius's rejection very "painful," her reply to him was defiant:

> You suggest to me that I put off accepting the Nobel prize that has just been awarded to me, and you give this explanation that the Academy of Stockholm, if it had been forewarned, would probably have decided not to give me the prize, unless I could publicly explain the attacks of which I have been the object. If that were the general feeling of the Academy, I would be profoundly disappointed. But I do not believe that it is up to me to surmise the intentions and opinions of the Academy. I must therefore act according to my convictions.

The action which you advise would appear to be a grave error on my part. In fact the prize has been awarded for the discovery of Radium and Polonium. I believe that there is no connection between my scientific work and the facts of private life. . . . I cannot accept the idea in principle that the appreciation of the value of scientific work should be influenced by libel and slander concerning private life. I am convinced that this opinion is shared by many people. I am very saddened that you are not yourself of this opinion.

Marie Curie informed Arrhenius that by the time he received her letter she would already have sent a telegram to announce that she would be in Stockholm for the ceremonies. "I wrote you earlier that I was disposed to follow your advice on this, but I have since received an opposing opinion." She added, however, that she was "so tired and so sick that I don't even know if it will be possible for me to make the trip."

Clearly, Marie Curie was in no mood to accede to Arrhenius's demand that she renounce the prize until after the Langevin trial cleared her name. But in any case, as she explained to him, it would no longer have been possible. Even though she believed, and her lawyer believed, that a trial "would have been the best way for me to defend myself," Paul Langevin and his wife had decided to settle out of court. There would be no divorce court or criminal court trial after all. "I consider," she told Arrhenius, "that I have nothing to reproach myself with, unless it is with having neglected my own self-interest in this situation."

The separation arrangement between Paul Langevin and his wife involved his admitting to be in the wrong. The custody of all four children went to Jeanne Langevin, but Langevin could have lunch with the two older boys when they were in school in Paris, and the children's time would be divided evenly between the two parents on Sundays and holidays. At age fifteen, the sons would come to live with their father. And he would be in charge of the "intellectual direction" of the children. Finally, there was a cash settlement of eight hundred francs a month, two hundred francs less than Jeanne Langevin had demanded a month earlier, before the letters were published.

According to Jean Perrin, Marie Curie "expressed *very clearly* her desire to allow the case to go to trial." And her lawyer, Alexandre Millerand, gave her "strong advice in the same direction." But Langevin, "fearing the new trouble that would come through publication of the proceedings and feeling a profound repugnance against exposing the miseries of his home life and against *taking sides publicly against the mother of his children,* decided to accept the arrangement that was proposed." Perrin had advised him to accept the arrangement, but he was not sure he was right, "particularly in view of the interests of Madame Curie."

Predictably, the right-wing press greeted the news of the settlement as a great victory for French motherhood. Maurice Pujo wrote in *l'Action française* that it was "the scandal alone which destroyed the insolent pretensions exhibited in the letters of the Foreign woman. . . . We can thus legitimately be proud of the result. It is not in vain that we have stood up to the Jewish hypocrisy . . . ; it is not in vain that several among us have gone in this connection to the field of battle, because it has brought about the triumph of the rights of an oppressed woman. As to our adversaries, as to the Sorbonne with its half-breeds and Jews, the defeat that they have experienced, despite all official power, has taught them that one doesn't succeed easily when one attacks . . . this still solid rock: French custom."

On December 10 and 11, despite ill health, Marie Curie attended the Nobel ceremonies in Stockholm accompanied by her sister Bronia and her daughter Irène. Notwithstanding the fears of some members of the Swedish Academy that it would be embarrassing for Madame Curie to "receive the prize personally from King Gustaf," she performed with her usual dignity and there were no awkward moments. On the contrary, the ordeal she had been through seemed to make her more assertive in her formal remarks, and more expressive in her informal ones. In thanking Mittag-Leffler at a private dinner, she spoke of Pierre, of her "worship of this beautiful life of disinterested work," and of the pride she felt "for myself and for my daughter who is here with me" in hearing him praised. At the banquet with King Gustaf, she spoke proudly of her own work. "Radioactivity is a very young science," she told the gathering. "It is an infant that I saw being born, and I have contributed to raising with all my strength. The child has grown; it has become beautiful. . . . One could not have wished for a more perfect blessing on it than the Swedish Academy of Sciences has given in conferring three Nobel prizes, one in physics and two in chemistry to the four names of Henri Becquerel, Pierre Curie, Marie Curie and Ernest Rutherford."

Marie Curie's formal Nobel lecture, like her informal speeches, made repeated mention of other workers, including not only Pierre Curie but also Rutherford, Soddy, Ramsay, and Debierne. But at the same time she laid claim, in reviewing the fifteen-year history of radioactivity, to the work that belonged to her alone. Much more than usual, she made use of the first person. "The history of the discovery and isolation of this substance," she told the Academy, "furnished proof of the hypothesis made by me, according to which *radioactivity is an atomic property of matter and can provide a method for finding new elements.*" And "isolating radium as a pure salt . . . was undertaken by me alone." Many of her paragraphs began with *Je.* "I determined the atomic weight several times," and "I thus obtained products of very great activity." "I was struck," "I measured," "I then thought," "I further thought." Let no one claim, the lecture implied, that Marie Curie was a mere appendage to gifted men.

If the scandal had made Marie Curie more assertive, it had also exacted a great toll. Even before she went to Stockholm, her friends were worried about her health. When she returned, her condition worsened until, on December 29, she had to be rushed to a hospital. For the next two years, she suffered from the effects of a severe and complicated kidney ailment, undoubtedly exacerbated by the pain of the scandal. She was unable to work. And indeed, she seems never to have felt robust again for the rest of her life.

Once the Langevins reached a settlement, the scandal died down. *L'Intransigeant* hoped "never to have to write another word about this affair, which returns now to the private domain." Only Gustave Téry persisted, attacking the "egoism" and "individualistic morality" of the Sorbonne one week, the "dirty foreigners" and "Jews" in the laboratories the next. Finally, near the end of December, *l'Oeuvre* announced the discovery that Marie Curie's middle name was Salomé and asked, "Is Madame Curie Jewish?" Although she had denied it in the past, *l'Oeuvre* claimed to have the proof: "Her father is in fact a converted Jew."

Not many people took Gustave Téry's ravings seriously. Nonetheless, Marie Curie would never be able to entirely obliterate the "stain" of the scandal. Only a few months before, in October, *le Figaro* had suggested that Marie Curie's chances of becoming a member of the Academy on her next try were excellent. Now it was clear there would never be a next try. And among the proper bourgeoisie of Paris, Marie Curie and her daughters' reputation could never be fully restored.

More important, from Marie Curie's point of view, the life she had hoped for with Paul Langevin was no longer a possibility. Langevin felt great remorse for what had happened to his friend. He tried to defend her to Arrhenius, explaining that Marie Curie was being "crucified for having tried to save, in the name of friendship . . . what she saw in me of a scientific future." And four years later, he wrote of his "constant remorse at not having been able to do anything to defend her against the intentionally false accusations which were published against her." Perhaps out of guilt, or because of the money he owed her, Langevin left a portion of his earnings from an invention to Marie Curie's daughters.

Back in the summer of 1910, when they exchanged the letters that were to bring them so much grief, Marie had written Paul Langevin that they were "linked by a profound affection that we must not allow to be destroyed." She compared the destruction of a "sincere and profound emotion" to the "death of an infant that one has cherished and seen grow," adding that it might be "an even greater misfortune than that in some cases." For a woman who had lost a baby, it was an especially forceful image, suggesting how deeply she cared for Paul Langevin. Perhaps the harshest consequence of the scandal was the mortal blow it dealt to what might have been, for both Marie Curie and Paul Langevin, a satisfying, loving life together.

Certainly all the evidence suggests that Marie Curie and Paul Langevin's love affair was over. Langevin wrote in 1915 that Marie Curie had "never ceased to show me affection and sympathy for my sorrows" and that he for his part had continued "friendly relations with her" and indeed "would not know how to continue" without her affection. But by that time, Langevin had "sought to achieve a little bit of a détente" with his wife, "only in the interests of our children." By 1914, according to his son André, Paul and Jeanne Langevin were back together. Later on, with his wife's acquiescence, Langevin had another mistress. But this time he chose a woman of the acceptable kind: she was an anonymous secretary.

Chapter Fifteen

RECOVERY

THOSE WHO KNEW Marie Curie well believed that her physical collapse at the end of 1911 was precipitated by the Langevin affair. "Obviously," Jacques Curie wrote her, "your illness results for the most part from the upset and the worries that you have had." Jean Perrin, looking back on her illness, concluded that "one can only attribute it to the terrible emotions endured by Curie, already weakened by overwork."

Undoubtedly the anguish of the Langevin affair made Marie Curie vulnerable. But it was a serious physical illness which sent her by ambulance to the maison de santé on rue Blomet on December 29, 1911. According to her doctors, a number of old lesions around her uterus and in the area of the kidney and ureter were causing a pyelonephritis (kidney infection). They recommended surgery, but waited to see if her condition would improve without it. Although the source of the troublesome lesions is not mentioned in the doctors' report, one possibility is that Marie Curie at one time had an asymptomatic tuberculosis which resulted in scarring without making her visibly ill. Tuberculosis, which she had dreaded all her life, may have paid her a silent visit after all.

Marie Curie stayed under the care of the Sisters of the Family of Saint Mary on rue Blomet for most of January 1912. When she returned home, it looked for a while as though she might be able to recover without the surgery the doctors had recommended. But in March she was back in the hospital again, this time for an operation performed by Dr. Charles Walther, apparently to remove the troublesome lesions. Afterward, she felt so ill that she believed death was imminent. She wrote a seven-page document giving the amounts and locations of all the radium in her possession, with instructions for its disposition. And she wrote Pierre's old friend Georges Gouy, asking him to help her plan the disposition of her affairs. Gouy wrote back reassuringly:

> Needless to say you can count on me to follow all the recommendations you will make. But the time has not come for that and you will live long enough to arrange everything as you deem right, to establish your children and to make the Radium Institute, which is now being built, prosper. This is a disagreeable moment to get through, and it is certainly permitted to a patient to have moments of discouragement, but there is not the least doubt that some time from now you will see things in a better light.

Gouy was right. But the recovery would take a very long time. After her operation, Marie Curie weighed only 103 pounds, twenty pounds less than she had weighed three years earlier, and she was subject to "attacks" in which she was overcome with paroxysms of pain. In April, after attending a conference which seemed to worsen her condition, she wrote to the dean of the Sorbonne asking for more time off. "I had hoped to take up teaching again after Easter," she explained. "To my great regret . . . it looks as though I won't be able to assume my duties again for a month or more." As it turned out, Marie Curie would be too ill to teach for another six months, and subject to relapses for many months after that.

In the meantime, she led the life of a convalescent—a life which bore a striking resemblance to her invalid mother's. At the time of what she called "ma grave maladie," Marie Curie was forty-four, just two years older than her mother had been when she died of tuberculosis. Like her mother before her, Marie traveled from one retreat to another in search of a cure. Like her mother, Marie worried about her daughters, who were often left behind. Like her mother too, she wrote discouraged letters to friends in which she imagined that her life would soon be over.

But unlike her mother, Marie kept moving not just to seek a cure but also to avoid prying eyes and gossiping tongues. Early in 1912 Jacques Curie wrote his sister-in-law, "Let us hope that the bad period is over. . . . This will be a bad year, of which you will retain a very unpleasant memory. . . ." But Marie still didn't feel safe from those who wanted to keep the scandal alive. Through most of 1912 and 1913 she traveled under other names; when she wrote to friends, she asked them not to reveal her whereabouts, and she took pains to ensure that her address would be unknown to the press wherever she went.

Already, in the weeks before her illness, she had moved out of her house in Sceaux, where neighbors had gathered to harangue her when the love letters were published fourteen months before. She seems to have spent only enough time at the Sceaux house to organize her belongings for the move to Paris, where she installed her family on the fourth floor of the graceful apartment building at 36 quai de Béthune on the tranquil Île St. Louis. According to Eve, who paid attention to such things, Marie never bothered to furnish this new home in the sumptuous style its ample rooms required. That quai de Béthune was a stylish address was less important to her than that it bordered the Seine and was situated right by the pont Sully, making it easy to walk across the river and climb the hill to the Sorbonne and the Radium Institute, now under construction. Of equal, if unspoken, importance, was the anonymity a grand apartment in a big city afforded. Here in the heart of Paris, vigilante neighbors weren't likely to gather outside her door.

And yet, even during her illness, Marie Curie was not out of reach of her tormentors. Apparently someone spread the rumor that she was in the hospital because she was pregnant with Langevin's child. The director and sister superior of the maison de santé where she was hospitalized wrote Marie Curie at the end of January about an "abominable insinuation" published in a newspaper about her. "Because of professional duty," they explained to Marie Curie, "we never reveal the diagnoses of patients," adding that the "allegation . . . is a lie which deserves the scorn of all honest people." Jean Perrin was equally indignant about the "absurd calumnies" that were spread about her illness. Finally, to dispel the rumors, *le Temps* published her doctors' diagnosis.

Soon after her operation in March, Marie left Paris for a little house in Brunoy, a charming village tucked into a bend in the Yerres River. Even though her sister Bronia didn't accompany her there (she had come earlier, during the initial crisis), Marie invoked her protection, renting under the name of Madame Długska. The Brunoy house was easy to reach, just a thirteen-mile train ride from Paris in the direction of Fontainebleau. And as a result, Marie's daughters could travel there, accompanied by their governess, when they weren't in school. In her notes on the children, Marie wrote of a week spent at Brunoy that spring with Eve, who was convalescing herself, and "likes keeping house but doesn't want to study."

When her condition didn't improve by summer, it was decided that Marie Curie should seek the higher altitudes and healthful waters of the Haute-Savoie region. In late June, accompanied by her friend Alice Chavannes, she made the long train trip from Paris to Thonon-les-Bains, a city at the edge of the French Alps whose climate and mineral waters were considered ideal for "hydrotherapeutic treatments." The Savoie region, as one guidebook noted, is cooled by the "glacial water which runs down from our snowy summits" and also could offer "almost all the varieties of mineral water known." The composition of the water in Thonon was considered particularly good for curing pyelonephritis.

However despondent Marie may have been when she wrote Georges Gouy in March, she had rediscovered her old determination by the time she arrived in Thonon-les-Bains. There she began to apply the same careful, scientific methods she used in the laboratory to the task of overcoming her illness. Every day for most of a month, she measured the cubic centimeters of water she took in, and recorded the amounts on a chart morning and evening. On the same chart she recorded urine output and made note of "crises" and signs of pus in her urine. She recorded her temperature, morning and evening, on the same chart, and to the side entered anecdotal observations. "Dull pain in the region of the ureter from two in the morning until noon," read a typical entry, "then lessened until evening. Urine slightly cloudy." Or, on another day, "Persistent pain from morning through the day (kidney and ureter). Cloudy urine in the morning, then clear the whole day."

Unfortunately, Marie Curie's careful observations pointed to only one conclusion: she wasn't getting much better. "I am pursuing my water cure in a tranquil place," Marie wrote her colleague Ellen Gleditsch in mid-July. "My health is improving very slowly and I won't have too much of my vacation to restore me to a condition in which I can work." As in Brunoy, she worried that her location would be discovered. This time, she used "Madame Skłodowska" and asked everyone she wrote to keep her address a secret. André Debierne, her devoted assistant, forwarded her mail from Paris and gave out her address only when he thought it urgent.

At the end of July, Marie traveled from Thonon, near the Swiss border, to England, where she was to spend the rest of the summer vacation with a friend and colleague named Hertha Ayrton, a woman uniquely qualified to provide her with the peace and anonymity she so desired. Marie Curie and Hertha Ayrton had first met in June of 1903, when Pierre Curie addressed the Royal Society on the subject of the discovery of radium. Hertha Ayrton was present that night in her role as wife of the physicist W. E. Ayrton. But she, like Marie Curie, was a scientist of importance in her own right. She had begun by inventing a measuring instrument, then made significant investigations into the hissing of the electric arc and the phenomenon of ripples caused by waves in sand. During their 1903 visit, the Curies were invited to the Ayrtons' for dinner, and Hertha and Marie began a friendship which was to last for life. Marie Curie once said to Hertha Ayrton, "I maintain a great affection for you, because you are not one of those people with whom one becomes disillusioned."

The parallels between the two women's experience as scientists are striking. Hertha Ayrton had sought membership in the Royal Society, as Marie Curie had in the Academy of Sciences, and been turned down—in her case on the grounds that she was a *married* woman (although, in fact, no woman was admitted to full membership in the Royal Society until 1945). Both women had two daughters and husbands who were extremely supportive of their work. Once, when Sir William Ramsay told a *Daily Mail* interviewer that "all the eminent women scientists have achieved their best work when collaborating with a male colleague," Hertha Ayrton, who once said she wished Marie Curie had won the 1903 Nobel Prize alone, responded with characteristic indignation. First she defended her friend Marie Curie, then went on to say that "all my scientific work has been carried out alone."

> My husband foresaw that if we collaborated any merit that might attach to our work would be attributed to him . . . and he therefore, out of chivalrous regard for my scientific reputation, refused ever to collaborate with me. . . . In later days he knew so little of what I was doing on the subject of sand ripples and oscillating water that he saw some of my experiments for the first time when I showed them in public.

She ended by pointing out that most of Sir William Ramsay's own work had been done "when collaborating with a male colleague."

Even in background, Marie and Hertha had something in common: both were outsiders in the dominant culture, Marie because she was Polish and Hertha because she was a Jew. Born Phoebe Sarah Marks, Hertha was the third child in the family of a Polish-Jewish refugee named Levi Marks, who struggled to make a living in the clock and jewelry trade in Portsea, England. After passing the Cambridge University Examination for Women, Hertha (as she renamed herself) entered the newly formed Girton College for women in 1876. There she came to the attention of a feminist named Barbara Bodichon, who in turn introduced her to Mary Ann Evans, known as Mrs. George Henry Lewes, and known to posterity as the great novelist George Eliot.

George Eliot wrote encouraging letters to Hertha Marks and may have helped subsidize her education as well. She also probably made use of the young Jewish girl in developing the character of Mirah in her last novel, *Daniel Deronda*. The idea of the novel, which involves an English gentleman's encounter with the Jewish world of London, predated George Eliot's encounter with Hertha Marks. But there is little doubt that Hertha influenced George Eliot's development of the character of Mirah. According to Hertha's biographer, the description of Mirah as "a girl hardly more than eighteen, of low slim figure, with most delicate little face, her dark curls pushed behind her ears under a large black hat, a long woollen cloak over her shoulders," bore a strong resemblance to the young Hertha in her homemade cloak. And Mirah's memories of the Hebrew melodies her mother sang resembled Hertha's own stories, always proudly told, of her mother's Orthodox practices.

In one important way, Marie Curie and Hertha Ayrton differed. Unlike Marie, Hertha was a political activist, a voice for the independence of Ireland who became deeply involved in the English suffrage movement. Marie, on the other hand, usually kept a distance from politics, insisting that she could make a more important contribution as a scientist. Both women were aware of this difference and looked with some longing and admiration on the path not taken. In a moment of discouragement, Hertha Ayrton once said, "I often think very sadly that perhaps I should have been more useful to the Cause if I had devoted myself to my own special work as Madame Curie has done." Marie Curie, for her part, found particular reasons to sympathize with the English suffragists, who during this period were being sent to jail for their demonstrations. She once told Hertha that Poles were sometimes viewed with suspicion if they *hadn't* been sent to prison for the cause of an independent Poland. And indeed, it was right around this time that Marie Curie's nephew Władek (Józef's son) was sentenced to prison for having written a patriotic verse.

Always extremely cautious about attaching her name to causes, Marie Curie readily agreed when the request came from Hertha Ayrton. "I accept your using my name for the petition of which you tell me," she wrote in the spring of 1912, "because I have great confidence in your judgment, and I am convinced that your sympathy must be justified." She added, "I was very touched by all that you told me of the struggle of English women for their rights; I admire them very much and I wish for their success."

The petition in question protested the imprisonment of leaders of the suffrage movement. "I am a member," Hertha Ayrton explained to Marie Curie, "of the association whose leaders are now in prison, and I know those leaders personally and look on them as persons of the utmost nobility of mind and greatness of purpose." During 1912 and 1913, events brought Hertha Ayrton into closer and closer involvement with the cause. In the spring of 1912, Hertha's daughter Barbara was locked up in Halloway prison for her suffragist activities. Hertha's response was to declare, "I am very proud of her."

Once in prison, many of the suffragists went on hunger strikes, and the English government, rather than force-feed them, adopted the policy of releasing the women when they were near starvation, allowing them to regain their strength, then rearresting them. Hertha Ayrton's house in Norfolk Square became a haven for the recovering hunger protesters, or "mice" as they were widely known. On several occasions she received Christabel Pankhurst, the leader of the movement, when she was so weak that she had to be carried up the stairs on a stretcher. "Many a militant suffragist of the rank and file," observed one of their number, "owed her health, if not her life, to the care and skill with which she was nursed at Norfolk Square." Clearly, Marie Curie was placing herself in capable hands.

The idea that she and her daughters would vacation in England with Hertha Ayrton predated Marie Curie's illness. It had been planned in the spring of 1911, when Hertha Ayrton visited Paris to present her work on sand ripples before the Société de physique. Marie Curie came to greet her friend at the train station and, after her presentation and a luncheon given by Alice Chavannes, invited her back to her house in Sceaux. "We saw her two daughters," Hertha reported to her daughter Barbara, "both very interesting children. . . . I spoke to Madame Curie about coming to see us this summer, but she says she has already arranged to go to her sister at her old home in Poland, this year, but would much like to come with the two children next summer."

In the intervening months, Hertha Ayrton kept up a steady flow of letters to her friend, congratulating her on the Nobel and deploring her attackers. "You have my sympathy in all your great and unmerited troubles as well as your well-merited triumphs," she wrote in January of 1912. Then, hearing of Marie's illness, she kept in touch through Bronia with her progress. "I would be very grateful to you," she wrote Bronia in February, "if you would have the goodness to send me a postcard to tell me if she is doing better and if she is no longer suffering these terrible attacks of pain."

In almost every letter, Hertha Ayrton urged her friend to come to her in England. "I shall take a house by the sea in Devonshire or Cornwall . . . ," she wrote in January, "for the months of August and September, so you and your daughters will be able to have two months of sea bathing. . . . You will not need to come to London before going there. I will meet you at Dover, or whichever port you come to, and we will all travel together along the coast. . . . In this way no one will know anything about your visit and if you come under another name you will be absolutely safe from intruding visitors." As usual, the trip is to have an educational dimension for Irène and

Eve. "It will be quite easy to get an English lady as holiday governess for the two girls," Hertha writes, adding, "that will be less expensive for you than bringing anyone from France, and much more efficacious as regards learning English. I am looking forward with great pleasure to learning to know your children, and if we can quite re-establish your health during your visit it will be a real joy to me."

At the end of July, the plan was realized; Marie Curie, traveling as Madame Skłodowska, crossed the channel to join her friend. Together they moved into to an old mill house at Highcliffe-on-Sea in Hampshire, on the edge of New Forest, "with nothing but a little wood between the garden and the sea shore." Soon after, they were joined by Marie's daughters, who had been in Brittany with their Polish governess.

In most respects, the visit was a success. No one in the press learned that Marie Curie was in England, even though she ended her visit with a few days at Hertha's house in Norfolk Square. Hertha's suffragist daughter Barbara, who had impressed Marie with her "pride and courage" on earlier occasions, was on hand some of the time to entertain Marie's daughters. And an English governess, Miss Manley, proved satisfactory. "Irène learns English," Marie wrote in her notes on the children, "and is in good health." Together, Marie and Irène spent time writing out poetry. Once, when they disagreed about a word in a Lamartine poem, they wrote asking Alice Chavannes to settle the dispute. Eve, who had been ailing off and on for months, seemed to recover at Highcliffe. "She takes baths in the sea despite the cold," her mother noted, "and returns [home] in good health."

The only person who didn't improve during the visit was Marie Curie herself. In mid-August, she wrote Ellen Gleditsch, "Unfortunately, I am still suffering and can't write at length." A month later, corresponding with H. A. Lorentz about the possibility of attending a meeting of the Solvay Commission in Brussels in October, she explained that "I am only beginning to recover very slowly. . . . I would probably be in a condition to make the trip—although certain days I am still very ill—but I fear that in any case this would be at the cost of a very great fatigue." In the end, after much vacillation, Marie Curie didn't make the trip to Brussels that year. It was a wise choice: the return trip from London to Paris was enough to send her to bed once again.

IN THE EARLY DAYS of Marie Curie's illness, Hertha Ayrton observed to Bronia that "science is always there, grand and calm, a refuge against all evils. That is what I feel when I settle into my laboratory and that is what Madame Curie must remember." But unfortunately, the solace Marie Curie might have found in her laboratory following the Langevin affair was denied her by her illness. Her letters are full of the frustration this caused her. To Georges Jaffé, who had spent the year 1911–12 in her laboratory, she wrote, "I regret very intensely having been prevented from taking an active part in this life of the laboratory that we all love." And to H. A. Lorentz, as she worried over whether she should attend the Solvay meeting in October 1912, she wrote, "I would not want to give a talk on general ideas. It has been so long that I no longer have the habit and I wouldn't know how to do it."

But it wasn't just the illness which interfered with Marie Curie's life as a scientist. All the reversals she suffered during these years, beginning with her rejection from the Académie des sciences in 1910, had adverse consequences. The experience with the Academy had the effect of silencing her voice in the most widely read scientific publication in France, the *Comptes rendus.* For the next eleven years, she did not ask to have her work presented at the Academy; therefore it was not published in the official organ of the Academy. Instead, her papers appeared in *le Radium* and the *Journal de physique,* where they might be read by those working in radioactivity, but not necessarily by the larger scientific community.

Important projects were interrupted by the maelstrom of the Langevin affair. Back in the spring of 1911, Marie Curie had traveled to Leiden, in Holland, to work with the Dutch physicist Heike Kamerlingh Onnes on observations of radioactive substances at extremely low temperatures. Their experiments, which demonstrated that the radioactive process was independent of temperature, were an important further proof that, in the words of Frederick Soddy, "Radioactivity . . . must be regarded as a process which lies wholly outside the sphere of known controllable forces." Marie Curie and Kamerlingh Onnes had stopped for the summer vacation in 1911, vowing to return in October. The Langevin affair intervened; it wasn't until 1913 that they were able to publish their findings. Even then, their paper, "The radiation of radium at the temperature of liquid hydrogen," explained that "as the continuation of the work has been prevented . . . by the long indisposition of one of us, we thought it best not to wait any longer in publishing our results."

More significant than the interruptions was the fact that Marie Curie's preoccupations kept her from participating fully in the burst of scientific discovery that took place during these years. It is a cruel irony that during the years 1911 to 1913, during which Marie Curie was least able to pay attention, the study of radioactivity, "this chemistry of the invisible," as she once called it, yielded its most stunning results.

The first breakthrough grew out of experimental work on alpha particles, which Rutherford had been studying off and on for several years. At McGill University in Canada in 1906, he had found that the relatively large, positively charged alpha particles could be deflected from a straight path by a magnetic field. In the process of that experiment, he noted that alpha particles also deflected slightly when passing through a thin sheet of mica.

In Manchester, England, Rutherford undertook further experiments with alpha particles, devising, with Hans Geiger, a method for actually counting them with the naked eye by shooting them at a screen of zinc sulfide which flashed each time a particle struck. This work of shooting beams of alpha particles at various materials and observing their deflections was continued by Geiger and a young assistant named Ernest Marsden. But they were troubled by stray particles that defied their expectations.

When they complained about it to Rutherford, he suggested that they try to see if, in fact, the "stray" particles were actually deflecting at wide angles or even bouncing back from the surface they were being aimed at. Very quickly, Geiger and Marsden were able to demonstrate that that was the case: a certain number of alpha particles were deflected at wide angles, and some came right back toward their source.

This was a surprising finding. If the tiny electrons were embedded, as the "plum pudding" model of the atom proposed by J. J. Thomson suggested, in a jelly of positive charge, then the relatively large alpha particles, traveling at great velocity, should shoot right through them, not bounce back. It was, as Rutherford was later to explain, "almost as incredible as if you fired a 15-inch shell at a piece of tissue paper and it came back at you."

The experimental observation was made early in 1909. On December 14, 1910, Rutherford wrote Bertram Boltwood that "I think I can devise an atom much superior to J. J.'s [J. J. Thomson's]. . . . It will account for the reflected alpha particles observed by Geiger, and generally, I think will make a fine working hypothesis." On March 7, 1911, speaking before the Manchester Literary and Philosophical Society, Rutherford proposed a new model for the atom, based on the deflection of the alpha particles. In Rutherford's model, most of the atom was empty space, which was why many alpha particles passed through the foil without being deflected. The atom's positive charges, according to Rutherford's theory, were all concentrated in a central core of the atom, which he called the nucleus. When the alpha particles came close to this nucleus, they met a strong repulsive force and a large deflection resulted. Rutherford's atom resembled the solar system, with a large sun in the middle (the nucleus) and much smaller electrons orbiting around it.

The idea that individual atoms might be replicas of the solar system had been proposed before. Jean Perrin had suggested in 1901 that "each atom might consist . . . of one or more positive suns and small negative planets." But Rutherford was the first to put forward experimental evidence to support this hypothesis. His talk in Manchester ushered in the nuclear age.

The next major breakthrough in understanding the structure of the atom occurred two years later, in 1913, when Niels Bohr, a young Dane working in England, wrote a series of three papers entitled "On the Constitution of Atoms and Molecules." Rutherford's atom had a central positive proton with negatively charged electrons orbiting around it at high velocity. The idea was that the force pulling the electrons toward the nucleus would be balanced exactly by the acceleration due to the circular motion of the electron. Bohr's scheme elaborated Rutherford's in a way that provided an explanation for phenomena that were already well known but only partially understood: Planck's quantum and line spectra.

The many-colored line spectra, it may be remembered, are lines along the spectrum which elements produce when heated to a gaseous state. Each element has its own series of lines, its own "signature," and new line spectra had been used to confirm the existence of new elements, including radium. Now Bohr turned to the work that had been done on the line spectrum of hydrogen, and suggested that each of its characteristic lines was caused by a discrete jump of the single electron in hydrogen from one orbit to the next, in much the same way a tennis ball might bounce from one stair to the next. Each jump represented the release of a "quantum" of energy—the same quantum Max Planck had observed when studying black-body radiation at the turn of the century.

At the subatomic level, it now seemed, not only matter but energy was divided into discrete packages, or quanta. Bohr's three papers laid out the rudiments of a new quantum physics, a physics in which older mechanistic models were inadequate. While explaining some phenomena, quantum theory raised new questions which would preoccupy physicists for decades to come.

It has become usual to suggest that these new developments passed Marie Curie by. But despite her personal difficulties during these years, she showed herself to be *au courant* in her correspondence and papers. She and Einstein corresponded, for instance, about Max von Laue's important research on gamma-ray diffraction in crystals. And at the Solvay Conference of 1913, she was the only participant, besides Rutherford himself, who paid any attention to Rutherford's hypothesis about the atomic nucleus.

Several historians have noted that, remarkably, no one who attended the 1913 Solvay Conference, two years after Rutherford proposed the nucleus, commented on the hypothesis. Abraham Pais points out that J. J. Thomson, in the paper he gave at Solvay, mentioned nothing about Rutherford's or Bohr's work; "Yet two years before, Rutherford had discovered the nucleus, while, earlier in 1913, Bohr had cracked the hydrogen atom!" Jagdish Mehra, in his history of the Solvay Conferences, writes that it is "remarkable . . . that the uniqueness of Rutherford's discovery of the atomic nucleus for such exploration was not yet generally appreciated by physicists" at the time of the 1913 meeting.

But one scientist, Marie Curie, *did* take note of Rutherford's nucleus at the 1913 meeting. In responding to J. J. Thomson's paper, Marie Curie had said that the work of Rutherford led to "important conclusions about . . . a central positive nucleus of small dimensions surrounded by a distribution of electrons." The year after, in an article for the educated lay readers of the *Revue du mois,* Marie Curie expanded further, noting that "Mr. Rutherford, based on the study of the dispersion of alpha rays, has concluded that this positive nucleus must be of extremely constrained dimensions, so that it presents itself almost like an isolated positive charge surrounded at a certain distance by a distribution of electrons which determine what we consider to be the diameter of the atom."

Marie Curie certainly understood complex issues of the time well. Take, for instance, a paper given before the Société de physique in 1912, in which she anticipates the vexed question of whether radiation consists of waves or particles:

> It is necessary . . . to note that the theory of the emission of continuous electromagnetic or luminous waves has recently come up against [the possibility of] discontinuities in the structure of these waves. . . . The future will show to what extent the two conceptions can come together and to what extent, as a consequence, the notion of a *ray* will become preponderant, and to what extent that of a straight trajectory . . . of matter or of energy moving at great speed.

And yet, despite her keen interest and understanding of the new developments in physics, Marie Curie's contribution after 1910, the year of her rejection from the Academy, came mainly through the work of others in her laboratory. Her own efforts would continue largely in the byways of radiochemistry. And while it is impossible to know whether she would have broken more new ground without the interruption of the Langevin scandal and her illness, her personal difficulties certainly affected her productivity. More important, all the hurt and humiliation accentuated her tendency to defensiveness. Much of the energy she had, during these critical years in radioactive research, was used up in defending her past accomplishments.

April of 1913, for instance, found her writing to Georges Jaffé, who had spent the previous year in her lab, to remind him that "the absolute value of a current produced in a vase of dimensions determined by a curie of emanation was determined not by Duane and Laborde but by me." Often, as with the dispute over polonium, there were good reasons for Marie Curie to defend her discoveries. Sir William Ramsay, for instance, published a paper in 1913 in which he claimed that his was the first good work on the atomic weight of radium. "You will perhaps have seen," Marie Curie wrote Rutherford soon after, "that M. Ramsay has published a work on the atomic weight of radium. He gets exactly the same result as me and his measures are less consistent than mine. In spite of that he concludes that his work is the first good work on this subject!!! I admit I was astonished." She adds that he "makes some malicious and inexact remarks" about her "experiments on atomic weight."

Certain male scientists were hostile simply because Marie Curie was a woman. Sir William Ramsay was one of them. Another seems to have been the American chemist Bertram Boltwood, who told Rutherford at one point that he had "always" thought of her as "a plain darn fool" and who was indignant when Yale later "voted the Madame an honorary degree of Doctor of Science!"

Ernest Rutherford, however, was different. He seems to have genuinely liked Marie Curie, and she him. He showed concern and sympathy for her when she was so cruelly treated by the French press during the Langevin affair. But during these years, Rutherford was working with Marie Curie on establishing a radium standard, an area in which she felt strongly that she had historic claims. And in this process, even Rutherford found her "a rather difficult person to deal with."

Rutherford broached the subject of a radium standard with Marie Curie in the spring of 1910. At the time, he was doing some comparisons of his own, between his "empirical" radium standard and one from Vienna, and he asked Marie Curie to send a sample from her lab for comparison. During the exchange, a discussion began about the possibility of appointing a committee to work on developing an international standard.

Such a standard was needed, as Marie Curie explained, in order to "assure agreement between numerical results obtained in different laboratories"; to assure accuracy in medical applications, which were increasing; and to provide stability and reliability in the manufacture of radium. Writing to Rutherford in August of 1910, Marie Curie approved the idea of "a committee which will discuss the question of a standard." She told him she would be happy to prepare the standard, but was concerned about how other secondary standards would be compared with the primary international standard, which would be "kept *chez moi.*" This was a first hint of the proprietary attitude which led to tensions during the two-year period in which the international standard was established.

At the Radiology Congress in Brussels in the fall of 1910, a committee was named with representatives from the United States and the major western European countries, and Marie Curie agreed to undertake the work of preparing the standard. By the fall of 1911, when the committee members gathered at the first Solvay Conference, Marie Curie had done it, but told Rutherford that she wanted "to retain it in her Laboratory partly for sentimental reasons and partly to continue observations on its activity." Rutherford told her that "the Committee could not allow the international standard to be in the hands of a private person." He insisted too that all the duplicate standards must be "sent in the name of the International Committee and not of herself as an individual." He added, in explaining the situation to Stefan Meyer, the Austrian scientist who was secretary of the International Radium Standard Committee, "I was not quite sure whether she had the idea of merely giving a personal certificate; but I pointed out to her that the International Committee existed for this purpose."

"As you know," Rutherford confided to Boltwood, "she is very obstinate, but after some discussion she suggested that it might do to place a duplicate in one of the French Bureaus to be taken as a standard." Others, however, were not happy with this solution; they wanted the *original* standard, not a duplicate, to be deposited at the Bureau of Weights and Measures at Sèvres. To this Marie Curie ultimately agreed. There seem to have been other points of contention as well. One was the not unreasonable question of reimbursement for the radium involved: Marie Curie wanted the radium that was being taken from her laboratory for the international standard to be replaced. Another disagreement had to do with the measurement itself; Stefan Meyer in particular seems to have doubted Marie Curie's results.

Through it all Rutherford acted as mediator—sympathetic to Marie Curie's sentimental attachment to radium, but firm in his insistence that the standard belonged to the committee. To Boltwood, he confided that he was "hoping to have Marie Curie over here in February at the opening of the new extension Laboratory, when we shall give her an Honorary Degree. I think that these little things will help to smooth matters over." At the same time, he encouraged Stefan Meyer to prepare his own radium standard and bring it to Paris for comparison. "I have not much doubt that the two standards will be found in very good agreement," Rutherford told Boltwood, "but it will be a devil of a mess if they are not. That is one of the reasons why I must be there to act as arbitrator between the two parties. . . . I think I can compare two nearly equal standards [to] an accuracy of 1 in 1000. I suppose, however, we shall not worry if the agreement of the two standards is within 1 in 300 or 400."

By the end of March 1912, when the comparisons were finally made, Marie Curie was too sick to take an active part. The committee members had lunch at Marie Curie's apartment, where Rutherford found her looking "rather feeble and ill," then repaired to the Curie lab, where the Viennese and Curie standards were found to be in satisfactory agreement. Rutherford said afterward that "I think perhaps we got through matters very much quicker without Mme. Curie, for you know that she is inclined to raise difficulties." Almost a year later, on February 21, 1913, Marie Curie was well enough to travel, with André Debierne, to Sèvres, carrying a glass tube, sealed with her own hands, containing twenty-one milligrams of pure radium chloride. There, at the Bureau of Weights and Measures, the tube was placed in a safe, ready to serve as the basis of comparison for radium standards on five continents. Marie Curie's radium had become the world's.

DURING 1913, Marie Curie's letters began to refer less often to illness and more often to her life as a scientist. To Georges Jaffé she wrote in May that "the construction of the new laboratory is going forward and we will probably be able to occupy it after the summer vacation," adding that her health was better, though she was still too tired to work in the lab as much as she would like. In October, despite a relapse some weeks before, she attended the Solvay Conference in Brussels. And in November she journeyed to Warsaw to dedicate a radium institute, built there in her honor. Even though she was still not entirely well, the plight of Poland aroused her indignation, as always. "This poor country," she wrote a colleague, "massacred by an absurd and barbarous domination, really does a great deal to defend its moral and intellectual life. A day may come perhaps when oppression will have to retreat, and it is necessary to last out until then. But what an existence! What conditions!" To Irène she wrote of her nephew, Józef's son Władek, an "excellent boy" who was working "as a simple laborer in a factory." "Can you imagine," she wrote her daughter, "that he is being tried for having written and signed some verses with a completely innocent patriotic passage in them! And he will be sentenced without doubt to fifteen days in prison!!! Can you imagine such practices? What's more he laughs about it and his family doesn't take the trouble to feel bad."

In Poland, strong memories tended to invade even official functions. One ceremony was held in the Museum of Industry and Agriculture, where the young Maria Skłodowska had first conducted chemistry experiments. A banquet sponsored by Polish women in Marie Curie's honor was attended by Jadwiga Sikorska, the subversive director of the elementary school Marie had attended. When she saw her teacher, now an old lady, Marie walked down among the tables to reach her and kiss her on both cheeks. "I have seen again the places to which my memories of childhood and youth are attached," she wrote a colleague. "I have seen the Vistula again and the tomb [of the family] in the cemetery."

That fall of 1913, Marie Curie also traveled to Birmingham in England to receive an honorary degree (too late to "smooth matters over" regarding the radium standard, as Rutherford had hoped) and reported to Irène on the event with rare lightheartedness. "They dressed me in a beautiful red robe with green trim" she wrote her daughter, "just like my companions in misery—that is to say the other scholars receiving the doctor's degree. We each listened to a brief discourse celebrating our merits . . . after which each of us took a place on the platform. Finally we left, taking part in a sort of procession composed of all the Professors and Doctors of this University in similar outfits to ours. All that was rather amusing; I used the solemn occasion to take note of the laws and customs of the University."

There began to be more social occasions also at Marie Curie's large apartment on quai de Béthune. In late 1912, H. A. Lorentz came for dinner while he was in Paris giving a series of lectures. In March of 1913, Albert Einstein and his wife Mileva paid a more extended visit. "Only a few days have passed," Einstein wrote her afterward, "since all these marvelous things took place so quickly and my little gray cells continue to be agitated by them."

> But there is one thing I feel quite clearly: I am profoundly grateful to you, as well as to your friends, for having allowed me, during these days, to truly share your existence. I know of nothing more inspiring than seeing beings of your quality live together so perfectly. Everything at your house appeared to me to be so natural, as though in the workings of different parts of

a beautiful work of art, so that despite my rudimentary knowledge of French the feeling of being a foreigner never took root.

I thank you warmly for the hours you gave over to me, and I
beg of you to excuse me if, at times, you felt disagreeably
shocked by the rudeness of my manners.

It was during this visit that Einstein and Marie Curie made plans
to hike during the summer vacation in one of the most beautiful of
the Alpine passes of Switzerland, near Engadine. The hiking group
would include Marie's two daughters, Einstein's son, Hans, and the
Curie girls' English governess. Eve remembered her mother, "ruck-
sack on back," hiking and talking with Einstein on the trail that summer. "In the vanguard gamboled the young ones," Eve wrote in her
biography of her mother, "who were enormously amused by this journey. A little behind, the voluble Einstein, inspired, would expound to
his confrère the theories which obsessed him."

The Engadine hike occasioned the most critical remarks Einstein
ever made about Marie Curie. He wrote his cousin Elsa Einstein
afterward that "Madame Curie is very intelligent but has the soul of a
herring, which means that she is poor when it comes to the art of joy
and pain." The main way she expressed her feelings, Einstein
claimed, was by grumbling. And Irène, in his opinion, was "even
worse—like a grenadier." It was what others criticized too, especially
in Marie Curie's later years: she could be dour, and stiff, as could
Irène. But Einstein, whose job in Zurich had come about in large
part because of Marie Curie's recommendation, was courting his
cousin Elsa, who would later become his second wife, when he wrote
the letter. And it is likely that he was trying to reassure her that his
hiking outing with another woman had not been any fun at all. In
any case, Marie Curie seems to have enjoyed herself in her serious
way, stopping at glacier mills along the path and discussing the forces
at work with Einstein, and asking him the names of all the peaks,
which she thought he should know, since he was a Swiss resident at
the time.

One of her great pleasures on the Engadine hike was observing
Eve in good health. In her notebook on the children, she noted that
her younger daughter "walks a lot and looks marvelous." Throughout
most of Marie's physical crisis, Eve had suffered from a variety of
mysterious symptoms. In May of 1912, Marie had written in her notebook that eight-year-old Eve had "a slight fever climbing to 100 . . .
in the evening without other symptoms." When Bronia's husband
Kazimierz Dłuski visited that same month, he had examined Eve's
lungs and found nothing. Yet Eve didn't feel well enough to go to
school (she was now enrolled with her sister at the Collège de Sévigné

in Paris). That summer, while her mother sought a cure in the mountains before going to England, André Debierne, who kept the lab going and played surrogate father as well, reported that Eve seemed "nervous" at times, and had a low fever. X rays were taken, but revealed nothing. Eve was still unwell at Christmas in 1912, prompting her mother to spend the holiday in Lausanne, Switzerland, "to restore her." It wasn't until the spring of 1913, when Eve was treated for worms, that she had regained her health.

While Eve languished, like her mother, Irène seemed to grow stronger. Fourteen to sixteen during her mother's crisis, Irène was at an age when some girls grow silent and passive. Irène instead became more sure of herself, and more able to express her wishes and opinions. It was during this period that Marie entered the only negative comment about her daughters that occurs anywhere in her notebooks. "Irène learns English and thrives," she wrote during their visit to Hertha Ayrton in England. "People find her too self-centered and not concerned enough with me and her sister, which causes me pain because it is obviously true." But what Marie and others criticized as self-centeredness seems at greater distance to have been a healthy effort to break loose from the ties which had bound her so tightly to her "sweet Mé," who had been her only care and concern when the crisis began.

Her mother's humiliation seemed to bring out a kind of defiant pride in Irène. In the spring of 1912, after all the attacks on the family name and after her mother's retreat behind other names, Irène became very interested in anything having to do with the Curie family. Marie described her daughter as "très patriote," using the word *patriote* idiosyncratically to describe pride of family rather than country. "She adores everything relating to the Curie family: the name that she bears and that she would not like to change, the family of her father." That March, as her mother recovered from surgery, Irène asked to go to Montpellier, where she spent an exuberant two weeks in the embrace of her uncle Jacques Curie and his family.

Irène's letters home are filled with enthusiasm. "At Montpellier, I met Uncle," she reports. "In the morning we walked in the town. In the afternoon we were in Palavas on the edge of the sea. We were together, uncle and I, all day long." Her aunt, her uncle's young dog Sultan, the pregnant cat, the chickens who give fresh eggs, the little house and charming garden—all delight the young voyager. "Uncle is so happy to have me here," she reports. "I'm not at all tired from the trip and I haven't even slept much." At the house of her cousin Madeleine, Jacques Curie's married daughter, there are more wonders: a garden which will grow plants thirty feet high and has two resident turtles; a big yellow dog and Madeleine's two-year-old daughter Annie, who is "much more agreeable than little children usually are" because she is fastidious.

It was on this visit that Irène got to know Maurice Curie, a cousin eight years older who was to become a close friend and colleague. For a time, some in the family even thought they were in love. Like Pierre and Marie before them, Maurice and Irène spent long hours together exploring the countryside on bikes, pedaling five miles to the seaside, snacking in the dunes, tromping through peat bogs. "We came back," Irène reported to her mother, "with four pounds of mud on our shoes and fifteen miles in our legs." The next day, they set out in the morning on their bikes and returned with "an extraordinary hunger in our stomachs, a second fifteen miles in our legs after having burned I don't know how many *milliards* of calories on a sun-drenched route."

It was during the Montpellier visit that Irène began to address her mother some of the time as "Ma chérie," a salutation which put the two on a more equal footing than "Ma douce Mé." It was then, too, that she proved capable of managing for herself, when she missed her stop on the train. Her cousin Madeleine had put her on the train for Montpellier, where she was to be met by her Uncle Jacques. When she found that the train had gone past the Montpellier station, she got off at the next stop, sent a telegraph to her uncle, and waited for the first train back, which didn't come until three in the morning. "I arrived at Montpellier at 3:30 [in the morning]," she wrote her mother, "and found uncle, who had been alerted by my telegram." In a postscript she added, "I beg you not to get upset about this business of the train since I handled it well."

As her mother pursued her cure in the French Alps, Irène wrote her regularly of new enthusiasms and friendships. "These English lessons are my happiness," she wrote, "I love English a lot right now." And three weeks later, "You know, *chérie,* that one of my needs is to read. When I have a book I devour it. Imagine what suffering to have books and not know the content." She is reading, "simultaneously," Minna von Barnhelm, Shakespeare's histories, the end of Giraudoux's *Ondine,* the beginning of Dickens's *David Copperfield,* "in English," Coleridge's "Rime of the Ancient Mariner," some little stories in German, and some other little stories. "That makes seven types of reading . . . I have a dictionary on my table at all times. Make a wish that I extricate myself from this muddle of English and German books!"

When Marguerite Chavannes visits Irène at quai de Béthune, they move Irène's bed into her mother's room and talk "indefinitely" into the night. Then, because the apartment is an ideal setting for watching the fireworks on Bastille Day, Irène is asked in her mother's absence to play hostess to the Perrins. Gleefully, she reports to her mother on the festivities:

> Once we got to our house, Mlle. Heichorn [the housekeeper] absolutely insisted on decorating a cake she had made. . . . Aline [Perrin] and I set the table and prepare our lanterns. Two rows of lanterns in my window and one row in Valentine's [the Polish governess]. Then M. Perrin, Mme Perrin and Francis arrived. We dined gaily. Each one of us two (Aline and I) took turns bringing the dishes from the kitchen: Mme Perrin took advantage of one of my absences to put salt in my water glass. François [Perrin] frightened us by saying that there were bugs underneath our plates: the bug was made of iron. We went out, Madame Perrin, Aline and I, to see the fireworks. This fireworks was superb. They set them off on the pont Sully.

Soon after, from the summer house in Brunoy, Irène planned and carried out a long bike ride by herself. "With the help of signs near the roads and landmarks that I had noted on my map," Irène wrote her mother proudly, "I got to Champrosay (near the Seine), by crossing the forest." After that, following bad roads and good ones along the river, crossing two bridges, and biking along the Paris–Geneva route, she regained the house in Brunoy. "I think I went about fifteen miles," she told her mother.

The next time Irène corresponded at any length with her mother was during the summer of 1914, a time when, as she noted, "the international situation is so disquieting." By then, Irène had passed both parts of the *baccalauréat* exam and was planning to enter the Sorbonne. From l'Arcouëst, where she had gone with Eve, the cook, and the governess to prepare the way for her mother and guests, she dispensed advice in the voice of a grown-up. "If you feel that you need to take care of yourself," she wrote her mother, "don't hesitate, I beg you, to delay your arrival to effect your cure. You understand that your health must take precedence over the desire that we have to see you again."

Discussing her sister Eve's education, she sounded like her mother:

> Eve works a lot. She doesn't want to do arithmetic, but one shouldn't bother her about that because she puts really a lot of good will into doing other things, even German. I believe that one has only to allow her to work a little at her pleasure because if one insists on requiring arithmetic, right now, perhaps she would lose her enthusiasm which would be too bad.

Already that summer, Marie Curie and her daughter Irène were becoming partners. "I feel already," Marie wrote Irène that summer, "how much you have become a companion and friend to me." Both mother and daughter assumed that they would eventually work together in the laboratory. But world events brought them into collaboration sooner than they had expected, not in the laboratory but along the embattled front lines of the French army in World War I.

Chapter Sixteen

SERVING FRANCE

SATURDAY, AUGUST 1, 1914, was a perfect summer day on the coast of Brittany. The sea skirting the jagged red rocks was green near the shore, blue at the horizon. In l'Arcouëst, "Captain" Charles Seignobos and the summer regulars—the Borels, the Perrins—climbed onto the sailboat *l'Eglantine* for the usual trip to a nearby island, where they would disembark to play games or swim or perhaps gather fennel. On most such days, the sound of singing on the *Eglantine* could be heard from afar; the captain, a collector of French and Canadian songs, taught them by the dozens to his crew. But on this day, the *Eglantine* was unusually somber. That morning, the socialist Jean Jaurès, brilliant orator, founder of the newspaper *l'Humanité*, which ultimately came to the defense of Dreyfus (as well as Marie Curie), had been assassinated. And there were rumors that France was about to go to war.

"During the whole boat trip," Irène Curie reported to her mother back in Paris, "no one was in good spirits and, if anyone said three words, two at least had to do with world events." All had been saddened by the news that morning of Jaurès's assassination. His last article had been, as Henriette Perrin observed, "so calm, so wise, so noble." Jaurès's death was further evidence, if more were needed, that the warmongers had triumphed: the conflict sparked by the assassination of Archduke Ferdinand and his wife by a Serbian nationalist in Sarajevo at the end of June was about to widen into a European and then a world war.

That afternoon, after the *Eglantine* crew returned to shore, an alarm bell sounded in the little cluster of houses which made up the town of l'Arcouëst. At 3:45 P.M., France had decreed mobilization.

The writer Colette, who was vacationing nearby, described the scene in the larger seaside town of St. Malo.

> —children in red *maillots* leave the sand for snacks and climb back into the clogged streets. . . . And in the middle of the city a cacophony of noises: the alarm bell, the drum, the shouts of the crowd, the tears of children. . . . Everyone crowds around the official with the drum, who reads; no one listens to what he reads because they know it already. Women leave the group running, stopping as though they had been struck, then running again, with a look of having passed an invisible barrier and bolted over to the other side of life. . . . Adolescent boys blanch and stare ahead like sleepwalkers.

From l'Arcouëst, Irène reported to her mother that she felt "excited and enervated, more by the uncertainty than by anything else. I think that if they do declare war, I won't panic and I won't cry either, because that would do nothing but panic the others." The sixteen-year-old Irène had gone to the seaside a week earlier, along with her nine-year-old sister Eve, a Polish housekeeper, and a Polish governess. Already, she told her mother, "people in the countryside are panicked. They confuse war and mobilization. . . . Eve arrived in the evening in tears because a little twelve-year-old imbecile who plays with her told her war had been declared."

In Paris, Marie Curie was hurrying to wind up her affairs so that she could travel to l'Arcouëst for a month's vacation with her daughters. But on that Saturday, August 1, she sat down to write them a letter.

> Dear Irène, dear Eve,
>
> Things seem to be going badly, we are awaiting the mobilization momentarily. I don't know if I will be able to leave because I won't be ready before Monday and transportation may be cut off. Don't panic. Be calm and courageous. If war doesn't break out right away, I will come to join you Monday. . . . If my departure becomes impossible, I will stay here and you will return here as soon as possible, that is when the mobilization is finished and the trains are able to bring back civilians.

Marie instructed Irène to do what the Perrins and Borels thought best, returning with them to Paris if it seemed wiser. "As for me, I persist in thinking that you can all stay there even in case of war, during the first two weeks at least." The next day, she wrote again to tell them that the Germans had entered France "without a declaration of war. . . . We won't be able to travel easily for some time, but after some days I will probably be able to see you again." But it was to be months, not days. The reunion, like so much else during World War I, took much longer than anyone had expected.

Soldiers on both sides went to war with high hopes that summer. The German Kaiser told his departing troops that they would be "home before the leaves have fallen from the trees." In France, a patriotic determination offset for the moment the fears of families saying goodbye to their loved ones, who departed in trains "armoured with bouquets, as though for a battle of flowers."

At the Paimpol station, where Irène went with Henriette Perrin and the children to see off Jean Perrin, the troops rolled out of town to the sound of music. "The departure was not too painful," Irène wrote her mother, "because at the moment when the train was going to leave and when everyone probably felt their heart heavy like lead (at least mine did), there was military music that began to play. . . . People who were on the platform to see their friends and their relatives off completely forgot to cry for a moment; people raised their hats, their hands, their hankies more to hail the music than to say goodbye and the train left without one feeling this pressure of the heart that I feel at separations and which was well-justified at that one."

One reason for optimism about the war was the belief that modern weaponry would deal quick knockout blows. Long wars, like the Hundred Years' War of the fourteenth century and the Thirty Years' War of the seventeenth, were thought to be impossible in the twentieth. But to most people's surprise, World War I turned into a four-year nightmare and took more lives than any catastrophe in Europe since the Black Death. Nor did it bring lasting peace. The punitive treaty which ended it contributed to World War II twenty-five years later. From a long perspective, it could be said that the shot fired at Sarajevo, setting off World War I, began the twentieth century's very own Thirty Years' War.

Marie Curie, who grew up with the sad object lessons of the Polish uprisings, was less sanguine than most about the coming war. "It is hard to think," she wrote her most political friend Hertha Ayrton, "that, after so many centuries of development, the human race still doesn't know how to resolve difficulties in any way except by violence." And to Irène, during the first week of war, she wrote that "all the French have high hopes and think that the struggle, although rough, will end well. But what massacre we are going to see, and what folly to have allowed it to be unchained!"

Whatever her reservations, Marie Curie was committed right from the start to making some contribution. "If we come to it," she wrote Hertha Ayrton, "it will certainly be necessary to put science aside and think only of the most pressing national interests." And in her letter to her children on the day of mobilization, she wrote, "You and I, Irène, we will try to make ourselves useful."

Irène seized on this idea with the enthusiasm and impatience of youth. From August 1, the day of mobilization, to October 8, when she finally left l'Arcouëst to join her, she begged her mother, using every argument she could conjure up, to allow her to return alone to Paris so that she could be "useful." The letters came daily, sometimes twice daily, all sounding the same note. In her tenacity, Irène proved to be her mother's daughter.

"I am tormented," she wrote her mother on August 1, "because they say to me that I must stay here . . . and not add uselessly to the crowding in Paris, but I don't know what will become of me here. . . . In case there is war try to find out . . . what I would be able to do, where I could go." And the next day: "my only desire is to return." And the day after: "Dearest, I know well that this is perhaps not reasonable but my only desire is to return. . . . I am very unhappy to find myself so far from Paris and so far from you in such a moment."

Marie replied that she would like very much for Irène to come, but that it was "impossible for the moment," assuring her that there wasn't any way to be useful yet, since "the nation's only effort for the moment is in mobilization." Irène should be patient, "gather strength by the sea," and take care of her little sister. "I charge you with your little sister," Marie admonished, "who wrote me a card full of despair . . . be maternal toward her in my absence."

But Irène didn't want to play mother to Eve, and assured her mother repeatedly that Eve was perfectly content with her newfound playmates, and "hardly thinks about world events now that we are adjusted to the situation." She even hinted that she was too obsessed to attend to her little sister anyway. "In recent days," she wrote on August 13, "I wasn't able to pay much attention to Eve because I could only deal with my preoccupation by working [on math problems] and going to Paimpol to seek news." At almost seventeen, Irène felt too old to be at the seashore with her little sister, the housekeeper, and the governess. "I am big enough," she wrote her mother, "not to have to cling perpetually to Walcia's [the governess's] skirts. I feel perfectly capable of returning alone to Paris and I suffer so much from my inaction."

Most difficult for Irène was not knowing what was going on. "We have had no mail, no papers . . . a profusion of the most fantastical news," she wrote her mother early on, ". . . I don't even know if war has been declared; one hears stupid things: destruction of six (or 12 or why not 100) German divisions . . . destruction of a Zeppelin . . . they say the Germans have invaded Luxembourg . . . but M. Seignobos doesn't believe that this would be true . . . I understand now the difficulty that historians must have in establishing the facts . . . when one can't even know what is happening at this very moment." And later, when war was under way, she reported that "we talk often of war but . . . have trouble thinking that it is a reality and not just a possibility."

Marie Curie, in Paris, was surrounded by evidence that the war was real. All her male students and colleagues had left, with the exception of Louis Ragot, a mechanic who couldn't serve in the army because of a heart condition. And very soon they were reporting back to her from their various stations. André Debierne was at Romainville, near Paris, for the moment. Her nephew Maurice Curie, who had been working in her laboratory, was assigned to Vincennes, where he was eagerly awaiting a call to action. Fernand Holweck, a tall blond Alsatian physicist, was part of the French offensive into German-occupied Alsace and Lorraine at the start of the war. From his position with the telegraph section of the Second Army in a reclaimed section of Lorraine, he reported that the "reception of the inhabitants . . . was rather cold, which is natural after all on the part of people who don't know what nation they will ultimately belong to." The army was holding the line well against the Germans, he assured her, "except in the north."

Despite censorship, which kept bad news from the French public, the high hopes of early August didn't last long. Within days, Marie reported to Irène that "the country of Poland is occupied by the Germans," adding, "I know nothing of my family." And even though "brave little Belgium" was "putting up a fight," everyone knew they were no match for the invaders. In eight days, the Germans crossed Belgium, burning and looting as they went. By the end of the month, the German divisions seemed likely to realize a modified version of the Schlieffen plan, which called for a wheeling counterclockwise movement southward to take Paris. Only one major waterway, the river Marne, stood between the German line and the city.

"Things aren't going well," Marie Curie wrote Irène on August 31, "and we all have heavy hearts and uneasy spirits. . . . We must keep our firm conviction that after the bad days the good times will come. It is in this hope that I press you to my heart, my beloved daughters."

As the threat of occupation loomed, Marie Curie's longing for her children intensified. "I burn with the desire to embrace you," she wrote Irène on August 29. And two days later: "I have such a desire to embrace you that I almost cried." And yet, even though much of the middle class left Paris, and even though the government removed to Bordeaux, Marie Curie felt, despite the urgings of her friends, that she must stay at her post.

To those who stayed in Paris, these days were unforgettable. "The overloaded trains took into the country a great number of people, mostly of the well-to-do class," she wrote later. "But, on the whole, the people of Paris gave a strong impression of calm and quiet decision . . . the weather was radiant, and under the glorious sky of those days the great city with its architectural treasures seemed to be particularly dear to those who remained in it."

"All that's left in Paris," wrote the journalist Jean Ajalbert, "is Paris, its monuments, squares, its hills, its river—and what a marvel, deserted Paris, the great boutiques closed, a rue de la Paix, a rue Royale, an avenue de l'Opéra traveled only by authorized military vehicles."

One reason Marie Curie stayed on was to watch over her new laboratory, now more or less complete, and in particular over the laboratory's precious supply of radium. As the Germans threatened Paris, the radium provided her with her first wartime assignment. Perhaps with a little prompting, the government that August decreed that "the radium in the possession of Mme Curie, professor of the faculty of sciences of Paris, constitutes a national asset of great value." As a result, an order was issued to transport it to Bordeaux for safe-keeping "for the duration of the war."

On September 3, accompanied by a government representative, Marie Curie braved the crowded trains to transport the radium, a heavy load in its lead casing, to Bordeaux. The next day, traveling back to Paris on a train which stopped mysteriously in the midst of fields, she learned the welcome news that "the German army had turned; the battle of the Marne had begun." She "shared the alternating hope and grief of the inhabitants during the course of that great battle, and had the constant worry of foreseeing a long separation from my children in case the Germans succeeded in occupying the city." But in the end, the French forces, fortified by reinforcements sent out from Paris in taxicabs, teamed up with the British Expeditionary Force to overwhelm the Germans. The victory at the Battle of the Marne meant Paris was safe from invasion, at least for the time being.

Soon afterward, Fernand Holweck wrote optimistically from the front: "I hope to have the pleasure soon of working in the new Institute." Marie Curie wrote Irène that "we all have great hope," noting that "the theater of war is changing right now." The change, however, was in the direction of paralysis. As winter closed in, the German and Allied fronts solidified along a line that extended from the English Channel all the way to the Swiss border, a line which would hardly vary by more than ten miles over the next three years. Previous assumptions had to be put aside. It was going to be a long war after all, a war of attrition requiring enormous amounts of ammunition and costing untold lives. Already that fall the first casualty reports were appalling: 850,000 French killed, wounded, or captured, and about 675,000 Germans. What's more, because of its length and consuming costs, it was a war which would be won or lost in large part on the home front.

From the start, President Raymond Poincaré had called on the French public to unite to bid "farewell to . . . all the hatreds and quarrels of yesterday." Now socialists and nationalists, priests and anticlerics should join together in supporting the war effort. To a remarkable extent, they did. Despite the war's shaky premises, only a few brave voices spoke out against it. In part, this had to do with draconian press censorship. Romain Rolland, one of the few critics, was able to voice his opinions only because he was in Switzerland. But even without censorship, anti-German sentiment was at such a fever pitch that most would have been willing to join the *union sacrée* in order to ensure victory. "The Barbarians," wrote Jean Ajalbert, "had believed stupidly that the French were going to destroy each other; they [the French] will make better use of their arms."

Feminists, too, put their struggle aside in order to fight the external enemy. Marguerite Durand revived her newspaper *la Fronde* "not to claim political rights for women but to help them accomplish their social duties." When peace returns, Durand promised, "all feminist theories will be energetically defended in this paper; but now we are in a time of war. We must submit courageously to adversity, give confidence to those who depart, watch maternally over those who remain. We must dress physical wounds and comfort moral pain. We must show ourselves . . . worthy of the rights we demand."

War provided many women with new possibilities. With men at the front, women were required to replace them in the munitions factories, making shells and guns, and in a wide range of jobs which kept the country and the economy moving. Women drove trams and loaded coal, became waiters and cabinetmakers. In the country, they did the farmwork their men had always done in the past.

For the sheltered women of the French middle class, the war opened a window into the real world. Louise Weiss, the protected daughter of a prosperous family, described her shock when her work with refugees placed her in an operating room with a woman's naked body. "I had never before seen a nude woman," she recalled. "I had scarcely looked at myself in the mirror." This "first real contact with human flesh" was "the revenge of matter on the unreality of the University."

Marie Curie was not nearly so sheltered as most middle-class women. She had been working in the world all her adult life alongside men, conferring with them at conferences, teaching with them at the university. But the war provided her, too, with new opportunities. The war meant that she could put the painful humiliations of the Langevin affair cleanly behind her. In war, the moral transgressions of Sorbonne professors became trivial. And even though she shouldn't have had to prove anything, her heroic efforts would be a retort to all those xenophobes who maligned her during the Langevin affair. The "foreign woman" had a chance now to demonstrate her loyalty to France.

Marie Curie also saw the war as an opportunity to serve her native country. Poland had become the battleground between Russia and Germany on the eastern front. While some Poles saw little difference between the two oppressors, Marie Curie placed her hope in the Tzar's announcement, made sixteen days after the war began, that he intended to give Poland autonomy. In a forceful statement to *le Temps,* she described this as "the first step toward the solution of the very important question of Polish unification and reconciliation with Russia."

> In our time, when the feelings of nationalities are particularly intense . . . one can only hope for a reconciliation and durable peace between the Poles, who number 25 million, and Russia, on the basis of an absolute respect for the rights of nationalities.

It would be many years, Marie Curie asserted, "before such a conception will be taken up by the German empire. Germany pursues the extermination of the Polish race by means even harsher than those used in Alsace and Lorraine against French sentiments."

> All the Poles for whom France is, as it is for me, an adopted country to which they are joined by profound ties of affection and gratitude, wish for the union of their compatriots so that they can join forces with France against Germany.

Writing to Paul Langevin, with whom she remained friendly despite the traumatic repercussions of their affair, she explained that she was "resolved to put all my strength at the service of my adopted country, since I cannot do anything for my unfortunate native country just now, bathed as it is in blood after more than a century of suffering."

As with everything she did, Marie Curie devoted herself to the war effort with enormous energy and thoroughness. Her expense notebooks for these years are replete with charitable donations. There are regular entries for Polish aid, for national aid, for "soldiers" and for "yarn for soldiers" (she seems to have been knitting for them), for shelters for the poor, as well as for causes with Polish names. In addition, according to Eve, she took the earnings from her second Nobel Prize out of a Swedish bank account and invested them in French war bonds, where they lost most of their worth. She would have contributed her medals as well, but officials at the Bank of France refused to melt them down.

After the war was over, Marie Curie wrote that she "had the good luck to find a means of action." In truth, however, luck had very little to do with it. Indeed, if some officials of the French army had had their way, she would have remained quietly in Paris, watching over her laboratory. But once she had determined that there were "grave omissions in the organization" of the French army's health service (service de santé), and once she had established, from conversations with the eminent radiologist of her acquaintance Dr. Henri Béclère that X-ray equipment was scarce and "when it existed was rarely in good condition or in good hands," she knew she had come upon her mission. She would find a way, despite official resistance, to make X rays available to wounded soldiers at or near the front.

Caring for the wounded was the accepted role for middle-class women in this as in previous wars. Marguerite Borel ran a hospital, and both Henriette Perrin and Alice Chavannes did volunteer nursing. It was natural for Marie to look in that direction as well. Besides, growing up under the shadow of illness had given her an acute sympathy for the sick, and having two siblings who were doctors gave her more familiarity with the world of medicine than most of her colleagues in physics and chemistry. What was ideal about the work in radiology was that it allowed her to use her scientific knowledge to ease suffering. It was a marriage of mind and heart. X rays, of course, were not the focus of Marie Curie's scientific work, but the phenomenon was part of the history that led to her discoveries. Like anyone working in radioactivity at the time, she knew how to produce X rays. And that knowledge, along with her determination, was all she needed.

By the second week of the war, Marie was writing to Irène that she had found something to do in "in the area of medical radiography." "My first idea," she wrote after the war, "was to set up radiology units in hospitals, employing the equipment that was sitting unused in laboratories or else in the offices of doctors who had been mobilized."

The hospital work served as an initiation. While doing it she learned the rudiments of X-ray examination from Dr. Béclère while, apparently simultaneously, passing them on to volunteers, often scientific colleagues "who applied themselves to acquiring radiological technique, while at the same time filling in their knowledge of anatomy." Meanwhile, her visits to the hospitals of the Red Cross around Paris convinced her that, given the lack of personnel and equipment, as well as the many emergency stations which had no electricity available, what was really needed was a "mobile post" which carried electricity and X-ray equipment to those in need.

And so, with this in mind, Marie Curie went about putting together her first radiology car. Later she would write about the need for X-ray workers to be *débrouillard*—a word that resists translation but means something like "able to figure things out." In the beginning, and indeed throughout these years, it was Marie Curie herself who had to be the most *débrouillarde* of all.

The first step was to find a benefactor who would donate an automobile—a small one which could easily maneuver narrow streets —and the funds for the equipment she planned to install in it. For this, she appealed successfully to the French Red Cross, the Union des femmes de France. The next step was to purchase or scavenge the elements essential to making X rays: equipment for converting the electricity available on site into the power required, along with several glass vacuum tubes through which the electrical charge would be fired to produce X rays; a lightweight table on which to lay the patient; a rolling rack for the glass vacuum tube, or ampoule, so that it could be easily moved to the area being examined; a small number of photographic plates and supplies; a screen for radioscopy; curtains to produce darkness at the site; an apron and other material for protecting the operator; and some insulated cable and a few other tools. The weight of all the equipment, according to Marie Curie's postwar book on the subject, would come to about five hundred pounds.

There was also the problem of electricity, which was lacking in many of the emergency stations. This was another reason the radiology cars were vital: they brought their electricity with them. "The production of current," Marie Curie explained, "can be assured by a generator installed . . . on the car." But such a generator was rather expensive and weighed about two hundred pounds. A lighter, cheaper solution was a generator which could be fastened to the running board of the car and hooked up to the car motor, whose power it converted to electricity. Above all, as Marie Curie instinctively understood, everything had to be as light and as cheap as possible, while at the same time tough enough to withstand rough transport. It was even possible, she suggested, in sites with electricity available, for the *voiture radiologique* to be replaced by a horse-drawn carriage.

After the war, Marie Curie looked back fondly on the first car she equipped. "This little car . . . carrying only the equipment that was strictly necessary, has without doubt left many memories in the Paris region. Manned in the beginning by voluntary personnel, former students at the École normale or professors . . . it alone provided service to the troops retreating to Paris during the greater part of the war, in particular at the time of the flood of wounded who arrived in September of 1914 following the Battle of the Marne."

She vividly describes how the *voiture radiologique* did its job in these early days:

> Advised of a pressing need, the radiology car departs . . . carrying all its supplies and its provision of gasoline. That doesn't prevent it from moving at the speed of 25 miles an hour when the state of the road permits it. The personnel consist of a doctor, a technician and a chauffeur, but on a good team each transcends his *métier*.

Once they arrive at their destination, where they have been "impatiently awaited for the examination of wounded newly arrived at the hospital," the technician and the doctor unload the equipment and carry it inside, while the chauffeur hooks up a long cable to his generator so that he can produce electricity. Inside, with the help of nurses, the radiology team covers the windows with the black curtains they have brought. "With one glance, the technician and his chief decide where the apparatus should go, place it, assemble the pieces of the folding table, install the ampoule and the valve and establish the connections." They test the equipment, perform the necessary "delicate adjustments." Finally everything is ready. "Barring difficulties, in a familiar place, the installation can be done in a half-hour. It is rare that it requires more than an hour."

Then the team goes to work with the doctors and surgeons of the hospital. The wounded are brought in, on stretchers or leaning on nurses. They are examined first with radioscopy (an outmoded exploratory process during which X rays are passed over the body while the examining doctor looks at the picture produced on a screen), then X-ray films are taken. An aide writes down all observations. "That lasts as long as is necessary," Marie Curie explains, "time is forgotten, all that matters is getting the job done with care. Sometimes, a difficult case slows things down, other times, the work proceeds rapidly. Finally the task is finished." The team "packs the equipment in the cases and returns to its base, to begin again the same day or else the next."

As the casualties of the Battle of the Marne made their way back to Paris and to the hospitals served by Marie Curie's little *voiture radiologique*, she became aware of the "truly striking" neglect at the front of the diagnostic benefits of X rays. "The lack of equipment and the lack of information at the beginning of the war permitted operations without radiological exam which, later, would have been considered criminal."

At that time, a wounded man was *never* examined with the help of X-Rays in the first days following the injury; he was thus *always* operated on and transported in conditions in which chance played a preponderant role. How many of the wounded were evacuated with an injury which required rest but which remained unknown; how many others died of infections that one would have been able to avoid with the help of an operation made at the time with the help of a radiological exam; how many were amputated for similar reasons; how many were operated on several times without success for lack of an examination, and had to stay for many months in hospitals; how many contracted illnesses which could have been prevented by more enlightened care.

At the start of the war, the army health service had X-ray equipment in some of the larger army hospitals to the rear of the front. It even had some mobile radiological posts. But the view adopted by "public powers" was that there was no need for such facilities nearer the battle zone. Surgeons operating at the front tended to share this official view, for reasons Marie Curie found understandable. "In general, at the very beginning of the war, they had very limited confidence in the utility of radiology. Sometimes they refused it outright, for fear of congestion and loss of time. Most often, they considered it applicable in the great centers only, to the rear of the front, conforming to the opinion then held by the directors of the health service." In such cases, she noted, "it wasn't enough to offer the radiological equipment . . . an entire education was required."

Fortunately for Marie Curie, she was not alone in her wish to reform the military health service. In October of 1914 a private organization, the *Patronage des blessés,* was founded for that purpose by M. E. Lavisse, one of the Sorbonne circle. Marie Curie, encouraged by Émile Borel to plead her case to the Patronage, was made "technical director of radiology" and began to receive funds for her project. At around the same time, she found an individual benefactor: an architect named Ewald, who was willing to donate his car for conversion into a second *voiture radiologique.* Then, with a second car equipped and with the Patronage des blessés and the Union des femmes de France in her corner, Marie Curie started on her campaign to win over the *service de santé* of the army.

She began by approaching someone she knew well, a Frenchman of Polish origin named Jean Danysz who had worked in her laboratory. Not long before the war, he had decided to return to Warsaw as co-director of the radium institute which had opened there under Marie Curie's aegis. In 1914, however, he was back in France, a second lieutenant fighting in the infantry at an undisclosed location on the western front. There, on October 23, he received a card from Marie Curie informing him that she had "an X-Ray car all ready to go" and asking him if he had "knowledge of needs of this sort. You could indicate the possibility of bringing this car to your major," she suggested, "while sending me a request for domicile, with which I could obtain authorization to come." Lieutenant Danysz wrote back optimistically. The medical major, to whom he had passed on the proposal, "thinks your proposition will be received with enthusiasm, all the more because at our military hospital the lack of X-Ray equipment is sorely felt."

But no one in the hierarchy of the *service de santé* wanted to deal with the request of a woman who, it was explained, "wants ardently to be put at the disposition of a service on the front." The request went from desk to desk until it reached the *médecin inspecteur chef supérieur* of the *service de santé,* who ruled that only the minister of war could decide such a matter. The minister of war, as it happened, was Alexandre Millerand, the lawyer who had represented Marie Curie in the Langevin affair. He informed Marie Curie that only General Joffre, commander in the combat zone, could respond to such a request. But he promised to ask Joffre to consider it "with all the seriousness it deserves." Apparently permission was finally granted. On November 1, 1914, Marie Curie, along with her daughter Irène (who by then had come to assist her), the mechanic Louis Ragot, and a chauffeur, arrived with radiology car number two at the Second Army's evacuation hospital at Creil, some twenty miles behind the front line at Compiègne, set up their equipment, and began taking X rays.

The first skirmish with army bureaucracy was won, but the battle wasn't over. During the next three years, Marie Curie would spend much of her energy overcoming various forms of resistance. Because she was a woman, because she was a volunteer and not part of the regular army, because she had something to offer which the army didn't provide—for all of these reasons and more, various pockets of the *service de santé* persisted in placing obstacles in her path. Four months after permission was granted for car number two, Marie Curie was informed that she could not receive a permit to travel with a radiology car because of new regulations concerning women. To M. E. Lavisse, president of the Patronage des blessés, she bemoaned the "growing difficulties that are put in our way. It seems that despite all the results obtained, one can never gain the confidence of the military chiefs and rely on their support. Every day new difficulties arrive to add to or replace the old ones, paralyzing all efforts . . . it is likely that we will be put in the position of not being able to respond to *an emergency call for service,* and that, because of this, we will have to regret the maiming or death of several of the wounded." Two and a half years later she was still fighting the same battle: yet another official order had come down forbidding her to travel to the front. In the end, however, Marie Curie "succeeded in winning a sort of official sanction from the *service de santé*. Some chiefs of army service addressed requests directly to me and regular relations based on my assistance were established with the headquarters of the *service de santé* in Paris."

Whatever its reservations, the military would have had a hard time denying that the unstoppable Marie Curie made a remarkable contribution to the war effort. With the support of the Patronage des blessés, which allocated most of its seven hundred thousand francs in donations to her cause, she procured and equipped eighteen radiology cars herself; some of the cars examined as many as ten thousand wounded. She established about two hundred permanent radiology posts as well. Dressed in her civilian clothes and wearing a Red Cross armband, she traveled all the way up and down the line on about thirty separate trips. Sometimes she traveled by train, carrying the components of an X-ray post to be set up at a permanent site. Other times, she went in one of the *voitures radiologiques,* to answer an emergency call, or to repair equipment that wasn't working well. "Sometimes it only took an hour," she wrote afterward, "to reestablish normal functioning; it was only a matter of making adjustments, whereas they had thought it was a punctured transformer or deteriorating ampoule." Usually, she was driven by a chauffeur or accompanied by a technician on her outings. But in July of 1916, she procured her own driver's license, so that she could drive herself when necessary.

It was important, she maintained, to spend time at the various radiological posts, "live their lives," and thus understand the problems. Many times, she acted as assistant to the radiologist examining wounded soldiers. Notebooks she kept throughout the war bear witness to hours of such collaboration. The knowledge of anatomy required to describe such complications as a "shell fragment under the scapula which had penetrated the external face of the arm and must have then passed through the axilla" seems to have been acquired on the job.

From the beginning, Marie Curie had understood that her most important task was training and educating others. Again and again in her postwar book on the subject, she emphasized that providing equipment was useless without training to go with it. Surgeons who thought they could pinpoint the location of a shell fragment, for instance, simply by looking at the X ray were sorely disappointed and concluded that "this radiology has completely tricked us." In order to pinpoint the location, it was often necessary to use a compass and make a geometric calculation. But those who asked for this compass were likely to be disappointed too if they didn't understand how to use it. It was "necessary above all to improve the knowledge of the operator." When doubters found themselves for the first time "working with some person able to localize a projectile exactly . . . the first successes achieved appeared to them to be a miracle, skepticism yielded to the most complete confidence."

As the war dragged on and the usefulness of X rays became obvious, there was a growing need for more radiologists and technicians. Dr. Béclère trained a group of about three hundred physicians at Val de Grace Hospital, and the army opened a school for X-ray technicians. But the army recruits, according to Marie Curie, were not selected because of aptitude for the work and were often mediocre. Finally, Marie Curie was asked by the army to conduct a course for technicians. As usual, however, the army's support was less than wholehearted: the locale provided for the training was a hangar at Neuilly with virtually no X-ray equipment, so that she had to transport her own with the help of her mechanic. Because of these difficulties, she gave up on the course after a few months and proposed an alternative: she would train nurses to be technicians instead. Reluctantly, "because the lack of personnel was a veritable menace," the army approved the project.

The school for *manipulatrices,* as the female X-ray technicians were called, opened in October, 1916, at a new training hospital in Paris named for Edith Cavell, the English nurse executed by the Germans in 1915. Women from a variety of backgrounds—some army nurses, some Red Cross nurses, some simply young women with a "rather solid" education—came in groups of twenty for an intensive six-week training. Between the time it opened and the end of the war, the school turned out about 150 *manipulatrices* who went immediately to assignments at radiology posts around the country.

Marthe Klein, a young scientist who had taught *manipulatrices* with her, afterward attested to Marie Curie's "great confidence" in "the good sense and the determination of women, whatever their social class. All these women, without any scientific background, some of them maids and some of them socialites, succeeded in acquiring the physics concepts they needed in order to operate and maintain the X-ray equipment."

Marie Curie's personal involvement in the training of these young women is apparent in the notebook she kept on their performance. "Mediocre in the beginning, has very much improved," she wrote about one student. And about another "good student, lively and intelligent." She took pride as well in their performance after graduation. "They gave, in general, entire satisfaction in their work. Some even found themselves obliged to provide radiological service in the absence of radiologists, and handled this task with such a conscientious effort that they earned the approval and entire confidence of their chiefs of service." This was a job women could do well, Marie Curie noted, in peace as well as war.

MARIE CURIE'S high praise for these young women was published in her book *Radiologie et la guerre*. Less publicly, she lavished even greater praise on her daughter Irène, who worked closely with her throughout the war and who became, at the young age of eighteen, a teacher of the course for *manipulatrices* at Edith Cavell Hospital. Although Irène's name doesn't appear once in the book, Marie Curie allowed herself "a few lines" about her daughter in an unpublished report about the activities of the Radium Institute during the war. She praised "the devotion and good will of this child, who was only seventeen and who had such a lively desire to fulfill her duty as a citizen." Irène "did her best to help me in the most varied conditions" and was "endowed with qualities of reason, energy and equilibrium rare in someone of her age." Perhaps Marie's praise in the report was calculated to win an official appointment of Irène to the post of *préparateur délégué* in her mother's laboratory at war's end. If that was the case, it succeeded. The partnership between mother and daughter, forged in war, was to continue in the laboratory for all the remaining years of Marie Curie's life.

As she waited impatiently in l'Arcouëst at the beginning of the war, Irène's unhappiness about not being able to do her patriotic duty was compounded by the fact that she was with a Polish governess and housekeeper who excited suspicion among the locals. "Actually, I regret that we have foreigners with us," she told her mother. She worried that people might think her unpatriotic "because they have accused you, yourself, of being a foreigner" and because "we don't have anyone in the army."

In early September, Irène wrote her mother that a drunk had come into the house and told Walcia (the governess) and Jozia (the housekeeper) "that they were Germans and should leave the country in three days." Worse still was "all the gossip which goes around about me. I am going to give you some examples: they say that I am a German spy. They say also that, when I leave in the morning with a little pail to gather some blackberries, I am carrying things to eat (in the little pail) for a hidden German spy. They say also that I am a German man disguised as a woman, etc. Naturally, I only learn about this indirectly. . . . It pains me to think that they have taken me for a foreigner, when I am so profoundly French and I love France more than anything. I can't keep from crying every time I think of it, so I will stop so that this letter is legible."

It was a familiar and painful subject for Marie Curie, but she responded with equanimity. "I was so sorry to hear that you have had some unpleasantness about your nationality," she wrote Irène. "Don't take these things too much to heart, but do your best to clarify things to people with whom you do business. Remember also that, not only should you endure these little problems with patience, but that it is in fact your duty to protect Josephine [Jozia] and Valentine [Walcia]. . . . This would be your duty even if they were Germans, because, even in that case, they would still have the right to visit in Brittany. Chérie, be more aware of exactly what your duty is, as a Frenchwoman, to yourself and to others. But since you are very young to keep your head about this, enlist the aid of M. Seignobos, who is so good and who will not refuse you his influence."

Irène's exile in l'Arcouëst was prolonged by yet another trial. In mid-October, just as her mother was finally giving her the all-clear to return to Paris, she injured her foot while rock climbing and had to stay on another two weeks. The accident brought at least one benefit, however: it gave Irène a chance to test her stomach. "I was rather amused," Irène wrote her mother as she described the first aid administered to her lacerated foot. "First I established that the view of my foot didn't bother me at all, and that gave me pleasure because I had often wondered if I was afraid of the sight of blood. I looked at my wound with much interest because one could see the tendon. I also saw how they put in the clips. Naturally, with each clip they put in (or took out if it was badly placed), I stiffened in order not to cry, but in the intervals, I laughed and I joked a lot better than all my audience gathered around." Irène would soon have other opportunities to test her sang-froid.

When she finally got back to Paris that October, she made up for lost time. With her mother's permission, she took a nursing course instead of going to university, and she quickly obtained a diploma. By November, she was traveling with her mother to the front, absorbing everything she could about radiological examination. They made stops at a string of hospitals not far behind the front lines—first at Creil, then at a Red Cross hospital in Montereau and another temporary hospital set up in a château near Mormont. In each place, Irène observed her mother entering the name of each soldier in her notebook, followed by a description of his complaint and of the radiological findings. "Tardy, Émile, Fourteenth chasseurs, examination of left forearm, bullet in forearm," her mother wrote. And "Decouzon, Jean Baptiste, 263rd infantry, pain in the leg, shell fragment in the right thigh removed . . . depth 10 cm."

By the time Irène turned eighteen, in September of 1916, she was on her own at a radiological post in Hoogstade, in the little triangle of Belgium that remained unoccupied by German troops. There she slept in a tent with other nurses while training the radiological team. She and her mother had become collaborators, trading news about their shared task. "I spent my birthday admirably," she wrote her mother, "except that you weren't there, my *douce chérie.*"

> To start, I found the [protective] apron that I accused you of having maliciously swiped. Then I made an X-ray of a hand loaded with four rather large shell fragments that I localized and that they extracted today. (In this regard I forgot to tell you that the projectile of Descamps has been extracted; they came upon it right away and Descamps is now walking around again.) In the afternoon I went to a soccer match and in the evening to a little concert; after that I slept in the tent under a beautiful starry sky.

Irene traveled from post to post, dealing with a variety of problems. In one place, there was a technician who couldn't do the geometry required to locate a foreign body, in another there was red tape that threatened to tie up a train shipment. One doctor was so clumsy he damaged the equipment. Or a transformer was malfunctioning. Or personnel who were promised never arrived. In addition to teaching *manipulatrices* at Edith Cavell, she also, incredibly, managed to obtain her *certificats* from the Sorbonne, with distinction, during the war years: in math in 1915, physics in 1916, and chemistry in 1917. During the summer of 1917, a year before the war finally came to a close, Irène returned to l'Arcouëst, the scene of her early exile. This time she was a willing vacationer, badly in need of a rest. "I eat well," she reported to her mother, "and sleep like a marmot."

FOR SOME WOMEN, including Irène and Marie Curie, World War I was a time of great excitement as well as pain and loss. Many women were freer than ever before to be out in the world doing things. Men, on the other hand, found themselves forced into a kind of nightmare passivity in the trenches, unable to move forward or backward, but only from side to side.

The contrast certainly holds when one compares the experience of Irène and Marie Curie with that of their closest correspondents at the front. There is no mistaking Marie Curie's sense of satisfaction when she writes that she has to hurry to the north because a radiology car has been knocked out of commission and needs her attention. Even the difficulties—tire blowouts, minor accidents, equipment failures, and bureaucratic roadblocks—presented new opportunities for triumph.

But there were very few such opportunities for the men at the front, particularly in the long war of attrition which followed the Battle of the Marne. Instead, as Maurice Curie reported, there was "always the monotony of the trench; one goes there like penpushers go to their offices and it seems that it will never end; the lines of barbed wire, the huts, the mines, the shells, the bullets . . ."

Of all the young men who corresponded with Marie Curie during the war, Maurice was the one she loved the most. "Dear Maurice," she wrote Irène when he left for the front, "I think often of him." Maurice, who had become so friendly with Irène when she visited his family in the south, had come to Paris the year before the war to study chemistry and to work in his aunt's lab. Now that he was assigned to munitions supply in the First Corps, he kept up a steady, sometimes playful, correspondence with Marie. "Irène tells me," he wrote her, "that you are in the neighborhood of Verdun. I stick my nose into every medical car that passes along the road but I never see anything but many-striped caps, and I don't imagine that the military authorities have taken steps to regularize . . . your coiffure, which is hardly according to regulations." Maurice ordered her to take care of her health; if he found her tired he would issue a "severe reprimand." Sometimes—under orders from Irène, who wanted the family to be more informal—he addressed Marie as *tu* instead of *vous*. Even his father Jacques Curie didn't do that.

Despite his aunt's best efforts to get him reassigned to the rear, Maurice Curie spent twelve months on the front lines, most of it near Verdun, scene of one of the war's longest and bloodiest battles. As a junior officer in charge of munitions supply, Maurice was certainly in less danger than those in the infantry—"except when one goes to resupply under fire." But he was close enough to see a great deal. His letters to his aunt provide an intimate view of one of the most savage wars of all time.

Like so many others, Maurice had begun the war as an enthusiastic patriot, eager to serve. That first October, following the German retreat from the Marne, he saw the terrible consequences of that battle as he walked north to join the front near Reims. "One hundred thirty kilometers on foot, sack on back, rain and mud, hardly any food, across the mass graves of Epernay, Montmirail, etc. It is unbearable." Still, Maurice wanted to be a part of the action. "I made a request to go with the firing batteries . . . and thus be able to take a more active part." He added that he was "happy to see Irène an active patriot."

By February of 1915, however, Maurice was sounding discouraged. "I should like to leave the village where I am," he wrote his aunt. "One winds up being a ruin living amid the ruins. This hole has been so thoroughly demolished that they are running a new train line through it in order to reprovision Verdun. I would give my blanket for an hour spent at the window of quai de Béthune [Marie Curie's apartment]."

Maurice was troubled by the senseless destruction he saw. From Reims, he wrote that the cathedral had been "profoundly damaged," the tower and apse burned; "I fear for it in the cold of winter." And six months later, he explained to his aunt that the village of Vauquois was a strategic point fought over with "incredible passion," even though it was so insignificant before the war that it didn't even have its own water supply. Most of the horses his artillery unit relied on to haul their guns were killed off. "Will we sign up on our return for a course on the systematic destruction of beings and of things?" Maurice asked his aunt.

Maurice's letters were a compendium of the excesses which made World War I unique. There was the ritual firing of enormous amounts of ammunition in the general direction of the enemy. "I am going back down now into the trenches," Maurice wrote, "in keeping with my custom of serving breakfast [mortar fire] daily to these Messieurs Boches [the Germans]; they are used to it and this morning they didn't respond, which makes the job much easier—because it has become a job, this war which never ends."

There was the demoralizing life in the trenches, where for weeks, or months, men were "confined to cold, water-logged, rat- and vermin-infested holes in the ground, constantly exposed to rifle, machine-gun, shrapnel and artillery fire without being able to fight back." In June of 1915, Maurice wrote that he was "very tired, with a touch of low spirits . . . I have had more than two months in the trenches in deep winter and confess that I have a certain apprehension about the new campaign, of which the evidence is palpable."

After the Germans introduced poison gas into the war, in April of 1915, Maurice was exposed to that as well. "Tomorrow morning," he wrote his aunt, "they will close us in a room and the atmosphere will be charged with asphyxiating gases, tear gases etc. We are trying on the new protective masks. If you knew what a headache that gives you."

Maurice was no longer at the front in March of 1917, when the French troops committed acts of open insubordination to protest the poor leadership of the high command. But he, too, grew to distrust his superiors. "As sergeant of lodging," he explained to his aunt, "I am in charge of the change of quarters and position in combat. I have to defend my men against these gentlemen soldiers, who want to shelter their pretentious uselessness in the best spots."

On rare occasions, Maurice was able to forget the war. A lover of nature like his father and his late uncle Pierre, he wrote his aunt about the countryside near the battlefields. "Have you seen our Argonne this spring?" he asked his aunt. "It is a fairy forest and when I am free, I use the horses of my comrades to ride through the woods."

Sometimes there were reunions with friends from the laboratory. In February, F. Canac wrote Marie Curie that he had run into both Maurice and another lab worker named Malfitano, who was fighting with the Italians. "You can imagine with what joy I had these two encounters and reconstituted thus the little scientific kingdom of Paris."

Maurice survived the war. After a year at the front he was reassigned, perhaps because of his aunt's intervention, to a powder-supply post behind the lines. But not all of the young men of Marie Curie's acquaintance were so lucky. F. Canac, who had written Marie Curie, "I no longer have any hope of returning from this war," survived long enough to return to the laboratory but died later of a tuberculosis contracted in the trenches. Fernand Lebeau, the nephew and adopted son of Marguerite and Emile Borel, was killed in the front lines, where he chose to fight in order to promote the cause of socialism. "We socialists," he had told his aunt, "who want to work for understanding among people and for peace have decided to place ourselves on the front lines to prove that we are just as courageous as anyone else."

Saddest of all for Marie Curie was the death of the Polish-French Jean Danysz, the second lieutenant she had asked to help her with her radiology car. Marie Curie's connection to Jean Danysz dated from her earliest days in Paris, when she lived in the "little Poland" of Bronia and Kazimierz's apartment; she had known his father, a biologist who worked with Pasteur and who, with Pierre Curie, had written one of the earliest papers on physiological effects of radium exposure. The son Jean had been a personal friend as well as colleague, keeping her informed about the birth of children, progress on his doctorate, and possible career choices. Danysz's work on beta rays, which is still cited, was important enough so that he was offered a job in America. But in the end, he decided to return to Warsaw to direct the radium institute which was to open there with Marie Curie's support. "There is only one thing that saddens me," Danysz wrote Marie Curie in the fall of 1912, "it is that . . . I will be obliged to leave your laboratory, where I have spent such good years, where I have felt so content."

On the other hand, he noted, one of the best things about a return to Warsaw was that "I won't be leaving you altogether," since he would still be working "under your direction."

In his letters from the front, Danysz had made light of the dangers and difficulties of his situation. But in retrospect, they were filled with ominous signs. On September 25, he wrote Marie Curie that he had already been in six or seven battles. "As a result of the disappearance of four-fifths of the officers of my regiment," he wrote, "I find myself *chef de compagnie.*" He was carrying the flag as well, "since my predecessor was killed by a mortar shell." Ten days later, he wrote again, describing the poignant attempt he and his comrades were making to create a little home for themselves in holes in the ground "which we have covered with branches and dirt."

> We have put straw inside and we sleep there with our clothes on. Every day we improve our setup by bringing everything that could be useful from a neighboring village: a chair, a table, a mattress, blankets—with the result that our holes become more and more habitable. The nights are becoming a little cold. Fortunately, there is no rain. . . . We are some hundreds of meters from the German lines, with the result that we hear gunfire or take shelling all the time. I am beginning to get used to it.

Two months later, Danysz was dead. "M. J. Danysz has been killed in combat," Marie Curie wrote her friend Ellen Gleditsch in Norway, "which for me is a great sorrow."

Jean Danysz died in the first year of the war. When it was all over, four years later, there were 1,375,800 French dead. France, Marie Curie observed, had "lost the elite of its youth." Germany's losses were even higher, and Britain, Russia, and Austria-Hungary had sustained huge numbers of casualties as well. Altogether, nine million died in combat and twenty million died as a result, directly or indirectly, of the war. Nor was it clear just what the purpose of it all had been.

In time, many survivors would come to feel, as the English diarist Siegfried Sassoon did, that "the war was a dirty trick which had been played on me and my generation." But when the German army collapsed following the Allied offensive in the fall of 1918, a mood of triumph prevailed. On November 11, 1918, after news came that the armistice had been signed, all of France erupted in a victory celebration. Church bells rang in small towns, and flags appeared everywhere. In Paris, the celebrating lasted two days. Traffic came to a standstill; crowds gathered at the place de la République and the place de la Concorde. When the band of the Republican Guard struck up all the Allied anthems on the steps of the Opéra, a huge crowd sang along and bystanders "were seen to burst into tears."

Marie Curie was working in her lab when the guns sounded over Paris heralding the signing of the armistice. Eager to join in the victory celebration, she went with Marthe Klein in search of flags. When there were none to be found, she bought material in red, white, and blue and hastily sewed flags, with the help of the cleaning lady, to hang from the windows of the Radium Institute. Then she and Marthe found a building attendant to drive them into the streets of Paris in her radiology car to join in the celebration. Up and down the crowded streets they went, through the masses of people. In the place de la Concorde, the crowd brought the old Renault, already battered from its service in war, to a stop. People clambered onto the roof and fenders; when the car took up its route again "it carried off a dozen such extra passengers who were to occupy this improvised 'imperiale' for the rest of the morning."

From the front, Canac reported that he and Holweck had "had a little laboratory meeting to celebrate the victory." And Holweck wrote that he was happy that life would now return to normal. "It is going to be so pleasant not to speak constantly of submarines, grenades and torpedos. Radioactive projectiles are much more *sympathiques*."

Chapter Seventeen

AMERICA

Aₓ FTER THE VICTORY celebrations, there was anger and remorse among the victors as well as the vanquished. Many who had watched their comrades die felt deep outrage, directed "not against the enemy but against the fathers." Henri Barbusse, whose novel *Le Feu* was dedicated to three fallen comrades, wrote, "After all, why do we make war?"

> We don't know at all why but we can say *who* we make it for
> . . . each nation presents the Idol of war with the fresh flesh of
> 1500 young men to tear apart each day . . . for the pleasure of
> a handful of leaders . . . an entire nation goes off to be butch-
> ered, . . . so that a caste in gold braid can write their names
> down as princes in history books; so that a caste with gold . . .
> can further line their pockets . . .

Mary Borden, an English nurse who worked near the front lines, compared the treatment of soldiers to the doing of laundry. "It is all carefully arranged," she wrote in *The Forbidden Zone,*

> . . . It is arranged that men should be broken and that they
> should be mended. Just as you send your clothes to the laundry
> and mend them when they come back, so we send our men to
> the trenches and mend them when they come back again . . .
> just as long as they will stand it; just until they are dead, and
> then we throw them into the ground.

Like Mary Borden, Marie Curie was appalled by the suffering at the front. "I can never forget," she wrote afterward, "the terrible impression of all that destruction of human life and health. To hate the very idea of war, it ought to be sufficient to see once what I have seen so many times, all through those years: men and boys brought to the front-line ambulance in a mixture of mud and blood, many of them dying of their injuries, many others recovering but slowly through months of pain and suffering."

And yet, unlike many critics of the war, Marie Curie refused to believe that all sides were equally culpable. From the first days of conflict, when she wrote Irène that she hoped the Germans would "see where their autocratic government has led them," she insisted on the moral superiority of the French Republic. To those who admired dictatorship, she had a ready response: "I have lived under a regime of oppression," she would say. "You have not. You don't understand your own good fortune in living in a free country."

Ever the positivist, she saw the Allied victory as the triumph of democracy over tyranny. And rather than dwell on the terrible losses, she looked for ways that the war experience had advanced knowledge. In the fall of 1916, she was working at X-ray posts in Amiens and Montdidier when the young casualties arrived from the Battle of the Somme. That first day alone, the British lost sixty thousand men. But when she looked back on that murderous battle, it was to note that it marked the first occasion on which the "crushing flow" of wounded was treated by "X-Ray teams working concurrently with surgical teams, transmitting the results of each radioscopic exam to the surgeons."

Furthermore, the benefits of X rays to the war wounded were yet another proof that "pure science" would continue to benefit mankind in unexpected ways. "All civilized groups have an absolute duty to watch over the domain of pure science . . . ," she concluded in *Radiology and the War*, "to protect and encourage its workers and to provide them with the support they need. It is only by this means that a nation can grow and pursue a harmonious evolution toward a distant ideal."

One ideal, dreamed of for many years, became a reality at the end of the war: as a result of the Treaty of Versailles, Poland became a sovereign nation for the first time in 123 years. Polish independence was not among the issues which ignited the war. But the conflict, once begun, "automatically breathed fresh life into the Polish Question." Right away, liberation organizations sprang up like mushrooms all over Europe.

Poland became the battleground on the eastern front, and a total of 1.9 million Poles served in the Russian, German, and Austrian armies. The great powers, in order to secure the loyalty of their Polish conscripts and the Polish population at large, made competing promises of autonomy after the war. When the war ended, national hero Marshal Piłsudski entered Warsaw and declared himself in command of a newly independent and still-nebulous Polish state. A series of small wars followed, with Ukrainian nationalists and with Russia. But in time a shaky but genuine Polish republic took hold.

"A great joy came to me," Marie Curie wrote in 1921, "as a consequence of the victory obtained by the sacrifice of so many human lives."

I had lived, though I had scarcely expected it, to see the reparation of more than a century of injustice that had been done to Poland . . . that had kept her in slavery, her territories and people divided among her enemies. It was a deserved resurrection for the Polish nation, which showed herself faithful to her national memories during the long period of oppression, almost without hope.

To Józef, she quoted the words of Mickiewicz, learned at their father's knee: "We, 'born in servitude and chained since birth,' we have seen that resurrection of our country which has been our dream." It is perhaps not surprising that the photographs Marie Curie carried with her in the large black briefcase she always took along to the front were not of her children but of her parents. It was their wish for a free Poland that she hoped the war would somehow fulfill. "It is true," she wrote Józef, "that our country has paid dear for this happiness, and that it will have to pay again. But can the clouds of the present situation be compared with the bitterness and discouragement that would have crushed us if, after the war, Poland had remained in chains and divided into pieces? Like you, I have faith in the future."

And yet, even though Marie Curie refused to share the disillusion of many intellectuals around her, she was changed by the war in important ways. Her belief that knowledge, and particularly scientific knowledge, conferred wisdom was shaken when a group of German scientists signed a document, called the Manifesto of the Ninety-three, in support of the autocratic Kaiser. In it, prominent German intellectuals declared that German victory was necessary to the progress of civilization and the well-being of the human race. For some years after the war, she judged German scientists according to whether they had signed the Manifesto of the Ninety-three.

To Romain Rolland, who asked her to sign a declaration calling on the intellectuals of the world to unite against war, she wrote in 1919 that "I entirely share your aspirations for the reign of peace and fraternity. However I can't join you in this instance because your point of view is not entirely the same as mine. Certainly, I have a horror of war and I deplore, like you, the subjection of intelligence to brute force." On the other hand, she pointed out, "the highest cultivation of intellect is not a guarantee of a just view of national and social problems. . . . Men whose minds deal in abstractions on the highest level and who produce admirable work have shown that they are ready to side with all kinds of acts of banditry committed on behalf of their country. A scholar who signs the Manifesto of the Ninety-three is humanly more remote from me than a simple citizen who is capable of seeking justice not only for himself but for others."

The letters Marie Curie wrote to Romain Rolland and to Henri Barbusse, who were seeking her adherence to a movement they named Clarté, reflect a shift in her attitude toward political issues. Before the war, she might simply have dismissed their pleas with the explanation that her life was entirely devoted to science. In the spring of 1919, her response was lengthier and more thoughtful. Clarté, which grew out of the revulsion of intellectuals against the slaughter they had witnessed in the war, published a manifesto in March 1918 entitled "For an International of the Mind." Before long, under the influence of Barbusse, Clarté became increasingly sympathetic to Bolshevism. But in the beginning, it was endorsed by intellectuals from many nations and with a broad panoply of views, including Einstein, Upton Sinclair, Heinrich Mann, and Selma Lagerlöf. It was just this that made Marie Curie unwilling, as she explained to Barbusse, to add her name to the list.

"I have a great apprehension about entering into a large group to undertake a public campaign. . . . It doesn't seem possible to form a homogeneous group among people who know each other a little or not at all and who have some very general principles in common. . . . I know that people who are used to speaking out in public unite willingly in a group . . . but it is precisely that that I don't want to do because there is in it a sort of opposition to the working methods that I am accustomed to." And to Romain Rolland, a novelist whose "beautiful literary works" she admired, she explains that she doesn't hold all sides equally responsible for the cataclysm of the war. "The difficulty that I have with the form of your appeal," she explains, "is that it does not require the signers to be in agreement on certain elementary principles of international and social justice. Thus the agreement would be illusory because differences would reappear at the moment of the first conflict. . . . For a useful common action, there needs to be a minimum of agreement on . . . precise problems (invasion of Belgium, torpedoing of the Lusitania, devastation of France, reconstitution of Poland, independence of Ireland, etc)."

And yet, even though the Clarté movement was not for her, Marie Curie no longer believed that it was enough to work for a better world through science. The old yearnings she had expressed to Bronia when she was a governess in Poland, "to work for the people, with the people," had resurfaced. "I still have not entirely figured out the form of participation in social action I would be able to take on," she wrote Barbusse. But she knew that she would prefer to work with "a small homogeneous group made up of people who know each other and who know in examining a question in common that they will be able to succeed in forming a clear and genuine opinion about it. In such a friendly group, I feel sustained and my faculties of reflection are increased." Whereas in a large group, "I feel isolated and lacking an organic link with my surroundings." In such a situation, "there is a sterility to my participation."

Three years after she wrote these letters to Henri Barbusse and Romain Rolland, Marie Curie found an organization she could believe in: the Commission on Intellectual Cooperation of the League of Nations. She did not choose to serve: she later noted that she had learned of the creation of the commission, and her appointment to it, from a newspaper article. But once chosen, she participated wholeheartedly in the organization, attending its meetings in Geneva and serving for a time as vice president. Characteristically, her influence worked in favor of action over talk. "We must avoid the illusion of effective activity," she insisted, "because it strangles real activity." The broader goal, as she noted in a 1930 report on the commission, was "to spread and reinforce beneficial habits of cooperation in this world, motivated by a great hope for peace." But in order to "obtain results which will serve as an example, it is necessary to limit the field of activity and to pursue with tenacity a certain number of tasks, sometimes humble in appearance, but of real intrinsic value."

Over her twelve years on the commission, Marie Curie worked on several such "humble" but important tasks: the establishment of an international bibliography of scientific publications; development of guidelines for international scholarships in science; an attempt to write rules for protecting scientists' claims to discoveries. She also found herself shoring up and defending an often contentious organization.

Her first such effort involved Albert Einstein. Though living in Berlin, Einstein was an internationalist and a pacifist who had not joined other German scientists in signing the Manifesto of the 93. When Marie Curie heard that he too had been invited to join the commission, she wrote encouraging him to do so. "I believe your acceptance, as well as mine, is necessary if we have any hope of rendering any real service. That is also the opinion of our mutual friends." While she didn't know yet what the commission could accomplish, "my feeling is simply that the League of Nations, although still imperfect, is a hope for the future."

In the beginning, Einstein decided to accept, even though Germany had not yet been admitted to the international body (that would occur in 1924). "I would be very happy, believe me," he wrote Marie Curie, "if you accepted . . . since I know that we already find ourselves in agreement on questions of this kind." Less than a month after he agreed to join, however, an ominous and shocking event occurred in Berlin: Walther Rathenau, a Jew who was a wealthy industrialist and who had been named foreign minister in the Weimar government, was assassinated by terrorists linked to the German Freikorps. At the time, Rathenau's death elicited great protests. But Einstein, more than others, sensed the ominous anti-Semitism of the act, anti-Semitism which would turn the assassins into heroes ten years hence.

He wrote to Marie Curie that the Rathenau assassination had convinced him he could not serve on a committee of the League of Nations, even though his "ideas concerning the importance of such an enterprise have not changed. . . . On the occasion of the tragic death of Rathenau as on various other occasions I have felt that a very strong anti-Semitism reigns in the milieu that I am supposed to represent to the League of Nations and . . . that I cannot agree to this role of representative or mediator. I think you will understand perfectly."

But Marie Curie didn't understand at all. "I received your letter which has caused me a great disappointment," she replied. "It is precisely because dangerous and harmful currents of opinion exist that it is necessary to combat them and you can, from this point of view, exercise an excellent influence by your own personal courage even without having to fight for the cause of tolerance. I believe that your friend Rathenau, whose sad fate I regret, would have urged you to make at least an effort at peaceful international intellectual collaboration. Couldn't you still change your mind?"

Einstein, however, persisted in his refusal to serve, sending a second letter elaborating on the first. "One finds among the intellectuals here," he wrote Marie Curie, "an indescribable anti-Semitism, reinforced especially on the one hand by the fact that Jews play a disproportionately large role in public life and on the other hand by the fact that many among them (me for example) fight for international objectives. It is for this reason that, from a purely objective point of view, a Jew is not the best person to serve as a liaison between the German intelligentsia and the international intelligentsia. It would be better to choose a man who has close and easy relations with the German intelligentsia, who is considered by it to be a 'true German' (I think of men like Harnack or Planck). . . ." In fact, other correspondence from this period reveals that Einstein believed his visibility placed him in physical danger.

Two years later, in a letter congratulating Marie Curie on the occasion of the twenty-fifth anniversary of the discovery of radium, he offered a quite different explanation. His refusal, he now said, had to do with the fact that the League of Nations persisted in excluding Germany and therefore, "under the guise of objectivity," became "a willing instrument of power politics." He also noted, in a bid for forgiveness, that she was a person who was "full of goodness and obstinacy at the same time, and it is for that that I like you, and I am happy that I have been able, during the peaceful days we spent together, to glimpse the depth of your mind where everything gets figured out in private."

Marie Curie responded warmly, citing their "ties of friendship." She noted that it would "certainly have been difficult for you to be part of the commission when Germany wasn't part of the League of Nations, and it seems to me that it would have been sufficient to give this reason for withdrawing." She noted that the League would be a better organization if Germany belonged. "I grant you willingly that the League isn't perfect. It has no chance of being so since men are imperfect. But it can improve things to the extent that poor human creatures recognize the necessity. It is the first attempt at an international understanding without which civilization is threatened with disappearing."

To Einstein's lament that intellectuals got along no better than the masses, she replied that "the contrary has happened. Ordinary mortals communicate rather freely, while the intellectuals have succeeded in erecting barriers between them that they don't know how to dissolve." Teaching, she suggested, was at fault, because it was "not sufficiently detached from politics. . . . Here is what one can gain from teaching: the doctor knows that he must care for a sick person without concern for his nationality. Doesn't that prove that the feeling of solidarity can and should be taught and that men are capable of accepting its international reach, even during war?"

IT IS DIFFICULT to reconcile Marie Curie's energetic advocacy in these letters to Einstein with the seeming passivity of her approach to the other major international adventure of her life after the war: her relationship with the youthful and radium-rich America.

The world war had given America new importance in the eyes of Europeans. U.S. troops, joining the conflict late, were seen by some as rescuers of a depleted Allied force. And it was the American president Wilson whose Fourteen Points became the basis for the League of Nations, even though, paradoxically, the United States refused to join the League in the end. Compared to a physically and economically devastated Europe, America was more than ever a land of plenty. It was also a land where women, as of 1920, had won the right to vote.

This was the context in which an editor of an American women's magazine paid a visit to Marie Curie one day in May of 1920. Marie Meloney, known to her friends as "Missy," had long been urging every writer she knew who went to Paris to interview Marie Curie. None had been able to penetrate the walls of privacy the famous scientist had built around herself. Finally, two years after the war's end, Missy Meloney herself traveled to Paris. Her note to Marie Curie said, "My father, who was a medical man, wrote: 'It is impossible to exaggerate the unimportance of people.' But you have been important to me for twenty years, and I want to see you a few minutes." For some reason, perhaps because the observation on the unimportance of people sounded like one she had sometimes made herself, Marie Curie granted Missy Meloney an interview.

"I waited a few minutes," Meloney wrote afterward, "in a bare little office which might have been furnished from Grand Rapids, Michigan. Then the door opened and I saw a pale, timid little woman in a black cotton dress, with the saddest face I had ever looked upon. . . . Her kind, patient, beautiful face had the detached expression of a scholar. Suddenly I felt like an intruder. I was struck dumb. My timidity exceeded her own. I had been a trained interrogator for twenty years, but I could not ask a single question of this gentle woman in a black cotton dress."

In these introductory words, we see a legend being born. A great woman, but also a humble woman, was this idealized Marie Curie— no strident feminist or careerist she. Rather, she was the tragic widow, self-sacrificing, detached from the material world, and above all impoverished. A few weeks before, Marie Meloney had seen Edison's laboratory and found him "rich in material things—as he should be." She had grown up near Alexander Graham Bell and "admired his great house and his fine horses." She was expecting to find Marie Curie installed "in one of the white palaces of the Champs d'Elysées." Instead, here she was face-to-face with "a simple woman, working in an inadequate laboratory and living in a simple apartment on the meager pay of a French professor." Very soon, Missy Meloney came to the conclusion that she was going to find a way to help.

The story of Missy Meloney's campaign for Marie Curie in America has usually been told as though it were all Missy's idea. The retiring scientist, it is said, was completely overwhelmed by the enthusiasm and energy of the journalist. Marie Meloney was simply an unstoppable force. Even Marie Curie tended to view the whole American encounter in that light.

But this is too simple. Marie Curie could be—as Einstein noted

—enormously stubborn. When it came to requests and propositions she found unworthy or pointless, she knew how to say no and did so more often than not. There was something about Missy Meloney, and about what she had to offer, that appealed to Marie Curie.

Early on, Marie Curie seemed to sense that Meloney might know the way to unlock some of America's wealth for her. "To put me at my ease," Meloney related afterward, "Madame Curie began to talk about America." She spoke of her wish to visit there, then she went on to talk about radium.

> "America," she said, "has about fifty grammes of radium. Four
> of these are in Baltimore, six in Denver, seven in New York."
> She went on naming the location of every grain.
> "And in France?" I asked.
> "My laboratory," she replied simply, "has hardly more than a
> gramme."

It didn't take much effort for Missy to figure out that a gram of radium from America would be a welcome addition to Marie Curie's laboratory.

Still, it would be wrong to suggest that Marie Curie was simply using Missy, just as it would be wrong to suggest the opposite. Marie Curie liked, and grew to love, Missy Meloney, a small, frail woman with a slight limp, and large black eyes set in a "lovely pale face." Eleven years younger than Marie Curie, Marie Mattingly was born in Kentucky, the daughter of a doctor who had conducted research on tetanus. Her mother, the doctor's third wife, was an unusual woman for her time, a college graduate who established a school for freed black slaves in 1876. Later, as a widow, she became president of the Washington College for Girls and did some writing for a women's magazine.

Her daughter Marie became a full-time journalist at seventeen, when she joined the staff of the *Washington Post*. She married an editor, William Brown Meloney, with whom she had one child. At the time of her encounter with Marie Curie, she was an associate editor of a Butterick publication called *Everybody's*. But soon after, she became editor of *The Delineator*, one of the six major women's magazines of the period, and it was there that she orchestrated the campaign to raise one hundred thousand dollars to buy Marie Curie, "The Greatest Woman in the World," a gram of radium.

Always, when she spoke of her to other friends, Marie Curie emphasized how "sincere" Missy was, how concerned for her. And Missy was sincere in her own way. She idolized and adored Marie Curie, and said so often. When Marie saw her off at the train station after a later visit, she wrote how touched she was. "There is no one living to whom you should pay this attention—least of all Missy."

Perhaps because of the humiliations she suffered during the Langevin affair, Marie Curie seems to have been particularly susceptible, at this stage in her life, to such hero worship. As a result, she tended to overlook the ways in which Missy's articles and fund-raising were creating a fictional version of her—a version which produced a brilliantly successful fund-raising campaign, but which gave a false impression of Marie Curie's situation and purpose.

Despite the example of her pioneering mother and despite her own successful career, Missy was a political and social conservative. And *The Delineator,* though once more daring, became a platform for such views after the war. The same issue of *The Delineator* which carried a lead editorial about radium for Marie Curie, for instance, carried a lengthy article by Calvin Coolidge warning about radicals (Charlotte Perkins Gilman was mentioned) infiltrating women's colleges. "With the greatly augmented power conferred by equal suffrage," Coolidge noted, "and with the predominance of the mother in the home, the instruction given in women's colleges will, more than ever before, create a mighty influence in the determination of America's future." And radicalism "means the ultimate breaking down of the old sturdy virtues of manhood and womanhood."

Missy Meloney believed in those sturdy virtues. She herself had left work for ten years to care for her child. Once, she sent Marie Curie a book she admired called *This Freedom,* by A. S. M. Hutchinson. It is a poisonous piece of fiction about a mother whose three children are destroyed—one becomes a criminal, one dies from a botched abortion, and one commits suicide—all because their mother goes back to work. Toward the end of the book, the mother says, "This is not the children's tragedy. This is my tragedy. These are not the children's faults. These were my transgressions. Life is sacrifice. I never sacrificed."

Marie Curie wrote Missy that she disagreed with the book. "I agree, of course, that it is not easy for a woman to bring up children and to work out of home," she wrote in her careful English, "but I don't believe either that the author is right in his conclusion. . . . I don't think that he has considered the rich women who leave the children to a governess and give most of their time to visits and dresses. And of course he never gave a thought to the condition of poor women, peasants or factory workers, who could not stop working, even if they wished ever so much."

Missy, however, was oblivious to differences between her views of motherhood and her idol's. In the issue of April 1921, which was largely devoted to the life and work of Marie Curie, Missy's lead article described her as "a woman of rare beauty. She has a classical head. The high, broad forehead, the full temples, the generous back, have the lines of an old Greek statue. But the face is not Greek. It is softer, fuller, more human. It has suffering and patience in it. It has the mother look." Later in the same article, commenting on Marie Curie's story of her separation from her daughters during the war, Missy comments, "She felt she had to apologize for being absent from her children, even in the war." In her activities at the front, Missy saw Marie Curie as "mother and minister to an agonized people." And once again, quoting Marie Curie's explanation that she could not come to America because she could not leave her children, Missy comments, "A volume in that sentence. She could not leave her children."

Of course this idea of Marie Curie hovering over her daughters is ridiculous. Some might even say that Marie's long absences from Eve, during which Eve was cared for by friends and governesses, bordered on neglect. But it is what Missy Meloney wanted to believe, and succeeded in getting others to believe. It coincided nicely with a conservative backlash against feminism following the leap forward provided by the war and suffrage.

Another piece of the myth which would cause some resentment in France was the idea that Marie Curie was impoverished. In fact, in the postwar years, she was better off than most other scientists in France: she had her own laboratory, designed to her specifications. "It is true," Marie Curie wrote Missy, in an effort to temper her exaggerations, "that I am not rich, but that is nearly always so for French scientists, and I live like other professors of the University; so I don't complain or feel unhappy about it."

But the whole campaign, and Missy's role in it, depended on Marie's being deprived and neglected. *The Delineator*, though devoted largely to fashion, sentimental fiction, and modernity in the home, had been publishing stories for some time about "a little corner of the war-devastated world which *The Delineator* has taken under its protection." There had been detailed descriptions of leveled French towns and of their inhabitants, liberated by American forces in the last days of the war. And at the end of each article, there was information about how to help, by sending a check to the magazine's "French-Relief Editor." Helping Marie Curie, a personification of ravaged France, would fit well with *The Delineator*'s charitable image.

And so, allusions to Marie Curie's poverty—and greatness—were sprinkled liberally throughout Missy's inflated prose. "France is poor," she wrote, "and there is less than a gram of radium at the Radium

Institute in Paris." And then, going to a wild extreme, "When Christ died on the cross, His name was not known five hundred miles from Calvary. And Madame Curie, who after long, hard years of struggle against resistant nature wrested from the earth the secret of radium, is too poor to purchase the precious stuff for further and much-needed experiments."

To some extent, Marie Curie herself participated in this poverty myth. It was then, as it is now, one of the ways of raising money for the laboratory and for research. And when asked by Missy Meloney to outline all her needs, she responded with a long list—she would like to expand her laboratory and she needed a secretary. "Right now, I am typing the letter I'm writing you myself." She would like a laboratory outside Paris where large quantities of radioactive material could be processed and where biological research could be done. She also would like it if there were some way to raise money for the radium institute in Warsaw. And since there was no hope of support from the French government, still recovering from the war, it would be wonderful to receive as much help as possible from American friends.

During this period, Marie Curie also wrote a biography of Pierre, and a brief autobiography (at Missy's suggestion), which emphasized the poor working conditions of the early years and laid particular stress on the sad fact that Pierre died without the laboratory he dreamed of. Furthermore, the idea that there was some virtue in poverty and struggle ran deep in Marie and in her Polish family, and made it hard for all of them to admit their own considerable prosperity. Józef's daughter, for instance, wrote after his death: "My father always said that the bravest people grow up in hardship, and I think he was right."

But as time went on, as her laboratory was enriched by foundation grants and her salary was supplemented by a special pension provided by the French government (partly in response to America's generosity), as she began to accumulate vacation properties around France, Marie Curie's poverty claims—and their perpetuation in the popular press—grew increasingly disconsonant with her situation. To some they came to seem ungrateful, or worse, hypocritical.

Yet another, more dangerous myth was promoted by Missy Meloney's campaign: that Marie Curie could find a cure for cancer. The April 1921 issue of *The Delineator* which orchestrated the campaign opened with an editorial headlined THAT MILLIONS SHALL NOT DIE! And Missy Meloney's hagiographic profile of Marie Curie in the same issue ended dramatically thus: "And life is passing and the great Curie getting older, and the world losing, God alone knows, what great secret. And millions are dying of cancer every year!" Further along in the magazine, there was an article on cancer by Dr. William J. Mayo of the famed Mayo clinic, subtitled "Half Those Who Die Might Be Saved." To his credit, Dr. Mayo made no inflated claims for radium treatment. But one had to read the fine print to find that out.

In June of 1921, after her fund-raising mission was largely accomplished, Missy Meloney ran another article in *The Delineator*, complete with an anecdote about an impoverished woman, dying of cancer, who gave the one hundred dollars she had planned to spend on her own burial to the radium fund to "help some other poor devil miss the agony I have known." Her contribution was not accepted, *The Delineator* hastened to add, but the amount was given in her name. "The foremost American scientists," the *Delineator* editorial declared, "say that Madame Curie, provided with a single gram of radium, may advance science to the point where cancer to a very large extent may be eliminated."

Of course, Marie Curie had never believed this or claimed it. On the contrary, she had made clear to Missy Meloney from the start that her contribution to the cancer effort was indirect. The radium she received from America was to be used for pure research. But it would replace the radium she had isolated years before, much of which was now being used in radium therapy.

Once again, however, there was enough of an overlap between her goals and Missy's to contribute to the confusion. Unlike most of her colleagues, Marie Curie had taken a keen interest in the medical applications of her discovery. She believed in pure research, but she was also pragmatic, like the family she came from. She was, after all, the daughter of a man who said, when he learned of her discovery of radium, that it was "a pity . . . that this work has only theoretical interest." She had experienced the loss of her mother from a disease which scientists had since demystified. And she was the sister of two doctors.

All of this made it natural for her to promote, from early on, the establishment of an institute in France for radium therapy, or curietherapy, as it was often called there. "Radium therapy," she wrote in 1915, "is a method of great value whose principles, technique and application originated in France." But because of lack of funding, the treatment "is now vegetating in the country where it was developed while it prospers in those into which it has been imported."

In these years, when the insidious effects of radioactivity were very partially understood, radium and other radioactive materials were held out as treatments not only for cancers, but for a wide range of other illnesses. Arthritis, lupus, surface ulcers, birthmarks, gout, even some forms of mental illness—all were thought to respond to radium therapy. The ways of taking in radium were as diverse as their targets: one could breathe in the emanation, swallow a radium liquid, be washed in a radium solution, or receive an injection. Cancers were generally treated with tiny quantities of radium or radon (radium emanation) sealed in minute glass or platinum tubes and placed near the malignant cells. Sometimes these tiny ampoules were inserted in the body around the cancerous tissue and left there to do their work.

Until the war, Marie Curie's connection to radium therapy was primarily through the measurements against the international standard which her lab provided to clinicians. But during the war she decided that her lab should try to make up for the "lacuna" caused by the lack of an institute for radium therapy. In 1916, she established a service at the Radium Institute, with the support of the military health service, in which she used her radium to prepare ampoules of radium and radon for the treatment of the wounded in military hospitals. After the war, a section for radium therapy, under the direction of Dr. Claudius Regaud, had been added at the Radium Institute.

Marie Curie's hopes for this new branch of her institute were high, though not as high as Missy Meloney's. "One of the most terrible of human scourges, cancer, is yielding more and more to increasingly refined applications of radium, which is coming to complement or to replace surgical skills . . . ," Marie Curie wrote in *Radiologie et la guerre.* "The cruel illness is not yet reduced to impotence, but it is fought effectively and all hopes are possible." Furthermore, she was proud that "the Radium Institute will have an important social role, in addition to its purely scientific task."

If Marie Curie's reasons for involving the institute in radium therapy were complex, Missy Meloney's motives for emphasizing radium's curative powers were obvious. It was much easier to raise a large sum of money for the purpose of curing cancer than for the purpose of probing the secrets of the atomic nucleus. "We may think," she wrote ingenuously in *The Delineator,* "that radium is too scientific for us to understand. And perhaps it is. But its uses and effects enter into our every-day life. Men on the battlefields and in the hospitals of France and all over the world bless the discoverer of radium."

Missy Meloney turned out to be a brilliant fund-raiser. Between May of 1920, when she left Marie Curie's office with the promise that "the women of America" would provide her with a gram of radium, and January of 1921, she had managed to raise the one hundred thousand dollars required to buy a gram of radium. Her fund-raising methods were a faithful mirror of the story she had chosen to tell about Marie Curie. She formed two committees, one male and one female. The female committee was made up of civic-minded nonprofessional women, including Mrs. Robert Mead, founder of the American Society for Control of Cancer. The male committee was composed primarily of medical men, many of them leaders in cancer research. Only a few of those on the male committee were engaged in the basic research for which Marie Curie's gram of radium was destined. Even more importantly, there was not a single working woman scientist anywhere to be seen.

Marie Curie insisted from the start that she would have nothing to do with soliciting funds. "I don't feel justified in asking unknown people in your country so far abroad," she wrote Meloney in November of 1920, "and I would not like to do it." But if Missy was successful, "I would of course do all I could to arrange for coming to America to receive the gift."

Right from the start, however, there was a huge gap between the way Marie Curie envisaged her tour of the United States and the way Missy Meloney did. Marie Curie wanted to come in October of 1921, so that she wouldn't be away from her laboratory during the school year. Missy Meloney wanted her to come much earlier, in May and June, so that she would be able to receive honorary doctorates in commencement exercises in a long list of universities and women's colleges she was lining up. Marie Curie wanted to stay no more than two weeks and insisted it would be "difficult to accept giving lectures, except for those which are absolutely necessary." Missy Meloney imagined, and had promised, innumerable appearances, including the ultimate spectacle, the presentation of the gram of radium by President Harding at the White House.

Convincing Marie Curie to go along with her program was one of Missy Meloney's hardest-fought battles. In January, she sent a telegram urging her to come in "May at latest," and assured her that she would come to France herself so that she could accompany Marie to America on the boat. In February, Missy managed to convince the venerable rector of the Academy of Paris, Paul Appell, to write Marie Curie urging her to take the trip for the good of French science.

In March, Marie Curie sent a partial capitulation. She would come in the spring, and she would stay a month. Her daughters would accompany her. "After all that you have written me," she wrote, "I don't doubt that my trip will be of the greatest usefulness to me and to my Institute." She would like to see parts of America where "nature is particularly beautiful," and she warned against too many meetings, since "prolonged conversation and noise" were very tiring for her.

But the closer Marie Curie got to the day of her departure for America, the more Missy Meloney's campaign snowballed. Everyone in America, it seemed, wanted to genuflect before the "great Curie." And news that the president of the United States was going to present her with a gram of radium even mobilized a French magazine, *Je sais tout,* which organized a gala to celebrate "one of the glories of French science, the discovery of Radium." On April 28, shortly before her departure for America, the highest dignitaries of France, including President Aristide Briand, gathered at the Opéra to hear Jean Perrin and others discourse on the accomplishments of Marie Curie and the promise of her discoveries. The great Sarah Bernhardt read an "Ode to Madame Curie," referring to her as "the sister of Prometheus."

> *No, you have never led an army,*
> *No voices whispered stern commands.*
> *But your sincere consuming ardor*
> *Far outshines the burning brands.*

The "foreign woman" of the Langevin scandal was forgotten; Marie Curie was now France's modern Joan of Arc.

By May 4, when Marie Curie, along with her daughters and Missy Meloney, departed Cherbourg on the *Olympic* of the White Star line for the ocean voyage to America, Missy had committed her to a seven-week stay, during which she would receive ten honorary degrees from colleges and universities as well as numerous medals and honorary memberships, and attend untold numbers of luncheons and dinners and assemblies. In between, there was to be time for some of the things that truly interested her: visits to laboratories, to Niagara Falls, and to the Grand Canyon. Missy assured her that all was being arranged "with the least possible pressure on your time and your strength."

But even before she arrived in New York, Marie Curie had misgivings. From the boat, she wrote Henriette Perrin that Missy was "full of devotion" and had provided everything possible to make the passage easy, including a luxury suite arranged by the president of the White Star line himself. But the passage had been rough, and "without being really sick," she had suffered from dizziness and mental fatigue. Longingly, she evoked the coming vacation in Brittany:

> I think of l'Arcouëst, of the good time we shall soon be having there with our friends, of the garden where you will come to spend a few peaceful hours, and of the sweet blue sea that we both love, which is more hospitable than this cold, taciturn ocean. I am thinking, too, of the child your daughter is expecting, who will be the youngest member of our group of friends, the first of the new generation. After this one, I hope, there will be born a great many more children of our children. . . .

Irène and Eve, Marie told her friend Henriette, seemed very happy so far, and Missy was "more good and kind than I can say, and I don't believe that she does it for selfish reasons; she is an idealist and seems very disinterested and very sincere. And yet, dear Henriette, that doesn't protect me from a dose of public appearances which make me tremble in advance. Perhaps, at least, I will find some resources for my laboratory."

The large crowds gathered at the pier to welcome her to New York could not have been reassuring, nor could the noise of bands playing three national anthems at the same time. Polish and women's organizations had waited for hours to greet her. Emerging from her cabin a half hour after the boat docked, Marie Curie, dressed in her usual black and sporting a round-brimmed taffeta hat which she no doubt thought a concession to fashion, was seated in an armchair on the deck so that two dozen or so photographers could take her picture. The beauty Missy had insisted on in *The Delineator* was less evident to the daily press than her plainness. She was a "motherly-looking scientist in plain black frock," declared the *New York Times,* although at fifty-three she was still "energy personified."

The headline on the story that day was: MME. CURIE PLANS TO END ALL CANCERS. According to the *Times,* the visitor said that "radium is a positive cure for cancer" and that she intended to use the radium she was given "to continue experiments to find better methods for the treatment of cancer." To those in the medical community who had expressed doubts, she responded that they "do not understand the method."

This last sentence sounds like something Marie Curie may have said. She had made similar points about radiology. But the claim about ending cancer was a clear distortion, and the next day, the *Times* printed her retraction. RADIUM NOT A CURE FOR EVERY CANCER, the *Times* headline read. But while the initial story ran on the front page, the retraction appeared on page sixteen.

So began a tour during which Marie was continuously assigned the familiar woman's role of healer rather than that of scientist. Typical were the remarks of Dr. Francis Carter Wood, head of Crocker Cancer Research Laboratory of Columbia University, who told an audience of chemists, "I do not welcome her as a scientist, but as the woman who has done more to comfort human beings than any one who has made important discoveries in this generation."

Dr. Wood's remarks were made before a meeting of chemists and physicists at the Waldorf Astoria, one of the many large gatherings Marie Curie dreaded the most. Fortunately, however, her visit began in surroundings she found much more sympathetic. After a little rest and recuperation at Missy's home in Greenwich Village, Marie Curie was whisked off by car to visit the campuses of women's colleges, whose graduates had been the principal donors to the Marie Curie Radium Fund.

Marie Curie was a great believer in exercise and healthy surroundings for young women. Two years earlier, when she learned that the University of Paris was planning a sport park for male students only, she had written an indignant letter to the rector. "Don't our daughters need exercise and good health?" she had asked. ". . . And isn't it the role of the University to combat prejudices that may exist in families about this?"

In the United States, the healthy environment at women's colleges made a great impression. That the schools were in the country, with lawns and trees, made them far healthier than those in cities like Paris, she noted afterward. She admired the modern bathrooms, complete with hot water, the meticulously clean dormitories, and the extensive sports programs. And she was struck, in her visits to Smith, Mount Holyoke, and Vassar, by the young women's *joie de vivre.* "They are so different from French students," she told the *Herald Tribune.* "Over there all are sad and most dressed in black from the war." "While an almost military order reigned in the organized ceremonies . . . ," she wrote afterward, "a youthful spontaneity and gayety showed up in the songs of welcome composed and sung by the students, in the aspect of smiling and excited faces, in the wild running across the lawns to come greet my arrival. It was, in truth, a charming impression that I won't soon forget."

There were quieter moments as well, as when the party en route from Smith to Vassar stopped along a brook in the Berkshires for a picnic lunch, and Marie and Irène wandered around picking violets and spring beauties. Or when she accompanied Margaret Hill, a senior majoring in physics, to the Vassar laboratory at ten-thirty at night because that was the best time to observe the workings of a new Curie electroscope. "I was so excited and awed by Madame Curie's coming to Vassar that I could hardly stand it," Margaret Hill Payor wrote seventy years later.

The climax of Marie Curie's visits to women's colleges occurred at Carnegie Hall on May 18, in what was, according to the *New York Times,* the "largest meeting of American college women ever held in this country." The thirty-five hundred women in attendance at the event, sponsored by the American Association of University Women, were crowded into an auditorium festooned with the banners of the colleges represented. Marie Curie, surrounded by dignitaries and flowers on stage, sat smiling as a line of young women who had distinguished themselves in scientific research at their colleges filed past her and presented her with orchids. The Naples Table Association, the oldest organization in America for the encouragement of women in the sciences, presented her with the Ellen Richards Research Prize of two thousand dollars. And leading women in science paid tribute.

Dr. Florence Sabin, of the Johns Hopkins Medical School, saluted Marie Curie for proving "that a woman could absorb herself in the hardest of all intellectual labor, scientific laboratory research, and at the same time be a simple wife and mother." Another speaker noted that Marie Curie had set a powerful example, even though she had not been in "the self-conscious woman movement."

The fireworks that evening were provided by a woman who was very much a part of the movement, M. Carey Thomas, president of Bryn Mawr and passionate advocate of women in the sciences. On this occasion, she chose to discuss the newfound power of women, provided by the vote. Women, she argued must remain politically separate from men if they wanted to bring about disarmament and peace on earth. "We women can and must stop war. Unless we stop it, no one will stop it. Why should we bear children to perish in indescribable torture?"

Marie Curie's remarks were brief and timid by comparison. In just twenty-nine English words (the *Times* was counting) she thanked her admirers in a speech that could barely be heard beyond the first few rows. The Vassar Choir, some fifty women strong, ended the ceremony with a rendition of "The Star-Spangled-Banner."

After she returned to France, Marie Curie told an audience of interested women that "the men, in America, approve and encourage the aspirations of women." And certainly, everything she experienced would have led her to that conclusion. But unbeknownst to her, there had been several instances in which men in power had reacted to news of her visit with discomfort or downright hostility. Bertram Boltwood wrote his friend Rutherford that when he learned that "the Madame" wanted to call on him, he went immediately to the Yale authorities and told them "that I had no desire to have the honor thrust upon me and that I considered that it was the duty of the institution to entertain her." When he learned that Yale, "on the recommendation of a couple of medical men," had voted to give her an honorary degree, he told them that they had been "a little hasty in their action." Marie Curie did visit Boltwood's laboratory, despite his protests, and he was "quite pleasantly surprised to find that she was quite keen about scientific matters and in an unusually amiable mood. . . . She certainly made a good clean-up over here. . . . But I felt sorry for the poor old girl, she was a distinctly pathetic figure. She was very modest and unassuming, and she seemed frightened by all the fuss the people made over her."

Boltwood, who was hostile to Jews as well as women, added that he was glad Yale hadn't given Einstein a degree when he visited in April. "Thank heaven. . . . We escaped that by a narrow margin. If he had been over here as a scientist and not as a Zionist it would have been entirely appropriate, but under the circumstances I think it would have been a mistake." Marie Curie, innocent of Boltwood's hostility, mentioned her visit to his laboratory as one of the highlights of her trip.

Similar sentiments may have been expressed by the members of the physics department at Harvard, who voted in private not to give Marie Curie a degree. When Missy Meloney pressed retired Harvard president Charles Eliot for an explanation, he replied that the physicists believed that the credit for the discovery of radium did not belong entirely to her and that, furthermore, she had done nothing of great importance since her husband died in 1906. Missy Meloney's indignant reply would not have impressed the physics department: ". . . the outstanding virtue of these years," she wrote President Eliot, "lies in the fact that having discovered radium and come into prominence she turned to her home as a normal mother and gave the intimate, minute attention to her children which motherhood should impose."

Another debate arose among executives of the National Academy of Sciences, one of whom queried others as to whether it would be "as wise as it would be graceful" to elect Marie Curie a foreign associate at its meeting in April, just prior to her visit. The queried leaders concluded, however, that it was not wise that "a general question, such as the admission of women to the Academy, whether as active members or associates, should be settled hastily, as many members would oppose such action. . . . Moreover," he added facetiously, "if we elect Mme. Curie in this way, we shall have to elect the Prince of Monaco." Instead, suggested George E. Hale, why not "arrange for a reception under the auspices of the Academy and . . . give her a medal or prize if one can be found or made available?" Since both Harvard and the National Academy of Sciences received her warmly —Harvard president A. Lawrence Lowell compared her to Isaac Newton—Marie Curie probably had no suspicion of these rumblings.

In retrospect, the most interesting speech occasioned by Marie Curie's visit was given at an event she did not attend. Dr. Simon Flexner, at Bryn Mawr's commencement exercises, addressed the girl graduates on "The Scientific Career for Women." Flexner, who was director of the Rockefeller Institute for Medical Research and a self-described "lover of opportunity for women," gave a thoughtful assessment of the difficulties they faced, beginning "in the intellectual atmosphere surrounding boys and girls in the home. While the girl is complacently occupied with dolls and miniature dressmaking and millinery, the boy's imagination is being excited by mechanical toys which his aroused interest impels him to destroy, in order that the inner mechanism may be laid bare." Furthermore, the boy, "once launched on a scientific pursuit . . . looks forward to a life's career and indulges the hope, if not the expectation, of being attended by some good woman." For women, a career in science means "too often . . . the denial of domestic companionships and compensations which men easily win and enjoy." All the same, Flexner insisted, "now that the doors of opportunity have been thrown open to women, one may expect that many more will pass their portals and enter upon a career of science."

Two days after Flexner delivered his address to the young women of Bryn Mawr, a *New York Times* editorial attempted to counter his enthusiasm. Though there were "many women, beginning with Mme. Curie as the most illustrious modern instance, who have attained eminence in some domain of science . . . instinct or something else must have told a good many of his young . . . hearers that such achievement was not for them." True, women can be "efficient in laboratories" and some are capable of doing original work. But "the majority of women are still to develop either the scientific or the mechanical mind."

> This is not an essential inferiority to men. Far from all men, indeed, have such minds. But more of men than women have latent capacities in those directions, and more of them have the power—a necessary qualification for any real achievement in science—of viewing facts abstractly rather than relationally, without overestimating them because they harmonize with previously accepted theories or justify established tastes and properties, and without hating and rejecting them because they have the opposite tendencies.

The *Times* concluded that Flexner "made a mistake" if he encouraged all of the young women graduates to go into science.

It was arguments like this one which led historian of science Margaret Rossiter to conclude, in *Women Scientists in America,* that Marie Curie's visit to the United States, far from opening doors, simply raised the threshold for women entering science. In the 1920s and 1930s, according to Rossiter, women scientists came to believe that in order to succeed, they had to be "Madame Curies." They "adopted a new, more conservative, and less confrontational strategy of deliberate overqualification and personal stoicism." Rossiter calls this the "Madame Curie strategy." In her view, Marie Curie's 1921 tour of America actually set women back.

The facts, however, suggest otherwise. In 1920, the year before Marie Curie's first visit to America, forty-one women in America were granted Ph.D.s in science. In 1932, three years after her second and last visit, there were 138. And while, as Rossiter points out, the women's doctorates didn't earn them the jobs they deserved, the fact remains that many more women were choosing to go into science. It is possible that Marie Curie's visits inspired them.

Two days after the remarkable gathering of college women at Carnegie Hall, Marie Curie attended a reception in the Blue Room of the White House. There President Warren G. Harding, after reaffirming the friendship of the American people for France and Poland, presented her with the key to a green leather case containing an hourglass with the "Symbol and volume of one gramme of Radium" in it. (The actual radium was safely stored at the factory until her departure.) True to Missy Meloney's script, President Harding spoke of the affection of "generations of men" for "the noble woman, the unselfish wife, the devoted mother. If, indeed, these simpler and commoner relations of life could not keep you from great attainments in the realms of science and intellect, it is also true that the zeal, ambition and unswerving purpose of a lofty career could not bar you from splendidly doing all the plain but worthy tasks which fall to every woman's lot." He presented her with "this little phial of radium . . . confident that in your possession it will be the means further to unveil the fascinating secrets of nature, to widen the field of useful knowledge, to alleviate suffering among the children of man."

Marie Curie's reply was brief, as usual:

> I can not express to you the emotion which fills my heart in this moment. You, the chief of this great Republic of the United States, honor me as no woman has ever been honored in America before. The destiny of a nation whose women can do what your countrywomen do to-day through you, Mr. President, is sure and safe. It gives me confidence in the destiny of democracy. . . . I thank your countrywomen in the name of France . . . I love you all, my American friends, very much.

After the ceremonies, the dignitaries moved outside for group photographs. It was, as Marie Curie remembered afterward, a "radiant day in May," and the White House appeared "peaceful and full of dignity, white in truth, among its green lawns with vast vistas." Marie Curie had put on her fancier black dress, with lace sleeves and neck, and a stole with ruffled white lace edges, for the special day. She looked almost exuberant as she walked down the White House steps on President Harding's arm.

In fact, however, she was not well. Already before the White House ceremony, her hand had been injured by an overzealous handshake and she had had to keep it in a sling. Increasingly, as the trip progressed, she had to curtail or cancel engagements, and Irène and Eve found themselves receiving degrees and holding press conferences in their mother's place.

All kinds of explanations were given, and chewed over in the press. The "small talk," it was said, was too much for her. The campaign was too strenuous: even so powerful a man as Teddy Roosevelt had collapsed under similar pressure. She was a woman who was unaccustomed to so much socializing "after being in her laboratory almost continuously for the last twenty years."

But the main source of her bouts of illness, including drops in blood pressure, dizziness, and anemia, was undoubtedly her long exposure to radioactivity. Marie Curie herself explained that "my work with radium . . . especially during the war, has so damaged my health as to make it impossible for me to see many of the laboratories and colleges in which I have a genuine interest."

Perhaps influenced by Missy Meloney's upbeat public relations campaign, doctors attending Marie Curie during her visit absolutely refused to admit a connection between radium and her illness. "There is nothing the matter with Mme. Curie at all," insisted Dr. E. H. Rogers, "except that she has been trying to do too much. . . . There is no case on record of any one being injured in health by radium. It causes slight burns, of course—that was the way it was discovered—but these have never had any after effects. Mme. Curie has now been working with radium twenty years. Many others have handled it constantly for about the same period. If it had any deleterious effects they would have been noted long ago. . . . Madame Curie is somewhat anemic, as nearly all persons of confined, studious pursuits are. . . . She will in all probability go as far west as the Grand Canyon . . . there [is] no reason on earth why she should not go."

Marie Curie and her daughters did go west, participating in more ceremonies and receptions along the way. Chicago, with its large Polish population, gave Marie Curie a reception that "surpassed all others in fervor." And honorary degrees were presented at the University of Chicago, at Northwestern University, and at the University of Pittsburgh.

Besides ceremonies, there were visits to laboratories which interested her, including one to Standard Chemical Company in Pittsburgh, where she noted with pride that the processes she had developed for isolating radium were still in use in the arduous process of extracting it from Colorado carnotite. And there were trips to two natural wonders she had wanted to see: the Grand Canyon and Niagara Falls.

According to Eve, Marie Curie was too sick to get excited about the Grand Canyon, although she spoke afterward of its "magnificent and savage appearance." But her daughters were "carried away by enthusiasm." Although they had often had to accompany or stand in for their mother, the girls had managed to escape once in a while. There had been tennis, boating, "an elegant week end on Long Island, an hour's swimming in Lake Michigan, a few evenings at the theater, and a night of wild delight on Coney Island."

But the West, where most official visits were canceled to preserve Marie Curie's health, had been the most fun for them. "Everything amused . . . ," Eve wrote afterward, "the three days on the train by the Santa Fe line, across the sands of Texas; the exquisite meals in solitary little stations under a Spanish sun; the hotel at the Grand Canyon, an islet of comfort on the edge of that extraordinary fault in the earth's crust." Irène and Eve rode ponies along the edge of the chasm and mules down to the bottom where "the young Colorado rolled impetuously."

On June 25, after returning to the East Coast for still more ceremonies, Marie Curie and her daughters boarded the *Olympic* once more to return to France. It had been a strenuous tour, subjecting Marie Curie to more public appearances than she could have imagined in her worst nightmares. But she had come away with a sense of the "immensity of spaces" and the "unlimited possibilities for the future" in America, with resources for her work and contacts which would, with Missy's help, bring more support in the form of money, equipment, and scholarships. In addition, locked away in the purser's safe was a wooden box with metal handles, no more than a foot square, with a hinged top that opened to reveal a heavy lead cylinder. And inside that cylinder was a half teaspoon of material which would yield up secrets, and sorrows, for many years to come.

Chapter Eighteen

A THOUSAND BONDS

MANY MATERIAL THINGS were of little interest to Marie Curie. She didn't care for "hangings, carpets and draperies," according to her daughter Eve, much preferring to keep the shining parquet floor of her grand Louis XIV–era Paris apartment bare, and the windows open to the magnificent views of the Seine and the Île de la Cité. Only reluctantly, at the urging of her American friends, did she use some of their money to install central heating against the chill and damp of Paris winters. Nor did she take any pleasure in self-adornment. When Eve began going out in the evenings, Marie would come to her room and watch in amazement as she dressed. Eve's high heels and bare-backed dresses shocked her, and she declared her makeup "dreadful." And when Eve took her shopping, "she never looked at the prices, but with infallible instinct she would point out . . . the simplest dress and the cheapest hat." Then once she found a dress she liked, "you had to peel it off her back."

One thing Marie Curie did care about, however, was real estate. After the war swallowed up much of her savings, she became increasingly interested in owning land, especially land with spectacular views. In l'Arcouëst, where she and her daughters had stayed for years in other people's houses, she bought a piece of land on a windswept moor high above the ocean and built a house of white plaster, with stone corners, in the Breton style. After she was introduced by a friend to the sun and warmth of the Midi, she bought property along the Mediterranean in a place called Cavalaire and built again.

Her requirements in houses were simple: they should be light-filled and well laid out. At least as important were the gardens and trees that surrounded them. When Irène went to l'Arcouëst without her, Marie wrote inquiring about "the health of the new little pines."

And when Marie went without Irène, she devoted much of her letters to the state of the garden. Similarly, in Cavalaire, she wrote Irène that although the house "seems very pretty and very convenient," it "still lacks plantings in the immediate surroundings." Before buying yet another piece of land, to build a house on outside Paris, she required information about the cost of "planting a tree of maximum height . . . such as a fruit tree" on the grounds.

The property to which Marie Curie devoted most of her energy was the cluster of tan brick and stone buildings on the rue des Nourrices (later rue Pierre Curie) which were the Institut du Radium. The Radium Institute was not really hers to own, of course, but she acted from the beginning as though it were. Even before construction began in 1912, she claimed the inner courtyard between the two original buildings by planting linden trees on it. And every year, she got out a string she had reserved for the purpose and used it to measure the girth of her trees and record their growth. She referred to the various and ever-expanding chemistry and physics laboratories and workshops of the institute as "my laboratory." Those who did research there were, by logical extension, "my workers." And the various Polish scientists whom she invited and found stipends for over the years were referred to, over dinner with Eve, as "my Poles."

When she was away on vacation, in l'Arcouëst or, increasingly, on the warmer Mediterranean coast, the lab—her lab—was never far from her thoughts. "I am a little preoccupied with what is going on at the laboratory," she wrote Irène from Cavalaire, ". . . It is sad that one can't be doubled and write at Cavalaire at the same time that one tends to experiments in Paris."

Of course there were other experienced people at the lab, most notably André Debierne, who was *chef de travaux*. And there was, after 1918, the increasingly capable Irène, who kept her mother informed and performed little tasks others couldn't have, like making sure that the Polish researchers, who came to Paris with less experience than others, presented their work in the best light. "I begged Pawlowski not to turn in his notes," Irène reported to her mother in Cavalaire, "because I saw that they were in a terrible shambles compared with the other authors'. I am going to look at that again with him now." But still Marie Curie worried that the lab didn't run quite as well without her. After an unexpected absence, she wrote Irène that she "tremble[d]" to think what she would find on returning to Paris. "I beg you to take care of Mlle Lub [a newcomer from another lab] so that she won't get an impression of disarray at the beginning of her stay."

The dream of a laboratory for research in radioactivity went back to the last years of Pierre's life, when a chair at the Sorbonne had been established in his honor with the promise of a laboratory to follow. After his death, it became Marie Curie's dream as well. In 1909, Émile Roux, a physician and advocate for Marie Curie who was head of the well-endowed Pasteur Institute, got the idea that his Institute could build a laboratory for her. That mobilized the university, which didn't want to lose a leading light to the institute. Louis Liard, vice-rector of the university, met with Émile Roux and together they came up with a plan for two separate laboratories. One, to study the physics and chemistry of the radioactive elements, would be directed by Marie Curie and funded by the university. The other, to study medical applications of radioactivity, would be funded by the Pasteur Institute and headed by a well-known medical researcher from Lyon, Dr. Claudius Regaud. Two buildings would be constructed, side by side, on land owned by the university. Together they would become the Institut du Radium.

Marie Curie was involved in every detail of the planning, and once the buildings began to go up she met regularly at the site with the architect, Henri-Paul Nénot, designer of the "new" Sorbonne of 1900. Claudius Regaud sometimes attended these meetings as well. But according to his assistant, Regaud was a younger man from "the provinces," and "listened to her as a student listens to his teacher." Regaud did contribute to the planning of the building which was dedicated to medical research. But the building called the Pavillon Curie, with its generous rooms and tall windows, reflected Marie Curie's ideas, as did its personnel.

Marie Curie liked to cite Pasteur, who spoke of laboratories as "sacred places" in which "humanity grows, fortifies itself, and becomes better." Marcel Guillot, a chemist who came to the Pavillon Curie in 1927, found that "the Laboratory of Madame Curie was for her a unique place of work and meditation, isolated from the world, within which she had gathered those she accepted as working companions, whether they were scientists of high quality, beginning researchers or modest technical collaborators."

Marie Curie's criteria for accepting researchers was one that minimized confrontation. She almost always took an applicant who was recommended by a colleague: even before they came for an interview, she would have made up her mind. If people wanted to work in her lab and had the credentials and projects that weren't outlandish, she took them. But then, according to Manuel Valadares, a Portuguese physicist who worked with her, she would watch them work "for a few months. If she became convinced that the 'new one' didn't have the necessary qualifications to be an experimenter (because it sometimes happened that someone entered the laboratory only to be able to brag that he had worked under Marie Curie's guidance) she would tell him that many people were waiting for the position he now occupied" and ask him—or her—to go.

From the early days, Marie Curie's laboratory had hosted an unusual number of women, including Ellen Gleditsch, Eva Ramstedt, Sybil Leslie, and many more. In 1931, for instance, out of the thirty-seven researchers working at the Curie lab, twelve—a remarkably high number for that period—were women. Some were consigned to the drudgery of the lab: the service of measurement against the radium standard and the lengthy, and dangerous, fractionations involved in purifying certain radioactive elements. But it was also possible for the women to grow: Marguerite Perey, who began at the lab as a washer of test tubes, discovered the element francium and became, fifty-one years after Marie Curie first tried to break the barrier, the first woman elected to the *Académie des Sciences*.

Her laboratory accommodated not only more women than most, but also more foreigners. One year there were, along with French workers, two Russians, a Pole, an Englishman, a Yugoslav, a Romanian, a German, a Belgian, three Chinese, an Iranian, an Indian, an Austrian, two Portuguese, a Swiss, and a Greek.

To all of them Marie Curie was "la patronne" (the boss). Some workers found her cold and dictatorial, particularly in her later years. Bertrand Goldschmidt, who entered the lab at the very end of Marie Curie's life, claims that she told him, "You will be my slave for a year, then you will begin work on a thesis under my direction, unless I send you to specialize in a laboratory abroad." And Fernand Holweck, the big blond Alsatian who had worked with her even before the war, was known at times to rage against her stubborn declarations. Another lab worker remembers him pounding on the door of her office and shouting "chameau!"

Particularly after her eyes became clouded by cataracts around 1920, those who met her for the first time were intimidated by her "glacial" expression. "The first contact with Madame Curie left a strange impression," noted Marcel Guillot, "because the appearance of this frail woman, all dressed in black, of such simplicity as to seem almost impoverished, made you feel pity and also her face was almost impassive, and her look abstracted to the point of total indifference."

But if Madame Curie felt that her visitor came to her motivated only by scientific ardour and that the only goal of entering in the Laboratory was Research, her expression . . . brightened and an extraordinary impression of human availability radiated from this woman, with her gentle voice, who then became capable of the greatest kindness. . . . Her concern for each of us had something of the familiar and almost maternal in it.

Lucien Desgranges, who began working as an apprentice to André Debierne at age thirteen and a half and who rose eventually to the position of chief mechanic, remembers Marie Curie's attention to him in his early years at the lab. At four every day, she insisted that he go outside to get away from the unhealthy air of the laboratory, "to breathe, to take the air, to eat something." He used to go out, with another boy from the laboratory for company, and play at throwing stones on a vacant lot which was destined for one of the ongoing additions to the lab. "Sometimes instead of staying fifteen minutes, we stayed a half hour, or three quarters of an hour . . . she was very tolerant of all that." Some years later, when Desgranges needed only to be married to live in the apartment two floors above the laboratory, she kept the apartment vacant for two years until he found a wife and qualified. "The fact that we had a place to move into as soon as we were married," Desgranges recalled, "was a true act of kindness." Both his children were born in the bedroom just above Marie Curie's office.

Marie Curie warmed instantly to stories of adversity. When Hélène Emmanuel-Zavizziano, a young woman of Greek origin, was unable to get results after several years' work on a doctoral thesis in another lab, she was introduced to Marie Curie by a Polish woman who was her assistant. "This first interview," Emmanuel-Zavizziano wrote nearly forty years later, "is still very vivid to me. This woman, pale and thin in a narrow black dress, who scrutinized with her cold, penetrating look, paralyzed me into timidity at first. But she began to ask me questions with such great simplicity, and her face relaxed into a smile so full of charm, that I allowed myself to go ahead and tell her of my disappointments as a beginning researcher and she decided to accept me into her Radium Institute." There "ZoZo," as everyone called her, began to work on one of the elusive daughter products of actinium Marie Curie was determined to describe: protoactinium.

From that time on, ZoZo saw "la patronne" every two or three days. "She appeared all of a sudden, noiselessly, always dressed in black, around six in the evening. She sat on a stool and listened attentively to the account of the experiments; she suggested others." Hélène Emmanuel-Zavizziano expressed suprise that Marie Curie took time for "a beginner like me. I wonder how many directors of theses . . . do as much."

Jean Perrin, who moved into the lab next to Marie Curie's in the 1920s and who enlisted her in his campaigns for government support, often told people she was "the greatest lab director I have ever known." At least one of the workers in her lab agreed. "She was a phenomenon," Moise Haissinsky recalled, "not only in her own time. She was able to direct the huge institute and its numerous physical and chemical laboratories, aware of all that was going on in them, mindful of every detail of the work we were involved in. She inspired, administered, and led, at the same time leaving young scientists to their own initiative and giving them the freedom to choose their subject matter and working methods."

"La patronne" observed a certain formality in her relations with the workers in the lab, never using first names, and always addressing everyone as Monsieur, Madame, or Mademoiselle regardless of their position and her history with them. According to Guillot, the atmosphere approximated that of a "religious convent. This comparison was reinforced by the extreme respect for Science and total devotion which every gesture, every word from Madame Curie manifested."

But there were also times and places for informality. Celebrations were held whenever someone in the lab presented their doctoral dissertation. And there was tea regularly in the late afternoons. There was also a particular hallway, with a staircase and radiator for sitting, where researchers used to gather to talk over scientific questions. When Marie Curie passed by this "parlor," as it was sometimes called, she would often join in. She would sit on the stair, surrounded by a large number of young scientists, and engage in sometimes lengthy discussion. "We called these occasions," Moise Haissinsky remembered, "the study of the science of radioactivity on the staircase."

The aspect of radioactivity which continued to most concern Marie Curie was the radioactive elements themselves: discovering them, measuring them, possessing them both physically and intellectually. It was a source of great pride that her lab had "one of the most beautiful supplies" of radioactive materials. Anyone going to a remote part of the world was likely to be charged by her with seeking out minerals which might be of interest. She had Ellen Gleditsch search for two particular minerals in Norway during the war. When Frantisek Behounek, a Czech who had worked in the lab, went to the North Pole with Roald Amundsen, he brought back mineral samples for her. Similarly, when Henri Pellard found himself in a remote part of Indochina, twelve days by horse from any other transportation, she wrote him that "if you find out about any beautiful radioactive samples, you could send them to me for the collection of the laboratory."

When she traveled, as she did increasingly after the war, the idea of procuring radioactive sources for her laboratory was never far from her mind. Even before the war ended, she had traveled to Italy to visit sites with radioactive deposits. She traveled to Oolen, in Belgium, to visit and woo the Union Minière du Haut Katanga, the company which was refining newly discovered rich deposits in the Belgian Congo. (Eventually, this company loaned radium to Claudius Regaud for his experimental work and gave Marie Curie residues for work on actinium). And of course there had been the American trip, which netted not only a gram of radium but also promises from physicians to collect the tiny ampoules or seeds that were left over from their treatment of malignant tumors. These seeds contained radon, which over time decayed to polonium, a strong source of alpha rays. Over the last years of her life, Marie Curie's correspondence is crowded with letters of thanks, typed by her secretary, to American doctors who had mailed her their radon seeds.

Marie Curie also took pride in the technical work of her laboratory, which prepared radon seeds for Regaud's use and which provided a service of measuring radium against the standard she had established. Although the work was usually done by others, Catherine Chamié remembers a time when Marie did a particularly important measurement herself. She worked during Easter vacation because there was less activity then to disturb the delicate process. And she worked in semidarkness, using the *quartz piézoélectrique* Pierre had invented. "The series of operations involved in opening the apparatus, pushing down the chronometer, lifting the weight, etc. as the piézoélectrique method requires, is accomplished by Madame Curie with a discipline and perfect harmony of movements. No pianist could accomplish with greater virtuosity what the hands of Madame Curie accomplish in this special kind of work. It is a perfect technique which tends to reduce the coefficient of personal error to zero." Afterward came the calculations, "which she did hurriedly to compare results," and if the measurements were within the allowable margin of difference, "one saw her sincere joy about it." When her experiments didn't go as planned, on the other hand, "she looked sad and desolate, as if she had just endured a terrible misfortune."

Young scientists coming into Marie Curie's lab were sometimes surprised and a little disappointed that she still directed so much of her attention to radioactive elements, rather than to the mysteries of the atomic nucleus which were the preoccupation of, for instance, Rutherford's laboratory. "She continued," observed Marcel Guillot, "to have the discovery of new radioactive elements as her principal object, and that by crystallizations or fractionated precipitations, thus remaining faithful to the method of work which had been fruitful in her hands in the beginning."

And yet Marie Curie's preoccupation with radioactive elements turned out to be crucial to the lab's most important accomplishments. It led a young woman named Marguerite Perey to discover a long-sought radioactive element she named francium in 1939. More significantly, the availability of strong radioactive sources made it possible for researchers at the Curie lab to observe phenomena others couldn't. And these observations, in turn, led to some of the most important discoveries of the interwar years.

The first such discovery, made by Salomon Rosenblum in 1929, is a perfect example of the way in which Marie Curie's obsession with strong radioactive sources contributed to a new revelation about the atomic nucleus. Rosenblum was a citizen of the world: born in Russia, he had been educated in Denmark, Sweden, and Berlin before he arrived at the Curie lab in 1924. There, according to Marie Curie, he had "learned to work," and had "attracted my attention with his aptitude for conceiving original ideas, which I hadn't entirely approved of but which interested me." One of the ideas was to subject alpha rays, given off in the decay of thorium, to the forces of a very strong electromagnet which had recently been constructed by Aimé Cotton, the husband of her former student Eugénie Feytis, five miles or so outside Paris, in Bellevue.

Marie Curie was vacationing at l'Arcouëst when Rosenblum got his first results in the spring of 1929. But Irène wrote to tell her the news: "we have seen with great interest the rays of Rosenblum," she wrote. "The phenomenon seems very clear and inspires complete confidence. It is a beautiful result. When you return to Paris, you should certainly put a little of your strong actinium in a favorable state to give off actinon and produce the ray of ac[tinium] C in collaboration with Rosenblum."

Using the strong Bellevue magnet and an alpha-emitting source, thorium C (a daughter product of thorium), Rosenblum had been able to curve the trajectories of alpha rays and analyze their spectrum. From this he concluded that not all alpha rays shot out of the nucleus with the same energy, and that their energies must correspond to events in the disintegration process within the nucleus of thorium C.

It was decided that in order to try the same experiments with other radioactive elements, the chemists at the Curie laboratory should put aside their work to prepare high-quality sources, all of which would be tried out on a date determined by "the boss." Moise Haissinsky, one of the chemists, remembers that they "appeared at the laboratory at 8 o'clock (Madame Curie had been there since six)." Then everyone, except Marie Curie, drove with the radioactive source to the electromagnet in Bellevue. "The first exposure lasted one hour," Haissinsky recalls, "and while Rosenblum continued to monitor the electromagnetic current, I went to develop the negative plate. Examining it under red light I noticed that the spectrum had six lines. We had expected, Madame Curie, Rosenblum and I, two at most!" Haissinsky called Rosenblum over to take a look. "When he saw the six spectral lines, [he] began to dance around in joy, like one possessed." Haissinsky rode back to Paris to get a second source which Madame Curie was preparing in the meantime. "I called to her from the doorway, 'Excuse me, Madame, the spectrum shows six lines!' "

"Madame Curie turned around abruptly, removed her glasses, and gazed at me with her most beautiful smile, which lit up her tired face, and she said, 'Six spectral lines, that is impossible, surely you must be joking, Sir!' "

"But because she knew I wasn't joking, she added, 'Well, so we will prepare an even better radioactive source for you immediately.' And she set to work right away."

BY THE TIME of Rosenblum's discovery in 1929, the twin buildings of the Curie and Regaud laboratories had expanded into a small city. The Curie lab had doubled in size, thanks to funds supplied by a pro-science French parliament, and the number of researchers there had grown from a handful just after the war to between thirty and forty. Regaud's Pavillon Pasteur had added an outpatient unit and was building another biology lab, partly with funds from the Curie Foundation, which had been established for the purpose. In addition, there were two ambitious plans for the future: a fifty-bed hospital and a small industrial laboratory, to be built on the outskirts of town, where large quantities of radioactive materials could be refined for use in the main Curie lab. Building had become so routine that Marie Curie held weekly meetings with the architect.

More and more, as the twenties progressed, Marie Curie's institute was becoming the locus for a realignment of power in French science. Her lab had long been a recipient of private grants, beginning with those from the Carnegie Foundation during Pierre's lifetime. And her institute, along with the Pasteur Institute, had set a precedent for scientific research independent of education. In the twenties, under the persuasive and energetic leadership of Jean Perrin, the Rothschild and Rockefeller Foundations made major donations which resulted in a cluster of additional institutes along rue Pierre Curie. Perrin worked next door to Marie Curie's lab, in the Institute of Physical Chemistry. And next to that building, across a courtyard, was the Henri Poincaré Institute of Mathematics and Mathematical Physics, headed by Émile Borel.

Spencer Weart, in *Scientists in Power,* documents the way in which the center of power shifted in the 1920s away from the older, more conservative Academy of Sciences toward this younger, more dynamic group assembled in the new buildings along rue Pierre Curie. Under the dynamic leadersip of Jean Perrin, and with the important political help of Émile Borel, who was elected to the Chamber of Deputies in 1924, the circle which included Perrin, Borel,

Marie Curie (and later Irène), and Paul Langevin gained more and more control over research funding. And although Marie Curie would not live to see it, Perrin eventually succeeded in shifting most of the funding of research in France from the Academy of Sciences to a new entity, the still-preeminent Centre national de la recherche scientifique (CNRS).

As THE LAB EXPANDED and as its wealth in radioactive sources grew, there was another, ominous and unwelcome, development. Paradoxically, the same "strong" sources which were Marie Curie's great pride and joy were prepared at a cost to the health of the lab's workers, a cost which became more and more difficult each year to deny.

When radiation energy enters the body, the effect is harmful to healthy cells. Large amounts of energy are transferred to individual molecules in the region through which the radiation passes, and these large energy transfers disrupt the molecular structure, which in turn affects the normal functioning of a cell. The cell suffers injury or dies. An analogous event, on a visible scale, is the entry of a bullet into the body. When the bullet fired from a gun enters the body, it dissipates its energy as it tears apart the tissue through which it penetrates. Particles shot from radioactive materials are destructive missiles, but they work silently and invisibly, and their damage is much more difficult to detect and measure.

This, more than anything else, was the reason that it took so long for Marie Curie—and all the scientists studying radioactivity—to realize the extent of radiation's harmful effects. There had never before been a poison quite like it: an unseen poison that acted on the body over many years and affected different people in different ways. But there were other reasons for the delayed recognition as well. For one thing, in the hands of doctors radiation had proved effective in the treatment of cancers. This should have been taken as evidence of danger, since the radiation worked by destroying cells, albeit malignant ones. But, during the early years of this century, there was a belief that science by definition meant progress, and therefore a natural tendency to assume that this new discovery must be part of the march toward a better tomorrow.

Pierre Curie's last papers had reflected this hopefulness. In one, he reported on the fatal effect of radon on mice and guinea pigs. But in others, he documented the radioactivity present in various thermal waters around Europe—waters that had long been believed to improve health. The unspoken assumption was that the waters' radioactivity must have some health-giving powers.

A wide variety of quacks and opportunists traded on this assumption, and on the Curies' good name. There were claims for a radioactive "Curie Hair Tonic" which not only stopped hair loss but restored hair to its original color, and for a "Creme Activa" which promised eternal youth, accompanied by the statement that "Madame Curie . . . promises miracles." A 1929 European pharmacopoeia listed eighty patent medicines whose ingredients were radioactive; they came in the form of bath salts, liniment, suppositories, toothpaste, and chocolate candies.

But reputable physicians also believed in "radium therapy" for a range of illnesses besides cancer. It is shocking now to read that World War I soldiers were subjected to intravenous injections of a radium solution in cases of extreme blood loss, and to external applications of radium and radon to soften scar tissue, loosen joints, and "stimulate nerve function." Marie Curie was proud of the "emanation service" she established at her lab during the war to provide ampoules for such treatment.

Not that Marie Curie was unaware of the dangers of radiation. She would have known of the severe injuries suffered by early X-ray technicians. Probably, she had heard about Thomas Edison's assistant, Clarence Dally, who died in 1904 of a cancer resulting from attempts to develop an X-ray-powered lightbulb. Certainly, she knew of doctors and technicians in France who had lost fingers and arms and eyesight from exposure to X rays, which resemble the gamma rays given off by radioactive sources. In her book *Radiology and the War,* Marie Curie cautions repeatedly against prolonged operations in which "the rays inundate the hands and face of the operator as well as the body of the patient." She notes that a severe "radiodermatitis" has in some cases led to "gangrene and death," even though "the person who receives the rays feels no pain to warn that he has been exposed to a noxious dose." And of course Marie Curie's own fingers, scarred by a sometimes painful radiodermatitis, were a constant reminder of radiation's destructive potential.

The issue was not whether radiation was harmful; that was well known. Rather, the question was one which continues to be asked: *How much radiation is too much?* The levels of exposure now considered "safe" are a small fraction of what Marie Curie and her colleagues lived with in their laboratory. To suggest just how much more stringent standards have become, it is enough to say that papers that were kept at the laboratory had to be decontaminated before they could be made available to researchers at the Bibliothèque nationale, and some of them still cannot be inspected unless the reader signs a waiver. The hope with which radioactivity was greeted in the early years has been replaced by a fear sometimes bordering on the irrational.

The cataclysm of Hiroshima and Nagasaki contributed, more

than any other event, to that change. But even before the atomic bomb, there was a growing understanding of radioactivity's power to do harm. If one year can be singled out in which the picture began to darken, it is probably 1925. That was the year a young woman named Margaret Carlough, who worked as a painter of luminous watch dials in a plant in New Jersey, sued her employer, U.S. Radium Corporation. She claimed that her work, which involved using her lips to point her brush, had caused irreparable damage to her health. With the suit, news began to come out about the fate of other women who had worked in the factory. At least nine dial painters had already died. Others were suffering from severe anemia and deterioration of the jaw, or "radium necrosis." Although the company steadfastly denied it, blaming the deaths on everything from poor hygiene to hysteria, responsible investigators concluded that the dial painters' deaths were caused by radiation. By 1928, fifteen dial painters were known to have died from radium exposure; there is no way of knowing how many more victims had been misdiagnosed.

The dial painters' deaths defied conventional wisdom about radioactivity. In the first place, radium was present in the luminous paint in extremely small proportions: one part radium to thirty thousand or more parts of zinc sulfide. Radium in such small doses had been assumed to be harmless, if not beneficial. Secondly, the ingestion of radium was not thought to incur great risks; although it meant that alpha particles which could not penetrate skin were introduced into the body, it was assumed that they would be quickly expelled. The radium-dial painters were living—and dying—proof that ingested radium, chemically similar to calcium, sought out and lodged in the bones, where it damaged blood-forming tissues and caused abnormalities, including anemia and leukemia.

By the time Missy Meloney wrote her about the dial painters, in June of 1925, Marie Curie was already dealing with another tragedy closer to home. Two engineers, Marcel Demalander and Maurice Demenitroux, had died within four days of one another from the radiation they were exposed to in preparing thorium X for medical use in a small factory on the outskirts of Paris. Demalander, who was thirty-five, had been sick for three months and died of "severe anemia," and Demenitroux, aged forty-one, succumbed to a leukemia after a year's illness.

The deaths of Demalander and Demenitroux forced a reexamination of the safety question both in the press and in the scientific community. *Je sais tout,* the weekly which had honored Marie Curie at the time of her 1921 visit to America, ran a front-page gallery of nine radiologists and researchers who had suffered the ill effects of radiation, calling it "The glorious martyrology of radium and X-

Rays." Along with Demenitroux, there was a radiologist who had undergone a "series of amputations, of fingers, of his hand, of his arm," another who had lost most of his eyesight, and several who had died after terrible suffering. "Can one be protected against the murderous rays?" asked *Je sais tout*.

The question was revisited in the scientific community as well. Marie Curie had known both Demenitroux and Demalander since before the war, when they passed through her laboratory as students. She asked their colleague I. Jaloustre to write a report for her on the circumstances of their deaths. Jaloustre pointed out in his report that the two engineers were by no means the first to die from exposure to radioactive elements. The daily newspapers had reported on the death of a London nurse; and a Frenchwoman, one Madame Artaud, charged with the care of the medical equipment used in mesothorium and radium treatments, had died of a serious anemia "which might very well have been caused by . . . radiation." As for Demalander and Demenitroux, "they didn't . . . perceive, except in the last days, that radioactivity could be the cause of the illness they were dying of."

The French Academy of Medicine responded to the deaths by appointing a commission to look into health standards in places preparing radioactive materials. The Academy had appointed a commission four years before. But the resulting report, presented by André Broca in 1921, addressed what were called "unjustified fears" in the general public about the "danger of penetrating rays." While acknowledging that precautions should be taken, Broca noted that there was radioactive gas "in the air we breathe, particularly in the neighborhood of certain mineral sources, and these places are inhabited by flourishing populations; many sick people even go there to reestablish their health." Indeed, Broca suggested that, as in homeopathy, small doses of radiation might be beneficial. "We would not be surprised if a weak dose of radioactive emanation was one day shown to be useful on a regular basis." The 1921 report recommended that the Academy "point out the possible dangers, but affirm that . . . well-known precautions make it possible to avoid them." It would not be wise, the report concluded, to impose encumbering regulations.

The 1925 commission praised the "excellent" report of 1921. But the tone of *this* report, prepared by Marie Curie, Antoine Béclère, Claudius Regaud, and others, was entirely different. Focusing on small industrial operations, the commission stressed the dangers inherent in preparing radioactive materials, particularly radium and thorium, without proper precautions. In particular, they emphasized the blood changes which could result from the inhalation of alpha particles. They recommended measures "already perfectly well-known": the envelopment of radioactive sources in a thick heavy metal and the interposition of lead screens between the worker and the source. In addition, the workers in the lab, factory, workshop, or hospital should undergo periodic blood tests to detect abnormalities.

"It is not enough," the commission warned, "to give out advice, even to give orders. It is necessary to make sure that the advice is listened to, that the orders are executed." To this end, they recommended that "industrial establishments which prepare, manipulate or transport radioactive bodies be classed as dangerous to health" and that they be regulated by the Minister of Work and Health.

In 1925, this recommendation appeared to some to be alarmist. An industrial chemist named Harlan Miner with whom Marie Curie was in regular correspondence wrote her that "we have been a little disturbed in America by a recent report from France . . . that the manufacture of radium is now classed as a dangerous operation by the French Academy. . . . We are, of course, keenly interested in this . . . and I am naturally wondering whether the report is authentic or whether it is somewhat exaggerated." He added that he was happy to say that there was "no evidence of serious effects" upon employees at the Welsbach Company, although they worked with mesothorium.

Marie Curie replied that deaths of the two engineers "demonstrated that it was necessary to warn of danger, to industrialists as well as to engineers." But she assured him that she knew of no "grave accidents due to radium or to mesothorium among the personnel of other factories . . . nor among the personnel of my Institute."

By the time Marie Curie's reply reached Harlan Miner, sometime in early June, the French Academy's warning no longer seemed exaggerated. One of the young men in his company, and a second working for a radium manufacturer had just died, quite suddenly, of an anemia. "As far as I know," he wrote her, "these are the first fatalities among chemists engaged in the manufacture of radium and mesothorium in the Country. I have been informed however that there have recently been several fatalities among operatives in a self-luminous paint factory." He asked her to send him everything available on the subject of "the effect of radio-active substances upon the worker in this field. . . . I am following this up in the interest of humanity and of our science." Throughout 1925, as news of radiation deaths accumulated, Marie Curie proudly maintained that "we have still not had anything serious in our Institute." She pointed out that Demenitroux and Demalander had been working with very strong solutions of radiothorium and mesothorium in "a defective installation," "a little room without aeration and without a protective screen. The poisoning was probably due partly to penetrating rays, but for the most part perhaps to thorium emanation which was being released constantly into the room." She also noted that, in the last months of their lives,

Demenitroux and Demalander lived in a house right near their laboratory "because they felt tired and didn't want to travel. Thus they didn't have a chance to get out and take the air."

By the standards of the day, Marie Curie's laboratory does seem to have been quite careful. Most of the methods of protection which are currently recommended in dealing with radioactive materials were in place in her lab, albeit in much less stringent form. Hoods "with good draught" had been installed in the lab to evacuate radioactive gases. Radioactive sources were encased in lead and a protective screen was maintained between the worker and the source. Workers were required to use forceps rather than their fingers in handling the sources. And as early as 1921 they had begun receiving periodic blood tests.

But on November 30, 1925, Irène received a letter from a Japanese scientist named Nobus Yamada, who had worked closely with her in preparing polonium sources. In July of 1924, Irène had written her mother that "Yamada has made some good plates with a new very strong source." Sixteen months later, Yamada wrote Irène that he had fainted suddenly two weeks after his return home to Japan and had since been confined to bed. "The cause of the illness still isn't clear. It is certain that I was very tired after the long stay abroad, but also there was a poisoning from the emanations. Here we don't have enough quantity of radioactive substances and as a result we have no descriptions of poisoning from these substances." He added his thanks "to Madame Curie and to you" for helping him to attain his doctorate. "It is very difficult to obtain this title here."

Two years later, Nobus Yamada was dead. "He seemed to be suffering from nervous debility when he came home," his widow wrote Marie Curie, "but one day he suddenly fell down senseless. Since then he has been totally confined to bed, and in spite of every effort and medical treatments he passed away forever."

Marie Curie was always enormously sympathetic to the sick and bereaved. Her response to the news of Yamada's death was a letter praising his "great qualities." For others she did more, organizing a collection for the widows of Demalander and Demenitroux, writing regularly to a former worker in her lab who was dying of tuberculosis, and then, after his death, leaning on the powers within the university to publish his unfinished doctoral dissertation to please his parents and honor his memory.

Yet she was unlikely, except in the most obvious cases, to make a connection between various illnesses and radiation. There were many reasons for this. One was the state of knowledge about radiation sickness at the time. The variety of ways radiation could affect health was not well understood. Nor was the long time lag between exposure and effect. Perhaps most importantly, individuals differed widely in their response to exposure. If Marie Curie used herself as a gauge, it was difficult to understand how others could become so ill.

Considering just how much radioactivity she had been exposed to, particularly in the early days when she was isolating radium without any protection, Marie Curie was remarkably resistant. So were some others in her lab. Lucien Desgranges, who started work in the lab at fourteen and rose to chief engineer, was given the assignment of decontaminating instruments in the lab, a job he performed with a scrub brush. Yet he lived into old age. So did Hélène Emmanuel-Zavizziano, the young woman who worked with protoactinium.

Others were not so fortunate. In the summer of 1927, while Marie Curie was vacationing in l'Arcouëst, Irène reported that Sonia Cotelle, a thirty-year-old chemist of Polish origin, was "in very bad health . . . she has stomach troubles, an extremely rapid loss of hair, etc." Cotelle was working with polonium, as Yamada had been. "It will be necessary to examine if, in the evaporation of strong solutions, there is not some polonium carried off in the air in a notable quantity," Irène wrote her mother. Then she added, "given that I have worked a lot on that without being made ill, I think more that she must have swallowed some polonium as the activity of her lips would lead one to think and her urine. What's more her present ill health perhaps has no connection with that but she is very uneasy, which is understandable." Even in this case, Irène was reluctant to conclude that there was a connection to radioactivity.

Sonia Cotelle's was one of a number of illnesses in the lab. Another worker had an accident which affected his eyes. And there were numerous cases of radiodermatitis which sometimes grew more serious and led to loss of fingers. Many others showed signs of abnormality in their blood: in 1931, for instance, seven out of twenty workers in the lab showed some sort of blood anomaly. When the doctors ordered it, those with abnormal blood tests were packed off to the country, where they would receive letters from "la patronne" encouraging them to stay as long as was necessary to effect a "cure." The belief that damage was not permanent, that fresh air could undo it, was reassuring to everyone. When Irène's blood count was abnormal in 1927, Marie wrote her brother Józef that "Irène doesn't feel well yet, she still doesn't have enough erythrocytes. She will be leaving soon for two weeks of winter sports and hopes that this stay in the mountains will be good for her anemia."

In addition to the blood disorders, there were a number of deaths which, with the benefit of hindsight, appear suspicious. For instance, two lab workers died of tuberculosis at ages thirty-three and forty-three after blood tests showed abnormalities. Another, aged thirty-one, died quite suddenly of a bronchitis. Might their resistance have been reduced by their exposure to radiation? Another young man whose work with protoactinium had caused anemia was killed in an apparent accident on vacation. Might his weakened condition have contributed to his death? There is no way of knowing now. But in our time we are as likely to suspect radioactivity as the Curies were to discount it.

Both Marie and Pierre Curie had more reason than most to downplay radium's pernicious effects. It was their precious discovery, a glowing thing that they had admired in the night. And if it was so dangerous, they were more likely than almost anyone else in the world to be its victims. Furthermore, they believed that risks had to be taken in scientific research, and shouldn't be complained about. "In fact," Pierre Curie had told a journalist in 1903 in discussing his skin lesions, "I am happy after all with my injury. My wife is as pleased as I. . . . You see, these are the little accidents of the laboratory: they shouldn't frighten people who live their lives among alembics and retorts." This heroic view of science contributed to Marie Curie's tendency to minimize the increasingly debilitating effects of radiation on her own health.

At times, Marie Curie was perfectly candid about it: when traveling in the United States, she stated simply enough that her health had been ruined by exposure to radioactivity, especially during the war years when she worked around X rays. At other times, she seemed reluctant to admit, even to herself, that radium was to blame. "My greatest troubles," she wrote Bronia in November of 1920, "come from my eyes and ears. My eyes have grown much weaker, and probably very little can be done about them. As for the ears, an almost continuous humming, sometimes very intense, persecutes me. I am very worried about it: my work may be interfered with—or even become impossible. Perhaps radium has something to do with these troubles, but it cannot be affirmed with certainty."

Always, in the last years of her life, Marie Curie insisted on secrecy about her ailments. "These are my troubles," she wrote Bronia. "Don't speak of them to anybody, above all things, as I don't want the thing to be bruited about."

According to Eve, Marie Curie went to absurd lengths to keep her illnesses secret, not only from the public but from others in the lab. Around 1920, when she began to develop cataracts as a result of radiation exposure, she invented tricks that allowed her to go on with her work, placing very visible colored signs on her instruments, and writing her lecture notes in huge letters. "If a pupil was obliged to submit to Mme Curie an experimental photograph showing fine lines, Marie by hypocritical questioning, prodigiously adroit, first obtained from him the information necessary to reconstruct the aspect of the photograph mentally. Then and then alone she would take the glass plate, consider it, and *appear* to observe the lines."

When at last surgery was required, she wrote to Eve in l'Arcouëst asking her to come back to Paris. "You must tell our friends at l'Arcouëst that I have not been able to get through a piece of editing that we were working on together and that I need you as I have been asked for it in a hurry." She checked into the clinic as Madame Carré, and sent Eve to be fitted for the thick glasses she needed. There were three more surgeries, all done without the knowledge of her friends and colleagues. As she told Eve, "Nobody needs to know that I have ruined eyes."

There were many reasons for what Eve described as "noble duplicity." Of course, Marie Curie hated publicity and she didn't want to be pitied. But she also didn't want the workers in her laboratory to view her as old and helpless. And perhaps most important of all, she didn't want to give in to debility herself. After her last cataract operation in 1930, she wrote proudly to Eve from Cavalaire that she was "acquiring the habit of going about without glasses. . . . I took part in two walks over awkward rocky mountain trails. That went off rather well, and I can walk fast without accidents."

Marie Curie didn't want to face the obvious: if radiation was ruining her health, then the best treatment was to retire. And this, as she confessed to Bronia in September of 1927, was the thing she could not bear to do. "Sometimes my courage fails me and I think I ought to stop working, live in the country and devote myself to gardening. But I am held by a thousand bonds. . . . Nor do I know whether, even by writing scientific books, I could live without the laboratory."

Chapter Nineteen

LEGACIES

THERE WAS SOMETIMES a contradiction between what Marie Curie chose to do herself and what she advocated for others. There was, for instance, the question of protecting discoveries. In the League of Nations' Commission on Intellectual Cooperation, she worked on a resolution which would give scientists and inventors property rights and allow them to profit from their discoveries. But she herself and Pierre had decided, twenty years before, not to patent the process by which radium was prepared, a process used in industry for many years. "I still believe what we have done right," she wrote in the 1920s. And yet, a note of regret can be detected in her observation that "it is a fortune which we have sacrificed in renouncing the exploitation of our discovery, a fortune that could, after us, have gone to our children." What's more, "we could have had the financial means of founding a satisfactory Institute of Radium, without experiencing any of the difficulties that have been such a handicap to both of us, and are still a handicap to me."

It was perhaps this thought which led Marie Curie to work on a resolution which would protect others' inventions. Certainly, it was the wish that her daughters be secure which led her to place one of the country houses in each girl's name (Eve was assigned the Cavalaire house and Irène the one in l'Arcouëst), and to place the gram of radium from America in Irène's charge in the last year of her life. As for her laboratory, which was another sort of child, she never ceased to campaign for it, at home and abroad. "I mostly think of what has to be done and not of what has been done," she wrote her friend Missy in 1929, "and it is because I am afraid that my strength could fail me, that I do not enjoy remembering my birthday.

I surely need several years of efficient work to take care of the Institution created by me and Dr. Regaud and to make it safe in the future."

It was this drive to ensure the laboratory's future which kept Marie Curie from taking the New Year's advice she gave Irène to "each day have the pleasure of living, without waiting for the days to pass to find pleasure in them, and without putting too much hope of pleasure uniquely in the days ahead." Either out of a sense of duty or to raise money, Marie Curie often found herself in a ceremonial role she hated. "I am stupefied by the life I lead and incapable of saying anything intelligent to you," she wrote Irène while a guest of honor in Prague in 1925. "I wonder what fundamental vice there is in human organization which makes this form of agitation necessary? 'Dignifying science' Madame Meloney would say. And what is beyond denying is the sincerity of all those who do these things and their conviction that they must do them."

Marie Curie was made especially uncomfortable by the solicitousness everyone showed the honored guest on these occasions. Once, during her first visit to America, Missy had come upon her washing her own underwear, insisting that "with all the extra guests in the house, the servants have enough to do." When she returned to America, in 1929, she complained again of the fuss people made over her. There didn't seem to be the same respect for privacy in America as in Europe, she wrote Irène. The houses were without gardens and trees to give "an impression of intimacy." And there were no keys or keyholes for the bedroom doors. "They come into your room," she wrote, "sometimes having knocked, other times not having taken the trouble. The maid thinks that she pleases me by moving my things around, displacing them, opening and closing the window ten times in an hour without consulting me, turning the fire when it isn't necessary; I spend my time keeping her from making me happy according to her personal views. My excellent friend Mme Meloney has the same tendency, but she tries hard not to annoy me and proves really touching in this way."

Marie Curie's second trip to America was designed to fulfill yet another obligation. A group of American women had raised enough money to buy a gram of radium for the institute that was to be established, with her encouragement and her sister Bronia's planning, in Poland. Reluctantly, after several postponements and a great deal of correspondence, Marie Curie had come in the fall of 1929, to be presented with a check for the radium by President Hoover. But except for seeing American friends, Marie Curie seems to have been too ill, on this second trip, to get much more from America than the financial support. At one point, she described herself to Irène as a "poor prisoner."

It was around the time of the second American trip, in 1929, that Marie Curie was asked to give her opinion on "surmenage"—overwork among students—and spoke out strongly in opposition to a "system of education which does not correspond to the normal conditions of physical and intellectual development," which kept students in school from early in the morning until four or five in the afternoon, and required them to study every night until "almost midnight," taxing their eyes and depriving them of sleep.

But Marie Curie, so adamant on the subject of *surmenage* in youth, was guilty of worse in age. Eve described coming home to the apartment on quai de Béthune and seeing a light on in her mother's study:

> The spectacle was the same every night. Mme Curie, surrounded by papers, calculating rulers, and monographs, was seated on the floor. She had never been able to get used to working in front of a desk. . . . She had to have limitless space to spread out her documents and her sheets of graphs. She was absorbed in a difficult theoretical calculation, and although she had noticed her daughter's return, she did not lift her head. Her brows frowned and her face was preoccupied.

Lucien Desgranges, who lived above the laboratory, remembered that she was often the first to arrive there in the morning and the last to leave. "Not infrequently . . . instead of returning home for supper, she satisfied herself with a piece of bread or a few cookies, along with a glass of tea warmed up on a hot plate." And Catherine Chamié remembers one particular time when she stayed most of the night to watch over the preparation of actinium X.

> The day of work isn't enough for the separation of this element, Madame Curie stays for the evening, without dinner, but the separation . . . is slow; so we stay the night, so that the intense source we're preparing won't decay too much. It is already two o'clock in the morning and the last operation has still to be done: centrifuging for an hour. . . . The centrifuge turns with an annoying noise, but Madame Curie stays beside it without wanting to leave the room. She contemplates the machine as if her ardent desire for the experiment to succeed can will the maximum amount of precipitation of Actinium X. For Madame Curie, nothing exists in this moment except this question, neither her daily life, nor her fatigue; it is a complete depersonalization and concentration of all her soul on the work she is doing.

Marie Curie had once told a reporter looking for color about her life, "In science, we must be interested in things, not persons," and she was capable of a deep absorption in the things of science which amounted to a waking dream. When a friend stopped by the laboratory one day to ask her about Irène, who was quite ill, she found the interruption wrenching: "Why can't people leave one alone to work?" she asked indignantly. Another time, when Eve was about fifteen, her mother was so preoccupied that she didn't notice her daughter had double pneumonia. A doctor who was staying at the house walked by the room, noticed Eve prostrate, and called an ambulance. "Then of course she felt guilty," Eve recalls, "and spent two nights at the hospital."

Oblivious though she often was, Marie Curie was interested in people as well as things. Her attachments to friends and family were deep. When, in 1930, she heard that Jacques Curie had been in bed for three weeks, she rushed to Montpellier to be by his side, despite her own fragile health. And when she learned that Bronia's daughter Hela died, an apparent suicide, in Chicago, she was deeply saddened. "We have had a deep family grief," she wrote an American friend, "because my sister has lost, by accident, her only daughter . . . I loved that girl."

As she grew older, Marie Curie felt the sadness of her physical separation from family more keenly. "There are three of you in Warsaw," she wrote Bronia in 1932, "and thus you can have some company and some protection. Believe me, family solidarity is after all the only good thing. I have been deprived of it, so I know."

One of the benefits of starting a radium institute in Poland was the opportunity it provided her to travel to her native country and take part in its new struggle. From Warsaw, where she went in 1921 to seek support from the government for an institute, she wrote enthusiastically to Irène about preservation efforts. "There is a picturesque old town," she wrote, "which contains ancient houses and squares which are being taken charge of by societies which provide the funds necessary for conservation. There is the Vistula . . . there are some beautiful very large parks as well as public and private gardens. . . . There is no doubt that they could, with all of this do very well in time." Eleven years later, thanks in large part to the organizational efforts of her sister Bronia, Marie Curie had the satisfaction of returning to Poland to celebrate the opening of the Warsaw Radium Institute. The president of the Polish republic was on hand for the dedication.

In France too, during these final years, there was recognition of a particularly satisfying kind. In February of 1922, in a rebuke to the Académie des Sciences, which had rejected her eleven years earlier, the Académie de Médicine made Marie Curie the first Frenchwoman to enter the Institute. "One would hope," Jacques Curie wrote her, "that the Academy of Sciences would learn its lesson and call you now to its bosom." That was not to be.

But the following year, in conjunction with a celebration of the twenty-fifth anniversary of the discovery of radium, the French parliament voted Marie Curie a substantial pension for life. Whatever might still be whispered in private about the Langevin affair, Marie Curie had become, with the help of the American tour and two Nobel Prizes, one of the few Frenchwomen in history to transcend a scandal.

What made the anniversary celebration especially sweet, as she later told a friend, was that all three of her siblings—Józef, Helena, and Bronia—came from Poland for it. Also, it was an occasion honoring not her but the discovery, and gave her yet another opportunity to recognize her closest collaborators and to proselytize for the laboratory. "Pierre Curie left us several years before the creation of the Laboratory which bears his name, where his elder daughter now works with me," she noted, and concluded with the wish that "the era of difficult beginnings has passed, and that our Institute will find the support it needs to fulfill its destiny."

For the most part, however, Marie Curie much preferred anonymity. Raymond Drux, her chauffeur for the last four years of her life, remembers stopping with her en route to l'Arcouëst and Cavalaire. Once, in a crowded restaurant in Caen, the owner recognized her. "Isn't that Madame Curie?" he asked. The driver denied it, but the owner persisted. While the travelers waited for their dinner, he walked up to Madame Curie with his guest book, spoke her name loudly (for the benefit of other diners), and asked her to sign. "Madame Curie got up, without a word laid down money for the uneaten meals, and we left."

Another time, heading south to Cavalaire, they stopped at a hotel with a lovely garden at the edge of the Rhône. "After dinner, she went into the garden, where roses were blooming, walked the paths and breathed in the aroma of the flowers. The following morning, the owner of the hotel cut several of the most beautiful of the roses, still wet with dew, and laid them next to the table setting of the anonymous silver-haired lady." Touched by the gesture, Marie Curie asked for his guest book, in which she signed her name, much to the hotelier's surprise and delight. "That was how Madame Curie was: she could not tolerate brazenness . . . but she rewarded emotional subtlety."

If there was a time, outside the laboratory, when Marie Curie could live intensely inside the moment, it was when she was in the country. Even in winter, her driver remembers, she "liked to spend Sundays taking long walks through the woods. In heavy shoes, with her ever-present backpack, she could spend the entire day wandering through the Fontainebleau, Rambouillet or Senart forests," often accompanied by Irène, who was "also a devotee of long hikes." In Poland, in Cavalaire, in l'Arcouëst, she was an energetic walker, swimmer, and observer. "We have had some sun today," she wrote Irène from Cavalaire in December of 1926, "which allowed me to take a walk of two and a half hours this morning on the mountain above Cavalaire. . . . The mimosas have their clusters of little balls all ready to open and those with the long simple leaf have decided to take the lead, especially where they are well protected in sunny spots, exhibiting a small number of particularly velvety open flowers of a delicious color."

After the war, Marie Curie took more frequent vacations, traveling in winter to the warmer Cavalaire and in summer to l'Arcouëst, where she took part in the joyful routine of Captain Seignobos and his crew. A typical day began, according to Eve, when Marie Curie joined the "initiates" gathered in front of Taschen, the captain's house, "dawdling as they waited for the daily embarkation for the islands. . . . She wore a hat of washed-out linen, an old skirt and the indestructible swanskin pea jacket. . . . Her feet were bare, in sandals. She placed in front of her a bag like fifteen other bags scattered about the grass, swollen with her bathrobe and bathing suit."

The group set out then, with two sailboats and five or six rowboats, for Roch Vras, a deserted island where they came to bathe nearly every morning. "The men undressed near the empty boats, on a beach covered with brown seaweed, the women in a corner carpeted with slick, rubbery weeds, which had been called 'the ladies' cabin' since the beginning. Marie reappeared among the first, in her black bathing suit, and made for the sea. The bank was steep, and no sooner had one plunged into the water than the bottom disappeared."

Taught to swim by Eve and Irène, she practiced an overarm stroke. "Her innate elegance and grace had done the rest. You forgot her gray hair, hidden under the bathing cap, and her wrinkled face, in admiring the slim, supple body, the pretty white arms and the lively, charming gestures of a young girl." For Eve, "the picture of Marie Curie swimming at Roch Vras in that cool deep water of ideal purity and transparence is one of the most delightful memories I have of my mother."

In the loving and vivid biography Eve wrote after Marie Curie's death, she insisted that her mother "never showed a preference" between the two "very different daughters whom she had brought into the world." Yet there can be little doubt that Marie had an easier relationship with her older daughter, who shared her passion for science. For a time, during Eve's adolescence, Marie talked to Irène about her as though they were raising her together. "I hope . . . our Evette will love us more in Paris than she did in l'Arcouëst," Marie wrote Irène in the summer of 1919, when Eve was fourteen.

As time went on, and Eve continued to show promise at the piano, Marie supported her by buying a grand piano and finding good teachers. And when concerts followed, Marie wrote Missy Meloney of her excitement. Yet there is always the impression, from Eve and her mother, that they lived in different worlds. Marie wrote Irène that she dreaded being cooped up with Eve's piano practicing if the weather was bad in l'Arcouëst. "We will have to reconcile the scientific work represented by us two with the musical art represented by Evette, which is much easier in good weather than in rain." Eve felt in retrospect that her mother didn't understand the intensity of training required for a concert career, encouraging her to get a general education first. Unlike Irène, who never waivered in her determination to be a scientist, Eve did a great deal of "veering and tacking," trying her hand at criticism and playwriting as well as music. Eve felt she could have used more guidance. Nor could it have been easy to endure the condescension of scientists, some of whom believed theirs was the only worthwhile calling. At the celebration of the twenty-fifth anniversary of the discovery of radium, the usually tactful H. A. Lorentz commented on "a new collaboration, which is full of promise" between Irène and her mother. "I am quite sure that Mlle. Eve Curie would like to do this as well as her sister, but in the end we can't all be physicists."

Yet there were many times when Eve and her mother seem to have simply enjoyed each other's company. Together, they traveled to Spain in April of 1931, on the eve of national elections which would transform the country from a monarchy into a republic. Marie Curie, who was sixty-four and ailing, was so touched by what she saw that she rarely complained. The days were beautiful and sunny, the people were "excellent," and tours of Madrid were "very agreeable." Rooms without heat and even crowds were endured cheerfully. "It is very moving," she wrote Irène, "to see what confidence in the future exists among the young and among many of their elders." And later, "what interests me a lot are the conversations with republicans and the enthusiasm that they have for revitalizing their country. May they succeed!" Afterward, Eve described the trip to Spain as a "dazzling, never-to-be-forgotten journey."

BY THE TIME of the Spanish trip, life at quai de Béthune had undergone a transformation. On October 9, 1926, at age twenty-nine, Irène

Curie had married Frédéric Joliot. Dinners after that became a duet, in which Marie discussed the laboratory, then asked Eve to "give me news of the world." Eve would talk of many things, including her little car, a *deux-chevaux,* and its gas mileage. After Fred and Irène's first child, Hélène, was born, Eve might have news of her. "Stories about her granddaughter . . . ," Eve recalled, "a quotation from the child's talk, could make her suddenly laugh to the point of tears, with an unexpected laugh of youth."

In March of 1932, a second child, a son, was born to the Joliot-Curies. When they decided to name him Pierre, Jacques Curie wrote how happy he was that the name "won't disappear from the family." But even before the arrival of baby Pierre, there were striking parallels between the partner Irène had chosen and her father, as well as her beloved grandfather. Frédéric Joliot was born in 1900, three years after Irène, into an activist family. His father, like Irène's grandfather Curie, had been a Communard, and was forced to flee to Belgium for some years to escape the subsequent crackdown. Like Pierre Curie, Joliot was educated outside the privileged *grandes écoles.* He studied at the École de physique et chimie, where Pierre's successor Paul Langevin steered him in the direction of physics as well as politics. In 1924, some years after Joliot graduated first in his class from the École de physique et chimie, Langevin suggested that he enter Marie Curie's laboratory. Irène, who was both older and more experienced in the lab, often had the task of teaching technique to the young Joliot.

It was an opportunity for the two young people to observe each other closely. "I didn't have the slightest idea that we might marry one day," Frédéric Joliot said later. "But I watched her. . . . With her cold appearance, her forgetting sometimes to say hello, she didn't always create sympathy around her at the laboratory. In observing her, I discovered in this young woman, that others saw as a little brutish, an extraordinary, poetic and sensitive being who, in a number of ways, was a living representation of her father. I had read a lot about Pierre Curie . . . I found in his daughter this same purity, this good sense, this tranquillity." In many ways they were a good match. Unlike Irène, Frédéric would never forget to say hello; he was as naturally gregarious as she was withdrawn. When Irène and her mother traveled to Brazil shortly before their wedding, Frédéric wrote that he found the laboratory "a fraud" without her. "I link myself more with human beings than with things; one can work anywhere . . . what gives interest in life in the lab are the people who animate it."

In the beginning Marie Curie seems to have been less than ecstatic about the match. To Józef she wrote, showing a little of ancient Polish prejudices, that Fred's family were "well-respected but they are industrialists." And to Missy Meloney she noted, with perhaps more than usual reserve, that "the esteem that exists between these two people allows one to believe in a favorable future." Mostly, as she told Józef a year or so after their marriage, "I miss Irène a lot. We were so close for such a long time. Of course, we often see each other, but it's not the same."

But as time went on, Marie Curie became more enthusiastic about her new son-in-law. She had lunch with the young couple four times a week, and, according to Irène, "my mother and my husband often debated with such ardor, answering back and forth so rapidly, that I couldn't get a word in and was obliged to insist on having a say when I wanted to express an opinion." To Jean Perrin Marie Curie confided, "That young man is a ball of fire."

In many ways, the team of Frédéric and Irène Joliot-Curie, as they chose to call themselves, must have reminded Marie Curie of her own partnership with Pierre. Frédéric, like Pierre, was a physicist and a tinkerer who loved playing around with instruments. Irène, like her mother, was more the chemist. And in 1931, the young couple began to collaborate, like their elders, in making a series of exciting discoveries.

The discovery of the neutron, as historians of science have noted, was an unusual one. Most of the important observations were made by one group of scientists; but the interpretation of those observations was made by someone else. Among those who prepared the way, the most important were undoubtedly Ernest Rutherford and Irène and Frédéric Joliot-Curie. Back in 1920, Ernest Rutherford had proposed something he called a "neutral doublet," a particle with no charge which would roughly double the mass of the nucleus. The next year, at the Solvay Conference of 1921, he reiterated this idea, using the word "neutron" to describe it. Such a particle, having no charge, would be difficult to detect. But it would go a long way toward explaining the fact that each element in the table of Mendeleev has an atomic mass roughly equal to twice its charge.

Marie Curie was present at the 1921 Solvay Conference where Rutherford mentioned the neutron, but her own interests didn't tend in that direction. Nonetheless, by a circuitous route, her preoccupation with the radioactive elements was important to the experimental proof of Rutherford's hypothesis. The experiments, which involved using alpha rays as projectiles to bombard nuclei of various elements, required a strong source of alpha rays which didn't give off gamma rays to confuse the picture. Polonium, the element Marie Curie had discovered first and named after her native land, was such a source. And it was polonium which made it possible to detect the neutron.

The first step was taken in Germany in 1930, when both Walther

Bothe and Herbert Becker got some surprising results from bombarding light elements with alpha particles from polonium. When they subjected beryllium to the rays, they produced a penetrating radiation of greater energy than the bombarding particles.

This was of particular interest to Irène Curie, who had been working for some years preparing strong sources of polonium. Because of Marie Curie's assiduous collecting of radon seeds, combined with the dangerous work of preparing it, the Joliot-Curies had, by 1931, the largest concentration of polonium in the world. Indeed, it was routine for them to prepare a polonium source almost ten times stronger than was possible anywhere else. In December of 1931, Irène Curie reported that beryllium, bombarded by alpha rays from her strong polonium source, gave off an even more penetrating radiation than the German experimenters had reported.

What was this penetrating radiation?

On January 18, 1932, the Joliot-Curies published a second paper about the effect of the beryllium radiation on a screen containing hydrogen (a layer of paraffin wax). By a series of "simple and elegant" experimental tests, the Joliot-Curies demonstrated that the radiation from the beryllium was knocking protons out of the hydrogen. At this point, they understood that what they were seeing were elastic collisions—like the collisions of billiard balls—between the beryllium radiation and the nuclei of hydrogen atoms. But the explanation they gave of the phenomenon was unconvincing: they attributed it to gamma rays, even though it was unlikely that massless photons could propel the much larger proton forward.

In England, however, Rutherford and a younger researcher named James Chadwick thought differently. "I don't believe it," was Rutherford's response when he heard the Joliot-Curies' explanation of their findings. Chadwick had recently obtained a good supply of polonium himself, thanks to a donation of radon seeds from an American hospital. He set up his own version of the Joliot-Curies' experiment and bombarded a range of elements with the beryllium radiation. "A few days of strenuous work were sufficient to show," Chadwick recalled, "that these strange effects were due to a neutral particle and to enable me to measure its mass: the neutron postulated by Rutherford in 1920 had at last revealed itself."

Privately, Frédéric Joliot noted that "it is annoying to be overtaken by other laboratories which immediately take up one's experiments." But publicly, he made the generous observation that "it is natural and just that the final step in the discovery of the neutron was taken in [the Cavendish Laboratory]. Old laboratories with long traditions have . . . hidden riches. The ideas put forward in other times by our masters, gone or still living, many times taken up then forgotten, penetrate consciously or unconsciously in the thought of those who frequent these laboratories."

For the same reasons, the Curie laboratory was the natural site for the next major revelation: the discovery of artificial radioactivity. "Everything," Frédéric Joliot observed afterward, "was favorable to facilitating the work and the interpretation of results: the existence of intense sources of polonium, as well as the knowledge of natural radioelements discovered by our illustrious teacher."

In California, in the summer of 1932, an American researcher named Carl Anderson had discovered a new particle in a shower of cosmic rays, a positively charged electron which was assigned the name "positron." The instrument he used to make the discovery was a Wilson cloud chamber, a twenty-year-old invention that made the invisible trajectories of particles visible by shooting them through a saturated vapor, in which they produced a line of droplets.

Frédéric Joliot was a devotee of the Wilson cloud chamber, and proud of the improvements he had made to the instrument at the Curie lab. When he had a free moment, he liked to take visitors down to the basement where he kept his modified version. "An infinitely tiny particle projected in this enclosed region can trace its own path thanks to the succession of drops of condensation. Isn't it the most beautiful experiment in the world?" he would ask.

And so, when the Joliot-Curies heard about the new particle Anderson had detected in his Wilson cloud chamber, they went immediately to their own photographs of particle tracks and discovered that they too showed evidence of positrons. They began bombarding a variety of elements with alpha particles from a polonium source to look for more positrons. They found that medium-weight targets ejected protons, but they noticed that lighter elements sometimes emitted a neutron and then a positron instead of a proton.

In October of 1933, Irène and Frédéric Joliot-Curie joined Marie Curie at the Solvay Conference in Brussels for the first time, and presented a paper on their findings. Once again, their preliminary explanation of the phenomenon they were observing turned out to be incorrect. They suggested that what they were seeing, when the bombardment produced a neutron and a positron, might be the breakup of the proton. Perhaps the proton was a compound, rather than an elemental particle. Lise Meitner, a German researcher who was highly respected for the precision of her work, doubted that the Joliot-Curies were really seeing neutrons, and others seemed to agree with her. "After the session," Joliot later recalled, "we were quite downhearted, but at that moment professor Niels Bohr took us aside, my wife and I, to tell us that he found our results very important. A little later Pauli gave us the same encouragement."

When they returned to Paris, the Joliot-Curies decided to vary the distance between the alpha emitter and the target they were bombarding, thinking that their results might vary with the distance the particles traveled through air. When the alpha particles struck aluminum, they definitely produced neutrons, contrary to Lise Meitner's doubts. And as the distance between the alpha source and the aluminum target increased, the neutron emissions fell off to zero. But something else, something entirely unexpected, happened as well: even after the neutron emission stopped, a positron emission continued, decreasing over a certain period of time in the same manner as radiation from a naturally radioactive element.

Now, Joliot forsook his beloved Wilson cloud chamber for a Geiger counter and called in Irène. Sure enough, when he irradiated the target with alpha rays, the Geiger counter crackled. But when he removed the alpha-ray source, the Geiger counter should have gone silent. Instead, it continued its crackling, losing its initial intensity in about three minutes. This was a complete surprise: ordinary, stable aluminum had become radioactive.

At this point, the international composition of the Curie laboratory worked to the Joliot-Curies' advantage. A young German physicist named Wolfgang Gentner who was an expert on Geiger counters happened to be working at the lab that year. Joliot, not quite believing what he had seen and heard, asked Gentner to check the Geiger counters while he and his wife went off to fulfill a social obligation. The next morning, when they returned to the lab, there was a note from Gentner: the Geiger counters were in perfect working order.

The Joliot-Curies were now beginning to comprehend what was happening: the aluminum, when bombarded by alpha particles, was capturing one of the alpha particles and then emitting one neutron, thus becoming an unstable, "radioactive," isotope of phosphorus, an isotope which didn't exist in nature and which decayed, over time, to stable silicon. When, through a chemical test, they were able to verify their hypothesis, Frédéric Joliot-Curie felt "a child's joy. I began to run and jump around in that vast basement . . . I thought of the consequences which might come from the discovery." Joliot told Wolfgang Gentner, "With the neutron we were too late. With the positron we were too late. Now we are in time."

The significance of the Joliot-Curies' discovery was manifold. They had shown that it was possible to force an element artificially to release some of its energy in the form of radioactive decay. Like Pierre Curie before him, Joliot was quick to see the power of this discovery, noting that "scientists, building up or shattering elements at will, will be able to bring about transmutations of an explosive type." In his history of modern physics, Emilio Segrè calls the Joliot-Curies' discovery of artificial radioactivity "one of the most important . . . of the century." In 1935, the Nobel Committee would recognize the significance of the discovery, awarding Irène and Frédéric Joliot-Curie the Nobel Prize in Chemistry.

On January 15, 1934, the day the Joliot-Curies made their discovery, Pierre Biquard received an excited phone call from his good friend Frédéric Joliot. In minutes, Biquard ran from his laboratory on rue Vauquelin to the Joliot-Curies' basement lab. He remembers that "the apparatus he wanted to show me consisted of equipment scattered over several tables. Its newness and apparent disorder revealed . . . an experiment set up in haste, to reproduce as a demonstration a discovery made several hours before with Irène." Joliot filled Biquard in on the background, then performed the experiment, irradiating the target with alpha rays, then removing the alpha source and holding the Geiger counter up to the target. Then, Biquard recalls, "the laboratory door opened . . . and Marie Curie and Paul Langevin came in."

Afterward, Frédéric Joliot recalled that moment. "I will never forget the expression of intense joy which overtook her when Irène and I showed her the first [artificially produced] radioactive element in a little glass tube. I can see her still taking this little tube of the radioelement, already quite weak, in her radium-damaged fingers. To verify what we were telling her, she brought the Geiger-Muller counter up close to it and she could hear the numerous clicks. . . . This was without a doubt the last great satisfaction of her life."

THERE WERE, however, a few family satisfactions yet to come. That same January, Marie Curie joined the Joliot-Curies on a trip to the mountains of the Savoie. Her grandchild Hélène was now seven, and Marie ice-skated with her and explored the terrain in snowshoes. "I remember being a little worried one night," Irène wrote later, "when she returned after dark . . . having gone quite a ways away to a place where one could see the sunset over Mont Blanc."

At Easter, Marie Curie took one more trip with her sister Bronia to the house in Cavalaire. But this time, her health turned the visit into a near disaster. Bronia, who had lost her daughter and more recently her husband Kazimierz, had reasons of her own to be sorrowful. But it was Marie who broke down. "When she reached her villa at Cavalaire . . . she was exhausted and had a cold," writes Eve. "Her house was icy when they arrived, and the heat . . . did not warm it fast enough. Marie, shaken by a chill, suddenly abandoned herself to an attack of despair. She sobbed in Bronia's arms like a sick child." Committed to writing a new edition of her two-volume book, *Radio-*

activity, Marie worried that "the bronchitis might deprive her of the strength to finish it."

"All things considered," her physician brother Józef wrote afterward, "that trip didn't do her any good. . . . After five weeks [Bronia] went back to Poland, leaving her sister in a worse condition than she had found her."

Still Marie Curie was full of projects. She wanted to finish her book, but she also wanted to build a house in Sceaux, away from the city, and planned to move into a modern apartment in a new building in university city. But she was increasingly beset with fever and chills which she couldn't overcome. "On one sunny day in May 1934," Eve wrote in *Madame Curie,* "she stayed until half-past three in the physical laboratory . . . exchanged a few words with her collaborators," and murmured " 'I have a fever and I must go home.' " On her way, she made a tour of the garden and noticed a sickly rambler rose. Her parting words were an order to the laboratory mechanic to take care of it. Later, she summoned Sonia Cotelle and asked her to put away the actinium she was working on until her return. But there was to be no return.

From then on it was Eve Curie who watched over her rapidly declining mother. Doctors in Paris saw old tubercular lesions on an X ray and advised that Marie Curie be taken to Sancellemoz, a sanatorium in the Savoy mountains. The trip was "sheer torture: in the train, arriving at Saint-Gervais, Marie collapsed, fainting, in the arms of Eve and the nurse." Once she was installed in "the best room at the sanatorium," the doctors took more X rays and found no evidence of TB. "The journey had been useless." A Swiss doctor, examining her blood tests, diagnosed "pernicious anemia in its extreme form."

"Then," Eve wrote afterward, "began the harrowing struggle which goes by the name of 'an easy death'—in which the body which refuses to perish asserts itself in wild determination." Eve, adhering to the conventional wisdom of the time, tried to keep her mother from the knowledge that she was dying. She encouraged Józef and Bronia not to rush to her bedside, as this would only frighten her.

But Marie, ever the scientist, insisted on reading her temperature. On July 3, she held the thermometer in her "shaking hand" and discerned that her temperature had dropped for the first time. "And as Eve assured her that this was the sign of her cure . . . she said, looking at the open window, turning hopefully towards the sun and the motionless mountains: 'It wasn't the medicines that made me better. It was the pure air, the altitude. . . .' " She died at dawn the next day "when the full light of a glorious morning had filled the room." The doctor gave the cause as "aplastic pernicious anemia of rapid, feverish development. The bone marrow did not react, probably because it had been injured by a long accumulation of radiations."

Marie Curie, who had always worn black in life, was laid to rest "all in white, her white hair laying bare the immense forehead, the face at peace. . . . Her rough hands, calloused, hardened, deeply burned by radium, had lost their familiar nervous movement. They were stretched out on the sheet, stiff and fearfully motionless—those hands which had worked so much."

TRIBUTES CAME to Eve and Irène from the humble and the great. Rutherford praised Marie Curie's "great abilities," and Niels Bohr wrote to Irène of her "kindness" on a recent visit. He added that "it must . . . be a great comfort to you to think of all the encouragement and pleasure Madame Curie in her last years had from the wonderful discoveries of you and your husband which . . . have crowned her great life work."

The most touching testimonials came from those who had known Marie Curie at her laboratory. Georges Fournier, one of her favorite students, wrote that "we have lost everything." And André Broca wrote from Copenhagen that "the idea that I will enter her office without finding her behind a mountain of well-ordered papers has made me cry like a child."

> How can one imagine the Institute without her? How can I think of this famous staircase—where one could so easily stop her as she passed—without seeing her leaning on the banister, her large forehead a little tilted and her hands in perpetual motion? It is in this Institute that . . . Madame Curie first spoke to me, with so much sweetness and understanding. . . . She had guessed my enthusiasm, and she spoke to me of her first encounter with Lippmann and of her first work. It seems to me that I see her still in the basement, discussing the virtues of a calorimeter; . . . or at that last Christmas eve party at the laboratory . . . where we spoke so much of the future of theoretical physics in France. The more I invoke these memories . . . the more difficult it is for me to imagine the house where she exhausted her strength and her life without her. And it seems to me that the stones and bricks are going to break apart.

On Friday, July 6, at noon on a hot, sunny day, the coffin of Marie Skłodowska Curie was lowered over Pierre Curie's in the small cemetery in Sceaux, where she had visited so faithfully over the years. There were no official speeches or ceremonies, and no important dignitaries came to pay their respects. Outside of the family, there were only close friends: the Borels, the Perrins, Langevin, Regaud.

The only pomp was a collection of great wreathes, including one from the president of the Polish republic. Incredibly, *le Journal* chose to criticize Marie Curie for the simple obsequies, calling it a sign of "the supreme pride which takes the form of voluntary effacement, of refusal of honors, of excessive simplicity." But this last little meanness was quickly refuted by Eve, who wrote that "my sister and I believed that we were respecting the intimate wishes of our mother, in burying her in the cemetery in Sceaux, in the tomb where Pierre Curie rests, and also in giving the ceremony a simple character."

Jacques Curie was too frail to come to the ceremony, and Marie's sister Helena, who was vacationing in the mountains with her granddaughter, couldn't be reached in time. But both Bronia and Józef had come from Warsaw, bringing with them, unbeknownst to each other, the tribute they knew would please their sister most. Over the coffin, they each sprinkled a handful of Polish soil.

NOTES

The early chapters of this biography rely on a number of texts translated for the first time from the Polish, including the memoirs of Maria Skłodowska's siblings Józef and Helena and the letters of her mother Bronisława. Translations into English were done by Alexandra Gordinier and Anna Sobczynski. Literal translations of poems were versified by poets Paula Bonnell and Jan Schreiber. On the other hand, letters written by Maria Skłodowska in Polish in her youth, and letters which she wrote to her Polish family from Paris in later years, no longer exist in their original Polish form. They were lost during the total destruction of Warsaw by the Nazis. Portions of these letters were quoted, however, in Eve Curie's biography of her mother, first published in French in 1937. Eve Curie Labouisse is unable at this point, sixty years after the fact, to remember whether she translated the letters from Polish herself (she spoke some Polish) or, which is more likely, got help from her then-living aunts, Marie Curie's sisters Bronia and Helena. Since the book was superbly translated into English by Vincent Sheehan, I am using his translations of the letters for the most part.

In Paris, I made extensive use of the Curie papers in the Salle des manuscrits of the Bibliothèque Nationale and of the archive at the Institut Curie. In connection with the Langevin affair, I was the first to be allowed to use the accounts written at the time by friends and kept in the library of the École de physique et chimie. Unless otherwise indicated, all translations from French into English are mine.

Abbreviations for frequently used sources:

BN: Bibliothèque Nationale, Paris.
CR: Comptes rendus, the publication of the Académie des sciences (also called during some of this period the *Comptes rendus hebdomadaires*).
CUL: Cambridge University Library.
DSB: Dictionary of Scientific Biography, ed. Charles Coulston Gillispie, New York: Charles Scribner and Sons, 1970.
EPC: École de physique et chimie.
IC: Institut Curie.
RAS (CHS): Royal Academy of Sciences, Center for History of Science, Stockholm, Sweden.
RUL: Royal University Library, Oslo, Norway.

CHAPTER ONE: A FAMILY WITH CONVICTIONS

17   Poland's fate: Davies, *God's Playground,* 2:19. From K. Kolbuszewski, ed., *Poezja barska* (Cracow, 1928), as translated by Davies.

"in a shining robe": Davies, *God's Playground,* 1:452. From Wespazjan Kochowski, *Annalium Poloniae Climacter Secundus* (Cracow, 1688).

Maria Salomea: Salomea was the name of a thirteenth-century Polish princess who founded a convent in Cracow and became Blessed Salomea. It was also the name of Maria's paternal grandmother.

"the patroness": letter from Władysław Skłodowski to Father Władysław Knapinski, the family priest and friend, regarding the baptism of a granddaughter, 19 February 1893. Archives of the Jagellonian University, Cracow.

18   "The name of Poland": Brandes, *Poland,* 47.

19   "Don't think": letter from Bronisława Skłodowska to Eleonora Kurchanowicz, 27 August 1860. Marie Skłodowska Curie Museum, Warsaw.

"the happiest time": unpublished memoir by Józef Skłodowski, Polish Scientific Academy, Warsaw.

"political events": Józef's memoir.

20   Bernardo Bellotto: This is the painter known to the Poles as Canaletto, though he is not the Canaletto renowned in Western Europe.

"The ceilings": Edwards, *The Polish Captivity,* 1:46.

"Even Copernicus": Davies, *God's Playground,* 2:111. Translation of a poem by Alexander Blok, "Voz'mediye" (Retribution).

"Even on making introductions": Brandes, *Poland,* 28.

21   Landed peasants: Adam Zamoyski, *The Polish Way,* 213.

"déclassé nobles": Simons, *Eastern Europe,* 9.

his grandson: Józef's memoir.

two strains of thought: Bromke, *Poland's Politics.*

22   "science, commerce": as quoted by Blejwas, *Warsaw Positivism,* 11–12.

"Separated, divided": poem in addenda of Helena Skłodowska Szalay's memoir, from the National Library, Warsaw. A shorter version of the memoir, entitled *Ze Wspomnien o Marii Skłodowskiej-Curie,* was published by Nasza Księgarnia in 1958. Versified by Paula Bonnell.

The "end of the age of error and treason" refers to the hope that Alexander II, who succeeded Tzar Nicholas in the year the poem was written, would bring about promised reforms.

23   "a powerful weapon": Blejwas, quoting from *Przegląd Tygodniowy* (Weekly Review) of 1870 in *Warsaw Positivism,* 135.

A privately circulated "Address": Edwards, *Polish Captivity,* appendix.

"One might ask": Józef Skłodowski memoir.

"For instance": Brandes, *Poland,* 35.

24   "He stopped": Józef's memoir.

"quite regular": ibid.

"My father": Marie Curie, *Pierre Curie* and autobiographical notes (New York: Macmillan, 1923), 161. Subsequent references to this work in these endnotes are by title only.

This book, which goes under the title *Pierre Curie,* contains an important addendum: an autobiography Marie Curie wrote in English in response to a request from her American admirer, Missy Meloney. Although the biography of Pierre was published first in France, Marie Curie refused to allow the autobiography to accompany it there, insisting that French colleagues would consider writing about oneself immodest. I have made extensive use of this autobiography in English throughout the book.

24   "Even when we were older": Józef's memoir.

25   Unlike his brother: Marie Curie, in her autobiographical notes in *Pierre Curie,* has her father attending the university in Petersburg, but I suspect this is wishful thinking. Józef's more detailed account, in Polish, seems more plausible.

     "Before he went": Józef's memoir.

     "You, Władysław Jósefowicz": ibid.

     "poor but ambitious": ibid.

26   "she had what was": *Pierre Curie,* 156.

     "It's hard": Bronisława Boguska to Eleonora Kurchanowicz, 22 August 1860.

     "Private schools": *Pierre Curie,* 156.

     a large barometer: Helena Skłodowska Szalay's memoir.

27   "My father": Józef's memoir.

     "for history lessons": Helena's memoir.

     "He had a rare gift": Józef's memoir.

     "the poet": Miłosz, *The History of Polish Literature,* 203.

     "great emotion": Helena's memoir.

     "strong taste for poetry": *Pierre Curie,* 160.

28   "We would arrange": Józef's memoir.

     "the soul of the house": *Pierre Curie,* 158.

     "religious without exaggeration": Józef's memoir.

     "a kind of ABC": Miłosz, 173. Julian Ursyn Niemcewicz (1757–1841).

     Poles "have cultivated": Brandes, *Poland,* 59.

29   "I think about it": Józef's memoir.

     parents "continued": *Pierre Curie,* 157. Marie Curie's *Autobiographical Notes* were written in her book-learned English. She has assumed that the word *villégiature* (summer holiday) has an equivalent in English.

     Józef remembers traveling: Józef's memoir. Chant is rhymed in Polish.

30   There, on the banks: In 1990, I visited Skłody and spoke with a descendant of the Skłodowski family (his great-great-grandfather and Maria's great-grandfather were brothers) who remembered and described the thatched manor house, now gone. Also Józef, in his memoir, described returning there for a visit.

     Boguski ancestors: Henryk Sadaj, "Polka, której drugą ojczyzną była francya," *Panorama Polska,* October 1982.

     "a heroic period": Agnieszka Morawińska in *Symbolism in Polish Painting,* 29.

     "beside a brook": as quoted in Morawińska, *Symbolism,* 29.

     "The periods of vacations": *Pierre Curie,* 161.

31   "On Saturdays": Józef's memoir.

     "That may be the reason": ibid.

32   The Polish Dr. Bujwid: Odo Feliks Kazimierz Bujwid (1857–1942). From *Encyklopedia Powszechna* (Warsaw: Państowowe Wydawnictwo Naukowe, 1973), 1:369.

     O you of Skalbmierz: versified by Paula Bonnell.

33   "This catastrophe": *Pierre Curie,* 157–58.

     "She would often sit": Helena's memoir.

     "a profound depression": *Pierre Curie,* 157.

     Władysław's account: as noted in Józef's memoir.

     two of the best doctors: Helena's memoir. Drs. Ignacy Baranowski and Tytus Chałubiński. Chałubiński was, according to Brandes, "long regarded as the leading physician of Poland."

     "an exceptional personality": *Pierre Curie,* 157.

34   "I am taking care": This letter and all those which follow from Bronisława

to Eleonora Kurchanowicz are from the archive of the Marie Skłodowska
Curie Museum in Warsaw. The nickname Małgosia mentioned by Zofia is
a diminutive of Margaret. It is not clear why her mother used it.

35   "grant me a recovery": This was a pilgrimage she never took, because it
was five miles and she feared exhausting herself.

37   Zosia and I broke our wafer: In Poland, a special large wafer, blessed by
the Church and picturing a Christmas scene, is shared by the family
around the table. The ritual includes breaking off each other's wafers,
greeting each other, and kissing.

38   "Up until that year": Józef's memoir.

39   typhus in general: Roderick E. and Margaret P. McGrew, eds. *Encyclopedia of Medical History* (New York: McGraw-Hill, 1985).

"I still can't think": Józef's memoir.

41   "Our sister's death": Helena's memoir.

Maria, too, wrote: *Pierre Curie,* 157.

Józef believed: Józef's memoir.

We are lonely: words on the stone, Powązki Cemetery, Warsaw.

"Cuckoos call": Władysław Skłodowski to Józef, 8 July 1877. Marie Skłodowska Curie Museum, Warsaw.

"he brought very discouraging news": letter from Ksawery to Eleonora
Kurchanowicz, 24 August 1876, as quoted by Maria Burdowicz-Nowicka
in "Nieznane materiały do dziejów rodziny Marii Skłodowskiej-Curie,"
Kwartalnik historii nauki i techniki, Rok XXI.

"We stood": Helena's memoir.

Bronisława Skłodowska: Powązki Cemetery, Warsaw.

42   An angel: poem among addenda to the unpublished version of Helena's
memoir.

CHAPTER TWO: A DOUBLE LIFE

43   dour Miss Tupalska: *The Republic,* no. 150, 1925 (a Polish journal).
Interview with Jadwiga Sikorska. Madame Sikorska suggests that Bronisława Skłodowska had already died when Maria attended her school, but
this is not the case. She died in the spring of that year. But I trust the
statement that "Each morning, Marya came to school with Miss Tupalska,
who still taught at my school, and at the end of the day's lessons she
returned home with her." The characterization of Miss Tupalska comes
from Eve Curie, *Madame Curie,* 17–19. Subsequent references to this
work in these endnotes are by title only.

"one of the finest parks": K. Baedeker, *West- und Mittel-Russland: Handbuch für Reisende* (Leipzig: Verlag von Karl Baedeker, 1883).

44   private school of Madame . . . Sikorska: at the corner of Marszałkowska
and Królewska Streets.

"I get so anxious": letter of Bronisława Skłodowska to Eleonora Kurchanowicz, 3 October, probably 1873. Marie Skłodowska Curie Museum, Warsaw.

"a hard life": *The School of Jadwiga Sikorska in Warsaw* (Szkola Jadwigi
Sikorskiej w Warszawie), published to celebrate the fiftieth anniversary of
Jadwiga Sikorska's work (Warsaw: 1927). Jadwiga Sikorska's diary is quoted
at length in the text.

45   "Something as small": speech of Pawel Sosnowski in *The School of Jadwiga Sikorska.*

45   "Only when I said calmly": Jadwiga Sikorska in *The School of Jadwiga Sikorska*.
"abnormal" situation: Marie Curie, *Pierre Curie*, 159.
"the youngest": ibid., 158.
"wanted always": Manuscript in English, BN, Paris.
"With my mind's eye": Helena's memoir.

46   "Since none of us": Józef's memoir.
"Seeing our parents' . . . faces": memoir of Helena Skłodowska Szalay.

47   "very violently": *Madame Curie*, 79. Letter of Maria to her cousin Henrietta, 25 November 1888.
The death of a parent: Martha Wolfenstein "How Is Mourning Possible?" in *The Psychoanalytic Study of the Child* 21 (New York: International Universities Press, Inc., 1966): 93–123; and Erna Furman, *A Child's Parent Dies* (New Haven: Yale, 1974).
headmistress's advice: *The Republic*.
There were a few good teachers: Józef's memoir.

48   even private conversations: in *Warsaw Positivism*, Blejwas dates the total ban on Polish from 1885, but Józef and Maria's memoirs suggest it was in place earlier.
"All that Russification": Józef's memoir.
Maria remembered: *Pierre Curie*, 159. Some of the difference in Maria and Józef's view may have to do with timing. Józef, two years older, completed most of his gymnasium education before the reign of the fanatical Aleksander Apuchtin as curator of the Warsaw School District. Apuchtin, who took over in the year after Maria entered gymnasium, used spies to inform on gymnasium students and generally intensified the pressure for Russification (Davies, *God's Playground*, 2:100).
"the touchstone of Nationality": ibid., 2:89–90.

49   "In strict contrast": ibid., 2:21.
nothing "riled so much": ibid., 2:99.
"In your letter": Władisław Skłodowski to his son Józef, July 8, 1877. Curie Museum, Warsaw.
"traditional [German] respect for learning": Józef's memoir.
"hostile to the Polish nation": *Pierre Curie*, 159.

50   "In spite of everything": *Madame Curie*, 36.
Maria's "chosen sister": *Madame Curie*, 78.
Kazia and Maria, for their part: *Madame Curie*. In an interview in 1988, Eve Curie Labouisse told me that she took this walk with Kazia in the 1930s as part of the research for her biography of her mother. The vivid details were provided by Kazia at that time.

51   In general, according to Helena: Helena's memoir.
"lemonade and chocolate ices": *Madame Curie*, 79. Letter from Maria to Kazia, 25 October 1888.

52   For the sisters Skłodowska: Józef's memoir.
"distinguished himself": Helena's memoir.
"the fatigue of growth": *Pierre Curie*, 163.

53   "The land": Morawińska, *Symbolism*, 24.
rutted roads: For a description of travel in the Polish countryside, see Hutchinson, *Try Cracow and the Carpathians*.
"Rich it is": Brandes, *Poland*, 111.
But she would also have passed: Images are drawn from Boyd, *Polish Countrysides*, and from Wunderlich, *Geographischer Bilderatlas von Polen*.
"oas[es] of civilization": Brandes, *Poland*, 111.

54   Their houses: Józef's memoir.
a woman with a dowry: Maria Milewska, actually a cousin of Władisław Skłodowski's.
"Ah how gay": *Madame Curie,* 40.
Kotarbiński: Józef Kotarbiński (1849–1928) was a prominent actor, director, and author. A number of photographs and paintings of Kotarbiński are included in the museum of the Grand Theater in Warsaw.
"He sang": *Madame Curie,* 40.

55   "Your home": Józef's memoir.
According to Józef: Józef's memoir.

56   "We could speak Polish": *Pierre Curie,* 161–62.
dance, "one of the Polish graces": Davies, 1:251.

57   "In Poland . . . the mazurka": Brandes, *Poland,* 37–38.
"I have been to a *kulig"*: *Madame Curie,* 43.
she told her sister Bronia: This letter to Bronia is in the French edition of *Madame Curie* (Paris: Gallimard, 1938, 39–40) but not the English. All the information on Polish customs, dances, and costume comes from Jacek Marek, who has a graduate degree in folkloric studies from the University of Poznan and is the founder of the Poznan Polytechnic Institute Folk Group.

58   "That summer": Helena's memoir.

59   "I ought to give you an account": *Madame Curie,* 43–44.
The "follies" involved: Helena's memoir.

60   "following your example": *Madame Curie,* 45.
Kind sir: Helena's memoir. Versified by Jan Schreiber.

CHAPTER THREE: SOME VERY HARD DAYS

62   noise, dirt, and sultry air: Helena's memoir. Like the school Władysław Skłodowski had headed earlier, this small apartment was on Nowolipki Street.
"The plants are healthy": *Madame Curie,* 51.
"I shall install myself": *Madame Curie,* 77. Letter from Maria to Henrietta, 10 December 1887.

63   iconoclastic *Life of Jesus:* Joseph Ernest Renan's *la Vie de Jésus* was published in France in 1863. Its portrayal of Jesus as a historic figure of merely human dimensions caused Pope Pius IX to call Renan the "European blasphemer." He was influenced by French positivism.
romantic poets: Mickiewicz and Słowacki.
"We have learned": Blejwas, quoting Aleksander Swiętochowski, in *Warsaw Positivism,* 248.
"When a bullet strikes": as quoted in W. F. Reddaway, J. H. Penson, O. Halecki, and R. Dyboski, eds., *The Cambridge History of Poland* (Cambridge, England: Cambridge University Press, 1941), 388.
Warsaw University: Actually called the Warsaw Central School because the Tzar, while allowing faculties of higher learning, would not permit them to be called a university.
"stubborn, clear-eyed . . . Swiętochowski": Brandes, *Poland,* 71.
"The ideals of the past": quoted in Blejwas, *Warsaw Positivism,* 135.
"Poets . . . what do you give": ibid., 139, quoting from *Przegląd Tygodniowy* (Weekly Reader).
"We believe . . . neither in revolution": As quoted in Bromke, *Poland's Politics,* 13.

64   statements should be "supported by evidence": Davies, quoting Julian Ochorowicz, a follower of Comte, in *God's Playground*, 2:51.

"I still believe": *Pierre Curie*, 168.

Comte, a believer in the "natural inferiority of women": as quoted by Londa Shiebinger in *The Mind Has No Sex?* (Cambridge, Mass.: Harvard University Press, 1989), 269.

"a woman possesses": quoted in Blejwas, *Warsaw Positivism*, 185.

Orzeszkowa deplored: Goscilo, *Russian and Polish Women's Fiction*, 30.

"You should be ashamed": quoted in ibid, 221–22.

65   "To an ideal positivist": *Madame Curie*, 55.

"the most educated of all" the women: Józef's memoir.

By the time Maria graduated: Sources of information on the Flying University were J. Mackiewicz-Wojciechowska, *Zagadnienia Pracy Kulturalnej* (Warsaw: 1933), as well as personal communications with Andrzej Piber, custodian of Manuscript Department, National Library, Warsaw, and Krystyn Kabzińska, former curator of the Marie Skłodowska Curie Museum in Warsaw.

66   Among the twenty-one Poles: Davies, 2:361–62.

"The men in Poland": Brandes, *Poland*, 53.

"A person . . . came to inquire about lessons": *Madame Curie*, 51.

"It was one of those rich houses": ibid., 60.

67   Being a governess: as quoted in M. Jeanne Peterson, "The Victorian Governess: Status Incongruence in Family and Society," in Vicinus, *Suffer and Be Still*, 11. From an essay by Elizabeth Eastlake in *Quarterly Review*, 84 (December 1848).

"In the end, my relations with Mme. B——": *Madame Curie*, 60.

"I shall not be free long": ibid., 62.

"That going away": *Pierre Curie*, 163. Draft at BN, in English, includes the last sentence.

68   "Loving the country": ibid., 164–65.

"Everybody says that I have changed": *Madame Curie*, 80. November 25, 1888.

69   "big, quiet and agreeable": ibid., 64. 3 February 1886.

"a whole collection of children": ibid.

"The Z. household": *Madame Curie*, 67. 5 April 1886.

"In this part of the country": ibid., 64. 3 February 1886.

"If you could only see": ibid., 67. 5 April 1886.

"I still don't know if my pupil": ibid., 76–77. 20 May 1887.

70   "His *nyanya*": ibid., 64, 3 February 1886.

"With all I have to do": ibid., 72. December 1886.

"The arrival of new guests": ibid., 66–67. 5 April 1886.

her continuing self-education: *Pierre Curie*, 166.

"At nine in the evening": *Madame Curie*, 72. December 1886. According to Helena, some of the math problems were sent by her father, to be solved and sent back to him. It was a practice she would repeat with her own daughter Irène, when they were apart many years later.

71   "A very nice old man": *Madame Curie*, 72. December 1886.

"I am very much afraid": ibid., 77. 20 May 1887.

"I was as much interested": *Pierre Curie*, 165–66.

"Bronka and I give lessons": *Madame Curie*, 68. 3 September 1886.

almost universal: According to Czesław Miłosz in *The History of Polish Literature*, ninety percent of Poles in this period were illiterate.

"For the girls and boys": *Madame Curie*, 67. 5 April 1886.

72   "You are probably unaware": ibid., 79. 25 November 1888.

72   "great joys and great consolations": ibid., 68. December 1886. The English translation has Maria living on the first floor, but I believe it was in fact the second (French *premier étage*).

"even this innocent work": *Pierre Curie*, 165.

"a young lady . . . privately teaching": Brandes, *Poland*, 18.

"I've been shaken": This letter appears in the French edition of *Madame Curie* but not in the English edition. *Madame Curie* (French edition), 67. 24 January 1888.

73   "an icy atmosphere": *Madame Curie*, 78. 18 March 1888.

"One week after my arrival": ibid., 64. 3 February 1886.

girls "all dance": ibid., 67. 5 April 1886.

74   "treated to the sight": ibid., 64. 3 February 1886.

"long sleigh rides": *Pierre Curie*, 164.

such pleasure: According to Helena's granddaughter, the sisters were opposed, at the time that Eve Curie wrote her book, to revealing that the romance occurred. That may account for the very discreet treatment of it in *Madame Curie*, including the selection of letters.

"I could have had a holiday": *Madame Curie*, 68. 3 September 1886.

"Some people pretend": ibid., 72–73. December 1886.

"Above all?": *Madame Curie*, French edition, 65. 1886.

75   "I think that if you borrowed": *Madame Curie*, 75. 9 March 1887.

"What suffering": ibid., 76. 4 April 1887.

"I can imagine": ibid., 77.

76   "Don't believe": ibid., 77. 10 December 1887.

last stamp she owns: ibid., 78. 18 March 1888.

"I am learning chemistry": ibid., 79. October 1888.

"nothing you could ever confide": ibid., 78–79. October 25, 1888.

77   keeps "the lamp . . . burning": "Miss Antonina" by Eliza Orzeszkowa, in Goscilo, *Russian and Polish Women's Fiction*, 206–230.

"then I give myself a shaking": *Madame Curie*, 80. 25 November 1888.

78   she can "think only of Easter": ibid., 82. 13 March 1889.

"The idea of socialism": Blejwas quoting Dłuski, 278–279.

"My journey": *Madame Curie*, 82. 14 July 1889.

"Mme. F., her husband, her mother": ibid., 83.

79   "If everything": ibid., 83–84. March 1890.

"Dear Bronia": ibid., 12 March 1890.

81   "tiring and unpleasant" job: Józef's memoir.

"Together we passed": *Pierre Curie*, 166–67.

"Chronicles": The novelist Prus's "Weekly Chronicles" were published in various Warsaw periodicals for forty years.

82   "to my great joy": *Pierre Curie*, 167.

Władysław's letter: *Madame Curie*, 87–88. September 1891.

83   One other document: Part of an unpublished reminiscence, written in verse, at the Archives of the Jagellonian University, Cracow.

84   ". . . Now Bronia": *Madame Curie*, 88–89. 23 September 1891.

CHAPTER FOUR: *A PRECIOUS SENSE OF LIBERTY*

85   one of three women: Charrier, *l'Évolution intellectuelle féminine*.

course catalogue: *annuaire, Université de Paris*, 1891–1892. Widener Library.

Warm wool dresses: This and the detail about the mattress brought from home are taken from *Madame Curie*.

86   Passengers in the better-class cars: William Sloane Kennedy, *Wonders and Curiosities of the Railway* (Chicago: S. C. Griggs and Co., 1884), 106.
the border police: K. Baedeker, *West- und Mittel-Russland: Handbuch für Reisende*, 1883.
The train carrying . . . Maria: *Bradshaw's Continental Railway, Steam and Transit Guide*, September 1890.
For the first few hours: Baedeker, 1883.

87   Rue d'Allemagne: now avenue Jean Jaurès.
"in the atmosphere": Sylvestre et al., *Paris au temps jadis*, 145, 147, 151.
Between visits from patients: The names of visitors are from *Madame Curie*.
stiff and haughty: Józef's memoir.

88   "Mademoiselle Marie": *Madame Curie*, 98.
"my little brother-in-law": ibid., 106. 17 March 1892.

89   A Russian who visited: N. Tchédrine, *Berlin et Paris: Voyage satirique à travers l'Europe* (Paris: Louis Westhausser, 1887).
"came to France": from a four-page handwritten discussion of French education which seems to have been a response to the old question, "How do we compare with the Germans?" Marie Curie refused to compare, preferring to describe her own educational experience. "I don't wish to discuss the relative value of French and German teaching . . . I don't believe discussions which require calm and leisurely reflection can be profitably undertaken just now." Perhaps written not long after World War I. BN.

90   "You have no doubt learned": *Madame Curie*, 106. 17 March 1892.
"gave me a very precious": *Pierre Curie*, 171.
An American woman: A. Herbage Edwards, *Paris through an Attic* (London: J. M. Dent & Sons Ltd., 1918). Although written twenty-seven years after Marie arrived in Paris, this book refers back to a time when the last Sorbonne construction was just completed, i.e., around 1890.
Many foreign students: Rofsmann, Ph., *Ein Studienaufenthalt in Paris; ein Führer für Studierende, Lehrer und Lehrerinnen*. (Marburg: 1900).
"Today I begin": *Marie Curie*, 115. 15 September 1893.

91   "The room I lived in": *Pierre Curie*, 170.
"Higher, higher": This version of the poem is from the unpublished addenda to Helena's memoir. Versified by Jan Schreiber.

92   She writes of "conversations": *Pierre Curie*, 171.
"French *male* students": This passage was written in English; otherwise the gender of the students would have been apparent.
"The worst fate": Jules Michelet in *la Femme*, 1860, as quoted in Moses, *French Feminism in the Nineteenth Century*, 35. See also Shapiro, ed., *Pleasures of Paris*, 32. "Women of the bourgeoisie and of the upper class were severely restricted as to where they could go. Unmarried young ladies never went out alone. In some cases even after they were married they did so rarely or not at all."

93   "The decline": Margadant, *Madame le professeur*, 15–16.
"Women without men friends": Abbot, *A Woman's Paris*.
"Woman is not a brain": as quoted in Gold and Fizdale, *Misia*, 80.
"the more advanced": as quoted in Margadant, *Madame le professeur*, from *la psychologie des femmes, cours professés pendant plusieurs années à la Sorbonne* (Paris: A. Colin, 1900).

94   Unlike the man: as quoted in Dijkstra, *Idols of Perversity*, 12.
a wife's adultery: Eugen Weber, *France: Fin de Siècle*, 92.
It would take fifty-seven years: Stetson, *Women's Rights in France*. Stetson puts the date of boys' and girls' curricula being made the same as 1924.

94   A *nouvelle doctoresse: l'Illustration,* 20 June 1896.
Frenchwomen surpassed . . . foreign: Charrier, *l' Évolution intel-lectuelle féminine,* 188.
95   "different from Parisians": Kauffman, *Paris of Today,* 40–41.
"What distinguishes": Sylvestre et al., *Paris au temps jadis,* 291.
"the kind who distracted": ibid., 290, as cited in Bourrelier, *La Vie du quartier-latin,* 162. Bourrelier was looking back on a much earlier period.
"girls in the Boul' Mich' ": Edwards, *Paris through an Attic,* 166 and 160.
96   The number of genuine *étudiantes:* Charrier, *l'Évolution intellectuelle féminine.*
the "presence of women": Bourrelier, *La Vie du quartier-latin,* 187–88.
It was not uncommon: Alexis Martin, *Paris: Promenades dans les vingt arrondissements* (Paris: A. Hennuyer, 1890).
police crackdown: The precipitating event was the accidental death of a student in prior demonstrations.
"Does it not seem strange": Henry, *Paris Days and Evenings,* 295.
97   "The cafés": Edwards, *Paris through an Attic,* 161, 163, 166.
"pleasant memories": *Pierre Curie,* 171–72.
98   "The survival of France": Paul, *The Sorcerer's Apprentice,* 4.
"above all an homage to science": André Tuilier in Rivé, ed., *La Sorbonne et sa reconstruction,* 37.
99   "one of the best housed": Terry Shinn, "The French Science Faculty System, 1808–1914: Institutional Change and Research Potential in Mathematics and the Physical Sciences," in J. L. Heilbron, ed., *Historical Studies in the Physical Sciences* (Berkeley: University of California Press, 1981), 305.
"In the life of the laboratories": Marie Curie on education, in handwritten document written around the time of World War I.
100   man of "wit and verve": Émile Roux, in a 1904 *Bulletin de l'Institut Pasteur,* as quoted in the *Dictionary of Scientific Biography* entry on Duclaux.
"a series of brilliant solutions": *Dictionary of Scientific Biography* entry on Appell.
"It is difficult": *Madame Curie,* 116. 18 March 1894.
101   "The lilacs": ibid., 113. 16 April 1893.
"Mademoiselle": letter from M. Lamotte to Maria Skłodowska, 26 June 1894. BN.
102   "Your last letter": *Madame Curie,* 103. 31 January 1894.
"keep the lodging": ibid., 111. 5 March 1893.
"Is your wife": ibid., 106. 17 March 1892.
103   "I hardly need say": ibid., 115. 15 September 1893.
"I am studying": ibid., 115. 15 September 1893.

CHAPTER FIVE: *A Beautiful Thing*

104   He seemed to me: *Pierre Curie,* 74.
"the cruel trials": *Madame Curie,* 88. 23 September 1891.
"I lack the courage": Pierre Curie to Maria Skłodowska, Marseille, 7 September 1894. BN.
105   "we quickly forget": Langevin, *Revue du mois,* Tome II, July–December 1906, 14.
École municipale: Later, "municipale" was removed from the name.

106   "I write to beg you": Pierre Curie to "Monsieur le directeur," n.d. BN.
"I have often wondered": letter from Pierre Curie to Marie Curie, 7 September 1894. BN.
"cherished child": Pierre Curie to Georges Gouy, 17 March 1892. BN.

107   "We can do in this life": André Brandt, *Le docteur Curie et le Saint-Simonism à Mulhouse* (Mulhouse: Bader & Co., 1938).
Ultimately he left: He may have left because the Saint-Simonians were publicly tried and found guilty of various crimes, including outrages against public morals, in Paris in 1832.

108   It was maintained in the family: An 1890 performance report in the Archives nationales describes Eugène Curie as "un médecin fort ordinaire, qui n'inspire aux familles qu'une médiocre confiance; il a le diagnostique hésitant et ne parait pas avoir une expérience bien sérieuse. Il est surtout homeopathe. Comme second médecin, il est suffisant, mais dans les cas graves, je me croirai obligé d'avoir recours à un practicien plus habile et plus clairvoyant." These remarks could reflect prejudice against homeopathy, as well as Curie's politics. But there may also have been nonpolitical reasons for his lackluster career.
According to Jacques: Jacques Curie's biographical notes, sent to Marie in 1920 for her biography, *Pierre Curie*. BN.
"Oh, what a good time": *Pierre Curie*, 42. Excerpt from an 1879 diary.

109   "irregular and incomplete": Jacques Curie's biographical notes.
"slow mind": *Pierre Curie*, 34.
"his dreamer's spirit": *Pierre Curie*, 33–34.
Pierre's "quite irregular" education: Langevin, *Revue du mois.*
"I don't dislike": *Pierre Curie*, 44.

110   Until he was fourteen: Jacques Curie's biographical notes.
"An object possesses": *Pierre Curie*, 58.

112   "Thanks to you": Curie to Gouy, 29 March 1882. BN.
"From the scientific point of view": Jacques Curie's biographical notes.
nonexperimental work: Pierre Curie wrote several papers in which he proposed general laws of symmetry.
"the time when": *Revue du mois.*

113   "In all scientific work": as quoted by Langevin, *Revue du mois.*
"Women of genius": *Pierre Curie*, 77.
"To drink, to sleep": fragments of a journal written by Pierre Curie in 1881. BN.

114   "exquisite": *Pierre Curie*, 31.
115   "We began": ibid., 74.
"I have just read": Pierre Curie to Marie Skłodowska, 10 August 1894.
"a blasphemy": F. W. J. Hemmings, *Émile Zola*, Oxford: The Clarendon Press, 1953. This is Hemmings paraphrasing Zola.
"I hope, my dear friend": Pierre Curie to Georges Gouy, 7 November 1905.
"If your life": literal translation of poem written to Kazia Przyborowska, who was engaged to a German, about 1887. Among the addenda to Helena's unpublished memoir.

116   totting up her scores: Scrap of paper in Pierre's hand. BN.
"Pierre Curie came": *Pierre Curie*, 75.
"vivacity and energy": *Pierre Curie*, 48. Marie Curie's description of Jacques.
Later, he would tell her: Marie Curie in the journal she kept after his death.
"Godspeed then": poem written by Maria to Kazia. Versified by Jan Schreiber.

117   "Nothing could give me more pleasure": letter from Pierre Curie to Marie Skłodowska, 10 August 1894. BN.
"It is possible": Nobel speech given 6 June 1905, in connection with the 1903 Nobel Prize.

118   "You see how": Pierre to Marie, 10 August 1894. BN.
"I couldn't decide": Pierre to Marie, 14 August 1894. BN.

120   "Why write that way?": Pierre to Marie, 17 September 1894. BN.
"As you can imagine": Pierre to Marie from Marseille, 7 September 1894. BN.

121   "So you are": Pierre to Marie, 17 September 1894. BN.
"I'm not coming": Pierre to Marie, n.d. BN.

122   "with beautiful blue eyes": *Pierre Curie*, 31.
"true discoveries": Paul, *Knowledge to Power*, 54.

123   "I was greatly impressed": *Pierre Curie*, 67.
From Józef: *Madame Curie*, 135–36. 14 July 1895.

124   "When you receive": *Madame Curie*, 136. July 1895.
"I came too late": Alfred de Musset, after George Sand rejected him. Letter from M. Lamotte to Marie Skłodowska, 10 July 1895. BN.
a "joyous atmosphere": Helena's memoir.

CHAPTER SIX: EVERYTHING HOPED FOR

125   "Our life": *Madame Curie*, 146. 18 March 1896.

126   took a look: expense entry in the 1896 *cahier de dépenses.*
They were subscribers: Rudorff, *Belle Époque*, 174.
"amazed" by their modest clothes: Borel, *A travers deux siècles*, 105.
"At Sceaux": *Madame Curie*, 146. 18 March 1896. Marie to Józef.
"The idea of rupture": Alfred Dupont Chandler, *A Bicycle Tour in England and Wales* (Boston: A. Williams & Co., 1881), 109–10.
Bécane: Shapiro, *Pleasures of Paris*, 98.
a two-volume scientific treatise: C. Bourlet, *Nouveau Traité des bicycles et bicyclettes* (Paris: Gauthier-Villars, 1898).
"a revolution": L. Baudry de Saunier, *Histoire générale de la vélocipédie* (Paris: Paul Ollendorff, 1891), xi.
"To the many": Ward, *Bicycling for Ladies*, 13.
"which will liberate us": Montorgueil, *Les Parisiennes*, 15.
"It is the bicycle": ibid., 14–15.

127   "in constant fear": Luther H. Porter, *Cycling for Health and Pleasure* (Boston: Wheelman Co., 1890), 52.
"a hat that will stay": Ward, *Bicycling for Ladies*, 99, 93, 94.
"We loved": *Pierre Curie*, 84.

128   a tiny village: Auroux.
"some with their heads": Louis Nadeau, *Voyage en Auvergne* (Paris: E. Dentu, Libraire-éditeur, 1862).
"Lingering until twilight": *Pierre Curie*, 83.
"the banks of the Loing": ibid., 84.
"We only take": *Madame Curie*, 146. 23 November 1895.
"Everything goes well": ibid., 145–46. 23 November 1895.

129   about three times: based on information in Weber, *France: Fin de Siècle*, 195.
"our means": *Pierre Curie*, 80.
"I took eight pounds": *Madame Curie*, 163.

129   Brillouin: Among pupils he influenced, along with Marie, were Charles Coulomb, Jean Perrin, and Paul Langevin.

"work I can do": *Madame Curie,* 146. 23 November 1895.

"To satisfy his need": Langevin, *Revue du mois.*

130   "the most complete": *Pierre Curie,* 82.

some interesting results: ibid., 81. These results were never published.

did not "interrupt our work": *Madame Curie,* 146. 23 November 1895.

"an exchange of energy": Poincaré tribute at the Académie des sciences, 23 April 1906.

"I am going to have a child": *Madame Curie,* 147. 2 March 1897.

"We are very depressed": ibid., 148. 31 March 1897.

"the moorland": Augustus J. C. Hare, *North-western France* (London: George Allen, 1895), 251. This describes the coast at Trégastel, some distance further west, but it applies to Port-Blanc as well.

131   "terrible" day: Pierre to Marie, 27 July 1897. BN.

"explaining to him": 17 July 1897. BN.

"I think of my dearest": Pierre Curie to Marie Curie, n.d. BN.

"I need your caresses": Pierre Curie to Marie Curie, 27 July 1897.

132   "a touching desire": *Pierre Curie,* 88.

"My little darling": Pierre to Marie, 17 July 1897. BN.

"My dear husband!": Marie to Pierre, 28 July 1897. BN.

"Maman is so sad": Pierre to Marie, 29 July 1897. BN.

"the good little student": from *cahier de Pierre,* the notebook Marie began after Pierre's death. ("petite étudiante bien sage.")

"Have you found": Pierre to Marie, 29 July 1897. BN.

"training on the coasts": Pierre to Marie, 19 July 1897. BN.

133   "I've sent you": Pierre to Marie, 29 July 1897. "Mme. P. and D." are used because I can't read the spelling of the names in Pierre's letters.

"I am still nursing": *Madame Curie,* 150. 10 November 1897.

"we have taken": entry in the *cahier des enfants* that Marie began at the time of Irène's birth. BN.

134   "The bear cub": *cahier de Pierre.*

"rays of a peculiar character": *Pierre Curie,* 94.

"replac[ed] Parliament": Weber, *France: Fin de Siècle,* 240.

135   While aristocratic Paris: Gold and Fizdale, *Misia.*

To certain social critics: Heilbron, "Fin-de-siècle Physics."

136   "Doom loomed": Weber, *France: Fin de Siècle,* 3.

Prejudice: ibid., 135.

137   The historian Fierens-Gevaert: Rudorff, *Belle Époque,* 174.

"The cult of reason": Henry E. Guerlac, "Science and French National Strength," as quoted in Paul, "The Debate over the Bankruptcy of Science," 300.

claimed that science should rule the world: Zola in a speech at Berthelot banquet, 1895, as paraphrased in Heilbron, "Fin-de-Siècle Physics."

"god of the day": Heilbron, "Fin-de-Siècle Physics."

138   "Bring up a woman": quoted in Heilbron, "Fin-de-Siècle Physics."

Henri Brisson: Nye, "Gustav Le Bon's Black Light," 166.

"the world is now": Harry Paul, "The Bankruptcy of Science in 1895," 310.

In general: Heilbron, "Fin-de-Siècle Physics."

"I did not think": as quoted in Pais, *Inward Bound,* 35.

139   Roentgen's work was contingent: I am indebted to Pais's *Inward Bound* for this approach to the subject.

"regardless of whether": Wilhelm Conrad Roentgen, *Eine Neue Art von Strahlen,* Würzburg, 1895.

139   couldn't be refracted: Later, Laue's experiments with crystals showed they could be refracted, but their wavelength was too short to be refracted by the usual prisms.
        Within weeks: *l'Illustration*, 1 February 1896. The photographs were made by Jean Perrin.
140   An X-ray float: photographs in Jacques Borgé et Nicolas Viasnoff, *Archives de Paris* (Paris: Éditions Balland, 1981).
141   "I thought immediately": as quoted in Pais, *Inward Bound*, 43.
        "a man of assured position": Romer, *Radioactivity*, 7.
        "One wraps a photographic plate": Henri Becquerel, "Radiations émises par phosphorescence," *CR* 122 (1896), 420. As quoted in Pais, *Inward Bound*.
142   "The sun persistently": W. Crookes, *Proceedings of the Royal Society* A 83, xx, 1910.
        "I shall particularly insist": Henri Becquerel, "Radiations invisibles émises par les corps phosphorescents," *CR* 122 (1896) 501–3.
        "All that he could say": Romer, *Discovery*, 21.
        "discovered radioactivity": Pais, *Inward Bound*, 42.
143   "a prisoner of the hypothesis": Jean Perrin, "Madame Curie et la découverte du Radium," in *Vient de paraître*, bulletin bibliographique mensuel, February, 1924.
        "something of a 'dead horse' ": Badash, "Radioactivity before the Curies," 134.
        Uranium was almost impossible: ibid.
        "The subject": *Pierre Curie*, 94.
        he suspected Becquerel: Pierre to Georges Gouy, 9 June 1902. BN.
144   "the beautiful experimental discovery": Kelvin to Pierre Curie. BN.
        "the best and most serious": Badash, "Radioactivity before the Curies," 131.
        Lord Kelvin, J. Carruthers Beattie, M. Smoluchowski de Smolan, "Experiments on the electrical phenomena produced in gases by Röntgen Rays, by Ultra Violet Light, and by Uranium," Proceedings of the Royal Society of Edinburgh, 21 December 1896, Vol. 21, p. 393.
        Lord Kelvin, J. Carruthers Beattie, M. Smoluchowski de Smolan, "On electric equilibrium between Uranium and an insulated metal in its neighbourhood," Proceedings of the Royal Society of Edinburgh, 1 March 1897, Vol. 22, p. 131.
        Kelvin's direction: See Badash, "Radioactivity before the Curies."

CHAPTER SEVEN: DISCOVERY

145   forty-three degrees: 6.25 C. The account which follows of the discovery of polonium, radium, and radioactivity is based on three laboratory notebooks, begun in December of 1897 and continued over the next three years. In addition, I have made extensive use of an annotated chronology written by Irène Joliot-Curie about the three notebooks, which is appended to the 1955 French edition of Marie Curie's biography of Pierre Curie. It is entitled "Les carnets de laboratoire de la découverte du polonium et du radium." I am grateful to Hélène Langevin, Irène's daughter, for recommending this important commentary to me.
        "a new method": Jean Wyart in the DSB entry for Pierre Curie.
146   the upper plate would become charged: An explanation in current terms: Radioactive substances emit alpha, beta, and gamma rays, all of which are

capable of ionizing air. This ionization diminishes the resistance of the air between the two plates, and redistributes the voltage between the two as a result.

146   "future truths": as quoted in Heilbron, "Fin-de-Siècle Physics."

no more charge can be transmitted: MC's thesis explains: "A preferable method of measurement is that of compensating the charge on plate A, so as to cause no deflection of the electrometer. The charges in question . . . may be compensated by means of a [piezo]electric quartz balance, one sheath of which is connected to plate A and the other to earth. The quartz lamina is subjected to a known tension, produced by placing weights on a plate; the tension is produced progressively, and has the effect of generating progressively a known quantity of electricity during the time observed. The operation can be so regulated that, at each instant, there is compensation between the quantity of electricity that traverses the condenser and that of the opposite kind furnished by the quartz." Thesis presented in 1903, reprinted in English in *Chemical News* (London: D. van Nostrand Co., 1904).

147   Jean Perrin: According to Langevin, Pierre did not know Perrin at the time, though they were to become friends. *Revue du mois,* July–December 1906.

148   "My dear friend": letter from Charles Friedel to Pierre Curie, 3 March 1898. BN.

against a *normalien:* Perrin was a graduate of the École normale supérieure, the most prestigious of educational institutions. Pierre of course was not.

"abandoned his work": *Pierre Curie,* 97.

149   "is very remarkable": Note de Mme. Skłodowska Curie, *CR* 126 (1898), 1101–03.

"novelty into physics": Pais, *Inward Bound,* 55.

"All uranium compounds": Note, *CR* 126. The next paper, in December, would refer back to the first and make the implication explicit: "One of us has shown that radioactivity seems to be an atomic property."

Other researchers: Badash, "Radioactivity before the Curies."

150   "I had a passionate desire": *Pierre Curie,* 97.

Pierre . . . claimed: ibid., 90.

Bémont: according to Paul Langevin, in "Discours prononcé le 30 Octobre, 1932" at the time of Bémont's death.

151   "We have not": Note de M. P. Curie et de Mme. S. Curie, "Sur une substance nouvelle radio-active, contenue dans la pechblende," *CR* 127 (1898): 175–78.

152   A notebook: *cahier des enfants,* BN.

as energetically as ever: This is based on the *cahiers de dépenses,* which has an entry for a new bicycle costume for Pierre, for maps and a Baedeker, and also for excursions to numerous places around Auvergne.

153   periodic table: The periodic table is now arranged on the basis of atomic number rather than weight, and looks somewhat different as a result.

"The result": "Prix Gegner" *CR* 127 (1898): 1133.

"I congratulate you": Marcelin Berthelot to Pierre Curie, date illegible, 1898. BN.

The paper read to the Academy: Note de M. P. Curie, de Mme P. Curie, et de M. G. Bémont, "Sur une nouvelle substance fortement radio-active, contenue dans la pechblende," *CR* 127 (1898): 1215–17.

"Demarçay's note": "Sur le spectre d'une substance radio-active," *CR* 127 (1898): 1218.

154   "There could be no doubt": *Pierre Curie,* 99.

154   Pierre Curie once confided: Borel, *A travers deux siècles*, 105.
"One can discern": Irène Curie, "Marie Curie, ma mère," 92.
"extremely handicapped": *Pierre Curie*, 99.
155   dissection room: Jozef Hurwic, *la Radioactivité: Découverte et premiers travaux* (Paris: Cahiers d'histoire et de philosophie des sciences, 1991), 66.
nearly worthless: i.e. pitchblende from which the uranium had already been extracted.
"How glad I was": *Pierre Curie*, 185.
"I had to work with:" *Pierre Curie*, 101.
156   "You can't imagine": *Madame Curie*, 162–63, 2 December 1898.
Bolesław Prus: "Weekly Chronicles," 18 June 1898.
"I miss my family": *Madame Curie*, 172. 1899.
"We have to be very careful": ibid., 180. 19 March 1899.
157   "We had an especial joy": *Pierre Curie*, 103.
Sometimes, after dinner: ibid., 104.
"We have abandoned": as quoted in *Pierre Curie*, 102.
One sample, she explained: letter in Polish to "Dear Sir," to be used for a conference, 18 July 1900. Archives of the Jagellonian University, Cracow.
"I am following": Georges Gouy to Pierre Curie, n.d. BN.
158   "was soon an intimate friend": *Pierre Curie*, 105.
"through beams": Shapiro, *Pleasures of Paris*, 15.
sitting "by the hour": Henry Adams, *The Education of Henry Adams* (Boston: Houghton Mifflin, 1918), 379.
"an opportunity": *Pierre Curie*, 103–4.
In their longest paper to date: "Les nouvelles substances radioactives et les rayons qu'elles émettent," rapport présenté au Congrès international de physique (Paris: Gauthier-Villars, 1900).

CHAPTER EIGHT: *A Theory of Matter*

160   "The Professor": as quoted in Pais, *Inward Bound* 39.
negatively charged particles: building on the work of Jean Perrin, who had found the cathode rays to be negatively charged.
"Thus on this view": J. J. Thomson, *The Philosophical Magazine*, 5 October 1897, 312.
161   "Who has ever seen": as quoted in Nye, "Molecular Reality, 7.
"The bodies": as quoted in Caullery, *French Science*, 186.
Those who accused: Nye, "Gustav Le Bon's Black Light," 164, 165, 168.
"The most diverse opinions": J. J. Thomson, *Philosophical Magazine* 44 (October 1897).
162   "the immutability": Bernadette Bensaude-Vincent, "L'éther, élement chimique: un essai malheureux de Mendéléev?" *Bulletin du Centre de recherche en histoire des sciences et des techniques,* 183.
"One of us has shown": CR, 26 December 188. Georges Gouy, writing to Pierre probably in 1899, tells him that he is "satisfied to see the facts marching in the direction of the materialist or ionic direction to which I've always been partisan." One can probably presume that he and Pierre thought alike on this, as on most scientific issues.
"the first time": Pais, *Inward Bound* 55.
"The emission of the uranic rays": Marie Skłodowska Curie, *Revue scientifique,* 3:14 (21 juillet 1900).
163   a suggestion . . . Georges Gouy had made: This was in connection with

the mysterious Brownian movement. The brilliant Gouy looked into it before Perrin and Einstein. See Pais, 108, and also Nye, *Molecular Reality*, 21.

163   "The truth is": PC to Edouard Guillaume, 30 December, 1898.

"all of space": Marie Skłodowska Curie, *CR* 126 (1898).

"From this research" J. Elster and H. Geitel, "Versuche an Becquerelstrahlen," *Annalen der Physik und Chimie*, No. 12 Band 66, 11 November, 1898. "Nach diesen Versuchen erscheint uns die Hypothese Erregung der Becquerelstrahlen durch andere im Raume existierende Strahlen im höchsten Grande unwahrscheinlich."

"Elster and Geitel": Pierre Curie to Charles Edouard Guillaume, 30 December 1898. BN.

164   "I am now busy": as quoted in Eve, *Rutherford*, 80.

"could never accustom": *Pierre Curie*, 136

165   "Electrification essentially": Pais, *Inward Bound*, 86.

Curie's radioactivity: The other rays Rutherford had detected and named "alpha" were not deciphered nearly so quickly. Indeed, it would take another ten years to understand that they were the helium nuclei, and still longer to puzzle out their place and role in the nucleus.

166   "had these experiments": Irène in her comments on her parents' laboratory notebooks.

"in response to events": Romer, *Radiochemistry*, 13.

"the radiation": Rutherford, "A radio-active substance emitted from thorium compounds," *The London, Edinburgh, and Dublin Philosophical Magazine and Journal of Science*, 5 (1900), 49:1–14.

Pierre and Marie Curie's paper: "Sur la radio-activité provoquée par les rayons Becquerel," *CR* 129.

"a persistent activity": "à la suite de la communication de M. et Mme Curie," *CR* 129.

167   Rutherford's second report: "Radioactivity produced in substances by the action of thorium compounds," *The London, Edinburgh, and Dublin Philosophical Magazine and Journal of Science* 5 (1900), 49:161–92.

"the enormous quantity": William Crookes, "Sur la source de l'énergie dans les corps radio-actifs," *CR*, 16 January 1899.

"went through every mineral": Sir William Crookes, "Radio-activity of Uranium," Proceedings of the Royal Society of London, 1899–1900, 66, 409–22.

168   "recent studies:" Henri Becquerel, *Nature* 63, 21 February 1901.

In a paper: André Debierne and Pierre Curie, "Sur la radio-activité induite et les gaz activés par le radium," *CR*, 25 March 1901. Two more papers during the year by Debierne and Pierre Curie, on 29 July 1901 and on 2 December 1901, also discuss induced radioactivity. The first makes the distinction again between the substance and a gas. The second examines induced radioactivity in enclosed spaces.

"M. and Mme. Curies": Ernest Rutherford, "Emanations from radioactive substances," *Nature*, 13 June 1901. This work was done with Miss H. T. Brooks, M.A., at McGill, to whom he gives credit here and in a subsequent paper in *Chemical News* on 25 April 1902.

Either "each radioactive atom": *CR*, 13 January 1902.

169   transformation: Rutherford, according to one anecdote, told Soddy not to call it "transmutation" because "they'll have our heads as alchemists."

"is at once": *Journal of the Chemical Society, Transactions* 81 (1902): 837–60.

"material nature of the emanation: *CR*, 26 January 1903.

169   a rejoinder: *Philosophical Magazine*, 1 April 1903.
170   "the so-called corpuscles": Georges Gouy to Pierre Curie, 27 July 1903. BN.

a "partisan": Gouy, n.d., probably 1899. BN.

"resolving the chemical elements": William Crookes in an address to the Congress of Applied Chemistry in Berlin, 5 June 1903, as reproduced in *Science*, Friday, 26 June 1903.

"all the most prominent workers:" *Philosophical Magazine* 4 (1902).

171   "substances in which". *Revue scientifique*, 70.

"decidedly limited knowledge": *Nuclear Almanac*, 470.

"Even more surprising": Badash, *Rutherford and Boltwood*, 4.

"Sometimes": *Pierre Curie*, 186.

172   "It had taken me": ibid., 188.

"according to its atomic weight": Marie Curie, "Sur le poid atomique du radium," *CR*, 21 July 1902.

"It is not an exaggeration": Jean Perrin in *Vient de paraitre*.

173   "Marckwald's polonium": A discussion of the Marckwald-Curie debate, along with the papers exchanged, is in Romer, *Radiochemistry*, 35–38 and 80–105.

174   "He deplores": Henri Becquerel to Pierre Curie, 27 October 1899. BN.

"You will be pleased to know": Pierre Curie to Georges Gouy, 20 March 1902. BN.

175   "would do well": Becquerel, to Pierre Curie, 27 October 1889.

"His sincerity": Paul Langevin's tribute in *Pierre Curie*, 148.

of "politics, of schools": excerpt from a proposal for the association, written by Pierre Curie. BN.

"The University of Geneva": Pierre Curie to Charles Guillaume, 31 July 1900.

176   Curie family sofas: *Madame Curie*, 231.

"deliberate ordinariness": Eugénie Cotton, *les Curie*, 54.

4,020 F: *cahier de dépenses*.

first woman: Eugénie Cotton, *les Curie*, 43.

"face the many anxieties": *Pierre Curie*, 114.

177   "few illusions": ibid., 107.

"repeatedly dismissed": Marcel Proust, *Remembrance of Things Past: The Guermantes Way* (New York: Vintage Books 1981 [1934]), 232.

about 150,000 francs a year: Crawford, *The Beginnings of the Nobel Institution*, 16.

"My dear friend": Pierre Curie to Georges Gouy, 9 June 1902. BN.

178   "After all": Georges Gouy to Pierre Curie, June 1902. BN.

Proust: *The Guermantes Way*, 231.

"allow me to put you *au courant*": Paul Appell to Marie Curie, 1903. BN.

179   "I'm studying": letter of Pierre Curie to Appell, 27 June 1903. BN.

"As you have seen": Pierre Curie to Georges Gouy, 13 November 1902. BN.

"The physical fatigue": *Pierre Curie*, 114.

ten pounds: 4.6 kilograms.

"struck in seeing Madame Curie": Georges Sagnac to Pierre Curie, 23 April 1903.

180   "The ends of fingers": *Pierre Curie*, 118.

one of their colleagues: J. Danysz, "De l'action pathogène des rayons et des émanations émis par le radium sur différents tissus et différents organismes." *CR*, 16 February 1903.

181   "very good health": *cahier des enfants*. BN.
182   "Maria was so happy": Helena's memoir.

182   struck by a truck: Józef's memoir.
        "And now you are in possession": *Madame Curie*, 190.
        "My father": *Pierre Curie*, 169.
183   "profoundly": Eugénie Cotton, "J'ai connu Pierre Curie," *Revue Horizons*, April 1956.
        "Our researches": "Recherches sur les substances radioactives," thèse presentée à la faculté des sciences de Paris pour obtenir le grade de docteur ès sciences physiques. (Paris: Gauthier-Villars, 1903).
        "congratulations on the defense": Georges Gouy to Pierre Curie, 27 July 1903.
        "brought out a tube": "The Sole Meeting of Pierre Curie and Ernest Rutherford," *The Lancet*, 21 November 1907.
184   she had a miscarriage: Pierre to Georges Gouy, January 1904. BN.
        "I am in such consternation": *Madame Curie*, 190–91.
        "I am quite overwhelmed": ibid., 191.
        "But Pierre Curie asked me": Eugénie Cotton in *Revue Horizons*.
185   "almost cured": Marie Curie to Robert Underwood Johnson, 20 September, 1903. BN.
        "on the other hand": *Madame Curie*, 210, 11 December 1903.
        "a most enthusiastic reception": *Pierre Curie*, 124.
        "was very moved": Marie Curie to Lady Huggins, 6 December 1903, BN.
186   "strict confidence": letter in French to M. and Mme Curie from Charles Aurivillius of the Swedish Academy.

CHAPTER NINE: *THE PRIZE*

187   Bouchard's endorsement: Crawford, in *The Beginnings of the Nobel Institution*. Crawford does not have him listed in 1901, apparently because he did not officially nominate them. But according to his 1902 letter, he proposed their names in 1901. Bouchard was an early student of radiology. Later, he and Pierre Curie collaborated on research on the physiological effects of radiation exposure.
        two . . . proposed: letters of 21, 29 January courtesy of the Royal Swedish Academy of Sciences, Center for History of Science.
        four members . . . wrote a nominating letter: n.d., RSA (CHS).
188   "more adventurous": Crawford, *The Beginnings*, 109. Arrhenius was out of the loop in 1903 because he was being considered for the chemistry prize.
189   If it is true": Mittag-Leffler Institute, Djursholm, Sweden.
        "A completely new field": report of Knut Ångström to the committee, RSA (CHS). Translated from Swedish.
        "their joint researches": as quoted in Crawford, *The Beginnings of the Nobel Institution*. The decision left open the possibility of awarding a Nobel in chemistry at a later date for the discovery of the radioactive elements. This was done in 1911, when Marie Curie was awarded a second Nobel in chemistry.
190   powers of inspiration: Londa Schiebinger, *The Mind Has No Sex?*, 150–51.
        We can't be gone: Pierre Curie to Carl Aurivillius, secretary of the Swedish Academy, 1 November 1903. BN.
        "We did not go": *Madame Curie*, 210–11, 11 December 1903.
        "didn't much want": Georges Gouy to Pierre Curie, 14 December 1903. BN.

191   "There is no doubt": Crawford, *The Beginnings of the Nobel Institution*, 193.
       "For the first time": Jean-Denis Bredin, *The Affair*, 517.
192   "This tale": *la Vie parisienne*, 19 December 1903. In January 1904 the judges of the Criminal Chamber heard the argument that Dreyfus's 1899 conviction was based on false accusations and forgeries.
       English or American: *l'Indépendence roumaine*, December 1903, and other newspapers.
       "miserable wooden hangar": *l'Echo de Paris*, 10 December 1903.
       "Eh bien!": *La Grande Revue*, January 1904.
       "even today": *le Rapide*, 26 December 1903, no. 5, p. 1.
       The "supremacy of France": *l'Éclair*, May 1905.
       "Madame Curie": *les Dimanches*, 20 December 1903.
193   "The truth is": *Chicago Evening Post*, March 1904.
       "The case of": *les Dimanches*, 20 December 1903.
       "Mrs Curie": *New York Herald*, 21 December 1903.
       "M. Pierre Curie": *The Vanity Fair*, 26 December 1903.
       "assisted him": *Truth*, 17 December 1903.
       "Radium, insisted *le Radical*": *le Radical*, July 1905.
       "It would be a mistake": *Nouvelles illustrées*, 17 December 1903.
194   "our opulent bourgeois salons": Marcel Villain, *Familia*, 27 December 1903.
       "delicious sentiments": ibid.
       "minute attentions": Verax, *Paris Sport*, 10 January 1904.
       the "example of Marie Curie": ibid.
       "It seems": Diogène, "Prix Conjugal" in *l'Independance roumaine*, December 1903.
195   "I hesitate": Christiane, *le Matin*, 20 December 1903
       "I see in my imagination": Flammarion, "les Conseils de la cousine," in *Annales politique et littéraires*, 27 Decembre 1903.
       "métal conjugal": Émile Gautier, *le Journal*, 21 December 1903.
       "singular and extra-scientific vogue": *l'Actualité*, 14 April 1904.
       "scarcely a person": Badash, "Radium," 147.
       "Medusa's Radium": *l'Actualité*, 14 April 1904.
       "fancy unison movements": Badash, "Radium," Quote is from *San Francisco Chronicle*, 29 May 1904.
196   "quite scientific": *New York Herald*, 13 December 1903. The spintharoscope had recently been invented by Sir William Crookes.
       "would not care": Badash, "Radium," 146–147
       "has a laboratory": *New York Herald*, 20 December 1903.
       "the great American inventor": *le Courier de l'Eure*, 3 December 1903.
       "rodent ulcer": *Daily Mail*, December 1903.
197   "Is the Monster Conquered?": *Le Petit Journal*, 19 January, 1904.
       "Just at present": Bernard Shaw, Preface to *The Doctor's Dilemma* (New York: William H. Wise & Co., 1936), 26.
       "after the physicians": Héloise Comtesse d'Alemcourt, *The New Orleans Daily Picayune*, 17 January 1904.
       "serious trouble": *Pierre Curie*, 190.
       "inundated with letters": *Madame Curie*, Marie Curie to Józef, 11 December 1903.
       "the stupid life": Pierre Curie to Georges Gouy, 22 January 1904. BN.
198   "I send you my most affectionate greetings": *Madame Curie*, Marie Curie to Józef, 19 March 1904.
       "I sense": *la Liberté*, 12 December 1903.
       "took advantage": *le Gaulois*, 14 December 1903.

198   "I had to ring": *le Temps,* 10 December 1903.
199   "I can give you": *l'Echo de Paris,* 30 December 1903.
        to "see a house": *la Presse.*
        "the frittering away": Pierre Curie to Georges Gouy, 24 July 1905.
        "Don't forget": *Madame Curie,* 210–11, 11 December 1903.
200   "They spent": The catalogue of their spending is from *Madame Curie;* the Frenchwoman was Madamoiselle de St. Aubin, who became Madame Kozlowska.
        "to wish": Pierre Curie to C. E. Guillaume, 15 January 1904. BN.
        "It was evident": *Philadelphia Evening Bulletin,* February 1904.
201   "Here is an absolutely unknown fact": *la Presse,* 12 January 1904.
        "you are naturally": Éleuthère Mascart to Pierre Curie, 22 May 1905.
        "Arrange it": Mascart to Pierre Curie, 25 May 1905.
        "As for the Academy:" Pierre Curie to Georges Gouy, 24 July 1905. Désiré-Jean-Baptiste Gernez was finally elected to the Academy in June of 1906. Alphonse-Théophile Schlösing was the son of Jean-Jacques. Both were engineers specializing in agriculture. The French words used to describe Pierre Curie were "un orgueilleux."
202   "little house": *la Patrie,* July 1905.
203   "discreet allusion": *le Journal,* 31 January 1904.
        "I pray you": *Pierre Curie,* 133.
        "all this noise": Pierre Curie to Georges Gouy, 22 January 1904.
        "They are going to create": Pierre Curie to Georges Gouy, 22 January 1904. Louis Liard was vice-rector of the Academy of Paris.
        "What with my courses": Pierre Curie to Georges Gouy, 13 January 1905. BN.
204   "defined a standard": Jean Wyart in DSB. Others seem to credit Rutherford for this.
        Papers referred to are 17 November 1902, "Sur la constante de temps caractéristique de la disparition de la radioactivité induite par le radium dans une enceinte fermée"; 9 February 1903, "Sur la disparition de la radioactivité induite par le radium sur les corps solides," both by P. Curie and J. Danne.
        "defied all contemporary scientific experience": *Pierre Curie,* 117.
        "the first appearance": *DSB.*
        "somehow ethereal waves": Kelvin, *Philosophical Magazine* 7, 1904.
        "the hypothesis": F. Soddy, *Radioactivity and Atomic Theory,* reprint edited by T. J. Trenn (New York: Wiley, 1975), 84.
        "This release": Curie and A. Laborde, "Sur la chaleur dégagée spontanément par les sels de radium," *CR,* 16 March 1903.
205   "When an atom": Georges Gouy to Pierre Curie, 27 July 1903. BN.
        "a new fact": Pierre Curie, *"Revue de recherches récentes sur la radioactivité,"* Journal de chimie physique 1:409–49, 1903.
        "I feel sure": Badash, *Rutherford and Boltwood,* 135.
        he published two more papers: Curie and J. Dewar, "Examen des gaz occlus ou dégagés par le bromure de radium." *CR,* 21 janvier 1904; and Curie and J. Danne, "Sur la disparition de la radioactivité induite par le radium sur les corps solides," *CR,* 14 March 1904. Curie and J. Danne, "Loi de disparition de l'activité induite par le radium après chauffage des corps activés," *CR,* 21 mars 1904. Papers on thermal waters and effects of exposure: Curie and A. Laborde, "Sur la radioactivité des gaz qui se dégagent de l'eau des sources thermales," *CR,* 9 May 1904; Ch. Bouchard, P. Curie, and V. Balthazard, "Action physiologique de l'émanation de radium," *CR,* 6 June 1904; Curie and A. Laborde, "Sur la radioactivité des gaz qui proviennent de l'eau des sources thermales," *CR,* 25 June 1906.

206   Pierre's "rheumatism": *Madame Curie,* 180. 19 March 1899.
        "violent crisis": Pierre Curie to Georges Gouy, January 1905. BN.
        "ever be able": Pierre Curie to Georges Gouy, September 1905. BN.
        "we have established": Bouchard, Curie, and Balthazar, "Action physi-
        ologique."
        "change the object": *Pierre Curie,* 135.
        "the considerable vogue": *Pierre Curie,* 136.
        "My brother": 27 September 1894.
207   "psychic phenomena": William Crookes, in *Nature,* 8 September 1898,
        447.
        "science, severe and inexorable": Richet, *Traité de métapsychique,* ii.
        "All the phenomena": Crookes, in *Nature,* 8 September 1898, 447.
        "everything around us": Henri de Parville, *le Correspondant,* 10 January
        1904, 188, 190.
        "we know little": Pierre and Marie Curie, "Sur les corps radioactifs," *CR,*
        13 January 1902.
208   "intermediaries": Richet, *Traité de métaphysique,* 42.
        Born in an Italian mountain village: Carrington *Eusapia,* 24.
        "studied": Richet, *Traite de métaphysique,* 38.
        "Eusapia is": Montorgueil, *les Parisiennes d'à present,* 91.
        "We have had a series": Pierre Curie to Georges Gouy, 24 July 1905.

CHAPTER TEN: TURNING TOWARD HOME

210   "We are": Pierre Curie to Georges Gouy, 13 January 1905. BN.
        "lovely jungle": Pierre's early journal. BN.
        "cut through": Alan Houghton Brodrick, ed., *Greater Paris and the Ile-
        de-France* (Hodder and Stoughton Ltd., 1952), 38.
211   "the monotonous region": Louis Barron, *les Environs de Paris* (Paris:
        Maison Quantin, n.d., but around 1886), 388.
        an hour by train: Baedeker, *Paris and Environs.*
        "children and the laboratory": Pierre Curie, to an unidentified woman of
        means who had offered to help build a laboratory in the country. 6 Febru-
        ary 1906. BN.
        scheduling of playmates: *Madame Curie.*
        "she finds": Pierre Curie, letter of 6 February to unknown woman.
        "very chubby": Marie's *cahier des enfants.* This and subsequent descrip-
        tions of the two girls in this chapter come from this notebook, unless
        otherwise indicated.
        "Existence is too hard": *Marie Curie,* 226.
        "Don't you find it": Marie Curie to Tatiana Jegorow, 25 December 1904.
        In an article by Jerzy Róziewicz, in *Kwartalnik Historii nauki i techniki,*
        "Listy Marii Sklodowskiej-Curie do Tatiany Jegorowej," R. XXV 1/1980.
212   "protests energetically": Marie Curie to Józef, 23 March 1905. *Madame
        Curie,* 226.
        traveling across town: *Madame Curie.*
213   "I have a great deal of work": *Madame Curie,* 227, 23 March 1905.
        "These pupils": *Pierre Curie,* 189.
        "The twentieth": Marthe Baillaud, in one of a series of reminiscences
        published in *Sévriennes d'hier et d'aujourd 'hui,* 50, December 1967, in
        connection with the hundredth anniversary of Marie Curie's birth.
214   "But in the case": Cotton, *les Curie,* 45.
        "the essential reference": Lucienne Goss Fabin, as part of a Cinquante-

naire du premier cours de Marie Curie à la Sorbonne, held on 12 January 1957. Proceedings later published.

214   "Until we came": Cotton, *les Curie,* 45–47.

215   "proud to hear": Cotton, *les Curie,* 45–46.

"like two shadows": Borel, *À travers deux siècles,* 68.

On at least one occasion: Marie Curie to Auguste Rodin 1 January 1905, from the archive of the Musée Rodin. Thanks to Ruth Butler, Rodin biographer, for finding this.

216   she and Pierre went: Cotton, *les Curie,* 61.

stop and buy caviar: *Madame Curie.*

"touching": Emile Gautier, *Echo du Nord,* Lille, 23 May 1906. Also Albert Laborde, *Pierre Curie dans son laboratoire,* Conférence faite au Palais de la Découverte, à l'occasion du 50ième anniversaire de la mort de Pierre Curie, 1956.

Paul Langevin, *Revue du mois.*

217   "fruitful conversations": Cotton, *les Curie,* 58.

escape to the Perrins': Ibid., 60.

closest woman friend: *Madame Curie.*

"the gaiety": Borel, *À travers deux siècles,* 85.

among the first: Bredin, *Dreyfus.*

218   "little colony": Langevin, *Revue du mois.*

"pile of mysterious things": *la République française,* 17 December 1903.

couldn't see much evidence: Albert LaBorde, "Pierre Curie dans son laboratoire," conference faite au Palais de la Découverte, on the fiftieth anniversary of Pierre Curie's death, 24 March 1956.

"certain eyes are not sensitive to them": Georges Gouy to Pierre Curie, 14 December 1903. BN.

"measures": Pierre Curie to Georges Gouy, 13 January 1904. BN.

"announced": Georges Gouy to Pierre Curie, March 1906 (approximately).

"frank gaiety": Cotton, *les Curie,* 58.

219   "very agreeable": Pierre Curie to Georges Gouy, 24 July 1905. BN.

Pierre's lecture to the Swedish Academy: Conférence Nobel de Pierre Curie, *les Prix Nobel en 1903* (Stockholm: Imprimerie Royale, 1906).

220   vividly recalled: Helena's memoir is the source for the entire Normandy description.

224   "Oh, she will be": *Familia,* 27 December 1903.

"Well then, I will ask grandpa": Cotton, *les Curie,* 60.

"My wife": Pierre Curie to Georges Gouy, 7, November 1905, BN.

225   In the laboratory: Laborde, "Pierre Curie."

"And in fact": *Madame Curie,* 240.

"Unless one acts": Pierre Curie to Georges Gouy, 14 July 1905. BN.

"I don't have a relationship": Pierre Curie to Georges Gouy, 6 October 1905, BN.

"at least": Pierre Curie to Georges Gouy, 24 July 1905. BN.

he himself presented: This was the last paper he would present.

226   "gros bonnets": "big shots"—actually Georges Gouy's words, in a letter to Pierre Curie around the end of March, 1906, regarding the association.

"We have had": Pierre Curie to Georges Gouy, 14 April 1906. BN.

"We were happy": from the journal Marie Curie kept during the year after Pierre's death (see Chapter 11).

CHAPTER ELEVEN: DESOLATION AND DESPAIR

227   "Poincaré made": From the journal Marie Curie kept during the year following Pierre's death, hereafter referred to as the mourning journal. BN.

"the fecundity": *Pierre Curie,* 147

He saw it: letters of Georges Gouy to Pierre Curie, March, 1906, of another correspondent (name undecipherable) to Pierre Curie on 8 April 1906, and Pierre Curie to Georges Gouy on 14 April 1906. BN.

228   A little before ten: The account of the events surrounding Pierre Curie's death is pieced together from accounts in twelve French and three English-language newspapers.

his pleas that day: Charles Barrois to Marie Curie on 20 April 1906. BN.

"Never," Paul Langevin remembered: *Revue du mois.*

229   out from behind: The carriage driver maintained that PC crossed in front of the carriage, not behind it.

230   "he wasn't careful": *Le Journal,* 20 April 1906.

"Pierre Curie . . . was a Parisian": Émile Gautier, *Écho du Nord,* Lille, 23 mai 1906.

"My son is dead": *Madame Curie,* 246.

231   I enter the room: mourning journal.

"brushed up": Jean Bernard, *la Vie de Paris 1906* (Paris: Alphonse Lemerre, 1907), 170–71.

"Physical forces": *Revue du mois.*

233   mahonia: also called Oregon Holly Grape. An evergreen shrub with holly-like leaves and dense yellow flower blooming in late winter and early spring.

marsh marigolds: in French, *renoncules d'eau.* The *ranunculus* family is vast, and includes many buttercups, but marsh marigold is an early spring variety common in watery places.

237   "brought glory": *CR,* Monday, 23 April 1906.

"All those who knew him": *Pierre Curie,* 147–48.

"His immense kindness": *Pierre Curie,* 150.

238   "genial inventor": Berthelot to Marie Curie, 21 April 1906. BN.

"although I only": Rutherford to Marie Curie, 26 May 1906. BN.

"Very near here": *Revue du mois.*

243   a commission of the Faculté: "M. Pierre Curie. Maintien de la chaire de P. Curie," a commission report. Members Bouty, Janet, Lippmann were present; the meeting was presided over by Dean Paul Appell. Archives nationales.

"unrelenting pain": Georges Gouy to Marie Curie, 30 April 1906. BN.

244   the first woman: Charrier, *l'Evolution intellectuelle féminine,* 407. The numbers would remain small for many years. In 1930, there were only six women on the faculty of the Sorbonne, two in science.

"men-about-town": The description, and the journalist's remark, are from a reminiscence delivered by Mademoiselle C. Schulhof on the occasion of the fiftieth anniversary of Marie Curie's first lecture. "Sévriennes d'hier et d'aujourd'hui," March 1957.

"almost furtively": description and quote from Marie Curie in Schulhof, "Sévriennnes."

245   Don't think: Marie Curie to Eugénie Feytis, 8 December 1906. École normale supérieure.

246   "I believe": Jacques Curie to Marie Curie, 18 April 1907. BN.

CHAPTER TWELVE: A NEW ALCHEMY

247   "Until the end": *Madame Curie,* 268.
"Pierre Curie observed": "Action de la pesanteur sur le dépot de la radio-activité induite" *CR* 145, 7 September 1907.
"power to exercise": "Préface aux Oeuvres de Pierre Curie," as it appeared in *Revue du mois,* April 1908.
"decorations in general": Marie Curie to Monsieur le Ministre, draft, 28 November 1910. BN.

248   "house without charm": *Madame Curie,* 263, 267.
"It is rather curious": Irène Joliot-Curie, "Marie Curie, ma mere," 94.

249   "If one of the apprentices": *Madame Curie,* 270–71.
"One had only to see their joy": Cotton, *les Curie,* 78.
"My mother": Irène Joliot-Curie, "Marie Curie, ma mère," 97.
"sent into the open air": *Madame Curie,* 267.

250   Marie Curie wanted: from an unpublished memoir written by Marie's namesake Maria Skłodowska Szancenbach, daughter of Józef. The memoir, written toward the end of Szancenbach's life, was translated from the Polish.
"of my mother collapsing": *Madame Curie,* 264–65.
"upset in such a way": *Madame Curie,* 265.
"The father and the wife": Cotton, *les Curie,* 75.
"The presence of Dr. Curie": *Madame Curie,* 266.

251   "Eu, eu, eu": Cotton 75–76
"decisive": *Madame Curie,* 266.
"He had me read": Irène Joliot-Curie, "Marie Curie, ma mère," 94.
"Rising at dawn": Alice Edouard Chavannes, July 1914. One of three testimonials written in defense of Marie Curie following the Langevin affair. The other two, written by Henriette Perrin and Jean Perrin, are extensively cited in the coming pages. EPC.
cooperative school ended: *Madame Curie,* 271.

252   "The struggle": ibid., 272.
"ever away": ibid., 266.
"less reliable": ibid., 265.
"her near ones": ibid., 264.
"I think": Irène Joliot-Curie, "Marie Curie, ma mère," 94.
"My mother": *Madame Curie,* 272–73.
"I will never forget": Marie Skłodowska Szancenbach's memoir.

253   "on the shore": Marie Curie to Ellen Gleditsch, 17 August 1908. RUL.
"My dear good Mé": Irène to Marie Curie, 1907. This and other letters between Irène and Marie Curie may be found in the Bibliothèque nationale; also in Ziegler, *Marie–Irène Curie Correspondance.* Subsequent references to their correspondence in these endnotes are by date only.
The Madeleine mentioned could be Irène's cousin, Jacques's daughter. But it seems more likely that it was Madeleine Langevin, age five. That would suggest that the Langevins were at Arromanches with the Curies not only in 1908 (see *cahier des enfants*) but also in 1907. Maybe that's when Paul and Marie got the idea for the school.
"I am taking": Arromanches, 1907.
"only missed": Arromanches, 1907.
"I have a good appetite": 1907.
"I love Mé": 1907.
"I read every day in Polish": August 1907.

254   "who barely knows": 22 September 1909.
"I couldn't do": 1907.
"I've forgotten": 1910.
"If they are still": 19 August 1909. A monkey puzzle tree is a Chilean pine, *Araucaria imbricata,* whose twisted branches puzzle even a monkey.
"I would like": 1907.
"It has been a long time": August 1907.
"Come back": 24 July 1908.
"I would like": 19 August 1909.
"I will be": 6 August, 1910.

256   "difficult": *Madame Curie,* 266.
"The little packets": Alice Chavannes' testimonial.
"preoccupied and saddened": Marie Curie to the Royal Society, which has requested her portrait, 7 March 1910.

257   "Fate did not": "Préface," *Revue du mois,* April 1908.
"Everybody said": Borel, *À travers deux siècles,* 105. Borel places this event in the spring of 1911, but all the evidence suggests it occurred a year earlier.
"His emotional state": ibid., 94, 103, 104.

258   "inexperience": testimonial of Jean Perrin about the Langevin affair, July 1914. EPC. When Paul Langevin and his wife decided to settle their differences out of court, Marie Curie was denied the opportunity to tell her side of the story. Paul Langevin, remorseful about the public disgrace she had been subjected to, asked his friends the Perrins to write down the versions of the story they would otherwise have provided in court, versions which were highly sympathetic to Marie Curie. These testimonials, which were written several years after the events, were in a file at the École de physique et chimie which had been kept closed for many years. When I visited the library there on 2 February 1990, somewhat in advance of a date set by the family for opening the files to researchers, I was allowed to see them. I am grateful to Bernadette Bensaude-Vincent and Monique Monnerie, the librarian at the École de physique et chimie, for making this possible.
"terrible scenes": testimonial of Henriette Perrin about the Langevin affair, April 1914. EPC.
"he complained": Jean Perrin testimonial.

259   "cared for her": Henriette Perrin testimonial.
"We found ourselves": Jean Perrin testimonial.
" 'harshness' ": Henriette Perrin.
"I grew": Henriette Perrin.

260   "He said later": Paul Langevin to a monsieur (possibly Gustave Téry) as part of a challenge to duel. n.d. EPC.
"Langevin is standing": Pierre Curie to Georges Gouy, 13 January 1905. BN.
"Langevin possessed": from a tribute which appeared in *la Pensée* at the time of Langevin's death in 1946. As quoted in *Correspondance françaises.*

261   "produced new insights": Bensaude-Vincent, *Langevin,* 30.
"greatly appreciated": Henriette Perrin testimonial.
"When he talks": Borel, *À travers deux siècles,* 104.
My dear Paul: All quotes from the correspondence between Marie Curie and Paul Langevin during this period are taken from the 23 November 1911 issue of a scurrilous weekly called *l'Oeuvre.* They were published with malicious intent, in an effort to publicly disgrace and humiliate Marie Curie. However, I have decided, on the basis of the style of the letters as well as their content and certain internal consistencies, that they are in

fact genuine excerpts from the letters. At the same time, however, it is important to point out that the excerpts were chosen by Gustave Téry, the editor of *l'Oeuvre*, in order to shock his readers and to show Marie Curie in the light he felt was least complimentary.

261   vacationed with the Langevins: They may also have vacationed together in 1907.

And as late as: Jean Perrin testimonial.

262   5 rue Banquier: according to *l'Oeuvre*.

"I write you": *l'Oeuvre*.

To Henriette Perrin: Henriette Perrin testimonial.

Jean Perrin: Jean Perrin testimonial.

264   "fell seriously ill": Jean Perrin.

"and found": Badash, *Rutherford and Boltwood*, 225. All quotations from the Rutherford–Boltwood correspondence are taken from this book; subsequent references are cited by the editor's name followed by page number.

"in honour of": Rutherford, "Radium Standards and Nomenclature," *Nature*, 6 October 1910. Chemistry texts in our time usually claim that the curie unit is named after Marie Curie, but in fact the name was chosen in honor of Pierre.

265   "nucleus of a second family": Borel, *À travers deux siécles*, 175.

It would be so good: *l'Oeuvre*.

267   "came to find me": Henriette Perrin.

"entirely illusory": *l'Oeuvre*.

268   Marie Curie told Henriette: Henriette Perrin.

269   "We can't go on": *l'Oeuvre*.

270   Paul Langevin sounds: ibid.

"Without speaking:" Letter from Jean Perrin to Paul Langevin, October 10, 1910. EPC.

271   "She was very changed": Henriette Perrin.

vacated by the death: 31 October 1910.

Marcel Brillouin had determined: Marcel Brillouin to Marie Curie, 10 November 1910, BN.

CHAPTER THIRTEEN: REJECTION

273   "For three years": Marie Curie to Jacques Danne, 18 June 1909. "Privileged" may refer to the fact that Danne was by then editor of *le Radium*.

274   "discovered five": *le Matin*, 17 August 1908.

"If R[amsay] is right": Badash, 60.

Ramsay "is very anxious": ibid., 158.

"I wonder": ibid., 182.

275   "The work": Unpublished reminiscence by Ellen Gleditsch. RUL.

"I decided": Marie Curie to Ellen Gleditsch, 27 August 1908. RUL.

"the residue": Madame Curie et Mademoiselle Gleditsch, "Action de l'émanation du radium sur les solutions des sels de cuivre," *CR* 147 (1908).

"riddled": Badash, 187.

"has been treed": ibid., 190.

"I must acknowledge": ibid., 196.

276   "very anxious": Badash, 234.

"the collection": *Traité, de radioactivité*, v, xi.

"In reading": Badash, 234–35.

"as there is": ibid., 244.

277   "a passionate researcher": Cotton, *les Curie,* 74.
        "A seat": *le Temps,* 31 December 1910.
278   "This beautiful result": as quoted in "Mémoires et Communications,"
        CR, 27 March 1940.
        "Branly would": Pierre Curie to Georges Gouy, 13 January 1905. BN.
        "I can't": Georges Gouy to Marie Curie, 13 November 1910. BN.
        "the joy of hostesses": Gaston Deschamps, *le Figaro,* 4 January 1911.
280   "admirable plea": Marguerite Durand, *Excelsior,* 4 January 1911.
        "serious and seductive". Jean-Paul Clébert, *les Daudet: Une famille bien
        française* (Paris: Presses de la Renaissance, 1988), 293–94.
        "Fifty years ago": Léon Bailby, *l'Intransigeant,* 6 January 1911. Baude-
        laire's lines in French: "Et se lançant, de loin, un regard irrité/Les deux
        sexes vivront chacun de leur coté."
281   "a paradise for women": B. Van Vorst, *le Figaro,* 24 Jan 1911. Same day
        as announcement of Branly election.
        "also a novelist" Henri de Regnier, 1864–1936, became a member of the
        Académie française himself in 1912.
        "A woman's book": *le Figaro,* 21 January 1911.
        "I began to laugh": Gérard d'Houville, *le Temps d'aimer,* Paris: Arthème
        Fayard & cie, Editeurs, 1907.
282   "Is Madame Curie": *le Figaro,* 21 January 1911.
283   "but what difficulties": *le Figaro,* 4 January 1910.
        "the women yet young": *le Figaro,* 21 January 1911.
        "Sévérine": Her real name was Caroline Rémy.
        "Our lady": René de Livois, *Histoire de la presse française,* vol. 2, (Lau-
        sanne: Éditions Spes, 1965).
284   "one of the most pretty": Sévérine, *l'Intransigeant,* 26 January 1911.
        "it was here": Shiebinger, *The Mind Has No Sex?,* 21. Among those
        nominated were Madeleine de Scudéry, Madame des Houlières, and Ma-
        dame Dacier.
285   five academies: The five were the Académie française, Académie des
        inscriptions et belles-lettres, Académie des beaux-arts, Académie des sci-
        ences morales et politiques, Académie des sciences.
        "for twenty years": from Pasteur's *Correspondence,* 2:281, as quoted in
        Crosland, *Science under Control,* 167.
        "Never in memory": *l'Intransigeant,* 5 January 1911.
        "had never been": *l'Action française,* 5 January 1911.
286   "The assembly": *le Figaro,* 5 January 1911.
        "at the risk": *l'Action française,* 5 January 1911.
        The result: There were actually three votes, one on the whole motion
        and one each on the first and second parts. The resulting totals varied by a
        few votes.
        "misogynous Institute": *l'Humanité,* 5 January 1911.
287   "want to respect": *le Paris-Journal,* 5 January 1911.
        "Madame Curie would be wise": *le Petit Parisien,* 5 January 1911.
        "No matter what": *le Temps,* 5 January 1911.
288   "Madame Curie had": unknown paper, date.
        "In the opinion": *l'Action française,* 23 January 1911.
        "Madame Curie has": ibid.
        "the most beautiful": *le Figaro,* 6 January 1911.
        "A whole long": *l'Action française,* 23 January 1911.
        "a master of invective": Alfred Cobban, *A History of Modern France*
        (Reading: Cox & Wyman Ltd. 1965) 3:86.
289   "Attendance at mass": Hause and Kenney, *Women's Suffrage and Poli-*

tics, Information on positions of newspapers on suffrage, as well as newspaper statistics, comes also from Hause and Kenney.

289   "The New Dreyfus Affair": *l'Humanité,* 4 January 1911.
"who doesn't": Henri Fournier in *l'Action française,* 5 January 1911.
Dreyfus Contra Branly: l'Action française, 23 January 1911. Tartuffe was Molière's religious hypocrite. The reference to "M. le Perpetuel" is to Curie supporter Darboux, who was permanent secretary of the Institute.

291   "Madame Curie": *l'Intransigeant,* 25 January 1911.
"One talks": *le Figaro,* 24 January 1911.

292   Charles Bouchard: letter to G. Retzius, 10 November 1911. RSA (CHS).
Comptes rendus noted: *CR,* 152, 30 January 1911.
"the defeat": *l'Action française,* 24 January 1911.
"a personal victory": Jean Bernard, *la Vie de Paris,* (Paris: Alphonse Lemerre, 1912), 40.
"the vote": *le Temps,* 25 January 1911.
"suffered": Charles Edouard Guillaume to Marie Curie, 26 January 1911. BN.
"I think": Georges Urbain to Marie Curie, 23 January 1911, BN.
"in no wise": *Madame Curie,* 278.

293   Others, most notably: According to a story in *l'Action française,* an academician named Radau told Marie Curie that he was opposed to admitting women to the Institute when she visited him. Then Darboux came to visit him. "I defended myself in vain, he was so pressing, so eloquent, and I ended by giving in to his entreaties and promising to come and vote in favor of his candidate." This story is the only evidence I could find that Marie Curie paid visits.
"lack of nobility": Paul de Cassagnac in *l'Autorité* 12 January 1911.
"beautiful gesture": Bernard, *la Vie de Paris,* 40. Since Marie Curie was not present at the vote, there is no way she could have made this ridiculous gesture, unless she deputized a colleague.
"In posing": Bailby, *l'Intransigeant,* 25 January 1911. Both Bailby and Darboux make reference to an apparent announcement Marie Curie made of her candidacy, probably in *le Temps,* but I have been unable to find it. I also have found nothing in newspaper reports which shows her affirming her candidacy directly to journalists.

CHAPTER FOURTEEN: SCANDAL

295   indulgent: A wife's single act of adultery could bring three months to two years in prison, while a husband was subject to a fine, and then only if he brought the mistress home. See Stetson, *Women's Rights in France.*
"Madame Curie should": Jean Perrin testimonial.
"Like venial sins": Berenson, *The Trial of Madame Caillaux,* Although the story is different, the same attitudes which fueled the drama of Madame Caillaux, who murdered the editor of *le Figaro,* came into play in the Langevin-Curie affair. Berenson's thoughtful analysis and the sociohistorical background he provides have been extremely useful to me in telling the Curie-Langevin story.

296   "judged very severely": Marie Curie to Paul Langevin, summer of 1910, as reproduced in *l'Oeuvre.*
Around Easter of 1911: Perrin testimonial.
"like two shadows": Borel, *A travers deux siècles,* 68.

297   Marguerite Borel remembered: *A travers deux siècles,* 106–7.
298 · "out of fatigue": Perrin testimonial.
        According to Jeanne Langevin: The story of the rupture is drawn from allegations made in the press by Jeanne Langevin and from the Perrin testimonial.
299   "to pay life insurance": from Marie Curie's *cahier de dépenses,* BN, and IOUs from Paul Langevin, EPC.
        she traveled to Leiden: The resulting paper was "Sur le rayonnement du radium à la température de l'hydrogène liquide," by Kamerlingh Onnes and Marie Curie, *le Radium* 10 (1913), 181.
        decay series of polonium: This was the work she corresponded with Rutherford about; he wanted to know if the end of the series was lead. "I am sure it is a very difficult piece of work," he wrote her in January of 1912. "If it does not turn out to be lead, what is it?" BN.
300   "We eat ice cream": Irène to Marie Curie, Zakopane, 1911.
        "I find": Irène to Marie Curie, Zakopane, 1911.
        "I love Poland": Irène to Marie Curie, Zakopane, 1911.
        "I kiss you": Irène to Marie Curie, Zakopane, 1911.
        When I see: Irène to Marie Curie, Zakopane, 1911.
301   "Eve very much": *cahier des enfants.*
        "needed all": ibid., xiii.
302   "Lorentz is a miracle": Einstein to Heinrich Zangger, director of the Institute for Forensic Medicine of Zurich University. As quoted in Mehra, *The Solvay Conferences,* xiv.
        "I spent": ibid.
        A STORY OF LOVE: *le Journal,* 4 November 1911.
304   "I would just like to say": *le Temps,* 5 November 1911.
        "Mme Curie didn't": ibid.
305   "A ROMANCE": *le Petit Journal,* 5 November 1911.
306   "saying softly": *l'Intransigeant,* 6 November 1911.
        "we know": *l'Intransigeant,* 7 November 1911.
307   I consider abominable: *le Temps,* 8 November 1911.
        agreed to represent: The letter in which Millerand agreed to represent her is dated 8 November, the same day as the statement in *le Temps.*
        "I am in despair": Fernand Hauser to Marie Curie, 5 November 1911. EPC. The letter was later reprinted in several newspapers.
308   "private life": Louis Depoully to Marie Curie, 6 November 1911, EPC.
        "whose violence": Albert et Terrou, *Histoire de la presse,* 65.
        "In the name of liberty": ibid., 66.
        bribe it: This was done during the Panama Canal scandal, when papers were paid about thirteen million francs to keep the risks of the venture quiet.
        obtained a pure enough sample: "Sur le poids atomique du radium" in *CR* 145 (1907).
        metallic state: "Sur le radium metallique," *CR,* 151, 1910.
309   Curies' discovery: Nobel Chemistry Committee report to the Swedish Academy of Sciences. RSA (CHS).
        "much greater": from the glowing nomination letter written to the Nobel Chemistry Committee by Svante Arrhenius. Received by the committee 28 January 1911. RSA (CHS).
        "special branch": Chemistry Committee report. RSA (CHS).
        "The said lady": Cables are from "Correspondence concerning the Nobel prize in chemistry of Marie Curie, 1911," in the manuscript collection of the RSA (CHS).
        "Madame Curie": *le Temps,* 9 November 1911.

309   "The Nobel Prize": *le Temps,* 15 November 1911.
310   "the thriller": Mehra, *The Solvay Conferences.*
        "so incensed": Einstein to Curie, in German, from Prague, 23 November 1911. Countway Library, Harvard University.
        "I know": CUL, probably 5 November 1911.
        "sure it is all": Badash, 257.
        genuinely pleased: See letter to Boltwood on December 5.
        asked Perrin: I have deduced this from a long letter Perrin wrote to Rutherford about the situation on around 20 December 1911. CUL.
        "I love you": Loie Fuller to Marie Curie, 24 November 1911. EPC.
311   "disgust": C. Mabus to Marie Curie, 17 November 1911, EPC.
        "May the vibrant sympathy": Weiss to Marie Curie, 15 November 1911, EPC.
        "just recompense": Émile Picard to Marie Curie, 9 November, 1911, EPC.
        "What a story": Jacques Curie to Marie Curie, 6 November 1911 (Jacques has written October, but it is clearly a mistake), EPC.
        To the Editor: Jacques Curie to "Monsieur le Directeur," 9 November 1911, EPC.
312   "by publishing": *le Petit Journal,* 6 November 1911.
        It may have been: The account which follows of the visit of Perrin and Borel to the Prefect of Police is taken from Perrin's testimonial.
313   "consorting": "d'entretien de concubine au domicile conjugale." "Marital dwelling" (*domicile conjugale*) apparently applied to any dwelling which Paul Langevin paid for.
        "Science and Virtue": *l'Action française,* 6 November 1911.
314   Even though: *l'Action française,* 18 November 1911.
315   A NEW AFFAIR: *l'Intransigeant,* 19 November 1911.
        "Priggish pedants": *l'Action française,* 20 November 1911.
        "What recourse": Maurice Pujo, *l'Action francaise,* 20 November 1911.
316   "only one piece": *l'Intransigeant,* 20 November 1911.
        Téry was a man of extremes: de Livois, *Histoire de la Prcssc,* 404–6.
317   "very beautiful": 27 Decembcr 1911, Jacques Curie to MC, EPC.
        "It no longer divides": *l'Oeuvre,* 23 November 1911.
318   "Chopin de la Polonaise": punning on "Polonaise de Chopin"; "chopin" was slang meaning, in this context, "easy mark" (Harrap's *New Standard French and English Dictionary*), and "Polonaise" of course here refers to Marie Curie herself.
        Women could be forgiven: See Berenson, *The Trial of Madame Cailloux* on the *crime passionel.*
        "This foreign woman": *l'Action française,* 22 November 1911.
        "right to happiness": *l'Oeuvre,* 23 November 1911.
        "scientific morality": ibid.
        "we have passions": *l'Humanité,* 9 December 1911.
319   "which had never been more": Cobban, *A History of Modern France,* 98.
        "impose respect": Weber, *The Nationalist Revival.* Quoting from debates in the Chamber of Deputies.
        "the birth": Weber, *France: Fin de Siècle,* 95.
        "revolutionaries": Hause and Kenney, *Women's Suffrage,* 13.
320   "Many of France's: Berenson, *The Trial of Madame Cailloux,* 11, 12.
        probably destroyed: Toward the end of her life, Marie Curie destroyed many letters and asked others to do so.
321   Marguerite Borel tells the story: the account which follows is taken from Borel, *A travers deux siècles.*

323   "There is . . . a man": *l'Oeuvre,* 23 November 1911.
324   "Duelling became": Berenson, *The Trial of Madame Caillaux,* 16.
       "a steam engine": as quoted in Berenson, *The Trial of Madame Caillaux,* 184.
       "Thank heaven!": Edwards, *Old and New Paris,* 345.
325   "scoundrel": Pierre Mortier to Marie Curie, 25 November 1911. The four duels, beside that between Langevin and Téry, were Leon Daudet v. Henri Chervet of *Gil Blas* on November 23, 1911; Pierre Mortier v. Gustave Téry on November 24; Comte Léon de Montesquiou v. Georges Breittmayer (representing the Daudet and *Gil Blas* factions) on November 28; and between Pierre Mortier of *Gil Blas* once again and Bainville of the Daudet faction on December 19.
       According to Marguerite Borel: Borel, *A travers deux siècles.*
       "Nervously tugging": The account of the duel is taken from *le Petit Journal* and *l'Intransigeant* of 26 November 1911.
326   I have no personal: *l'Oeuvre,* 30 November 1911.
       "delicate matter": Marie Curie to Svante Arrhenius, 22 November 1911, RSA (CHS).
       "chicanery" . . . "lies": Arrhenius to Marie Curie, 1 December 1911. EPC.
327   A letter attributed to you: Arrhenius to Marie Curie, 1 December 1911. Mittag-Leffler Institute, Djursholm. Apparently, Arrhenius sent another, similar, letter to Marie's colleague Urbain, which he later refused to share with her, probably to spare her feelings.
       "You know": Marie Curie to Mittag-Leffler, 19 December 1911, Mittag-Leffler Institute.
       You suggest: Marie Curie to Arrhenius, 5 December 1911, RSA (CHS).
328   According to Jean Perrin: Perrin testimonial.
329   "the scandal": *l'Action française,* 21 December 1911.
       "receive the prize: Draft of a letter from G. Retzius to Charles Bouchard, 14 November, 1911. Also see letter from Olof Hammarsten to Aurivillius, November 15, 1911. RSA (CHS).
       "worship": Rough draft, BN.
       "Radioactivity is": Rough draft written in Bronia's hand on Grand Hotel, Stockholm stationery. 10 December 1911.
       formal Nobel lecture: *Nobel Lectures in Chemistry 1901–1921* (New York: Elsevier, 1966), 202–212.
330   "never to have to": *l'Intransigeant,* 3 December 1911.
       "individualistic morality": *l'Oeuvre,* 6 December 1911.
       "dirty foreigners": *l'Oeuvre,* 13 December 1911.
       l'Oeuvre announced: 20 December 1911.
       proper bourgeoisie: In the 1920s, a young American woman named Theodora Mead (later Abel), whose mother had been a principal fund-raiser for Marie Curie in the United States, stayed for a year with a proper French family in Paris. She visited often with the Curies, and played violin with Eve at the piano. When she suggested inviting the Curies to her house, her hostess refused because of Marie Curie's reputation. Personal interview with Theodora Mead Abel.
       "crucified": Paul Langevin to Svante Arrhenius, 6 December 1911, EPC.
       "constant remorse": Paul Langevin testimonial, 24 September 1915.
331   "linked by a profound affection": Marie Curie to Paul Langevin, summer of 1910. *L'Oeuvre.*
       "never ceased": ibid.
       By 1914: André Langevin, *Paul Langevin mon père* (Paris: les Éditeurs

français réunis, 1971). He puts it in the negative: "Mon père et ma mère allaient vivre separés jusqu'à la guerre de 1914." Although Marie Curie and Paul Langevin's liaison was broken off, the families were ultimately linked. Irène's daughter, Hélène Joliot, married André Langevin's son Michel.

CHAPTER FIFTEEN: RECOVERY

332   "Obviously": Jacques Curie to Marie Curie, 10 January 1912. EPC.
"one can only": Perrin testimonial.
According to her doctors: from a one-page description of Marie Curie's illness, signed by three doctors. 26 February 1912. BN.
seven-page document: handwritten on 3 March 1912. IC.
333   Needless to say: Georges Gouy to Marie Curie, 17 March 1912.
"I had hoped": Marie Curie to Appell, 15 April 1912.
"ma grave maladie": from a chronology at the end of the *cahier des enfants*.
"let us hope": Jacques Curie to Marie Curie, 4 February 1912. EPC.
334   move to Paris: In her *Autobiographical Notes* in *Pierre Curie*, which make no mention of the Langevin affair, Marie Curie explains move as a result of her "grave illness" and the children's education program.
"abominable insinuation": letter addressed to Madame Curie by the manager and the sister superior of the maison de santé, Vaugirard, 27 January, 1912.
"hydrotherapeutic treatments": Gabriel de Mortillet, *Guide de l'etranger dans les départements de la Savoie et de la Haute-Savoie* (Chambéry: J. Perrin, 1861).
335   The composition of the water: *Savoie, les guides bleus* (Paris: Librairie Hachette, 1961).
recorded the amounts: From a three-page chart kept by Marie Curie at Thonon. BN.
"I am pursuing": Marie Curie to Ellen Gleditsch, 15 July 1912, RUL.
336   "I maintain": Sharp, *Hertha Ayrton*, 242.
full membership: In 1945, Kathleen Lonsdale and Marjory Stephenson were elected.
"all my scientific work": ibid., 246.
337   "a girl": George Eliot, *Daniel Deronda* (London: Penguin Books, 1967), 227. (First published in 1876.)
"I often think": Sharp, *Hertha Ayrton*, 240.
"I accept": ibid., 237
"I am a member": Hertha Ayrton to Marie Curie, 28 May 1912. BN.
338   "Many a militant suffragist": Sharp, *Hertha Ayrton*, 239.
"We saw": ibid., 230.
"You have": Hertha Ayrton to Marie Curie, 2 January 1912, BN.
"I would be very grateful": Hertha Ayrton to Bronia Dłuski, 18 February 1912. BN.
"I shall take": Hertha Ayrton to Marie Curie, 28 February 1912, BN.
339   "with nothing": Sharp, *Hertha Ayrton*, 241.
they wrote asking Alice: The question was whether Lamartine had written "Créature d'un jour qui t'agites une heure" or "Créature d'un instant . . . " Alice Chavannes replied that "Créature d'un jour" was correct, because the hemistich in an alexandrine required six beats, not seven. Chavannes to Marie Curie, 5 September 1912. BN.

339   "She takes baths": *cahier des enfants.*

       "Unfortunately": Marie Curie to Ellen Gleditsch, 19 August 1912. Chewtonmill House, Highcliffe. RUL.

       "I am only": Marie Curie to Lorentz, 15 September 1912. Algemeen Rijksarchief, The Hague, Netherlands.

       "science is always": Hertha Ayrton to Bronia, 7 January 1912. BN.

340   "I regret": Marie Curie to Georges Jaffé, 14 August 1912.

       "I would not want": Marie Curie to H. A. Lorentz, 22 September 1912. Alg. Rijks, The Hague.

       For the next eleven years: The first paper published in the *Compte rendus* following her rejection was *"Sur le rayonnement G et le dégagement de chaleur du radium and du mésothorium."* It was presented by M. G. Lippmann and published in *CR* 172 (1921).

       "Radioactivity . . . ": E. Rutherford and F. Soddy, *Philosophical Magazine* 5, 1903.

       "as the continuation": The paper was published as *"Sur le rayonnement du radium à la température de l'hydrogène liquide"* in *le Radium* 10 (1913), 181.

       Marie Curie, "les Radio-elements et leur classification," *Revue du mois* (1914).

341   "almost as incredible": E. N. da C. Andrade, *Rutherford and the Nature of the Atom,* Doubleday, New York, 1964. This statement, frequently attributed to Rutherford, may not be authentic (Ruth Sime, personal communication). Nonetheless, it seems too vivid and useful to give up.

       "I think": in Badash, 235, 14 December, 1910.

342   "each atom": as quoted in Pais, *Inward Bound,* 183.

343   "Yet two years before": ibid., 188.

       "remarkable . . .": Mehra, *The Solvay Conferences,* 76.

       "important conclusions": Marie Curie, "Sur la loi fondamentale des transformation radioactives," Curie, *Oeuvres,* 507–10. This article first appeared in 1921 in a publicaton of the Institut Internationale de Physique Solvay, Paris.

       "Mr. Rutherford": Marie Curie, "Les radioelements . . . ,"*Revue du mois* (1914). Marie Curie's emphasis on the smallness of the nucleus is a little off; in fact, the nucleus is very large compared to the electrons. It would have been more accurate to speak of it as compact. Furthermore, the empty space in the atom is enormous, not just a "certain distance."

       "It is necessary . . .": Marie Curie, conference given in 1912, published by the Société de physique, 1913.

344   "the absolute value": Marie Curie to Georges Jaffé, 17 April, 1913.

       "You will": Marie Curie to Rutherford, 17 October 1912.

       "plain darn fool": Boltwood to Rutherford, 5 December 1911. Badash, 260.

       "voted the Madame": Boltwood to Rutherford, 14 July 1921, Badash, 346.

       "a rather difficult person": Rutherford to Boltwood, 20 November 1911. Badash, 258.

       a discussion began: Rutherford to Marie Curie, 9 May 1910, BN; Marie Curie to Rutherford, 6 August 1910, CUL.

345   "assure agreement": Marie Curie, "les Mesures en radioactivité et l'étalon du radium," *Journal de physique* 2 (1912).

       "a committee": Marie Curie to Rutherford, 6 August 1910.

       "to retain": Rutherford to Boltwood, 20 November 1911. Badash, 257.

       "sent in the name": Rutherford to Meyer, November 8, 1911. CUL.

345   "As you know": Rutherford to Boltwood, 20 November 1911. Badash, 258.
       sympathetic to: Rutherford wrote to Meyer, "For sentimental reasons, which I quite understand, she wished to retain this standard for her own Laboratory." November 8, 1911. CUL.
346   "hoping to have": Rutherford to Boltwood, November 20, 1911. Badash, 258–59. As it turned out, Marie Curie's illness caused a postponement to the fall of 1913, well after the issues about the standard had been resolved.
       "I have not much doubt": Rutherford to Boltwood, 18 March 1912. Badash, 264.
       "I think perhaps": Rutherford to Boltwood, 22 April 1912. Badash, 270.
       "the construction": Marie Curie to Jaffé, 17 April 1913.
       radium institute: This institute was the result of the offer, made by Sienkiewicz and others in a Polish delegation, to build her a laboratory in Warsaw. She had agreed to be its titular head.
       not entirely well: She was suffering, as she wrote Irène, from a tooth abcess.
       "This poor country": Marie Curie to a colleague, *Madame Curie*, 283.
       To Irène she wrote: 26 November 1913. BN.
347   "I have seen again": *Madame Curie*, 283.
       "They dressed me": Marie Curie to Irène, 15 September 1913. BN.
       "Only a few days": Einstein to Marie Curie, 3 April 1913. In Michel Biezunski, ed., *Albert Einstein: Correspondances françaises*.
348   "In the vanguard": *Madame Curie*, 284.
       critical remarks: Martin Klein et al., eds., *Collected Papers of Albert Einstein* (Princeton: Princeton University Press, 1987), 5:554.
349   seemed "nervous": André Debierne to Marie Curie, 12 July 1912.
       "to restore her": *cahier des enfants*.
       "très patriote": ibid.
       "At Montpellier": Irène to Marie Curie, 31 March 1912.
350   "much more agreeable": Irène to Marie Curie, 2 April 1912.
       in love: from an interview with Eve Curie Labouisse, who took it back as soon as she said it.
       "We came back": Irène to Marie Curie, 11 April 1912.
       "I arrived": Irène to Marie Curie, 3 April 1912.
       "These English lessons": Irène to Marie Curie, 10 July 1912.
351   "Once we got": Irène to Marie Curie, 18 July 1912.
       "With the help": Irène to Marie Curie, 19 July 1912.
       "the international situation": Irène to Marie Curie, 27 July 1914.
       "If you feel": Irène to Marie Curie, 24 July 1914.
352   "I feel already": Marie Curie to Irène, 6 September 1914.

CHAPTER SIXTEEN: SERVING FRANCE

353   The sea: Colette, *les Heures longues* (Paris: Fayard & cie, 1917), 6. Colette was in St. Malo.
       In l'Arcouëst: details from Borel, *A travers deux siècles*, 175–83.
       "During the whole": Irène to Marie Curie, 2 August 1914.
       "so calm": Henriette Perrin to Marie Curie, 1 August 1914. BN. Marie Curie wrote to Irène the same day: "You saw Irène that this poor Jaurès was assassinated. It is sad and abominable."
354   children in red *maillots*: Colette, *les Heures longues*, 7.

354   "excited and enervated": Irène to Marie Curie, 2 August 1914.
       Dear Irène, dear Eve: Marie Curie to children, 1 August 1914.
355   "home before": As quoted in Barbara Tuchman, *The Guns of August*
       (New York: The Macmillan Company, 1962).
       "armoured with bouquets": Ajalbert, *Dans Paris,* 9.
       "The departure": Irène to Marie Curie, 3 August 1914.
       "It is hard to think": Marie Curie to Hertha Ayrton, 1 May 1913, as
       quoted in Sharp, *Hertha Ayrton,* 248.
       "all the French": Marie Curie to Irène, 5 August 1914.
       "If we come to it": Marie Curie to Hertha Ayrton, 1 May 1913, in Sharp,
       Hertha Ayrton, 248.
356   "You and I": Marie Curie to Irène, 1 August 1914.
       "I am tormented": Irène to Marie Curie, 2 August 1914.
       "my only desire": Irène to Marie Curie, 3 August 1914.
       "impossible for the moment": Marie Curie to Irène, 6 August 1914.
       "In recent days": Irène to Marie Curie, 13 August 1914.
       "I am big enough": Irène to Marie Curie, 7 August 1914.
       "We have had": Irène to Marie Curie, 3 August 1914.
357   "reception": Holweck to Marie Curie, 14 August 1914. IC.
       "the country of Poland": Marie Curie to Irène, 6 August 1914.
358   "The overloaded trains": *Pierre Curie,* 206.
       "All that's left": Ajalbert, *Dans Paris,* 9.
       "the radium": order signed by Pierre Guesde, *résident supérieur,* August
       1914. Part of an exhibit at the Bibliothèque nationale, Paris, 1967. See
       catalogue *Pierre et Marie Curie* (Paris: Bibliothèque Nationale, 1967), 62.
       "the German army": *Pierre Curie,* 208.
       "I hope": Fernand Holweck to Marie Curie, 8 September 1914. IC.
       "we all": Marie Curie to Irène, 6 September 1914.
359   "farewell": as quoted in Thébaud, *la Femme au temps de la guerre de 14*
       (Paris: Éditions Stock: 1986), 26.
       "The Barbarians": Ajalbert, *Dans Paris,* 9.
       "not to claim": as quoted in Thébaud, *la Femme au temps de la guerre
       de 14,* 27.
       "I had never before seen": Weiss, *Mémoires d'une Européenne,* 184.
360   "the first step": *le Temps,* Monday, 17 August 1914.
       "resolved": *Madame Curie,* Marie Curie to Paul Langevin, 1 January
       1915, 298.
361   In addition: *Madame Curie,* 301.
       "had the good luck": Marie Curie, *la Radiologie et la guerre* 2.
       "grave omissions": Marie Curie, handwritten "Rapport sur l'activité du
       laboratoire de physique générale (Institut du Radium) pendant la guerre,"
       BN.
       "when it existed": ibid.
       "in the area": Irène to Marie Curie, 11 August 1914. Irène was repeating
       back her mother's phrase.
       "My first idea": "Rapport sur l'activité du laboratoire,"
       "who applied themselves": Marie Curie, *la Radiologie et la guerre,* 103.
362   "The production": ibid., 33.
       "This little car": ibid., 35–36.
363   Advised: ibid., 37–40.
       "The lack of equipment": ibid., 70.
364   At that time: ibid., 115–16.
       "public powers": ibid., 14.
       "In general": ibid., 104.
365   "an X-Ray car": *Bibliothèque nationale* catalogue, 63.

365   "thinks your proposition": Danysz to Marie Curie, October 1914. BN.
"wants ardently": BN catalogue, 62.
"with all the seriousness": ibid., 62–63.
"growing difficulties": Marie Curie to Lavisse, 14 February 1915, BN.
366   yet another official order: Dr. Haret to Marie Curie, 21 October 1917,
BN.
"succeeded": "Rapport sur l'activité du laboratoire."
"Sometimes it only took": *Marie Curie, la Radiologie et la guerre,* 107.
"shell fragment": ibid., 53.
"this radiology": ibid., 72–73.
367   "necessary above all": ibid., 85–86.
"working with some person": ibid., 90.
"because the lack": "Rapport sur l'activité du laboratoire."
"rather solid": Marie Curie, *la Radiologie et la guerre,* 111.
"great confidence": As quoted in Cotton, *les Curie,* 85–86.
"Mediocre": ibid., 111–12.
368   "They gave": ibid., 111.
a teacher: a third teacher was Marthe Klein, who later married the physicist Pierre Weiss. Formerly a student at Sèvres, she taught in the lycee at
Versailles.
"the devotion": "Rapport sur l'activité du laboratoire."
"Actually I regret": Irène to Marie Curie, 8 August 1914.
"that they were Germans": Irène to Marie Curie, 3 September 1914.
369   "I was so sorry": Marie Curie to Irène, 6 September 1914.
"I was rather amused": Irène to Marie Curie, 24 September 1914.
370   "I spent my birthday": Irène to Marie Curie, 13 September 1915.
obtain her *certificats:* Math with *mention très bien,* physics and chemistry with *mention assez bien.*
"I eat well": Irène to Marie Curie, 3 August 1917.
371   "always the monotony": Maurice to Marie Curie, 30 August 1915, BN.
"Dear Maurice": Marie Curie to Irène, 6 September, 1914.
"Irène tells me": BN catalogue, 65.
"severe reprimand": Maurice to Marie Curie, 16 October 1915, BN.
"except when": Maurice to Marie Curie, 12 September 1914, BN.
"One hundred": Maurice to Marie Curie, 19 October 1914, BN.
"I made": Maurice to Marie Curie, October 31, 1914, BN.
372   "I should like": Maurice to Marie Curie, February 23, 1915, BN.
"incredible passion": 19 October 1914.
"Will we": Maurice to Marie Curie, 9 April 1915, BN.
"I am going": Maurice to Marie Curie, 4 October 1915, BN.
"confined": Kirchberger, *The First World War,* 189.
"very tired": Maurice to Marie Curie, 11 June 1915, BN.
"Tomorrow": Maurice to Marie Curie, 14 November 1915, BN.
"As sergeant": Maurice to Marie Curie, 15 August 1915, BN.
373   "Have you seen": Maurice to Marie Curie, 9 April 1915, BN.
"You can imagine": Canac to Marie Curie, Feb 1, 1915. IC.
"We socialists": *À travers deux siècles,* 165–66.
Danysz' work: See Pais, *Inward Bound,* 155. Also, Ruth Sime in type-
script copy of her biography of Lise Meitner.
"There is": Danysz to Marie Curie.
374   "As a result": Danysz to Marie Curie, 26 September 1914, IC.
"which we have covered": Danysz to Marie Curie, 4 October 1914. IC.
"M. J. Danysz": Marie Curie to Ellen Gleditsch, 2 November 1914.
RUL.
"lost the elite": Marie Curie, *la Radiologie et la guerre,* 121.

374   "the war": Sassoon, *The Memoirs of George Sherston,* 244.
375   'were seen to': as quoted in Becker, *The Great War,* 320–21.
       "it carried off": *Madame Curie,* 305.
       Canac reported: Canac to Marie Curie, 12 November 1918.
       "It is going to be": Holweck to Marie Curie, 12 November 1918.

CHAPTER SEVENTEEN: AMERICA

376   "not against": Paxton, *Europe in the Twentieth Century,* 122.
        "After all": Barbusse, *le Feu,* 281.
        "It is all": Mary Borden, *The Forbidden Zone* (London: Heinemann, 1929), 17.
        "I can never forget": *Pierre Curie,* 216.
377   "see where": Marie Curie to Irène, 6 August 1914.
        "I have lived": *Madame Curie,* 356.
        "crushing flow": Marie Curie, *la Radiologie et la guerre,* 50–51.
        "All civilized groups": *ibid.,* 143.
        "automatically": Davies, 2:378.
378   "A great joy": *Pierre Curie,* 221–22.
        "We, 'born in servitude' ": *Madame Curie,* 305.
        she judged: ibid., 308.
        "I entirely": Marie Curie to Romain Rolland, 26 June 1919. BN.
379   a movement they named Clarté: Nicole Racine, "The Clarté Movement in France, 1919–21," *Journal of Contemporary History* 2 (2) (April 1967). 195–208.
        "I have": Marie Curie to Henri Barbusse, 15 May 1919. BN.
        "The difficulty": Marie Curie to Romain Rolland, 26 June 1919. BN.
        "to work": Marie Curie to Bronia, *Madame Curie,* French Edition, 67.
380   "I still have not": Marie Curie to Barbusse, 20 June 1919.
        "a small homogeneous group": Marie Curie to Barbusse, 15 May 1919.
        "We must": Marie Curie, "Sur la Commission internationale et l'Institut internationale de cooperation intellectuelle." A typed report written in 1930. BN.
        "I believe": Marie Curie to Einstein, 27 May 1922. In Biezunski, *Einstein: Correspondences françaises.*
381   "I would": Einstein to Marie Curie, 30 May 1922. Ibid.
        "ideas concerning": Einstein to Marie Curie, 4 July 1922. Ibid.
        "I received": Marie Curie to Einstein, 7 July 1922. Ibid.
        "One finds": Einstein to Marie Curie, 11 July 1922. Ibid.
        other correspondence: Clark, *Einstein,* 361.
382   "under the guise": Einstein to Marie Curie, 25 December 1923. Ibid.
        "ties of friendship": Marie Curie to Einstein, 6 January 1924. Ibid. Einstein eventually participated in the efforts of the commission.
383   "My father": Missy Meloney in introduction to *Pierre Curie,* 15.
        "I waited": Missy Meloney in *Pierre Curie,* 16–17.
        "rich": ibid., 15–16.
384   "To put me": ibid., 17–18.
        "lovely pale": *Madame Curie,* 32.
        Eleven years younger: Much of the background of Missy Meloney, as well as other important facts and insights about Marie Curie's trips to the United States, comes from a dissertation written by Judith Magee: "Marie Curie: A Study of America's Use of Marie Curie as a Devoted Wife and

Mother, Saintly Scientist, and Healer of Humanity" (Department of Women's History, Sarah Lawrence College, 1989).

385   "There is": Missy Meloney to Marie Curie from on board the *S.S. Homeric*, 14 November 1924. BN.

"With the greatly": Calvin Coolidge, *The Delineator*, June 1921.

"This is": A.S.M. Hutchinson, *This Freedom* (Boston: Little, Brown, 1922), 369.

"I agree": Marie Curie to Missy Meloney, 11 January 1923. Columbia University Library.

386   "It is true": Marie Curie to Missy Meloney, 7 November 1920. BN.

"a little corner": *The Delineator*, January 1920.

"France is poor": *The Delineator*, April 1921.

387   "Right now": Marie Curie to Missy Meloney, 9 March 1921. BN.

hard for all of them: Later in life, Bronia wrote to her sister Maria, insisting that she was in fact quite well off in Poland.

My father": Unpublished memoir in Polish by Maria Skłodowska Szancenbach, Józef's daughter.

388   "a pity": *Madame Curie*, 190.

"Radium therapy": Marie Curie, "Des raisons motivant la creation d'un institut officiel de radiumtherapie en France," a typed report written in 1915.

389   "lacuna": Marie Curie, *la Radiologie et la guerre*, 137–39.

"We may think": *The Delineator*, April 1921.

390   "I don't feel": Marie Curie to Missy Meloney, 7 November 1920. BN.

"May at latest": Missy Meloney to Marie Curie, 25 January 1921. Western Union. BN.

"After all": Marie Curie to Missy Meloney, 4 March 1921. BN.

"one of the glories": From a pamphlet published by *Je sais tout*, "En l'honneur de Madame Pierre Curie et de la découverte du radium." Poem by Maurice Rostand. Versified by Jan Schreiber.

391   "with the least": Typed "Tentative Program" sent to Marie Curie by Meloney prior to the trip. BN.

"full of devotion": Marie Curie to Henriette Perrin, 10 May 1921, from on board the *Olympia*. BN and *Madame Curie*, 326.

392   "motherly-looking": *New York Times*, 12 May 1921, 1.

"I do not": *New York Times*, 18 May 1921, 17.

393   "Don't our daughters": Marie Curie to the rector (Paul Appell). 12 June 1919. BN.

"They are": *Herald Tribune*, 15 May 1921.

"While an almost": Marie Curie, "Ma reception aux États-Unis," *Conferencia, Journal de l'université des annales*, 15 August 1922.

"quieter moments": *New York Tribune*, 15 May 1921.

"I was so excited": Margaret Hill Payor, personal correspondence.

"largest meeting": *New York Times*, 19 May 1921, 15:1.

394   "that a woman": *Star*, 19 May 1921. In addition to Florence Sabin and M. Carey Thomas, those on the platform included Alice Hamilton, professor of industrial medicine at Harvard, and Margaret Washburn, professor of psychology at Vassar.

"the self-conscious": as quoted by Judith Magee, in "The Discoverer of Radium," *The Outlook*, 25 May 1921, no author.

"We women": *New York Times*, 19 May 1921, 15.

"the men": Marie Curie, "Ma reception."

"the Madame": Badash, 346–47.

395   he replied: Eliot to Missy Meloney, 18 December 1920, Columbia University Library.

395   "the outstanding virtue": Missy Meloney to Eliot, 24 December 1920. Columbia University Library.
"as wise": letter of Home Secretary C. G. Abbot to George E. Hale, 28 February 1921. Archives of the National Academy of Sciences.
"a general question": George E. Hale to C. G. Abbot, after talking over the suggestion with Noyes and Millikan, 7 March 1921. Archives of the National Academy of Sciences. The first woman to be elected to the Academy was Florence Sabin, in 1925.
Lowell compared her: *New York Times*, 24 June 1921.
"The Scientific Career": Simon Flexner, "The Scientific Career for Women," an address given at the commencement exercises of Bryn Mawr College, 2 June 1921. Reprinted in *The Scientific Monthly*, August 1921.

396   "many women": *New York Times*, 4 June 1921, 12:6.
"adopted a new": Rossiter, *Women Scientists*, 129.

397   "generations of men": *New York Times*, 21 May 1921.
I can not express: As quoted in *Science*, 27 May 1921.
"radiant day": Marie Curie, "Ma reception."

398   "after being": *New York Times*, 28 May 1921.
"my work": ibid., 25 June 1921.
"There is": ibid., 29 May 1921.
"surpassed": *Madame Curie*, 334.
"magnificent": Marie Curie, "Ma reception."

399   "carried away": *Madame Curie*, 334.
There had been, ibid., 333.
"Everything amused": ibid., 334.
more ceremonies: including the Harvard and Wellesley commencements.
"immensity": Marie Curie, "Ma reception."

CHAPTER EIGHTEEN: *A Thousand Bonds*

400   She didn't care: *Madame Curie*, 350.
"dreadful": ibid., 359.
"she never": ibid., 352.
"you had to peel": interview with Eve Curie Labouisse, February 1990.
"the health": Marie to Irène, 7 September 1924.

401   "seems very pretty": Marie to Irène, Cavalaire, 24 September 1926.
"planting:" Marie to Irène from Prague, 14 June 1925. Marie Curie purchased land in Fontenay-aux-Roses in September 1925 with the idea of moving there from Paris, but she never got around to doing it.
every year: These details of laboratory life are taken from *Madame Curie*, as well as from interviews and reminiscences of lab workers.
"I am a little": Marie to Irène, 13 April 1929.
"I begged": Irène to Marie, 9 March 1929.
"trembled": Marie to Irène, 9 May 1932.

402   "the provinces": Antoine Lacassagne, in "Pięć wspomnień z różami," (Five memories with roses), written by Halina Kowzan for the Polish magazine *Swiat*, 1967, number 44. In the article, five former workers in the laboratory reminisce about Marie Curie. Translated from the Polish.
"sacred places": as cited in *Pierre Curie*, 146.
"the Laboratory": Marcel Guillot in *Swiat*.
"for a few months": Manuel Valaderes in *Swiat*.

403   One year: Haissinsky interview, *Swiat*.

403   "You will be": Goldschmidt, *Pionniers de l'atome*, 20.

"chameau!": camel, as in beast. Interview with Hélène Emmanuel-Zavizziano, October 1989.

"The first contact": Marcel Guillot, "Marie Curie-Skłodowska," *Nuclear Physics* A103 (1967).

404   "to breathe": interview with Lucien Desgranges, 30 January 1990.

"The fact": Desgranges interview, *Swiat*.

stories of adversity: Hélène Emmanuel-Zavizziano, *Journal de l'association des anciennes élèves de l'école Vinet*, 9 November 1970.

"the greatest": *Madame Curie*, 364.

"She was": Haissinsky interview, *Swiat*.

405   "religious convent": Guillot, *Nuclear Physics*.

"We called": *Swiat*.

"one of the most beautiful": *Conferencia, Journal de l'universite des annales*, 1 June 1925.

"If you find": Marie Curie to Henri Pellard, 1923. IC.

406   Catherine Chamié remembers: from an unpublished reminiscence by C. Chamié, a docteur ès sciences who was in charge of measures at the lab. Written in 1935.

"She continued": Guillot, *Nuclear Physics*.

407   "learned to work": Marie Curie in "Note de Madame Curie relative à M. Rosenblum", 31 May 1930. According to his widow, Eva Rosenblum, Salomon Rosenblum believed Marie Curie treated him unfairly, downplaying his discovery in order to ensure a Nobel Prize for Irène. I have not found any evidence to bear this out, however. On the contrary, Marie Curie sought support for his work from an American benefactor and from Albert Einstein, and seemed in private correspondence to have been pleased at his triumph, writing to Irène that "the results of Rosenblum have filled me with satisfaction" (13 April 1929), and "our Rosenblum was in seventh heaven" (4 August 1929). To Einstein she wrote that she had been able to find funds to support Rosenblum's work for five years but that she had run out of resources. "I haven't told M. Rosenblum that I was going to speak to you of his situation and he has not asked it of me in any fashion. If I do speak to you, it is only because I know how much your name is used to raise funds for the Jewish cause and that I wonder if there might not be means there to help a young Jew [*un jeune israélite*] for whom I have a very great respect" (30 August 1929). Throughout the writing of this book, I have looked carefully for any evidence of anti-Semitism in Marie Curie and have found none. Nor does Rosenblum's widow allege anti-Semitism. Salomon Rosenblum ultimately committed suicide. Interview with Eva Rosenblum in October, 1989. Correspondence with Abraham Pais.

"we have seen": Irène to Marie Curie, 9 March 1929.

Moise Haissinsky . . . remembers: *Swiat*.

408   weekly meetings: Interview with Lucien Desgranges.

409   An analogous event: The explanation and the analogy come from Shapiro, *Radiation Protection*.

"Pierre Curie's last papers": *CR*, 6 June 1904 and 25 June 1906.

410   Curie Hair Tonic: BN correspondence, 26 December 1924.

"Madame Curie . . . promises": BN correspondence.

European pharmacopoeia: Weart, *Nuclear Fear*, 50.

soldiers were subjected: Edward R. Landa, *Buried Treasure to Buried Waste*, 23. In a discussion of treatments in British and American army hospitals.

"emanation service": Marie Curie, *la Radiologie et la guerre*, 137.

410   "the rays": ibid., 91.
severe "radiodermatitis": ibid., 93–94.
had to be decontaminated: *CR,* 17 February 1958, "Contamination radioactive de manuscrits de Pierre et Marie Curie, relatifs aux expériences ayant suivi la découverte du radium." Note of M. Frédéric Joliot.

411   That was the year: The dial painters' story has been taken from Hilgartner, Bell, and O'Connor, *Nukespeak;* and from Caulfield, *Multiple Exposures.*
"The glorious martyrology": *Je sais tout,* 15 February 1925.

412   "which might": report of L. Jaloustre to Marie Curie, 15 January 1925. BN.
the resulting report: M. Broca, "Sur les dangers des radiations pénétrantes et les moyens de les éviter," *Au nom de la Commission du Radium, Bulletin de l'Académie de médecine,* III, 85, (1921).
this report: "Rapport sur le contrôle et la réglementation des établissements industriels qui s'occupent de la préparation des corps radio-actifs," présenté au nom d'une commission composée de MM. d'Arsonval, Béclère, A. Broca, Mme Curie et M. Regaud, rapporteur, *Bulletin de l'Académie de médecine,* 10 February 1925.

413   "we have been": Harlan S. Miner, Welsbach Company, Gloucester, N.J., to Marie Curie, 12 May 1925. BN.
"demonstrated": Marie Curie to Harlan S. Miner, 29 May 1925. BN.
"As far as": Harlan S. Miner to Marie Curie, 16 July 1925. BN.
"we have still": Marie Curie to Stefan Meyer, 9 January 1925. BN.
"a defective": Marie Curie to Harlan S. Miner. BN.

414   "because they": note handwritten by Marie Curie at the end of a report by L. Jaloustre, on the death of his "friends and collaborators", 15 January 1925. BN.
"Yamada": Irène to Marie Curie, July 1924.
"The cause": Nobus Yamada to Irène Curie, 30 November 1925. IC.
"He seemed": Namie Yamada to Marie Curie, 29 December 1927. IC.
Her response: correspondence at the Institut Curie. The former worker whose dissertation she managed to get published was Jean d'Espine.

415   "in very bad health": Irène to Marie Curie, Brunoy, 5 August 1927.
affected his eyes: Wolfers, October 1923. IC.
grew more serious: Marguerite Perey eventually had a necrosis of her right hand and lost a finger; for the most part, her illness occurred after Marie Curie's death.
seven out of twenty workers: from a single-page typed report of "Examens hématologiques" performed between January and July of 1931. IC.
"Irène doesn't": Marie Curie to Józef, 5 December 1927, letter in Polish from the National Museum in Warsaw. Irène's first child, Hélène, was born 19 September 1927, and the anemia was probably being ascribed to that event. However, Irène was also affected by this time by exposure, especially from the X-ray work during World War I.
Two lab workers: Jean d'Espine died in 1930, and Paul Kerromes died 6 July 1932.
Another, aged thirty-one,: Émile Regnier died 1 April 1933.

416   Another young man: M. Reymond, who drowned August 1932.
"In fact": *la Liberté,* 12 December 1903.
she stated: This seems to be the only time Marie Curie mentions the harmful effects of X rays, which probably were a major contributor to her health problems, as well as Irène's.
"My greatest troubles": *Madame Curie,* 371.
"These are": ibid.

416   "If a pupil": *Madame Curie,* 372.
417   "You must": ibid.
        "Sometimes my courage": *Madame Curie,* 373.

CHAPTER NINETEEN: *LEGACIES*

418   "I still believe": *Pierre Curie,* 226–27.
        "I mostly think": Marie Curie to Missy Meloney, 12 November 1929.
419   "each day": Marie Curie to Irène, 19 December 1928.
        "I am stupefied": Marie Curie to Irène from Prague, 13 June 1925.
        "with all": *Pierre Curie,* introduction, 24.
        "an impression": Marie Curie to Irène: 18 October 1929. BN.
420   "poor prisoner": ibid.
        "system": "Opinion sur le Surmenage Scolaire," four handwritten pages,
        1929. BN.
        The spectacle: *Madame Curie,* 360.
        "Not infrequently": Lucien Desgranges in *Swiat.*
        The day: reminiscence of C. Chamié, 1936. BN.
421   "In science": *Madame Curie,* 222.
        "Why can't": ibid., 374.
        "Then of course": Interview with Eve Curie Labouisse, February 1990.
        "We have had": Marie Curie to Elsie Mead, 16 November 1921.
        "There are three": *Madame Curie,* 358.
        "There is": Marie Curie to Irène, 6 October 1921.
        The president of the Polish Republic: Ignacy Mościcki.
422   "One would hope": Jacques Curie to Marie Curie, 14 February 1922.
        That was not to be: Nor was Irène Curie admitted to the Académie des
        sciences, though she had won a Nobel Prize and tried for admission on
        two separate occasions. The first woman to be admitted to the Académie
        des sciences was Marguerite Perey in 1962.
        Pierre Curie: Typescript of remarks made by Marie Curie at the anniver-
        sary. BN.
        Raymond Drux . . . remembers: *Swiat.*
423   "We have had": Marie Curie to Irène, 28 December 1926.
        A typical day: *Madame Curie,* 313–316.
        "never showed": ibid., 310.
424   "I hope": Marie Curie to Irène, 3 September 1919.
        "We will": Marie Curie to Irène, 4 August 1922.
        Eve felt: interview with Eve Curie Labouisse.
        "veering and tacking": *Madame Curie,* 310.
        "I am quite": H. A. Lorentz, tribute at the twenty-fifth anniversary cele-
        bration, December 1923. BN.
        "excellent": Marie Curie to Irène, 22, 24, 30 May 1932.
        "dazzling": *Madame Curie,* 339.
425   "Stories about": ibid., 356.
        "won't disappear": Jacques to Marie Curie, 26 March 1932. Catalogue of
        Bibliothèque nationale.
        "I didn't": As quoted by Eugénie Cotton, *les Curie,* 113.
        "a fraud": Goldsmith, *Frédéric Joliot-Curie,* 32.
        "well-respected": Marie Curie to Józef, 13 June 1926. Letter in Polish,
        National Museum, Warsaw.
426   "the esteem": Marie Curie to Marie Meloney, 23 June 1926. Columbia
        University Library.

426   "I miss Irène": Marie Curie to Józef, 5 December 1927. Letter in Polish, National Museum, Warsaw.

"my mother": Irène Joliot-Curie, "Marie Curie, ma mère."

"That young man": as quoted in Cotton, *les Curie,* 114.

427   it was routine: Norman Feather, "The experimental discovery of the neutron," Proceedings of the Tenth International Congress of the History of Science (Paris, 1964).

"simple and elegant": ibid.

"I don't believe it": Sir James Chadwick, "Some personal notes on the search for the neutron," in the Proceedings of the Tenth International Congress of the History of Science (Paris, 1964).

"it is annoying": Frédéric Joliot to D. Skobeltsyn in Moscow, 2 April 1932. As quoted in Goldsmith, *Frédéric Joliot-Curie,* 42.

"it is natural": Frédéric Joliot-Curie, "Les grandes découvertes de la radioactivité," *la Pensée,* 74, 1957.

428   "Everything": ibid.

"An infinitely tiny particle": P. Biquard, 36

"After the session": as quoted in Weart, *Scientists in Power,* 44.

429   "a child's joy": as quoted in Biquard, *Joliot-Curie and his theories,* from interview in Portuguese newspaper, *Republica,* 10 January 1955.

"with the neutron": oral history interview with Wolfgang Gentner by C. Weiner, Center for History of Physics, American Institute of Physics, New York, November 1971.

"scientists": Nobel Prize speech, *les Prix Nobel en 1935* (Stockholm: Imprimerie Royale, 1937).

430   "one of the most important": as quoted in Rhodes, *The Making of the Atom Bomb,* 202.

Pierre Biquard received: Biquard, 40–41.

"I will never forget": *la Pensée.*

"I remember": Irène Joliot-Curie in "Marie Curie, ma mère."

"When she reached": *Madame Curie,* 378.

431   "All things considered": Józef's memoir.

"On one sunny day": *Madame Curie,* 379–81.

"sheer torture": ibid., 382.

"that her temperature": ibid., 383.

432   "all in white": ibid., 384–85.

"great abilities": Rutherford to Irène Joliot-Curie, 3 July 1934 (must be July 4). BN.

"kindness": Niels Bohr to Irène Joliot-Curie, 22 September 1934. BN.

"lost everything": *Madame Curie,* 384.

"the idea": A. Broca to "Mes chers amis," Copenhagen, 6 July 1934. BN.

433   "the supreme pride": Clément Vautel in *le Journal,* 9 July 1934.

"my sister and I": Eve Curie in *le Journal,* 11 July 1934.

unbeknownst to each other: Józef's memoir.

BIBLIOGRAPHY

BOOKS

Abbot, Mary. *A Woman's Paris: A Handbook of Every-day Living in the French Capital.* Boston: Small, Maynard & Co., 1900.

Abir-Am, Pnina G., and Outram, Dorinda, eds. *Uneasy Careers and Intimate Lives: Women in Science 1789–1979.* New Brunswick, N.J.: Rutgers University Press, 1987.

Ajalbert, Jean. *Dans Paris, la grande ville (sensations de guerre).* Paris: Éditions Georges Crès et cie, 1916.

Albert, Pierre, et Terrou, Fernand. *Histoire de la presse.* Paris: Presses universitaires de France, 1979.

Badash, Lawrence. *Radioactivity in America: Growth and Decay of a Science.* Baltimore: Johns Hopkins, 1979.

————, ed. *Rutherford and Boltwood: Letters on Radioactivity.* New Haven: Yale University Press, 1969.

Baedeker, K. *Paris and Environs.* Leipzig: Karl Baedeker, 1891.

Barbusse, Henri. *Le Feu.* Paris: Flammarion, 1965.

Becker, Jean-Jacques. *The Great War and the French People.* St. Martin's Press: New York, 1986.

Bellanger, Claude. *Histoire générale de la presse française.* Paris: Presses universitaires de France, 1969–.

Bensaude-Vincent, Bernadette. *Langevin: Science et vigilance.* Paris: Belin, 1987.

Bensaude-Vincent, Bernadette, and Stengers, Isabelle. *Histoire de la chimie.* Paris: Éditions la Découverte, 1993.

Berenson, Edward. *The Trial of Madame Caillaux.* Berkeley: University of California Press, 1992.

Bibliothèque nationale: *Pierre et Marie Curie.* Paris, 1967.

Biezunski, Michel. *Albert Einstein: Correspondances françaises.* Éditions de Seuil, 1989.

Biquard, Pierre. *Frédéric Joliot-Curie: The Man and his Theories.* London: Souvenir Press, 1965.

Blejwas, Stanislaus Andrew. *"Warsaw Positivism: 1864–1890: Organic Work as an Expression of National Survival in Nineteenth-Century Poland."* Dissertation, Columbia University, 1973.

Bohning, Daryl E., et al. *The Nuclear Almanac.* Reading, Mass: Addison-Wesley, 1984.

Borden, Mary. *The Forbidden Zone*. London: Heinemann, 1929.

Borel, Marguerite [Camille Marbo, pseud.]. *A travers deux siècles 1883–1967*. Paris: Éditions Bernard Grasset, 1968.

Borgé, Jacques, et Viasnoff, Nicolas, *Archives de Paris*. Paris: Éditions Balland, 1981.

Bourrelier, Henri. *La Vie du quartier-latin*. Paris: Éditions Bourrelier et cie, 1936.

Boyd, Louise. *Polish Countrysides*. New York: American Geographical Society, 1937.

Brandes, George. *Poland: A Study of the Land, People and Literature*. New York: Macmillan, 1903.

Bredin, Jean-Denis. *The Affair*. New York: George Braziller, 1986.

Bromke, Adam. *Poland's Politics: Idealism versus Realism*. Cambridge, Mass.: Harvard University Press, 1967.

Carrington, Hereward. *Eusapia Palladino and Her Phenomena*. New York: B. W. Dodge & Co., 1909.

Caulfield, Catherine. *Multiple Exposures: Chronicles of the Radiation Age*. New York: Harper & Row, 1989.

Caullery, Maurice. *French Science, and its Principal Discoveries*. New York: Arno Press, 1975.

Charle, Christophe, and Telkes, Eva. *Les Professeurs de la Faculté des sciences de Paris: Dictionnaire biographique 1901–1939*, Paris: Éditions du CNRS, 1989.

Charrier, Edmée. *L'Évolution intellectuelle féminine*. Thèse pour le doctorat en droit. Paris: Éditions Albert Mechelinck, 1931.

Clark, Ronald William. *Einstein: The Life and Times*. New York: World Publishing Co., 1971.

Cobban, Alfred, *A History of Modern France*. Reading, England: Cox & Wyman, 1965.

Colette. *Les heures longues*. Paris: Fayard & cie, 1917.

Cotton, Eugénie. *Les Curie*. Paris: Editions Seghers, 1963.

Crawford, Elisabeth. *The Beginnings of the Nobel Institution: The Science Prizes, 1901–1915*. Cambridge, England: Cambridge University Press, 1984.

Crawford, Elisabeth, Heilbron, J. L., and Ullrich, Rebecca. *The Nobel Population 1901–1937*. Berkeley: Office for History of Science and Technology, 1987.

Crosland, Maurice. *Science under Control*. Cambridge, Mass.: Cambridge University Press, 1992.

Curie, Eve. *Madame Curie,* New York: Doubleday, 1937.

Curie, Marie. *L'Isotopie et les éléments isotopes*. Paris: Librairie Scientifique Albert Blanchard, 1924.

———. *Oeuvres de Marie Skłodowska Curie*. Warsaw: Państwowe Wydawnictwo Naukowe, 1954.

———. *Pierre Curie. With Autobiographical Notes*. New York: Macmillan, 1923.

———. *La Radiologie et la guerre*. Paris: Librairie Félix Alcan, 1921.

———. *Traité de radioactivité*. 2 vols. Paris: Gauthier-Villars, 1910.

Curie, Pierre. *Oeuvres de Pierre Curie*. Paris: Gauthier-Villars, 1908.

Davies, Norman. *God's Playground: A History of Poland*. 2 vols. New York: Columbia University Press, 1982.

de Livois, René. *Histoire de la presse française*. Vol. 2. Lausanne: Éditions Spes, 1965.

de Saunier, Baudry, L. *Histoire générale de la vélocipédie*. Paris: Paul Ollendorff, 1891.

Dijkstra, Bram. *Idols of Perversity*. New York: Oxford University Press, 1986.

Edwards, H. Sutherland. *The Polish Captivity: An Account of the Present Position of the Poles*. 2 vols. London: William H. Allen & Co., 1863.

———. *Old and New Paris*. Cassell and Company, 1893.

Evans, Richard J. *The Feminists: Women's Emancipation Movements in Europe, America and Australasia 1840–1920.* London: Croom Helm, 1977.

Eve, A. S. *Rutherford: Being the Life and Letters of the Rt Hon. Lord Rutherford, O.M.* New York: The Macmillan Company: 1939.

Fox, Robert, and Weicz, George, eds. *The Organization of Science and Technology in France 1808–1914.* Cambridge, England: Cambridge University Press, 1980.

Giroux, François. *Une femme honorable.* Paris: Fayard, 1981.

Gold, Arthur, and Fizdale, Robert. *Misia: The Life of Misia Sert.* New York: Alfred A. Knopf, 1980.

Goldschmidt, Bertrand. *Pionniers de l'atome.* Paris: Éditions Stock, 1987.

Goldsmith, Maurice. *Frédéric Joliot-Curie.* London: Lawrence and Wishart, 1976.

Goscilo, Helena, ed. *Russian and Polish Women's Fiction.* Knoxville: University of Tennessee Press, 1985.

Grigg, E. R. N., *The Trail of the Invisible Light: From X-Strahlen to Radio(bio)logy.* Springfield, Illinois: Charles C. Thomas, 1965.

Hause, Steven C., with Kenney, Anne R. *Women's Suffrage and Social Politics in the French Third Republic.* Princeton: Princeton University Press, 1984.

Henry, Stuart. *Paris Days and Evenings.* Philadelphia: J. B. Lippincott Co., 1896.

Hilgartner, Stephen, Bell, Richard C., and O'Connor, Rory. *Nukespeak.* San Francisco: Sierra Club Books, 1982.

Hurwic, Józef, *Importance de la thèse de doctorat de Marie Skłodowska Curie pour le développement de la science sur la radioactivité.* Thesis presented to the Faculté des sciences de Paris, 1992.

———. *la Radioactivité: Découverte et premiers travaux.* Paris: Cahiers d'histoire et de philosophie des sciences, 1991.

Hutchinson, Alex H. *Try Cracow and the Carpathians.* London: Chapman and Hall, 1872.

Institut de France. *Index biographique de l'Académie des sciences.* Paris: Gauthier-Villars, 1979.

Joliot-Curie, Irène. "Les Carnets de laboratoire de la découverte du polonium et du radium." An appendix to the French edition of Marie Curie's *Pierre Curie*, 1955 edition.

Kauffman, Richard. *Paris of Today.* New York: Cassell Publishing Co., 1891.

Kevles, Daniel J. *The Physicists.* New York: Alfred A. Knopf, 1978.

Kirchberger, Joe H. *The First World War: An Eyewitness History.* New York: Facts on File, 1992.

Kuhn, Thomas S. *The Structure of Scientific Revolutions.* Chicago: University of Chicago Press, 1962.

Landa, Edward R. *Buried Treasure to Buried Waste: The Rise and Fall of the Radium Industry.* Colorado: Colorado School of Mines, 1987.

Langevin, André. *Paul Langevin mon père.* Paris: Les Éditeurs français réunis. 1971.

McMillan, James F. *Twentieth-Century France: Politics and Society 1898–1991.* London: Edward Arnold, 1992.

Manuel, Frank. *The Prophets of Paris.* New York: Harper & Row, 1965.

Margadant, Jo Burr. *Madame le Professeur.* Princeton: Princeton University Press, 1990.

Martin, Alexis, *Paris: Promenades dans les vingt arrondissements.* Paris: A Hennuyer, 1890.

Mehra, Jagdish, *The Solvay Conferences on Physics: Aspects of the Development of Physics since 1911.* Boston: D. Reidel Publishing Company, 1975.

Miłosz, Czesław. *The History of Polish Literature.* New York: Macmillan, 1969.

Montorgueil, Georges. *Les Parisiennes d'à présent.* Paris: H. Floury, 1897.

Morawińska, Agnieszka. *Symbolism in Polish Painting 1890–1914.* Detroit: Detroit Institute of Arts, 1984.

Moses, Claire Goldberg. *French Feminism in the Nineteenth Century.* Albany: State University of New York, 1984.

Myers, Denys P. *Handbook of the League of Nations.* New York: World Peace Foundation, 1935.

Nye, Mary Jo. *Molecular Reality: A Perspective on the Scientific Work of Jean Perrin.* New York: American Elsevier Inc., 1972.

Ogilvie, Marilyn Bailey, ed. *Women in Science: Antiquity through the Nineteenth Century.* Boston: MIT Press, 1986.

Pais, Abraham, *Inward Bound.* New York: Oxford University Press, 1986.

———. *Subtle Is the Lord.* New York: Oxford University Press, 1982.

Paul, Harry W. *From Knowledge to Power: The Rise of the French Science Empire in France, 1860–1939.* Cambridge, England: Cambridge University Press, 1985.

———. *The Sorcerer's Apprentice: The French Scientist's Image of German Science, 1840–1919.* Gainesville: University of Florida Press, 1972.

Paxton, Robert O. *Europe in the Twentieth Century.* New York: Harcourt Brace, 1985.

Pestre, Dominique. *Physique et physiciens en France, 1918–1940.* Paris: Éditions des archives contemporaines, 1984.

Pflaum, Rosalynd. *Grand Obsession: Madame Curie and her World.* New York: Doubleday, 1989.

Prost, Antoine. *Histoire de l'enseignement en France 1800–1967.* Paris: A. Colin, 1968.

Proust, Marcel. *Remembrance of Things Past: The Guermantes Way.* New York: Vintage Books, 1981 [1934].

Radvanyi, Pierre, and Bordry, Monique. *La Radioactivité artificielle et son histoire.* Paris: Seuil/CNRS, 1984.

Reid, Robert William. *Marie Curie.* New York: Saturday Review Press, 1974.

Rhodes, Richard. *The Making of the Atom Bomb.* New York: Simon & Schuster, 1988.

Richet, Charles. *Traité de métapsychique.* Paris: Librairie Félix Alcan, 1922.

Rivé, Philippe, ed. *La Sorbonne et sa reconstruction.* Paris: La Manufacture, 1987.

Romer, Alfred, ed. *The Discovery of Radioactivity and Transmutation.* New York: Dover, 1964.

———. *Radiochemistry and the Discovery of Isotopes.* New York: Dover, 1970.

Rossiter, Margaret W. *Women Scientists in America: Struggles and Strategies to 1940.* Baltimore: Johns Hopkins University Press, 1982.

Rudorff, Raymond. *Belle Époque: Paris in the Nineties.* London: Hamish Hamilton, 1972.

Sassoon, Siegfried, *The Memoirs of George Sherston.* New York: The Literary Guild of America, Inc., 1937.

Shapiro, Barbara Stern, ed. *Pleasures of Paris: Daumier to Picasso.* Boston: Museum of Fine Arts, 1991.

Shapiro, Jacob. *Radiation Protection: A Guide for Scientists and Physicians.* Cambridge, England: Harvard University Press, 1990.

Sharp, Evelyn. *Hertha Ayrton: A Memoir.* London: Edward Arnold & Co., 1926.

Shiebinger, Londa. *The Mind Has No Sex?* Cambridge, Mass.: Harvard University Press, 1989.

Simons, Thomas W., Jr. *Eastern Europe in the Postwar World.* New York: St. Martin's Press, 1991.

Stetson, Dorothy McBride. *Women's Rights in France.* New York: Greenwood Press, 1987.

Sylvestre, Arman, et al. *Paris au temps jadis.* Paris: Bibliothéque en couleurs, 1897.

Thébaud, Françoise. *La Femme au temps de la guerre de 14.* Paris: Éditions Stock: 1986.

Tuchman, Barbara. *The Guns of August.* New York: The Macmillan Company, 1962.

Vicinus, Martha, ed. *Suffer and Be Still: Women in the Victorian Age.* Bloomington: Indiana University Press, 1972.

Ward, Maria E. *Bicycling for Ladies.* New York: Brentano's, 1896.

Weart, Spencer R. *Nuclear Fear: A History of Images.* Cambridge, Mass.: Harvard University Press, 1988.

———. *Scientists in Power.* Cambridge, Mass.: Harvard University Press, 1979.

Weber, Eugen. *France: Fin de Siècle.* Cambridge, Mass.: Harvard University Press.

———. *The Nationalist Revival in France, 1905–1914.* Berkeley: University of California, 1959.

Weicz, George. *The Emergence of Modern Universities in France, 1863–1914.* Princeton: Princeton University Press, 1983.

Weiss, Louise. *Mémoires d'une Européenne. Tome I: Une petite fille du siècle.* Paris: Albin Michel, 1968.

Woznicki, Robert. *Madame Curie: Daughter of Poland.* Miami: The American Institute of Polish Culture, 1983.

Wunderlich, E., ed. *Geographischer Bilderatlas von Polen.* Potsdam: Edmund Stein, 1917.

Zamoyski, Adam. *The Polish Way: A Thousand-Year History of the Poles and their Culture.* New York: Franklin Watts, 1988.

Ziegler, Gilette, ed. *Marie–Irène Curie Correspondence: Choix de lettres, 1905–1934.* Paris: les Éditeurs français réunis, 1974.

ARTICLES

Badash, Lawrence. "Radioactivity before the Curies." *American Journal of Physics* 33 (2) (1965): 128–35.

———. "Radium, Radioactivity, and the Popularity of Scientific Discovery." *Proceedings of the American Philosophical Society* 122, (June 1978).

Chadwick, Sir James. "Some personal notes on the search for the neutron." Proceedings of the Tenth International Congress of the History of Science. Paris, 1964.

Feather, Norman. "The experimental discovery of the neutron." Proceedings of the Tenth International Congress of the History of Science. Paris, 1964.

Heilbron, J. L. "Fin-de-siècle Physics." In *Science, Technology and Society in the Time of Alfred Nobel.* Oxford: Pergamon Press, 1982.

Joliot-Curie, Irène. *"Marie Curie, ma mère." Europe* 108, (1954): 89–121.

Langevin, Paul. "Pierre Curie." In *Revue du mois,* Tome II, juillet–décembre 1906.

Malley, Marjorie. "The discovery of atomic transmutation: Scientific styles and philosophies in France and Britain." *Isis* 70 (1979).

Nye, Mary Jo. "Gustav LeBon's Black Light." In *Historical Studies in the Physical Sciences.* Princeton: Princeton University Press, 1974, 163–195.

Paul, Harry. "The Debate over the Bankruptcy of Science." *French Historical Studies 1967–68* 5:299–327.

Perrin, Jean. "Madame Curie et la découverte du Radium." In *Vient de paraitre,* Bulletin bibliographique mensuel, February 1924.

Racine, Nicole. "The Clarté Movement in France, 1919–21." *Journal of Contemporary History* 2 (2) (April 1967) 194–208.

Regaud, Cl. "Marie Skłodowska-Curie." *Notice nécrologique,* read at the Conseil de la Fondation Curie, 24 October 1934.

INDEX

PHOTO CREDITS

The photographs in the picture section appear through the courtesy of the following institutions or individuals:

PAGE 1: *top,* Marie Skłodowska Curie Museum; *two bottom,* Archives Curie et Joliot-Curie, Paris.

PAGE 2: *all three,* Archives Curie et Joliot-Curie, Paris.

PAGE 3: *top left,* Archives Curie et Joliot-Curie, Paris; *top right* and *bottom,* Marie Skłodowska Curie Museum.

PAGE 4: *both photos,* Archives Curie et Joliot Curie, Paris.

PAGE 5: *top left* and *bottom,* Archives Curie et Joliot-Curie, Paris; *top right,* Institut de France, Archives de l'Académie des sciences.

PAGE 6: Archives Curie et Joliot-Curie, Paris.

PAGE 7: *top,* The Burns Archive; *bottom,* Archives Curie et Joliot-Curie, Paris.

PAGE 8: *top left* and *center,* Roger Viollet, Paris; *top right,* from *Die Berühmten Erfinder, Physiker, und Ingenieure,* Aulis Verlag Deubner, Köln, Germany; *bottom,* Archives Curie et Joliot-Curie, Paris.

PAGE 9: *top, center* and *bottom left,* Archives Curie et Joliot-Curie, Paris; *bottom right,* Marie Skłodowska Curie Museum.

PAGE 10: Archives Curie et Joliot-Curie, Paris.

PAGE 11: *both photos,* Roger Viollet, Paris.

PAGE 12: *top left,* Roger Viollet, Paris; *top right* and *bottom right,* Archives Curie et Joliot Curie, Paris; *bottom left,* from *The History of the Institution of Electrical Engineers, 1871–1931,* published by the Institution of Electrical Engineers, London. Courtesy of the History of Science Collections, University of Oklahoma.

PAGE 13: *all photos,* Marie Skłodowska Curie Museum.

PAGE 14: *three photos,* Archives Curie et Joliot-Curie, Paris.

PAGE 15: *top,* Archives Curie et Joliot-Curie, Paris; *center,* Rare Book and Manuscript Library, Columbia University, New York; *bottom,* Stefan Batuk, Warsaw, Poland.

PAGE 16: *top,* Archives Curie et Joliot-Curie, Paris; *bottom left* and *right,* Roger Viollet, Paris.